NEW DOCUMENTS ILLUSTRATING EARLY CHRISTIANITY

A Review of the
Greek Inscriptions and Papyri
published in 1979

by

G. H. R. Horsley

with the collaboration of
A. L. Connolly and others

The Ancient History Documentary Research Centre
Macquarie University
1987

The Ancient History Documentary Research Centre (Director: E.A. Judge, Professor of History) has been formed within the School of History, Philosophy & Politics at Macquarie University to focus staff effort in research and professional development and to coordinate it with the work of other organisations interested in the documentation of the ancient world.

This volume has been produced with the support of Avondale College, the Macquarie Greek Summer School, the Macquarie University Research Grant, the Society for Early Christianity, Trinity Grammar School, and the following individual donors: D. Cameron, N.M. Cameron, D. Claydon, P. Geidans, B.F. Harris, P.E. Hollingdale, B.R. Horsley, P. Mathers, A.F. and M. Pennington, H.W. Piper, W. Ritchie, D.W.B. Robinson, and J.G. Sperling.

Editorial correspondence should be addressed to Dr G.H.R. Horsley, School of History, Philosophy & Politics, Macquarie University, N.S.W. 2109, Australia.
Business address: The Ancient History Documentary Research Centre, Macquarie University, N.S.W. 2109, Australia.

SUGGESTED CATALOGUING DATA:

Horsley, G.H.R.
New Documents illustrating early Christianity. A Review of the Greek inscriptions and papyri published in 1979.

Bibliography.
Includes index.
ISBN 0 85837 599 0
ISBN 0 85837 600 8 (pbk)

1. Bible. New Testament — Language, style. 2. Inscriptions, Greek. 3. Manuscripts (Papyri). 4. Greek language, Biblical. 5. Church History — Primitive and early church. I. Macquarie University. Ancient History Documentary Research Centre. II. Title.

PA 810 1987 487.4

Typeset by All Language Typesetters, 10-14 Mitchell Street, Marrickville, N.S.W. 2204.
Printed by Southwood Press, 80-82 Chapel Street, Marrickville, N.S.W. 2204.

CONTENTS

LIST OF ENTRIES

A. New Testament Context

B. Minor Philological Notes

C. Biblical and Related Citations

INTRODUCTION

This Review is primarily a reporting service, designed to make more widely known especially to biblical scholars published texts of philological and historical interest. Those who follow up the bibliographies to particular items will therefore find that much in these pages is derivative, although independent suggestions and comments are also offered. Entries in MM and BAGD are again supplemented/qualified considerably. The character and objectives of the Macquarie-based project to rework MM, for which *New Docs* is intended to serve as a preliminary contribution, is explained in the Preface to *New Docs 1976*. See also C.J. Hemer, 'Towards a new Moulton and Milligan', *Novum Testamentum* 24 (1982) 97-123. The fifth volume in the *New Docs* series will consist of several linguistic studies which take their rise from the first four volumes. A new, cumulative set of indexes to the set of five volumes will also be included, bringing this phase of the project to an end. Work on the new MM is now under way.

The reader who has been mainly kept in mind during the writing of entries has been the NT researcher, teacher, or student. While the main focus is upon the NT and the first four centuries, texts of later date have been included if it is judged that they may be of interest to students of that era (e.g., liturgical and homiletical texts; biblical citations). Some entries (e.g., **2**, **23**, **24**, **27**) have been included simply because they treat texts representative of the times in some way, and make a general contribution to understanding the background of the NT and the world of early Christianity.

This volume treats texts published during 1979, either for the first time or as re-editions, in corpora and 'conspectus' volumes (such as *AE*, *BE*, *SEG*). Occasionally such a text will render necessary a more-than-passing discussion of texts published at some earlier date, which were not re-published in 1979. Following the practice of *SEG*, we have not refrained from including occasional references to texts and discussions published after 1979, where they are relevant. The emphasis is heavily upon Greek texts, although Latin documents and occasionally ones including Semitic words are noticed. Corpora consisting entirely of, e.g., Latin inscriptions, or hieroglyphic, demotic or Coptic papyri have not been taken into account.

The inscriptions of Ephesos, collected in eight volumes in the *Inschriften von Kleinasien* series and published between 1979-84, have naturally provided a major focus for the present Review. This Repertorium contains over 3,500 items. Although vols. Ib (commentary to the texts in Ia) and VIII.3 (the last of the index volumes) are still awaited, it was decided to cull the whole set of these inscriptions in this present volume.

Listed below are all collections for the year 1979 which have been read, arranged according to the abbreviations used in this volume. Where the abbreviation is bracketed, the work was read, but no texts were selected for noting here. Volume number and date are provided throughout the Review for all texts from non-1979 corpora. Where no volume number and date are given, the reference is to a publication of 1979 as listed below. Occasional publications from 1976-1978 which were missed have been included.

List of works read

Actes Constantza	— *Actes du VIIe Congrès international d'épigraphie grecque et latine, Constantza, 9-15 septembre 1977*, ed. D.M. Pippidi (Bucharest, 1979)
AE	— *L'Année épigraphique 1979* [1982]
BE	— *Bulletin épigraphique*, by J. and L. Robert, in *Revue des études grecques* 92 (1979) 413-541
BE Index	— *Index du Bulletin épigraphique de J. et L. Robert, 1966-1973*, by J. Marcillet-Jaubert/A.-M. Vérilhac (Paris, 1979)
[*BL*]	— *Berichtigungsliste der griechischen Papyrusurkunden aus Ägypten* 6, edd. E. Boswinkel/P.W. Pestman/H.-A. Rupprecht (Leiden, 1976)
[*BL Index*]	— *A Cumulative Index to Berichtigungsliste Vols. 1-6*, by J.W. Shumaker (*TLG Publications Series* 9; Irvine, 1979)
Chiat, *Synagogue Art*	— *A Corpus of Synagogue Art and Architecture in Roman and Byzantine Palestine*, by M.J.S. Chiat (4 vols; Diss. Minnesota, 1979)
[*Ch.L.A.* 10, 11]	— *Chartae Latinae Antiquiores*: *Facsimile-Edition of the Latin Charters Prior to the Ninth Century* 10. *Germany* I. *Berlin* (*DDR*); II. *Bundesrepublik Deutschland und Deutsche Demokratische Republik,* edd. A. Bruckner/R. Marichal (Zurich, 1979)
Christophilopoulos, *Νομ. Ἐπιγ.*	— *Νομικὰ Ἐπιγραφικά*, by A.P. Christophilopoulos (2 vols; Athens, 1977, 1979)
CIL III Add.	— *Inscriptiones Latinae in Graecia repertae. Additamenta ad CIL III*, ed. M. Šašel-Kos (*Epigrafia e Antichità* 5; Faenza, 1979)
CMC (ET)	— *The Cologne Mani Codex* (*P.Colon.inv.nr. 4780*). *'Concerning the Origin of his body'*, trans. R. Cameron/A.J. Dewey (*SBL Early Christian Literature* Series 3, *Texts and Translations* 15; Missoula, 1979)
CPR	— *Corpus Papyrorum Raineri* VII. *Griechische Texte* IV, edd. H. Zilliacus/J. Frösén/P.Hohti/J.Kaimio/M. Kaimio (2 vols; Vienna, 1979)
Didymos, *Eccl.*	— *Didymos der Blinde, Kommentar zum Ecclesiastes* (*Tura-Papyrus*) I-VI, edd. G. Binder/M. Gronewald/J. Kramer/B. Krebber/L. Liesenborghs (*Papyrologische Texte und Abhandlungen* 9, 13, 16, 22, 24, 25, 26; Bonn, 1969-1983)
[Drew-Bear, *Nome Hermopolite*]	— *Le nome Hermopolite: toponymes et sites*, by M. Drew-Bear (*American Studies in Papyrology* 21; Missoula, 1979)
Garbrah, *Erythrae*	— *A Grammar of Ionic Inscriptions from Erythrae*, by K.A. Garbrah (*BeitrWge zur klassischen Philologie* 60; Meisenheim am Glan, 1978)
Guarducci, *EG* IV	— *Epigrafia greca* IV. *Epigrafi sacre pagane e cristiane,* by M. Guarducci (Rome, 1978)
[HWusle, *Formen des gr. Epig.*].	— *Einfache und frühe Formen des griechischen Epigramms*, by H. HWusle (*Commentationes Aenipontanae* 25, *Philologie und Epigraphik* 3; Innsbruck, 1979)
Helbing, *AGI*	— *Auswahl aus griechischen Inschriften*, by R. Helbing (Berlin, 1915; repr. Chicago, 1977)
I.Apollonia	— *Apollonia, the Port of Cyrene. Excavations by the University of Michigan 1965-1967*, by R.G. Goodchild et al. (*Supplements to Libya Antiqua* 4; Tripoli, 1976 [1978]) ['The inscriptions of Apollonia', by J. Reynolds, pp.293-333]
I.Berenike	— *Excavations at Sidi Khrebish, Benghazi* (*Berenice*), by J.A. Lloyd/R. Reece/J.M. Reynolds/F.B. Sear et al. (2 vols; *Supplements to Libya Antiqua* 5; Tripoli, 1977, 1979) ['The Inscriptions', by J.M. Reynolds, I.233-54]
I.Ephesos I-VIII	— *Inschriften griechischer StWdte aus Kleinasien* XI-XVII. *Die Inschriften von Ephesos* I-VIII, edd. H. Wankel/C. Börker/R. Merkelbach et al. (Bonn, 1979-1984)
IG XIV *Suppl.*	— *Inscriptiones Graecae Galliae Hispaniae Britanniae Germaniae,* ed. G. Kaibel/A. Lebegue (Berlin, 1890; repr. with suppl. by Al. N. Oikonomides, Chicago, 1978)
[*IGA*]	— *Inscriptiones Graecae antiquissimae praeter Atticas in Attica repertas*, ed. H. Roehl (Berlin, 1882; repr. Chicago, 1978)
IGB	— *Inschriften griechischer Bildhauer*, by E.M. Loewy (1885; repr. Chicago, 1976)
IGM	— *Inscriptiones Graecae Metricae ex Scriptoribus praeter Anthologiam Collectae*, ed. Th. Preger (Leipzig, 1891; repr. Chicago, 1977)
IGUR	— *Inscriptiones Graecae Urbis Romae* III, ed. L. Moretti (Rome, 1979)

IMS — *Inscriptions de la Mésie supérieure* IV. *Naissus – Remesiana – Horreum Margi*, ed. P. Petrović (Belgrade, 1979)

I.Nikaia I-II.2 — *Inschriften griechischer StWdte aus Kleinasien* IX-X.2. *Katalog der antiken Inschriften des Museums von Iznik* (*Nikaia*) I-II.2, ed. S. Şahin (3 vols; Bonn, 1979-1982)

Lodi, *Enchiridion* — *Enchiridion euchologicum fontium liturgicorum,* by E. Lodi (*Bibliotheca 'Ephemerides Liturgicae', Subsidia* 15; Rome, 1979)

[*O.Lund*] — *Ostraca Lundensia. Ostraka aus der Sammlung des Instituts für Altertumskunde an der UniversitWt zu Lund*, ed. C. Tsiparis (Lund, 1979)

O.Tebt.Pad. — *Ostraka da Tebtynis della Università di Padova* I, ed. C. Gallazzi (Milan, 1979)

P.Col. — *Columbia Papyri* VII. *Fourth Century Documents from Karanis*, transcribed by R.S. Bagnall/N. Lewis, edited with translation and commentary by R.S. Bagnall (*American Studies in Papyrology* 20; Missoula, 1979)

P.Köln — *Kölner Papyri* II, ed. B. Kramer/D. Hagedorn (*Papyrologica Coloniensia* 7; Opladen, 1978)

P.Laur. — *Dai papiri della Biblioteca Medicea Laurenziana* III, ed. R. Pintaudi (*Papyrologica Florentina* 5; Florence, 1979)

P.Oxy.Hels. — *Fifty Oxyrhynchus Papyri*, edd. H. Zilliacus/J. Frösén/P. Hohti/J. Kaimio/M. Kaimio (*Commentationes Humanarum Litterarum* 63; Helsinki, 1979)

PSI — *Papiri greci e latini* XV.1, edd. V. Bartoletti/M. Manfredi (Florence, 1979)

P.Soterichos — *Das Archiv des Soterichos*, ed. S. Omar (*Papyrologica Coloniensia* 8; Opladen, 1979)

P.Strasb. — *Papyrus grecs de la Bibliothèque Nationale et Universitaire de Strasbourg* V. 5, edd. J. Schwarz et al. (Strasburg, 1979)

P.XV Congr. — *Actes du XVe Congrès International de Papyrologie* 2. *Papyrus inédits*, edd. J. Bingen and G. Nachtergael (*Papyrologica Bruxellensia* 17; Brussels, 1979)

Pallas, *Monuments paléochrétiens* — *Les monuments paléochrétiens de Grèce découverts de 1959 à 1973*, by D. Pallas (*Sussidi allo studio delle antichità cristiane* 5; Vatican City, 1977)

[*Pap.Brux.* 15] — *La collection Marcel Hombert* I. *Timbres amphoriques et autres documents écrits acquis en Egypte* (*Papyrologica Bruxellensia* 15; Brussels, 1978)

Pap.Brux. 16-19 — *Actes du XVe Congrès International de Papyrologie*, edd. J. Bingen/G. Nachtergael (4 vols; *Papyrologica Bruxellensia* 16-19; Brussels, 1978-1979) [see also under *P.XV Congr.*]

[Pflaum, *Narbon.*] — *Les fastes de la province de Narbonnaise,* by H.-G. Pflaum (*Gallia* Suppl. 30; Paris, 1978)

Pfuhl/Möbius — *Die ostgriechischen Grabreliefs,* edd. E. Pfuhl/H. Möbius (2 vols, and 2 vols of plates; Mainz am Rhein 1977-1979)

Pircher — *Das Lob der Frau im vorchristlichen Grabepigramm der Griechen*, by J. Pircher with G. Pfohl (*Commentationes Aenipontanae* 26, *Philologie und Epigraphik* 4; Innsbruck 1979)

Reilly, *Slaves* — *Slaves in Ancient Greece. Slaves from Greek manumission inscriptions*, by L.C. Reilly (Chicago, 1978)

RIS — *Römische Inschriften in der Schweiz,* ed. G. Walser (3 vols; Bern, 1979, 1980)

[*SB*] — *Sammelbuch griechischer Urkunden aus Ägypten* XIII. *Index zu Bd. XII*, ed. H.-A. Rupprecht (Wiesbaden, 1979)

SEG — *Supplementum Epigraphicum Graecum* 29 (1979 [1982])

SGPI — *Sammlung griechischen PtolemWer-Inschriften*, by M.L. Strack; originally published as an appendix in his *Die Dynastie der PtolemWer* (Berlin, 1897; repr. separately Chicago, 1976)

SIA II — *Inscriptiones Atticae, Paraleipomena et Addenda. Supplementum Inscriptionum Atticarum* II, ed. A.N. Oikonomides (Chicago, 1979)

SIA III — *Inscriptiones Atticae, Paraleipomena et Addenda. Supplementum Inscriptionum Atticarum* III, ed. A.N. Oikonomides (Chicago, 1979)

Speidel, *Dolichenus* — *The Religion of Iuppiter Dolichenus in the Roman Army*, by M.P. Speidel (*EPRO* 73; Leiden, 1978)

Tibiletti, *Lettere* — *Le lettere private nei papiri greci del III e IV secolo d. C. Tra paganesimo e cristianesimo,* by G. Tibiletti (*Pubblicazioni della Università Cattolica di Milano, Scienze filologiche e letteratura* 15; Milan, 1979)

Tod, *PGE* — *The Progress of Greek Epigraphy 1937-1953,* by M.N. Tod (repr. from *JHS* 54 [1939] - 75 [1955]; Chicago, 1979)

Tsigaridas, *Κατάλογος* — *Κατάλογος χριστιανικῶν ἐπιγραφῶν στὰ μουσεῖα τῆς Θεσσαλονίκης*, by E. Tsigaridas and K. Loverdou-Tsigarida (*Μακεδονικὴ Βιβλιοθήκη* 52; Thessalonica, 1979)

Tuchelt, *DenkmWler* — *Frühe DenkmWler Roms in Kleinasien. BeitrWge zur Überlieferung aus der Zeit der Republik und des Augustus* I. *Roma und Promagistrate,* by Kl. Tuchelt (*Istanbuler Mitteilungen* Beiheft 23; Tübingen, 1979)

[Wouters, *Gramm.Pap.*] — The *Grammatical Papyri from Graeco-Roman Egypt. Contributions to the Study of the 'Ars Grammatica' in Antiquity*, by A. Wouters (*Verhandelingen van de koninklijke Akademie voor Weterschappen, Letteren en Schone Kunste van België, Klasse der Letteren* 41.92; Brussels, 1979)

Abbreviations

Other abbreviations follow standard conventions, except where altered for clarity.

Journals — as in *L'Année philologique* (but note, e.g., *RAC* = *Reallexikon für Antike und Christentum,* not *Riv*(*ista*) *di Ant*(*ichità*) *Crist*(*iana*)).

Papyrological works — as S.R. Pickering, *Papyrus Editions* (North Ryde, N.S.W., 1984).

Epigraphical works (for which no standard guide exists) — according to generally used conventions (see LSJ), preceded where necessary by *I.* (e.g., *I.Apollonia*).

Ancient authors, biblical and patristic works — generally as in LSJ, BAGD, and Lampe (see below).

Some other abbreviations used, occasionally frequently, in this volume:

Aland, *Repertorium* — K. Aland, *Repertorium der griechischen christlichen Papyri* I. *Biblische Papyri* (Berlin, 1976)

BAGD — Bauer/Arndt/Gingrich/Danker, *A Greek-English Lexicon of the New Testament and other Early Christian Literature* (Chicago, 1979^{2})

BDF — Blass/Debrunner/Funk, *A Greek Grammar of the New Testament and other Early Christian Literature* (Chicago, 1961)

Bib.Pat. — *Biblia Patristica. Index des citations et allusions bibliques dans la littérature patristique* (Centre d'analyse et de documentation patristiques; 3 vols; Paris, 1975-81)

CIJ — J.B. Frey, *Corpus Inscriptionum Judaicarum* (2 vols; Rome, 1936, 1952); vol. 1 repr. with Prolegomenon by B. Lifshitz (New York, 1975)

CPJ — V.A. Tcherikover, A. Fuks, et al., *Corpus Papyrorum Judaicarum* (3 vols; Cambridge [Mass.], 1957-64)

DACL — Cabrol/Leclercq, et al., *Dictionnaire d'archéologie chrétienne et de liturgie* (15 vols; Paris, 1907-1953)

Deissmann, *Bible Studies* — G.A. Deissmann, *Bible Studies* (ET: Edinburgh, 1923; repr. Winona Lake, 1979)

Deissmann, *LAE* — G.A. Deissmann, *Light from the Ancient East* (Grand Rapids, 1980^{4})

ECL — Early Christian Literature

Foraboschi — D. Foraboschi, *Onomasticon Alterum Papyrologicum* (4 vols; Milan, 1966-71)

Gignac, I/II — F.T. Gignac, *A Grammar of the Greek Papyri of the Roman and Byzantine periods* I. *Phonology*; II. *Morphology* (Milan, 1976, 1982)

Hatch and Redpath — Hatch and Redpath, *A Concordance to the Septuagint and other Greek Versions of the Old Testament* (Oxford, 1897; 2 vols. repr. Graz, 1954)

Lampe — Lampe, *A Patristic Greek Lexicon* (Oxford, 1961, repr.)

LSJ/LSJ Suppl. — Liddell/Scott/Jones, *A Greek-English Lexicon* (*Oxford*, 1940^{9}, repr. with supplement ed. E.A. Barber, 1968)

LXX — Septuagint (Rahlfs' edition)

Migne, *PG*/*PL* — Migne, *Patrologia Graeca*/*Patrologia Latina* (Paris, 1857-87/1844-64)

MM	— Moulton and Milligan, *The Vocabulary of the Greek Testament* (London, 1930; repr.)
Naldini	— M. Naldini, *Il Cristianesimo in Egitto. Lettere private nai papiri dei secoli II-IV* (Florence, 1968)
N/A^{26}	— Nestle/Aland, *Novum Testamentum Graece* (Stuttgart, 1979^{26})
NB	— F. Preisigke, *Namenbuch . . . enthaltend alle . . . Menschennamen . . . in griechischen Urkunden . . . Ägyptens . . .* (Heidelberg, 1922)
Peek, *GVI*	— W. Peek, *Greichische Vers-Inschriften* I (Berlin, 1955)
Solin, *GPR*	— H. Solin, *Die griechischen Personennamen in Rom. Ein Namenbuch* (3 vols; Berlin, 1982)
Spicq, *NLNT* I/III	— C. Spicq, *Notes de lexicographie néo-testamentaire* (2 vols, plus Suppl. vol.; *Orbis Biblicus et Orientalis* 22.1-3; Göttingen, 1978-1982)
Spoglio	— S. Daris, *Spoglio lessicale papirologico* (3 vols; Milan, 1968)
UBS^3	— *The Greek New Testament* (New York; United Bible Societies, 1975^3)
Turner, *Typology*	— E.G. Turner, *The Typology of the Early Codex* (Pennsylvania, 1977)
van Haelst	— J. van Haelst, *Catalogue des papyrus littéraires juifs et chrétiens* (Paris, 1976)
WB	— F. Preisigke, et al., *Wörterbuch der griechischen Papyrusurkunden* (Heidelberg, et alibi, 1924-)

An asterisk (*) beside a reference in the bibliography for an entry signifies, where more than one edition exists, which has been reprinted; otherwise the *editio princeps* has been followed.

Dates are AD unless otherwise marked. IV^1 = 'first half IVth century', IV^2 = 'second half IVth century'; etc.

Textual sigla used are as follows:—

α̣β̣	— letters not completely legible
. . . .	— 4 letters missing
- - - -	— indeterminate number of letters missing
[αβ]	— letters lost from document and restored by editor
[±8]	— about 8 letters lost
<αβ>	— letters omitted by scribe and added by editor
≪αβ≫	— editorial correction of wrong letters in the text
(αβ)	— editor has resolved an abbreviation in the text
{αβ}	— letters wrongly added by scribe and cancelled by editor
[[αβ]]	— a (still legible) erasure made by scribe
\`αβ´	— letters written above the line
α´ or ᾱ	— letter stands for a numerical equivalent
v., vv., vac.	— one, two, several letter spaces left blank (*vacat*) on document
m.1, m.2	— first hand (*manus*), second hand
front/back	— writing along the fibres/across the fibres of a papyrus sheet.

The **format of most entries** is as follows:—

Item no. Short title
Provenance Date
editio princeps
Text
Brief descriptive comment
Bibliography (very selective, normally including only actual references to the text)
Translation
Comment

Where a text is not quoted in full or at all this format is somewhat modified, but should still be clear (e.g., Section B, *Minor Philological Notes*). Within the larger subdivisions of the Review items have usually been arranged chiefly by genre (e.g., letters, epitaphs), and within that, chronologically. This arrangement does not apply to Section B, where entries are alphabetical; nor, of course, to Section F (*Varia*). In Section C entries follow canonical book order with liturgical/credal material at the end. Where an entry deals with a diversity of texts, it is placed in the genre grouping to which the first, usually the main, text belongs.

The **indexes** are to be regarded as an integral element in the Review. They will usually provide the easiest means of discovering which biblical words and passages are discussed, what ideas and institutions, etc.

Item numbers are in bold type throughout the Review, for cross-referencing.

The following individuals have contributed separate entries to this volume: D.C. Barker (**21**), R.J.S. Barrett-Lennard (**123**), P.M. Brennan (**27**), A.L. Connolly (**23-26**, **29**, **30**, **45**, **55**, **66**, **72**, **78**, **91**, **96**, **97**, **103-106**, **108**, **117**, **134**), E.A. Judge (**80**), R.A. Kearsley (**14**), R.Oster (**19**), R. Tracey (**111**). All other entries are by the undersigned. Translations have been made by the author of the entry.

For those wishing to refer to this Review, the **abbreviation** *New Docs 1979* is suggested.

Acknowledgements

Advice from colleagues on specific matters is acknowledged in the appropriate entry. Detailed responses to draft entries by the consulting editors and by E.A. Judge have both averted numerous *faux pas* and suggested new leads to pursue. A.L. Connolly, a colleague specialising in *koine* philology, has collaborated in the production of this volume to a far greater extent than the score of entries by him may indicate. He undertook a considerable amount of the preliminary reading of texts in the earliest stage of preparation for the book. He was also the problem-solver as our project switched over to being written on an NEC APC machine, using Gramedit software. Very considerable advice and help was provided about the latter by its developers in North America, D.A. Carson and P. Miller. E. Smith learned Greek especially to equip herself to handle keying-in of the entries. The accuracy and speed which she attained was a marked help in getting the manuscript finished by early 1987. M.F. Curran, P. Geidans and S.P. Swinn helped with proof-reading. As ever, staff of the Macquarie University Library have been cheerfully efficient in dealing with the needs of the project. Finally, although too young to appreciate anything yet about this book except that 'Dad is always busy', *New Docs 1979* is dedicated to our three children, with the wish that they may one day gain as much enjoyment out of their own vocation as their father derives from his.

G.H.R. HORSLEY

* * *

Dr C.J. Hemer, Research Fellow at Tyndale House, died in Cambridge on 14 June, 1987, at the age of 57. E.A. Judge writes, 'Colin Hemer came to Macquarie as a Visiting Fellow for two months in 1980. It was his idea that we should publish the *New Documents* series to re-awaken interest in the relevance of documentary texts for the language and culture of the NT. In his own work he showed how one might open up a bridge of understanding from Classical into NT studies. Until this disciplinary gulf was crossed there was bound to be an important element of historical realism missing. His book, *The Letters to the Seven Churches of Asia in their Local Setting*, appeared at Sheffield in 1986, and he leaves close to completion a two-volume work on the historicity of Acts.'

A. NEW TESTAMENT CONTEXT

1. The silversmiths at Ephesos

Ephesos — time of Claudius, or later

ed. — *I.Eph.* VI (1980) 2212

ἡ σορός ἐ<σ>τιν καὶ
ὁ περὶ αὐτὸ τό-
πος καὶ τὸ ὑπό-
γειον ἡρῷον Μ.
Ἀντωνίου Ἑρμεία
ἀργυροκόπου νεο-
ποιοῦ καὶ Κλαυδίας
Ἐρ̣ωτίου γυναικὸς αὐτοῦ.
ἐν ᾗ σορῷ οὐδεὶς
βληθῇ ἢ οἱ προγε-
γραμμένοι· εἰ
δέ τις τολμήσει
πτῶμα βάλαι ἢ
γράμμα ἐκκόψαι,
δώσει τοῖς ἐν Ἐφέσῳ
ἀργυροκόποις ✕ ,α.
ταύτης τῆς σοροῦ κήδε̣ται τὸ συνέδριον τῶν ἀργυροκόπων καὶ καθιέρωσεν Ἐρώτιν ✕ πεντακόσ<ι>α
<ἐ>δόθη δὲ ὁ κλῆρος (*leaf*) ≪μ≫ηνὶ ≪ς´≫ ἡ(μέρ̣ᾳ) (*leaf*) η´ ἱσταμένῃ. (*leaf*)

(*Col.*1) This tomb and the area around it and the subterranean vault belong to M. | Antonius Hermeias, silversmith, *neopoios*, and Claudia daughter of Erotion, his wife. (*Col.*2) No one is to be put in this tomb | except the aforementioned. If anyone does dare to put in a corpse or excise this text, | he shall pay to the silversmiths at Ephesos 1000 denarii. (*Beneath both cols.*) Responsibility for this tomb rests with the association of silversmiths, and Erotion dedicated 50,000 denarii. The legacy was provided in the 6th month, on the appointed 8th day.

This text reflects a common phenomenon: a legacy provided by a relative of the deceased is managed by some corporate body to ensure the proper upkeep of the grave-site. But in this particular case the managing society is the silversmiths' guild at Ephesos, known above all for the instigation (at the behest of one of its members) of the demonstration in the theatre recorded at Acts 19.23-41.

MM, followed by BAGD, offers mainly papyrus attestations of ἀργυροκόπος (NT, only Acts 19.24), the only inscription adduced being *SIG*[3] 1263 from Smyrna. With the publication of the *I.Eph.* Repertorium we may now provide examples far 'closer to home'. As well as the text quoted above, the following may be noted from *I.Eph.*, all generally of Imperial date unless further specified:

— II.425.10, honorific inscription set up by the ἀργυροκόποι (for this reading, which corrects the text as printed in vol.II, see the ed. n. *ad* III.636) for Tib. Claudius Aristio, a man much mentioned in inscriptions as well as in Roman literature (e.g., Pliny, *Ep.* 6.31.1). Some dateable events for this man place him in Domitian's reign, others in the time of Trajan. On this man see **14** below.
— II.547, the word ἀργυροκόπων ('place of the silversmiths') on two columns in Arkadiane street, and so not far from the theatre and the Lower Agora.
— II.585, an acclamation: αὔξει τ[ὸ] πλῆθος [τ]|ῶν ἀργυ|ροχόων | τῶν ζών|τω[ν], 'may the guild of silversmiths flourish . . .!' Ἀργυροχόος is to be taken as synonymous with ἀργυροκόπος.
— II.586, dedication to Artemis, Antoninus Pius, καὶ τοῖς [ἀργυ]|ροκόποις (5-6).
— III.636 (III[1](?)), τὸ ἱερὸν συνέδριον τῶν ἀργυροκόπων honours its *prostates*, Claudius Acilius Julius (on προστάτης cf. **122** below).
— VI.2441 (n.d.), very fragmentary epitaph mentioning τὸ συνέδριον] τῶν ἀργυροκόπων [. . ., (*l*.3).
— Too late for inclusion in *I.Eph.* is D. Knibbe/B. İplikçioğlu, *JÖAI* 55 (1984) Hauptblatt 130-31 (III[1], time of Elagabalus?), a complete, brief honorific inscription set up by οἱ ἀργυροχόοι of Ephesos to honour the proconsul Valerius Festus, their *soter* and benefactor.

In our text the deceased is a *neopoios* (see the index vol. to *I.Eph.*, VIII.1, for many attestations of this word); for these officials see **28** below. Still worth reading is W.M. Ramsay's discussion of an inscription — now repr. as *I.Eph.* V.1578 — which mentions a Demetrios who is a *neopoios*: *The Church in the Roman Empire before AD 170* (London, 1903[7]) 112-45, especially 113-34, where he rejects the conjecture of Hicks that this Demetrios was the silversmith mentioned in Acts 19, with the participle ποιῶν at 19.24 being a confused reminiscence of νεοποιῶν.

The noun πτῶμα (*l*.13) occurs very frequently in this formula about adding other cadavers to private tombs. In the NT the word is found several times with this meaning: Mk. 6.29 (par. Mt. 14.12); 15.45; Mt. 24.28; Rev. 11.8, 9. MM, s.v., supplies two epigraphical examples of π. = 'corpse', to both of which BAGD refers without providing further documentation. The word is quite common: merely from *I.Eph.* the following funerary texts may be listed in addition to the text printed above. Some come from the *territorium* of Ephesos, various sites in the Kaystros valley to the NE. The list includes: VI.2222, 2226, 2304; VII, 1.3215, 3216, 3224, 3225, 3260 (largely restored, but not in doubt because of the presence of the formula), 3287A, 3291, 3322. From Yeniköy, west of Nikaia, we may add *I.Nikaia* II, 1.766, a grave relief (III) belonging to Aurelia Longina and her family, on which the formula is repeated (*l*.8).

The establishment of foundations for various purposes is well attested among the inscriptions of Ephesos. Cf. B. Laum, *Stiftungen in der griechischen und römischen Antike* (Leipzig, 1914) vol. I, nos. 74-77. Pride of place must go to *I.Eph.* Ia.27 (VI.6027; and see the *Addenda et corrigenda* supplement to *I.Eph.* Ia-VII, 1 [1981], p.2), erected in 104 AD by C. Vibius Salutaris. One feature of this long text — 568*ll.* survive; text, translation and commentary in J.H. Oliver, *The Sacred Gerusia* (*Hesperia Suppl.* 6; Princeton, 1941) 55-85 — is treated at **14** below. This inscription is of considerable interest for the information it yields about the organisation, status and importance of the silver trade at Ephesos (e.g., *ll.*470-476, where it is laid down that a silver statue of Augusta Homonoia Chrysophoros, dedicated to Artemis, is to be placed above the theatre seating where the *hieronikai* sit at every assembly of the people; cf. *ll.*437-43). More superficially, a gauge of the importance of the silver trade at Ephesos is provided by the word-index in *I.Eph.* VIII.1, where a dozen ἀργυρο- words are listed spread across over 40 inscriptions. The Vibius Salutaris inscription is one among several texts which disclose explicitly that the theatre was the regular place for the *ekklesia* (*ll.*22, 54, 91-92, 123, 557-58, etc.). Cf. *I.Eph.* Ia.28, a bilingual inscription of the same year concerning the dedication of silver statues κα|τ' ἐκκλησίαν ἐν τῷ θεάτρῳ (*ll.*21-22; = *omni ecclesia* | *in theatro* [*ll.*8-9]). The Vibius Salutaris inscription receives brief mention in Guarducci's chapter on foundation inscriptions, *EG* III

(Rome, 1974) 246-62 (at 258-59). More recently, C.P. Jones, *JRS* 73 (1983) 116-25 (cf. *BE* [1984] 402), has associated *I.Eph.* VII, 1.3334 with 3214, an inscription (I fin.) in which a certain Peplos establishes an association of *herostai* to perpetuate his memory with certain rites and to oversee the proper upkeep of his tomb. Among other foundation documents we may note I.Eph. VII, 1.3216 (Tire, n.d.), establishing the arrangements for an annual funeral banquet (εὐωχίαν, *l.*6; this NT *v.l.* at Jude 12 — no entry in MM — is also attested by *I.Eph.* Ia.26.10, 16 [time of Commodus]; VII, 2.3860.9-10 [n.d.], 4123.15 [n.d.], these last two establishing a foundation to memorialise the deceased).

Returning to the tense situation narrated in Acts 19, it should not be overlooked that those working in other crafts were also involved (Acts 19.25); by way of analogy, in *SIG*[3] 1263 (from Smyrna; noted above) the guild is ἡ συνεργασία τῶν ἀργυροκόπων καὶ | χρυσοχόων (*ll.*1-2). R. Oster has provided (*per litt.* 5 Nov., 1986) the following note: 'Artifactual evidence shows the participation of related industries in the production of devotional items for the goddess Artemis. There is a small lead idol of Artemis, clearly a devotional object like those made by the Ephesian silversmiths, in the Vienna Museum: W. Oberleitner, *Funde aus Ephesos und Samothrake* (*Kunsthistorisches Museum, Wien, Katalog der Antikensammlung*, II; Vienna, 1978), 57, no.22. To my knowledge, no ναοὺς ἀργυροῦς 'Αρτέμιδος (Acts 19.24) have been discovered, but there are artifactual remains of a miniature marble temple of Artemis, patently manufactured for devotional purposes (Oberleitner, 56, no.20). There are also gems engraved with iconography of the Artemis cult which had devotional significance (ibid., 57, no.24, fig.37)'. Oster also notes Lucian, *Alex.* 18 as roughly contemporary literary testimony for the use of silver devotional objects in newly founded cults.

While on the subject of silver objects a rescript of the joint emperors Marcus Aurelius and Lucius Verus in 162/3 refers to silver images of themselves: ὃ δὲ πρῶτον ἡμῖν ἐκοίνωσας, | τὸ περὶ τῶν ἀργυρῶν εἰκόνων, πρᾶγμα ὡς ἀληθῶς τῆς ἡμετέρας συνχωρήσε|[ως] προσδεόμενο≪ν≫, 'the question which you first communicated, the one concerning the silver images, is a matter that truly needs our agreement', *I.Eph.* Ia.25.8-10 (pls. 25-27; =*I.Eph.* VI.2023). Though we are dealing with small statues here, coinage carried the εἰκών of the emperor, the nub of the trap-question to Jesus about paying taxes (Mk. 12.16 = Mt. 22.20; Lk. 20.24). In this quotation the verb κοινόω may be noted in passing: this is not the sense it carries in the NT, where it always has the secondary notion 'make/declare common, viz. unclean' (Mt. 15.11; Acts 10.15, etc.). Neither MM nor BAGD provides any documentary parallel for such a usage. A little further on *I.Eph.* Ia.25 provides the following imperial decision: τὰς οὖν εἰκόνας τῶν αὐτοκρατόρων, ἃς ἀποκεῖσθαι λέγεις ἐν τῷ συνε|[δρί]ῳ τούτῳ, παλαίας, ἑνὶ μὲν λόγῳ πάσας δοκιμάζομεν φυλαχθῆναι τοῖς ὀνόμασιν, ἐφ' ο|[ἷς] γέγονεν αὐτῶν ἑκάστη, εἰς δὲ ἡμετέρους χαρακτῆρας μηδέν τι τῆς ὕλης ἐκείνης | [μ]εταφέρειν (*ll.*11-14), 'so as for the statues of the emperors which you mention are stored away in this *synhedrion*, old (as they are), to put it briefly we approve that they have been preserved for the names for which each of them (the statues) was made; and (we approve) of you changing nothing at all of that material into our likenesses'. For the literal use of ἀπόκειμαι cf. in the NT Lk. 19.20. Λέγω + acc. and infin. is well attested in the *koine*: for NT references see BDF §397(3). The passage gives us an excellent further example of χαρακτήρ to illustrate its sole NT occurrence at Heb. 1.3.

The motive of the craftsmen for precipitating the Acts 19 incident (portrayed by the writer as a near-riot and lynching) was economic, the protection of their jobs (Acts 19.25, 27). The riot/strike of the bakers' guild at Ephesos (*I.Eph.* II.215) provides an analogy to what happened here to this extent, the involvement of the guilds in engendering urban strife: . . ὥστε συμ]|[βαί]νειν ἐνίοτε τὸν δῆμον ἰς ταραχὴν καὶ θορύβους ἐνπίπτειν διὰ τὴν σ[ύλ]|λ̣ο̣γον καὶ ἀθρασίαν τῶν ἀρτοκόπων, ἐπὶ τῇ ἀγορᾷ, κτλ, (1-3), 'with the result that it happens that sometimes the *demos* falls into confusion and uproar because of the assembling together and insolence of the bakers at the agora'. This inscription, which is a proconsular decree and was in fact found at Magnesia on the Maeander, was treated in a classic article by W.H. Buckler in id./W.M. Calder (edd.), *Anatolian Studies Presented to W.M. Ramsay* (Manchester, 1923), 30-33 (pl.2). The *I.Eph.* text of this inscription includes some readings suggested more recently, mainly by R.Merkelbach, *ZPE* 30 (1978) 164-65. But the issue concerning the silversmiths is made more emotive by its being couched primarily in terms of a threat to the status of Ephesian Artemis. The narrative in Acts sits comfortably with the suggestion that this threat to religious (and economic) stability was perceived to have come from Jews (cf. Acts 19.34). Whether or not the author of Acts correctly interpreted (19.23) the disturbance as the result of successful inroads being made by Paul and his companions, it is probably too early for the Christians to have been identified as a separate group by those outside Judaism who had no close contact with Christians.

I.Eph. II.215, mentioned above, has two words worth noting to parallel the single occurrence of each in the NT. At *ll.*5-6 the proconsul says that he issues his edict as a way of bringing the strikers to their senses: ἀναγκαῖον ἡγησάμην διατάγ[ματι] | αὐτοὺς σωφρονίσαι. The sole documentary text noted by BAGD, s.v. σωφρονίζω — NT: only at Tit. 2.4 — refers by another nomenclature to the same papyrus as MM's *P.Oxy.* 1 (1898) 33 *back* (late II). This inscription is quoted by MM, s.v. πειθαρχέω, to illustrate the use of the verb with the dative, as in the NT at Acts 27.21; but the line number on which the word occurs is 7 not 8.

For a coppersmith at Ephesos note *I.Eph.* II.554, Διογένου[ς] | χαρκωμα|τᾶδος, '(work place) of Diogenes the coppersmith'; the form χαρκ- is equivalent to χαλκ- (see ed. n., ad loc.). In the NT the only person with such a trade, Alexander (2 Tim. 4.14) is described by the briefer term χαλκεύς.

2. ' . . . in memory of her'

Kyzikos in Mysia — I, second quarter
ed.pr. — E. Schwertheim, *ZPE* 29 (1978) 213-28 (pls. 11, 12)

Ὁ δῆμος
καὶ οἱ πραγματευόμενοι ἐν τῇ πόλει
Ῥωμαῖοι
Ἀπολλωνίδα Προκλέους διά τε τὴν
τῶν γονέων καὶ τὴν τοῦ ἀνδρὸς ἀρετὴν
καὶ τὴν ἴδιον αὐτῆς σωφροσύνην.
I [- -] Στρατίου
[- -]
[- -]ΤΟΣ
[- -]
[- -]
[- -]\ΟΤΟΣ
[- -]
[- -] _\ΟΥΜΕΝ
[- -]Ο̣ΤΟΣ
[- -] π̣ολλάκις
[- - - - - - -πρεσβεύσαντος πρὸς το]ὺς ἡγεμόνας
[- -] κ̣αὶ αὐτοῦ
[- -σ]τ̣εφανηφορίαις

[- - - - - - - - - - - - - - - - - - - ἀποδ]εδειγμένου, βίον τε
[- - - - - - - - - - - - - - - - - - -] δ̣ημοκρατικώτατον
[- - - - - - - - - - - - - - - - - - μ]η̣τρὶ σωφρονεστάτῃ
[- - - - - - - - - - - - - - - - - - -]δι τῇ Καβηρίδου
[θυγατρί - - - - - - - - - - - διὰ] παντὸς χρόνου
[- - - - - - - - - - - - - - - γυναῖκ]α οὐ μόνον φιλανδροτάτην
[ἀλλὰ καὶ - - - - - - - - - - - - τῶ]ν ποτε γυναικῶν
[-] ⁻ΟΝΟΙΣ καὶ ἐν οἷς
[-] ἀνανκαιοτάτοις
[καιροῖς - - - - - - - - - - - - - - - -]σα καὶ ἐπιδοῦσα
[-]νους καὶ παραμύθιον
[-] κοινὴν ἐλπίδα τίθεται
[-] τ̣αύτης ἄχθεται μὲν
[- - - - - - - - - - - - - - - - - - - π]έ̣νθος, οἶται δὲ δεῖν
[- - - - - - - - - - - - - - - - - - - τ]οῦ ἀνδρὸς καὶ τῶν τέκνων
[- - - - - - - - - - - καὶ εἰς ἀμοι]β̣ὴν τῆς περὶ ἐκείνην ἀρετῆς
[- - - - - - - - - - - - - - - -]Λ̣ Α̣ . . . · *v.* ἐφ' οἷς συνδραμὸν
[εἰς - - - - - - - τὸ τῆς] π̣όλεως [π]λ̣ῆθος προσέταξε
[τοῖς ἄρχουσι πᾶσι τὰ]ς̣ προσηκούσας αὐτῇ τειμὰς εἰσηγήσασθαι·
[δι' ἃ δὴ δεδόχθαι τῷ δήμῳ·] π̣ενθῆσαι μὲν πανδημεὶ πάντας
[τοὺς κατοικοῦντας τὴν] π̣όλιν ἄνδρας τε καὶ γυναῖκας,
[κλεισθῆναί τε τὰ ἱερ]ὰ̣ καὶ τὰ τεμένη καὶ πάντας τοὺς
[ναοὺς - - - - - - - - μέχρι] τῆς ἐκκομιδῆς, ἀκολουθῆσαί τε
[τῇ κηδήᾳ τοῦς πρυτανεύ]ο̣ντας καὶ τοὺς ἐπωνύμους
[ἄρχοντας καὶ τούς τε] π̣αῖδας καὶ ἐφήβους καὶ τοὺς πολείτας
[καὶ τοὺς ἐλευθέρους ἄνδρα]ς̣ τῆς πόλεως πάντας, ὁμοίως δὲ
[καὶ τὰς παρθένους] κ̣αὶ τὰς πολείτιδας καὶ τὰς λοιπὰς
[τὴν πόλιν κατοικούσας ἐλευ]θ̣έρας γυναῖκας·
II καὶ ἐπειδὴ τὴν ἐν τοῖς κάλλεσιν ἐκκομιδὴν ἔχει συνκεχωρημένην,
δεδόσθαι αὐτῇ καὶ ἐνταφὴν ἐν τοῖς προγονικοῖς τοῦ ἀνδρὸς
αὐτῆς μνήμασιν τοῖς οὖσιν ἐπὶ τοῦ μεγάλου λιμέν[ο]ς·
τοὺς δὲ πρυτάνεις τοὺς πρυτανεύοντας τὸν μῆνα τὸν ᾿Ανθεστηριῶνα
στεφανοῦν αὐτὴν ἀνὰ πᾶν ἔ[το]ς ἐν τοῖς ᾿Ανθεστηρίοις τῇ δωδεκάτῃ
καὶ τῇ τρισκα̣[ιδ]ε̣κάτῃ χρυσῷ στε[φά]νῳ, ἀνανγέλλοντος τοῦ ἱεροκήρυκος
μετὰ τοὺ̣[ς προ]τε[τ]ειμημένους· *v.* ῾Ο δῆμος στεφανοῖ ᾿Απολλωνίδα Προκλέους
διά τ̣ε τὴν τῶν γονέων καὶ τὴν τοῦ ἀνδρὸς ἀρετὴν
καὶ τὴν ἰδίαν αὐτῆς σωφροσύνην ἀϊδίῳ τῷδε τῷ στεφάνῳ·
κατασκευάσαι δὲ αὐτῆς καὶ ἀγαλματοθήκην ἐν τῷ Χαριτησίῳ,
εἰσερχομένων ἐκ τῆς ἱερᾶς ἀγορᾶς ἐν δεξιᾷ, ἐν ᾗ καὶ ἀναστῆσαι
αὐτῆς ἄγαλμα· *v.* ἐπεὶ δὲ καὶ τὴν ἱερωσύνην εἶχεν τῆς ᾿Αρτέμιδος
τῶν Πυθαϊστρίδων, εἰς μαρτυρίαν τῆς περὶ τὰ ἱερὰ αὐτῆς εὐσεβήας
τῇ ἑβδόμῃ τοῦ ᾿Αρτεμισιῶνος ἀνὰ πᾶν ἔτος, ὅταν συνελθῶσιν
εἰς τὸ Χαριτήσιον αἵ τε ἱέρηαι καὶ αἱ Πυθαϊστρίδες κ(α)ὶ αἱ ἱεροποιοί,
στεφανοῦν αὐτῆς τὸ ἄγαλμα· *v.* ἵνα δὲ καὶ τῆς σωφροσύνης αὐτῆς
ὑπόμνημα ἐνφανὲς ᾖ πάσῃ τῇ πόλει, ἀνατεθῆναι αὐτῆς ἄγαλμα
ἐν ἑνὶ τῶν οἰκημάτων τῆς τετραγώνου ἀγορᾶς ἐν τῇ στοᾷ
τῇ ἀπὸ τῆς ἀνατολῆς, τῷ ὄντι μεταξὺ τοῦ τε τῶν τειμητῶν ἀρχήου
καὶ τοῦ ἀγορανομίου, κοσμηθέντι δὲ αὐτῷ χρῆσθαι εἰς τὸν ἀεὶ χρόνον

ἀρχήῳ τόν τε κοσμοφύλακα καὶ τοὺς ἀεὶ κοσμοφυλακήσοντας·
τοὺς δὲ ἀπογραφομένους πρὸς τὸν κοσμοφύλακα τὰς τῶν γάμων
συντελήας στεφανοῦν ἐπάνανκες τὸ ἐν τῷ ἀρχήῳ καθιερωμένον
III 'Απολλωνίδος [ἄγαλμα· *v.* ἀναστῆσαι δὲ αὐτῆς]
καὶ ἄλλα ἀγάλμ[ατα, - - - - - - - - - - - - - - - -]
'Αφροδείτης τῆς [- - - - - - - - - - - - - - - - - -]
ἐν τῷ ναῷ τῆς 'Αρτ[έμιδος - - - - - - - - - - - -]
καὶ ἀνδριάντα ἐν τ[- - - - - - - - - - - - - - - - -]
τόπῳ ταῖς νενεικηκυίαις [- - - - - - - - - - - - - - - - -]
αὐτὴν ὑστερεῖν ΤΕ[- - - - - - - - - - - - - - - - -]
καὶ συνγενίσιν δεδ[όσθαι - - - - - - - - - - - - - -]
ἐν τῷ τεμένει τῆς 'Α[- - - - - - - - - - - - - - -]
ἀνδριάντα ἐπίχρυσ[ον ἀναστῆσαι ἐν ᾧ ἂν]
οἱ προσήκοντες αὐτ[ῆς προαιρῶνται τόπῳ·]
ὑπό τε τὰ (ἀ)γάλματ[α ἐπιγραφὴν ἀναγράψαι τήνδε·]
'Ο δῆμος καὶ οἱ πραγμ[ατευόμενοι ἐν τῇ πόλει]
'Ρωμαῖοι 'Απολλωνί[δα Προκλέους διά τε τὴν τῶν]
γονέων καὶ τὴν τοῦ ἀ[νδρὸς ἀρετὴν καὶ τὴν ἴδιον]
αὐτῆς σωφ<ρ>οσύνην· [*v.* ἀναγράψαι δὲ καὶ τὸν ταμίαν]
ἐπὶ τὸ μνημῆον τόδε [τὸ ψήφισμα· *v.* τὸ δὲ ψήφισμα]
εἶναι περὶ φυλακῆς [τῆς πόλεως.]

Large block of marble (1.41 max. surviving width x .675H m.), found in the village of Hamamlı. *Ll.*1-6 form a separate panel in the centre top portion of the face, with lettering more than twice the size of the letters in the rest of the text. *Ll.*7-88 (letters 1cm. high) are arranged in three columns, to the left of the central panel and running the full height of the stone (*col.*I, *ll.*7-47), roughly below the central panel (*col.*II, *ll.*48-70), and to the right of it (*col.*III, *ll.*71-88) running down to a level just below that of *l.*6. A considerable portion of *col.*I is broken away, as is the right side of *col.*III. There are few errors, and there is evidence of correction (e.g., τόπῳ was omitted and later added in the blank space to the left of *col.*III, at *l.*76).

Bib. — L. Robert, *CRAI* (1978) 553-56; BE (1978) 393; *SEG* 28 (1978) 953; *M. Sève, *BCH* 103 (1979) 327-59 (pls. 1-3); *BE* (1980) 424; E.A. Judge, *TynB* 35 (1984) 21-22.

The *demos* and the Romans engaged in business in the city honoured Apollonis, daughter
5 of Prokles, because of her | parents' virtue and that of her husband, and because of her own moderation.
(*Col.*I; *ll.7-35 too lacunose for translation*)
36 In view of these things at a meeting in the . . . the citizenry instructed all the magistrates to inaugurate appropriate honours for her. As a result, indeed, the *demos* has resolved:
40 the totality of all | men and women who live in the *polis* are to be in mourning. The temples, sacred areas and all the shrines are to be closed . . . until her burial. The presidents and the eponymous magistrates are to follow the cortège, as also are the boys,
45 ephebes, citizens, | and all free males in the city; likewise unmarried girls, female citizens, and the remaining free women who live in the city. (*Col.*II) Since she has been granted the privilege of a funeral dressed in beautiful (clothes [i.e., dressed in purple]), she is to
50 be interred in her husband's ancestral | vault, near the Great Harbour. The presidents

who hold the presidency for the month of Anthesterion are to crown her (i.e., her statue) annually with a gold crown at the Anthesteria festival on the twelfth and thirteenth days, while the sacred herald proclaims, after those who have been previously honoured: 'The *demos* crowns Apollonis, daughter of Prokles, | because of her parents' virtue and that of her husband, and because of her own moderation, with this perpetual crown'. A place for her statue is to be provided at the Charitesion, on the right side where people enter from the Sacred Agora in which also stands her statue. And in view of the fact that she also held the priesthood of Artemis | among the Pythaistrides, as a testimony of her piety concerning religion, on the seventh day of Artemision annually when the priestesses, the Pythaistrides and the temple overseers assemble in the Charitesion, they are to crown her statue. Additionally, in order that the remembrance of her moderation may be visible to all the city, a statue of her is to be erected | in one of the rooms on the Square Agora on its eastern portico, which lies between the office of the *timetai* and the *Agoranomion*. The *kosmophylax* and his successors in this magistracy are to have the use of this office in perpetuity once it has been decorated. Those who register with the *kosmophylax* the formalisation of their marriage | are required to garland the statue of Apollonis which is dedicated in the office. (*Col.*III) And other statues of her are to be set up . . . of Aphrodite . . . in the shrine of Artemis; . . . | and a statue in . . . (*ll.76-79 too lacunose for translation*) | A gilded statue is to be set up in whatever location her relatives choose. Beneath the statues the following inscription is to be recorded: 'The *demos* and the Romans engaged in business in the city honoured Apollonis, daughter of Prokles, because of her | parents' virtue and that of her husband, and because of her own moderation'. The treasurer is to record this decree on her tomb. May the decree be for the safeguarding of the city.

This inscription, originally attached to the tomb of the deceased, gives us a very detailed example of a posthumous honorific decree. Though badly lacunose in *col.*I and partly so in *col.*III, its very unadorned detailing of the honours which are to be provided for her is one indication of a first-century date (Schwertheim, 226). Sève (334-35) is able to narrow this date down to the second quarter of I AD by his consideration of two factors: the letter shapes, some of which (especially *rho*) are distinctive; and relations between the Romans and Kyzikos. Sève's article is virtually a simultaneous *ed.pr.* for, although it appeared after Schwertheim's and takes account of it, both were in the press at the same time. Between these two articles the inscription for Apollonis has been accorded a very comprehensive initial treatment.

The inscription consists of the wording of the motion passed by the citizens (*ll.*1-6, repeated at *ll.*54-56, 83-86), followed by a decree which first mentions the past contributions of Apollonis' nusband or father (to *l.*20) and those of herself (*ll.*25-30). It then proceeds to set out in detail the ways in which her memory will be kept before the city: arrangements for the funeral (*ll.*39-50), an annual crowning of her statue and public recitation of the motion at the Anthesteria festival (*ll.*51-56), the erection of a special edifice within the temple of the Graces to house another(?) statue of her, which is also to be crowned every year by holders of the priesthood she once had (*ll.*57-63). A further statue of her is to be placed in a room adjoining the Square Agora, which is to be refurbished (68) and serve as the premises of the *kosmophylax*. Those who come to register their marriage are to crown the statue (*ll.*63-71). From what survives of the fragmentary *col.*III it is clear that other statues are to be erected in various locations, the supporting bases of which are to carry the text given as *ll.*1-6 (*ll.*71-86). The treasurer is responsible for having the present entire decree carved on Apollonis' tomb (*ll.*86-87).

Two other posthumous honorific inscriptions have been included in previous Reviews, and both belong also to I AD Asia Minor. *New Docs 1978*, **9** (Ayazviran in Lydia, 96/7) is a brief tribute by family members and co-participants in a private religious association in which the deceased Apollonios is accorded gold crowns. That document is the result of private initiative. The text reprinted at *New Docs 1978*, **18** (Iulia Gordos, 75/6) provides a number of parallels with the new Kyzikos inscription. It, too, is issued by the city and by the Romans involved in commerce there. The dead man's civic contributions are enumerated (magistracies, embassies), and his domestic relations are praised. The cortège is to be escorted to the tomb by the citizens; and the dead man is to have a statue and other remembrances set up. Yet the new Kyzikos text is on a quite different scale in the details it sets forth concerning the memorialising of Apollonis. The frustrating feature in this case is its lacunose state in *col.*I: we can only infer in very general terms something of what she did to earn this posthumous recognition.

It is normal that, where such an honour is voted for a woman, male relatives will also figure large. Hence in the brief motion Apollonis' parents and husband are honoured for their *arete*, she for her *sophrosyne*. Entirely clichés as they are, they suggest what we may in any case glean from the surviving words in *ll.*7-20, that her husband or father takes precedence in having his achievements recounted. The masculine participle in *l.*20 shows that this section of the decree extends at least to there. That this man had participated in embassies to the Roman governor is implied by ἡγεμόνας (17); and there was apparently more than one occasion when he held the stephanephorate (19). This widely-attested magistracy in Asia Minor appears from other evidence to have been at least partly a religious post at Kyzikos, and its holders were looked to for the provision of liturgic benefactions to the city (Sève, 352). The adjective δημοκρατικώτατος in its political sense is difficult to fit in here (21); but Sève (336 n.26) provides examples from Plutarch where it means 'affable, unaffected in manner', a usage not listed in LSJ.

By *l.*25 this very lacunose section has turned to Apollonis herself. Her domestic faithfulness is noted (φιλανδροτάτην, 25) as so complete that it is explicit she was pre-eminent among women (26); for this adjective cf. *New Docs 1978*, **11**. It appears that she may have provided some benefaction at a critical time (27-29). It goes without saying, of course, that the very existence of such an inscription for a woman implies that she had wealth at her disposal. Yet this section which deals with Apollonis' qualities appears to end by *l.*30; its brevity contrasts with the preceding lines devoted to her male relative. For by *l.*30 the decree has moved on to offer official consolation to her family. The noun παραμύθιον here occurs in the NT only at Phil. 2.1, for which MM (followed by BAGD) notes one papyrus and one verse inscription. This new attestation is nearer in date to the time of the NT and is well worth recording for a new MM entry. Spicq, *NLNT* II.658 n.4 and 659 n.3, provides a few further documentary references for the noun. The name Paramythios occurs at Pfuhl/Möbius II.2139 (provenance unknown, within Bithynia(?), III[1]; pl.307; = *SEG* 1695). On the related noun παραμυθία see **75**, below. The grief which Apollonis' death evoked is emphasised (32, 33). As for ἀμοιβή — a reasonable restoration in view of the following words — it is often used where a city honours someone in return for philanthropic benefactions conferred.

*Ll.*37-38 signal that the decision to honour Apollonis was one of popular initiative. She is to be accorded a state funeral (39-47), at which there is public and general mourning by all free people, adult and child, citizen and non-citizen of Kyzikos. The procession to her tomb is officially organised. The closure of the temples (41-42) is not unparalleled, but is certainly a rare distinction to be accorded. Sève notes (342 and n.58) for comparison *CIL* XI, 1 (1888) 1421.20-24 (Pisa) a Latin text in which the temples are closed as a mark of respect at the death of C. Caesar.

The wording in *l.*48 suggests what we may have in any case suspected: that this is not the first time Apollonis has received public recognition. The decision, taken before her death, to grant her a special funeral is by no means unique. What is unparalleled, however, is the mention of the funeral clothing in which her body is to be dressed. Sève argues persuasively (342) that τὰ κάλλη refers to the right to wear purple clothes, a privilege reserved not for just any benefactor of the city. If it is wondered why a public decree should concern itself with the place of burial (*ll.*49-50), the answer lies in the rarity with which burials were allowed inside a city. Graveyards were situated outside. Yet occasionally, and as a special honour, individuals were accorded the right of burial within the city (so Sève, 344). K.L. McKay has suggested to me (*per litt.*) that in *l.*48 we may not necessarily have a periphrasis for the perfect. With the sense 'have received', ἔχω/ἀπέχω is common in papyrus sales formulae; and this meaning is found in the NT at Rom. 5.1. The literal sense of the line in our text would be, 'she has received the funeral . . . as agreed'. Ἔχω + perf. pass. participle is a rare construction in both literary and non-literary texts, but is attested in the Classical period at Hdt. 1.60.1. As McKay correctly points out at *TynB* 23 (1972) 42-43, N. Turner's treatment — in Moulton's *Grammar*, III (Edinburgh, 1963) 88-89 — of periphrastic forms of the perfect is misleading; see also McKay, *BICS* 12 (1965) 17.

So much for the burial itself. The decree next addresses the question of the perpetuation of Apollonis' memory, and this occupies the remainder of the text (51-88). Among the less common honours awarded to her are the decision to house one of her statues in a specially constructed edifice, apparently a free-standing *aedicula*, roofed over but with no side-walls to allow the statue to be visible. The word ἀγαλματοθήκη (57) has not been attested before. The other rarity among these posthumous privileges is recorded in some detail in *ll.*63-71. A room apparently already in use for some other function is to be redecorated for the use of the *kosmophylax*, with whom newly-weds are to register their marriage. It is required (70) of the latter when they come to do this that they crown the statue of Apollonis which is specially placed there. This public official has been attested hitherto only in one other inscription which is also from Kyzikos (Sève, 354). For ἀπογράφομαι (69) Sève provides a number of documentary parallels, useful for illustrating the NT at Lk. 2.3, 5. The use of passive κοσμέω at *l.*67 of the decorating of a building provides a good parallel for Mt. 12.44; Lk. 11.25, and 21.5. This text should not be taken as typical for its evidence of the registration of marriages with a civil authority. Athenian law, for example, did not require this, though dowries could be registered on a voluntary basis (Sève, 354-55).

In the following very fragmentary lines (71-81) provision is made for the erecting of other statues, all of which will carry (82) the dedication whose wording forms *ll.*1-6. In contrast to ἀνδρίας (75, 80), the usual term for the statue of a mortal, ἄγαλμα (72, 82) is normally used of a marble statue of a god or hero. On this distinction see L. Robert, *Hellenica* 11/12 (Paris, 1960) 124 n.2. This would mean that the restoration αὐτῆς at the end of *l.*71 is unlikely. Yet in *l.*82 ἄγαλμα seems to be employed as a general term for any type of statue.

Associations exclusively for women, such as the Pythaistrides (60, 62) appears to be (judging from its name), are rare. This cult of Artemis Pythia whose priesthood Apollonis held (59-60) is well attested at Miletos, the mother-city of Kyzikos; and Sève suggests (358) that it came to Kyzikos when the latter was established as a colony of Miletos. This association, which had a college of priestesses, members and *hieropoioi* (62; the term is attested of women only in one other inscription, again from Kyzikos: Sève, 358), meets in the temple of the Charites. Cults to the Graces alone (i.e., not in association with other deities) are rare; and the implication of *ll.*57-59 is that this is a building of some size (so Sève, 356-57).

In addition to the information which this text yields *en passant* about various cults and civil magistracies — the inscription provides us with our first attestation of a *timetes* (= Latin *censor*) at Kyzikos, for example (*l*.66) — we learn something of the topography of the I AD city. Sève's article is useful on this question; he identifies the 'Great Harbour' (*l*.50) with the western of the two ports of Kyzikos (349-51). More than two agoras are known; here we have the names of two: the 'sacred' (i.e., the civic?) and the 'square' agoras (*ll*.58, 65; cf. Sève, 346-49).

A few lexical items may be noted for the NT or ECL. For σωφροσύνη (6, 56, 63, 86; cf. 22) cf. **56** below. The verb πραγματεύομαι (2, 83), common enough in inscriptions, occurs in the NT only at Lk. 19.13; BAGD gives no specific examples. The context in which ἀναγγέλλω (53) occurs offers a useful parallel to Acts 19.18, ἀναγγέλλοντες τὰς πράξεις αὐτῶν. At Heb. 7.11, 12, 24 ἱερωσύνη is used of the Levitical priesthood; but a text like this present one shows that it is the general term (*l*.59) with no such restrictions of meaning placed upon it except by context. Cf. the similar use of ἱερατεύω discussed below at **62**. For ἐμφανής (64) see **52**. The phrase at *l*.66, ἀπὸ τῆς ἀνατολῆς, is worth noting in relation to Rev. 21.13; and μεταξύ + gen. (66) provides an excellent parallel for Mt. 23.35 (cf. BAGD, s.v., 2a). The presence of the noun συγγενίς in the fragmentary *col*.III, at *l*.78 — cf. Lk. 1.36 — confirms the view (noted at BAGD, s.v.) that the word was disavowed by the Atticists. Μνημεῖον (87) is very common in the Gospels. In the last clause of the text, φυλακή is used somewhat unusually, not as in the NT. With ἐκκομιδή at *ll*. 42, 48 we may compare the related verb ἐκκομίζω, only found at Lk. 7.12 in the NT.

'Αρχεῖον here (66, 68, 70) refers to a building, an office, not as in ECL to the records stored there. Christophilopoulos, *Νομ. 'Επιγ.* II.9-69, is a wide-ranging essay on archives (both public and private) in Greek cities; cf. *SEG* 1723. *I.Eph*. VII, 2.3850 (Kürdülü, 45km. NE of Ephesos, II init.) is a typical example of a well-preserved private document, a copy of which was lodged in the ἀρχεῖον at Hypaipa. This funerary monument provides very full details of who may be buried in the tomb, and in exactly which section of it. In excavations beneath an ancient mosaic floor at Nea Paphos in W. Cyprus over 11,000 clay seals have been found: see I. Michaelidou-Nicolaou, *Actes Constantza*, 413-16. The date range of these items is mid II BC-I AD. They were once attached to papyrus texts, rolled up, tied and sealed with a signet ring impression into clay. This find must comprise material from a public archive. For the metaphor of sealing a book (i.e., a roll) in the NT cf. Rev. 5.1, 2, 5, 9; 6.1, etc.

A further useful parallel to the new Kyzikos text is the exactly contemporary *I.Eph*. III.614B (mid-I). This is also a posthumous honorific inscription, for Laevia Paula; although much briefer (23*ll*.) than that for Apollonis, this complete text follows a similar pattern. Some points of comparison are the enumeration of her husband's achievements as a reason for honouring her (*ll*.10-13), and the *boule*'s authorisation of the burial procedures with a civic herald reading the city's motion at the funeral (*ll*.13-19). On another face of the same stone there survives in good condition *I.Eph*. III.614C, providing similar honours for Laevia's husband, M. Antonius M. *f*. Albus, at his death. Here there is no mention of the wife (except that he is to be buried in the grave previously authorised for her, *ll*.24-26).

Honours accorded a wife because of her husband's achievements are by no means reserved to a posthumous context. For example, *I.Eph*. III.683A honours Herakleides Didymos, and then proceeds to praise his wife Ammion for her *sophrosyne* 'and on account of her husband Herakleides' goodwill towards the *demos*', καὶ διὰ τὴν τοῦ ἀνδρὸς αὐτῆς | 'Ηρακλείδου πρὸς τὸν δῆμον εὔνοιαν (*ll*.11-12). As well as the standard terms in which Herakleides is praised we may note a less common reason at *l*.5, 'the depth of his knowledge', διὰ τὴν ἐν τῷ μαθήματι δύναμιν. Given the context of his being honoured for his piety towards Artemis in the preceding line, this statement may be an acknowledgement of his learning in matters about cult practice involving the goddess. The noun μάθημα is found in ECL, but not in the NT.

The financial patronage accorded by women to the ministries of Jesus and Paul has often been noted for the NT. Apollonis provides us with a signal analogy, exactly contemporary, though her beneficence is not directed to individuals. On patronage by women see further **122**, below.

3. A society of friends

Saittai in Lydia 170/1

ed.pr. — S. Bakır-Barthel/H. Müller, *ZPE* 36 (1979) 171-72 no. 29 (pl.6)

ἔτ(ους) σνε´ μη(νὸς) Ἀπ[ελλαίου]
η´ Γλάφυρον Δ[ιογέ-]
νους οἱ συνβιω[ταὶ τὸν]
ἑαυτῶν φίλ[ον̣ ζήσαν-]
τα ἔτη ιη´.

White marble stele, with a wreath.

Bib. — *SEG* 1188; *BE* (1980) 466.

In the year 255, month of Apellaios, on the 8th day, the associates (honoured) Glaphyros son of Diogenes, their friend, who lived | 18 years.

A considerable number of funerary inscriptions from the necropolis at Saittai have been published in recent years. The article by Bakır-Barthel/Müller includes over two dozen, whose numbering follows on from an earlier group of texts published by G. Petzl, *ZPE* 30 (1978) 249-76. A further 22 have been published by H. Malay/Y.Gül, *ZPE* 44 (1981) 81-90 (pls.7-9). One of the most interesting features among these short epitaphs is the erecting of posthumous honorific monuments by the deceased's fellow-craftsmen or associates in some club. Trade guilds represented in the group of inscriptions published by Bakır-Barthel/Müller include, e.g., no.28 (165/6; pl.6; = *SEG* 1186), ἡ σύνοδος τῶν τεκτόνων (carpenters), and no.30 (183/4; pl.6; = *SEG* 1191), ἡ συνεργα|σία τῶν λεινοργῶν (linen workers). In no.27 (156/7; pl.6; = *SEG* 1185), the group is left undefined: ἡ συμβίωσις τὸν | ἴδιον συμβιωτὴν ἐ|τείμησαν (*ll.*3-5). Similarly, the nature of the association to which Glaphyros belonged is not made explicit in the text printed above. From the subsequent publication of Saittai epitaphs, Malay/Gül, no.7 (162/3; pl.7; = *SEG* 31 [1981] 1026) is erected by ἡ πλατεῖα τῶν | λεινουργῶν, 'the street of linen-workers'.

Of particular note in the initial text above, for Glaphyros, is the term φίλος used here of a member of an association. No.31 in the same article (194/5; pl.6; *SEG* 1195) provides another instance: after the date the text reads ἡ συνεργα|σία τῶν πιλοποιῶ|ν τὸν φίλον Ἀττα|λιανὸν ἐτείμησαν | ζή(σαντα) ἔτ(η) κζ´ (2-6), 'the felt-makers' co-operative honoured their friend

Attalianos who lived 27 years', an inscription which yields our first evidence from Lydia of this particular industry. In the Malay/Gül article, their no.19 is also relevant to note (223/4; pl.9; = *SEG* 31 [1981] 1038): (date) ἐτείμησαν οἱ | φίλοι τὸν φίλον Ἀρ|τεμυλλιανὸν | ζή(σαντα) ἔτ(η) κη′ (2-5), 'the friends honoured their friend Artemyllianos who lived 28 years'. This delimited use of φίλος serves as a parallel, at least at a general level, for 3 Jn 15, ἀσπάζονταί σε οἱ φίλοι. ἀσπάζου τοὺς φίλους κατ' ὄνομα. At Acts 27.3, where Paul is allowed to go πρὸς τοὺς φίλους, it is unlikely that a similar sense should be pressed; though perhaps it cannot be ruled out altogether. The further references noted as having this meaning by BAGD, s.v., 2a, are rather more doubtful. These latter passages, Jn 11.11 and 15.14, 15, were so interpreted by H.J. Cadbury, himself a member of the Society of Friends, a title which preserves the same semi-technical use. The presence of this usage in the Johannine corpus alone in the NT is suggestive; for if 3 Jn was written at Ephesos in Lydia, with Saittai not so far away, perhaps the writer adopted this local currency of the word as it suited his own purposes well.

A note to *SEG* 1188 provides several more references to this use of φίλος in inscriptions from Lydia, though part of the reference has become confused. For 'C. Naour, *ZPE* 44 (1981) 89 no.19' read 'H. Malay/Y. Gül, . . .'; and add 'C. Naour, *ZPE* 44 (1981) 34 no.15'. Similar confusion occurs in *SEG*'s n. ad 1191.

4. A gladiator meets his match

Kyzikos in Mysia — II

ed. — L. Robert, *Les gladiateurs dans l'Orient grec* (Limoges, 1940; repr. Amsterdam, 1971) 228 no. 293.

Ἑορτὴ ἡ γυνὴ αὐτοῦ καὶ Ἀσκλη-
πιάδης ὁ ὑὸς αὐτοῦ Δανάῳ δευ-
τέρῳ πάλῳ Θρᾳκῶν μνείας
χάριν.
[ἐ]ννεάκις πυκτεύσας ᾤχετο εἰς
Αἴδην.

Pedimental-shaped stele, showing a bas-relief scene of a funeral banquet, with the deceased and his son reclining and his wife seated to the right. The family dog sits in front of the couch. Below this, the text, with a gladiator's helmet on a pedestal to its right.

Bib. — Pfuhl/Möbius II.1267 (pl.188); *E. Schwertheim, *Die Inschriften von Kyzikos und Umgebung* I (*IK* 18; Bonn, 1980) 144 (incl. further bibliography).

Heorte his wife and Asklepiades his son to Danaos, a member of the second squad of Thracians, as a memorial. | Having been in combat nine times he went to Hades.

This brief epitaph for a gladiator is entirely typical of the funerary monuments erected for these men. Robert's book, first published nearly half a century ago, remains the definitive treatment. Though reprinted unchanged, Robert has provided many supplementary notes on the subject in subsequent volumes of *BE*, and several longer discussions in certain volumes of his *Hellenica*.

From the present year's reading a considerable troupe of gladiators has been netted. Pfuhl/ Möbius' corpus provides most, with an entire section devoted to them: II.1196-1268, eight of them not previously published. Not all are funerary monuments, in fact. For comment on aspects of this group of seventy-odd items see *BE* 13 (pp.416-18). One of these, no.1247 (Pergamon, late Imperial; pl.187; Robert, no.263), is for a certain Chrysomallos; another gladiator with this same name is memorialised in an inscription reprinted as *I.Nikaia* I.276 (not dated; Robert, no.81). A considerable number of these monuments carry striking relief sculptures depicting the gladiator with his net, trident, or other arms, or combatants in action. Several gladiator inscriptions appear in *I.Eph.*, too: IV.1170-82 (cf. *BE* [1981] 465); V.1620, 1621; VII, 2.4346. Of these nos.1171 (time of Septimius Severus), 1182, 1620 (another copy of no.1182, both from the time of Commodus?), 1621 (*c.*154-70), and 4346 indicate that the gladiator troupe was funded by an asiarch. A statue base for T. Flavius Montanus (*I.Eph.* VI.2061, no.II) refers to gladiatorial combats and beast hunts — μ]ονομαχίας καὶ κυνήγια (*l.*10) — in an unmistakably early (Trajanic) II AD context.

The colourful wording of *I.Nikaia* I.277 makes the following Imperial-period epitaph for Melanippos of Tarsos more memorable than most of the texts for these men (pl.24; Robert, no.298).

τὸν θρασὺν ἐν σταδίοις ἐσο-
[ρᾷ]ς με νέκυν, παροδεῖτα, Ταρ-
[σέ]α ῥητιάριν, δεύτερον πάλον,
[Μ]ελάνιππον. οὐκέτι χαλκε[λ-]
άτου φωνὴν σάλπιγγος ἀκο[ύω]
[οὐ]δ' ἀνίσων αὐλῶν κέλαδον ἀ-
[εθ]λῶν ἀνεγείρω· φασὶν δ' Ἡρα[κ-]
[λ]έα δυοκαίδεκα ἆθλα τελέσσ[αι]·
[τα]ὐτὰ δ' ἐγὼ τελέσας τρισκαιδέκατ[ον]
τέλος ἔσχον.
Θάλλος καὶ Ζόη Μελανίππ[ῳ]
μνείας χάριν ἐκ τῶν ἰδίων
ἐποίησαν.

I who was brimful of confidence in the stadium, now you see me a corpse, wayfarer, a *retiarius* from Tarsos, a member of the second squad, Melanippos (by name). No longer do I hear the sound of the beaten-bronze | trumpet, nor do I rouse the din of flutes during one-sided contests. They say that Herakles completed 12 labours; but I, having completed the same (number), | met my end at the thirteenth. Thallos and Zoe made this for Melanippos as a memorial at their own expense.

For πάλος in these two texts quoted above see Robert, 28-31. On Ταρσεύς in the latter see **87** below; in that entry another epitaph for a gladiator, from Cilicia, is reprinted. The phrase φωνὴ σάλπιγγος (or other grammatical combinations of these words) is found with some frequency in the NT: 1 Cor. 14.8; Rev. 1.10; 4.1; 8.13.

One word in the first inscription deserves brief comment, πυκτεύω (*l.*5). In the NT this verb occurs once, metaphorically, at 1 Cor. 9.26, where Paul speaks of 'making every punch count' in his ministry: οὕτως πυκτεύω ὡς οὐκ ἀέρα δέρων. Robert has discussed this verb, *RA* (1929) 24-42 (= *Opera Minora Selecta* I [Amsterdam, 1969] 691-708), showing that it is by no means confined to a boxing context, but is employed as a technical term in texts relating to gladiators. MM cites one example only of this verb, a reference taken over in BAGD's entry. This text is repr. with a better reading as Pfuhl/Möbius II.1196 (Tralles, II; pl.181; Robert, no.149): - - - ὁ πυκτεύσας πολλάκις ἐν στ̣[αδίοις], | [νίκην δ' ἀ]π' ἐμοῦ λάβεν οὐδείς. Μοῖρα δ' [ἐμὲ] | [δάμασε]ν, κτλ (*ll.*1-3), 'I fought often in the stadium, and no one gained a victory over me.

But Fate conquered me, . . .'. In no.1197 (pl.181; Robert, no.148) the participle [πυκτεύ]ων has been restored at the beginning of the text. These two epitaphs, which share the same provenance and date, are companion pieces to such an extent — as the plate shows — that Robert suggests (*BE* 13, *ad fin.*) that they emanated from the same atelier and honour two combatants perhaps killed in the same *spectaculum*. Other instances of πυκτεύω in these gladiatorial memorials are: Pfuhl/Möbius, II.1228.3 (Tripolis in Lydia, late Imperial; pl.184; Robert, no.146) for Chrysopteros who succumbed in his thirteenth contest; 1249 (Ankyra region, later Imperial; pl.186; Robert, no.89), the *retiarius* Kallidromos whose eighth contest was his last; and 1263 (Alabanda, late Imperial; pl.187; Robert, no.169), epitaph for Polyneikes who died in his twentieth bout, not because he lacked the skill but because his old body was overborne by a younger man: εἰκοστὸν πυκτεύσας, | οὐχὶ τέχνῃ λειπφθεὶς, | ἀλλὰ νέος γεραρὸν σῶ|μα κατειργάσατο (*ll*.4-7).

It is clear that these epitaphs use the verb in a formulaic way to indicate the number of contests fought. This is borne out by the other examples in Robert, *Gladiateurs* (all of Imperial date): nos.20 (Edessa), 30 (Plotinopolis), 76 (Amasia), 141 (Philadelphia in Lydia). Note also a text from Amphipolis, partly quoted at *Gladiateurs*, 16 n.4, πολλάκι πυκτεύσας καὶ πολλάκι νικήσας. Perhaps the most interesting inscription involving a gladiator which carries this verb is Robert no.65 (Gortyn). This honorific text employs the participle — abbreviated as πυκ(τεύσας) — nine times in its list of the places where the man fought, the names of his opponents, and the outcome on each occasion: a victory (νεικῶ), a convincing victory (νεικῶ λαμ(πρῶς)), or a draw (στάνς; note the Latin loanword).

5. 'Physician, heal yourself . . .'

Stratonikeia in Caria — Later II

ed.pr. — W. Peek, *AM* 56 (1931) 123-24 no. 7 (*non vidi*)

Κυπρογένους Παφίης ὁ ἐπώνυ|μος ἐνθάδε κεῖμαι,
ἠΐθεος κοῦρο[ς], | προλιπὼν ὥραν βιότοιο.
θρέψας μοι Κάρπος στήλην μνήμης ἐπέθη|κεν,
πάντα ὀλέσας καρπὸν τῶν ἐπ' ἐμο[ὶ] | καμάτων.

πολλοὺς Ἐπαφρόδε<ι>τε σ[ὺ] | μὲν νοσέοντας ἔγειρας,
εἰητρὸς | γεγαὼς πᾶσιν ἑταιρότατος,
ἀμ|φότερον τέχνην τ' ἀγαθὸς καὶ ἤθεα | κεδνός,
τῆς γὰρ ἐπιστήμης μαλλο|φρονεῖν ἔμαθες
ἀλλ' οὔτοι σεαυτὸ[ν] | νούσου ἐδυνήσαο σῶσαι,
ἰητρῶν γὰρ | ἔφυ Μῦρα κραταιοτέρα.

Metrical inscription surmounted by bust of the deceased carved in relief. Beneath the bust stand two birds. Vertical bars mark line divisions on the stone. In *l*.10 read Μοῖρα.
Bib. — Peek, *GVI* 1934; *Pfuhl/Möbius II.2112 (pl.304).

Taking my name from the Cyprus-born lady of Paphos here I lie, a god-like youth, after abandoning prematurely (προ-) the bloom of life. Karpos who reared me set up the remembrance stele for me, having lost all the fruit of his toils for me.

| Epaphroditos, you raised many who were sick; having become a doctor you were most companionable to all, both good at your craft and diligent in character, for you learned to be wiser than your knowledge. But you could not save yourself from sickness, | for Fate is stronger than doctors.

The two distinct epigrams are redolent of Homeric language, as so often in the Roman period. Unlike the two epigrams on a funerary stele for Theodosia (**114** below) there is not much overlap between the pair here. Epaphroditos has died of some illness; though his death is premature, to call him a *kouros* (2) is an idealising feature, since the second epigram indicates that he must already have been some years into adult life if already a practising doctor. He is a *threptos*, and the point of *l*.4 — apart from the play on words with the name of the man who brought him up — is that Karpos has worked to secure a good future for Epaphroditos, but now it is to no avail. (It is equally possible that Karpos' purpose in rearing his *threptos* was to ensure his *own* security in old age.)

The phrase νοσέοντας ἔγειρας (5) has no exact parallel in the NT. The verb used most commonly of Christ healing the sick is θεραπεύειν (Mt. 4.23; 9.35; 10.1, etc.), whereas ἐγείρω in such a context mostly is reserved for raising the dead (Mt. 10.8; 11.5; 14.2, etc.). The only NT instances of ἐγείρω in the sense of raising from a sick bed (and thereby curing the ill person) are the incident involving Peter's mother-in-law, where Jesus προσελθὼν ἤγειρεν αὐτὴν κρατήσας τῆς χειρός· καὶ ἀφῆκεν αὐτὴν ὁ πυρετός, κτλ (Mk. 1.31); and Jas. 5.15, ἐγερεῖ αὐτὸν (*sc.* τὸν κάμνοντα) ὁ κύριος. As K.L. McKay points out to me, the use of the imperative at Mt. 9.5, 6, preserving the literal sense in a healing context, shows how the word is undergoing a semantic shift.

Epaphroditos is praised for his good bedside manner (if this is the sense of *l*.6), his professional skill and his ethics (7). The point of *l*.8 appears to be that his was no mere book-learned knowledge, but he relied to good effect upon his intuition in diagnosing and treating patients. The verb μαλλοφρονεῖν is not listed in any of the lexica (LSJ, Lampe, Sophokles); it may be wondered whether there is an error in the text: μᾶλλο<ν> φρονεῖν, 'for rather than knowledge, you learned to be wise'.

The sentiment of *l*.9 will immediately bring to mind the words ἰατρέ, θεράπευσον σεαυτόν (Lk. 4.23), which appears from its context to have been an aphorism in general currency which Jesus used for the occasion. But the actual wording in the epigram may recall us to quite a different context in the Synoptics: ἄλλους ἔσωσεν, ἑαυτὸν οὐ δύναται σῶσαι (Mk. 15.31 = Mt. 27.42; cf. Lk. 23.35). The epigram then concludes with the gnomic comment that no one can overcome fate, here couched in wording appropriate to the deceased.

The name Epaphroditos is exceedingly common — at Rome the thirteenth most frequently attested Greek personal name (Solin, *GPR* III.1439) — and it may be appropriate to list attestations noted from the texts culled for this present Review:

SEG 152, *col*.V.36, 93 (Athens, 175/6), ephebic list.

1354 (area of Prusias ad Olympum, III init. AD [*sic* — *SEG* misprints as BC]), epitaph set up by E. to his wife Eia (= Pfuhl/Möbius II.1708).

IGUR 1254 (Rome, dated II by Solin, *GPR* I.323), Marcus Clodius E. sets up epitaph for himself, his wife, his freedmen καὶ ἀπελευ<θ>έρων ἀπε[λ]|ευ<θ>έροις (5-6).

1366 (Rome, n.d.), very fragmentary metrical epitaph.

Pfuhl/Möbius I.244 (Rhodes, Imperial period), E.'s epitaph for his *threptos* Zosimos.

639 (east of Patara in Lykia, Imperial period), epitaph for E.

700 (probably Nisyros, I BC), epitaph for E.

735 (Byzantion, I BC), epitaph for E., aged 4.

740 (Kyzikos, 'late' [Imperial]), epitaph; for text see II, p.569.

876 (Chios, late Hellenistic), epitaph for E.

II.1708 (= *SEG* 1354, above).

1977 (area of Miletopolis, III-IV), epitaph for E.

2112, the text printed at start of this entry.

I.Eph. Ia.20A.57-58, B.46 (54-59 AD), building inscription for fisheries' customs house listing fishermen, including L. Consius E., and [P]omponius Epaphro[ditos]. On this text see *New Docs 1978*, **4**, pp.18-19.

47.69 (time of Commodus), document detailing *prytaneis'* expenses, and listing among the *kouretai* M. Ulp(ius) E. This same man may occur at V.1600.61.

III.666a.22 (n.d.), the *epimeletes* Metrodoros son of E. is mentioned in an honorific text for someone else.

IV.1030.10 (*c.*120 AD), Diadoumenos son of E. in a list of *kouretai.*

V.1602c.5, 24 (n.d.), two men called E. in a list of Dionysiac initiates.

VI.2243 (n.d.), funerary altar for a Corinthian, Cn. Cornelius E., trainer in a gymnasium (ἀλείπτης), set up by another Corinthian.

2272 (n.d.), epitaph for C. Julius [Epaphro]ditos, a member of the *familia Caesaris.*

2502 (n.d.), very fragmentary epitaph for(?) [An]tiochos son of E[paphr]oditos.

2935 (n.d.), fragmentary text mentioning [ ]nius Epaphrodi[tos].

VII,1.3280.2 (n.d.), fragmentary epitaph mentioning E]paphrodi[.

IG XIV *Suppl.* 2468 (Aquae Sextae, n.d.), epitaph for Ἀκῖλις E., a Roman citizen.

Reilly, *Slaves*, 897-907, all ex-slaves in manumission texts from Delphi, Kalymna and various locations in Thessaly, ranging in date from 181/0 BC-II AD.

In the case of Rome, Solin, *GPR* I.320-24, lists 294 attestations of the name, ranging from I BC-III/IV, though with a relative preponderance in I AD. Of these, there is only one person certainly of free-born status; it is a name used for slaves and ex-slaves. At *GPR* III.1360 two further examples are noted, one a citizen from the time of Marcus Aurelius or Commodus.

While the name Epaphras is to be regarded as a hypocoristic form of Epaphroditos (cf. BDF §125(1)), the frequency of attestation shows that it has an independent existence (*pace* Lightfoot, *Comm. on Colossians*, ad 4.27, '(Epaphras') full name would be Epaphroditus, but he is always called by the shortened form Epaphras'). There is no instance known to me where both these names are used of the same person. As the NT commentaries recognise, the Epaphras of Col. 1.7 and 4.12 is certainly to be distinguished from the Epaphroditos of Phil. 2.25 and 4.18. From the 1979 culling we may note the following occurrences of the name Epaphras:

SEG 152, *col.*II.92 (Athens, 175/6), ephebic list.

786 (Thasos, n.d.), epitaph on a sarcophagus fragment.

IGUR 1358 (Rome, dated III AD by Solin, *GPR* I.326), Ἐ<πα>φρᾶς (reading not certain; see Moretti's app. crit.), a citizen of Alexandria, makes a tomb for his wife.

I.Eph. Ia.20A.47, B.25 (54-59 AD), building inscription for fisheries' customs house listing fishermen, E. son of Tryphon, and [. . .]is E.

III. 803.2 (n.d.), honorific text for [ ] | [Ep]aphras, priest for life of the Imperial cult.

VI.2900.16 (n.d.), the name E. on ceramic ware (potter's signature?).

Reilly, *Slaves*, 895, 896, two ex-slaves in manumission inscriptions from Hypata (*c.*40 AD) and Kyretiai (I BC) in Thessaly.

Note also *I.Eph.* IV.1007 (time of Claudius or Nero), a *kouretes* Smyrnaios son of Epaphr[; and V.1945a (n.d.), fragment with Epaphr[; which of the two names was originally here is in both cases indeterminate. Again, Reilly, *Slaves*, 908-09, attest the name Ἐπαφρῶ (Delphi, I AD init., Hypata in Thessaly, *c*.130). Whether this name is complete or is to be taken as an apocopation of Epaphroditos is unclear.

Of 107 attestations listed in Solin, *GPR* I.324-26, the majority are of servile or freed status (only two certain freedmen); there are no examples of free status. Within the chronological spread of I BC-III AD for this name, there is a marked relative predominance of attestation during I AD.

Epaphras is less common than Epaphroditos in the Greek inscriptions (mostly from Asia Minor) surveyed (almost 1:4), compared with the (largely Latin) examples from Rome collected by Solin (1:2.75). This may suggest, as E.A. Judge says in a note to me, that 'it was commoner for hypocoristic forms to penetrate into formal (i.e., tombstone or other public record) use in Roman slave households. This could mean that the hypocoristic form was more commonly used there, or that (if the two names could be concurrently used of the one person) it was less likely to rise to formal use in non-servile families'. With this epigraphical evidence from Asia Minor and Rome, plus some from elsewhere, we may note briefly the Egyptian attestations, where the ratio appears to be considerably higher (8+:1). From Foraboschi and *NB* we find upwards of 40 instances of Epaphroditos (in various spellings), and 5 of Epaphras; the date range is I-III AD.

Although the names Epaphroditos and Epaphras are both sufficiently common for us to think of the latter as having an independent existence by the Roman period — even if in origin it is an apocopation of Epaphroditos — yet there are firm examples of people possessing rarer names who also have a hypocoristic form. In a series of papyrus letters to a certain *dioiketes* called Akousilaus, *P.Tebt.* 2 (1907) 409 (5 AD) addresses him in *l.*1 as Ἀκουσιλάωι, but the address on the back has Ἀκοῦτι. Two years before, another letter to this man, *P.Tebt.* 2.408, has Ἀκουσιλά|ῳ (*ll.*1-2), and Ἀκ[ο]υ[σιλάῳ restored on the back (though the surviving letters could equally have been restored to yield Ἀκ[ο]ῦ[τι). In *P.Tebt.* 2.289 we have a letter (23 AD) probably to the same man, now a *toparch*, addressed as Ἀκοῦτι in *l.*1 (name lost completely on the back). In another letter four years later, in 27 AD, we may well have the same man addressed, *P.Tebt.* 2.462 (description only given of this text by edd.). A further example of this phenomenon is provided by the famous and often-quoted letter of the boy who writes to his father, *P.Oxy.* 1 (1898) 119 (II/III), in which Theon (*l.*1) calls himself Theonas on the back. For further discussion of hypocoristic forms see **101**, below.

The theme of the doctor who could not save himself is found also in an epitaph for a midwife, *IGUR* 1240 (Rome, early Imperial?; pl. on p.96; vertical bars mark line divisions on the stone):

Θ(εοῖς) (*leaf*) Δ(αίμοσι).
Ἰουλία Πρειμιγένει|α μαῖα πολλὰς σώ|σασα γυναῖκας
οὐκ ἔ|φυγον Μοίρας· ζήσα|σα καλῶς ἀνέλυ|σα
εἰς οἶκον, ὅπου | μοι τόπος εὐσεβί|ης ἀπέκειτο.
| Τι. Ἰούλις Ἱέραξ ἀν|νὴρ τῇ γαμετῇ
| μνημοσύνης | ἀγαθῆς ταῦτ' ἐ|πέγραψε φιλῶν.

To the divine spirits. I, Julia Primigenia the midwife, saved many women, yet I did not escape the Fates. After a good life I departed home, where a place of piety has been reserved for me. | Tiberius Julius Hierax her husband inscribed this for his wife for the sake of a good remembrance, since he loved (her).

Since both people are Julian freedmen an Imperial date is at least plausible for this epigram. Childbirth was the greatest cause of adult female mortality in antiquity, though it is by no means explicit on epitaphs. For four Jewish examples where this is mentioned as the cause of death note *CIJ* II.1481, 1510, 1515 (all from Tell el-Yehoudeh, ranging from 25-5 BC), and *IGUR* 1268.9-11 (Rome, n.d.), a probably Jewish epigram for a woman who died 11 days after the birth of her third child. Quite what the statement means at 1 Tim. 2.15, σωθήσεται δὲ διὰ τῆς τεκνογονίας, is not fully clear; but it certainly reflects this same awareness of the high risk always accompanying a confinement. Euripides' Medea gives telling expression to this: '(Males) say that we (women) live a life free from danger at home, while they go off to war. Fools! I would prefer three times over to stand in the battle line than give birth (even) once!' (*Med.* 248-51). The presence of ἀναλύω in *l*.3 parallels Paul's intransitive, figurative use of the verb at Phil. 1.23, τὴν ἐπιθυμίαν ἔχων εἰς τὸ ἀναλῦσαι καὶ σὺν Χριστῷ εἶναι. The inscription also illustrates the use of ἀπόκειμαι at 2 Tim. 4.8, since both passages include the term in a context where a reward is reserved after death. The inscription thus offers informative parallels worth including in a new MM.

It is possible that the *IGUR* inscription quoted just above may also be Jewish, in view of the phrase τόπος εὐσεβίης in *l*.4. T. Muraoka suggests to me, further, that the genitive phrase in *l*.6 is strongly reminiscent of the Hebrew funerary formula, זִכְרוֹנוֹ לִבְרָכָה 'of blessed memory' which, along with its variations, is apparently based on Prov. 10.7, זֵכֶר צַדִּיק לִבְרָכָה, 'the memory of the just is blessed'. Some Jewish inscriptions in Greek quote or allude to this verse as it is found in the Greek versions: the wording of *CIJ* I.201.2-3 (Rome, n.d.), μνήμη δικαίο[υ] σ[ὺ]ν | ἐνκωμίῳ, closely resembles the text of the LXX, μνήμη δικαίων μετ' ἐγκωμίων; and *CIJ* I.370.6-7 (Rome, n.d.) quotes the version of Aquila, μν(ε)ῖα δικαίου εἰς | εὐλογίαν (cf. *CIJ* I.119 and 343). Features of both the LXX text and Aquila are found in *CIJ* I.86.2-5 (Rome, n.d.) which reads μνήμη | δικαίου [ε]ἰς εὐλογίαν | οὗ ἀληθῆ τὰ ἐνκώ|μια, 'may the memory of the just be blessed, whose praises are true'. Cf. *CIJ* I.731c (Kisamos in Crete, IV or V), an epitaph for Sophia the presbyter and *archisynagogissa* of Kisamos, in which occurs the phrase μνήμη δικέας ἰς ἐώνα, '(may) the memory of (her) righteousness (last) forever'. On the woman's title see no.13 in the discussion below at **113**. In *CIJ* I.661 (a trilingual text in Hebrew, Latin and Greek; Tortosa in Spain, VI?) the Hebrew clause זִכְרוֹנָהּ תְּהִי לִבְרָכָה, 'may her memory be blessed', is translated in the Greek by the adjective παμμνη[στός], 'wholly worthy of remembrance' (cf. LSJ *Suppl.*, s.v.). The Latin version of the text has *benememoria* here, which is found as the translation of the Hebrew of Prov. 10.7 in *CIJ* I.629 (bilingual Hebrew and Latin; Calabria, n.d.). A similar expression occurs in a text which may be Christian, *P.Oxy.* 50 (1983) 3599 (9 Dec., 460), a letter addressed to Flavius Dorotheos, υἱῷ τοῦ τῆς ἀρίστης μνήμης Ἰωσήφ, 'son of Joseph of excellent memory' (*ll*.4-5). A VI AD Christian epitaph from Cappadocia for Maria 'the *diakonos* of pious and blessed memory', ἡ τῆς εὐλαβοῦς κὲ | μακαρίας μνήμης διάκο|νος (*ll*.2-4), was reprinted at *New Docs 1977*, **109**. The presence of ΘΔ (= *Dis Manibus*) in *l*.1 of the memorial for Julia Primigenia is no absolute bar to these individuals being Jewish: see *New Docs 1976*, **76**, for several Jewish and Christian texts which include the formula, which is not attested before Augustus.

On the subject of doctors, at Ephesos they formed a 'faculty' centred upon the Mouseion. In *I.Eph.* VI.2304.6 this council is responsible for the upkeep of the tomb of a doctor who was a former member and his wife: τῆς σοροῦ κήδονται τὸ συνέδριον, οἱ ἐν Ἐφέσῳ ἀπὸ τοῦ Μουσείου ἰατροί. Another medical member is referred to at VII, 1.3239 (Imperial period); cf. also IV.1162.9-10 (time of Antoninus Pius; the restoration ἰατροῖς *l*.10 is certain, given the context). An edict of a triumvir, *I.Eph.* VII, 2.4101 (I^2 BC), concerns in part the freeing of doctors from liability to taxes and liturgies (cf. *New Docs 1977*, **2**, p.12).

6. 'Do not disturb' in Nikaian epitaphs

Nikaia II/III

ed. — W. Peek, *GVI* I.1946

[Σε]κοῦνδος ἐσθλὸς χερσὶ κηδευθεὶς πατρὸς
[ἐ]νθάδε κατοικῶ, νέος ὑπάρχων καὶ καλός.
οὐκ ἔστ' ἐν ἀνθρώποισι πλησμονὴ βίου,
ἀλλ' ὅταν ἐπέλθῃ τοῦ βίου τὸ λείψανον,
δεῖ κατθανεῖν σε· τοῦτο γὰρ Μοιρῶν μίτος
ἐπέκλωσεν ἡμεῖν, πάλι μολεῖν πρὸς Ἄϊδαν.
εἰκοσαετὴς γὰρ ὢν ἐγὼ θνήσκω ταχὺ
καὶ τοῦ πόλου τὸ λαμπρὸν ἡλίου σέλας
λιπὼν εἰς αἴθραν ἀλλαχοῦ στρατεύομαι.

Φούλβιος Ἄλφιος τεῦξεν τόδε σῆμα Σεκούνδῳ
τέκνῳ γλυκυτάτῳ· τοῦτο [γὰ]ρ δαίμων πικρὸς
[προ]σέταξεν ἡμεῖν, ἵνα ποιῶ κἂν μὴ θέλω.
[σκύ]λῃ δὲ μηδεὶς ξένος ὑπάρχων τὸν νέκυν·
[τίς] γὰρ θελήσῃ σῶμά μου σκυλᾶν τέκνου,
[δώσ]ει ταμείῳ ἀττικὰς δισχιλίας·
[ἢν δ]ή τις ἄρα γνησίων ἀφ' α≪ἵ≫ματος
[θάπ]τειν θελήσῃ, τοῦτο συγχωρεῖ νόμος.
χαῖρε.

White marble, pediment-shaped stele (55B x 80H cm.). The metre is mostly iambics, but a hexameter occurs at *l.*10.

Bib. — **I.Nikaia* I.195 (pl.17); W. Peek, *Griechische Versinschriften aus Kleinasien* (*ErgWnzungsbWnde zu den TAM*, 8; *Denkschr. Öst. Akad. der Wiss., phil.-hist. Kl.*, 143; Vienna, 1980) 38 no.21a.

Secundus the good, buried by his father's hands, here I dwell, a young man and good-looking. People never have enough of life, but whenever the last portion of life arrives, you | must die. For this is what the Fates' thread spins for us, to come once more to Hades. For in my twentieth year I die quickly, and leaving the sky's radiance, the bright light of the sun, I go on campaign elsewhere in the sky. | Fulvius Alphius constructed this tomb for Secundus his sweetest child; for bitter Malevolence gave me this order, so that I am doing it even though I do not want to. Let no one who is a stranger disturb the corpse; for whoever wants to disturb the body of my child | shall pay two thousand Attic (drachmai) to the treasury. If, in fact, some one of his blood-relatives perhaps wants to bury (someone here), custom concedes this. Farewell.

We appear to have two separate funerary epigrams here (1-9, 10-17) — for other examples see **5** above, and **114** below — though neither yields much information about the father and his deceased son. All we are told are their names, and that Secundus died in his twentieth year. The remaining verses are devoted to gnomic comments (3-6, 8-9, 11-12), and a warning against reuse of the tomb except by relatives.

In the year before *I.Nikaia* I appeared, L. Robert coincidentally published a discussion of the verb σκύλλω in funerary texts, demonstrating that it was employed with distinctive frequency at Nikaia and in epitaphs for Nikaians buried elsewhere. An instance of the latter, *IGUR* II.2 (1973) 837 (Rome, Imperial period), provided the starting-point for his comments, in *CRAI* (1978) 269-76 (cf. *BE* 543; ibid., [1980] 510). The word is by no means confined to a Nikaian context, as he shows with attestations from Thera, Elis, Salamis on Cyprus, Syracuse and Akrai in Sicily, as well as other places in Asia Minor (271 n.7). Furthermore, the presence of the verb occasionally in papyri indicates that it is not limited to use as a formula on funerary monuments. BAGD, s.v., notes only some of the instances quoted by MM. Tibiletti, *Lettere*, no.19 (= *P.Oxy.* 34 (1968) 2727; late III/early IV) provides a further such example: ἐὰν ᾖ σοι ἀβαρές, | σκυλεὶς πρὸς Θέονα τὸν σκυ|τέα καὶ Γερόντιον ποίησον | αὐτοὺς γενέσθαι πρὸς μέ, κτλ (18-21), 'if it's no bother to you, trouble yourself to go to Theon the bootmaker and Gerontios and make them come to me . . .' The aorist passive participle here thus offers a parallel to Lk. 7.6, κύριε, μὴ σκύλλου.

MM fails to provide any epigraphical examples of the verb, though it is more frequently attested in fact on stone than on papyrus. BAGD acknowledges this with the general siglum 'inscr.', but gives references only to papyri. So it may be in order to itemise a number of instances here, from the *I.Nikaia* volumes alone. In so doing, it will emerge how a stock formula in funerary texts becomes adapted by Christians from the fourth and fifth centuries onwards. If not dated more specifically all these texts are to be taken as belonging to the Imperial period. All the texts are from Nikaia or its near environs. A confusing feature is the form σκυλῆ as printed in the *I.Nikaia* volumes and accepted by *SEG*. A note at *SEG* 1295 sees this as from σκυλέω, a verb otherwise not certainly attested. However, σκύλη as the aorist subjunctive of σκύλλω is entirely appropriate in grave warnings/curses (cf. Robert, 271 n.6). Yet there are some texts where futures are used in the following clause (δώσει, etc.); and in these instances σκυλῆ may have been written for σκυλεῖ. In the catalogue below the form given is σκύλη, altering what is usually printed in *I.Nikaia*; but it should be borne in mind that the future may sometimes have been intended. (A good case for the latter can be made out for no.1331 in the list, with the following ἢ θάψει.)

I. 98 fragmentary end of an epitaph, ἐὰν δέ τις | αὐτ[ὴ]≪ν≫ [σκ]ύλη, ἀποδώσε, προ[στείμου] τῷ ταμε[ίῳ . . .

117 sarcophagus (pl.10), εἴ τις δὲ ἂν σκύ[λη, κτλ (*l.*5).

120 (= *SEG* 1295), concluding portion of an epitaph, perhaps from a sarcophagus, for Aurelius Ion and his wife, ἐπὶ [τ]|ῷ μετὰ τὸ κατατεθῆ[ναι] | ἡμᾶς ἀμφοτέρους μ[η]|δενὶ ἐξὸν ἔστα<ι> σκῦλ[α]|ι· ὃς δὲ ἂν σκύλη ἢ ἀπ[αλλ]|οτριώση, δώσει προ[στεί]μου τῷ ἱερωτάτῳ [ταμεί]ῳ ✱ ͵βφʹ (*ll.*5-12).

128 fragmentary conclusion of an epitaph, probably from a sarcophagus, μετὰ] τὸ κατατεθῆναι | [ἡμᾶς μηδένα ἕτ]ερον σκῦλαι τὴν | [σκάφην· εἰ δέ τ]ις σκύλη, δώσει | [τῷ φίσκῳ ✱ ͵β]φʹ καὶ τῇ πόλει ✱ ͵β (*ll.*2-5).

136 (part of this text is printed as Pfuhl/Möbius I.339), fragmentary portion of text from a sarcophagus(?), ὃς ἂν σκύλη, δώσ|[ει, κτλ (*ll.*3-4).

142 (= *SEG* 1331), the verb is fully restored.

193 (III; pl.17; = *SEG* 1293), grave for a family, with the ὃς δὲ σκύ̣λ̣η̣ clause at *l.*9.

195 the text printed at the beginning of this entry.

217 (pl.21; = *SEG* 1302) epitaph for Asklepiodotos and his family, εἰ δέ τις μὴ πρ|οσήκων σκύ|λη τὸ μνημεῖον, | δώσει, κτλ (17-20). On the wording μὴ προσήκων, referring to one who has no rights to the tomb, see Robert, 273 n.14. Other examples in *I.Nikaia* are I.142; II, 1.1355 and 1587. See further on no.555 below.

353 (pl.26), [ἐὰ]ν δὲ σκύλη τὸ μν[ημεῖον], | [δώσ]ει, κτλ.

552 (pl.28), aedicula, beginning of this Christian text lost. *Ll.*6-11 read: εἴ τις δὲ ἕτε|ρος σκύλῃ τὸ | κυμητήριν, δώ|σι λόγον θεῷ | ἐν ἡμέρᾳ κρί|σεος (*sic*).

555 (pl.30; = *SEG* 1321; cf. *BE* [1980] 516), Christian epitaph for Aurelius Chrysanthos and his family, *ll.*14-19 of which read: εἴ τις δὲ σκύλῃ τὸ | κοιμητήριν, ὁ | ἀνόμως δώσι | λόγο(ν) θεῷ ἐν ἡ|μέρᾳ κρίσεως | κὲ τῷ ταμίῳ ✱ ρ´. Here ἀνόμως (= -ος) appears to act as an equivalent of μὴ προσήκων (see no.217 above).

556 (IV/V; pl.31) Christian epitaph, εἰ δέ τις | ἕτερος σκύλῃ, δώσει λό|γον τῷ θεῷ ἐν ἡμέρᾳ κρίσ[εως] (*ll.*10-12).

557 family grave, Christian, τίς ἂν σκύλῃ τὸ | κοιμητήριον, δώσει λόγον θεῷ (*ll.*11-12). τίς here is equivalent to ὅστις or ὅς: see BDF §298(4).

573 fragmentary Christian epitaph, restored as ἐ[άν τις δ]|ὲ σκύλῃ, δ[ώσει λό]|γον θεῷ [ἐν ἐκεί]|νῃ τῇ ἡ[μέρᾳ, καὶ] | δώσει, κτλ (*ll.*3-7). Robert, 274 n.21, doubts the plausibility of the restoration in *ll.*5-6; but see *BE* (1980) 517, where it has come to be accepted, apparently.

II, 1.559 (on p.323; probably V; pl.29), Christian epitaph for a family, μηδινὶ ἐξὸν εἶναι σκῦ|λαι· εἰ [δ]έ τις τολμήσει, δῶσι προσ|τε[ί]μου τῷ ταμείῳ δηναρίων | ✱ μυ(ριάδος) κ´ καὶ λόγον θεῷ ἐν ἡμέρᾳ | κρίσεως (*ll.*9-12).

2.1250 (II; pl.4), εἴ τις δὲ ἂν σκύλῃ ἢ ἀπαλ|[λο]τριώ[σῃ, ἀπόδωσει, κτλ (*ll.*9-10).

1251 (III?; pl.6), funerary epigram for Bassa: εἴ τις ἔτι σκύλῃ, λυμῷ (*read* λοιμῷ) γε[. . .]τ[. .] δὲ ἐξαπόλοιτο, 'if anyone disturbs it further, may he be . . . and destroyed by plague' (*l.*4).

1331 (probably III; pl.11), εἴ τεις δὲ ἕτερος εἰσκύλῃ οἶκον τὸν | ἀνεξοδίαστον ἢ θάψει τεινὰν ἄλ|λον εἰς ὑμᾶς (*read* ἡμᾶς), δώσει τῷ ταμίῳ τρίσ|δεκα μυριάδας καὶ τῇ Εἰκραλη|νῶν κώμῃ ἐγδεικείου (*read* ἐγδικίου) δηνάρεια | πεντακειχείλεια· καὶ κίνου (*read* ἐκείνου) γε|νεὴ .υ. . . ἐξαπολεῖτε, εἴ τεις | δὲ ἕτερος εἰσκ[ύλῃ, 'and if anyone else disturbs this inalienable home (of the dead), or buries someone else on us, he will pay to the treasury 130,000 (denaria), and to the village of the Ikralenoi 1005 — 5000, reading πεντακει(σ)χείλεια, would be a less peculiar amount — denaria, as his punishment. And may his family . . . be destroyed if anyone else disturbs (the tomb)' (*ll.*10-17).

1355 εἰ δέ τις εἰσκύλῃ {σ} | τῷ μὴ προ<σ>ήκοντι, δώσι, κτλ (*ll.*8-10). On τῷ μὴ προσήκοντι see comment above on no.217.

1378 (III-IV), ὡς μηδενὶ ἑτέρῳ ἐξὸν | ε[ἶ]ναι σκοῖλαι ἢ διαδό|χοις αὐτῶν· ὃς δὲ ἂν σκοίλῃ χωρὶς τῆς τῶν δια|δόχων γνώμης ἀποδώ|σει, κτλ (*ll.*10-15), 'since no one else is permitted to disturb (the grave) except their successors, whoever does disturb it without the successors' permission shall pay . . . '

1472 (III; pl.29), μετὰ δὲ ταῦτα εἴ | τις τολμήσει σκῦ|λαι, δώσι τῦς κληρονό|μυς, κτλ (*ll.*7-10), 'after this, if anyone dares disturb (the grave) he shall pay to the heirs . . . '

1587 εἰ δέ τις ἂν σκύλῃ μὴ | προσήκων, ἀπόδωσει, κτλ (*ll.*6-7). On μὴ προσήκων see comment above on no.217.

Several brief observations may be made on this catalogue. The formula is occurring at least by II AD (no.1250); it is employed primarily, and predominantly, in the context of a financial penalty imposed for tomb disturbance. Yet the apodosis clause which may follow occasionally consists of a curse formula (no.1251; in no.1331 both a fine and a curse are specified). *IGUR* II, 2.837, mentioned earlier, is another example where the apodosis takes the form of a curse: ὃς δὲ | ἂν σκύλῃ μ<ή>τε αὐ|τῷ θάλασσα πλω|τὴ μηδὲ γῆ βατή (*ll.*10-13), 'whoever disturbs (the deceased), may the sea not be navigable for him nor the earth passable'. On this particular formula and its variants see Robert, 270 n.5. Helbing, *AGI* 30 (near Kephisia in Attika, *c.*160; = *SIG*^{3} 1238) includes one of these variants in an epitaph for a woman who is described as τὸ | φῶς τῆς οἰκίας (*ll.*1-2): whoever interferes with the tomb's memorabilia (statues, etc.) 'may his land not bear fruit and the sea not be navigable for him . . .', τούτῳ μήτε γῆν καρ|πὸν φέρειν μήτε θάλασσαν πλωτὴν εἶναι, κτλ (*ll.*6-7). The phrase by which the woman is described offers an interesting analogy to those used in the NT of people, such as τὸ φῶς τοῦ κόσμου (Mt. 5.14; used twice in the Fourth Gospel by Jesus to describe himself: Jn 8.12; 9.5; cf. 11.9 where it is used literally), τὸ φῶς τῶν ἀνθρώπων (Jn 1.4, of Jesus), τὸ φῶς τῆς ζωῆς (Jn 8.12, of Jesus). Dedications thanking a god for a successful and safe voyage (εὔπλοια) are the opposite side of the coin to the phraseology in these curse formulas just noted: see H.S. Versnel, in id. (ed.), *Faith Hope and Worship. Aspects of Religious Mentality in the Ancient World* (*Studies in Greek and Roman Religion* 2; Leiden, 1981), 9. See further **26**, below.

It is of interest to see how Christians adapted the σκύλλω formula: divine retribution becomes a sanction now, with (nos. 555, 573, 559) or without (552, 556, 557) retention of the financial penalty. On the formula δώσει λόγον τῷ θεῷ south of Nikaia in E. Phrygia see briefly *New Docs 1978*, **98**, p.136. As for the σκύλλω clause itself, we may note the variations employed. The object may be personal (the deceased: no.98, 195, etc) impersonal (the tomb: no.217, 552, etc.) or unstated (no.556, 1250, etc.). The first of these uses offers a parallel for the NT occurrences at Mk. 5.35 and Lk. 8.49. Furthermore, the σκύλλω clause nearly always employs an aorist subjunctive, introduced by a variety of wordings: conditionals with (no.98, etc.) or without (no.128, etc.) ἄν, indefinite relatives (nos. 120, 136, etc.). In no.557 τίς serves the function of ὅστις, thus providing a useful parallel to such NT passages as Mk. 14.36, οὐ τί ἐγὼ θέλω, ἀλλὰ τί σύ, and Lk. 17.8, ἑτοίμασον τί δειπνήσω. The indefinite pronoun τις is often present, but not mandatorily, as is the particle δέ; and the fluidity in the order of these may be noted (compare nos. 552 and 555 with no.556).

There are other features also deserving of mention in the text which has provided the starting-point for this entry. κηδεύω (*l*.1) is not rare — NT: only as a *v.l.*, at Mk. 6.29 — but MM lacks an entry. Neither MM nor BAGD gives any documentary attestation of πλησμονή to illustrate the NT *hapax* at Col. 2.23, πρὸς πλησμονὴν τῆς σαρκός. That phrase is usually seen as pejorative, 'indulgence of the flesh', *vel sim.*; but πλησμονή is not in itself pejorative, and the context in which it occurs in our inscription (*l*.3) does not provide an exact semantic parallel, therefore. BAGD follows MM, s.v. ἀλλαχοῦ, in citing the latter's sole testimony to ἀλλαχοῦ, to which the instance in our inscription (*l*.9) may be added to illustrate its single occurrence in the NT, at Mk. 1.38. The inscription also provides us with a good example of στρατεύομαι used metaphorically (*l*.9), as in such NT passages as 2 Cor. 10.3 and 1 Tim. 1.18. Cf. *IG* XIV *Suppl.* 2461 (Massilia, Imperial period), a clearly non-Christian verse epitaph (in view of the reference to the saviour gods in *l*.4) at the end of which the deceased young man — who at *l*.2 calls himself θεῷ φίλος; cf. the slightly differently nuanced φίλος θεοῦ, said of Abraham at Jas. 2.23 — says ἧς στρατιῆς εἷς εἰμ[ι], λαχὼν θεὸν ἡγεμονῆα, 'I am a member of this host — viz, those who dance with the heavenly (beings), *l*.11 — having obtained God as my commander' (*l*.12).

For the idea implied in *l*.9 of the text from Nikaia with which we began, that the deceased has a continued existence εἰς αἴθραν, cf. *ll*.8-9 of the epigram from Ephesos for a six-year-old girl quoted at *New Docs 1977*, **14**, p.51, ἠέρι δ' ἐμ[πεπό]|τηται κατ' οὐρανόν, 'and in the air her soul is in flight through heaven'. Pfuhl/Möbius I.808 (pl.117) reprint this text as it occurred in the *ed.pr.*; but it has been improved upon (cf. W. Peek, *ZPE* 28 [1978] 178-79), and *I.Eph.* VI.2104 includes several different readings again from the text given in the *New Docs 1977* entry. A Christian epitaph for a certain Photios — included twice in *SIA* III, at xiii (= *IG* III, 2.x.1386), and at p.129 (= C. Bayet, *De titulis Atticae Christianis antiquissimis* [Paris, 1878] no.38) — mentions that 'earth hides his body here but at least his soul has flown into the sky and is in the company of those (who have gone) before', γῆ σῶμα κρύπτει τῇ|δέ γ' ἀλλ' εἰς αἰθέρα | ψυχὴ διέπτη καὶ σύ|νεστιν οἷς τὸ πρίν. These last words appear to be an allusion to the 'Communion of Saints'. Similarly, in *IGUR* 1321 (Rome, III or IV) — repr. and discussed at **10** below — the deceased says that 'after he died he gave back his soul to the air, and his body to the earth', ἀλλὰ νεκρωθεὶς | τὴν ψυχὴν ἀπέδωκεν ἐς ἀέρα, σῶμα δὲ πρὸς γῆν (5-6).

Of interest, too, is *IGUR* 1326 (Rome, II/III, or later; pl. on p.180), an epitaph for M. Sempronius Nikokrates, a man who was once a musician (μουσικὸς ἀνήρ, *l.*2), poet and lyre-player, as well as possibly having been an actor in a Dionysian troupe (συνοδείτης, 4; see Moretti's n. ad loc.). Then he turned his hand to slave-trading, ἔνπορος εὐμόρφων γενόμην, | φίλοι, μετέπειτα γυναικῶν (7-8). He puns on his career as a merchant in the following lines: πνεῦμα λαβὼν δάνος οὐρανόθεν | τελέσας χρόνον αὖτ' ἀπέδωκα (9-10), 'receiving my spirit as a loan from heaven, now that I have completed my time I have repaid it'. The poem concludes with a neat *kyklos*, as Nikokrates indicates (11-12) that the Muses to whom he had devoted the earlier part of his life now adorn the sarcophagus in which his body rests. The adjective εὔμορφος (7) may be noted here, as BAGD has no epigraphical references to illustrate this word found in ECL. At least in this much-employed *topos*, it is clear that there is no real distinction made between πνεῦμα and ψυχή (on these words see **11** below), nor between ἀήρ and οὐρανός. A further variant of the motif is to be seen in *IGUR* 1329.4 (Rome, Imperial), where the *psyche* is said to go πρὸς Ὄλυμπον. In contrast to this view that the soul goes up to heaven mention may be made of *IGUR* 1204 (Rome, probably II; pl. on p.65), in which two friends originally from the same city of Termessos in Pisidia are commemorated by the son of one of the deceased. In this epigram one of the dead men says, 'fire has destroyed our flesh, and this all-nourishing earth conceals our bones, but our divinely-sent souls have departed on that voyage common (to all) below the earth, (having experienced) the one (i.e., same) fate', σάρκας μὲν πῦρ νῶ[ιν ἐδαί]σατο, | ὀστὰ δὲ κεύθ[ει] | ἥδε χθὼν πάμφορβο[ς], ἀτὰρ | ψυχαὶ θεόπεμπτοι | οἴχεσθον κατὰ γῆς ἐνὶ δαίμονι | ξυνὰ κέλευθα (*ll.*19-24). This notion, that the soul is implanted in the body by God, is paralleled in the NT, though in different wording: note, e.g., Jas. 4.5, τὸ πνεῦμα ὃ κατῴκισεν (*sc.* ὁ θεὸς) ἐν ἡμῖν; and cf. 1 Cor. 3.16, τὸ πνεῦμα τοῦ θεοῦ οἰκεῖ ἐν ὑμῖν.

Reverting once more to our initial text, in *l.*12 ἵνα is probably consecutive — cf. in the NT Lk. 9.45 and the somewhat ambiguous examples noted by BAGD, s.v., II.2 — but in view of the preceding προστάσσω it may serve here to introduce an indirect command (cf. BAGD, s.v. ἵνα, II.1.a.ε). If correctly accented by the editor, ἄρα (16) must be equivalent to ἄρα; for this use after a conditional conjunction (restored here in the inscription) cf. LSJ, s.v. ἄρα, B.6. The form πάλι (*l.*6) for πάλιν has been discussed briefly at *New Docs 1977*, **106**, p.190 (NT: only in the W text of Jn 1.35). Further examples, in *I.Eph.* VII, 2.3901 and *P. Würzb.* (1934) 21, are noted below at **18** and **128** respectively.

The notion of the Fates spinning one's alloted thread of life is a widely-attested cliché. T. Drew-Bear has collected numerous versions of this motif in G.W. Bowersock, et al. (edd.), *Arktouros. Hellenic Studies presented to B.M.W. Knox* (Berlin, 1979), 308-16. The earliest known examples come from IV or III BC Rhodes. In addition to the sentiment expressed here at *ll.*5-6, cf. from the present year's culling *I.Nikaia* II, 2.1298 (pl.7), οὐ τὸ θανῖν ἀλ|γινόν, ἀλλ' ὅ γε | Μοῖρ' ἐπέκλω|σε (*ll.*1-4); and no.1326 (pl.13), where the deceased tells the passer-by not to grieve ἐπὶ (read ἐπεί) τόδ' Μο(ĩ)|ρ' ἐπέκλωσεν (6-7). In an epitaph for a young Jewish woman — *IGUR* 1231, quoted below at **114** — the phraseology is also being recalled: [π]ονηρὲ δαῖμον, ὅς . . . | . . . ἔκλωσας (*ll.*4-5). There, though, it is not Moira, but Daimon which has settled the length of life. The phrase there provides an additional link with our Nikaian epitaph, whose *l.*11 has δαίμων πικρός. The thread of the Fates is mentioned also in *IGUR* 1243 and 1321, quoted at **9** and **10** respectively. Two epitaphs for gladiators reprinted as Pfuhl/Möbius II.1249 (region of Ankara, later Imperial; pl.186) and 1258 (Kyzikos, later Imperial; pl.187) also employ this *topos*. The first does not include the verb (ἐπι)κλώθω, but mentions the Μυρῶν μείτυν (*l.*12); the second speaks of the deceased's inability to escape the Μυρῶν μίτον ὅς μοι ἐπεκλώσθη (*l.*5). For further discussion of gladiators see **4** above.

Finally, two of the texts in the list above include a prothetic vowel in the form εἰσκύλῃ, *I.Nikaia* II, 2.1331 and 1355. Another example was noted at *New Docs 1978*, **69**, ἰστοργῆς, in a fourth-century epitaph from Saqqara. Concerning that instance G. Mussies has pointed out to me (*per litt.*, 9.8.85) that it 'proves that prothetic vowels occurred in Egypt and parallels the variant reading ἐστιβάδας (for στιβάδας) at Mk. 11.8D*. This inscription therefore seriously weakens the hypothesis that the copyist of Codex Bezae was either a Spaniard or a Provençal who introduced here the well-known ε- prothesis from his Romance vernacular into Greek'. Another likely instance occurs in an honorific inscription from the Athenian Agora: J.S. Traill, *Hesperia* 47 (1978) 295-97 no.21 (*c*.30 BC; pl.80). At *l*.11 the text contains the lettering ΕΙCΤΗΙΛΗΝΛΙΘΙΝΗ[Ν, which Traill reads as εἰς <σ>τή{ι}λην λιθίνη[ν. But the form εἰστήλην is quite to be expected at this period: so *BE* 151, where the medial parasitic *iota* is noted in this word, and also in στεφανῶ{ι}σαι at *l*.8.

7. A Roman Job

Rome III
ed. — *CIG* 4 (1877; repr. 1977) 9668

A Σύνοιδα ἐμαυτῷ μηδέν ποτε δράσας | κακόν·
εἱμαρμένῃ δὲ περιπεσὼν κακῇ | καὶ βασκάνῳ πικρῷ
ἔπαθον τοιαῦτα | οἷα μηδεὶς πώποτε.
ὁ γὰρ περὶ τέκνα | πλούσιος γεγὼς
ἐστερήθην μετὰ | μητρὸς αὐτῶν, συμβίου σεμνῆς καὶ | σώφρονος.
ὁποῖα δ' ἦσαν ἐπὶ τόπῳ βλέψον τέκνα·
| πατὴρ δ' ὑπάρχων καὶ γηρῶν κακῶς ὀδύρο|[μαι]
[- -]
B Ὅ ποτε πλούσιος | περὶ τέκνα, νῦν | κακὸν κακῶς
| τηρῶν ὡς Τάνταλος | κολάζομαι.

Opisthographic verse inscription, broken off at the bottom. Letter height of side A is .025m., of side B .045m. Vertical bars mark line divisions on the stone.
Bib. — **IGUR* 1490 (figs. on pp.282, 283).

A **I know in myself that I have never done anything evil, but encountering evil fate and bitter malevolence, I suffered such things as no one ever has (suffered). For I, who became wealthy in regard to children, | was deprived of them along with their mother, my honourable and chaste wife. The children which I had, see them on the tomb: I was their father and as I grow old I grieve terribly - - -**

B **I, once wealthy in regard to children, keeping a wretched watch in my wretchedness, am now being punished like Tantalos.**

This inscription is a curiosity in its preserved form, for texts written on both sides of a gravestone are not common. More than that, though, both sides were clearly carved by the same mason (so Moretti, ad loc.; the *kappa* is particularly distinctive), yet a different letter height has been used on each side. This might be explained by the mason's realisation that he did not have as much text left to carve on side B as he had anticipated, and so enlarged the lettering for the remaining words.

In its general content we have a striking parallel to the OT situation of Job, primarily because of the repeated phrase περὶ τέκνα πλούσιος (4, 8). There is no hint that the inscription reflects a Christian or Jewish milieu; and a parallel with the Job story is quite coincidental. Like Job, this man has a clear conscience (*l*.1, exactly paralleling what Job has to say at LXX Job 27.6, οὐ γὰρ σύνοιδα ἐμαυτῷ ἄτοπα πράξας: cf. also the wording at 1 Cor. 4.4); his suffering is unique and extreme (*l*.3) for he has not only lost his children (images of whom he has placed on the tomb, *l*.6; for other instances of this practice see **12** below) but also his wife. What is left to him now is an old age filled with lamentation.

For the figurative use of πλούσιος here we may compare Eph. 2.4, of God who is πλούσιος . . . ἐν ἐλέει, and Jas. 2.5, of those who are poor by the world's standards who are nevertheless πλουσίους ἐν πίστει. Περιπίπτω (2) is employed with the dative in two of the three NT places where it occurs: Lk. 10.30, and Jas. 1.2, of which the latter (πειρασμοῖς π. ποικίλοις) is the closer parallel to the phrase in the inscription.

The wording βασκάνῳ πικρῷ in *l*.2 may be a reference to Hades. Compare a funerary epigram for Apollodoros, Pfuhl/Möbius I.1021 (pl.153; = E. Schwertheim, *Die Inschriften von Kyzikos und Umgebung*, I [*IK* 26.1; Bonn, 1980] 493 [pl.34]), in which Hades is described as ὁ πᾶσι θνητοῖς ἄκριτος βίου βραβεύς, | ὁ πικρὸς Ἅδης, ὃς τὰ σέμνα βασκαίνει (1-2), 'Indiscriminate arbiter of life for all mortals, bitter Hades, who casts his envious eyes upon honourable things . . .' (Kyzikos, I BC). For the everyday presence of Christian amulets warding off the evil eye at early VII AD Anemorion in Isauria see J. Russell, *JÖB* 32 (1982) 539-48. One of these has the Trishagion on one side, ἅγιος | ἅγιος | ἅγιος | [κ]ς σαβ|[αο]θ; the other side contains the wording σφραγ[ὶς] | [Σο]λομῶνος [ἔ]χι τὴν βα|σκανίαν, 'the seal of Solomon holds (in check) the evil eye'. For the notion of Solomon as an efficacious magician in Jewish and Christian popular thought, see Russell's discussion (540) and the references mentioned there. The verb βασκαίνω here offers a useful parallel to the sole NT occurrence, Gal. 3.1. While Paul uses the verb there figuratively — so H.D. Betz, *Comm. on Galatians* (*Hermeneia series*; Philadelphia, 1979) 131 with n.32; *pace* B.H. Brinsmead, *Galatians — Dialogical Response to Opponents* (*SBLDS* 65; Chico, 1982) 79 — it cannot be doubted that he is entirely alert to its association with the evil eye, in view of his inclusion of the words κατ' ὀφθαλμούς in the following vivid clause. For Trishagia see **108** below.

The collocation κακὸν κακῶς (9; cf. κακὸν . . . κακῇ at *ll*.1-2) is common in Greek Tragedy and other classical literature, but also occurs in later Greek which is not particularly pretentious. In the NT, for example, note Mt. 21.41, κακοὺς κακῶς ἀπωλέσει αὐτούς. See MM's useful comment, s.v. κακῶς, where the relevant lines from our inscription are quoted. J.A.L. Lee has drawn my attention to the form κακινκάκως in *Vita Aesopi* G19; for discussion (together with some remarks in general on κακὸς κακῶς) see B.E. Perry, *AJP* 60 (1939) 33; Ch. Charitonides, *Πλάτων* 4 (1952) 105; and G.P. Shipp, *Antichthon* 17 (1983) 99.

8. Beloved in name and nature

Rome later III/IV init.

ed. — *IG* XIV (1890) 2068

Θ(εοῖς) Κ(αταχθονίοις).
ἤμην ὡς ἤμην φων`ὴν´ καὶ πνεῦμα καὶ εἶδος,
ἀρτιτόκου φωτὸς ψυχίον ἔνδοθ' ἔχ≪ω≫ν,
αἴσιος ἐμ φιλότητι καὶ ὄλβιος ἐμ πραπίδεσσι,
μηδὲν ἄγαν φρονέων, θνητὰ δὲ πάνθ' ὁρόω<ν>·
ἦλθον, ἀπῆλθον ἄμεμπτος, ἃ μὴ θέμις οὐκ ἐδόκευσα,
εἴτ' ἤμην πρότερον, εἴτε χρόνοις ἔσομαι·
παιδεύθην, παίδευσα, κύτος κόσμοιο πέδησα,
θείας ἐξ ἀθανάτων φωσὶ φράσας ἀρετάς.
κεύθι γαῖα φίλη με· τί δ' ἁγνὸν ὅμως ὄνομ'; ἤμην
πᾶσι Φίλητος (*vac.*) ἀνήρ, τῆς Λυκίης Λιμύ-
(*palm frond*) ρων. (*palm frond*)

Nearly square stele (34B x 29H cm.); text carved with considerable lack of care, despite the seeming regularity of the lettering. The underlined letters printed at the end of *ll.*6, 8, 10 are carved very small and below the line, roughly centred across the stele.
Bib. — Peek, *GVI* 1113; **IGUR* 1351 (pl. on p.205).

To the underworld gods. I was like I was in my speech, spirit, and form, possessing the implanted soul of a person just born, happy in friendship and fortunate in my mind, | holding the view 'nothing in excess', and viewing everything as mortal. I came (i.e., into the world), I departed blameless, I did not think about things which I ought not to: whether I had a previous existence, whether I shall have one in time (to come). I was educated, I educated (others), I shackled the vault of the universe, declaring to men the divine virtues which proceed from the gods. | The dear earth conceals me; yet what was my pure name? I was Philetos, a man beloved by all, from Limyra in Lykia.

The content of this epitaph is of considerable interest. Philetos, who puns on his name in the final verse (and cf. φιλότητι in *l.*4) died at Rome though originally from Lykia. The most obvious inference from *l.*8 is that he was a schoolteacher (so Moretti, n. ad loc.); yet the possibility that he was a professional philosopher cannot be excluded altogether. The trouble with this latter interpretation is that the allusions he makes add up to a philosophical pot-pourri. Taken in conjunction with *l.*7, the first couplet of the poem is suggestive of Pythagoreanism; *l.*5 quotes one of the most famous Classical Greek maxims of popular philosophy. The second half of *l.*8 is not really clear, but *may* allude to an interest in natural science or astronomy. The next line indicates that Philetos sought to draw attention to the gods by writing aretalogies: on these see *New Docs 1976*, **2**. Given his philosophical interests, it would not be inappropriate to consider him as a *theologos*, an expounder of the numinous to others. For similar activity by a first-century philosopher, and his potent effect on at least one person in Athens, see **18** below. The name Philetos appears in the NT only at 2 Tim. 2.17.

Returning to the first couplet, we have here an allusion to the trichotomy of body, soul and spirit, dealt with briefly at **11** below. Yet there is a fourth element drawn in here, φωνή. It is unclear what Philetos — whom we should doubtless consider to have composed this epitaph for himself — means by the word here: is it a hint perhaps that he was a native Lykian, for whom Greek was a learned language? If so, he has thoroughly mastered the latter. If we are to think of Philetos as a Lykian philosopher who went to Rome and mastered Greek to establish himself we have a precedent several centuries before. Diogenes Laertius mentions (4.67) that in II BC the Carthaginian philosopher Hasdrubal, who taught philosophy there in Punic (τῇ ἰδίᾳ φωνῇ κατὰ τὴν πατρίδα ἐφιλοσόφει), would have remained obscure had he not gone to Athens and become Karneades' most famous student. Karneades helped Hasdrubal learn Greek; and under the name Kleitomachos he wrote over 400 *biblia*, succeeding his mentor as head of the Academy in 129 BC.

This inscription offers a most instructive example of a letter-cutter's negligence. After the initial formulaic dedication in *l*.1 each succeeding line on the stone was intended to contain a complete verse, either hexameter or pentameter. The omission of the last two letters in φωνήν (*l*.2), subsequently carved above the line, is a common enough phenomenon. Between *l*.2 and *l*.4 is an especially wide gap, in which the mason has carved in smaller letters the first two words of *l*.3. These are roughly centred across the line. Clearly the line was omitted, and these words subsequently added, or at least after *l*.4 had been carved. Why the mason did not cut the whole verse along this line is unclear; the remaining words are jammed in the bottom right corner of the stele, in small, untidy lettering. Between *ll*.4 and 5 there is another large gap: Moretti thinks there may have been a line erased here. It is a common stylistic feature of many letter-cutters' work to carve certain letters, like *omicron* or *iota*, much smaller in size. But the presence of the phenomenon on this stele is not due to any aesthetic judgement by this mason; for all the instances are near the right edge of the lines, indicating that he was forced to cramp his letters by having misjudged his space. This is not the only sign of such misjudgement. The final letters of *ll*.6, 8 and 10 (i.e. those letters underlined in the text above) could not be fitted on to the ends of those lines, and were carved in very tiny script below the line and very approximately centred across the stone. The final letter of *l*.5 was merely omitted, rather than treated in this way. As another mark of the mason's poor workmanship, there is a large *vacat* of at least three letters after Φίλητος (*l*.11); this may have been left to allow the spillover letters MHMHN from the end of *l*.10 to be read more easily, for they are carved immediately above that space. But the result is that when he reached the edge of the stone he still had the last three letters of Λιμύρων to carve. (Actually, the *rho* could have fitted, but was held over with the other two letters in obedience to the rules of syllabification applying to the inscribing of words which have to be broken across two lines.)

9. 'Dearer than my mother . . .'

Rome III/IV(?)
ed. — *IG* XIV (1890) 1728

Θ(εοῖς) [Κ(αταχθονίοις)].
Τῷδ' ἐνὶ τύμβωι̣ [ἐγὼ κ]ε̣ἶ̣μαι παίδων ὄχ' ἄριστο̣[ς]·
οὔνομά μοι Κάλλισ̣τ̣ος, ἔ̣χ̣ω δὲ γένος Συρίηθεν,
ἕνδεχ' ἔτη [ζ]ή̣σας, δωδ̣εκάτου δ' ἐπιβάς·

μηδὲν ἐν ἀνθρώποισι κ̣ακὸν γνούς, μηδὲ βίοιο
π̣ικροτάτου μύστης, ἀλλ᾽ ἀκέραιος ἔτι,
παιδείαισι καλαῖς καὶ γυμνασίοις παρεδρεύων
ἔσχα τέλος ζωῆς Μοιράων ὡς ἐπέκλωσαν.
μνημεῖον τόδε μοι π̣οῖσεν θρέψασα γλυκεῖα
Φαυστεῖνα, μητρὸς πλ̣εῖον ἐμοὶ φιλίη,
ἣ καὶ ζῶντα φίλησεν ἀεὶ θανέοντά τ᾽ ἔτεισε.

Limestone stele (47B x 24.5H cm.) broken in the centre in antiquity; the few letters lost can be restored with confidence to yield a complete text. The text is mostly hexameters, with three pentamenters (*ll.* 4, 6, 10); each line on the stone constitutes a complete verse.

Bib. — Peek, *GVI* 745; H.W. Pleket, *Epigraphica,* II. *Texts on the Social History of the Greek World* (*Textus Minores* 41; Leiden, 1969), no.60; **IGUR* 1243 (pl. on p.102).

To the [underworld] gods. I who lie in this tomb was by far the best of children. My name was Kallistos, and my family came from Syria. I lived for eleven years, and was coming near to the twelfth. | Although I knew nothing of men's wickedness, nor was I an initiate of life's utmost bitterness, but was still undefiled, concerning myself with a good education and attending the gymnasium, I attained to the end of my life from the Fates, since they spun (my allotted thread). The woman who reared me made this memorial for me, sweet | Faustina, dearer than my mother, who both loved me constantly while I was alive and fulfilled her obligation to me now I have died.

This epitaph for a *threptos* is of interest particularly in that it shows that the child, of Syrian parentage, was brought up at Rome and given the opportunity of a thorough-going Greek education: not only *paideia* but also access to the gymnasium (the plurals here in *l.*7, or at least παιδείαισι καλαῖς, are poetical). Faustina is spoken of in most affectionate terms (10), which may call to mind Paul's parenthetical comment at Rom. 16.13, where Rufus' unnamed mother is called τὴν μητέρα αὐτοῦ καὶ ἐμοῦ. Yet the statement in the inscription may be taken *cum grano salis*, since Faustina herself will have commissioned the text. This epitaph, with its advertisement of the educational opportunity afforded to the boy by Faustina, thus provides a parallel to those memorials erected by masters to their slaves, discussed at *New Docs 1977*, **15**, pp.52-53.

Although μύστης does not occur in the NT, its presence in this inscription (*l.*6) is worth mention, since it provides a good example of the metaphorical use of this pre-eminently cultic word. This usage is not unique: Peek, *GVI* 956 (= Pleket, *Epigraphica* II, no.52) is the fragmentary beginning of a funerary epigram for Longeia, carved on an altar (Tomis, II), in which the four-year-old child says she died πρίν με μυηθῆ|ναι κακίης (*ll.*2-3), 'before I had any acquaintance with evil'. These passages provide a useful general analogy for Paul's frequent employment of μυστήριον in over a score of passages in a deliberately non-cultic way, at Rom. 11.25; 1 Cor. 15.51, etc.

The common, figurative force of ἀκέραιος here (6) parallels the NT usage at Mt. 10.16; Rom. 16.19; and Phil. 2.15. As for παρεδρεύω, this verb is found in the NT only at 1 Cor. 9.13 where its cultic association is clearly in view. In the Kallistos inscription the usage is more generalised; but although both nouns in that line are to be taken with it, a somewhat different meaning is required in each case, as is suggested in the translation given above. The motif of the thread of life spun by the Fates (8) has been noted at **6** above.

Finally, the negatives formed with μή in *l*.5 call for brief comment. In the *koine* μή becomes the usual negative particle used with participles; this is one element in the significant simplification of the classical distinction between οὐ and μή (cf. BDF §426). Yet our poem, as with so many of the funerary monuments in verse from the Imperial period, imitates epic in its vocabulary and syntax. Just in this one aspect, however, the composer of the epigram has let his guard drop, and the *koine* feature has slipped in.

10. A judicial career cut short

Rome III or IV
ed. — *IG* XIV (1890) 1976

῾Ρουφείνου τάφος οὗτος, ὃν ᾿Αστέριόν ποτ᾿ ἔκληζον·
ὃς προλιπὼν ῾Ρώμης δάπεδον Νείλου πόλιν ἐλθὼν
καὶ προκοπαῖς λάμψας, πολλοῖσι δὲ πολλὰ παρασχών,
μηδένα λυπήσας, ἀλλ᾿ εἰς τὸ δίκαιον ἀθρήσας,
Μοιρῶν οὐκ ἔφυγεν τρι<σ>σῶν μίτον, ἀλλὰ νεκρωθεὶς
τὴν ψυχὴν ἀπέδωκεν ἐς ἀέρα, σῶμα δὲ πρὸς γῆν.
ἀλλὰ καὶ εὐσεβίης ἔσχεν κρίσιν ἐν φθιμένοισιν
καὶ πάλιν εἶδε τὸ φῶς νεκρὸς ὢν καὶ πόντον ἔπλευσε
καὶ χώρης ἰδίης ἐπέ<β>η· σὺν παισὶ δὲ κεῖται,
ὧν οὐκ εἶδε τέλος θανάτου· πρῶτο<ς> γὰρ ἔθνησκε.
ἡ δὲ τέκνων δισσῶν μήτηρ, σεμνὴ <ἡ>δὲ φίλανδρος,
καὶ πέλαγος διέπλευσε καὶ ἤγαγε σῶμα βυθοῖσιν
καὶ καμάτους ὑπέμεινε καὶ ἐν θρήνοις διέμεινε
καὶ τύνβῳ κατέθηκε καὶ αἰῶσιν παρέδωκε.
Δαμοστρατείας ταῦτα τῆς φιλανδρίας.

Fairly large, rectangular marble stele (45B x 108H cm.). Each line contains a complete verse. The letters POY are carved in much larger size at the top of the block, presumably in error.
Bib. — **IGUR* 1321 (pl. on p.177).

This is the tomb of Rufinus, whom once they used to call Asterios. He left the land of Rome and went to the city of the Nile; and shining out in the progress he made, he provided many things for many people, causing distress to no one, but considered what was just. | Yet he did not escape the thread of the triple Fates, but died and gave his soul back to the sky, his body to the earth. But even among the dead he had the judgement of piety; and once more he saw the light of day, although he was a corpse, and sailed the sea and came back to his own land. And he lies with his children, | whose mortal end he did not witness; for he predeceased them. And the mother of the twin children, a fine woman who loved her husband, sailed across the ocean and brought his body over the deep, and endured difficulties and continued in her grieving and laid him down in this tomb and bequeathed him to eternity. | This monument is (testimony to) the wifely devotion of Damostrateia.

The situation reflected in this verse epitaph is by no means unprecedented. A man whose home was in Rome moved to Egypt — the 'city of the Nile' may indicate Alexandria — but died there, and his widow transported his remains back to Italy for final burial. An analogous instance is provided by *IGUR* 1151, where a young man from Rome had died and was buried at Antioch in Mygdonia in early II AD, but his ashes were later taken back to Rome. Another instance is afforded by *IGUR* 1323 (Roman Imperial period) where the bereaved mother indicates on the stele that she will send her child's ashes to her homeland, clearly somewhere other than Italy.

Speculation though it be, a guess may be hazarded that Rufinus, who mentions that he had the nickname Asterios, was a government official sent to Egypt for work in judicial administration. What we are told about him is very generalised, but *ll.*3-4 bespeak rapid advancement in a career (3), a position able to confer patronage (3), and a concern for justice (4). This last point is picked up in the claim at *l.*7 that at the judgement in the underworld his *eusebeia* was given due recognition. In the NT these sentiments come together in the recommendation at 1 Tim. 6.11, δίωκε δὲ δικαιοσύνην εὐσέβειαν πίστιν.

Among lexical items here προκοπή (3) may take our attention first. The use here is a generalised one (possibly alluding to the advancement of Rufinus' career) and so parallels that in the NT, at Phil. 1.25 and 1 Tim. 4.15. At *New Docs 1977*, **71**, it was stated that this noun is a Hellenistic coinage (cf. MM, s.v.). Strictly, this is not so, as examples are known from Xenophon and Eur. *Hipp.*: see the discussion by M. Smith in J. Jervell/W.A. Meeks (edd.), *God's Christ and his People. Festschrift for N.A. Dahl* (Oslo, 1977), 261-64. A papyrus example was noted in passing at *New Docs 1978*, **2**, p.12: *P.Giss.* 1 (1910) 27 = *CPJ* II.439 (Hermopolis, beginning of 117?), from a private letter referring to a slave 'bringing the good news of his victory and success', εὐαγγελίζοντι τὰ τῆς νείκης | αὐτοῦ καὶ προκοπῆς (*ll.*6-7). This is one of the several papyrus texts quoted by MM, s.v. Neither their entry, nor BAGD's cites any epigraphical attestations. Three of the latter have been noted in the reading done for the present Review. Pfuhl/Möbius, I.546 (Arablı, near Philadelphia in Lydia, probably I BC; pl.85) is a stele carrying a posthumous honorific inscription and a funerary epigram for Menekrates son of Diodoros. After mention of his good fortune in life he says in *l.*13 — *l.*6 of the epigram — 'but suddenly in (the midst of) my successes I left this life at the behest of Fate', ἄφνω δ' ἐν προκοπαῖς ἔλιπον βίον εἵνεκα Μοίρης. The noun is also found in the Vibius Salutaris inscription of 104 AD, *I.Eph.* Ia.27 (= VI.2027), which speaks of him 'embellishing by his dignified behaviour the progress towards betterment which Fortune has bestowed', τὰς ἀπὸ τῆς τύχης ἐπὶ τὸ κρε[ῖσ]|[σον] προκοπὰς κοσ[μεῖν τ]ῇ τῶν ἤθων σεμνότητι, κτλ (18-19). It is also partly restored in the very fragmentary remains of a civic decree, *I.Eph.* IV.1383a (Imperial period?).

The verb λάμπω has been noted previously, at *New Docs 1978*, **15**; and this passage provides another illustration of its use with a personal subject, as in the NT at Mt. 17.2 (and perhaps Mt. 5.16). It is apposite to mention here an occurrence of ἐπιλάμπω, found in the NT only as a *v.l.* for λάμπω, at Acts 12.7D, at *IGUR* 1287 (Rome, Imperial period; pl. on p.145). This is an epitaph for Olympia who died at the age of 22, apparently unmarried. Her memorial was erected by her brother: between them there existed στοργὴ | . . . μεγάλη (6-7). In Acts 12.7 the subject is φῶς, and so in this epigram, though the wording appears to be ungrammatical: στοργὴ | γὰρ μεγάλη τῶν ἀμφοτέρων διέμεινεν ὡς ὅπου φῶς | τὸ γλυκὺν παρέμεινε ἀκτεῖσι ἐπιλάμπων ἡδὺν ἀπὸ | στόματος καὶ γλυκὺν ὡς μελίτιν (6-9), 'for a great affection continued between them both, just as where the sweet light remained, shining forth with its rays sweetly from her(?) mouth, and lovely like honey(?)'. Near the end of this epitaph occurs a variant of the Osiris 'cold water' formula discussed briefly at *New Docs 1978*, **100**, pp.144-45: ψυχῇ διψώσῃ | ψυχρὸν ὕδ≪ωρ≫ μετάδ≪ο≫ς (10-11), 'may you (Osiris, or Aidoneus) give cold water to a thirsty soul'. Aidoneus is mentioned explicitly in *IGUR* 1269 (Rome, Imperial; pl. on p.129) where the ψυχρὸν ὕδωρ phrase recurs.

Rufinus' wife, who is responsible for burying him and setting up the epitaph, is called φίλανδρος in the poem with which we began (*l*.11; cf. τῆς φιλανδρίας at *l*.15). At *New Docs 1978*, **11**, p.42, half a dozen examples of these forms were noted, to illustrate the adjective found in the NT only at Tit. 2.4. Considerably more attestations have turned up in the texts read for the present volume, and may be noted briefly. The adjective occurs at *SEG* 1199 (Saittai in Lydia, after 212); Pfuhl/Möbius, I.447 (Telmessos, Imperial); ibid., II.2160 (Dorylaion, late Imperial); *I.Nikaia* II, 2.1251 (III?), 1296 (II), 1297 (IV?), 1315 (II/III; an attempt was made to erase the entire epitaph, but the wording remains visible), 1352 (II/III; superlative), 1483 (I/II; superlative); *IGUR* 1279 (Rome, Imperial), 1331 (Rome, Imperial); Guarducci, *EG* IV.522-23, no.1 (Catania in Sicily, IV[1]; Christian). The noun turns up less often, at Pfuhl/Möbius, II.2282 (Apamea Myrleia, late Imperial); and *I.Nikaia* II, 1.1201.13 (Imperial). In *I.Eph.* Ia.47.107 (time of Commodus) there is mention of a man called T. Aelius Philandros, a very rare instance where the word is not used of a wife.

As with so many funerary epigrams of the Imperial period, this one is imbued with many epic features and other highly stylised elements. Merely two examples may be noted: the series of three poetic synonyms for sea (8, 12 *bis*), and the employment of verbs with a common stem (8 and 12; 13 *bis*). The composer of the poem exhibits a touch of humour in *l*.8; and we may note there and in *l*.12 the loose use of νεκρός and σῶμα to refer to the ashes of the deceased, since it would be impracticable for a cadaver to be transported. (J.A.L. Lee points out to me, however, that the possibility that Rufinus was embalmed should not be ruled out, given his death in Egypt, the home of this practice.) Yet for all these features, we may note the superabundance of participial clauses (especially in *ll*.2-4, with which the six-fold paratactic καί in *ll*.12-14 jars sharply (cf., too, paratactic καί four times in *ll*.7-9). Although the person who composed this epigram was familiar enough with the conventions of the genre at a lexical level, the poet lacked sufficient experience of creating such verses to be able to make the poem read smoothly. This suggests that it may not have been commissioned by the widow from a professional; and, certainly, it is generally too specific to the individual being commemorated to allow it to be considered as a concoction from a mason's catalogue (see **12** below). It may be a reasonable inference, then, to conclude that Damostrateia herself wrote the poem. The possibility that Rufinus composed it in advance for himself is ruled out by the mention of the death of his children whom he predeceased (*ll*.9-10). *Ll*.12-14 perhaps reflect the instructions which he gave to his wife about his mortal remains, which she subsequently fulfilled as a final token of her *philandria*.

There is no complaint in this poem that death has come to Rufinus despite his living a good life. In an epitaph for Popilia, *IGUR* 1310 (Rome, Imperial period; pl. on p.167), the dead woman advises her husband: καὶ λέγε Ποπιλίην εὕδειν, ἄνερ· οὐ θεμιτὸν γὰρ | θνήσκειν τοὺς ἀγαθούς, ἀλλ' ὕπνον ἡδὺν ἔχειν (*ll*.7-8), 'and say that Popilia is sleeping, my husband; for it is not right (to say?) that the good die, but that they enjoy sweet sleep'. The 'sleep of death' is a common motif, of course, in later, Christian contexts, taking its rise from such a NT passage as the Lazaros story (cf. esp. Jn 11.11-14). But an inscription such as this indicates the non-Jewish ancestry of this notion. Cf. the wording ὕπνος αἰώνιος on a sarcophagus inscription, *I.Eph.* VII, 2.3828 (Hypaipa, after 212), where there is nothing to indicate a link with Judaism or Christianity. G. Petzl, *Die Inschriften von Smyrna*, I (*IK* 23; Bonn, 1982) 557 restores a funerary epigram to include similar wording. The 'sleep of death' is sometimes taken a step further, as in a III BC epigram from Melos — *IG* XII, 3 (1898) 1190, repr. and discussed at Pircher, no.19, pp.58-61 — in which the deceased wife is represented as saying, 'I love my husband even though I am dead', στέργω καὶ φθιμένα τὸν ἐμὸν πόσιν (*l*.1).

In *l*.6 Rufinus is said to have restored his *psyche* to the air and his body to the earth after he died. This comment provides a further parallel to the usage of νεκρόω at Rom. 4.19, in addition to the one cited by MM., s.v. See further the discussion at **6** above, about the continued existence of the dead after their physical death.

11. 'Body, soul and spirit . . .'

Rome | Imperial period

ed. — *IG* XIV (1890) 1720

Θ(εοῖς) Κ(αταχθονίοις).
[- - -]ρίου σῶμα νέρθεν, | πνεῦμα καὶ ψυχὴ μένει·
| ἡρπάγη νέος φίλοισιν | Ἱπποθόῃ καὶ συνβίῳ.

Metrical epitaph (two trochees). Vertical bars mark line divisions on the stone.
Bib. — Peek, *GVI* 1770; **IGUR* 1369 (pl. on p.216).

To the underworld gods. The body of . . . rios is below; his spirit and soul remain. He was snatched while still young from his friends and his wife Hippothoe.

In view of the dedication in *l*.1, a very common Greek rendering of the Latin *D*(*is*) *M*(*anibus*), the epitaph is unlikely to be Jewish or Christian. Yet occasionally other internal evidence in texts suggests that this formula was used by Jews and Christians: for a possible Jewish example see *IGUR* 1240, reprinted and discussed at the end of **5** above (cf. *New Docs 1976*, **76**, p.119 for other instances). Since the formula *D.M.* does not occur before the time of Augustus this short epigram may be taken to belong to the Imperial period. The presence of the trichotomy is therefore all the more striking as a parallel for 1 Thes. 5.23. A further instance of the trichotomy, apparently, may be seen in **8** above. The three known papyrus examples (all Christian) are discussed briefly at *New Docs 1976*, **64**. The distinction between πνεῦμα and ψυχή is by no means always observed: see the brief discussion in **6** above.

Much more common is the dual combination of σῶμα/ψυχή. In this regard, four honorific texts included in *I.Eph.* Ia may be instanced. No.5 (Astypalaia, probably II BC fin.) is a decree of Ephesos honouring the Astypalaioi who stood by the Ephesians and sailed against their enemies: 'hazarding their lives they did not spare either body or soul', παραβαλόμ[ενοι τῶ]ι ≪β≫ίωι οὔτε σ[ώματος] | οὔτε [ψ]υχῆς ἐφείσαντο, κτλ (*ll*.22-23). No.6 (II BC; pl.7), found at the city's Baths of Scholastica, praises a gymnasiarch called Diodoros. This text informs us that 'he provided also for the manliness of the *neoi*, inclining them both to gymnastics and to diligence, both physical and spiritual, deeming them of the utmost importance for the sake of having the reputation of the *neoi* increased both in theory and in practice', προ|[ενό]ησεν δὲ καὶ τῆς τῶν νέων εὐανδρίας προτρεπόμενο[ς] | [αὐ]τοὺς πρός τε τὰ γυμνάσια καὶ φιλοπονίαν σωματι|κήν τε καὶ ψυχικὴν περὶ πλείστου ποιούμενος ἕνεκεν τοῦ | καὶ λόγωι καὶ ἔργωι συνεπαυξηθῆναι τὸ τῶν νέων ἀξίωμα, κτλ (*ll.*15-19). For σωματικός cf. 1 Tim. 4.8; but ψυχικός here does not really parallel any of the NT uses of this adjective. The third item, *I.Eph.* Ia.11 (found at Aphrodisias, Hadrianic period; pl.12), records the Ephesians' decision to honour the Aphrodisian athlete Kallikrates. At *ll.*15-18 the wording runs: σώματι γὰρ [ὑ]|περβάλλων ἅπαντας ἀρχαίους ἐθαυμάσθη [τὴν] | [φύ]σιν, ψυχῆς τε ἐπιμελούμενος ἐμακαρί|ζετο τὸν τρόπον, 'surpassing all his predecessors in physique he was admired for his natural (strength), and taking care of his soul he was considered blessed in his character'. Finally, *I.Eph.* Ia.12 (II; pl.13) is a copy of a city decree which was found in the Baths of Hadrian at Aphrodisias. This honours an athlete, Aurelius Achilleus, of whom it is said: ὡς ἐν αὐ|τῷ πᾶσαν κεκρᾶσθαι τὴν ἀρετὴν ὅσην | ψυχῆς ἐστιν καὶ σώματος (*ll.*19-21), 'thus is there blended in him every virtue of soul and body'. All four of these inscriptions have numerous other words worth noting for the NT. MM picked up the first, s.v. εὐσχημοσύνη referring to the text as 'Cagnat [= *IGRR*] IV.1029.35' (*l.*36, in fact). In the section quoted from no.11 above μακαρίζω may be specially noticed, as neither MM nor BAGD provides any documentary references to illustrate Lk. 1.48 and Jas. 5.11.

An Athenian funerary epigram reprinted twice in *SIA* III (p.xi = *IG* III, 2.x.1383; p.166 = C. Bayet, *De titulis Atticae Christianis antiquissimis* [Paris, 1878], no.118) is at least plausibly Christian, if not unambiguously so. It appears to be for an unmarried woman — there is nothing to suggest she was only a girl (no parents are named) — and the passer-by is asked to 'gaze upon the holy beauty of the immortal soul and body of Asklepiodote', 'Ασκληπιοδότη[ς] ἱερόν, φίλε, δέρκεο κάλλος | ψυχῆς ἀθανάτη[ς] καὶ σώματος (*ll.*1-2). This presumably alludes to a portrait or image of the deceased set up on the tomb; cf. **7** and **12** for instances of this practice. Some further instances of the body/soul dichotomy are mentioned at **6**. From the papyrus texts of the year we may note the soul/body combination in Tibiletti, *Lettere*, no.27 (Hermopolis Magna, IV[1]; = *P.Herm.Rees* [1964] 5). This is a letter from Hermodoros to Theophanes, the latter of whom is known not to have been a Christian, though some of his correspondents may have been: see **124** below. Hermodoros hopes and prays that almighty God will restore Theophanes to them well in soul and body, ἀπολαβόντες | σε ἐρρωμένον ψυχῆι τε καὶ σώματι, κτλ (*ll.*13-14).

A magical gem from Asia Minor with a figure of Eros carries the inscription, 'give to me the wearer the life of Secundilla, δὸς τὴν ψυχὴν ἐμοὶ τῷ φοροῦντι Σεκουνδίλης: Guarducci, *EG* IV.276 (date not given). Here the noun must indicate the whole person whom the man wishes to possess. A similar meaning may be appropriate for ψυχή in a binding charm quoted at **13**, ad fin. At **46** below a phrase is discussed in which ψυχή appears to mean 'life'. Another text in which the word ψυχή occurs warrants mention here. Pfuhl/Möbius II.1775 (Perre in the Tauros mountains of Kommagene, n.d.) is a bas-relief featuring a reclining man and a seated woman. The text reads: ψυχὲ (*read* -αὶ) | Γαιανοῦ καὶ | Μαρ[θ]άνης· | ταῦτα γάρ, 'souls of Gaianos and Marthane; for this (is what they are)'. Here ψυχή is to be understood as a Greek equivalent for *nefeš*, which may designate the funerary stele, or the relief on the stele, as well as the more usual 'soul' (so edd. n. to *IGLS* 1 [1929] 48). The last of these senses is of course frequent in the LXX (Gen. 12.5, etc.). For the epithet θεόπεμπτος applied to the soul see *IGUR* 1204, quoted in part at **6** above.

For misplaced καί in *l.*3 of the epitaph with which we began, cf. an inscription on the plinth of a statue of Leto (Cremna in Pisidia, III(?)), Λ. Αἰλ. 'Ιουλιανὸς ὁ ἱερεὺς ἀρχιερεὺς κτίστης φιλό[δο]|ξος μετὰ καὶ τῶν τέκνων αὐτοῦ 'Ροτειλίου Λο[υ]|κίλλης καὶ τὰ ἀγάλματα ἀνέθηκαν τῇ γλυκυτά|τῃ πατρίδι, 'L(ucius) Ael(ius) Julianus, priest, high priest, fame-loving founder, together with his children Rutilius and Lucilla set up the statues to their most sweet country'. This inscription, along with others found in a 1970 rescue dig at the site, was first published by G.E. Bean, *TAD* 19 (1970 [1972]) 99-102; improved editions of some of these will be given in a forthcoming article in *AS* 37 (1987).

12. Tasting life

Rome Imperial period

ed. — *IG* XIV (1890) 1607 + 2171

῎Αρτι με γευομένην ζωῆς βρέφος | ἥρπασε δαίμων
καὶ οὐ πατρὸς | εἶδον ἐγὼ τύπον, ἀλλ' ἔθανον
| ἕνδεκα χρησαμένη μηνῶν φάος | εἶτ' ἀποδοῦσα (*leaf*)
κεῖμαι ἐν τύμ|βοισι τὸν ἀεὶ χρόνον, μηκέθ' ὁρῶ|σα
τὸ φῶς (*leaf*) σὺ δ' ἀναγνοὺς κλαῦ|σον,
ξεῖν<ε>, τὸν Εὐνόης τύμβον | [ἐ]π[ε]ρ̣χ̣ό̣[μ]ενος.

Nearly complete inscription, somewhat irregularly metrical in *ll*.4-5. Vertical bars mark line divisions on the stone.
Bib. — **IGUR* 1216 (pl. on p.77).

When I had just tasted life fate snatched me, an infant, and I did not see my father's pattern; but I died after enjoying the light of eleven months, then I returned it. I lie in the tomb forever, no longer seeing | the light; but you, stranger, read this and weep as you come upon the tomb of Eunoe.

Here is an epitaph for an infant who did not reach her first birthday. In the NT βρέφος refers almost always to an unborn child (Lk. 1.41, 44) or a new-born baby (Lk. 2.12, 16; Acts 7.19; cf. the figurative use at 1 Pet. 2.2). Only at 2 Tim. 3.15 does a slightly wider range of usage come into view, referring to early childhood; this sense would be apposite for Lk. 18.15, though 'new-born baby' cannot be ruled out there. At Pfuhl/Möbius I.392.5 (Smyrna, II BC; = G. Petzl, *Die Inschriften von Smyrna*, I [*IK* 23; Bonn, 1982] 520) this noun is used in a metrical epitaph for a two-year-old; while at no.480 (Kotiaion in Phrygia, 'pre-Byzantine' [edd.]) it occurs of a child who did not reach the age of three (οὔπω τριέτιν ἤδη, *l*.2). In an epitaph for a child aged 4 years and 4 months, *IGUR* 1272 (Rome, Imperial?), he is called υἱός in the prose section, βρέφος and νήπιος in the following epigram. Thus we appear to be getting beyond infancy for some attestations of this word. This phenomenon should not cause surprise: for a spreading 'downwards' in age, note the use of παιδάριον of an unborn child in a lead tablet used for a question to an oracle, repr. at **32** below.

Yet a caution needs to be sounded, which the text printed above illustrates well. It is well known that many epigrams chosen for tombstones are an amalgam of frequently-used lines and phrases selected as appropriate to the particular circumstances. A striking illustration of this is provided by T. Drew-Bear in G.W. Bowersock et al. (edd.), *Arktouros. Hellenic Studies Presented to B.M.W. Knox* (Berlin, 1979), 308-16 (pl.7). He publishes a metrical epitaph for Demosthenes (near Hasanlar in N-W Phrygia, II^2/III^1; = *SEG* 1401), the first two verses of which he traces in 18 other inscriptions (including one Christian text) ranging geographically from Boubon in North Lykia to Euboia and Crete, and chronologically from the early Hellenistic period to Gallienus' reign. See further **6** ad fin. In the present case, the first line of *IGUR* 1216 (above) appears also as *l*.1 of Pfuhl/Möbius 480, and as the first verse line in *IGUR* 1272. These instances perhaps also attest the geographically far-flung currency of such tags: Rome and Phrygia. In such contexts, therefore, it may not be so staightforward to say that βρέφος can refer to a child aged up to four. Rather, the parents (or the mason) have selected from a 'catalogue' this line of verse (which coincidentally contained the word) for their child's epitaph.

In this same first line of the inscription printed above, the infant is said to have 'tasted life'. Apart from the already-noted replication of this line in other texts, attention may be drawn to the incipit μήπω γευσάμενος ἥβης at *IGUR* 1228 (Rome, n.d.), an epitaph for a child of seven who is already an initiate of the Dionysiac mysteries. These phrases may call to mind the NT wording γ. θανάτου, used by Jesus of certain disciples (Mk. 9.1 = Mt. 16.28 = Lk. 9.27), by Jewish opponents at Jn 8.52, quoting supposed words of Jesus in response to his statement that the person who observes his *logos* will not *theorein* death forever; and it is used of Jesus at Heb. 2.9. The occurrence in three different NT contexts, together with the parallel turns of phrase in these funerary epigrams, suggests that the figurative use of γεύομαι was in general vogue. The active voice of the verb is much less commonly used, but also may be employed metaphorically. From this year's culling may be mentioned Pfuhl/Möbius II.1310 (pl. 193), a verse epitaph (Miletopolis in Mysia, II) for a teacher, which concludes: πρῶτος ὃς ὑμετέρους υἷας γεῦσε λόγων, 'he was the first to give your sons a taste of literature' (8; for this meaning of λόγος see *LSJ*, s.v., VI.3.e). Under the influence of the NT the phrase γ. θανάτου is found in a Christian epitaph from Egypt, reprinted and discussed briefly in *New Docs 1978*, **89**, p.107.

Three other philological features of the epitaph for Eunoe may be noted. First, in *l*.2 the child says she did not live to see her father's *typos*. Given that an eleven-month infant would certainly be able to recognise her father *l*.2 must mean more than 'I didn't see what my father looked like'. E.A. Judge suggests to me that 'recognise my father's pattern', i.e., follow in his ways(?), is the appropriate way to understand it. In view of the meaning of *typos*, we ought to be expecting the child to be *receiving* her father's imprint. Seeing it *in him* would be an inversion of the idea; so perhaps she means that she did not live long enough to see her father's *typos* in herself. For this sense cf. BAGD, s.v., 5b. Illustration of another meaning of this noun (BAGD, s.v., 2) occurs in *IGUR* 1268 (Rome, n.d.), a funerary epigram for Marcia, a Jew(?) — see ed. n. ad loc.; text discussed briefly at *New Docs 1977*, **15**, p.54; cf. **5** above — who is said to have had 'the *typos* of golden Aphrodite' (*l*.4). MM, s.v. τύπος, offer no illustration to parallel the sense 'statue' (BAGD, s.v., 3) which occurs at Acts 7.43 (quoting Amos 5.26). As an instance of this we may note *I.Eph.* II.286, a short funerary epigram (originally located in the Celsus Library — see the *Addenda et Corrigenda* Supplement [1981] to *I.Eph.* I-VII.1, p.8 — and therefore to be dated early II(?)) mentioning a τύπον ὄρθιον. L. Robert, *Hellenica* 13 (1965) 179 n.3, mentions that this meaning is commonly attested in epigrams. The phrase τὸν τύπον | τοῦτον occurs at *CPR* 54 (provenance unknown, II) in a fragmentary portion of a letter; it is possible that the words may refer to this letter itself, in which case we have a further useful illustration of the use at Acts 23.25 (cf. *New Docs 1976*, **26**, pp.77-78; BAGD, s.v.,4). At Pfuhl/Möbius I.480.7 (already mentioned above), the parents are said to have 'set up this image of me (on this tomb)', μ' ἐ[τύ]πωσαν [τῷδ' ἐπὶ τύμβῳ]. For this practice we may compare *IGUR* 1490.6 (quoted above at **7**). Note also *SIA* III, p.166 no.118 (quoted in part at **11**). At one remove from this is the statement ἧασέ τε εἰκόνας ἀντιτύπους, 'she left portraits which were exact copies', at *IGUR* 1327.5 (Rome, n.d.), a reference to the children the deceased woman had borne. Perhaps this usage helps us to understand *typos* in the Eunoe epitaph with which this entry began: the father is the *typos*, the daughter has not yet formed herself into his *antitypos*. At *IGUR* 1167.3-4 (Rome, III fin.(?)) we have what is probably another adjectival use of ἀντίτυπος: 'now I shall set up this inscription as an act of thanks to you, the corresponding thank-offering of which, made from wax, you will make flow with my tears', νῦν δέ σοι τήνδε γραφὴν θήσω χάριν, ἧς ἀπὸ κηροῦ | ἀντίτυπον ῥεύσει τοῖς δακρύοις χάριτα. The sense of this text is difficult; Moretti, n. ad loc., understands ῥεύσει as fut. midd. 2nd pers. sing.; for ῥέω transitive see LSJ, s.v., 2. I take it that the brother who erects this epitaph means that he will retain its wording on a wax tablet (the exemplar from which the inscription was copied on to the stone), and whenever he looks at it the memory of his sister will make him shed tears over it. MM have no entry for ἀντίτυπος, so these two epigraphical attestations are well worth including in a new entry to illustrate 1 Pet. 3.21. Likewise, their entry for the neuter noun ἀντίτυπον provides no documentary illustrations. From this year's collection of texts we may note the formula τούτου (*sc.* the epitaph, mentioning a penalty for interfering with the tomb) ἀντίτυπον ἀπετέθη εἰς τὸ ἀρχεῖον, 'a copy of this was lodged in the archives office', *I.Eph.* VI.2535 (n.d.; very similar wording at VII, 1.3230, dated II or III). These attestations offer good parallels for the sole NT occurrence of the noun at Heb. 9.24, χειροποίητα . . . ἅγια . . . ἀντίτυπα τῶν ἀληθινῶν.

More briefly, note χράομαι + accusative in *l.*3 of the Eunoe inscription, a good parallel to the use at 1 Cor. 7.31, καὶ οἱ χρώμενοι τὸν κόσμον ὡς μὴ καταχρώμενοι. Finally, attention may be drawn to the interchange of singular and plural forms of τύμβος (*ll.*4, 6), *metri causa*, as also the alternation between the forms φάος/φῶς (*ll.*3, 5).

13. Speak no evil

Rome — Imperial Period
ed. — *IG* XIV (1890) 1201

Οὐκ ἤμην, γενόμην· | ἤμην, οὐκ εἰμί· τοσαῦτα·
| εἰ δέ τις ἄλλο ἐρέει, ψεύσεται· | οὐκ ἔσομαι.
| Χαῖρε δίκαιος ὤν.
Ὦ παῖ, φυλάσσου μὴ σφαλῇς· ἡ γλῶσσά τοι
αὐτὴ μὲν οὐδέν, ἡνίκ' ἂν λέγῃ, πονεῖ,
ὅταν δὲ ἁμάρτῃ, πολλὰ προσβάλλει κακά.

Herm, with large intervals on the stone separating the three metrical parts of the text (2 hexameters, dochmius, 3 senarii). Letter height of the hexameter section is half that of the other wording, and may not be contemporary.
Bib. — Peek, *GVI* 1959; **IGUR* 1398 (pl. on p.235).

I did not exist, I was born; I existed, I do not exist; so much (for that). If anyone says anything different he will be lying: I shall not exist.
Greetings, if you are a just person.
My child, guard yourself lest you trip: the tongue | itself is not troubled, indeed, whenever it speaks; but whenever it errs it contributes many evils.

Of considerable interest for the NT is the epigram which comprises *ll.*4-6. The use of ὦ παῖ as a way of introducing moral advice suggests an analogy with OT Wisdom Literature, and with Proverbs in particular; υἱέ is normally employed there (1.10; 2.1; 3.1, 11, 21, etc.), though cf. παῖδες at 4.1. On τέκνον, παῖς and related words in *koine* see G.R. Stanton's paper forthcoming in the *Acta* of the XVIIIth International Congress of Papyrology, held in Athens in 1986. For the related τεκνίον — NT: Jn 13.33; Gal. 4.19; 1 Jn 2.1, 12, 28, and four further places in that short letter — cf. the discussion at *BE* 514.

The warning against troubles caused by the tongue is reminiscent of Jas. 3.2-12. The most recent major commentary on James in English, by P.H. Davids (*NIGTC*; Exeter, 1982), draws many parallels with Graeco/Roman and Jewish literature for specific features of this section of the letter, but no relevant documentary references are included. Davids argues (144) that Dibelius' claim is not proven, that James was dependent on a diatribe for some of his material in ch.3. In this, as in his general doubting of the presence of diatribe in James, he depends heavily (note especially 12 with n.40) on a brief comment made in another context by H.D. Jocelyn, *LCM* 43 (1979) 145-46, that 'diatribe' does not describe any ancient sub-genre of writing. Unfortunately, Davids did not note N.M. Horsfall's rejoinder (ibid., 170), in which he points out that it is used from the time of Plato (of Sokrates' discourses) onwards. The term is used as the title of works by various writers, such as the III BC Stoics Zenon and Kleanthes. Davids was unable to take account of the nearly simultaneously appearing S.K. Stowers, *The Diatribe and Paul's Letter to the Romans* (*SBLDS* 57; Chico, 1981). For a survey of literature on 'diatribe' in the NT see most recently K. Berger, *ANRW* II.25.2 (1984) 1124-32. Whether or not it is admissible to use the word 'diatribe' to describe the Jas. 3 polemic, it cannot be thought that this passage was composed *a nihilo*. The existence of the closely similar sentiment in a documentary text such as this inscription bears popular witness to the same moralising concern in the Roman world as James had.

The first two lines of the poem reflect commonly-expressed sentiments. With *l.*1 we may compare *IGUR* 1397 (Rome, n.d.), [οὐκ ἤ]|μη[ν, γε]νόμην, | οὐκ ἰμί, οὐ μέλι μοι, 'I had no existence, I was born, I do not exist, I don't care'; cf. the similar no.1283.6-7 in an epitaph for a doctor (n.d.). A gladiator's epitaph from Amasia (Imperial period) includes similar wording (*ll.*5-8), οὐκ ἤμην, οὐκ ᾔ|δειν, ἐγενόμην | οὐκ οἶδα, οὐκ εἰμί, οὐ μέλει μοι: repr. with bibliographical references for the motif in L. Robert, *Les gladiateurs dans l'Orient grec* (Limoges, 1940; repr. Amsterdam, 1971) no.76. With the strong denial of life beyond the grave (*l.*2) compare *IGUR* 1245 (n.d.), where the deceased tells the passer-by that 'in Hades there exists no boat, no ferryman Charon, no custodian Aiakos, no dog Kerberos; all we who are dead below have become bones, ashes, and nothing else' (*ll.*3-6).

There is no indication of the identity of the deceased in the inscription with which this entry began. This is by no means unprecedented. Attention may be drawn here to Pfuhl/Möbius I.847 (pl. 123), a carefully inscribed verse inscription surmounted by a bearded man seated in profile, his staff resting on a skull in front of his feet (Smyrna, II; text also in G. Petzl, *Die Inschriften von Smyrna*, I [*I.K.* 23; Bonn, 1982] 558). Vertical bars mark line divisions on the stone.

Ἄνθρωπος τοῦτ' ἐσ|τί. τίς εἶ, βλέπε, καὶ τὸ | μένον σε·
εἰκόνα τήν|δε ἐσορῶν σὸν τὸ τέ|λος λόγισαι
καὶ (*leaf*) | βιότῳ· χρῆσαι μή|θ' ὡς ἰς αἰῶνας ἔχων | ζῆν,
μηθ' ὡς ὠκύμο|ρος, ἵνα γηράσαντά | σε πολλοὶ
μαστί|ξωσι λόγοις θλειβόμε|νον πενίῃ.

This is a human being; consider who you are and what awaits you. As you look at this image reflect upon your end and do not treat your life as though you had forever to live, nor as though you are short-lived, with the result that many | will scourge you verbally when you have become old and are afflicted with poverty.

Here is another reflection on mortality, but the moralising tone of this epigram is made more striking by the accompanying relief of the philosopher-figure and the nearby skull. This latter motif may recall us to such stories as the anecdote in Hdt. 2.78 concerning the parading of a wooden corpse in a coffin after banquets to remind participants of their mortality. For a more hackneyed expression of the sentiment, 'Your turn will come too', cf. from this year's culling *IMS* 120 (Veliki Trnovac in the valley of S. Moravia in Moesia, n.d.), *fui quod tu es, | eris quod ego sum* (*ll*.6-7), 'I was what you are, you will be what I am'. On the Smyrna monument the non-identification of the deceased is to be explained (so Pfuhl/Möbius, following *ed.pr.*) by the fact that the monument had been prepared to this stage of completion and was awaiting a purchaser, who would have added, in the large blank area remaining on the stele below the text, details specific to himself or the person being memorialised.

While the first two verses and the last two are in elegiac metre, *l*.3 does not form part of this scheme (unless a hexameter was intended — scanning ἱς αἰῶνᾰς — as W. Ritchie suggests to me). Although there is no apparent reason for this metrical switch here, occasionally the rationale may be explicit: note, for example, *IGUR* 1189 (Rome, n.d.), where after two elegiac couplets *l*.5 is a trimeter, followed again by a pentameter in which the deceased says that his name, Taxiarches (incorporated into *l*.5), could not be fitted into a hexameter line. Returning briefly to the Smyrna epigram, we may note the presence of consecutive ἵνα (*l*.4), well-attested in the NT (Lk. 9.45; Jn 9.2; cf. BAGD, s.v., II.2). The claim of BDF §391.5, that 'Jewish teleology [contrast 'die jüdische Theologie', BDR §391, n.10, on p.318, surely a misprint?] in general has contributed to the blurring of the distinction between purpose and result', should be treated with some caution. The vivid figurative use of μαστιγόω in this epigram may be noted as a parallel of a general kind for Heb. 12.6, quoting Prov. 3.12, μαστιγοῖ (*sc.* ὁ κύριος) δὲ πάντα υἱὸν ὃν παραδέχεται.

The moralising poem from Smyrna is attributed to Bias of Priene (Pfuhl/Möbius, following *ed.pr.*), one of the so-called Seven Sages of the Archaic and Classical Greek world. As evidence of the widespread influence of such popular philosophy in brief form we may compare Guarducci, *EG* III (Rome, 1974) 78-80 (fig.38), a set of aphorisms concerning the Five 'Ages' of Man.

παῖς ὢν κόσμιος γίνου,
ἡβῶν ἐγκρατής,
μέσος δίκαιος,
πρεσβύτης εὔβουλος,
τελευτῶν ἄλυπος.

While a child (try to) be well-behaved; while a youth, well-disciplined; in middle age, just; wise in counsel when an old man; | dying with no regrets.

This inscription is one of two found on a stone base at Baktriane on the river Oxus in Iran, and published by L. Robert, *CRAI* (1968) 421-57 no.2 (figs.2-6), who dates it III BC init. To the left of this set of maxims is a four-line epigram in which a certain Klearchos says that he saw at Delphi these wise sayings of men of a past age, copied them down and had them carefully (ἐπιφραδέως, 3) inscribed in the *temenos* of Kineas. The *temenos* refers to the *heroon* where this man, probably the founder of the town, was buried (Robert, 431-38, who argues that Kineas may have been a Thessalian). As for Klearchos, Robert argues persuasively (442-49) that he may well have been Klearchos of Soloi, the Peripatetic student of Aristotle mentioned by Josephus, *Ap.* 1.22.

Robert shows that the set of maxims which survive is the last of a series of 147 such items preserved by Stobaios under the heading *Sosiades' 'Counsels of the Seven Wise Men'.* Sosiades is to be thought of as the editor of this collection, one of several revisions of which circulated in antiquity. Robert argues that, as the stone found at Baktriane preserves only the last item of the series together with a record of who had it erected, we should infer the presence originally of a larger monument which contained the entire collection. This inference receives confirmation from a stone fragment which appears to preserve parts of maxims nos. 47 and 48 in the list as preserved in Stobaios (Robert, 430). The use of γίνου in *l.*1 of the maxim quoted above has numerous parallels in the NT, e.g., Mt. 6.16; 10.16; 1 Cor. 11.1; 14.20; Gal. 4.12, etc.

In the same article Robert publishes (417-21, fig.1) a short dedicatory inscription to Hermes and Herakles which testifies to the existence of a gymnasium at Baktriane. The latter is well-known to be one of the best indicators for the spread of Hellenic social *mores.* Together with the surviving portion of the text erected by Klearchos, whose contents attest the penetration of Greek *paideia* into a remote corner of the Seleucid domain at the beginning of III BC, this inscription may be of some comparative interest when the question is being considered, how early Hellenism permeated Palestine.

Returning to the question of the tongue, its power is recognised in SIG^3 1175, a magical binding charm engraved on a lead tablet, *ll.*32-39 of which are reprinted as Helbing, *AGI* 36 (Piraieus, late IV/early III BC):

'Αριστὼ ἐγὼ ἔλαβον καὶ ἔδη[σ]α τὰς χεῖρας καὶ τοὺς πόδας καὶ τὴν γλῶσσαν καὶ τὴν ψυχήν· καὶ μὴ δύναιτο ὑπὲρ Φίλωνος φθένγεσθαι ῥῆμα πονηρόν, ἀλλὰ ἡ γλῶσσα αὐτῆς μόλυβδος γένοιτο· καὶ κέντησον αὐτῆς τὴν γλῶσσαν.

It is Aristo whom I have seized, and bound her hands and her feet and her tongue and her soul; and may she not be able to speak an evil word about Philo, | but may her tongue become lead; and stab her tongue.

This is the last of three binding texts on this lead sheet. The earlier two (not included in Helbing) are virtually identical in their form and terminology, with merely the names altered. Occasionally these charms may be rather more extensive, for example, the one reprinted at *New Docs 1976*, **8** (Antinoopolis region, III/IV). The discussion there reported the view of *ed.pr.* that the Antinous to whom appeal was made was probably not Hadrian's lover. Yet R. Lambert,

Beloved and God. The Story of Hadrian and Antinous (London, 1984) 192 and n.39 on p.271, has more recently argued that this identification is indeed plausible. In the present text we may note that in addition to mention of parts of the woman's body, Philo also seeks to control her soul; so also in the previous adjurations (*ll.*4, 16-17). However, ψυχή may be better understood here as a reference to the 'whole person'; cf. **11** above. But the emphasis is on the tongue, and reflects the widespread fear of the power of the word. The tongue as lead is a striking figure for such an unpretentious text, yet it is very apposite given the material on which it is written; the same phrase occurs earlier, at *ll.*6-7, 20-22. In the final sentence it is probably Hekate who is being invoked to act against Aristo (so Helbing, ad loc.).

14. Some asiarchs of Ephesos

Ephesos 104
ed. — *I.Eph.* Ia.27.220-46 (pls. 35,36)

[ ] τῶν δὲ καθιερωμένων ὑπὸ Σαλουτα-
[ρίου δην. β´] μ̣(υρίων) τ[ε]λέσει τόκον Σαλουτάριος δραχμιαῖον καθ' ἕκαστον ἐνι-
[αυτὸν] τὰ γει[ν]όμενα δηνάρια χίλια ὀκτακόσια, ἀφ' ὧν δώσει τῷ γραμμα-
[τεῖ τῆς β]ουλῆς δηνάρια τετρακόσι[α π]ε̣ντήκοντα, ὅπως ἐπιτελεῖ διανομὴν
[τοῖς] βουλευταῖς ἐν τῷ ἱερῶι ἐν τ[ῶι πρ]ονάωι τῆι γενεσίωι τῆς μεγίστης θεᾶς Ἀρ-
[τέμιδος,] ἥτ̣ις ἐστὶν μηνὸς Θαργη[λι]ῶνος ἕκτῃ ἱσταμένου, γεινομένης τῆς διανο-
[μῆς ἤδη τῆ]ς πέμπτης, διδομένο[υ ἑ]κάστῳ τῶν παρόντων δηναρίου ἑνός,
[μὴ ἔχον]τος ἐξουσίαν τοῦ ἐπὶ τῆς διανομῆς ἀπόντι δοῦναι̣, ἐ̣π̣εὶ ἀποτεισά-
[τω τῆι β]ο̣υλῆι ὑπὲρ ἑκάστου ὀνόματος τοῦ μὴ παραγενομένου καὶ λαβόντος
[προστείμου δην. ̣ · ἐὰν δὲ μείζω]ν γεί[νηται ὁ κόλλυβος, ὥστε]
[εἰς πλείονας χωρεῖν, ἐξέστ]ω καὶ [ ]
[ ]α ἀνὰ κυ[....]ν. ὁμοίω̣[ς δώ-]
[σει τῷ τοῦ συνεδρίου τῆς] γερουσ[ίας γ]ραμματεῖ κ[ατ' ἐνι-]
[αυτὸν ἕκαστον ἀπὸ τοῦ προγεγραμμέν]ου τόκου δη. [τπβ´]
[ἀσσάρια θ´, ὅπως ἐπιτελῇ κλῆρον τῇ] γενεσίῳ τῆς θεο̣[ῦ]
[ἡμέρᾳ τοῖς τοῦ συνεδρίου μετέχουσι]ν εἰς ἄνδρας τθ̣´ [ἀνὰ δη. α´· ἐὰν]
[δὲ μείζων ᾖ ὁ γενόμενος κόλλυβος,] ὥστε εἰς πλείο̣[νας]
[χωρεῖν, κληρώσει καὶ πλείονας, ἑκ]ά̣στου τῶν λαχ[όν-]
[των ἀνὰ δηνάριον ἓν λαμβάνοντ]ος. διδόσθ[ω δὲ καὶ]
[τοῖς τοῖς νεοκοροῦσι παρὰ] Σα[λ]ουταρίῳ τ[ῷ καθιερω-]
[κότι εἰς διανομὴν δη. καὶ το]ῖς ἀ̣σιαρχ̣ή̣[σασι] τ̣οῖς
[ἀναγραψαμένοις δη. εἰς κλῆρον] ἀ̣ν̣ὰ [δηνάρ]ι̣α ι≪α´≫, ᾧ καὶ
[τὰ εἰς τὴν θυσίαν ἀγοράσουσιν,] τοῦ κ̣λ̣ήρου γεινομένου
[τῆι πέμπτηι, μὴ ἔχοντος ἐ]ξουσία≪ν≫ τοῦ γραμματέος τῆς
[γερουσίας τοῦ παριέναι τὴν δ]ιανομὴν ἢ ἀναγραφὴν μετὰ
[τὴν Σαλουταρίου τελευτή]ν̣, ἐπεὶ ἀποτεισάτω πρόστειμον
[τὸ ἐν τῇ διατάξει ὡρισ]μ̣ένον.

The entire inscription (494B x 208H cm. [left] and 430H cm. [right]) from which the above lines are extracted consists of fragments of fifteen blocks of an inscribed panel of white marble, which originally covered about sixteen blocks of the south face of the southern retaining wall of the theatre at Ephesos. One block is completely lost. For a reconstruction of the whole inscription field see the diagram included in the introduction to *I.Eph.* Ia.27.

| . . . From the 20,000 denarii donated by Salutaris he will pay 9% interest, a yearly sum of 1800 denarii, from which he will give to the secretary of the council 450 denarii so that he may distribute them to the members of the council in the sanctuary in the vestibule (of the temple) on the birthday of the greatest goddess Artemis, | which is the sixth day of the month Thargelion; the distribution being conducted already during the fifth. To each of those present is given one denarius, and he who is responsible does not have the right to give (money) to anyone absent at the time of the distribution; since (otherwise) he shall pay to the council for each person who was not present and who received something . . . denarii. If the rate of exchange is better so as | to extend to a greater number of people this is permitted also . . . In the same way he will give to the secretary of the synedrion of the gerousia in each year from the aforementioned interest, 382 denarii and 9 asses in order that he may distribute them by lot on the birthday of the goddess | to members of the synedrion, to 309 men each receiving 1 denarius. If, however, the rate of exchange is better and permits the distribution to be extended among a greater number, he will draw lots for the increased number with each of those successful receiving one denarius. Moreover, let there be given to . . ., who fulfil cultic duties in the house of Salutaris, the | donor, . . . denarii and to those former asiarchs who have registered, . . . denarii by lot 11 denarii to each with which they will buy the supplies for the sacrifice, the drawing of the lot taking place on the fifth. The secretary of the gerousia does not have the right to suspend the distribution or the registration after | the death of Salutaris, since (otherwise) he is to pay the fine stipulated in the bequest.

These lines occur in the long inscription recording the perpetual foundation (διάταξις) of C. Vibius Salutaris, a Roman *eques* who had been an imperial procurator, but who was also a citizen of Ephesos and a member of its council. Such perpetual endowments (which differed from a testamentary bequest in that the benefits commenced during the lifetime of the donor) were not uncommon in the Greek East during the early Roman Empire. A general discussion of their form may be found in K.M.T. Atkinson, *RIDA* 9 (1962) 261-89. A study and catalogue of such foundations was published over seventy years ago by B. Laum, *Stiftungen in der griechischen und römischen Antike* (2 vols; Berlin, 1914): for the Salutaris bequest see II.82, 212-14. Text, translation and detailed commentary on the Salutaris bequest, which is especially long and detailed in its stipulations concerning use of the money provided, can be found in J.H. Oliver, *The Sacred Gerusia* (*Hesperia Suppl.* 6; Princeton, 1941) 55-85. Two more recent studies of individual foundations are those of T. Drew-Bear, *Chiron* 10 (1980) 509-36; (Hypaipa, early IV; = *I.Eph.* VII, 2.3803; cf. *SEG* 30 [1980] 1385), and C.P. Jones, *JRS* 73 (1983) 116-25, dealing with *I.Eph.* VII, 1.3334 and improving the text (Tire in the Kaystros Valley, late I; pl.2; cf. *BE* [1984] 402).

The text includes seven documents and is arranged in six columns of differing width and length. The documents are:

A (*ll.*1-133): a decree of the people concerning the endowment of Salutaris and awarding honours to him;

B (*ll.*134-332): the endowment itself, the letter sent at the time when the offer was made to the council and people (the extract printed above comes from this section);

C (*ll*.333-69): a letter of the proconsul C. Aquillius Proculus ratifying the endowment;
D (ll.370-413): a letter of the propraetorial legate, P. Afranius Flavianus, ratifying the endowment;
E (*ll*.414-30): a decree of the council about the participation of the goldbearers in the procession of the statues donated by Salutaris;
F (*ll*.431-46): a decree of the council about the honorary seats in the theatre for the goldbearers; and
G (*ll*.447-568): a supplement to the main endowment.

The Salutaris document is of twofold importance for the particular question of the asiarchy. First, it is among the earliest epigraphic references to the presence of asiarchs in Ephesos and is unlikely to date more than fifty years after the NT allusion to them in Acts 19.31. It is also of special interest because it provides a rare glimpse of certain former asiarchs included in the activities of city life amid the varied array of civic and sacred officials.

The official promulgation of the Salutaris document is dated to 104 by the names of the Roman consuls in *ll*.134-36. The endowment was designed to benefit the citizens of Ephesos and the personnel of the Artemision by gifts of money. It also provided funds for the manufacture of thirty-one gold and silver statues of Artemis, the emperor Trajan and his wife, and personifications of various aspects of the Ephesian and Roman constitutions, together with instructions for the occasions of their use and for their care at other times. Where the text is sufficiently well-preserved, it reveals that Salutaris gave precise instructions on the amount of the donations due to specific individuals or groups, and the way in which the distribution was to be made. These details are tabulated in Oliver (83-84). It is among these groups of recipients that the reference to the former asiarchs is to be found in *ll*.240-45. The secretary of the gerousia is given the power to make a distribution to them, provided that they have registered with him in advance. The money they were given was to be used to buy supplies for the sacrifice on the birthday of Artemis.

Asiarchs are most frequently attested in purely honorary inscriptions. These have been found all over the province of Asia, but by far the greatest number comes from the large cities on the coast and in the hinterland, such as Ephesos itself, Thyatira and Pergamon. According to the most recently-published list of known asiarchs by M. Rossner, *StudClas* 16 (1974) 101-42 — reported in *New Docs 1976*, **32** — well over a hundred asiarchs are recorded in inscriptions ranging in date from late I to *c*. mid-III; and these have been found in more than forty cities scattered about the province. Rossner's list also contains another large group of office-bearers in addition to the asiarchs: men and women who are known to have been *archiereus* or *archiereia* of Asia. By her inclusion of both asiarchs and *archiereis* of Asia, Rossner aligns herself with the majority of scholars studying the imperial cult in Asia in her belief (102) that the title asiarch was synonymous with that of *archiereus* of Asia.

However, it has not been possible to substantiate this view unequivocally, despite a century and a half of research (Rossner, 101). Even among those who have supported the identification of the asiarch with the *archiereus* of Asia there are significant differences in the interpretation of the actual relationship of the two titles: see, e.g., L.R. Taylor in F.J. Foakes-Jackson/K. Lake (edd.), *The Beginnings of Christianity*, I.5 (London, 1933) 256-62, and J. Deininger, *Die Provinziallandtage der römischen Kaiserzeit von Augustus bis zum Ende des 3. Jh. n. Chr.* (Munich, 1965) 36-50. Taylor believes that, initially, the *archiereus* of Asia was chosen from a college of asiarchs who were the foremost men of the province, and that not every asiarch was an *archiereus* of Asia until the second century when there were enough provincial temples in the various cities to allow an asiarch to be appointed to each, together with one supreme asiarch serving the whole province. Deininger, on the other hand, envisages a college of equal-ranking *archiereis* of Asia, which evolved from the single asiarch/*archiereus* of Asia who existed during I AD. In contrast to the pro-identity view, there have always been some who have maintained that the *archiereus* of Asia and the asiarch were not identical at all. According to one such view, the asiarch was an official who was responsible for the production of the festival of the provincial imperial cult (P. Le Bas/W. H. Waddington, *Inscriptions grecques et latines recueillies en Asie Mineure* [Paris, 1870] II.885). For D. Magie, *Roman Rule in Asia Minor* (2 vols; Princeton, 1950) I.449-50, the asiarchs were not provincial officials at all, but purely city benefactors and unrelated to the imperial cult. The ambiguity of much of the evidence relating to the asiarchy has certainly contributed to the variety of present views on its nature, and the difficulties of comprehensive research on the subject have been compounded by the fact that publications of epigraphic material from Asia Minor have generally been unsystematic and diffuse.

For this latter reason, the recently-published repertorium of Ephesian inscriptions has provided a welcome opportunity to reassess earlier conclusions and adopt a new approach to the study of the asiarchy. This collection contains approximately 3500 previously-known and new inscriptions from Ephesos in seven volumes, together with two index volumes (a third is anticipated). As the largest single group of asiarchs and *archiereis* of Asia is attested from Ephesos and its territory, the city is of central importance in resolving the debate over the function of the asiarchs. In 1974 Rossner was able to list 74 asiarchs or *archiereis* of Asia from Ephesos; but on the basis of the *I.Eph.* series this catalogue may now be enlarged to 106 men and women. Thus there has been a significant increase on the evidence available to Rossner; and therefore the new catalogue will provide the basis for a major study of the Ephesian office-bearers.

Four individual careers

A brief survey follows of the careers of four asiarchs who are so far the earliest securely-dated and designated by name at Ephesos. It is these who are closest in time to the early Christian community there with which Paul lived and worked.

The earliest and best attested of the four is Ti. Claudius Aristio who appears in approximately 25 inscriptions from Ephesos so far. He appears initially as asiarch in 92/93, but is documented in Ephesian public life at least four years before that. For example, Aristio was designated as *archiereus* of Asia for 88/89 and he officiated as high-priest of the provincial temple of the imperial cult in Ephesos at the time of a dedication by the people of Keretapa (*I.Eph.* II.234). Many such dedications from far-flung parts of the province were prompted by the construction of Ephesos' first temple of the imperial cult; and this inscription is only one of about ten similar texts in this and the immediately following years (see, e.g., *I.Eph.* II.235-41; V.1498). From dedications made by Klazomenai and Hyrkanis it emerges that Aristio was also provincial high-priest in the following year, 89/90 (*I.Eph.* II.235; V.1498); while in the next year, 90/91, another man held the office of *archiereus* of Asia and Aristio was *neokoros* of the temple (*I.Eph.* II.237, 241). The functions of the latter position are not known; however, it was clearly a prestigious one since it is known to have been hereditary later on in one prominent family of Ephesos (*I.Eph.* VII, 1.3038).

From 92/93, Aristio played an active role in the administration of the city. Two inscriptions of that year record that he held one of the eponymous magistracies of Ephesos, the *grammateia* of the *demos*; and in both cases Aristio is simultaneously named asiarch (*I.Eph.* II.461, 508). One of these two inscriptions is known to have come from the base of a statue found in a large building complex known now as the Harbour Gymnasium; and dedications on several other statue bases from there should probably also be restored with Aristio's name as *grammateus* of the *demos* (*I.Eph.* IV.1128, 1129, 1129a). Aristio's connection with the Harbour Gymnasium was not only an official one, however, for a third inscription reveals that he contributed to the cost of its construction. At that time he was holding another eponymous office of the city, the prytany, and on this occasion also was asiarch at the same time (*I.Eph.* II.427). Although the date of this inscription is unknown, because the building of the Gymnasium no doubt preceded the erection of the decorative statues which were provided during Aristio's *grammateia*, it may reasonably be supposed that his prytany was the earlier of the two offices. Elsewhere, again, it is recorded that at some point in his career Aristio had served the city as a gymnasiarch (*I.Eph.* III.638). While the details are not specified, it does seem likely that he would have served as gymnasiarch of the Harbour Gymnasium after its completion since he had been so closely connected with it from its inception.

After the year 92/93, the chronology of Aristio's career becomes much vaguer due to the lack of proconsular dates in the relevant inscriptions. It is clear, however, that he continued as a leading figure in Ephesos. His philanthropic activity towards the city is documented many times over the next twenty-five years or so. Especially important were his efforts to improve the water supply. He donated money for the construction of a long stretch of canal from the Kaystros River into the city (*I.Eph.* VII, 1.3217a, 3217b; VII, 2.4105). Together with his wife he financed a monumental street fountain in Kouretes Street, as well as a nymphaeum dedicated to Trajan (*I.Eph.* II.424, 424a). The aqueduct appears to have been at least partly completed by 113/14 since the earliest inscription relating to its maintenance dates to that year (*I.Eph.* VII, 1.3217a). Both the fountain-houses also belong to Trajan's reign and, according to the imperial titulature, date between 102 and 114. Yet the relative order of their construction is not known. Another important project of this period in Ephesos, the Celsus Library, was completed under Aristio's supervision although it had actually been donated by another. This building may be dated to the final years of Trajan's reign, or perhaps the beginning of that of Hadrian (*I.Eph.* VII, 2.5101, 5113; V.M. Strocka, *Proc. Xth International Congress of Classical Archaeology: Ankara-Izmir, 1973* [Ankara, 1978] 893-900). Despite the vagueness of the relative chronology, the dedicatory inscriptions of all three constructions make it clear that Aristio continued to undertake public offices in Ephesos during the early part of the second century. He bears two different titles. When the street fountain was completed, he was described as *archiereus* of Asia and *neokoros*. In both the dedication of the nymphaeum of Trajan and that of the Celsus Library, on the other hand, he is named asiarch for the third time.

It was some years before the completion of these magnificent projects on the city's behalf that Aristio was forced to appeal to the emperor for justice against certain malicious accusations made by his fellow-citizens. For a general discussion of trials such as this see J.H. Oliver, *AJP* 100 (1979) 543-58; and cf. **20** below where a set of similar appeals adjudicated by Marcus Aurelius is discussed. Pliny, who records the incident in a letter dated *c.*106/07 (*Ep.* 6.31.3) does not state the reasons for the attack in specific terms; but jealous rivalries between competing aristocratic families of the Greek *poleis* are well documented (Pliny, *Ep.* 10.81; cf. P. Garnsey, *Social Status and Legal Privilege in the Roman Empire* [Oxford, 1970] 69-70). At any rate, Aristio was honourably acquitted of the charge by Trajan; and from what is known of his subsequent financial contributions to the construction of an efficient water-supply in Ephesos, the episode did not cause his desire to be a leading citizen of the city to slacken. Perhaps, indeed, the elaborate and grandiose nymphaeum bearing a dedication to Trajan as well as to Artemis and the Ephesian people might have been Aristio's expression of gratitude to the emperor for his acquittal (*I.Eph.* II.424). Similarly, the statue erected by one of Aristio's freedmen and the latter's three sons to the imperial procurator in Ephesos, L. Vibius Lentulus, may have been inspired by their gratitude for Lentulus' support of their patron during the troubled period of the accusations and the trial in Rome (*I.Eph.* VII, 1.3046).

A contemporary of Aristio was T. Flavius Pythio. He was asiarch in 104/05, the proconsular year following that in which the Salutaris foundation was published. Like Aristio, Pythio served the city as *grammateus* of the *demos*. In fact he held the office twice, and it was in his second term as secretary that he is documented as asiarch concurrently in an inscription recording the dedication of a statue group in the Harbour Baths (*I.Eph.* III.858). In an inscription of the year 109/10, Pythio is again named asiarch, although not this time *grammateus* also. On this occasion he, his wife and their four children erected two statues in honour of the proconsul of Asia, C. Antius A. Iulius Quadratus, and his sister, Iulia Polla (*I.Eph.* VII, 1.3033, 3034). At some point in his career Pythio also served Ephesos as a *neopoios* (*I.Eph.* V.1578a). The *neopoioi* formed a board which was connected with the administration of the Artemision; on these officials see further **28** below. Two other members of Pythio's family, his father and his brother, also held this position (*I.Eph.* IV.1044). Some eleven years after he is first documented as asiarch, in 115/16, Pythio was *archiereus* of the city's imperial cult. By that year Pythio and his wife had also performed the exceptional service of undertaking not once only, but on six occasions, the expenses for one of the city's gymnasia which would otherwise have fallen to the treasury of Artemis (*I.Eph.* V.1500).

This same year, 115/16, is also that in which the third asiarch, Pythio's son T. Flavius Aristoboulos, was both *grammateus* of the *demos* and asiarch (*I.Eph.* V.1500). In his youth the name of Aristoboulos had appeared with those of other members of his family when his father as asiarch had erected statues to the proconsul of Asia and his sister (*I.Eph.* VII, 1.3033, 3034). Then Aristoboulos bore no title, but in 115/16 father and son again appear in the same inscription; and it was Aristoboulos who was then asiarch, not his father. Aristoboulos is known from one other inscription to have been *prytanis* in Ephesos the following year, 116/17 (*I.Eph.* IV.1384c), but no details of his activities are preserved.

The fourth asiarch known to have lived in Ephesos during late I/early II is P. Vedius Antoninus. He is documented first as *prytanis* some time between the years 93-103 (*I.Eph.* IV.1016). He next appears in the epigraphic record in the year 117/18, as *grammateus* of the *demos* for the second time and asiarch at the time of the dedication of the Temple of Hadrian in Kouretes Street (*I.Eph.* II.429; see M. Wörrle, *AA* 88 [1973] 470-77 for an extensive discussion of this inscription). There are also some very poorly-preserved fragments concerning certain building accounts of 116/17 which bear Antoninus' name (*I.Eph.* IV.1384c and 1384c, frags. A and B; three fragments from a single inscription); but there is no indication preserved of Antoninus' role in the matters which form the subject of the decrees. However, the man already known as asiarch, T. Flavius Aristoboulos was named as *prytanis* in one of them (*I.Eph.* IV.1384c). No other contemporary evidence for the activities of Antoninus is extant, but an honorary decree erected to his son P. Vedius Antoninus Sabinus some time later reveals that Antoninus had also been gymnasiarch, panegyriarch of the Great Epheseia and the Pasitheia, as well as an ambassador to Rome during his lifetime (*I.Eph.* III.728; cf. Wörrle, 473-74).

Despite the obviously restricted nature of the evidence concerning these four asiarchs, it is possible to draw some general conclusions about the nature of the asiarchy from their position in Ephesian society and their public careers.

The asiarchs and their families

The possession of the *tria nomina* by all four indicates they were Roman citizens. Indeed, in the case of Pythio, Aristoboulos and Antoninus, the name of their Roman tribe is also known (*I.Eph.* VII, 1.3033, 3034; IV.1016), fully confirming their status. An appeal such as that by Aristio to the jurisdiction of the imperial court at Rome is usually an indication of Roman citizenship. Their very possession of Roman citizenship suggests that the four asiarchs belonged to the highest échelon of society in Ephesos; and this view is supported both by the range of high city or provincial offices they themselves held and also by the information which is preserved about their immediate families. For example, Aristio's wife is known by name as Iulia Lydia Laterane. She had attained the position of *archiereia* of the imperial cult of the city of Ephesos and had also received the title of honorary adoption by the provincial *koinon*, 'daughter of Asia' (*I.Eph.* II.424a; cf. on the *archiereiai* of Asia, R.A. Kearsley, *GRBS* 27 [1986] 182-92). Iulia too, like her husband, had been a *prytanis* in Ephesos (*I.Eph.* V.1601e). The number of children born to Aristio and Iulia is not known; but it appears that they may have had a son at least, for the name of a Ti. Claudius Aristio junior appears as a member of the *hymnodoi* in one inscription dating to the reign of Hadrian (*I.Eph.* IV.1145). This choral group was formed from the elite of the province to sing on important occasions such as the birthday of the emperor. Aristio *neoteros* was among the performers, when the choir sang for the emperor Hadrian during his visit to Ephesos in 123.

Flavius Pythio's family is relatively well documented also. As noted above, his wife, Flavia Myrton, shared with him in his extended term as gymnasiarch in place of the goddess Artemis. His father, T. Fl. Perigenes, was a *bouleutes* and *neopoios* of Artemis, as was his brother who bore the same name (*I.Eph.* IV.1044). This brother may have been asiarch in Ephesos some time during the reign of Trajan (*I.Eph.* IV.1270); and certainly at least two of Pythio's three sons, Aristoboulos (see above) and Iulianus (*I.Eph.* III.712b), were also asiarchs during early II. Pythio's grandson, Flavius Iulianus the younger, was publicly honoured several times by the council and people of Ephesos (*I.Eph.* III.674; VII, 2.4342; for the stemma of this family see *I.Eph.* VII, 1, p.63).

Like Pythio, Vedius Antoninus belonged to a family which established a tradition of pre-eminence in Ephesos. The name of Antoninus' wife is not known so far; but an adopted son, whose full name was M. Claudius P. Vedius Antoninus Sabinus, is documented as both *archiereus* of Asia and asiarch (*I.Eph.* III.732; VI.2039). He is also known to have commenced an equestrian military career (*I.Eph.* III.726, 726a; cf. D. Knibbe, *JÖAI* 50 [1972-75] Beiblatt 72). Antoninus' sister, Vedia Marcia, was both an *archiereia* of Asia and a *prytanis* of Ephesos (*I.Eph.* IV.1017), while his grandson, Phaedrus Sabinianus, attained senatorial rank. Among his other achievements, Sabinianus was chosen quaestor of Cyprus (*I.Eph.* VII, 2.4110), and he was also praised on more than one occasion by the emperor Antoninus Pius for his generosity in paying for the erection of public buildings in Ephesos (*I.Eph.* V.1492-93; for the stemma of the family see *I.Eph.* VII, 1, pp.88-90).

Three of the four asiarchs, Aristio, Pythio and Antoninus, are also documented as benefactors of Ephesos by the provision of money for public works, the erection of honorary statues of civic or Roman officials, or the performance of embassies to Rome on the city's behalf. Such public beneficence is not characteristic only of asiarchs and their families. All families comprising the aristocratic elites of the Greek cities competed with each other during the early imperial period to achieve renown and status within their own communities, the province, and eventually, in the imperial service. In turn, they themselves were honoured with statues, such as those to Aristio (*I.Eph.* II.425; III.638, 638a), or those to the descendants of Antoninus and Pythio, which bear their names as well (*I.Eph.* III.728; VII, 2.4342). It is this extremely common pattern of participation in city life which tends to conceal what differences exist between the functions of the asiarch and the *archiereus* of Asia, for both offices were filled by members of exactly the same group of aristocratic families (F. Quass, *Historia* 31 [1982] 200-04).

Is *archiereus* of Asia to be equated with asiarch?

There are, nevertheless, features in the careers of Aristio, Pythio, Aristoboulos and Antoninus which suggest that there are identifiable characteristics in their activity as asiarchs within Ephesos which set them apart from the provincial *archiereus*, and indicate that the titles actually did refer to two distinct offices, at least in late I/early II.

The first point, exemplified by all four asiarchs, is the very strong link between the highest city magistracies, like the *grammateia* of the *demos*, and the asiarchy. On the importance of the *grammateus* of the *demos* in the Roman period, and his relationship to other officials of the city, see A.H.M. Jones, *The Greek City from Alexander to Justinian* (Oxford, 1940; repr. 1979) 239. This connection is so consistent that it suggests the asiarchy involved some executive power in the city allied to that of the *grammateus*. This same link may perhaps also be observed in Acts 19.31 where, during Paul's visit to Ephesos, out of the large range of officials in the city, it is the *grammateus* of the *demos* and the asiarchs who are together depicted as taking action to defuse the uproar of the silversmiths' riot (on silversmiths at Ephesos see **1**).

The contrast formed by the asiarch's close link with the highest magistracies of the city and the sort of activity documented for the *archiereus* of Asia can best be appreciated in this period by examination of the inscriptions relating to Ti. Claudius Aristio, since he is documented in both offices. When he was archiereus of Asia between 88-90, Aristio appeared in several inscriptions as the head of the provincial temple of the imperial cult and as the official by whose term of office the dedications of the cities or towns of the province were to be dated (*I.Eph.* II.234, 235; V.1498). The city of Ephesos itself and its magistrates, however, did not play any part. On the other hand, when Aristio was *grammateus* of the *demos* and asiarch, or prytanis and asiarch, he was officiating in decrees of the city concerned with the day-to-day management of internal affairs, such as the dedication of buildings or the erection of statues. The same is true of the other three asiarchs. In each case their term of office is used to date the actions of other citizens or public bodies of the city of Ephesos, and no connection with the affairs of the province is evident.

Finally, if consideration is given to the chronology of inscriptions relating to the career of Aristio, the distinction between the asiarchy and *archierosyne* of Asia is underlined further. He bears the title *archiereus* of Asia in several inscriptions dating to 88/89 and 89/90, but the first datable occasion on which he is named asiarch is 92/93. This chronological gap in the application of the two titles to Aristio during the reign of Domitian is indisputable because of the proconsular dating formula contained in the inscriptions themselves. Later in his career, however, in several inscriptions which cannot be dated precisely but which probably all belong to the reign of Trajan, Aristio is called both three-times *archiereus* of Asia (*I.Eph.* II.425, 425a) and three-times asiarch (*I.Eph.* II.424; VII, 2.5101, 5113). There is no evidence that the inscription describing Aristio as *archiereus* of Asia for the third time should be dated to the same year as those naming him asiarch for the third time; but the tendency has been to suggest that such is the case, and to conclude that the two different titles borne by Aristio actually refer to the same position, namely the high-priesthood of the provincial imperial cult (so, e.g., Quass, 193 n.56). This interpretation appears to be based on the assumption that the circumstance of one man holding either office three times, which is indeed rare (see Magie, II.1601-07), is unlikely to extend to the situation where Aristio could have held *each* title three times. However, the firm chronological information for the early part of Aristio's career indicates that this is just what must have happened. Aristio's three datable terms as *archiereus* of Asia and asiarch within the reign of Domitian (88/89; 89/90; 92/93) mean that by the reign of Trajan (if the two titles had been identical) Aristio's term of office would have been his fourth and not his third. Therefore, the well-attested chronological differences in Aristio's terms of office as *archiereus* of Asia and asiarch under Domitian must reflect a true distinction between the two offices in the late-first and early-second centuries.

Unlike Aristio, none of the other three asiarchs is known to have held both offices. It has been claimed by Rossner (130) that Pythio also held both offices. Yet there is no indication that Pythio is actually the anonymous grandfather referred to as *archiereus* of Asia in *I.Eph.* II.674. The reference may equally well apply to the maternal grandfather of the honorand. In *I.Eph.* VII, 2.4342 when exactly the same man is honoured again and Pythio is named as his grandfather he is specifically called asiarch. Thus, of the four asiarchs, only Aristio is indisputably documented as having held both titles. This is in accord with the general pattern of the evidence from Ephesos; for the number of men known to have held both the office of *archiereus* of Asia and that of asiarch is only a small proportion of the total of all office-bearers recorded for the city. In fact, less that one-tenth of the currently known asiarchs falls into this category over the two and a half centuries covered by the epigraphic evidence. Therefore, the number of cases belonging to any period where the two titles could arguably have been interchanged during the course of an office-bearer's career is very small. And in the only example from the period under discussion here it is clear that such a proposition is untenable.

Thus both the content and the chronology of the inscriptions documenting these four Ephesian asiarchs lead to the same conclusion, namely, that the asiarchy was a separate office from that of *archiereus* of Asia. This evidence is confirmed by the Salutaris foundation text also. In it the separate spheres of activity for the former asiarchs and the *archiereus* of Asia are apparent in a manner which is very similar to that in the inscriptions of the individual asiarchs. In the Salutaris text, for example, the former asiarchs are grouped with various administrative bodies of the city, while the *archiereus* of Asia is only referred to some eighteen lines further on and is included among the religious personnel of the temple of Artemis (*ll.*258-63).

In the attempts noted above to explain away the sort of differences between the asiarchs and *archiereis* of Asia, it has sometimes been proposed that the title asiarch was used to denote only certain aspects of the provincial *archierosyne*. It has been suggested, for example, that the title asiarch was held by the *archiereus* of Asia both during the short period of his presidency of the *koinon* festival and also after his term of office as a life-long title (R. Merkelbach, *ZPE* 32 [1978] 288). Others interpret the title solely as one retained for life after a man had served a term as *archiereus* of Asia (e.g., Rossner, 107). However, the inscriptions from Ephesos relating to Aristio, Pythio, Aristoboulos and Antoninus appear to invalidate both these points of view. First, the inscriptions provide no evidence of a connection between these four men in their capacity as asiarch and the festival of the *koinon* of Asia. Of the four only Antoninus is documented as a festival official of any sort, and he was panegyriarch of two local Ephesian celebrations, not of the provincial festival. In any case the reference to the panegyriarchy of Antoninus comes in an honorary inscription only; while in those inscriptions which portray an asiarch in action as, for example, the dedications of buildings or statues, there is nothing in the inscriptions to suggest that the focus of the asiarchs' activities was other than the magistracy they held and the city which they served.

Second, the inscriptions indicate in a variety of ways that the asiarchy was not a life-long title but a clearly-defined position with a fixed term. The use of the phrase τρὶς ἀσιάρχης for Aristio at the time of the building of the nymphaeum (*I.Eph.* II.424), for example, provides a direct comparison with the repeated tenure of the *grammateia* by Pythio and Antoninus. The reference in *l.*240 of the Salutaris endowment to the *former* asiarchs leads to the same conclusion. Finally, although Pythio had been asiarch in 104/05 and in 109/10, he is not so named in the inscription of 115/16 when his son, Aristoboulos, bears that title instead (*I.Eph.*

V.1500). Similarly, Aristio is not designated asiarch in 113/14 (*I.Eph.* VII, 1.3217a), although he had certainly borne the title in 92/93 at least.

The possibility that there was more than one asiarch officiating at any given time is likely since it is indicated to be the case at Tralles during I BC (Strabo, 14.1.42: 'some of [the Trallians] are always the foremost of the province, being called asiarchs') and at Ephesos in I AD (Acts 19.31). The evidence of the four asiarchs discussed above does not reveal whether any of them were contemporaries in office or how long their term was; but it does indicate, as does the Salutaris document in *l.*240, that there were at least several former asiarchs in the city at the same time. It is not possible to determine the exact number from the Salutaris inscription because of textual problems (cf. Oliver, 81-82).

It has been claimed by some who favour the identification of the asiarchy and the *archierosyne* that Acts' reference to asiarchs is an anachronism. Deininger, for example, holds (50) that use of the title asiarch lapsed between Strabo's mention in I BC and the epigraphic evidence beginning in late I AD. Yet there is firm evidence to the contrary. A group of inscriptions already published reveals beyond any doubt that the title was being used not only throughout I AD but also in late I BC as well. A full discussion of the relevant inscriptions is forthcoming in *AS.*

In summary, the Salutaris foundation document and the evidence concerning the earliest four asiarchs of Ephesos attested in that city's inscriptions is in accord with the view which distinguishes between the functions of the asiarch and the provincial *archiereus* in late I/early II AD. There is no indication at all that the asiarch was a priest, although it is true that the role assigned to the asiarchs in the Salutaris document does suggest they had some religious functions. Religious duties, however, were quite frequently attached to magistracies in the Greek cities cf. Jones, *Greek City*, 229); and this is well illustrated at Ephesos by the relationship of the *prytanis* to the city cult of Hestia (R. Merkelbach, *ZPE* 37 [1980] 77-90).

Finally, it must be emphasised that none of the four asiarchs considered above bears the extended title 'asiarch of the temple(s) in Ephesos'. It is the occasional presence of this so-called 'temple-title' after the word asiarch that has encouraged some scholars to identify the asiarchs with the provincial *archiereis* (Rossner, 102-03). Since none of the asiarchs known from late I/early II bears this title, the possibility of such an equation does not exist. In any case, the same phrase is occasionally to be found attached to other indisputably administrative officials (e.g., *I.Eph.* VII, 1.3080, a *grammateus* 'of the temples of Asia in Ephesos'), and thus cannot in itself constitute evidence that the asiarchy was a priesthood. Moreover, in the case of asiarchs of all periods, use of the temple-title was limited. It does not occur at all during the first neokorate, and when it does begin to appear attached to the title asiarch from the reign of Hadrian onwards, it is only found with approximately a quarter of the total number of asiarchs of Ephesos. By way of contrast, the phrase is a regular and very frequent feature of the provincial *archiereus* from the earliest phase of the imperial cult in Ephesos. In fact, *archiereis* of Asia in Ephesos are just as likely to bear the temple-title as not.

Thus, the individuality of the asiarchy is confirmed by the lack of evidence for the asiarchy as a priesthood in late I/early II. Moreover, the testimonies for asiarchs in the late Republican period, well before the institution of the imperial cult in Asia, and throughout the first century show that the title was not replaced by *archiereus* of Asia at the time of the institution of the cult (cf. Deininger, 50). All this indicates that the asiarchy was quite separate from the provincial high-priesthood, at least during the period covered by the evidence considered above.

(R.A. KEARSLEY)

15. Letter requesting help for a brother

Oxyrhynchos II
ed.pr. — M. Kaimio, *P.Oxy.Hels.* 47a (pl.33)

Διονύσιος Νικά-
νορι τῷ φιλτά-
τῳ χαίρειν.
παρακαλῶ σε, ἄ-
δελφε, τῷ ἀδε-
λφῷ μου Δημη-
τρίῳ συνλαβέσ-
θαι, ἄχρι ἂν τὰ σι-
τάρια μετρή-
σῃ. ἐγὼ γὰρ ἔτι
καὶ νῦν ἐπικιν-
δύνως ἔχωι.
οἶδας δὲ ὅτι οὐ-
κ ἀχαρίστῳ πα-
ρέχεις. τὸ δὲ σπου̣-
δαῖόν σου ἐπίστα̣-
μαι.

(*vacat*)

ἔρρω(σο), φίλτατε.
κα[ὶ] γὰρ ἐγὼ π̣α̣ρ̣ῶ̣ν
π̣ά̣λιν σοι προσεῖ-
χ̣ο̣ν.

Clearly written letter (6.5B x 21H cm.) on the back of a piece of papyrus cut from a list containing names arranged in several columns.

Dionysios to Nikanor his dearest friend, greetings. I request, brother, | that you help my brother Demetrios, until he gets the grain measured. | For I am still in a critical state even now. And you know that you are not providing (help) to a person lacking in gratitude. | I know your goodness. Farewell, dearest friend. | And further, when I was with you I paid attention to your interests.

This short letter is one of three written by Dionysios to various friends on behalf of his 'brother' Demetrios. The other two (*P.Oxy.Hels.* 47b, c) are in similar vein, but the wording varies slightly between them. No.47c, the most fragmentary of the group, is closer in wording to the text above than is 47b. It is not certain whether Demetrios is an actual brother, or whether ἀδελφός here (5-6) is simply reflecting ties of friendship, as must be inferred to be the case with its use (4-5) of the bond between writer and addressee. These letters offer in their own unassuming way a useful general parallel to the NT letter of Philemon. Like Paul, Dionysios makes a request of a friend on behalf of a third party, reminding the addressee of past indebtedness as a means of ensuring a proper response.

A few words may be noted briefly. For συλλαμβάνω + dative (47a, *ll.*5-8; 47c, *ll.*4-6) see BAGD, s.v., 1c (ECL, not NT). The adjective ἀχάριστος (47a, *l.*14; possibly to be restored at 47c, *l.*11) occurs at Lk. 6.37 and 2 Tim. 3.2. J.D.Denniston, *The Greek Particles* (Oxford, 1954^2) provides useful comment (109) on the particle combination καὶ γάρ (47a, *l.*20). The usage προσέχω + dat. at the end of 47a is common: see BAGD, s.v., 1a, α; 1b. In 47b πείθομαι ὅτι (instead of the infinitive) occurs twice (*ll.*6-7, 21), paralleling the use in the NT at Rom. 8.38; 2 Tim. 1.5, 12; and Heb. 13.18. In *l.*12 ἔχωι is a commonly attested mistake by hyper-correction for ἔχω. For some further examples note *P.Soterichos* 12.4, 19.3, 20.3 (ἀπέχωι at each place), 24.33-34 (ἐγ|καλῶι); all these texts from the same archive are from Theadelphia and fall within the period I^2-II^1.

16. Cannibalism at Alexandria?

Oxyrhynchos III
ed.pr. — P.J. Parsons, *P.Oxy.* 42 (1974) 3065

Ἄρει[ος] Ἀγριππίνῃ καὶ Κορνηλίωι τοῖς γονεῦσι
πολλὰ χαίρειν.
πρὸ μὲν πάντων εὔχ[ο]μαι τῷ θεῷ περὶ τῆς σωτηρίας
ὑμῶν καὶ τοῦ ἀδελφοῦ μου Στεφάνου. ἤδη πολλὰς ἐπιστο-
λὰς ὑμῖν ἔγραψα δηλῶν ὅτι μ[έλλ]ω πλέειν καὶ σωθῆ-
ναι τῆς πόλεω[ς] τάχα δὲ . . . . . . περὶ τῶν ἐνθάδε
γενομ[έ]ν[ω]ν· τοιαῦ[τ]α γέγονεν οἷα οὐδέποτε ἐκ τοῦ
αἰῶν[ο]ς γέγονεν· νῦν ἀνθρωποφαγεία ἐστὶν καὶ οὐ πόλε-
μος . [.] . . . . . οσεστ . . . . . της πόλεως εὑρεθεὶς νῦν
ηομ . . λω π . . . . [. .] . δε . ω τῷ Ἐπείφ· δηλ[ώ]σει
δέ σοι Αὐξάνουσα τὴν ἡμέραν ᾗ [ἀ]ν[απλ]εύσω καὶ τὸ ὄνο-
μα δι' ο[ὗ] ἐάν σοι πέμψῃ ἃ [κ]ατέλιπ[ο]ν τραγήματα· ἔστιν δέ·
κάροια διακόσια καὶ ἰσχάδες διακοσίας καὶ γραφῖα δύο·
αὐτὰ λήμψῃ μετὰ καὶ ἐπιστολῆ . . [. .]ης· διὸ κυρία μου
μήτηρ [.] εν . ακη . . . . λεον χαίρου ὅτι ἔξω τῆς
πόλεώς εἰμι· ἐγὼ γὰρ ἤθελον [π]ρὸς σὲν ἐλθεῖν, ἡ δὲ τῆς
πόλεως ἀνθρω . . . ια οὐκ ἀφῆκέν με· ἀλλὰ ἐὰν ζῶ-
μεν . . οκαισ . . . . . [· ἄ]σπασαι τὸν ἀδελφόν μου
Στέφανον καὶ . . . . ν σου· ἄσπασαι πρὸς ὄνομα
πάντας τοὺς ὑμᾶς φιλοῦντας πολλά.
ἐ[ρρῶσθ]αι ὑμᾶς εὔχομαι πολλοῖς χρόνοις
. . . . . . ουντας καὶ ὁμονοοῦντας.
. . . . Ἐπεὶφ ε´´
(*Back*) ἀπόδος . . . . ρσα μυροπώλῃ ἵνα ἀπ[οδῷ Ἀ]γριπ'πίνῃ μητρὶ
π(αρὰ) Ἀρείου υἱοῦ.
ἀπ[ό]δ(ος) εν . . [. .] . . χει . . . . [.] μυροπώλῃ εἶν' ἀποδ(ῷ)
Ἀγριπ'πίνῃ μητρὶ π(αρὰ) Ἀρείου.

Largely complete letter on a large sheet of papyrus (19.8B x 25H cm.). The letter was folded, with the address on the back added twice (24-25, 26-27) on each exterior surface. At *l.*6 τάχα δὲ ἠκού[σα]τε is a suggested reading mentioned in *P.Oxy.*, n. ad loc. At *l.*13 read κάρυα; at *l.*15, [π]λέον.
Bib. — Tibiletti, *Lettere*, 147-48, no.10.

Areios to his parents Agrippina and Cornelius, many greetings. Before everything I pray to God for your (good) health, as well as for that of my brother Stephanos. By now I have written many letters | to you, indicating that I intend to set sail and be brought safely out of the city. Possibly you have heard(?) about the events that have occurred here. Things have occurred such as never happened since the world began. Now it is cannibalism and not war . . . | . . . Auxanousa will indicate to you the day on which I will sail up river, and the name of the person through whomsoever she sends to you the dried fruits which I left behind, namely two hundred nuts and two hundred dried

figs and two writing implements. You will receive these with the letter as well. Accordingly, my lady | mother, . . . be glad the more that I am outside the city. For I wanted to come to you, but the cannibalism(?) of the city would not let me. Well, if we live . . . Greet my brother Stephanos and your . . . Greet warmly by name | all those who love you. I pray you may be well for many years . . . and being of one accord. Epeiph 5th. (*Back*) Give (this letter) to . . . the myrrh-seller so that she may give it to my mother Agrippina, | from her son Areios.

The first editor's suggestion, that this letter may have emanated from Alexandria, is attractive: Areios speaks of sailing up the Nile (*l.*11) to get home to his family in Oxyrhynchos, and mention of 'the polis' (6, 15-16) makes the reader think naturally of the most important city in Roman Egypt.

It is the allusion to cannibalism (*l.*8; possibly also *l.*17) that makes this letter memorable. Although there is clearly some kind of disturbance occurring where Areios is (*ll.*8-9), the question should be left open whether such phraseology may have been mere exaggeration, rumour-mongering (cf. especially *ll.*7-8). An alternative, figurative way to understand the word may be more appropriate, although such usage is not attested. In contrast to πόλεμος (8-9) the noun may be suggesting rather some kind of *stasis*, or civil war, which has become a 'dog eat dog' situation. Cf. use of the phrases ἐμφύλιος πόλεμος and ἐμφύλιος στάσις, noted at S.C. Barton/ G.H.R. Horsley, *JbAC* 24 (1981) 20 n.64. This figurative sense fits *l.*17 better than a literal sense, if the noun is indeed to be restored there. Pliny, *Ep.* 10.96.7, *rursusque coeundi ad capiendum cibum, promiscuum tamen et innoxium*, hints indirectly at the claim that Christians were participating in cannibalistic meals together (cf. A.N. Sherwin-White, *The Letters of Pliny* [Oxford, 1966] 707). On the occurrence of actual cannibalism (rare though it was) in the Graeco-Roman world see O.Montevecchi, *CISA* 5 (1978) 94-95.

Although the opening greeting is to both parents (and cf. *ll.*5, 20, 21), the writer has his mother primarily in mind (11, 12, 14-15, 16, 18, 19, 24, 27). There are several words and phrases worth quick comment. Passive σῴζομαι + gen. of being brought out of serious danger has no formal parallel in the NT; for σῴζω ἐκ in such contexts, however, note Jn 12.27; Heb. 5.7; Jude 5. In *ll.*7-8 the wording οὐδέποτε ἐκ τοῦ | αἰῶνος offers an excellent parallel to Jn 9.32, ἐκ τοῦ αἰῶνος οὐκ ἠκούσθη, κτλ. The same prepositional phrase is found at Gal. 1.4, but there the force is rather different. Neither MM nor BAGD, s.v., la, provides any documentary illustration of the Johannine usage. For the fairly uncommon occurrence of middle χαίρομαι (15), Acts 3.8D χαιρόμενος is noted in *ed.pr.* (cf. BDF §307). For θέλω (16), commonly attested in the sense of βούλομαι, note the comments and biliography at BDF §101, s.v. θέλω. The verb ὁμονοέω occurs in ECL, not NT; the instance here (*l.*22) offers a documentary illustration. Another from the year's culling of texts is *I.Eph.* Ia.8.24-25, ἀναγκαῖόν ἐστι | πάντας ὁμονοήσαντας ὑ[πο]στῆναι τὸν κίνδυνον, 'it is essential that all withstand the danger in united fashion', in a decree concerning war against Mithridates (86/5 BC). *SEG* 399 (Orchomenos in Arkadia, n.d.) is an inscription on an altar of Homonoia.

This text is one of 34 papyrus letters reprinted in Tibiletti, *Lettere*. Some may consider that the study of Greek epistolography, especially the relationship between papyrus letters and the NT epistles, has been comprehensively explored already. Items this century of note include: F.X.J. Exler, *The Form of the Ancient Greek Letter. A Study in Greek Epistolography* (Washington, 1923); G. Ghedini, *Lettere Cristiane dai papiri greci del III e del IV secolo* (Milan, 1923); M. Naldini, *Il Cristianesimo in Egitto. Lettere private nei papiri dei secoli II-IV* (Florence, 1968); J.L. White, *The Form and Function of the Body of the Greek Letter: A Study of the*

Letter-body in the non-literary Papyri and in Paul the Apostle (*SBLDS* 2; Missoula, 1972); C.-H. Kim, *Form and Structure of the Familiar Greek Letter of Recommendation* (*SBLDS* 4; Missoula, 1972). Whereas the last two of these works draw upon papyrus texts to illustrate and parallel the NT forms, the first three focus their attention upon the post-NT age (as also does Tibiletti), and do not show much interest in the NT *per se*. A supplement to Kim's collection is provided in H. Cotton, *Documentary Letters of Recommendation in Latin from the Roman Empire* [*BeitrWge zur klassischen Philologie* 132; Königstein, 1981) 53-54 (19 items). The most two most recent anthologies of letters are by S.K. Stowers, *Letter Writing in Greco-Roman Antiquity* (Philadelphia, 1986), and by J.L. White, *Light from Ancient Letters* (Philadelphia, 1986). The first provides translations but no texts of both documentary and literary letters; the second, Greek texts and translations of papyrus letters only. In addition to these books, the following selection of articles may be noted: J. O'Callaghan, *Estudios Eclesiasticos* 34 (1960) 391-402; id., *Aeg.* 41 (1961) 26-36; id., *Estudios Biblicos* 29 (1970) 153-55 (these three on Christian papyrus letters of V-VI); E. Wipszycka, *JJP* 18 (1974) 203-21 (review article of Naldini, containing many useful observations); Naldini, *CCC* 2 (1981) 167-76 (partly responding to Wipszycka, but also mentioning Christian letters published since his book); White, *Semeia* 22 (1981) 89-106 (epistolary forms and formulae); Kim, ibid., 107-12 (list of Greek papyrus letters by corpus and volume). Nor should Deissmann's contribution in *LAE* be forgotten; for although his book was not devoted exclusively to letters, he gave considerable attention to them and popularised for NT studies the distinction between popular letters as against epistles.

Naldini's collection is modelled on that of Ghedini, but publications of the intervening half-century enabled him to more than double the number of texts included as coming — in his judgement — from a Christian hand (Ghedini: 44; Naldini: 97). He includes all such letters up to V/VI, except for a few from certain archives (e.g. no.40 is the only one from the Abinnaios archive). Not all of the texts included by Ghedini are retained by Naldini (omitted are G. nos. 9, 10, 18, 33, 37). Nevertheless, he does incorporate a number of texts about which there is a doubt whether the writer was Christian. Thus, Wipszycka's judgement is that the certainly Christian letters down to the fourth century in Naldini's collection only total 46, half of those he has included. Those she rejects are in her view definitely pagan (N., nos. 14-17), uncertainly Christian (N., nos. 1-3, 7-12, 18, 22, 27, 32, 38, 44-46, 55, 57-59, 62, 63, 65, 66, 69, 70, 72, 73, 76, 81), or beyond the scope of the collection chronologically (N., nos. 82-97).

Tibiletti's approach is rather different. He provides, first, a very useful tabulation of over 500 letters dated III-IV/V, arranged chronologically, with provenance shown together with an indication whether the text is 'securely Christian', 'securely pagan', or uncertain. The provision of this information makes his list immediately of greater usefulness than the very bald collection by Kim (1981), which lists text numbers only. However, no siglum is provided to indicate the admittedly tiny number of Jewish letters surviving from the period (cf. *New Docs 1978*, **100**, pp.142-43). Inevitably for such a large list, some slips occur: on p.7 in his table *P.Laur.* 2 (1977) 41 is marked as securely Christian, though at 118 n.34 it is rightly noted as securely pagan. Tibiletti reprints this letter as no.5 in his selection; for a brief note on some of its wording see *New Docs 1978*, **100**, p.144. Further, although the aim is nearly achieved of including all letters of III-IV except very fragmentary items, a few have escaped the net, e.g., *P.Oxy.* 14.1763 (= Ghedini, no.10), 1764-1772, 1776, 1777 (all III or IV); *PSI* 8.979 (= Naldini, no.64; IV).

There follows the body of the book, a discussion of the criteria by which Christian/non-Christian attribution may be established. This includes comment on many individual lexical items (ἀγάπη, ἀδελφός, πρεσβύτερος, etc.), phraseology (salutations and farewells, *proskynema* formulae, etc.), *nomina sacra*, and biblical quotations/reminiscences — Tibiletti no.22 (Herakleopolite nome, 330-40; = *P.Lond.* 6 [1924] 1915 with corrections from *BL* 3.1 [1926] 100) provides a useful example of the phenomenon; see further *New Docs 1977*, **97**, pp.157-58. Tibiletti also gives consideration to the actual content of the letters, including the general theme of allusions to, or display of religiosity. Though some names are given attention, the onomastic criterion, as a way of helping to establish whether certain texts may be referring to Christians, is not sufficiently explored.

In contrast to Naldini's book, which gives much greater space to the texts themselves (more are reprinted, and fuller discussion is given), Tibiletti's selection serves as an appendix to the body of his book. These 34 letters offer a very representative sample of well-preserved letters spanning the two centuries; they illustrate many of the features he has already discussed. Securely pagan in his view are nos. 1-3, 5 (see comment above), 6, 9, 12-14, 16, 20; securely Christian are nos. 21-26, 28, 31-34; while those in the 'twilight zone' are nos. 4, 7, 8, 10 (printed at the beginning of this entry), 11, 15, 17-19, 27, 29, 30.

A tabulation may help to clarify certain differences between Ghedini, Naldini, and Tibiletti. The following list contains letters from III or IV whose Christian link is disputed. A dash indicates that the item was not included by Ghedini or Naldini, nor discussed by Wipszycka because it was not in the latter. All texts listed in the Tibiletti and Wipszycka columns are considered uncertain by them, except those marked (p)agan. A date is specified *N*(aldini)/*T*(ibiletti) where they differ. The starting point for this list is one prepared by S.R. Pickering (privately circulated within Macquarie University); cf. *New Docs 1977*, **97**, p.158.

no.	Text	Date	Ghedini (*item*)	Naldini (*item*)	Wipszycka (*page*)	Tibiletti (*page*)
1.	*P.Iand.* 2 (1913) 11	III	5	7	221	7
2.	*P.Oxy.* 9 (1912) 1120	III*T*	9	—	—	8
3.	*P.Oxy.* 14 (1920) 1678	III	7	9	221	9
4.	*P.Lund.* 2 (1937) 4 (= *SB* 5.2 [1938] 8091)	III	—	11	221	11
5.	*P.Princ.* 2 (1936) 73	III	—	12	221	9
6-9.	*P.Mich.*3 (1936) 216, 218, 219, 221 (= *SB* 3.2 [1927] 7248, 7250, 7251, 7253)	III fin.*N*/296*T*	—	14-17	205-06, 221(p)	12
10.	*PSI* 4 (1917) 299	III*N*/III fin.*T*	6	8	221	12
11.	*P.Oxy.* 14 (1920) 1773	III*N*/III fin.*T*	8	10	221	13
12.	*P.Giss. Univ. Bibl.* 3 (1931) 30	III/IV	—	22	221	13
13.	*P.Oxy.* 12 (1916) 1593	III/IV	33	—	—	14
14.	*P.Oxy.* 14 (1920) 1680	III/IV	15	32	221	14
15.	*P.Oxy.* 20 (1952) 2276	IIIfin.*N*/III/IV*T*	—	18	221	14
16.	*PSI* 8 (1927) 895	III/IV	—	27	221	14
17.	*P.Ant.* 1 (1950) 44	IV/V*N*/IV[1]*T*	—	92	(Xn)	16
18.	*P.Herm.Rees* (1964) 4	IV, 1st decades *N*/IV[1]*T*	—	38	213-15, 221	16
19.	*BGU* 3 (1903) 984	IV	28	55	221	17
20.	*P.Fay.* (1900) 136	IV	37	—	—	17
21.	*P.New York* 1 (1967) 25	IV*N*/mid IV*T*	—	73	221	17
22.	*PSI* 7 (1925) 825	IV[1]	—	44	221	17(p)
23.	*PSI* 14 (1957) 1423	IV*N*/IV[1]*T*	—	45	221	17
24.	*PSI* 7 (1925) 830	IV*N*/mid IV*T*	—	46	215, 221	17
25.	*P.L.Bat.* 13 (1965) 18	IV	—	81	221	18
26.	*P.Lond.* 3 (1907) 982	IV	27	54	(Xn)	18
27.	*P.Lips.* 1 (1906) 111	IV	30	57	221	18

28. *P.Lond.* 3 (1907) 1244	IV	31	58	221	18
29. *P.Oxy.* 1 (1898) 120	IV	36	62	221	19
30. *P.Oxy.* 10 (1914) 1299	IV	—	76	221	19
31. *P.Oxy.* 14 (1920) 1682	IV	26	52	(Xn)	19
32. *P.Oxy.* 14 (1920) 1775	IV	40	66	221	19(p)
33. *P.Princ.* 2 (1936) 101	IV	—	70	221	19
34. *PSI* 10 (1932) 1161	IV	—	72	221	20
35. *SB* 10.1 (1969) 10279 (= *P.Treccani* 1)	IV	—	69	221	20
36. *P.Oxy.* 10 (1914) 1298	IV*N*/IV fin.*T*	38	63	217-18, 221	21
37. *P.Oxy.* 14 (1920) 1683	IV*N*/IV fin.*T*	39	65	221	21

Two general observations may be offered on this list. First, none of these 37 texts is represented in Tibiletti's selection of letters at the end of the book. This is unfortunate, as it misses an opportunity to draw attention more sharply to the question of disputed criteria for assessing whether a text may be Christian or not. All the 'uncertain' letters he includes are ones which are excluded both from Ghedini and Naldini, or which were published since Naldini's book appeared in 1968. Second, comparison of the last two columns in this table show that Tibiletti's judgement is very nearly identical with Wipszycka's. She offers no comment on nos.26 and 31 in the list, thus implicitly accepting them as Christian. Similarly, by her silence about no.17 she seems to accept that it is Christian, although it is chronologically beyond the scope of Naldini's collection. And the two items which Tibiletti regards as securely pagan (nos.22 and 32) are treated by her as uncertain. As for nos.2, 13 and 20, these are not addressed by her since they were not included in Naldini's book, which serves as the focus of her article.

These differences of viewpoint between Wipszycka and Tibiletti may engage our attention. First, nos.6-9 are part of the Paniskos archive. Naldini does not include in his selection *P.Mich.* III.214 in view of its demonstrably non-Christian phraseology. Given that these letters are dated too closely together to allow as plausible Ghedini's theory (accepted by Naldini) that Paniskos was converted between the writing of no.214 and some of the other letters, the suggestion noted at *New Docs 1977*, **22** remains attractive, that the differing phraseology reflects the faith of the scribes who wrote the letters for Paniskos, who was himself illiterate, not the outlook of Paniskos himself. This gives considerable force to the view that Paniskos was unlikely to have been a Christian. That said, however, the point at issue here is whether any of those letters may have emanated from a Christian hand, not whether Paniskos was himself a Christian. Accordingly, *P.Mich.* III.216, 218 and 219 — all written by the same scribe — may well deserve to be considered as Christian in view of their phraseology. *P.Mich.* III.221 is rather more doubtful, and should be left as one of the 'uncertain' texts. A related problem arises with no.18 in the list above, for which see **124** below.

Second, nos.17, 26 and 31 contain the formula θεία πρόνοια or a variant of it; and the presence of this phrase is the basis for Naldini's inclusion of these letters as Christian (see his introductory comment to each). At *New Docs 1978*, **100**, pp.143-44, all papyrus examples of this phrase from the period mid-III-IV fin. were catalogued; and it was determined that as the phrase occurs in both Christian and non-Christian documents it is an inconclusive criterion. For these items therefore, Tibiletti's position is to be preferred.

Finally, nos.22 and 32 in the list above also contain a common feature, a *proskynema* formula; and it appears to be for this reason that Tibiletti classifies them as securely pagan. These letters do not mention Sarapis or a plurality of gods in the formula: in no.22 we have προσκύνημα . . . | παρὰ τῷ κυρίῳ θεῷ (*ll.*3-4), while the wording of no.32 is προσκύνημα . . . | παρὰ τῷ δεσπότῃ θεῷ (*ll*.3-4). Tibiletti (55 n.10) compares also *P.Oxy*. 33 (1968) 2682 (III/IV), π. . . . παρὰ τῷ θεῷ, and *P.Alex*. (1964) 30 (IV), π. παρὰ τῷ κυρίῳ θεῷ. Yet he acknowledges that the more recently published *P.Mich*. inv. 346 — *ed.pr.*: H.C. Youtie, *ZPE* 28 (1978) 265-68 — is Christian; its formula reads π. . . . | . . . κατ' ἑκάστην ἡμέραν (*ll*.2-3). Here, all divine allusion has been omitted, and the much blander nature of the formula confirms for Youtie (followed by Tibiletti) a suggestion made sixty years ago by Wilcken that the writer of such a text may have been a recent convert 'merely continuing old mental habits' (Youtie, 265). Although the wording in the Michigan papyrus differs from our nos. 22 and 32 that is, I suggest, only a matter of degree. There is simply insufficient information in nos. 22 and 32 to be able to decide either way whether there is a Christian association or not. It should be admitted, of course, that a monotheistic outlook does not automatically establish the text as Christian. But the use of the formula in a demonstrably Christian letter does bring into question the usefulness of the phrase as a criterion for establishing whether a text is Christian or not. In sum, these two letters should be marked as 'uncertain' rather than 'securely pagan'.

It should be mentioned, perhaps, that a papyrus which gives clear evidence of a link with Christianity does contain the apparent abbreviation ὑπὲρ προσκν[(for προσκ(υ)ν[ήματος?) at *l*.21. This item is *SB* 5.2 (1938) 7872, and the restoration is Deissmann's, who also restored *ll*.14-15 to read ὀφείλω γὰρ ποιῆσαι [τὸ προσκύνημά σου παν?]|σάββατον. Naldini includes this text as no.75, though without the restorations; and he queries whether it is even a letter. Even if the word may be accepted in *l*.21, we do not have anything resembling a *proskynema* formula here; nor should the restoration in *l*.14 sway us into presuming that there was a Christianised version of one there. On this text see further G. Geraci, *Aeg*. 51 (1971) 201.

Does the onomastic factor help resolve some of the uncertainties? In Tibiletti's sample of texts at the end of his book, his no.19 — = *P.Oxy*. 34 (1968) 2727 (III/IV) — is a letter from Basos to Eulogios (the latter a very rare name, if Solin, *GPR* II.705 is any guide), in the course of which a certain Theodoros is mentioned. Solin, *GPR* I.74-76 lists *c*.90 attestations of Theodoros from Rome, ranging from the beginning of the Principate to VII/VIII. From the third and fourth centuries (i.e., including those Solin marks as III/V, IV/V and IV/VI) there are 35 instances of which 17 are certainly Christian. This name appears to be in the process of being appropriated by Christians, but in the period of interest to us it has not yet become monopolised by them. Thus, in the case of the Tibiletti text this occurrence of the name offers us no help to weigh the scales in either direction. Analysis of the names which occur in the 37 texts listed above provides the same result: that for the period III-IV onomastics is of little help in being able to differentiate a Christian from a non-Christian, unless Bible names occur, in which case we are dealing with either Jews or Christians. As has been noted at *New Docs 1978*, **100**, and as is mentioned in the present Review (**112**, below), there are particular, localised reasons why the occurrence of Bible names in papyri of the fourth century is more likely to point to Christians than Jews.

Finally, it is a particular merit of Tibiletti's treatment that he remains explicitly agnostic about the religious affiliation of the writers or recipients of so many of the letters of this period. The third and fourth centuries were a time of great flux politically, socially and economically, no less than in the matter of religious faith (both institutional and individual). The temptation is always great to try to reduce the shadowy areas, to settle for a 'Christian or pagan' judgement. (Jewish letters are not a separate issue, but their near dearth in the period under discussion here inevitably makes them an insignificant category.) To see things in such black and white terms may appease the mind's desire for tidiness, but it is historically unhelpful.

That said, however, it would be useful to distinguish a fourth category of documents, as A.L. Connolly has observed to me. Apart from explicitly Christian letters and those which explicitly are not, other texts may be divided between those which are ambiguous as to religious affiliation and those which give no hint of this whatever. The value of this further subdivision ought to be immediately apparent. For since the ambiguous texts have occasionally been allowed to become a 'battle-ground' in research on the gradual 'Christianisation' of Egypt as evidenced by the letters, to be able to isolate this group from the much larger number of such texts which are entirely uninformative will allow a clearer sense of the proportions between the categories to emerge. It would be of interest, surely, to know what percentage of non-Christian letters evince any interest in religion at the level of phraseology employed. This same question can be applied to other genres of (semi-)private documentary texts, such as epitaphs. Accordingly, of the twelve papyri reprinted at the end of his book which Tibiletti classes as 'uncertain' the following seem to me to be entirely silent as to religious adherence: Tibiletti, nos. 7 (*P.Oxy.* 14.1667), 8 (*P.Oxy.* 14.1681), 10 (*P.Oxy.* 42.3065, printed above), 11 (*P.Oxy.* 42.3067), 15 (*SB* 12, 2.11243), 17 (*P.Tebt.* 2.424). This leaves us with a reduced group in the 'twilight zone', whose position vis-à-vis religion is ambivalent: 18 (*P.Oxy.* 8.1160), 19 (*P.Oxy.* 34.2727), 27 (*P.Herm.Rees* 5), 29 (*P.Strasb.* 3.286), 30 (*P.Herm.Rees* 11). Two other papyrus letters from this year's culling may also be grouped with this class. *CPR* 56 (provenance unknown, III/IV) is very fragmentary, but does preserve the phrase σὺν θεῷ at *l.*11. *CPR* 57 (Hermopolis, III/IV) is more interesting, a letter from a woman to her sister. It is not certain that these women are sisters: that they may be nuns would only be a conceivable alternative if the dating of this papyrus could be narrowed to no earlier than *c.*325. No names survive and there are no certain indications of Christianity; but as a subjective reaction to the text it could be said to have a 'resonance' of a Christian circle.

17. 'The mouse that roared'

Arsinoite nome mid-III

ed.pr. — G. Rosenberger, *P.Iand.* 6 (1934) 97 (pl.19)

Αὐρήλιος Ζωΐλος] Διογένει.
ἐδεξάμην σο]υ τὰ γρά[μμα]τα τῇ β καὶ εὗρον αὐτὰ
. .] . ι̣α̣[. . . . μα]θών σου τ̣ὴν μωρ[ί]αν. ἐγ[ὼ] μ̣ὲν
ὑπηρετῶ̣ν̣ ἐπ̣ιονειδ̣ί̣ζ̣[ο]μαι· οὔ̣κ ε̣ἰ̣μ̣ι ἀπονενοη-
μένος κα̣ὶ ο̣[ὔκ] ε̣ἰ̣μι ἀνα̣ί̣σ̣χυντος κ̣α̣ὶ̣ οὔκ̣ [εἰ]μι μῦς.
σὺ φιλοπ[όνει] τὰ γράμματά μου· μάθε οὖν ὅτι ἐ-
γ]ὼ πεποί[η]κά μου τὰ ἔτη ιδ̣ λοιπὸν ὑπηρε-
{ρε}τῶν τοὺς γονέας σου, καὶ ο̣ὐκ ἦν̣ ἀναίσχυ̣ν-
τος] κ̣α̣ὶ̣ οὐχ ὅμοιός σου ἐγενόμην οὐδὲ τῇ ἀδελ-
φῇ] μου. οὐκ̣ ἔδει σ̣ε τα̣ῦ̣[τα π]ρ̣ά̣ττειν καὶ ἀπελ-
θ]εῖν ἐτῶν ι̣β καὶ μ̣ο̣ιχάζειν εἰς Κυνοπο-
λ̣είτην. ἐὰν δὲ πάντα ποιήσῃς, οὐ δύνασαί μαι
δε]ῖ̣ραι. ὅτε γ̣ὰρ μ̣ε̣ι̣κ̣ρὸς ἦμ̣[ην], ἀ̣νάπαλιν ἐδε-
ήθ]ης σ̣ε ἄρα̣ι̣· λοιπὸν ὅτε νεανίσκος ἐγ̣ε̣ν̣ά̣-

μ]ην, μέλ<λ>ις με δεῖραι. ἐγ̣ε̣ν̣ά̣μην σου λοιπὸν
ἀνεχόμενος, οὐ μέ̣λ̣λ̣ω̣ σε λοιπὸν ἀνέχε-
σθαι. μαρτυρήσω δὲ καὶ τῇ ἀδελφῇ [μου
Θαήσιδι, ἐὰν παραγένηται πρὸ̣[ς ἐμ]ὲ [σὺν] θ̣ε̣οῖς.
(ἔτους) ε// Χοίακ γ̄
ἐ̣δόκουν γὰρ ὅτι μέλλις με φιλοστοργεῖν· ὅτ' ἐκεκινδυ-
νεύ̣κει ἡ μήτηρ μου, εὗρον ὅτι, ἐὰν γένηται
αὐτὴ μετὰ ἑκατὸν ἔτη, ἔμελλές με ἀλιστά̣σ̣τ̣ως
ἐκβαλεῖν πρὸς τῇ θύρᾳ. // // // //
τῷ ἀδελ]φ̣ῷ̣ Διογένει ἀπ(ὸ) Αὐρηλίου Ζωΐλου. //

Well preserved papyrus letter (20B x 22H cm.) whose folds are still visible. In *l.*10 the papyrus has π]ρατ'τειν. *Ed.pr.* reads ι̣θ̄ and [ἀπ]ι̣χ̣άζειν (*l.*11). *L.*24 is written sideways along the left margin.
Bib. — *Tibiletti, *Lettere*, 135-36 no.2.

Aurelius Zoilos to Diogenes. I received your letter on the second and found it . . . when I learned of your stupidity. I am reproached though I serve (you). I have not lost my senses | and I am not impudent and I am not a mouse. Give heed to my letter. Understand, therefore, that I have spent my 14 years now serving your parents, and I was not impudent and I was not like you or my sister. | You ought not to have done this, and gone away for 12 years and committed adultery(?) in the Kynopolite district. Whatever you do, you cannot beat me. For when I was young you begged me to pick you up over and over again; now, when I have become a young man | you intend to beat me. In this connection, I put up with you, (but) I do not intend to put up with you in future. And I shall also give witness (of this decision) to my sister Thaesis, if she comes to me with the help of the gods. Year 5, Choiak the 3rd. | For I used to think that you intended to show me affection. When my mother was in danger I discovered that even if she lives to be more than a hundred, you were intending inexorably to throw me to the door. (*Left margin*) To his brother(?) Diogenes, from Aurelius Zoilos.

It was too quickly assumed by the first editor that the fracas reflected by this angry letter concerns two brothers. Rosenberger restored the address running down the left margin to indicate that Diogenes was a brother (only the *omega* is certain) of Zoilos. Yet when other sections of this letter are considered that appears unlikely. Zoilos describes himself as a *hyperetes*, who has served Diogenes' parents for 14 years (7-8); moreover, he acknowledges his inferior status to Diogenes (3-4, taking ὑπηρετῶν concessively). He has received an abusive letter the day before from Diogenes, and in the heat of the moment gives him a piece of his mind, defending himself at the same time. 'My mother' in *l.*21 need not be one of 'your parents' (*l.*8). It may be suggested that the members of the *oikos* discussed here are: Diogenes and his parents; Zoilos, a house-born slave, perhaps; his mother and sister, the latter probably called Thaesis (if μου is accepted as the restoration at the end of *l.*17). Zoilos' mother and sister appear to be part of the household, too, and so are to be presumed to be of like status to Zoilos. *Ll.*13-15 are not altogether clear, but appear to suggest that Zoilos is older than Diogenes and had an affectionate relationship with him when they were children (cf. *l*.20). Rosenberger read [ἀπ]ιχάζειν as the infinitive in *l*.11, the suggestion being that Diogenes had absconded to the Kynopolite district. This seems more attractive than the otherwise grammatically unclear μοιχάζειν εἰς. It should be acknowledged, however, that the possibility that Diogenes and Zoilos are brothers cannot be completely ruled out. As E.A. Judge has pointed out to me, since the participle ὑπηρετῶν (4, 7-8) does not establish Zoilos' social rank clearly (as the noun would), inferior status may not be involved. On this view, Zoilos repudiates his absent brother's right to criticise him since he has had the burden of caring for their parents.

The baldness of the opening, the lack of a farewell, and the postscript (*ll*.20-23) contribute to the overall tone of frustrated anger. In *ll*.4-5 Zoilos is clearly replying to a series of reproaches made in the letter he has received. He denies acting crazily, impudently and as a coward (if this is what is suggested by μῦς). This offers a useful approximation to the situation in 2 Cor. 10, if not an exact parallel. There, Paul is responding to various accusations and innuendoes. But it is not certain that these charges have been transmitted to him by letter: they may have been passed on orally. Note 2 Cor. 10.10, and the possible allusions in *vss*. 1, 14, 15.

What has occasioned Zoilos' response? If we may read between the lines, Zoilos has run away from the house where he has served, fearing harsh treatment from Diogenes (12-13, 22-23). Diogenes must have accused him of impertinence and cowardice in so doing (5), and Zoilos points out that Diogenes absented himself from home for many years (10-12), leaving the care of Diogenes' parents to Zoilos (7-8). He is thus defending himself as a loyal family servant who regards himself as unjustly treated. Perhaps the parents have died and Diogenes has returned home to establish himself as the heir, but Zoilos has not adjusted easily to his new master's style.

This letter offers quite an *embarras de richesses* philologically. It is not written by a person totally lacking in education. Yet although Zoilos is acquainted with some 'good' forms, he is by no means in control of upper-register grammatical and lexical usage.

Although LSJ has picked up this text, s.v. φιλοπονέω, yet there is no entry for ἐπιονειδίζομαι (4; *ed.pr.* notes that it cannot be read ἔτι ὀνειδίζομαι; note, however, ἐπονειδίζω in LSJ *Suppl.*), or ἀλιστάστως (22; yet cf. LSJ, s.v. ἄλλιστος); and no attestations are listed s.v. μοιχάζω (11; admittedly, this reading is not certain). Confusion occurs between the oblique cases: ὁμοιός σου . . . τῇ ἀδελ|[φῇ, (9-10); ἐτῶν (11, for ἔτη); σου . . . | ἀνεχόμενος, . . . σε . . . ἀνέχε|σθαι (15-17); πρὸς τῇ θύρᾳ (23, which may, however, provide an instance of loss of the final *nu* on the accusative — so, *ed.pr.*). Genitive/dative confusion in later *koine* is a well-known phenomenon. From the present year's culling we may note in addition several texts from *P.Soterichos*, a family archive whose 28 texts from Theadelphia range in date from perhaps as early as 65/6 to 133 AD. In no.12 Gaion writes for his illiterate sister Tamystha to Σωτηρίχωι Λύκου γ[[ε]]εωργ`ῷ´ (*l*.3); but in 13.4 the genitive Σωτη[ρ]ίχου is wrongly given by the same Gaion, as also in 16.3. (This same Gaion has trouble with the morphology of his own name: Γαίων ἔγραψα, correctly at 12.14; but Γαίωνος αἴγραψεν at 13.13.) The reverse phenomenon, dative for genitive, occurs at 14.2, ἔχω παρὰ σοί. This particular group of texts from *P.Soterichos* spans the period 83-87 AD. A V AD Christian epitaph from Thessalonike — Tsigaridas, *Κατάλογος*, 22 (= *IG* X 2, 1 [1972] 786) — requests that Christ 'who made everything by his word' (ὁ | ποίησας | ἐνὶ λόγου | τὰ πάντα, *ll*.2-4) will grant repose and forgiveness to the deceased. Again, in no.1 of the same volume a tomb of the same provenance and century is said to belong to Eleutherios the sub-deacon, δι|αφέροντα Ἐλευ|θερίου οἰποδι|ακόνου (*ll*.1-4), where the dative would normally be expected. *BE* 276 quotes a Christian mosaic inscription from Philippi which includes the wording [Χ]ριστὲ βωήθι τ<ο>ῦ δούλου σου Πρίσκου. Note also *P.Abinn.* 32.6-10 (= Tibiletti, *Lettere*, no.24), quoted below at **124**, no.13. Some other examples of this syntactic feature which have surfaced in previous volumes are *New Docs 1977*, **116**, p.209, σύ(ν) τοῦ δούλου σου; *New Docs 1978*, **12**, p.46, Greek text *l*.2, for which G. Mussies suggests (*per litt.* 9.8.85) that the word division should be ἐλευθερᾶς αὐτοῦ; ibid., **82**, no.2, Greek text *l*.2, ἐν θαλάσης (*sic*). As Mussies notes, such examples illustrate the phenomenon in the Alexandrinus text of Rev. 1.1, τοῦ δούλου [αὐ]τοῦ Ἰωάννῃ. The verb μέλλω is used with aorist infinitive (15), present infinitive (16-17, 20) and future (or aorist) infinitive (23). With the form ἔμελλες (23) cf. ἤμελλα . . . πέμπιν at Tibiletti no.18 (= *P.Oxy.* 8 [1911] 1160, with corrections; III/IV), *l*.15. On the fluctuation in the augment of this verb see B.G. Mandilaras, *The Verb in the Greek Non-Literary Papyri* (Athens, 1973) §248. δοκέω ὅτι (20) is not classical.

The common *koine* use of πράττω as an equivalent of ποιέω may be noted (10); and the Atticistic -ττ- may be observed, but not given much weight as it is common for this particular verb in Ptolemaic as well as Imperial-period papyri (Gignac, I.150-51). On the use of an apostrophe to separate two identical consonants, as here in πράτ'τειν (10), see Gignac, I.163-64. (The apostrophe occurs also in the papyrus letter repr. at **16**, above, Ἀγριπ'πίνῃ [*ll*.24, 27, though not in *l*.1].) For ποιέω itself (7) with the meaning 'spend (time)', see BAGD, s.v., Ie, δ, where a few other papyrus examples are noted. This appears to be a usage which developed in the *koine*; in the NT note, e.g., Acts 20.3 and Jas. 4.13, for both of which our text offers a good parallel. The verb ὑπηρετέω occurs in this letter both with an accusative of person (7-8) and absolutely (4). For the former cf. the double accusative at *P.Oxy.* 6 (1908) 929.5-6, ἓν τοῦτό με ὑπη|ρετήσεις, 'provide me this one act of service' (late II or III). This is not the way the verb is employed in the NT (dative of person/thing: Acts 13.36; 20.34; 24.23). The weakened use of δέρω, 'beat' (13, 15), occurs in Old Comedy (see LSJ, s.v., II), but appears otherwise to be attested only in later Greek. BAGD, drawing on MM, provides only one papyrus and one epigraphical instance, to which this example may therefore be added to illustrate the frequent occurrence in the NT (Mt. 21.35, etc.). A very clear parallel for the NT chronologically comes in a sexual proposition made by two men to another, couched in the form of a letter: *P.Oxy.* 42 (1974) 3070 (I): οὐκέτι οὐ μὴ | δείρομέν σε ἐὰν δώσῃς | ἡμεῖν τὸ ποιγίσαι (6-8; *read* πυγίσαι). This text provides the starting point for J.E.G. Whitehorne's assessment of sexual mores in Graeco-Roman Egypt, *Pap.Brux.* 19, pp.240-46.

For μίκρος, 'young' (13), see BAGD, s.v., 1, b; again, this sense is one which develops in the Hellenistic period, with Menander a precursor, as often (*Sam.* 39-40). Another example, from *CIJ* II.1510, is quoted at **71** below. In the NT note Mt. 18.6, 10, 14. An imperfect might have been expected for aorist ἐδεήθης (13-14), given the iterative context. No specific documentary parallels are provided by BAGD, s.v. νεανίσκος, 1, since the word is quite common (here, at *l*.14). At *l*.17 the construction μαρτυρέω τινί offers a parallel to Heb. 10.15 and Rev. 22.18 (cf. BAGD, s.v., 1a). In contrast, παραγίνομαι πρός + acc. (18) is not a NT usage; but cf. 2 Tim. 4.16, οὐδείς μοι παρεγένετο for a similar sense for the verb. The simple form γίνομαι merits comment in this letter, too: note ἐγενόμην at *l*.9, but ἐγενάμην, apparently, at *l*.15. Of more interest is the use of γίνομαι in *l*.15 as a periphrastic tense: ἐγενάμην . . . ἀνεχόμενος. On this construction in the NT see BDF §354; N. Turner in Moulton's *Grammar of NT Greek*, III (Edinburgh, 1963) 87, 89, attributes the popularity of the construction in the NT to 'the influence of Semitic speech', particularly Aramaic. (T. Muraoka tells me that it is equally common in post-classical Hebrew.) The occurrence in our papyrus militates against his claim, though does not disprove it. Whether some half dozen instances constitute it as a popular NT construction is a moot point, given that it is thinly spread between four writers in the NT (Mk. 9.3, 7; 2 Cor. 6.14; Col. 1.18; Heb. 5.12; Rev. 3.2; 16.10). BAGD appears not to distinguish this usage of γίνομαι. As well as ἦν (8), the longer imperfect form ἤμην may have occurred at *l*.13. Paratactic καί is frequent at certain points in the letter (4-5, 8-9, 10); cf. BDF

§471. The pluperfect ἐκεκινδυνεύκει (20-21) is probably best translated as an imperfect since, as K.L. McKay points out to me (*per litt.*), 'the verb being stative the perfect aspect is most likely to have the same meaning, but with an intensified force, as the imperfective corresponding forms'. For the absolute use of this verb cf. 1 Cor. 15.30. At *l*.22 αὐτή provides a good example of unemphatic αὐτός in the nominative (see BAGD, s.v., 2). Another instance of this feature occurs in the text repr. at **18**, *l*.23.

Whereas λοιπόν at *l*.16 means 'in future' (cf. BAGD, s.v., 3a, α), in *ll*.14 and 15 the sense required seems rather to be 'furthermore, accordingly'. BAGD, s.v., 3b, notes 1 Cor. 4.2 as the only NT instance where it is so used, but offers no documentary parallels. For another example of τὸ λοιπόν, 'in future', note *AE* 565 (Thasos, time of Vespasian), a letter — first published in 1958 — from the procurator L. Vinuleius Pataicius to the archons, *boule* and *demos* of Thasos, in which he grants them release from postal charges in future except for those items which pass through their territory: καὶ τῆς ἀνγαρείας ὑμᾶς τὸ λοιπὸν ἀπολύω παρὲξ ἂν | διὰ τῆς ὑμετέρας χώρας (*ll*.4-5). Pfuhl/Möbius, I.301 (Kyzikos, dated III in the edition repr. in E. Schwertheim, *Die Inschriften von Kyzikos und Umgebung* I [*IK* 18; Bonn, 1980] 513) preserves an example of λοιπόν in the sense, 'finally', followed by an imperative. After the deceased identifies himself and his home city (Ravenna) and mentions his military career, he goes on to warn against the insertion of another body in his grave, λοιπὸν φυλάσσου, μή τινα ἐνθήσεις τάφῳ (*l*.6). This use of λοιπόν followed by the imperative occurs in the NT at 2 Cor. 13.11; Phil. 4.8 (though the imperative is far removed in position); and in 2 Thes. 3.1. At 1 Thes. 4.1 the imperatival idea after the adverb is expressed by another construction. Cf. *New Docs 1977*, **106**, pp.188-89.

Finally, concerning this letter from Zoilos, if this text concerns two men who are not brothers, but perhaps in a master/house-born slave relationship, then the attitude reflected in *l*.20 is of some small interest: φιλοστοργεῖν offers confirmation of the suggestion at *New Docs 1977*, **80**, pp.102-03, that φιλόστοργος and its related forms appears to be used more loosely in Egypt than of intra-familial relationships. On the word group see further at **33** below.

Another letter in Tibiletti's selection (no.30; = *P.Herm.Rees* [1964] 11 with some corrections) begins with a tone of upbraiding: θαυμάζω πῶς | ἐπελάθου τῶν ἐμῶν | ἐντολῶν ὧν πολλά|κις σοι κατ' ὄψιν ἐ|νετειλάμην (2-6), 'I am amazed that you have forgotten my commands, which I have often given you personally, . . .' (Hermopolis Magna, IV). Though little of the wording is in common, there is a similarity of tone with Gal. 1.6. For the phrase κατ' ὄψιν (MM, s.v., ὄψις provides several papyrus examples) cf. Jn 7.24, κατ' ὄψιν κρίνειν, where the meaning is slightly different.

18. Encouragement to a philosopher

Oxyrhynchos III/early IV
ed.pr. — P.J. Parsons, *P.Oxy.* 42 (1974) 3069

Ἀκύλας Σαραπίωνι
χαίρειν.
κομισάμενός σου τὰ γράμ-
ματα πάνυ ἥσθην· ἧ μάλιστα
ὁ ἡμέτερος Καλλίνεικος ἐμαρ-

τύρει περὶ τῆς διαίτης σου ἧς ποιῇ καὶ ἐν τοιούτοις ὢν πράγμασι[[ν]], μάλιστα μὴ ἀφιστάμενος τῆς ἀσκήσεως· ἄξιον οὖν ἐστιν ἐπαινεῖν ἑαυτούς, οὐχ ὅτι ποιοῦμεν ταῦτα ἀλλὰ ὅτι μὴ ἐξαγόμεθα ὑφ' ἑαυτ[ῶν]· ἀνδραγάθε̣[ι] οὖν καὶ τὰ λοιπὰ ἐπιτέλεσον ὡς ἀνὴ[ρ ἀ]γ̣α̣θός, καὶ μ[ή σ]ε̣ ταρασσέ[τ]ω̣ ἢ πλοῦτος ἢ ὥρα ἢ ἄλλο τ[ι τ]ῶν τοιού[[ν]]των, ὡς οὐδὲν ὄ̣φ̣[ελ]ός ἐστιν ἀρετῆς μὴ παρούσης, ἀλλὰ φροῦδα καὶ οὐδενὸς ἄξια. θεῶν σῳζόντων προσδέχομαί σε ἐν τῇ Ἀντινόου. τὸ σκυλάκιον πέμψον Σωτηρίδι, ἐπεὶ αὐτὴ νῦν ἐν ἀγρῷ διατρείβει. ἔρρω{σ}σο σὺν τοῖς σοῖς.

ἔρρω{σ}σο.

(*back*) Σαραπίωνι φιλοσόφωι
παρὰ Ἀκύλ̣ο̣υ̣
φίλου.

Well preserved papyrus (10B x 22.2H cm.). In *l.*5 a rough breathing mark was written over the definite article.

Bib. — Tibiletti, *Lettere*, no.20; S.K. Stowers, *Letter Writing in Greco-Roman Antiquity* (Philadelphia, 1986) 99 (translation).

Aquila to Sarapion, greetings. When I received your letter I was very glad. | Our Kallinikos has been giving extensive testimony concerning your way of life which you are leading even though you are in such circumstances, particularly as you are not abandoning your self-abnegation. | So it is appropriate to 'pat ourselves on the back', not because we do this (i.e. practise austerity) but because we are not led astray by ourselves. So act like a man, and finish what remains | like a good man. And do not let wealth distract you, or the (charm of) youth, or anything else like these; since they bestow no benefit if virtue is not present, but they are evanescent and | worthless. The gods preserving us, I expect you at Antinoopolis. Send the puppy to Soteris, since she now lives in the country. Good health to you, together with your (friends?). | Good health to you. (*back*) To Sarapion the philosopher from Aquila his friend.

The very fact that Sarapion is addressed as a philosopher suggests — even allowing for the very self-conscious nature of the letter — that his is a full-time vocation. This was by no means a rarity under the Second Sophistic; indeed, as Parsons notes (ad loc.), official support was expressed for such individuals by their being exempted from civic duties (liturgies, etc.). But

Sarapion seems to have encountered difficult circumstances; and Aquila has been anxious — if we may read between the lines of this letter — to hear that his friend at Oxyrhynchos has not abandoned his calling. The letter he has received has laid to rest his fears, as has the verbal confirmation brought by Kallinikos, presumably the bearer of the letter and a mutual friend (judging by ἡμέτερος, 5).

Though Aquila is an intellectual peer, the loaded sense of φίλος (28) ought not to be missed: he is claiming association with a man of some standing. We may compare the similarly-weighted use in the phrase φίλος τοῦ καίσαρος, of Pilate at Jn 19.12 (cf. the discussion at *New Docs 1978*, **75**). Philosophical terms are well represented: δίαιτα, ἄσκησις, ταράσσω, ἀρετή. Perhaps ἀνδραγαθέω and ἀνὴρ ἀγαθός should also be so considered in the particular context of this letter, not that the verb need carry such a connotation everywhere. At *P.Oxy.* 2 (1899) 291 (25/6 AD) an official writes to a subordinate concerning the need to demand payment from those in arrears: καὶ προέγρα|ψ[ά σοι] ἀνδραγαθῖ[ν] καὶ ἀπαιτεῖν | μ[έχ]ρι ὑγια[ί]νων παρ[α]γένωμαι (7-9), 'I wrote to you before to act like a man and demand payment until I get well and come'. It is no surprise that one who is instructed in philosophy should himself be employing some higher-style turns of phrase: e.g., ἡμέτερος (5, for ἡμῶν; cf. BDF §285), τοιοῦτος perhaps (7, 17: for the article accompanying it in the latter place cf. BDF §274), genitive absolute used according to classical criteria (18-19), φροῦδος (19; see Parsons' n. ad loc.). Yet there are features of his language which betray Aquila as a man of his times: μή + participle (8-9); the post-classical use of μή at *l.*12 (so *ed.pr.*, n. ad loc.); -σσ- in ταρασσέτω (16); and unemphatic nominative αὐτή (23; another instance is noted in *l.*22 of the text repr. at **17**). One particularly interesting indication that Aquila is aiming at a high style is the use of θεῶν σῳζόντων (20) in place of the more usual θεῶν θελόντων which is found in *P.Ross.Georg.* 3 (1930, repr. 1966) 2.5 (provenance unknown, III; = Tibiletti, *Lettere*, no.1), briefly discussed at **45** below; for a Christian version cf. *P.Oxy.* 12 (1916) 1494.4 (early IV; = Tibiletti, no.21), θεοῦ θέλοντος. For an example which uses both the plural and singular forms and may therefore be either pagan or Christian see Tibiletti, no.12 (*ed.pr.* — *P.Ross.Georg.* 3.3 [Arsinoite nome, III]), briefly discussed at **59** below. A more elevated form of this expression occurs in *P.Oxy.* 14 (1920) 1666.15 (mid-III; = Tibiletti, no.3), θεῶν οὖν βουλομένων; and an elegant variation is found in *P.Oxy.* 4 (1908) 935 (III): θεῶν συνλαμβανόν|των ἡ ἀδελφὴ ἐπὶ τ[ὸ] | κομψότερον ἐτράπη, | καὶ ὁ ἀδελφὸς δὲ Ἁρπο|κρατίων σώζεται | καὶ [ὑγι]αίνει, συνλαμβ[ά]|νο[υσι] γὰρ ἡμεῖν ἀεὶ ο[ἱ] | π[άτ]ριοι θεοὶ ἡμῶν | δ[ιδό]ντες ἡμεῖν ὑγία[ν καὶ] | σω[τ]ηρίαν, 'the gods assisting, our sister has taken a turn for the better, and our brother Harpokration is safe and well, for our ancestral gods always assist us, giving us health and safety' (*ll.*3-12). The use of κομψότερον here parallels Jn 4.52. Another variant, ἐὰν θεὸς θέλῃι, occurs at *col.*iv.9 in *P.XV Congr.* 22 (Panopolis, IV[1]; pls.11-12), a very long (nearly 200*ll.*) but fragmentary and abraded letter which belongs to an archive. In this letter Ammon, writing from Alexandria to his mother, indicates what he has been doing to try to revive the family's former prosperity and prestige. He gives her advice concerning the estate at Panopolis and ends with a very long list of greetings. Since in *P.Oxy.* 3069 Aquila adopts a conscious variation of the usual cliché we might speculate whether in this context the phrase should be given more than its usual weight: a conscious assertion of solidarity in their religious adherence in the face of the rise of Christianity, perhaps?

C. Préaux, *CE* 52 (1977) 175, has offered the suggestion that there are neo-Platonic nuances in this letter from Aquila to Sarapion. The content is insufficient to allow this possibility to be established. But the presence of ταράσσω (16) may hint at an Epicurean outlook, for ἀταραξία was a particularly important principle for that group. Furthermore, the concluding vague greeting to the recipient καὶ τοῖς σοῖς (24) might be consistent with our knowledge that the Epicureans adopted a household structure as a basis for their communities. See generally on this W.A. Meeks, *The First Urban Christians* (New Haven, 1983) 83-84 with the notes. Although it belongs to a later period, therefore, this little text may well prove of more than passing interest for those examining both the models for the Pauline groups, and his competitors.

Another third-century philosopher may also be mentioned briefly. *SEG* 32 (1982) 1255 is a dedication from Nikomedeia to Zeus on the base of a fragmentary statuette of the god with his eagle beside him: Ζηνὶ τοῦδε τοῦ κόσμου | πατρί· Αὐρ. Δημήτριος | φιλόσοφος καὶ βουλευτής. Demetrios was a councillor of his city. As *ed.pr.* notes — S. Şahin/M.H. Sayer, *ZPE* 47 (1982) 43-44 no.1 (pl.1a); cf. *BE* (1983) 424 — the notion of God being father of the *kosmos* has a philosophical ancestry going back to Plato. This text is reprinted in S. Öğüt-Polat/S. Şahin, *Epig. Anat.* 5 (1985) 110 no.14.

A Platonic link is explicit in a very interesting inscription from Ephesos, *I.Eph.* VII, 2.3901, first published by J. Nollé, *ZPE* 41 (1981) 197-206 (pl.5a; cf. *SEG* 31 [1981] 951), whose commentary is fundamental.

Ὀφέλλιον Λαῖτον Πλατωνικὸν φιλόσ[οφον]
ἐπιδειξάμενον λόγων καὶ ἠθῶν πᾶ[σαν]
ἀρετήν·
εἰ κατὰ Πυθαγόραν ψυχὴ μεταβαίνει ἐς ἄλλον,
ἐν σοί, Λαῖτε, Πλάτων ζῇ πάλι σωζόμενος.

(They set up the statue of) Ofellius Laetus, the Platonic philosopher, who displayed every virtue both in his speech and in his behaviour. If, according to Pythagoras, the soul transmigrates to someone else, | then preserved in you, Laetus, Plato lives again.

A nearly identical version of the last two lines is preserved on an Athenian inscription, *IG* II^2 3816 (cf. *SEG* 31 [1981] 168; *BE* [1981] 481, a long and useful discussion):

θειολόγου Λαίτοιο μετάρσιον ὕμνον ἀκούσας
οὐρανὸν ἀνθρώποις εἶδον ἀνοιγόμενον·
εἰ κατὰ Πυθαγόραν ψυχὴ μεταβαίνει εἰς ἄλλον,
ἐν σοί, Λαῖτε, Πλάτων ζῇ πάλι φαινόμενος.

After hearing the exalted hymn of Laetus who speaks of God, I saw heaven opening to men. If, according to Pythagoras, the soul transmigrates to someone else, then making his epiphany in you, Laetus, Plato lives again.

Nollé shows (199) that the term θε(ι)ολόγος serves to make a link with Plato, a connection which becomes explicit in the last verse. The author of the epigram has been so uplifted by what he has heard from Laetus that he has had a divine vision. The opening of heaven to reveal a vision to someone has close parallels in the NT, of course, particularly Jn 1.51 and

Acts 7.56. But Nollé (201 n.11) finds other useful analogies, in the OT (Ezek. 1.1), ECL (Hermas, *Vis.* I.1.4) and the *Corpus Hermeticum*. It is unclear whether Laetus was originally from Asia Minor, perhaps Ephesos itself, and went to Athens to pursue his philosophical vocation; alternatively, he may have been an Athenian who, already of eminence in this sphere, visited Ephesos. Whereas the *IG* inscription has usually been dated to III AD, Nollé (204-05) agrees with Dittenberger (in *IG* III[1] [1878] 270) that it belongs to I AD, as does also the Ephesian dedication. Accordingly, this philosopher thus provides a most interesting contemporary analogy for Paul's visit to Athens and his debate with philosophers, Stoics and Epicureans among them, before the Areiopagos council. Clearly Laetus had deeply affected more than one of his hearers. Another man who may also be classed as a *theologos* — he wrote aretologies and had pronounced philosophical interests — is discussed at **8** above. On the occurrence of the word in *I.Eph.* see **60** below. For πάλι in these inscriptions cf. **6** above. In contrast to the allusion here to Pythagorean transmigration of souls, a caustic attitude to it is expressed in a verse epitaph for Eutyches, *IGUR* 1221 (Rome, Imperial; pl. on p.81): ὃς θνητοῖς ψυχὴν πεί|σας ἐπὶ σώμασιν ἐλθεῖν | τὴν αὑτοῦ μέλεος οὐκ ἀν|έπεισε μένειν (5-8), 'whoever is of the view that his soul comes to (other) mortal bodies, the poor wretch has not persuaded his own soul to stay with him'.

The *I.Eph.* volumes include inscriptions for several other philosophers. A (neo-)Platonist from Tralles is commemorated by a pupil: *I.Eph.* VII, 2.4340 (Imperial), [. . . .]λ̣ι̣[ον] | Σεκουνδῖ̣ν̣[ον] Τραλλιαν[όν], | φιλόσοφ[ον] | Πλατωνικὸν | Κοίλιος | Μαρκελλεῖνο[ς] | [τ]ὸν ἑαυτοῦ | [δι]δάσκαλον. An 'eclectic' philosopher from Alexandria is honoured by the Ephesians: *I.Eph.* III.789 (Imperial), ἡ βουλὴ [καὶ ὁ δῆμος] | ἐτίμησαν Π[- - -] | 'Αλεξανδρέα, ἀπὸ [τοῦ Μουσείου] | [φ]ιλόσοφον ἐγλεκ̣[τικόν]. Finally, in *I.Eph.* III.616 (III[1], after 212) the asiarch M. Aurelius Daphnos honours Appius Alexandros, a man who had a public career as imperial procurator and who was also τὸν φιλόσοφον (*l.*6). It is interesting that Daphnos, himself of no mean standing, concludes his text for Alexandros by describing him as τὸν ἐν πᾶσιν τῆς πατρίδος | καὶ ἑαυτοῦ εὐεργέτην, 'the benefactor in all things of his state and of himself (viz., Daphnos)' (*ll.*12-13).

Returning to the comment earlier about a possible Epicurean flavour in *P.Oxy.* 3069, a more recently published, fragmentary letter of recommendation which alludes explicitly to Epicureanism deserves quotation. The text is *P.Oxy.* 51 (1984) 3643 (II[2]). The translation given below incorporates those readings and restorations which J.R. Rea regards as likely in his notes (in *ed.pr.*).

Οὐαλέριος . . . . . [. . . . .
'Οφελλιανῶι τῶ[ι . . . . .
ἀδε[λ]φῶ̣ι̣ [. . . . .
πάντες ἴσασιν [. . . . . .] . [
. εις. διόπερ ἐπιστέλλω
σοι ὑπὲρ Διογένου[ς] . εω . ος,
ἀδελφιδοῦ ὄντος [ἀνα]γ̣κ̣αιο-
τάτου μοι φίλου, ἀνδρὸς
φιλοσόφου γενομένο̣υ̣ τ̣ὰ̣
'Επικούρια, Θε . [.] . ς
τοὔνομα. διχόθ̣[εν] [. .] . ν
τὸν νεανίσκον, καὶ δ`ι´' ἐκε̣ῖ-
νον καὶ δι' αὐτὸν ἐπάξιο̣ν̣
ὄντ[α τῆς] παρ' [.]μεῖν . . [. .
σεως [. . . .]ς̣ δὴ ουκε̣[. . .
αυτ . [. . . .]σθα . [. . . . . . .
σοι[*c. 16 letters*
. . . .

Valerius Diodoros(?) to Ophellianos his . . . brother. All people know . . . | . . . Accordingly I am writing this letter to you on behalf of Diogenes Theon(?) who is a nephew of a very close friend of mine, a man who has become a philosopher in | Epicureanism, whose name is Theon(?). Treat the young man kindly for two reasons, both for that man and for his own sake, as he is worthy of . . . from us(?) . . . | . . .

For the possibility that the writer may be Valerius Diodoros, an Alexandrian scholar at the time of Marcus Aurelius, see Rea's introduction to this text in *P.Oxy.*, ad loc., and his n. to *l.*1. In *l.*9 γενομένου could imply that the philosopher is already deceased (so Rea, n. ad loc.); alternatively, that he has become (and therefore now is) a philosopher. This example of a second-century letter of recommendation possibly emanating from within a circle of people bound by ties of philosophical kinship is of considerable analogous interest for the connections between Paul and his friends. On Christian letters of recommendation see **124** below.

Not surprisingly, Epicurean sentiments occur in epitaphs. In the second of three elegiac couplets which constitute *IGUR* 1159 (Rome, Imperial period) it is said of the deceased: 'his name was Apollophanes, noted still for his trustworthiness and his (good) reputation, who exhorts mortals to get their share of gladness', τοῦ|νομ' Ἀπολλοφάνης, | πίστει μέγας ἠδ' ἔτι δό|ξῃ, ὃς προλέγει θνατοῖς | εὐφροσύνης μετέχειν (*ll.*4-8). This poem was composed as a funerary gift (τὴν δ' ἐπιτυμβίδιον | . . . χάριν, 9-10) by Apollophanes' *threptos*, who identifies himself as a poet in an allusive manner: τοὔνο|μα καὶ τέχνην ἦν Διό|δωρος ὅδε (11-13), 'in name and in craft he was Diodoros'. The allusion is to poetry as a gift of Zeus (see Moretti's n. ad loc.). Note the use here of προλέγω, 'exhort, warn', paralleling well the NT usage at 2 Cor. 13.2; Gal. 5.21; and, less certainly, at 1 Thes. 3.4 (where a 'prophetic' connotation may be present). MM provides one example only of εὐφροσύνη as a common noun, so the instance in this epigram deserves passing notice to illustrate the NT occurrences (Acts 2.28, quoting LXX Ps. 15.11; and 14.17). On this noun see further **58** below.

Much more explicitly Epicurean in their nihilism are the Greek verses included in a long Latin prose epitaph for M. Antonius Encolpus and his *libertus* Antonius Athenaios, granting space in the vault to their freedmen and freedwomen and their descendants: *IGUR* 1245 (Rome, II fin./III init.; pl. on p.104). In the section composed in iambics the deceased informs anyone who cares to read that now he is dead he can categorically deny the existence of the river of Hades, of Charon, Aiakos and the hound Kerberos (*ll.*14-15). In the elegiacs which follow, Encolpus requests that no perfumes or garlands be offered, or sacrifices burned at the tomb for the expense is wasted. 'If you have anything share it with me while I am alive; but when you make my ashes drunk (with wine offerings) you (simply) make mud, as a dead person does not drink', μὴ μύρα, μὴ στεφάνους στήλλῃ χαρίσῃ· λίθος ἐστίν· μηδὲ τὸ πῦρ | φλέξεις· ἰς κενὸν ἡ δαπάνη. ζῶντί μοι, εἴ τι ἔχεις, μετάδος· τέφραν δὲ μεθύσκων | πηλὸν ποιήσεις καὶ οὐκ ὁ θανὼν πίεται (*ll.*17-19). In the preceding Latin section of the gravestone one *libertus* is explicitly excluded from a burial portion in the vault (*ll.*4-5). It was not unprecedented for freedmen to lose the patronage of the master who had emancipated them. A Latin epitaph from Ostia (II^2) provides that the tomb may be used by the freedmen and women of the deceased and their descendants *excepto Hilaro liberto | meo abominando . . .* (*ll.*6-7), 'except my accursed freedman Hilarus': *ed.pr.* — M. Cébeillac-Gervason, in *Φιλίας χάριν. Miscellanea di studi classici in onore di E. Manni*, II (Rome, 1979) 453-61; cf. *AE* 94. The factitive verb μεθύσκω in *IGUR* 1245 is found in the NT only in the passive (Eph. 5.18; 1 Thes. 5.7, etc.).

A final epitaph to be noted in this context is Helbing, *AGI* 29 (Brundisium III/II BC; = *SIG*[3] 1227): Εὐκρατίδας Πεισιδάμου, | ῾Ρόδιος, | φιλόσοφος ᾿Επικούρειος, | τὸν τόπον τῆς Βρενδεσίνων βουλῆς | εἰς ταφὴν ψηφισαμένης, 'Eukratidas of Rhodes, son of Peisidamos, the Epicurean philosopher; the council of the Brindisii decreed (this) place for his tomb'. The text is of interest for the way it testifies to the value placed by a city on having a resident philosopher. Though an alien he was accorded burial at public expense.

This entry provides the opportunity to mention T. Flavius Damianos, 'the Sophist', whose memory is preserved both in Philostratos, *Vitae Soph.* II.23.605-06, and in a number of inscriptions from Ephesos. This man held various public offices, including *grammateus* of the *demos* in 167, and was a significant benefactor of the city. A statue of him is on show in Izmir Museum (E. Akurgal, *Ancient Civilizations and Ruins of Turkey* [Ankara, 1985[6]] pl.52). The near-dozen inscriptions referring to him are listed in the *I.Eph.* index vol. VIII.2, p.206, under his name. Most of these texts are honorific (e.g., III.672, 672A, 672B; VII, 1.3080), but no. VI.2100 is the exceedingly fragmentary remains of the funerary epigram for him and his wife, Vedia Phaedrina. By this marriage, Damianos became son-in-law to one of the most notable of all Ephesos' benefactors, M. Claudius P. Vedius Antoninus Phaedrus Sabinianus, who built the so-called 'Vedius gymnasium' and provided numerous other monuments. It is not certain whether this Vedius provided patronage for the 'professors' based at the Mouseion, οἱ περὶ τὸ Μουσεῖον | παιδεῦται (*I.Eph.* VI.2065): see further R.A. Kearsley, *GRBS* 27 (1986) 187 n.19. For the family tree of the Vedii, showing Damianos and his descendants, see *I.Eph.* VII, 1, pp.88-90.

It is appropriate to conclude this entry with a brief survey of recent publication of portions of the massive inscription set up at Oinoanda in Lykia by the Epicurean philosopher Diogenes. M.F. Smith has published 63 new fragments in *AS* 28 (1978) 39-92, and three previously known ones in *AS* 29 (1979) 70-85 (surveyed together at *SEG* 1444-1512). The new pieces bring the total of known fragments to just over two hundred. Smith had already published 51 new finds in six articles which appeared in the years from 1970 to 1976 (see *SEG*, p.363 for details). Recent editions of the 88 fragments recorded in the nineteenth century are both entitled *Diogenis Oenoandensis fragmenta*, by A. Grilli (Milan, 1960) and C.W. Chilton (Leipzig, 1967). The latter has also published a translation and commentary, *Diogenes of Oenoanda. The Fragments* (Oxford, 1971). For information about new readings and restorations of the fragments see *SEG* 19 (1963) 873; 20 (1964) 53; 26 (1976/77) 1437; 27 (1977) 934; and 31 (1981) 1296. Guarducci, *EG* III (Rome, 1974) 110-18, describes the inscription and reprints a part of it in which Diogenes explains why he set it up. She also discusses two fragments from a letter to the mother of Diogenes or perhaps that of Epicurus himself. All the fragments are parts of the enormous inscription (approx. 40m. long) which Diogenes set up in a stoa at Oinoanda; it included philosophical treatises, several letters and a collection of Epicurean maxims, and its purpose was to disseminate Epicurean teachings. The importance of Diogenes' writings lies in their orthodoxy, according to Smith, because 'when Diogenes gives us information not found in other sources, as he quite often does, we can be confident that he is accurately reporting Epicurean (if not Epicurus') views' (*Proceedings of the Xth International Congress of Classical Archaeology, Izmir, 1973* [Ankara, 1978] II.846 n.29). The possible identification of Diogenes with several men of that name in Oinoanda during II/early III is discussed by A.S. Hall in *JHS* 99 (1979) 160-63 (cf. *SEG* 1443). Arguing from epigraphical evidence Smith favours a date for Diogenes in the time of Hadrian or soon after (*PICCA*, II.846-47).

For an epitaph for a nun, described as φιλοσόφισσα, see **126** below.

19. Holy days in honour of Artemis

Ephesos *c.*162-64

ed.pr. — E.L. Hicks, *The Collection of Ancient Greek Inscriptions in the British Museum*, III.2 (Oxford, 1890) 482 (+ addendum on p.294)

A [Γ(άϊος) Πο]πίλλιος Κᾶρος Πέδω[ν] ἀνθύπατος λέγει· [ἔ]μαθον ἐκ τοῦ πεμφθέντος [πρός] με ψηφίσματος ὑπὸ τῆς λαμπροτ[ά]της Ἐφεσίων βουλῆς τοὺς πρὸ ἐμ[οῦ] κρατίστους ἀνθυπάτους ἱε[ρὰς] νομίσαι τὰς ἡμέρας τῆς π[α]ν̣η[γύρεως] τ̣ῶν Ἀρτε[μισίων] καὶ τοῦτο διατάγματι δεδηλωκέναι· ὅθεν ἀναγκαῖον ἡγησάμην καὶ αὐτὸς ἀποβλέπων εἴς τε τὴν εὐσέβειαν τῆς θεοῦ̣ καὶ εἰς τὴν λαμπροτάτης Ἐφεσίων πόλεως τειμὴν φανερὸν ποιῆσαι διατάγματι ἔσεσθαι τὰς ἡμέρας ταύτας ἱερὰς καὶ τὰς ἐπ' αὐταῖς ἐκεχειρίας φυλαχθήσεσθαι· προεστῶτος τῆς πανηγύρεως Τίτου Αἰλίου Μαρκιανοῦ Πρίσκου τοῦ ἀγωνοθέτου, υἱοῦ Αἰλίου Πρίσκου, ἀνδρὸς δοκιμωτάτου καὶ πάσης τειμῆς καὶ ἀποδοχῆς ἀξίου.

B [ἔδ]οξεν τῆς πρώτης καὶ με[γίστης] [μητρ]οπόλεως τῆς Ἀσίας καὶ δὶς νεωκ̣[όρου τῶν] [Σεβα]σ̣τῶν καὶ φιλοσεβάστου Ἐφε̣[σίων πόλεως] [τῇ βο]υ̣λῇ καὶ τῷ δήμῳ περὶ ὧν εἰσηγή[σατο] [. . . Λ]αβέριος Ἄμοινος φιλοσέβαστος, ὁ γραμμ[ατεὺς] [τοῦ δ]ή̣μου· ἐπεψήφισαν δὲ οἱ στ[ρ]ατηγοὶ τῆς πόλεως φιλοσέβαστοι· [ἐπειδὴ ἡ π]ροεστῶσα τῆς πόλεως ἡμῶν θεὸς Ἄρτε[μις] [οὐ μόνον] ἐν τῇ ἑαυτῆς πατρίδι τ̣ε̣ιμᾶται, ἣν ἁ[πασῶν] [τῶν πόλεων] ἐνδοξοτέραν διὰ τῆς ἰδίας θειότητ[ος πεποίη]κεν, ἀ]λλὰ καὶ παρ̣ὰ̣ [Ἕλλησίν τε κ]α̣ὶ̣ [β]α̣ρ̣βά̣ρ̣[ο]ις, ὥ[στε πανταχοῦ ἀνεῖσθαι αὐτῆς ἱερά τε κα[ὶ τεμένη, ναοὺς δὲ] αὐτῇ τε εἱδρύσθαι καὶ βωμοὺς αὐτῇ ἀνακεῖσθαι διὰ τὰς ὑπ' αὐτῆς γεινομένας ἐναργεῖς ἐπιφανείας, καὶ τοῦτο δὲ μέγιστον τοῦ περὶ αὐτὴν σεβασμοῦ ἐστιν τεκμήριον, τὸ ἐπώνυμον αὐτῆς εἶναι μῆνα καλούμενον παρ' ἡ̣[μ]ῖν μὲν Ἀρτεμισ[ι]ῶνα, παρὰ δὲ Μακεδόσιν καὶ τοῖς λοιποῖς ἔθνεσιν τοῖς Ἑλληνικοῖς καὶ ταῖς ἐν αὐταῖς πόλεσιν Ἀρτεμίσιον, ἐν ᾧ μηνὶ πανηγύρεις τε καὶ ἱερομηνίαι ἐπιτελοῦνται, διαφερόντως δὲ ἐ̣ν [τῇ] ἡμετέρᾳ πόλει τῇ τροφῷ τῆς ἰδίας θεοῦ τῆς Ἐφ[εσί]ας, προσῆκον δὲ εἶναι ἡγούμενος ὁ δῆμος [ὁ] Ἐφεσίων ὅλον τὸν μῆνα τὸν ἐπώνυμον τοῦ θ̣[είου] ὀνόματος εἶναι ἱερὸν καὶ ἀνακεῖσθαι τῇ θεῷ ἐδοκίμασεν διὰ τοῦδε τοῦ ψηφίσματος [διατιθέ]ναι τὴν περὶ αὐτοῦ θρησκείαν· διὸ δεδόχ[θαι] [ὅ]λον τὸν μῆνα τὸν Ἀρτεμισιῶ̣να εἶνα[ι ἱερὸν πάσας] [τ]ὰς ἡμέρας, ἄγεσθαι δὲ ἐπ' αὐταῖς μην[ός τε καὶ]

[δι'] ἔτ̣ους τὰς ἑορτὰς καὶ τὴν τῶν 'Αρτεμ[ισίων πανή-]
[γ]υριν καὶ τὰς ἱερομηνίας, ἅτε τοῦ μηνὸς ὅ[λου ἀνακειμέ-]
ν̣ου τῇ θεῷ· οὕτω γὰρ ἐπὶ τὸ ἄμεινον τῆς [θεοῦ τιμωμέ-]
[ν]ης ἡ πόλις ἡμ[ῶν ἐ]νδοξοτέρα τε καὶ εὐδ[αιμονεστέρα]
εἰς τὸ[ν ἅπα]ντα διαμενεῖ χ[ρόνον.]

C ἡ πατρὶς
Τ. Αἴλιον Τ. υἱὸν Κλ(αυδία)
Μαρκιανὸν Πρίσκο[ν τὸν]
ἀγωνοθέτην καὶ πα[νηγυριάρχην]
τ̣ῶν μεγάλων 'Αρτ[εμισίων]
[κα]ὶ̣ πρῶτον αὐτ[ὸν ποιήσαντα]
τὴν πανήγυριν κατὰ τέλειο[ν]
καὶ ἐκεχειρίας εἰς ὅλον τὸν
ἐπώνυμον τῆς θεοῦ μῆνα
τυχόντα καὶ τὴν 'Αρτεμισι-
ακὴν κρίσιν καταστήσαντα
καὶ τὰ θέματα τοῖς ἀγωνισ-
ταῖς αὐξήσαντα καὶ ἀνδρι-
άντας τῶν νικησάντων
ἀναστήσαντα·
τὴν τειμὴν ἀναστήσαντο[ς]
Λ. Φαινίου Φαύστου
τοῦ συνγενοῦς αὐτοῦ.

Statue base (48B x 112H x 48D cm.), with three sides inscribed.

Bib. — While portions of frags. A, B and C were discussed as far back as the XVIIth century, Hicks' edition was the first for the whole text. The most recent discussion of the inscription's history and interpretation is **I.Eph.* Ia.24 (further bib. given there); cf. R. Oster, *HTR* 77 (1984 [1986]) 233-37.

A The proconsul Gaius Popillius Carus Pedo states: 'I learned from the decree which was sent to me by the most illustrious | council of the Ephesians that the honourable proconsuls before me regarded the days of the festival of the Artemisia as holy and have made this clear by edict. This is why | I considered it necessary, since I also have regard for the reverence of the goddess and for the honour of the most illustrious city of the Ephesians, to make it known by decree that these days shall be | holy and the festal holidays will be observed on these days'. (This edict was promulgated) while Titus Aelius Marcianus Priscus, son of Aelius | Priscus, a man very well thought of and worthy of all honour and acceptance, was leader of the festival and president of the athletic games.

B It was decreed by the council and people of the patriotic city of the Ephesians, first and greatest metropolis of Asia, temple-warden of the Augusti two times, concerning the things about which | the patriotic [*N*] Laberius Amoenus, secretary of the people, made the motion. The patriotic *strategoi* of the city voted upon it. 'Since the goddess Artemis, leader of our city, is honoured not only in her own homeland, which she has made | the most illustrious of all cities through her own divine nature, but also among Greeks and also barbarians, the result is that everywhere her shrines and sanctuaries have been established, and temples have been founded for her and altars dedicated to her because of the visible manifestations effected by her. | And this is the greatest proof of the reverence surrounding her, the month named after her, called Artemision among us, and Artemisios among the Macedonians and among the other Greek nations, and among the cities within their borders. | During this month festivals and sacrifices are performed, particularly in our city, the nurturer of its own Ephesian goddess. The Ephesian people regard it as appropriate that the entire month named after the divine | name be sacred and dedicated to the goddess, and through this decree approved that the religious ritual for her be stipulated. Therefore, it is decreed that the entire month Artemision be sacred for all its

days, and that on the same (days) of the month, and | throughout the year, feasts and the festival and the sacrifices of the Artemisia are to be conducted, inasmuch as the entire month is dedicated to the goddess. For in this way, with the improvement of the honouring of the goddess, our city will remain more illustrious and more blessed for all time'.

C **His own city honours Titus Aelius Marcianus Priscus, son of Titus, of the Claudian tribe, the president of the athletic games and the leader of the festival | of the great Artemisia, (because) he was the first to conduct the festival in its entirety and obtained festal holidays for the entire month named after the goddess and | established the Artemisiac contest and increased the prizes for the contestants and erected statues of the ones who won. | L. Faenius Faustus, his relative, erected this in his honour.**

This mid-II inscription contributes important information in three areas: Roman involvement in local religious matters; the cult of the Ephesian Artemis; and philological notes for the NT.

Imperial involvement

As the edict of the proconsul C. Popillius Carus Pedo (frag.A) reveals, both he and his predecessors enacted διατάγματα that related directly to the veneration of Artemis. An inscription from nearby Aphrodisias documents Roman intervention in such matters from the late Republic (39 BC). The Roman Senate granted sanctuary privileges and asylum rights to the temple of the goddess Aphrodite at Aphrodisias, conferring the same 'rights and the religious sanctity which pertain to the temple or precinct of Ephesian Artemis at Ephesos', ἐκεῖνο τὸ ἱερόν, ἐκεῖνο τὸ τέμε|νος ἄσυλον [ἔ]στω τούτῳ τῷ δικαίῳ, ταύτῃ τε δ(ε)ισιδαιμονίᾳ ᾧ δικαίῳ καὶ ᾗ δεισιδαιμονίᾳ τὸ ἱερὸν εἴτε καὶ τέμενος 'Αρ|τέμιδος 'Ε[φε]σίας ἐστὶν ἐν 'Εφέσῳ, κτλ: J. Reynolds, *Aphrodisias and Rome* (*JRS Monograph* 1; London, 1982) no.8.55-57 (cf. *ll*.40-41, heavily restored). A contemporary inscription at Pergamon from the Asian proconsul P. Servilius Isauricus (46-44 BC) relates an ἐπίκριμα περὶ τῆς ἀσυλίας of the city's Asklepian sanctuary: C. Habicht, *Die Inschriften des Asklepieions* (*Altertümer von Pergamon*, 8.3; Berlin, 1969) no.1 (48-46 BC). For further discussion of *asylia* see **78** below.

There was often joint veneration of the Emperor and the Ephesian goddess and, significantly, the *Augusteum* was erected inside the *peribolos* of the temple of Artemis (see especially *I.Eph.* V.1522, to be dated 6-5 BC). Nevertheless, the Roman authorities never evinced a sycophantic attitude toward the goddess and her cult. Sometimes the legislation was supportive, as seen in the edict of Pedo, while at other times it was restrictive and censorious. Tacitus reports (*Ann.* 3.61) that Tiberius threatened to revoke the asylum privilege of Artemis' temple as well as that of numerous other temples and shrines because of their abuse of sanctuary rights in providing aid to criminals (*complebantur templa pessimis servitiorum*, 3.60). Only by persuasive petition before the Roman Senate was the city able to preserve this long cherished right of the goddess' temple.

Another Ephesian inscription (Ia.17-19), records a lengthy edict (dated *c*.44) of the proconsul Paullus Fabius Persicus who intervened in the affairs of the goddess. This inscription contains several decrees, four of which relate to the Artemis cult, two protecting and two censuring her. Other evidence for imperial involvement includes several sacred boundary stones (ὅρος ἱερός) demarcating Artemis' territory, which were set in place κατὰ τὴν διαταγήν of various emperors of the first and second centuries (e.g., *I.Eph.* VII, 2.3506-3512). No.3511 is reprinted and discussed briefly below at **28**, ad fin. An Ephesian inscription (*I.Eph.* II.213, repr. and discussed below at **22**) dated 88/9 AD records a petition to the proconsul Lucius Mestrius Florus seeking permission to continue the annual celebration of the 'mysteries and sacrifices' (*ll*.3-4) in honour of Demeter Karpophoros and of the Imperial cult. In order to secure his request the petitioner (employing a technique similar to the one used in *I.Eph.* I.24) refers to endorsements and sanctions from earlier governmental administrations (*ll.*8-10).

All of Rome's actions toward the Artemis cult are characterised by its well-known pragmatism in legal and religious matters. These inscriptions provide analogies for the pragmatism seen in the Pliny-Trajan correspondence regarding Christians in adjacent regions (Pliny, *Ep.* 10.96-97); they also illuminate certain parts of Acts where proconsular attitudes towards local religious matters are recounted, e.g., Acts 18.12-17, and especially Acts 19.38. Although always essentially pragmatic, proconsular involvement was occasionally more active than at other times. When faced with a crisis or a deteriorating social or economic situation, the proconsul's role would be more active. When a local council wanted to bolster its own programs or receive ratification for its own decrees, the proconsul's involvement was more passive. Plutarch complained (*Mor.* 814F-815A) that too many Greek cities had trivialised the process of seeking Rome's ratification by asking that virtually every municipal decree be approved by Rome's representative. Even though the proconsul's involvement in this petition for the Ephesian Artemis was relatively passive, it would be inappropriate — in view of the urban significance of the Artemis cult — to consider it as trivial. On our inscription in this regard see D. Nörr, *Imperium und Polis in der hohen Prinzipatszeit* (*Münchener BeitrWge zur Papyrusforschung und antiken Rechtsgeschichte* 50; Munich, 1969[2]) 24-26.

The Cult of the Ephesian Artemis

The name of Titus Aelius Marcianus Priscus appears at the end of frag. A, and he is the person honoured in frag. C. Noteworthy is the correlation of his recognised position of public leadership and urban patronage with his devotional and moral character, couched in terms entirely typical for such texts. In such a context προεστώς connotes leader, patron, supervisor, and director (see below). This is not only borne out by other literary and epigraphical data, but also by the synonymous use of the phrases προεστὼς τῆς πανηγύρεως (A.16-17) and πανηγυριάρχης (C.4; almost entirely restored). The laudatory terms used of Priscus (A.20-21) occur in the NT, employed admittedly in a variety of contexts, e.g., ἀνὴρ δόκιμος, Jas. 1.12; cf. Rom.14.18; πάσης τιμῆς/ἀποδοχῆς ἄξιος, 1 Tim. 1.15; 4.9; 5.17; 6.1; 1 Cor. 11.19; cf. 2 Cor. 10.18; 13.7.

The celebration of ἱεραὶ ἡμέραι (A.14-15) and ἱεροὶ μῆνες (cf. B.20-21, 25-26, 28) in classical religion, both pagan and Jewish, was commonplace. Even though the term ἐκεχειρία (C.8) was frequently used to designate a military truce in antiquity, L. Robert sensibly argues in regard to this inscription that it was a matter of a judicial holiday during which one could not conduct any legal business (*Etudes Anatoliennes. Recherches sur les inscriptions grecques de L'Asie Mineure* [Paris, 1937] 178). Robert's conclusion represents, however, only part of the truth. It is clear from this document and from literary sources that the celebrations of Artemis in the month Artemision included games, festivals, banquets, sacred processions, and sacrifices (Thuc. 3.104.3-4; D.H., *Ant. Rom.* 4.25.4; cf. I.R. Arnold, *AJA* 76 [1972] 17-22). Moreover, it probably included Saturnalian elements such as the temporary freeing of slaves and dismissal of schools, elements which occurred during the ἐκεχειρία at nearby Magnesia (*SIG*[3] 695, after 129 BC) when it honoured its own tutelary deity, Artemis Leukophryene. Clearly, the holiday included more than the cessation of legal activities.

Apparently, the fidelity and scrupulousness with which the sacred time and accompanying festivals of Artemis had been kept were waning. Either the proconsul himself had been negligent in honouring the ἐκεχειρία (the usual interpretation) or the populace in general had grown remiss in its reverence towards the goddess' liturgical calendar. Whatever the cause, the *boule* of the

Ephesians solicited from the proconsul a reaffirmation of a longstanding policy. With imperial support; the *boule* and *demos* of the local government could feel more secure in their punitive responses to violators. This temporary disregard for Artemis' holy days ought not to be interpreted as a tacit indication of the ascendancy of Christianity, as it was by Hicks: cf. R. Oster, *HTR* 77 (1984 [1986]) 233-37. General apathy of devotees explains much of the ebb-and-flow that characterised ancient religions. The neglect of pious activity on holy days is well attested in both Jewish and other documents of the era.

The social character and cultural significance of these sacred days is instructive in the analysis of Judaising Christianity in Anatolia. An appreciation of two facets of pagan thought is fundamental for understanding this Judaising issue. In the first place, the Sabbath was well known, even proverbial, among non-Jews, as a Jewish day for leisure: see M. Stern, *Greek and Latin Authors on Jews and Judaism*, III (Jerusalem, 1984) 146, s.v. 'Sabbath'. Second, the pagan world also had its own holy days typified by leisure, e.g., the Roman *dies nefasti*.

Against this backdrop, the writings of first-century Hellenistic Jews provide important insight into the possible reasons for Gentile Christian attraction to Judaising theology. While the LXX never employs the term ἐκεχειρία in any context, both Josephus (*Ant*. 1.1.1) and Philo (*de Vita Mosis* II.22, 211) used this term taken from Graeco-Roman religious practice to describe the Sabbath. In fact, Philo's description of God's ordained ἐκεχειρία (ibid., 211) sounds suspiciously like the procedures for the religious ἐκεχειρία in Hellenistic cities. Josephus even claims that Gentile interest in Judaism could be traced back to prior imitation of Sabbath piety that eventuated in holy days for leisure among non-Jews (*Ap*. 2.282; cf. Juv. 14.105-06).

Accordingly, when one considers the social matrix of Gentile Christians in western and central Anatolia who later embraced Judaising Christianity, this inscription is noteworthy evidence that Graeco-Roman culture was already quite accustomed, by legal practice, by civil religion, and by basic piety, to the phenomenon of leisured sacred days. Since nascent Pauline Christianity regarded holy days at best as *adiaphora* (Rom. 14.5-12) and at worst as antithetical to the Gospel (Gal. 4.8-10; Col. 2.16), a Christian living in the shadow of Paul's Gospel would have little hope of finding an equivalent to this regulated component of his previous piety.

The inscription printed above includes a description of the goddess which very aptly reflects her function as the tutelary deity of Ephesos: ἡ προεστῶσα τῆς πόλεως ἡμῶν (A.8; cf. R. MacMullen, *Paganism in the Roman Empire* [New Haven, 1981] 142 n.17). Other phraseology reflects the close bond between Artemis and the city, e.g., ἡ ἑαυτῆς πατρίς (A.9); the city as ἡ τρόφος τῆς ἰδίας θεοῦ τῆς Ἐφ[εσί]|ας (B.22-23). It is also reflected in numismatic iconography (B.V. Head, *Catalogue of the Greek Coins of Ionia* [London, 1892; repr. Bologna, 1964] nos.314, 346, 384; B. Pick, *JÖAI* 7 [1904] 1-41) depicting the female personification of Ephesos holding the cult statue of the goddess in the palm of her outstretched hand. In the present text the goddess reciprocates by making the city ἐνδοξοτέρα through her own divine nature (B.8). Eph. 5.27 depicts a church made ἔνδοξον through the benefaction of Christ, while this inscription depicts the city of Ephesos made ἐνδοξοτέρα through the benefaction and divinity of the Ephesian Artemis, the city's προεστῶσα.

To perceive in Artemis the patron goddess of the city of Ephesos is of course crucial for the interpretation of Acts 19.23-40. But there is more to it than this, for in Acts 19.27 Demetrios states that Artemis is worshipped not only in Asia, but throughout the whole world, an estimate endorsed by Pausanias (4.31.8). This inscription reveals that the urban officials responsible for the welfare of the cult affirmed a multi-racial clientele for their goddess. This was not unique since the idea of a bond between Greeks and non-Greeks is often thought to go back to Alexander, at least; cf. F. Bömer, *Untersuchungen über die Religion der Sklaven in Griechenland und Rom* (*Forschungen zur antiken Sklaverei* 14.1; Wiesbaden, 1981[2]) 175. In addition to this document (B.11), the phrase 'both Greeks and barbarians' (cf. Rom. 1.14) is used in a sermonette of Apollonios of Tyana (*Ep.* 67) regarding the various strata of society welcome in Artemis' temple.

It is not always possible to determine whether there were only individual devotees of Artemis at a particular location or whether a shrine and priesthood also existed there. Pilgrims, for example, came from regions where there was not a shrine and priesthood (cf. non-Israelite pilgrims in Jerusalem in 3 Kgdms 8.41-42). The term πανταχοῦ (B.11-12) bespoke the idea of universal devotion to the goddess. The concept of worldwide devotion was a standard part of religious hyperbole of the era and was employed variously by Jews, Christians, and others. NT examples of this theme would include Acts 28.22; Col. 1.23; 1 Tim. 3.16.

The goddess' spheres of influence included not only dozens of locations in Asia Minor — R. Fleischer, *Artemis von Ephesos und verwandte Kultstatuen aus Anatolien und Syrien* (Leiden, 1973) map II, indicates over fifty Anatolian cities where the *Artemis Ephesia* type was minted on coins — but numerous other regions around the Mediterranean basin. A representative list of sites where devotees of Artemis (and often shrines) were located includes the following.

1. A significant shrine of the Ephesian Artemis was located in Sardis: D.Knibbe, *JÖAI* 46 (1961-63) 175-82; G.M.A. Hanfmann, *Sardis from Prehistoric to Roman Times* (Cambridge [Mass.], 1983) 91.
2. Smyrna possessed a sacred precinct for the Ephesian Artemis: *CIG* II.3155.
3. An inscription from Aphrodisias records the dedication of a female cultic official (κοσμήτειραν, *l.*3) of the Ephesian Artemis who is also high priestess of the city cult: *CIG* II.2823.
4. A Carian site on the Halikarnassos peninsula between Dirmil and Farilya yielded an Imperial-period funerary monument for a devotee of the Ephesian Artemis: *SEG* 16 (1959) 698.
5. Herakleia Lynkestis in Macedonia (southern Yugoslavia, along the ancient *Via Egnatia*) yielded a monument (200 AD) pointing to the presence of a cult of the Ephesian Artemis: L. Robert, *Hellenica* 1 (Limoges, 1940) 71.
6. The Ephesian goddess had devotees on Chios: *CIG* II.2228.
7. A statue of the Ephesian Artemis was situated in the Corinthian agora, where most of the sanctuaries were located (Paus. 2.2.6).
8. Skillous in the western Peloponnese, approx. 4 km. south of Olympia and adjacent to the Ionian Sea, was where Xenophon built a temple with a sanctuary and sacred enclosure in honour of the Ephesian Artemis (Xen., *Anab.* 5.3.9; Paus. 5.6.5; Strabo 8.7.5, §387).
9. Alea in Arkadia possessed a sanctuary of the goddess Artemis of the Ephesians (Paus. 8.23.1).
10. An image of the Ephesian Artemis was erected in one of the rooms of the municipal building in Megalopolis in Arkadia (Paus. 8.30.6).
11. An important cult statue of the Ephesian goddess was located on the Aventine Hill in Rome (Sextus Aurelius Victor, *de viris illustribus* 7; Livy 1.45.2; cf. D.H., *Ant.Rom.* 4.26.4). An inscription to the virgin goddess Artemis of Ephesos was discovered in the Esquiline sector of Rome: *IGRR* 1 (1911, repr. 1964) 35.
12. Massilia possessed an *Ephesion* dedicated exclusively to the Ephesian Artemis (Strabo 4.1.4, §179).
13. Strabo (4.1.8, §184) mentions a temple of the Ephesian Artemis at the mouth of the Rhône River along the Mediterranean coast of France.
14. Emporion and Rhode (both on the NE coast of Spain) maintained cults of the Ephesian goddess (Strabo 3.4.8, §160; cf. 4.1.5, §180; cf. A. García y Bellido, *Les religions orientales dans l'Espagne romaine* [*EPRO* 5; Leiden, 1967] 18-20).
15. Hemeroskopeion, south of the river Sucro on the Spanish littoral, possessed a shrine of the Ephesian Artemis (Strabo 3.4.6, §159).
16. Saguntum (on the E. Spanish littoral) possessed a *templum Dianae* (Pliny, *HN* 16.216), identified as a temple of Ephesian Artemis: A. García y Bellido, *Madrider Mitt.* 4 (1960) 87-98.

17. Berezan (in the modern Ukraine), located on an island in the north Black Sea, preserves a graffito (V BC) to the Ephesian Artemis: *SEG* 32 (1982) 741.
18. Pantikapaion, a port city of the Crimean Bosporus in the north Black Sea, yielded an inscription dedicated to the Ephesian Artemis: N.P. Rozanova, *VDI* 73 (1961) 130-32 (in Russian).
19. Caesarea Maritima has yielded a miniature cult statue (II AD) of the goddess unearthed during excavations: A. Frova, *IEJ* 11 (1961) 196; cf. L.I. Levine, *Caesarea Under Roman Rule* (*Studies in Judaism in Late Antiquity* 7; Leiden, 1975) 43.
20. Merchant pilgrims from Phoenicia worshipped Artemis at her temple in Ephesos according to their native customs: A. Bammer, *AS* 35 (1985) 103-08.

The text of the inscription with which this entry began is explicit that the widespread veneration of the goddess is a direct result of her many palpable manifestations (διὰ | τὰς ὑπ' αὐτῆς γεινομένας ἐναργεῖς ἐπιφανείας, B.13-14). The motif of epiphanies was a commonplace in religions of the Graeco-Roman era and especially in their 'Missionssagen', many of which contain verbal similarities to this inscription; cf. F. Pfister, 'Epiphanie', *RE* Suppl. 4 (1924) 298. *I.Eph.* Ia.27.385 uses the epithet ἐπιφανεστάτη for Artemis. It has been suggested that this superlative epithet was often used of a deity in order to praise the power by which the god rescued or aided an individual or community (F. Steinleitner, *Die Beicht im Zusammenhange mit der sakralen Rechtspflege in der Antike* [Munich, 1913] 19). Bodily or palpable manifestations were rather commonplace in ancient folklore (Plato, *Soph.* 216a-c; Petronius, *Sat.* 17; Acts 14.11). In many faiths they were viewed by some as sufficient grounds for confirming faith (cf. Cic., *de nat. deorum* 2.2.5-6; 1 Cor. 15.1-8; Jn 20.24-29).

Discussion and advocacy of an epiphany often became necessary when a significant privilege or dramatic claim was made. Thus, when seeking ecumenical recognition of their games, sacrifices, contests, and truces, the advocates of Artemis Leukophryene from Magnesia on the Maeander ἀπελογίσαντο διὰ πλειόνων τήν τε τῆς θεᾶς ἐ|πιφάνειαν, 'recounted at length the manifestation of the goddess' (*OGIS* 233.35-36, dated to the reign of Antiochos III, 223-187 BC), since this far-reaching privilege rested upon the veracity of their claim of the goddess' epiphany. The term ἐναργής was also used by nationalistic devotees in a defensive spirit. The Egyptians, for example, contrasted the πράξεις ἐναργεῖς of Isis with the inferior μυθολογία of Greek deities (D.S. 1.25.4; cf. the pejorative use of μῦθοι in 1 Tim. 1.4; 4.7; 2 Tim. 4.4; Tit. 1.14; 2 Pet. 1.16). In frag. B of our Ephesian inscription reference to palpable manifestations is related to a city's or nation's obligation to defend and promote its tutelary deity. 'Εναργής is used here (B.14) in an apologetic context to exalt Artemis by emphasising the reality of her manifestations, thereby sustaining the truth of the city's cause against impiety.

Ancient polytheism had limits to its pluralism, and cults such as that of the Ephesian Artemis which had pretensions to worldwide influence evinced a spirit of ecumenism only so long as the goddess' prestige was not threatened. When the cult was threatened, the city quickly assumed the posture of advocate and defender. This is clearly depicted in *I.Eph.* Ia.2, a Hellenistic inscription (350-300 BC) which records the sentencing to death of dozens of men for their impious disruption of one of the goddess' festivals.

It would be imprudent to limit the goddess' revelations to physical appearances alone. Closely akin to the concept of ἐπιφάνεια was the epithet ἐπήκοος, found, e.g., at *I.Eph.* II.504 (114/15). This adjective characterises Artemis' accessibility through the prayers of her devotees. For examples beyond Ephesos see O. Weinreich, *AusgewWhlte Schriften* (repr. Amsterdam, 1969) I.138-39. Inscriptional documents attest that the goddess was wont to respond positively to the prayers and thanksgiving of her suppliants for safety, healing, and the like. For thanksgivings to Artemis employing εὐχαριστέω note *I.Eph.* III.940, 943, 957, 958, 960; V.1578b, 1587, 1588 (mainly II-III); see further below at **28**. Dedications in which εὔχομαι occurs are found at *I.Eph.* Ia.27.526, 529 (104 AD), and V.1448 (302 BC). For Artemis' healing power see E. Varınlıoğlu, *ZPE* 44 (1981) 62-66 no.2 (Keramos in Caria, *c.*III init.; pl.6). Numismatic, artefactual, and epigraphical sources reveal that the goddess likewise manifested herself to her worshippers through the medium of oracles (θεσμῳδοί): see, e.g., *I.Eph.* Ia.27.457; II.533; III.645.7; cf. D.G. Hogarth, *Excavations at Ephesos* (London, 1908) 190-92, for possible divination with *astragali*. Iconography on the cult statue of the goddess shows that devotees made weary by their struggles with the cosmic forces of astrological Fate also received succour from Artemis (Fleischer, 70-72, 410; R. Oster, *JbAC* 19 [1976] 41). The epiphany door on the *tympanon* of the temple, where a statue or priestess of the goddess stood, is an architectural expression of this belief concerning the goddess. This door can be seen on various coins minted at Ephesos: see P. Hommel, *Ist. Mitt.* 7 (1957) 29-55.

A narrative from Strabo regarding the place of epiphanies in the dissemination of the Artemis cult is instructive. The goddess personally appeared in a dream (παραστῆναι κατ' ὄναρ τὴν θεόν, 4.1.4; cf. Acts 23.11; 27.23) to a prominent Ephesian woman and at the same time by oracle to a ship of Phokaians sailing nearby. The purpose of this co-ordinated revelation is patently for the dissemination of the goddess' cult and influence. There are points of similarity between this narrative concerning Artemis and the co-ordinated revelation in the missionary narrative of Peter and Cornelius (Acts 10.1-33). In Strabo's account, the religion of the Ephesian Artemis reaches not only to the northern Ionian city of Phokaia, but also to her colony at Massilia, and in turn to the latter's colonies at the Iberian sites of Hemeroskopeion, Emporion, and Rhode (see nos. 12, 14, 15 in the list above). The synergism of divine revelation and human response was also operative in Xenophon's attribution to divine revelation of his selection of a temple site for Artemis in Greece (*Anab.* 5.3.7). On divine appeareances to authorise the establishment of a cult see *New Docs 1976*, **10**.

Divine commissioning terminology such as ἀποστέλλω is employed for various clerical representatives of the Ephesian Artemis. The 'Mother-Church' of Artemis at Ephesos sent θεωροί (*I.Eph.* Ia.2.3-4; [350-300 BC]; cf. P. Boesch, *ΘΕΩΡΟΣ. Untersuchungen zur Epangelie griechischer Feste* [Berlin, 1908]) to conduct sacred services at Sardis (Hanfmann, 91), and also stationed a group of νεωποιοί at the nearby suburb of Phygela to oversee sacrifices to the goddess: *I.Eph.* IV.1408.5-6 (300-250 BC), καὶ τῶν νεωποιῶν τῶν ἀπο|στελλομένων ὑπὸ τῆς πόλεως ἐπὶ τὰς θυσίας ἐμ Φυγέλοις, 'the *neopoioi* who were sent by the city for the sacrifices at Phygela'; on this text cf. L. Robert, *RPh* 41 (1967) 36-40. For *neopoioi* see **28** below. These two examples clearly show instances where, as in the NT, ἀποστέλλω need not imply far-flung itinerancy, but only appointment.

Though the epiphanies of Artemis provided a crucial component for the city's *apologia* for the goddess, the greatest proof (καὶ τοῦτο δὲ μέγιστον . . . | . . . τεκμήριον, B.15-16) of the honour due her was the widespread recognition of her majesty reflected in the adoption of her name into the calendars of the Greek speaking world. (The influence of the Ephesian calendar is discussed in A.E. Samuel, *Greek and Roman Chronology. Calendars and Years in Classical Antiquity* [*Handbuch der Altertumswissenschaft* I, 7; Munich, 1972].) This strategy of finding world-wide Hellenistic acknowledgement of one's own religion had analogies in the apologetic techniques of hellenised Judaism and of hellenised Christian authors.

Fragment B concludes by emphasising the reciprocity between the welfare of Ephesos and the honour shown to its tutelary deity (cf. U. Brackertz, *Zum Problem der Schutzgottheiten griechischer StWdte* [Diss. Berlin, 1976]), a concept of reciprocity well known in Jewish Zion-covenant theology and likewise seen in NT texts treating the fall of Jerusalem in 70.

Philology

Finally, a small number of comments on the language of this inscription is appended.

1. ἀποβλέπω εἴς τι (A.10-11): this is the sole epigraphical example noted by MM (whence BAGD), s.v. ἀποβλέπω, to illustrate the NT's use of this idiom at Heb. 11.26.
2. Ἕλλην/βάρβαρος (B.11): This ocurrence of the common contrast is much closer to Paul's use chronologically, geographically, and conceptually than examples given in MM. For the use and meaning of this distinction see I. Opelt/W. Speyer, *JbAC* 10 (1967) 251-90; and more recently M. Hengel, *Jews, Greeks and Barbarians* (Philadelphia, 1980) 55-66.
3. ἐπιτελέω (B.21): The use of ἐπιτελέω for the performance of sacred rites in Heb. 9.6 is illustrated in our text by ἱερομηνίαι ἐπιτελοῦνται. Strabo recounts (14.1.20) that during the nativity celebrations of Artemis at Ephesos, the priesthood of the Kouretes συνάγει συμπόσια καί τινας μυστικὰς θυσίας ἐπιτελεῖ. The verb appears in a similar context also at *I.Eph.* II.213.4, repr. below at **22**.
4. εὐσέβεια (A.11): Since this term is characteristic of 1 Tim. (2.2; 3.16; 4.7-8; 6.3, 5, 6, 11), whose destination was Ephesos (1 Tim. 1.3), its place in this inscription reflecting piety towards Artemis is noteworthy. The words τῆς θεοῦ should be taken as an objective genitive.
5. ἡμέρα (A.7): The use of the noun here in reference to sacred times is parallel to its use in Lk. 4.16; 22.7; Jn 19.31; Acts 13.14; 21.26; Rom. 14.5; Gal. 4.10; and Rev. 1.10.
6. κράτιστος (A.6): Employed similarly in Acts 23.26; 24.3 and 26.25. This use in *I.Eph.* I.24 provides a useful instance for an MM entry.
7. προΐστημι (A.16-17): The participial form in our inscription manifests the semantic complexity of this verb as it has been discussed by NT scholars. According to BAGD, s.v., προΐσταμαι can mean both 'be at the head (of), rule, direct', and 'be concerned about, care for, give aid', in both non-Biblical and Biblical texts. This variety of meaning has contributed to the 'lively debate' (B. Reicke, *TDNT* 6 [1968] 702) regarding Paul's use of this word in passages such as Rom. 12.8 and 1 Thes. 5.12. The debate in interpretation has arisen in large measure from the ostensible tension that exists between the concepts of care and concern on the one hand and offical rule and authority on the other hand. This inscription, neglected by MM in this regard, reflects the ease with which Graeco-Roman urban dwellers accepted the compatibility of the two notions of benevolent actions and structured authority. In fact, much of the political theory of Jewish, Greek and Roman cultures was based upon the concept of benevolent *imperium*. In our inscription both A.16-19 and C.4 clearly point to Priscus' directive and ruling function. While authority and leadership in urban celebrations secured one's reputation and prominence, this authority required one's care and patronage of the city, usually expressed financially. Certain Romans (e.g., Cicero, *de off.* 2.15-18) decried the ostentation, self-aggrandisement, and prodigality that characterised the urban liturgies (cf. A.H.M. Jones, *OCD*², s.v. 'Liturgy'), like those financed by Priscus. These liturgies continued, nevertheless, as an unavoidable part of urban life. *I.Eph.* V.1491 contains a reprimand from Antoninus Pius in 145 to the archons, *boule* and *demos* of the Ephesians that they had not acknowledged adequately the generosity of Vedius Antonius when he provided numerous buildings for the city. The emperor then contrasts (*ll.*12-18) the enduring worth of Vedius' benefactions with the ephemeral contribution of those who endow the city with only 'bread and circuses'.
8. τὸ θεῖον ὄνομα (B.24-25): Although this phrase is not used in the NT, wording such as ἅγιον τὸ ὄνομα (Lk. 1.49), τὸ καλὸν ὄνομα (Jas. 2.7), δοξάζειν τὸ ὄνομα (Rev. 15.4), μεγαλύνειν τὸ ὄνομα (Acts 19.17), and τὸ ὄνομα τὸ ὑπὲρ πᾶν ὄνομα (Phil. 2.9) all bespeak the same general concept of the Sacred Name. See further below at **117**.
9. φανερὸν ποιῆσαι (A.13-14): This idiom is used at Mt. 12.16 and Mk. 3.12 with the same meaning as here, namely, 'to make known'. This inscription is closer chronologically to the Gospel texts than the examples listed in MM.
10. φυλάσσω (A.16): A new MM entry for this verb could well include this occurrence to illustrate the meaning found in the NT, 'observe/keep (sacred law)', e.g., Mt. 19.20; Lk. 11.28; Jn 12.47; Acts 7.53; 21.24; Rom. 2.26. It is also a commonplace in the LXX.

(R. OSTER)

20. An imperial appeal for reconciliation

Athens 174/75

ed.pr. — J.H. Oliver, *Marcus Aurelius. Aspects of Civic and Cultural Policy in the East* (*Hesperia Suppl.*13; Princeton, 1970), especially 1-84 (pls.1-6)

Λάδικος Πολυαίνου ὁ ἐκκεκλημένος πρὸς Σωφάνην Σω[φά-]ν̣ους ἀπὸ Ἰουλ. Δαμοστράτου τοῦ ἄρχοντος τῶν Πανελλήνων φαίνεται κατὰ τὸν ὡρισμένον χρόνο[ν ἤδη] ἐ̣ν̣τ̣ὸς οὗ ἔξεστιν δικάζεσθαι πρὸς τοὺς κεχειροτονημένους Πανέλληνας κληθεὶς ἐπὶ τὴν κρίσιν, ἀπ[ελεγ-]χθεὶς δέ, καίτοι μετὰ τὴν νενομισμένην προθεσμίαν τῆς χειροτονίας γεγενημένης, οὔπ̣ω τὴν ἔννο[μον] ἡλικίαν γεγονὼς οὐδὲ τότε καὶ οὐδεμίαν ἀρχὴν πρότερον ἄρξας ὡς ὁ θεὸς πάππος μου ὥρισεν, ἀδίκως [ἐφει-]κέναι̣ [δ]οκεῖ.

. . .

Ἡγοῦμαι δεδηλῶσθαι, δι᾽ ὧν ἀπεφηνάμην, ὅτι ἕκαστα π[ρ]οϊδόμην ο[ὐ διὰ] πε̣[ρ]ιουσίας μᾶλλον ἢ φροντίδος, ἵνα πρὸς τὸ μέλλον Ἡρώιδηι τε ὑπάρχοι παρὰ Ἀθηναίοις συνευφρ[οσύ-]νηι περί τε τὰ θεῖα καὶ τὰ ἀνθρώπινα ἔχειν σὺν τῆι εὐκλεεῖ περὶ παιδείαν σπουδῆι, καὶ Ἀθηναῖοι τῆς πρόσ[θεν] γνωστῆς εἰς αὐτοὺς εὐποιίας τοῦ κρ. Ἡρώιδου μεμνημένοι τὸ θάρσος τῆς πρότερον περὶ ἀλ̣λ̣ή̣λους [οἰκει-]ότητος ἀναν̣εώσαιντο, δι᾽ ἣν οὐδὲ ἐμοῦ διαλλακτοῦ δέονται. Τί γὰρ ἂν ἔτι ὑποκαθέζοιτο ἐ̣ν̣ γνώμ[ηι τι-]νός, μετὰ τὸ ἀ̣παλειφθῆναι τὴν ἐπὶ [τ]αῖς αἰτίαις μνήμην, τῆς θεραπείας ἐπὶ πᾶσιν ἐκπεπον̣ημένης [ἵνα] Ἀθην[α]ίοις ἐ̣ξ̣ῆ̣ι̣ τὸν ἐμὸν καὶ τὸν ἴδ[ι]ον αὐτῶν Ἡιρώιδην στέργειν, οὐδενὸς ἔτι ἑτέρου τῆι εὐνοίαι με[γάλου] ἀντικρούοντος;

A long inscription on two plaques: I, incomplete but consisting of five (A-D, F) surviving fragments; II (= frag. E), reused as a paving slab and restored from its *c.*200 small pieces. Both were found in the Roman Market Place in Athens. Dimensions of II are .88B x 2.31H m. The extracts above are from II.

Bib. — The bibliography on this inscription is large, including several subsequent articles by Oliver. Of particular note are: C.P. Jones, *ZPE* 8 (1971) 161-83; W. Williams, *ZPE* 17 (1975) 37-56; *S. Follet, *RPh* 53 (1979) 29-43 (plaque II); Oliver, *AJP* 100 (1979) 543-58 (especially 543-48); *SEG* 127 (both plaques), with other bibliography; *BE* (1980) 208.

|. . . Ladikos son of Polyainos who has appealed (against the verdict on his lawsuit) against Sophanes, son of Sophanes, from (the court of) Julius Damostratos the archon of the Panhellenes, has manifestly been summoned for judgement at the time now laid down within which it is permissible for court cases to be made against the elected Panhellenes.

He was rejected, although the customary period of time for the vote had come and gone, since he was not yet of legal age even at that time, nor had he held any previous magistracy, as my deified grandfather had ruled (was required). | He appears to have made an unjustified appeal.

. . .

87 **I think it has been demonstrated by the declarations I have made that I have devoted my attention to each of the matters not so much out of superfluity as of caution, in order that in future it might be possible for Herodes, with his renowned enthusiasm for culture, to join with the Athenians in their enjoyment of religious and secular matters. And (I acted in this way) in order that the Athenians, | keeping in mind the previous well-known beneficence of the most esteemed Herodes towards them, might restore the confidence of their previous friendship with one another, a friendship because of which they do not need me as a mediator. For what could still be lying in the mind of anyone after the memory of these accusations has been effaced, now that his service in all things has been laboured over, in order that it may be possible for the Athenians to cherish my own — and their own — Herodes, given that no other significant impediment to goodwill still remains?**

The extracts above come from the second plaque (= frag. E) which forms the latter half of a very long inscription of Marcus Aurelius for the Athenians. The other fragments, parts of the first plaque, are too broken to yield any connected sense. Relatively little of the 102 lines of plaque II is missing and nearly all of that can be restored with confidence. This is one of the most important inscriptions to come to light in recent years from Imperial-period Athens. It provides considerable information about the relations between the emperor and a free city of major status, and about certain questions of Athenian constitutional law. What makes it particularly interesting, however, is its link with what Philostratos (*Vitae Soph.* II.1.559-61) tells us of the quarrel between the sophist and benefactor Herodes Attikos (*c.*101-77) and his fellow-Athenians, and the attempt of Marcus Aurelius to reconcile them.

The first 57 lines of plaque II consist of the emperor's summary verdicts on a variety of legal appeals which were addressed to him for adjudication by Herodes' enemies. These eight cases, of which *ll.*15-20 printed above is the second, involve complex legal questions, such as the right to membership of the Areiopagos. Some are appeals by defendants, others by plaintiffs; and in some instances the emperor adjudicates appeals concerning lawsuits the outcome of which has not yet been decided. There follows an extended section (*ll.*57-87) in which Marcus lays down new criteria for membership of both the Areiopagos and the *boule* at Athens. The inscription concludes (87-94) with an appeal by the emperor that the Athenians and Herodes should forget their differences: Herodes, whose friendship with Marcus was very close (he had been responsible for teaching Marcus), ought to be valued by his fellow-citizens for his real worth, namely, his 'renowned enthusiasm for *paideia*' (89). Appended to the end of the text is an imperial after-thought (94-102) on the new rules for *boule* membership.

There has been considerable debate since the text was published, whether this document is an edict or an imperial letter. It is composed in the first person singular, and so is clearly from the emperor himself, dictated to an amanuensis; but the lack of the standard closing salutation εὐτυχεῖτε argues against its being a letter. In the *ed.pr.* Oliver argues that it is a 'general epistle', an 'epistle in edict form' (35-37). His case was based partly on the reading μετὰ τὴν ἐπ[ιστο]|λ̣ὴ̣ν ἐ<μ>ὴν ἑτέραν at *l.*67, which he took to refer to an epistle of the year 165 from Marcus to the Areiopagos. A fragment of this text survives: see most recently the discussion of Oliver, *AJP* 101 (1980) 304-13 (cf. *SEG* 30 [1980] 87). But Williams has shown that the correct reading should be μετὰ τὴν ἐπ[ιστο]|λὴν τὴν ἡμετέραν, which thus disposes of the implication that the present document is also an epistle. Williams himself holds that on formal grounds it must be thought of as an edict (37, 40-51). The fact that it was dictated by the emperor personally, not composed on his behalf, is indicated by the presence of the postscript (94-102), which should otherwise be expected to have been worked into the relevant place earlier in the text.

Furthermore, it appears from *ll.*94-95 that the document was actually composed in Greek, and is not a translation from a Latin original for the Athenian recipients (so Williams, 52-56): 'Indeed, I have had a further thought in addition to all these cases which have been set out together in the Greek language concerning questions for adjudication', ὅ γε μὴν ἐπὶ πᾶσι τούτοις κατὰ τὴν Ἑλλήνων φωνὴν περὶ τῶν δικασθέντων συντετ[αγμέ]|νοις προσενεθυμήθην, κτλ. There is only one Latin loan-word in the text, [τῶν] | καλουμένων κωδικίλλων (35-36). The scenario which we are to envisage from Philostratos' account is that Marcus, after adjudicating this series of appeals at Sirmium (all of which concerned Herodes at least indirectly because his friends and enemies were involved) issued this imperial statement which was to be placed on public and permanent display at Athens.

The extract above, concerning Ladikos son of Polyainos, provides the emperor's judgement of an appeal made by a man whose attempt to gain a seat in the Panhellenion had been rejected in an Athenian court. On this and the details of the other cases under review see Oliver's *ed.pr.*, 37-42. The verb ἐκκαλοῦμαι occurs here as a term for an appeal to the emperor in *l.*15, and also in *l.*20 where the next case is adjudicated. Oliver, *AJP* 100 (1979) 556-57, argues that this verb with a personal direct object (omitted in the present case, since the object, Marcus, is obvious) is synonymous with ἐπικαλοῦμαι, such as is found in Acts 25.11, 12, 25; 26.39; 28.19: Καίσαρα ἐ. says Paul in the first of these passages. It is true that these two compounds are translation equivalents of the technical Latin term *appellare* in the second century; but Oliver is misleading to equate them with the usage in Acts. For in the latter ἐπικαλοῦμαι = *provoco*, the *appellatio* procedure not being clearly attested before the time of Marcus Aurelius. On this subject see A.N. Sherwin-White, *Roman Society and Roman Law in the NT* (Oxford, 1963) 68-69, 115. Spicq, *NLNT* III.288 with n.4, appears to blur the chronological distinction between *provocatio* and *appellatio*. Oliver (ibid.) provides some further documentary references to the use of these verbs and their related nouns. His 1979 article deals with Greeks applying to be tried by Roman courts. By no means always could Roman citizens request such a trial (for the limitations see ibid., 555); and, indeed, Greeks with political influence could obtain such a hearing even where they lacked Roman citizenship (ibid.). The evidence of *I.Eph.* Ia.15 + 16, two copies of an imperial letter probably from the time of Antoninus Pius discussed by Oliver (ibid., 556), indicates that a Roman citizen could not request trial by the emperor 'when the emperor had appointed a special agent, either a *legatus pro praetore* or a *curator civitatis* to reorder the affairs of a city'.

The main surviving fragment of this inscription (frag. E) abounds in words which provide parallels to the NT vocabulary. It also contains several words attested here for the first time: ἀντεισπράττω (82), εἰσφυγαδεύω (46), ἐννόμως (5), ἱεροκηρυκεία (11), συνευφροσύνη (88-89; with this word cf. συνευφραίνομαι, found in ECL; see also **58**). The first verb in this group preserves Atticistic -ττ-; and there are other indications of Atticism elsewhere, mostly further instances of this feature, but also the form τήμερον (77). Atticistic influence in a formal, legal document like this does not occasion surprise, especially in one from the second century. Another indication of higher style in the text is the proliferation of optatives, over a dozen of them in frag. E.

Among words in Follet's revised text which also occur in the NT the following may be noted:

ἀδίκως (19) — only at 1 Pet. 2.19; but cf. the legal context of the phrase τῷ κρίνοντι ἀδίκως, used of Pilate in the variant reading at 1 Pet. 2.23;

αἰτία (92) — as a legal technical term, 'charge', cf. Mk. 15.26 (= Mt. 27.37); Jn 18.38; 19.4, 6; Acts 13.28; 23.28; 28.28;

ἀναγινώσκω (37) — 'read aloud', i.e., in public; see references in BAGD, s.v., 2;

ἀναγκάζω (27) — passive; cf. Acts 28.19, of being compelled to appeal to Caesar;

ἀνθρώπινος (89) — explicitly in contrast to θεῖος here, implicitly at Acts 17.25; 1 Cor. 2.13; 4.3; 1 Pet. 2.13; cf. BAGD, s.v., 3;

ἀξιόω + infin. (21) — Acts 13.43 (*v.l.*);

ἀπέχω — in *l.*11 the sense is 'refrain (from seeking office)', cf. BAGD, s.v., 3; in *l.*47 it means 'keep away' physically, for which BAGD, s.v., 2, provides parallels;

ἀποδείκνυμι — 'be appointed' (6-7; cf. BAGD, s.v., 1); 'prove' (99), for which cf. Acts 25.7;

ἀπωθέω (29) — the common figurative sense, 'reject, repudiate'; cf. BAGD, s.v., 2;

ἀριθμός (13) — Lk. 22.3;

ἀφοράω (64) — for the meaning 'consider' cf. Phil. 2.23;

βραδύτης (43) — once only in the NT, 2 Pet. 3.9;

γε μήν (42, 71, 94) — cf. (εἰ) μήν, once only in the NT, in an LXX quotation at Heb. 6.14;

γνώμη — used both as a legal term, 'verdict, judicial opinion' (14, 61, 95) and more generally, 'mind' (14);

γνῶσις — at *l.*25 the sense is 'result (of an investigation)', at *ll.*56, 73 'decision'; no parallel for NT 'knowledge';

τὰ γράμματα (69) — plural of a letter, as at Acts 28.21;

δέησις (44) — 'petition', here addressed to the emperor. In the NT God is always the addressee; so the instance here offers a useful analogy.

διάγνωσις (53) — *cognitio*, the judicial decision of an emperor, as at Acts 25.21;

διάστημα (40) — 'interval' (of time), as at Acts 5.7; BAGD provide no epigraphical attestations;

δικάζω (17, 30, 43, 81, 85, 94) — 'judge, condemn'; NT, only in the 𝔓[75] text of Lk. 6.37;

ἐγγράφω (78-79), 'enrol', as at Lk. 10.20;

ἔγκλημα (frag. C, *l.*15) — legal technical term, as at Acts 23.29; 25.16. The noun occurs also in an agreement between Sardes and Ephesos, *I.Eph.* Ia.7 (98/7 or 94/3 BC; pls. 8, 9) at part II.22, as does also the related verb ἐκκαλοῦμαι in the same line. MM's entry for this noun includes no epigraphical examples.

τὸν ἑξῆς χρόνον (44) — cf. Lk. 7.11, ἐν τῷ ἑξῆς (*sc.* χρόνῳ);

ἐξωθέω (65, 69) — 'expel, drive out', Acts 7.45;

ἐπανάγω (59) — transitive here, only intrans. in NT;

ἐπιχειρέω + infin. (41) — Acts 9.29; 19.13;

εὐποιΐα (90) — 'beneficence, the doing of good deeds', as in the NT at Heb. 13.16. The possibility that the meaning here is 'good deeds' (ECL only) should not be ruled out.

ζήτησις (36) — '(judicial) investigation', as at Acts 25.20;

θάρσος (90) — 'confidence'; perhaps this is an appropriate meaning for the word at Acts 28.15 (or 'courage');

ἱερωσύνη (5, 13-14) — Heb. 11.7, 12, 24;

κανών (65) — 'rule, standard', Gal. 6.16;

καταλέγω (73, 80) — 'select, enrol', 1 Tim. 5.9;

κοινωνία (21, 29) — κ. of the Panhellenion, cf. examples at BAGD, s.v.,1;

λογισμός (83) — 'accounts' (pl.); this sense of the noun not found in the NT;

παρίημι (95) — 'neglect, leave undone', Lk. 11.42;

προγράφω (75) — παρὰ τὰ προγεγραμμένα, 'against public regulations'; cf. Gal. 3.1;

προθεσμία (18, 39) — 'period of time', NT *hapax* at Gal. 4.2;

προσδέομαι + gen. (96) — 'need in addition'; at Acts 17.25 the force of the prefix is not felt, according to BAGD, s.v. But this may be doubted, as K.L. McKay points out to me (*per litt.*). While English idiom may not need to translate the προσ-, the nuance is present: 'God needs nothing (beyond what he has) from anyone . . .'

προϋπάρχω (7) — here without a following participle, 'the pre-existing contribution', unlike the NT occurrences (Lk. 23.12; Acts 8.9);

σεμνότης (58) — 'dignity', here used of a city; in the NT of people only: 1 Tim. 2.2; 3.4; Tit. 2.7;
συντάσσω (94-95) — 'prescribe, order, direct'; NT, only at Mt. 21.6;
τάξις — at *l*.56 the sense 'proper order, arrangement' provides a good parallel for 1 Cor. 14.40; cf. Col. 2.5. Later in the inscription (72, 76), the meaning is 'post, position', a use attested in ECL (see BAGD, s.v.,3).

A number of other words are found in ECL only, including διορίζω (97), ἐξήγησις (96), ἐπανήκω (43), and στρατιωτικός (26).

On Marcus Aurelius' attitude to the Christians see P.A. Brunt in C. Deroux (ed.), *Studies in Latin Literature and Roman History*, I (*Coll. Latomus* 164; Brussels, 1979) 483-520. In the second century, according to Brunt, the persecution of Christianity as a crime (atheism) resulted from complaints and pressure exerted by individual Jews and others rather than being organised at an official level.

Guarducci, *EG* IV.230-32 reprints with discussion *IG* II/III^2 13200 (near Athens 160; also repr. as Helbing, *AGI* 30), an inscription from a sepulchral monument honouring the wife of Herodes, Appia Annia Regilla, called τὸ | φῶς τῆς οἰκίας (*ll*.1-2; for more on this phrase see **6** above). Most of the text is devoted to a cursing/blessing formula directed at those who seeked to destroy/preserve safe any of the statues which form part of the tomb. For a member of Herodes' circle who uses a similar formula which is claimed to reflect knowlege of LXX Deut. 28.22, 28, cf. *New Docs 1978*, **96**; to the bibliography given there add *BE* 352.

21. Census returns and household structures

Oxyrhynchos Feb./March 34
ed.pr. — J. Frösén, *P.Oxy.Hels.* 10 (pl.7)

αλς´
Σαμβᾶι στρατηγῶ̣ι
παρὰ Παυσᾶτος τοῦ Ἡφαιστᾶτ[[ιων]]ος
εἴσ̣ιν οἱ καταγεινόμενοι ἐν τῇ ὑπα̣ρχ(ούσῃ) μ̣[οι]
πατρικῆι οἰκίᾳ̣ ἐν κώμῃ Σιν̣[αρ]ὺ̣ τῆς̣ κά[τω]
τοπαρχίας [Π]α̣υσᾶς [Ἡ]φ̣αισ̣τ̣ᾶ̣[τος]
μητ(ρὸς) Ἡ̣ρ̣α̣[κλ]είας ὡ̣ς (ἐτῶν) [̣ ̣ οὐ]λ̣ὴ̣ γέν[υι ἀρι-]
σ̣τ̣ερᾷ̣, Ἡ̣φ[α]ι̣σ̣τ̣ᾶς `ὑ̣ι̣´ὸ̣[ς] μητ(ρός) Σ̣ο̣ῃ̣[ροῦτος (?) (ἐτῶν) ̣ ̣,]
Ἑρμογένης ἀδ[ε]λφὸ(ς) μ̣[η]τ(ρὸς) τ̣ῆ̣[ς] α(ὐτῆς) [(ἐτῶν) ̣ ̣,]
Ἀμόις ἕ̣τ̣ε̣ρο(ς) μητ(ρὸς) τῆ[ς] α̣(ὐτῆς) (ἐτῶν) ̣, Αρ ̣[̣] ̣[
ἀδελφὸ(ς) μητ(ρὸς) τῆς α(ὐτῆς) (ἐτῶν) ̣, Ἑ̣ρ̣[μο]γ̣έν̣[ης](?)
ἐπικα(λούμενος) Ἄωρος(?) α (ἔτους), [̣] (*vacat*)
γυναικῶν Σοηρ̣[οῦς(?) Ἑρ]μ̣ογένου̣ς̣
μητ(ρὸς) Πλουτάρχ(ης) (ἐτῶν) ̣ ̣[̣] ̣[̣ ̣ ̣ ̣ ̣ ̣]με̣ ̣ ̣ ρ̣π[̣ ̣ ̣ ̣ ̣]
Παυσᾶς Ἡφαισ̣τ̣ᾶ̣[τος ὁ προγεγρα(μμένος) ὁ]μ̣[νύω]

Τιβέριον Καίσαρα Σεβασ[τὸν Αὐτοκράτορα]
θεοῦ Σεβαστοῦ υἱὸν εἶ μὴν ἐξ ὑγ[ιοῦς]
καὶ ἐπ' ἀληθείας ἐπιδ[ε]δ(ωκέναι) τ[ὴν γρ]αφ[ὴν]
τῶν παρ' ἐμοὶ οἰκούντω[ν] καὶ μή[τε]
[ἐ]πίξενον μήτε Ῥωμαῖον μ[ήτε Α]ἰγύπ[(τιον)]
[μ]ήτε Ἀλεξανδ(ρέα) μήδ(ε) <ἄλλον> μηδ(ένα) οἰκε[ῖ]ν {π[αρ']}
[παρ'] ἐμοὶ παρὲ{κ}ξ τῶν προγεγρα[μ(μένων)·]
[εὐο]ρκοῦντι μέν μοι εὖ εἴη, ἐπ[ιο]ρκ[οῦν-]
[τι] δὲ τὰ ἐναντία. (ἔτους) κ Τιβερί[ο]υ [Καίσαρος]
(*vacat*) Σεβαστοῦ Φαμενὼθ ‾ (*vacat*)
(*m.2*) [Παυ]σᾶς Ἡφαιστᾶτος ἐπιδέδωκα [τ]ὴν [γραφ]ὴ[ν]
[καὶ ὀμώμοκα] τὸν ὅρκον. Δι[. .] [*c*.12 *letters*]
[*c*.16 *letters*] ἔγραψ[α ὑπὲρ αὐτοῦ διὰ τὸ]
[μὴ εἰδέναι γράμματα (*vacat* ?)]
. . . .
(*back*) (*m. 3*)] κάτω{ι} τοπαρχ(ίας) Σιναρύ

A fragmentary portion (10B x 24H cm.) of a roll from official archives — hence the volume and page number at the beginning of the document — containing the original of a census declaration (thus, the declarant's signature in *l*.26).

(Volume) 1 (page) 36. To Sambas, *strategos*, from Pausas son of Hephaistas. Those who are living in the | paternal house belonging to me in the village of Sinary in the lower toparchy are: Pausas son of Hephaistas whose mother is Herakleia, aged about . . . with a scar on his left cheek; Hephaistos, my son, whose mother is Soerous(?), [aged . . .]; Hermogenes, his brother, whose mother is the same woman, [aged . . .]; | Amois, another (brother), whose mother is the same woman, aged . . .; Ar. . ., a brother whose mother is the same woman, aged . . .; Hermogenes(?) called Aoros(?), aged 1 year. Of the womenfolk (there are): Soerous(?), daughter of Hermogenes, whose mother is Ploutarche, aged . . .; . . . | I, the aforementioned Pausas, son of Hephaistas, swear by Tiberius Caesar Augustus Imperator, son of the deified Augustus, that I have indeed honestly and truthfully made the declaration of those dwelling with me, and that no | non-family member is living with me, whether Roman, Egyptian, Alexandrian or anyone else except those listed above. May it be well with me if I have sworn aright, but the opposite if I have sworn falsely. Year 20 of Tiberius Caesar | Augustus, Phamenoth . . . (*m.2*) I Pausas, son of Hephaistas, have made the declaration and have sworn the oath. I Di. . . wrote for him because he is illiterate. | (*back, m.3*) Sinary in the lower toparchy.

Every fourteen years the Roman governor of Egypt ordered the district officials to carry out the household census of the whole population to serve as a basis of taxation. Under threat of penalty for incomplete reporting, heads of households (or in some cases landlords) listed each member of the household. In addition, those owning property would also have to declare it. This was either done in the household census or in a separate property return. G. Nachtergael, *P.Brux.* (1974) 1, pp.51-58 gives a full listing of census returns of both property and persons

— the two are often consolidated into a single document — together with a bibliography on the subject. A recent general discussion is that of O. Montevecchi, *Aevum* 50 (1976) 72-84; see also M. Hombert/C. Préaux, *Recherches sur le recensement dans l'Egypte romaine* (*P.L.Bat.* 5; Leiden, 1952). For a popular discussion of the problem concerning the difference between the Egyptian census procedure and that outlined in Lk. 2.4-5 see D.J. Hayles, *Buried History* 9 (1973) 121-26.

From publications of the year 1979 we may note the following other census documents. *P.XV Congr.* 13, 14 (both from Philadelphia, dated after 37, and 41-48/9, respectively) preserve a fragmentary list of house owners, and a list of names indicating parentage and age. *P.Laur.* 66 (pl.56) is from the same town and preserves a property return prepared for the year 188/9. *P.Col.* 124, 125 (Karanis, IV init.) are extracts from census declarations for taxation purposes concerning the various holdings of a certain Atisios.

The census returns from Roman Egypt provide unique evidence as to the types of household structures that existed in at least one part of the Empire. Approximately 270 of these household census returns have been preserved, covering the period between 5/6-257/8. Of this number only 131 are sufficiently intact to be able to be used in a study of the structure of households in Roman Egypt. The census documents provide evidence of several different types of household. The ideographs below do not necessarily represent actual households but are idealised structures of the different types of households found in the census returns. The households can be divided into two main categories, simple (53.4%) and complex (46.6%). The former term may be defined as households where the only relatives involved are either offspring or unmarried siblings. Complex households are so called because they consist of (a) more than one nuclear family; or (b) relatives in addition to the nuclear family. Included under this category are those 'simple' households which contain residents who, because there is insufficient information in the returns, cannot certainly be identified as relatives. The largest complex household attested in these returns consisted of 27 people (*BGU* 1 [1895] 115 [117/8 AD]). In the table below △ = male, ○ = female.

A. Simple (70 usable cases — 53.4%)

1. Single person (15 cases, 21.4%)

△

2. Single persons living together (2 cases, 2.9%)

△ △

3. Husband + wife, no offspring (1 case, 1.4%)

△——○

B. Complex (61 usable cases — 46.6%)

1. Parent/s + married offspring (19 cases, 31.1%)

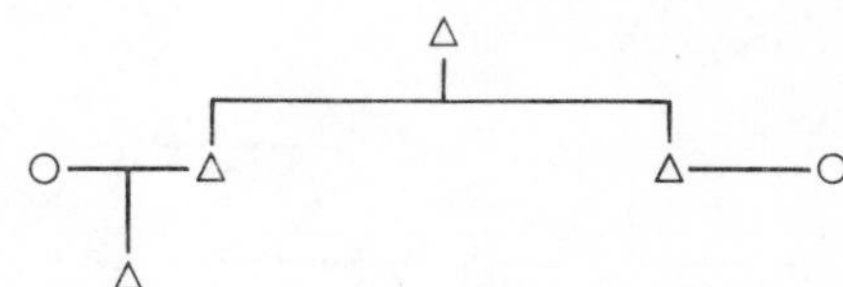

2. Siblings married or unmarried, with or without children (12 cases, 19.7%)

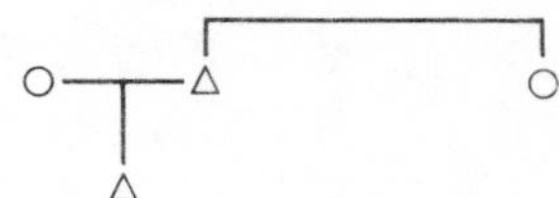

3. Husband + wife + relatives/residents (1 case, 1.6%)

△——○ △

4. Husband + wife + offspring (23 cases, 32.9%)

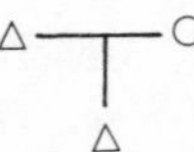

5. Single parent + offspring (24 cases, 34.3%)

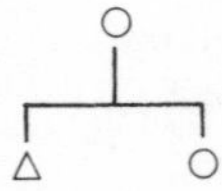

6. Siblings (5 cases, 7.1%)

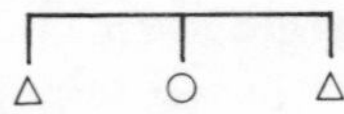

4. Nuclear family (including single parents) + relatives/residents (12 cases, 19.7%)

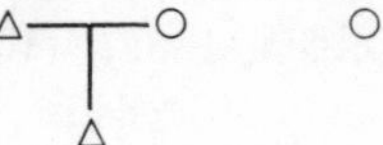

5. Parent/s + married offspring + relatives/residents (10 cases, 16.4%)

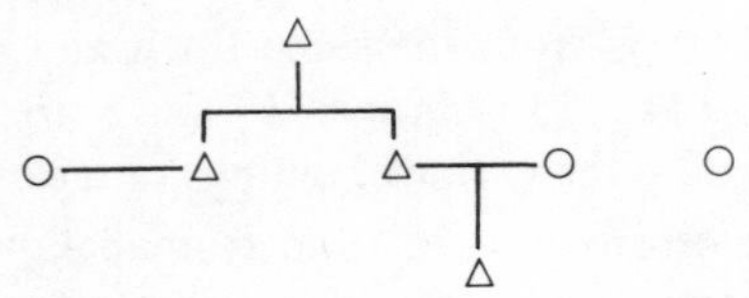

6. Siblings (married or unmarried) + relatives/residents (7 cases, 11.5%)

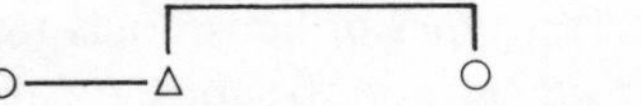

At the time of the census of 34 AD the family represented in *P.Oxy.Hels.* 10, with which we began, falls into the category of simple household, type 4. Those mentioned in the document are listed below, with names italicised of those living in Pausas' house. At *l.*14 the lacuna may have listed a daughter, given that women are listed from *l.*13.

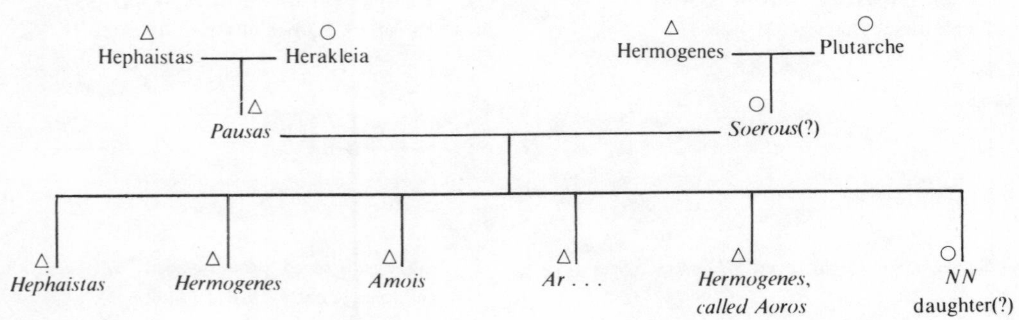

This nuclear family of parents plus their children can be expected to have developed into an extended, or complex household as the sons proceeded to marry and bring their wives into the home. Such a situation is reflected in *Stud.Pal.* 20 (1921; repr. 1969) 11 (Memphis, 175), a return for the year 173/4.

Ἀπολλωνίῳ στρατηγῷ
Μεμφίτου
[π]αρὰ Πετεαμουνις Πετε-
[α]μουν̣ι̣ς μητρὸς Ταμασις
[ν]εκροτάφου τῶν ἀπὸ Μοι-
[θ]υμεως τοῦ αὐτοῦ νομοῦ
[ἀπ]ογράφομαι καὶ τοὺς
[ἐ]μοὺς ἰς τοὺς ἀσκήνους
[ἰ]ς τὴν τοῦ ἐνεστῶτος ιδ (ἔτους)
Αὐρηλίου Ἀντωνίνου Καίσ[α-]
[ρος τοῦ κυρίου] κατ' οἰκίαν ἀπογρα-
[φήν·]
[Πετ]ε[αμο]υνιν τὸν προγε-
[γραμ]μένον νεκροτάφον
[ὡς (ἐτῶν)] οε οὐ`λ΄(η) μετώ`π΄(ῳ)·
Ἀμμωνᾶς υἱὸς ἐ̣γ̣ μητρὸς̣
[Σε]ναμουνις τελε`λ΄(ευτηκυίας) νε-
[κ]ροτάφος (ἐτῶν) με ἄση`μ΄(ος)·
[αὐ]τοῦ γυναῖκα
[Ἶ]σ̣ιν Ἰσᾶτος ἀρ`γ΄(ὴν) (ἐτῶν) μ̣
ἄσημον·
[ἀμ]φοτέρων θυγατέρα
[. . . . . .]ν̣ (ἐτῶν) δ·
[Ἀμμ]ωνᾶτος ἀδελφὸν
[Ὧρον] ν̣εκροτάφον (ἐτῶν) λ
[καὶ] Ὥρου γυναῖκα
[Τα]ωριν Ὥρου ἀρ`γ΄[ὴν] (ἐτῶν) λα·
[ἀμ]φοτέρων θυγατέρα
Ἀμουνιν (ἐτῶν) δ·
[ ]ις ἀδελφὸς το[ῦ] Ὥρο̣υ̣
[ν]εκροτάφος (ἐτῶν) λ·
[. . .]ασιν ἀργὴν θυγατέρα
[Πα]σίωνος Ὥρου τετε`λ΄(ευτηκότος) ἐ̣γ
[μη]τρὸς Ἀμμωναρίου (ἐτῶν) ιθ
ἄσ̣η`μ΄(ος).
[ὀ]μνύω τὴν τοῦ κυρίου
[Αὐρ]ηλίου Ἀντωνίνου Καίσαρο[ς]
[τοῦ] κυρίου τύχην ἀληθῆ
[εἶναι] τὰ προκίμενα
[(ἔτους) ιδ] αὐτοκράτορος Καίσαρος
[Μάρκ]ου Αὐρηλίου Ἀντωνίνου
[Σεβαστ]οῦ Ἀρμενιακοῦ Μηδι`κ΄(ου)
[Παρθ]ικ[οῦ] Γερμανικοῦ
[Μεγίστ]ο`υ΄, Ἐπειφ κθ. (*m.2*) Πετεα(μουνις)
[Πετεαμ(ουνις)] ἐπιδέδ`ω΄(κα) ὡς πρό(κειται)
Ἅθρης
[ ]̣ ἔγραψα ὑ`π΄(ὲρ) αὐ`τ΄(οῦ) μὴ εἰ`δ΄(ότος)
γρ(άμματα).

To Apollonios, *strategos* of Memphis, from Peteamounis son of Peteamounis and whose mother is Tamasis, grave-digger, who are (all) from Moithumis, the same nome. I register myself and my family who are not living in tents for the house-to-house registration of the current 14th year of Aurelius Antoninus Caesar the Lord: Peteamounis, the aforementioned grave-digger, aged about 75, with a scar on the forehead; Ammonas, my son, whose mother is the deceased Senamounis, grave-digger, aged 45, no identifying mark; his wife, Isis, daughter of Isas, having no trade, aged 40(?), no identifying mark; their daughter *N*, aged 4; the brother of Ammonas, Horos, grave-digger, aged 30, and the wife of Horos, Taoris, whose father is Horos, having no trade, aged 31; their daughter, Amounis, aged 4; . . .is, brother of Horos, grave-digger, aged 30; . . .asis, having no trade, a daughter of Pasion son of the deceased Horos and whose mother is Ammonarios, aged 19, no identifying mark. I swear by the *genius* of the Lord Aurelius Antoninus Caesar the Lord that the foregoing is true. Year 14 of Imperator Caesar Marcus Aurelius Antoninus Augustus Armeniacus Medicus Parthicus Germanicus the Greatest. Epeiph 29th. (*m.2*) I, Peteamounis son of Peteamounis provided the information as has been laid out above. I, Hathres *N*, wrote for him since he is illiterate.

The household represented in this text represents complex type 5; and the following family tree may be extrapolated (members of the household are italicised, and their age given below the name, where indicated).

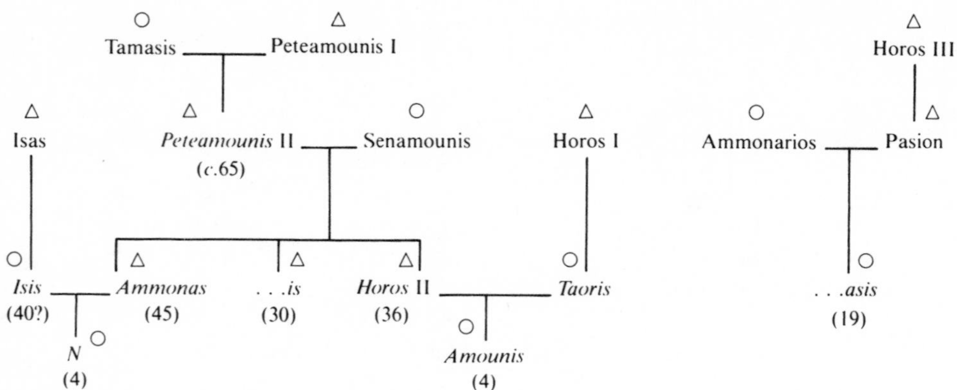

In this extended household the two wives, Isis and Taoris, have entered the paternal home of their husbands. In fact, all newly-married couples in the census returns follow this pattern. Nowhere do we have examples of a newly-married couple living by themselves, and all the examples we have testify to the fact that the wife on marriage entered into the paternal/maternal household of her husband. B.J. Malina, *The NT World. Insights from Cultural Anthropology* (Atlanta, 1981) 101-02, observes that this pattern was widespread in the first-century Mediterranean world. He draws attention to Jesus' saying in Mt. 10.35: ἦλθον γὰρ διχάσαι ἄνθρωπον κατὰ τοῦ πατρὸς αὐτοῦ καὶ θυγατέρα κατὰ τῆς μητρὸς αὐτῆς καὶ νύμφην κατὰ τῆς πενθερᾶς αὐτῆς. No mention is made here of a son-in-law, since it was the new wife who moved into her husband's house, not the husband into the wife's family.

In fact, whether the same types of family structures (especially the extended households) prevailed in other parts of the Empire is a matter for debate, as there has been some recent questioning of the widely-held belief that the extended family was the dominant domestic structure in antiquity. Using the evidence provided by tombstone inscriptions R. Saller/B. Shaw, *JRS* 74 (1984) 124-46, claim that the extended family was not the prevailing form of family structure in Rome and her western provinces. Their argument is based on the observation that the majority of the funerary inscriptions found in the Western Roman Empire give expression to nuclear relationships. However, although these same nuclear relationships are reflected in a large majority of Roman Egyptian dedicatory inscriptions, yet as the ideographs above indicate the extended family was very much a part of the culture of Roman Egypt.

Similarly, B. Rawson, in ead. (ed.), *The Family in Ancient Rome* (London, 1986), 4 is also of the opinion that the extended family in Roman society was rare. To support this assertion she refers to Cic., *de off.* 1.53. Yet it is not at all certain whether this statement of Cicero reflects the reality of the situation or his own ideals. It may, in fact, represent what he thinks should occur rather than what does happen. Furthermore, Cicero is not actually stating that a single household consisted of a married couple and their children; rather he is outlining the hierarchy of family obligations which, in his opinion, consisted first of the bond between husband and wife, next of the ties between parent and child, and thirdly of the bonds linking those within the household. Thus, from Cicero's point of view the household consisted of more than just the nuclear family. Therefore, to suggest as Rawson does that the extended family in Roman society was rare cannot be substantiated from Cicero's statement.

From *P.Laur.* 66, a property return noted above, we learn that the grandmother Nemmia had owned property which another person has inherited. In census returns where the owner of the house can be determined (124), 32% are owned or partially owned by females. Of these, 14.3% are owned by the wife, 5.7% are owned by the wife and husband together, 11.4% are owned by sisters and brothers, and 5.7% are owned by daughters; but by far the largest percentage (62.9%) are owned by a woman with no spouse. Three factors contributed to the high proportion of women in this last category owning the principal house.

i. *Death of a husband*
When the husband died, in some cases the wife could inherit the house in which the family lived. That this was not often the case can be observed from extant contemporary wills. In these documents there is only one clear case of a husband bequeathing all the property to the wife, *P.Oxy.* 3 (1903) 493 (11 AD). Usually the property is bequeathed to the children, and the wife is given the right to occupy the house. Cf. *P.Oxy.* 3.489 (117); *CPR* VI.1 (1978) 1 (125); *P.Oxy.* 1 (1898) 105 (117-38); *SB* 8.1 (1965) 9642 (117-38); *BGU* 1 (1895) 85 (155); *P.Ryl.* 2 (1915) 153 (138-61).

ii. *Married women owning the principal house*
As has been noted above, in some cases the husband resided in the house owned by his wife. We may add to these examples *P.Oxy.* 1 (1898) 104 (96 AD), a will in which a testatrix bequeaths to her son her house with the condition that her husband has the right to live in it. From this provision in the will we may deduce that the husband has no property of his own and is residing in the house owned by the wife. That this was not a general occurrence can be seen from the fact that we have only five examples of this type of arrangement from the census returns: *P.L.Bat.* 3 (1942; = *P.Oxford*) 8 (103/4); *P.L.Bat.* 11 (1963; = *P.Vindob. Sijpesteijn*) 24 (131/2); *BGU* 1 (1895) 95 (145/6); ibid., 54 (159/60); *P.Brux.* (1974) 7 (173/4).

iii. *Divorce*
When a wife was divorced from her husband it meant that she and her children (if she had custody of them) would have to leave the home of the former husband and either live with her parents or in her own house, if she had one. Given that not many wives inherited the principal house from their husbands when they died, and that not many married women owned the principal house, it seems reasonable to conclude that divorce accounts for the greatest percentage of women without spouses living in their own house. For an example of a divorce agreement from the present year's publications see *P.Oxy.Hels.* 35 (Oxyrhynchos, August 151). In this case the husband has custody of the child. Divorce was initiated by either party simply by separation; but a formal document was usually drawn up reflecting both parties' agreement concerning return of dowry, possession of other property, and custody of children.

Therefore, although nearly a third (32%) of principal houses are owned or part-owned by women, we cannot draw the conclusion that wives had an equality with their husbands when it involved ownership of the family house. Furthermore, it can be observed from the census returns that when the wife and the husband both owned property the choice was always made to live in the husband's house rather than in the wife's.

If the above factors may legitimately be applied generally to the Mediterranean world, it is quite likely that Lydia, Paul's first convert in Europe, who appears to be head of a household (Acts 16.14, 15, 40), was in fact divorced: cf. *New Docs 1977*, **3**, pp.31-32.

(D.C. BARKER)

22. Petition concerning Ephesian mysteries

Ephesos 88/9

ed. — *SIG*³ 820

Λουκίῳ Μεστρίῳ Φλώρῳ ἀνθυπάτῳ παρὰ
Λουκίου Πομπηίου Ἀπολλωνίου Ἐφεσίου·
Μυστήρια καὶ θυσίαι, κύριε, καθ' ἕκαστον
ἐνιαυτὸν ἐπιτελοῦνται ἐν Ἐφέσῳ Δήμητρι
Καρποφόρῳ καὶ Θεσμοφόρῳ καὶ θεοῖς
Σεβαστοῖς ὑπὸ μυστῶν μετὰ πολλῆς
ἁγνείας καὶ νομίμων ἐθῶν σὺν ταῖς
ἱερίαις, ἀπὸ πλείστων ἐτῶν συντετηρημένα
ἀπὸ βασιλέων καὶ Σεβαστῶν καὶ τῶν
κατ' ἐνιαυτὸν ἀνθυπάτων, καθὼς αἱ
παρακείμεναι ἐπιστολαὶ αὐτῶν περιέχουσιν·
ὅθεν, ἐπειγόντων καὶ ἐπὶ σοῦ τῶν μυστηρίων,
ἀναγκαίως, κύριε, ἐντυγχάνουσί σοι δι'
ἐμοῦ οἱ ὠφείλοντες τὰ μυστήρια ἐπιτελεῖν,
ἵνα ἐπιγνοὺς αὐτῶν τὰ δίκαια [- - - - -

Marble statue base.
Bib. — **I.Eph.* II.213.

To Lucius Mestrius Florus, proconsul, from Lucius Pompeius Apollonius of Ephesos. Mysteries and sacrifices are performed every year at Ephesos, sir, to Demeter | Karpophoros and Thesmophoros and to the divine Augusti by initiates with much propriety and lawful customs, together with the priestesses; (the mysteries) have been watched over for very many years by kings and emperors and the | annual proconsuls, just as their appended letters say. Accordingly, since the mysteries are soon upon us during your term of office, sir, those who ought to perform the mysteries necessarily petition you through my agency | in order that you, recognising their rights - - -

The proconsul to whom this petition was directed was known to Plutarch (see *I.Eph.*, n. ad loc.). The coupling of the Imperial cult with the celebration of the mysteries of Demeter may be suggestive of the Romanisation of the latter. Even though we lack the complete text of this inscription it provides an interesting indication of relations between a local citizen and the imperial representative. Though the proconsul is addressed courteously, Apollonius' points are so weighted that for Florus not to give his assent to the annual performance of the rites would be to break with documented precedent (8-11) and to deny the rights of those who should take responsibility for their organisation (13-15).

A few words may claim brief notice. For ἁγνεία (7) with the sense 'propriety', indicating that the whole ceremony is arranged properly, cf. 1 Tim. 5.2. ἐντυγχάνω τινί (13) is commonly used of petitioning someone. For this construction in the NT note Acts 25.24 and Rom. 11.2. Intransitive περιέχω (11) provides a good parallel to 1 Pet. 2.6, περιέχει ἐν γραφῇ (cf. BAGD, s.v., 2b). Rom. 7.18, 21 are the only verses where παράκειμαι (11) occurs in the NT, and though the context is somewhat different, it serves as a useful illustration. Indeed, the date of this text makes its vocabulary and syntax so nearly contemporaneous with the NT that numerous entries in a new MM could gainfully refer to it. On ἐπιτελέω (4) cf. item no.3 in the philological comments towards the end of **19** above.

In *I.Eph.* VII, 1.3059 (III or later?), a priestess of Artemis is praised for 'having restored all the mysteries of the goddess, and rendered them in accordance with ancient custom', ἀνανεωσαμένην πάντα | τὰ μυστήρια τῆς θεοῦ | καὶ καταστήσασαν τῷ | ἀρχαίῳ ἔθει, κτλ (*ll*.3-6).

23. A troublesome worker

Oxyrhynchos — 23 April, 212

ed.pr. — H. Zilliacus, *P.Oxy.Hels.* 23 (pl.16)

Κ̣[αλπουρν]ί̣ῳ [᾿Ισ]ι̣[δώρ]ῳι τῷ κ̣α̣ὶ̣
[῾Αρποκρατ]ί̣ωνι στρ(ατηγῷ) Μ̣ε̣μφίτου
παρ̣ὰ̣ Θ[έω]νος ῾Αρμ̣α̣ίωνο̣ς̣
γυμνασιαρχήσαντ̣[ο]ς̣ τῆς
Μεμφιτῶ̣ν̣ πόλεως. ἐπε̣ὶ̣
ἀπὸ το[ῦ] Μεχεὶρ μηνὸς
τοῦ ἐνεστῶτος (ἔτους) ἐπηρί̣α̣ν̣
π̣α̣θὼν ὑπὸ ᾿Απίωνός τ̣ι̣ν̣ο̣ς̣
κ̣αμηλείτου μου τυγχάνον̣-
τος καὶ π̣ά̣ντα τὰ ἀργαλεῖα τῶν
κτηνῶ̣ν̣ μου ὑπ' αὐτὸ̣ν̣ ὄ̣ν̣τ̣α̣
οὐ μόνον, ἀλλ̣ὰ̣ κ̣αὶ προχ̣ρ̣ε̣ί̣α̣ν̣
ἔχοντος, μηδενὶ λόγ̣ῳ̣ χ̣ρησά-
μενος κλέψαντο̣ς̣ ἔ̣νια τῶν
ἀργαλείων καὶ ἀπέδρασεν,
μαθὼν τὴν ἀπόνοιαν αὐ-
τοῦ κ̣α̣τ̣ε̣φρόν̣ησα τ[ῶ]ν ἐ-
μῶν μ̣ὴ̣ ἐπεξελθών, ἵνα
μὴ τὰ χείρονα πάθω ὑπ' αὐ-
τοῦ. σήμερον δὲ εὑρὸν α[ὐ-]
τὸν ἐνθάδε ἐργαζόμεν[ον]
μεθ' ἑτέρων καμήλω[ν] τ̣[ο]ῦ̣ [2-3 *letters*]
νώφιος γυμνασιαρχ[ήσαν]τ̣ο̣ς̣
τῆς α̣ὐ̣τῆς πόλεως ἐν̣ε̣π̣ο̣ι-
ησάμην αὐτῷ τῷ ᾿Α̣π̣ί̣ω̣[νι]
περί τε τῶν ἐμῶν κ̣[α]ὶ̣ τ̣[ο]ῦ̣
ἀνόμου αὐτοῦ ἐξόδου κ̣α̣θ̣' ὅ̣τ̣ι̣
εὗρον αὐτὸν πρὸς τῷ ἐμῷ καμ̣η̣-
λῶνι ὄντι ἐπὶ τοῦ α . . . . δρό-
μου ἐξαγορευτικοῦ ᾿Αφροδείτης
θεᾶς μεγίστης, οἰόμενος ὅτι δύ-
ναται παύσασθαι, ὃς δὲ τῇ αὐτῇ
ἀπονοίᾳ `ἐ΄χρήσατο καὶ πολλά μοι
ἀπαγγέλλει. εὐλαβούμενος οὖν
μὴ καὶ ἐν ἔργῳ γένηται τὸ
τῆς ἀπαγγελείας αὐτοῦ, ἀσφαλι-
ζόμενος οὖν ἐμαυτὸν ἐπιδίδωμι
τόδε τὸ βιβλίδειον. ἀξιῶ τὸν ᾿Απί̣-
ωνα ἀχθῆναι, ἵνα ἀκριβῶς ἐ̣ξε-
τάσῃς τὸν βίον αὐτοῦ, καὶ ἐγ-
γυήτην παρασχεῖν, ἵνα μηδεμί-
αν βλάβην ἐκ τῆς ἐπαγγελίας
αὐτοῦ βλάβω.
(ἔτους) κα Αὐτοκράτορος Καίσαρος
Μάρκου Αὐρηλίου Σεουήρου ᾿Αντωνίνου
Παρθικοῦ Μεγίστου Βρετανικοῦ
Μεγίστου Εὐσεβοῦς Σεβαστοῦ, Φαρμοῦθι
κη. (*m.* 2) Θέων ῾Αρμαίωνος γυμνασιαρ-
χήσας ἐπιδέδωκα ὡς πρόκιται.

Papyrus sheet (11B x 14H cm.), back blank. The translation below attempts to convey the fact that in places the expression is confused (*ll*.8-15) or at least awkward (*ll*.34-48), perhaps reflecting the dictation of unrehearsed thoughts rather than lack of competence. The full-stop of the *ed.pr.* after ἀπέδρασεν in *l*.15 has been changed to a comma in accordance with the suggestion of K.L. McKay (*per litt.*) that *ll*.5-20 are better read as one sentence. For ῾Αρμαίωνος (*ll*.3, 48) read ῾Ερμαίωνος, and for ἀργαλεῖα (*l*.10; cf. *l*.15) read ἐργαλεῖα; and perhaps also ἐπαγγ- should be read for ἀπαγγ- in *ll*.34, 36 (cf. ἐπαγγελίας at *l*.42 where the first ε has been corrected from α). On α for ε, particularly in the word ἐργαλεῖον, see Gignac, I.283-86. Read ι for ει in καμηλείτου (*l*.9), Ἀφροδείτης (*l*.30) and βιβλίδειον (*l*.38), and *vice versa* in πρόκιται (*l*.49). At *l*.20 εὑρών ought perhaps to be read.

To Calpurnius Isidoros also called Harpokration, *strategos* of the Memphite (nome), from Theon son of Harmaion, former gymnasiarch of the city | of Memphis. Because, suffering (as I did) from the month of Mecheir in the current year insulting treatment at the hands of a certain Apion who happened to be my camel driver | and who had all the tools for my cattle under his control, and not only these, but also pay in advance(?), he having no reason stole some of the | tools and ran away, having learnt of his recklessness I did not care about my possessions, and did not pursue him, so that I might not suffer worse things at his hands. | But today I found him here working with some other camels belonging to . . .nophis, former gymnasiarch of the same city, and I pressed my | claims with this Apion concerning my property and his illegal departure, seeing that I found him near my camel stable which is close to the . . . | confessing(?) way of the greatest goddess Aphrodite. And I thought that he was able to restrain himself, but he acted in the same reckless manner and made many threats against me. Therefore, taking care | lest what he threatened should actually come about, by way of safe-guarding myself therefore I am presenting this petition. I request that Apion be brought (before you) in order that you may closely investigate | his manner of life, and that he provide surety in order that I may suffer no harm from his threats. In the 21st year of Imperator Caesar | Marcus Aurelius Severus Antoninus Parthicus Maximus Britannicus Maximus Pius Augustus, Pharmouthi 18. (*m*.2) I, Theon son of Harmaion former gymnasiarch have presented the petition as is written above.

The purpose of Theon's petition is to restrain Apion from carrying out unspecified threats against him, and to this end Theon paints his former employee as untrustworthy, dishonest, abusive and potentially violent. Because the notion of threatening seems to be required by the context, the translations of ἀπαγγέλλω/ἀπαγγελία (*ll*.34,36; cf. *l*.42) follow the tentative proposals in the *ed.pr.* As J.A.L. Lee has suggested to me (*per litt.*), ἀπαγγελ- appears to be a distortion of ἐπαγγελ- and the development from 'promise', which is the prevailing sense of ἐπαγγέλλω/ἐπαγγελία, to 'threaten/threat' would be an easy one. Theon claims that Apion is such a desperate character that previously he was unwilling to prosecute Apion for an alleged theft for fear of suffering more trouble. (The ἵνα clause of *ll*.18-20 is to be understood as explaining his reason for not pursuing Apion, rather than what his purpose in prosecuting him would have been had he undertaken it; but cf. the translation given at *ed.pr.*, p.83: 'nor did I intervene against him in order to deter him from doing worse things'.) At the same time Theon's account implies that he himself was not provocative: he only pressed his claims when he came upon Apion near his own stables, where he himself might reasonably expect to be (especially as it is close to a public place?), and he had not expected such threatening behaviour from him. Theon, therefore, portrays himself as a quiet and inoffensive person in fear of a lawless scoundrel. For examples of 'the quiet life' being used in the rhetoric of petitions see **30**, below.

Theon's story is certainly plausible and may be largely accurate, but it cannot be accepted without question. One wonders why Theon did not act against Apion at first: perhaps he did not have sufficient resources to find and prosecute him (even though he may have been of the bouleutic class; cf. the Theon in *P.Oxy.* 31 [1966] 2584 [211] and see *ed.pr.*, n. ad. loc.), and perhaps he really was frightened of Apion. On the other hand Apion may have had good cause to run away and Theon felt he was not in a position to prosecute. For even in this petition he makes no attempt to recover the equipment allegedly stolen and concentrates only on Apion's threatening behaviour; nor had Apion felt it necessary to leave the district. When, therefore, Theon complains that Apion 'ran away' (*l*.15), it may be that Apion, nursing a genuine grievance, was only refusing to go on working for Theon. He did not flee to where he might not be found, but on the contrary turns up where he could expect Theon to come across him.

In such a context 'to run away' can mean 'to leave one's work (in breach of contractual obligations)', in which case it is usually expressed by ἀποτρέχω (aorist ἀπεδραμ-) rather than by ἀποδιδράσκω (aorist ἀπεδρ-). The form in *l*.15 does not belong strictly to either verb, but it may be, as K.L. McKay points out to me (*per litt.*), a regularisation of ἀπέδρα based on the 3rd person pl. ἀπέδρασαν. An example of ἀποτρέχω in the meaning 'leave work' occurs in the letter, *PSI* 4 (1917) 421 (Philadelphia, III BC), addressed to Zenon by some *chomatophylakes* who claim that he has not paid them for two months, nor sent them their corn allowance for one month. In *ll*.7-9 they write: ὥστε εἰ | μὲν διδοῖς ἡμεῖν· εἰ δὲ μή, ἀπο|δραμούμεθα· οὐ γὰρ ἰσχύομεν, 'Consequently if you give it to us [it is well?]; but if not, we shall run off. For we cannot go on.' In another letter to Zenon, *P. Col.* 4 (1940) 66 (Philadelphia, *c*.256/5 BC), one of Zenon's employees stationed in Syria (probably on the coast — see *ed.pr.*, pp.16-17), whose name is lost, complains that Zenon's agent in Syria refused to pay him and he fell into straitened circumstances: ἠναγκάσθην ἀποτρέχειν εἰς Συρίαν ἵνα μὴ τῶι λιμῶι παραπόλωμαι, 'I was forced to run off into Syria so that I might not perish through hunger' (*ll*.11-12). J.A.L. Lee has shown (*A Lexical Study of the Septuagint Version of the Pentateuch* [*SCS* 14; Chico, 1983] 125-28) that in III-II BC ἀποτρέχω largely took the place of ἀπέρχομαι (present and imperfect) in literary and documentary texts and could mean simply 'depart' or, in the context of manumissions, 'go free'. Ἀπέρχομαι (present and imperfect) is rare in the NT (only Mt. 8.19; 25.10; Lk. 9.57; Acts 23.32) having been replaced principally by ὑπάγω. For examples of ἀποδιδράσκω see a letter from Zenon, *P.Cair. Zen.* 1 (1925) 59015 *back* (Philadelphia, 259/8 BC [pl.5]), in which he speaks of the location of οἱ παῖδες οἱ ἀποδράντες (*l*.3); and *P.Oxy.* 3 (1904) 472 (an advocate's speech, *c*.130) mentioning a runaway slave. Also worth mention here is *UPZ* 1 (1927) 121 (provenance unknown, 13 Aug., 156 BC), a warrant for arrest in which the second of two runaway slaves, whose descriptions are given, is called ὁ συναποδεδρακώς (*l*.17); cf. two other 'Wanted' notices for slaves: *P.Oxy.* 51 (1984) 3616 (III? ; in the introduction to which are given further examples of runway slaves and bibliographical details on this topic), and 3617 (III). In *UPZ* 121 the verb ἀναχωρέω is used of the slaves' flight; on the word ἀναχώρησις and groups of free workers leaving their employment as a means of protest see W.L. Westermann, *AHR* 43 (1937/38) 270-87 and especially 276-77. The application of similar terminology to describe both slaves running away and free men leaving their work may be a sign that *de facto* the gap between slaves and the poor free was a narrow one.

Because it is Theon's aim to portray Apion as a dangerously violent character, it is not clear whether ἄνομος in *l*.27 has the strongly pejorative, but non-technical, sense of 'lawless', or the more specific meaning of 'illegal'. The latter would be intended if Apion had not only stolen goods, but also breached his terms of employment. For a brief description of the various conditions which could apply in cases of *locatio conductio operarum*, i.e., the hiring of labour, see R. Taubenschlag, *The Law of Greco-Roman Egypt in the Light of the Papyri 332 BC — 640 AD* (Warsaw, 1955²; repr. Milan, 1972) 371-83. G.E.M. de Ste Croix points out (*The Class Struggle in the Ancient Greek World* [Ithaca, 1981] 199) that the hired labourer was despised in antiquity and that his status 'was as low as it could well be — only a little above that of a slave, in fact'. For a discussion of the position of wage-labourers see also M.I. Finley, *The Ancient Economy* (London, 1985²) 62-94, and on the sometimes tenuous distinction between slaves and the economically dependent see I.F. Fikhman, *VDI* 155 (1981) 77-99 (in Russian). Though de Ste Croix makes little use of NT evidence in his section on 'Hired Labour' (179-204), he conveniently collects (at 580 n.52) all references to hired labour in the NT: Mt. 20.16: Mk. 1.20; Lk. 10.7; 15.7, 19; Jn 4.36; 10.12-13; Jas. 5.4; cf. also Lk 3.14; 2 Cor. 11.8; 2 Pet. 2.15; Rom. 6.23. Free persons who contracted to do work sometimes entered into conditions of service not unlike those of slavery. An example of this is the copy of a contract, *PSI* 8 (1927) 902 (Tebtynis, I), agreed to by a weaver who, it must be noted, had fallen into debt (if indeed this is the significance of the term Πέρσης τῆς ἐπιγονῆς, for which see P.W. Pestman, *Aeg.* 43 [1963] 15-53 and J.F. Oates, *YCS* 18 [1963] 119). In return for measures of wheat, an allowance for clothing and oil, and payment by his employer of certain taxes and sundries, the weaver gives these undertakings:

παρέξεσθαι ἐμαυτὸν ἐφ' ἔτηι δύο ἀπὸ τοῦ προκειμένου
χρόνου διατρίβωντα καὶ ποιοῦντα πάντα τὰ [ἐπ]ιτασσό-
μενα καὶ ὑφαίνων οὗ ἐὰν βούληται ὁ προγεγραμμένος
Ἥρων Ἁρυώτου καθ' ἡμέραν ἑκάστην·
. . . .
οὐ γινόμενος δὲ ἀφήμερος ἀπὸ τῶν τοῦ Ἥρωνος, ἀλλὰ καὶ συνα-
κ<ο>λουθῶν αὐτῷ πανταχῆι κατὰ τὸν νόμον· ἧς δὲ ἡμέρας
ἧς ἐὰν μὴ παραμείνωι, ἐκτίσω τῷ Ἥρωνι ἀργυρίου δραχμὰς
δύο· καὶ ἕκαστα ποήσωι καθὼς πρόκιται.

. . . that I shall present myself staying for two years from the aforementioned time and doing all that is instructed, and weaving wherever the aforementioned | Heron son of Haryotos wishes each day . . . And (I shall present myself) without being away for a day from the affairs of Heron, but accompanying him | everywhere according to the law. And for whatever day I do not remain in service, I shall pay Heron two silver drachmai and I shall perform each point as described above.

Of particular interest for the present discussion is the sense 'to continue to serve' which παραμένω takes on in such contexts. It is used with this meaning with reference to freed slaves in Helbing *AGI* 34.8 and to a slave or freedman in *P.Oxy.Hels.* 26.13 (both reprinted at **24** below), a meaning that is found in the NT at Heb. 7.23, though in a different context. A lengthy study of the usage of this verb and the noun παραμονή has been carried out by A.E. Samuel, *JJP* 15 (1965) 221-311. He concludes that the obligation to remain at someone's disposal was a contractual one imposed on free persons and freed slaves, and was not a type of quasi-slavery or a relationship into which slaves could enter (282-84, 311). Another example of its use in a contract for employment is found in *P.Oxy.* 8 (1911) 1122 (407), in which Aurelius Phoibammon says in *ll.*8-13:

ὁμολογῶ ἑκουσίᾳ καὶ αὐθαιρέτῳ γνώ-
μῃ συντεθῖσθαί με πρὸς σὲ ἐπὶ τῷ ἐμαὶ
παραμένιν παρὰ σοὶ καὶ συναποδημῖν
σοι ἐπὶ τῆς ἀλλ[ο]δαπῆς καὶ ὑπακούειν σοι
εἰς ἅπαν[τα τὰ ἐπιτραπησόμενά μοι
ὑπὸ σοῦ.

I acknowledge that willingly and by my own choice I have made an agreement with you to | remain in service to you and to travel with you in foreign parts and to obey you in respect of all instructions given to me by you.

From what remains of this papyrus it appears that this employer was at least obliged to feed and clothe his employee. For other documentary examples of this use of παραμένω see MM, s.v., where attention is drawn to the nuance it would bring to Phil. 1.25 and Jas. 1.25. See also *New Docs 1976*, **27**, an undertaking by shopkeepers to continue to work, in which this sense of παραμένω should perhaps be understood.

P.Oxy.Hels. 23, with which this entry began, has several words found in the NT. At *ll.*39-40 ἀκριβῶς ἐξε|τάσῃς is another parallel for the phrase — one only is given in MM, s.v., ἐξετάζω — which occurs in Mt. 2.8, where, however, the verb is followed by περί instead of the direct object. The word χείρων (*l.*19) is used in the sense 'more serious', which is the meaning found in all eleven NT examples except 1 Tim. 5.8 and 2 Tim. 3.13, where it is usually taken to mean 'morally inferior' (see BAGD, s.v. — MM does not comment on the distinction). For the word ἔξοδος (*l.*27) in the meaning 'departure', which is found at Lk. 9.31 and 2 Pet. 1.15, MM offers no example earlier than VI fin. Καταφρονέω (*l.*17) parallels the use in Heb. 12.2. Ἄνομος (*l.*27) here means 'illegal' (though 'lawless' is possible), but in the NT it refers exclusively to transgression of God's law. The meaning of εὐλαβηθείς in Heb. 11.7 is disputed (see BAGD, s.v.), but may have the same meaning as here in *l.*34 (cf. Acts 23.10 *t.r.*). In Mt. 27.64-66 and Acts 16.24 ἀσφαλίζομαι has a concrete sense as opposed to the figurative meaning here in *ll.*36-37 — MM provides documentary examples of this verb in concrete senses, but none is a very close parallel of the NT uses. J.A.L. Lee has pointed out to me (*per litt.*) that the construction αὐτῷ τῷ Ἀπίωνι (*l.*25) is probably an example of αὐτός being used in a way similar to οὗτος or ἐκεῖνος (cf. MM, s.v. αὐτός, and Moulton's *Grammar of NT Greek* I [Edinburgh, 1908[3]] 91). N. Turner in Moulton's *Grammar* III (Edinburgh, 1963) 194 (cf. 41) briefly discusses the view that this use results from Aramaic influence. Examples in papyri, such as this one, which are unlikely to be under Aramaic or NT influence, suggest that the construction was part of colloquial *koine* Greek.

From *PSI* 8.902 above may be noted in *ll.*2-3 the words παρέξεσθαι ἐμαυτόν with a participle which provide another example of the expression 'to show' or 'present oneself' found a Tit. 2.7. Other words from this text which occur in the NT vocabulary are διατρίβω (*l.*3) and συνακολουθέω (*ll.*14-15) — see BAGD s.vv. — for both of which MM gives no examples from I AD.

It is worth noting in passing the appearance in *P.Oxy.Hels.* 23-30 of the word ἐξαγορευτικός where the context is unfortunately obscured by the damage to *l.*29. The meaning of this word is not clear and the editor has sought a parallel in ἐξαγόρειος which occurs in *P.Lond.* inv. 2554.9-10, a request for cancellation of a deed of lien (Oxyrhynchos, 28 Aug., 249; *ed.pr.* — C.H. Roberts, *JEA* 20 [1934] 20-27). Roberts draws on the meanings of the verb ἐξαγορεύω ('to reveal', 'to confess') to elucidate the meaning of ἐξαγόρειος and translates θεαγῶν Θοηρείου ἐξα|γορείων by '*theagoi* at the temple of Thoeris of the revealing gods'. He prefers to link the word with the 'oracular powers of Egyptian deities', but concedes that the verb in the sense 'to confess' is commonly found in Lydian confessions. On confession texts from Lydia and central Asia Minor see *New Docs 1978*, **6**, pp.26-28.

(A.L. CONNOLLY)

24. A slave's bid for freedom

Oxyrhynchos 13 June, 296

ed.pr. — J. Frösén, *P.Oxy. Hels.* 26 (pl.17)

ἐπὶ ὑπάτων τῶν κυρίων ἡμῶν Αὐτοκράτορος Διοκλητιανο`ῦ´
Σεβαστοῦ τὸ ϛ̄ καὶ Κωσταντίου ἐπιφανεστάτου Καίσαρος τὸ β̄.
Αὐρηλίοις Διονυσίῳ τῷ καὶ Ἀπολλωνίῳ καὶ Δημητριανῷ Πλουτί[ωνο]ς
ἀμφοτέροις γυμ(νασιαρχήσασι) βουλευταῖς τῆς λαμπρᾶ`ς´ καὶ λαμ(προτάτης)
Ὀξυρυγχιτῶ[ν π]όλ(εως)
τοῖς ἀξιολογωτάτοις νυκτοστρατηγοῖς.
παρ' Αὐρηλίας [Τ]απάμμωνος Θωνίου μη(τρὸς) Ἀλλοῦτος ἀπὸ τῆς [α]ὐτῆς
πόλεως χωρὶς κυρίου χρημα(τιζούσης) τέκνων δ[ικα]ίῳ δ[ι]ὰ [τ]οῦ τροφίμο`υ´
πατρὸς Αὐρηλίου Σαραπιάδους Διδύμου τοῦ κ[α]ὶ Ἱέρακος ἀπὸ τῆς αὐτῆς πόλ(εως).
ἐκ διαδοχῆς τῶν γονέων μου κέκτημαι ἅμα τῇ ἀδελφῇ μου Διοσκου-
ριαίνῃ δοῦλον ὀνόματι Σαρμάτην οἰκογενὴν ἐκ δούλης Θαήσιος,
καὶ ἀπὸ τοῦ χρόνου τῆς τελευτῆς τῶν γονέων μου οὗτος ἀποφορὰς
ἡμῖν χορηγῖ. νῦν δὲ, οὐκ οἶδα πόθεν κινηθείς, ἀποσπᾶται(?) καὶ
οὐ βούλεται παραμένειν τῇ ἡμῶν ὑπηρεσίᾳ οὐδ' αὖ ἀποφορὰς διδόναι,
τί θηρώμενος οὐκ ἐπίσταμαι. (*vacat*) ὅθεν μὴ φέρουσα τὴν
οἰκέτου θρασύτητα ἐπιδίδωμι τάδε τὰ βιβλία ἔγγραπτα ἐντευξομένη(?) καὶ
ἐπαξιοῦσα διὰ τῆς ὑμῶν ἐπιμελείας ἐπαναγκασθῆναι τὸ παιδάριον τὰς
ὀφελομένας ὑπ' αὐτοῦ ἀποφορὰς ἀποδοῦναι καὶ ἐπιταχθῆναι ἵνα(?)
παραμίνῃ τῇ ὑπηρεσίᾳ ἡμῶν.
[(ἔτους)] ι̅β̅ καὶ (ἔτους) ι̅α̅ τῶν κυρίων ἡμῶν Αὐτοκρατόρων Διοκλητιαν[οῦ]
[καὶ Μ]αξιμιανο`ῦ´ Σεβαστῶν καὶ δ̄ (ἔτους) Κωσταντίου καὶ Μαξιμιανο`ῦ´
[τῶν] ἐπιφανεστάτων Καισάρων Παῦνι ι̅θ̅.

Αὐρηλ(ία) Ταπάμμων δι' ἐμοῦ Αὐρηλ(ίου) Σαραπιάδους ἐπιδέδω(κε). Αὐρήλ(ιος) Ἰσχυρίων
ἔγρα(ψα) ὑπὲρ αὐτῆς.

A papyrus sheet (13B x 25H cm.) with margins surviving at top and bottom and on the left. New sections in the sense are indicated by the first word being written out in the left margin (*ll.*1, 3, 6, 9, 19). New lines and new sentences begin with capital letters. In accordance with a suggestion from K.L. McKay (*per litt.*) the full-stop in the *ed.pr.* after διδόναι (*l.*13) has been replaced by a comma.

In the consulship of our lords the Emperor Diocletian Augustus for the 6th time and Constantius the most noble Caesar for the 2nd time. To the Aurelii Dionysios also called Apollonios and Demetrianos son of Ploution, both former gymnasiarchs, councillors of the illustrious and most illustrious city of the Oxyrhynchites, | the most worthy *nyktostrategoi*. From Aurelia Tapammon daughter of Thonios, whose mother was Allous, from the same city acting without a *kyrios* by the *ius liberorum* through her foster-father Aurelius Sarapiades son of Didymos also called Hierax from the same city. By inheritance from my parents I own with my sister Dioskouriaina | a slave by the name of Sarmates, house-born from the female slave Thaesis, and since the time of the death of my parents

he has been providing us with income. But now, from I do not know what motive, he is withdrawing from his work(?) and is not willing to remain in our service or, moreover, to pay dues, with what purpose I do not understand. Therefore, since I cannot endure | the insolence of a servant, I am presenting this written document with the intention of making a petition(?) and requesting that through your attention the slave be compelled to pay the income owed by him and be ordered to remain in our service. In the 12th year and 11th year of our lords the Emperors Diocletian | and Maximian Augusti, and in the 4th year of Constantius and Maximian the most renowned Caesars, Pauni 19th. Aurelia Tapammon has presented (this) through me, Aurelius Sarapiades. I, Aurelius Ischyrion, wrote for her.

The petition is addressed to two *nyktostrategoi*, who were minor officials responsible for public order and for receiving complaints about assault (see J. Lallemand, *L'Administration civile de l'Egypte de l'avènement de Dioclétien à la création du diocèse (284-382)* [Brussels, 1964] 164-65) and, as this text shows, about other matters. On the changing role of this office see J.D. Thomas, *CE* 44 (1969) 347-52. Aurelia Tapammon, the author, should be added to the list of women at *New Docs 1977*, **3**, pp.30-31 who held the *ius* (*trium*) *liberorum* (cf. *New Docs 1978*, **3**), as should two other women from the texts culled this year, Aurelia Eus (*CPR* 14, a copy of a landsale; Hermopolis, 28 April, 305), and Aurelia Aleka (*P.Col.* 185, a receipt for rents and taxes; Karanis, 319). Both are described as acting without a *kyrios*. These three women are mentioned at nos. 54, 78 and 86 respectively in the updated list of women who are known from the papyri to have held the *ius* (*trium*) *liberorum*, which has been published by P.J. Sijpesteijn in *P.Mich.* 15 (1982) App.II, pp.158-71. Three more women may be added to his list from texts published since 1981: Aurelia Petronia who is jointly making a declaration of *aparche* with her husband and who is illiterate (*P.Oxy.* 49 [1982] 3476 [17 Sept., 260]); a woman (name lost) purchasing some land (*P.Oxy.* 49.3498 [27 Oct., 274]); and Aurelia Tasia, also illiterate, who is seeking a lease for a room (*P.Haun.* 3 [1985] 55 [Dinneos Koite, 16 June, 325]). None is said to be acting with assistance. Cf. *P.Köln* 100 (Oxyrhynchite nome, 24 August, 133; *ed.pr.* — D. Klamp, *ZPE* 2 [1968] 81-150), a will in which Taarpaesis (also called Isidora) declares that she has the right to dispose of her property as she wishes (*ll.*4-5), even though her half-brother is acting as her *kyrios* (this clause is restored at *ll.*3 and 18). She makes no appeal to the *ius liberorum*, but she has three children (*ll.*5-6). For a female orphan and minor who appears to present a petition without sponsorship see *P.Köln* 173, discussed at **71** below. It is worth noting here that even when women are not said to be acting with a *kyrios*, they may have had one. *P.Soterichos* 18-21 are four receipts for rent issued by Sentia Asklatarion during the years 127/28-133 (Theadelphia; pls. 9, 10): in the first this woman makes no mention of a *kyrios*, but in the other three she specifies that she is acting with Lucius Egnatius Crispus; so either she simply did not mention him (or another *kyrios*) in the first receipt or her relationship with him began after the time of that transaction. These texts are also noteworthy in that Sentia apparently signed the documents in her own hand.

It is interesting that Aurelia Tapammon in *P.Oxy.Hels.* 26, though holding the right to conduct her own affairs, makes her petition through her foster-father, Aurelios Sarapiades (*ll.*7-8, 22). Since another man actually wrote the petition (*ll.*22-23), διά in *ll.*7 and 22 must indicate that Sarapiades' role was more than that of scribe. Among the 114 women in Sijpesteijn's list about a quarter are said to have assistance from a man (usually the husband), but in only one other case is this expressed by the use of διά: in *P.Michael.* (1955) 22 (Tebtynis, 29 Sept., or 9 Oct., 292) Aurelia Teieous acts διὰ τοῦ ἀνδρὸς Ζωτίκου (*l.*3). In this case, however, since the husband is writing for his illiterate wife, his role may be limited to that of scribe (see ed. n. *ad loc.*). In his list Sijpesteijn does not record the assistance rendered by Sarapiades in *P.Oxy.Hels.* 26, but the assistance of the husband in *P.Michael.* 22 is mentioned. (Note, too, that the reference for his no.96 should read *P.Mich.* 15.719.)

In the introduction to *P.Oxy.Hels.* 26 Frösén states that the text is a reply in the form of a petition to another petition (presumably one from the slave Sarmates), but does not indicate what evidence there is for this in the document. It is not clear, for example, what Sarmates would have filed a petition about. Frösén speculates that Sarmates may have believed himself freed by testamentary disposition (on which see below) upon the deaths of Aurelia Tapammon's parents; but he would only have petitioned to protect his freedom if Aurelia had already made efforts to enforce ownership, and this she does not seem to have done previously. Moreover, Aurelia claims that Sarmates has actually been making payments since her parents' deaths and has only recently 'withdrawn' (*ll.*11-12). Therefore, it is at least equally likely that Aurelia did have some rights over Sarmates and that for reasons unknown he was attempting to throw them off. Perhaps she had no husband, since the petition is made through her foster-father and not her husband, and Sarmates thought her too weak to pursue her claims. The use of παραμένειν (*ll.*13, 18) may suggest that Sarmates was a freedman, upon whom continuing service had been imposed as a condition of freedom. This would follow from the argument of A.E. Samuel, *JJP* 15 (1965) 221-311, that remaining in someone's service (παραμένειν) was a contractual obligation which was imposed only on free persons (see **23** above). However, Aurelia Tapammon nowhere calls him a freedman, but refers to him as τ̣ὸ̣ π̣α̣ι̣δ̣ά̣ρ̣ι̣ο̣ν̣ (*l.*16); and perhaps *paramenein* is not being used in a strict legal sense. If the reading ἀποσπᾶται (*l.*12) is correct Sarmates seems confident enough of his freedom to remain at hand and not run away; however, the reading is most insecure and there is no clear parallel to this use. Most documentary examples of ἀποσπάω occur in the active and refer to withdrawing people from work (see MM, *s.v.*, for examples), although in *BGU* 2 (1898) 467.9 (provenance unknown, II^{2}?) it is used of stealing camels; but in *Chrest. Wilck.* I (1912, repr. 1963) 70.24-26 (Fayum, 57/6 BC) the middle occurs: οὐ δυνάμενοι δὲ τοῦ ἱεροῦ ἀποσπᾶσθαι | διεδώκαμεν τὴν περὶ τούτων ἐπιτροπὴν Σωκράτῃ τῷ μάλιστα τοῦ ἱεροῦ | διὰ παντὸς προϊσταμένῳ, 'and since we cannot withdraw from (the work of) the temple, we have handed over the responsibility concerning these things to Sokrates who in particular continually looks after the temple'. Wilcken argues against the view that ἀποσπᾶσθαι means physically leaving the temple precincts. If he is right, this provides adequate sense for ἀποσπᾶται in *P.Oxy.Hels.* 26.12; but perhaps a part of ἀποτρέχω or ἀποδιδράσκω could also be read here. In the NT ἀποσπάω occurs four times; once of the drawing of a sword (Mt. 26.51), once of Jesus withdrawing a certain distance (Lk. 22.41), once of the seduction of the faithful (Acts 20.30) and once of a parting of friends (Acts 21.1). For another example of ἀποσπάω see *SB* 12.1 (1970) 10841.11 (Oxyrhynchos, IV; repr. at *New Docs 1976*, **85**) where it is used of withdrawing friendship (= *PSI* 8 [1927] 972 [IV]). On ἀποτρέχω see the discussion at **23**.

Sarmates had stopped paying ἀποφοραί (*ll.*11, 13, 17), payments made by slaves or conditionally freed slaves to their owners. Slaves who worked and earned money outside the household usually had to pass over a part of their earnings to their owners; freed slaves often gained their liberty on the condition that they continued to serve their household by paying ἀποφοραί or performing other services (R. Taubenschlag, *The Law of Greco-Roman Egypt in the Light of the Papyri 332 BC — 640 AD* [Warsaw, 1955^{2}; repr. Milan, 1972] 78 n.50, 80). Emancipation in wills is well known from the papyri, for example *P.Oxy.* 3 (1903) 494 (156), in which Akousilaos sets free under the sanction of Zeus, Earth and Sun two adult males, two adult females and the daughter of one of these women (*ll.*5-7), on condition, however, that the five freed slaves continue to provide δουλεία and ἀποφοραί to Akousilaos' wife until her death (*ll.*13-16). His other slaves and any more children born to the two women to be freed are part of the property to be inherited by his son (*ll.*11-13). For other examples of slaves freed in wills see Taubenschlag, 96 n.147; for the sanction of Zeus, Earth and Sun, *ibid.*, 97 n.151 (cf. *New Docs 1978*, **46**, p.74). For slaves apportioned in a will see *New Docs 1976*, **24**.

A manumission text from this year's culling is Helbing, *AGI* 34.3-19 (Steiris in Phokis, not before 250 BC; *ed.* — *IG* IX, 1 [1897] 42), a marble plaque which is headed by an unrelated dedication in *ll.*1-2 (= *IG* IX, 1.41), omitted here. The NW Greek forms should be noted: ἀφίητι for ἀφίησι; 3rd pl. verb endings in -ντι for -σι (e.g., ζῶντι); ποτ(ι)- for προσ-; ᾱ for η; προστᾶμεν for προστῆναι; ὑπέρ + acc.

Θεὸς τύχαν ἀγαθάν· ἄρχοντος ἐν Στείρι
Κάλλωνος τοῦ Ἀγήσωνος μηνὸς τετάρ-
του· Πραξίας Θέωνος ἀφίητι ἐλευθέρους Εὔπραξιν
καὶ τὸ ἐξ αὐτᾶς παιδάριον, ᾧ ὄνομα Δωρίων. μὴ κα-
ταδουλιξάσθω δὲ αὐτοὺς μηθεὶς μηδὲ καθ' ὁποῖ-
ον τρόπον. οἳ καὶ παραμεινάτωσαν πραξίᾳ καὶ τᾷ
γυναικὶ αὐτοῦ Ἀφροδισίᾳ, ἕως ἂν ζῶντι, καὶ θαψάντω καὶ τ[ὰ]
ὥ[ρ]ια αὐτῶν ποιησάτωσαν· εἰ δὲ μὴ θάψωντι καὶ ποιήσω[ν-]
τι τὰ ὥρια αὐτῶν, καθὼς προγέγραπται, ἀτελὴς ἔστω ἁ ἀ-
νάθεσις, καὶ ποταποτισάτωσαν ἀργυρίου μν-
ᾶς τριάκοντα. εἰ δέ τις ἐπιλαμβάνοιτο αὐτῶ-
ν ἢ καταδουλίζοιτο, ἅ τε γενηθ(ε)ῖσα δουλαγω-
γία αὐτῶν ἄκυρος καὶ ἀρμένα ἔστω, καὶ ποτα-
ποτισάτω ὁ καταδουλιζόμενος μνᾶς τριάκοντα
[κα]ὶ τὸ μὲν ἥμισον ἔστω τοῦ προστάντος, τὸ
[δὲ] ἥμισον τοῦ Ἀσσ(κ)λαπιοῦ. ἐξέ(σ)τω δὲ προστ-
[ᾶ]μεν ὑπὲρ (α)ὐτοὺς τὸν θέλοντα Φωκέων.

(May) the god (grant) good fortune. In the archonship in Steiris of Kallon son of Ageson during the fourth month: | Praxias son of Theon sets free Eupraxis and the child born to her, whose name is Dorion. Let no one enslave them, not in any way. But let them remain in the service of Praxias and his wife Aphrodisia, as long as they (the latter) live, and let them bury them | and perform their rites. If they do not bury them and perform their rites, as is written above, let the disposition be unfulfilled, and let them pay thirty mnas of silver besides. If anyone should seize them for himself or enslave them, let the resultant enslavement | of them be invalid and done away with, and let the one enslaving them pay thirty mnas besides, and let half belong to their protector and half to Asklepios. Let it be permissible for whoever of the Phokians wishes to act as protector on their behalf.

This text illustrates well some of the typical characteristics of conditional manumissions which are described by K. Hopkins in his survey of known manumissions at Delphi during II-I BC (*Conquerors and Slaves* [*Sociological Studies in Roman History* 1; Cambridge, 1978] 149-54; cf. *SEG* 1744 *bis*): continued service until the deaths of the owners as well as the obligation to attend to their burial and the rites of the dead, with the threat of re-enslavement for failure to comply with the conditions. For an example of a monument erected to a deceased master by a freedman see *New Docs 1977*, **19**, and for one by a slave, *New Docs 1978*, **74**. Noteworthy in the case of this manumission is Eupraxis' ability to take her child with her. For a possible example of a manumission of a slave couple with their child see **29**. Frequently, manumitted slaves were required to leave their children in slavery, or even to bear children to hand over as one of the terms of their release (cf. the dispositions in Akousilaos' will described above). In effect, some women slaves gained release by replacing themselves with their children. Further examples of this manner of gaining freedom are discussed by Hopkins (155-58), who notes that unlike all other relationships between slaves the one between mother and child was acknowledged by slave owners. This came about because most slave relationships, if recognised, would prevent separation by sale, whereas the recognition of slave motherhood (encouraging as it did the birth of household slaves) was motivated by economic benefits for the owner (163-68). Observing also that in the surviving Delphic texts slaves bought their release at prices approximating those of the slave market (158-60), Hopkins reaches the conclusion that 'market forces both systematically overrode affective ties between masters and slaves and disrupted the slaves' ties with their families' (134). Even the home-born slaves in Hopkins' survey, who might have been expected to receive favoured treatment, appear to have paid on average only a little less for their freedom (166-67).

This does not mean, however, that market forces necessarily prevented relations between slaves and their owners from being affectionate. In *P.Oxy.* 3.494, noted above, Akousilaos says in his will that he is setting free the five slaves κατ' εὔνοιαν καὶ φιλοστοργίαν, 'in accordance with my goodwill and affection' (*l.*6). Of course, this is as much an advertisement of Akousilaos' apparent generosity as an indication of the feelings between him and his slaves. For examples of masters erecting epitaphs for slaves out of such motives, see *New Docs 1977*, **15**, p.53 and *New Docs 1978*, **10**.

From the documents discussed above come a number of words found in the NT. In *P.Oxy. Hels.* 26.10 the word χορηγέω occurs with the same meaning as at 2 Cor. 9.10 and 1 Pet. 4.11; it is already well attested in MM. At the end of *l.*15 ἐντευξομένη, the future participle of ἐντυγχάνω, is insecurely read. The word is used in a similar context in Acts 25.24 where the Jews are said to have appealed to Festus; the other four occurrences in the NT (Rom. 8.27, 34; 11.2, and Heb. 7.25) are all used of appeals to God. The noun ἔντευξις is found in 1 Tim. 2.1 in the plural meaning 'prayers', and in 1 Tim. 4.5 in the singular with the sense of 'the action of praying'. BAGD, s.v., does not make explicit this distinction between 'a prayer' and 'the action of prayer'. On the legal process of *enteuxis* in Ptolemaic Egypt see O. Guéraud, *ENTEYΞIΣ. Requêtes et plaintes adressées au roi d'Egypte au III*[e] *siècle avant J.-C.* (2 vols; Cairo, 1931, 1932), a collection of 113 petitions from Magdola and Ghoran. Helbing, *AGI* 34.13 provides a near parallel to the use of ἐπιλαμβάνομαι in Lk. 23.26 (though in the latter with the accusative), where Simon of Cyrene is seized and pressed into service. See also the other uses of this word in the NT to indicate the seizing of a person with violence at Acts 16.19; 18.17; 21.30, 33 (the last two being with the genitive). None of MM's three examples of this word as used in the middle has the meaning found in the NT. The meaning of προΐστημι in *AGI* 34.17, 18-19 is not paralleled by its uses in the NT, where it usually has the sense of presiding over activities in the Church. On this verb see further **19** above, ad fin.

(A.L. CONNOLLY)

25. Standing on sacred ground

Smyrna I BC
ed. — *SIG*^{3} 997

[ἰ]χθῦς ἱεροὺς μὴ ἀδικεῖν,
μηδὲ σκεῦος τῶν τῆς
θεοῦ λυμαίνεσθαι, μηδὲ
[ἐ]κφέρειν ἐκ τοῦ ἱεροῦ ἐπ[ὶ]
κλοπήν· ὁ τούτων τι ποιῶν
κακὸς κακῇ ἐξωλείᾳ ἀπό-
λοιτο, ἰχθυόβρωτος γενόμε-
νος. ἐὰν δέ τις τῶν ἰχθύ-
ων ἀποθάνῃ, καρπούσθω
αὐθημερὸν ἐπὶ τοῦ βωμοῦ.
τοῖς δὲ συμφυλάσσουσιν
καὶ ἐπαύξουσιν τὰ τῆς
θεοῦ τίμια καὶ τὸ ἰχθυο-
τρόφιον αὐτῆς βίου καὶ
ἐργασίας καλῆς γένοιτο
παρὰ τῆς θεοῦ ὄνησις.

Stele. The date has been proposed by Sokolowski.
Bib. — *F. Sokolowski, *Lois sacrées de l'Asie Mineure* (Paris, 1955) no.17; Guarducci, *EG* IV.23-25.

Do not harm the sacred fish, nor damage any of the goddess' utensils, nor carry anything out of the sanctuary to | steal it. May the one who does any of these things be destroyed wretchedly by a terrible destruction, being eaten by fish. But if any of the fish dies, let it be offered | on the same day on the altar. And may those who join in watching over and who increase the valuables of the goddess and her fish-pond | have from the goddess enjoyment of life and successful labour.

This text is one of just over twenty which Guarducci reprints, in full or in part, or simply describes in a chapter on sacred laws (*EG* IV.3-45). Her selection of texts ranges in date from VI BC to late Imperial and includes a variety of types of sacred law which illustrate the ways in which the sanctity of holy places and of their activities was created and maintained. The law above concerns the sanctuary of an unknown goddess. Artemis, Kybele and the Syrian goddess Atargatis (who is known from elsewhere to have had sacred fish) have been suggested as appropriate deities (Guarducci, 24). The threat of retribution by being eaten by fish signifies being deprived of burial (Sokolowski, 49). MM cites the occurrence of ἰχθυόβρωτος in this text in their discussion of σκωληκόβρωτος, s.v. Cf. *New Docs 1978*, **65**.

It clearly emerges from this inscription that, while there were people who would respect the sanctuary and support it (*ll.*11-14), at least in return for the goddess' blessing (*ll.*14-16), there were others who might dare to steal, poach or vandalise the goddess' possessions (*ll.*1-8). Either, therefore, the cult was not a widely respected one in its district and was liable to suffer such depredations; or there were marginalised people in the community who did not share the values which the cult represented and whose loyalties were not aroused by it (for example, the poor who might want fish to eat). Cf. another text, reprinted by Guarducci at *EG* IV.18-19 (Attica, IV BC; = *IG* II/III^2 1362), which is an attempt to protect the sanctuary of Apollo Erithaseos by prohibiting under threat of punishment (a whipping for slaves and a fine for a free man) the removal of any timber or fallen branches and leaves from the sanctuary.

The text from Smyrna also contains instructions for sacrificing the sacred fish (*ll.*8-10). Sacred laws laying down regulations about the nature and time of sacrifices are common. Such a text is *I.Eph.* Ia.10 (a stele, 90B x 156H cm., found in the square in front of the theatre in Ephesos; pl.11) which though inscribed in late II or III probably dates from an earlier time, as the opening indicates:

ἀγαθῇ τύχῃ.
κεφάλαιον νόμου πατρίου·
τὸν πρύτανιν αἴθειν πῦρ ἐπὶ τῶν βω-
μῶν πάντων καὶ ἐπιθυμιᾶν τὸν λιβα-
νωτ̣ὸν καὶ τὰ ἱερατικὰ ἀρώματα, ἱερεῖα
προσάγοντα τοῖς θεοῖς νενομισμέ-
ναις ἡμέραις τὸν ἀρι≪θμ≫ὸν τξε´, καρδιου[ρ-]
γούμενα μὲν καὶ ἐκμηριζόμενα ρϙ´, κα-
τατελισκόμενα δὲ ροε´, ἐξ οἰκείας δυ-
νάμεως, περιηγουμένου καὶ διδάσκοντος
αὐτὸν τοῦ δημοτελοῦς ἱεροφάντου καθό-
τι ἕκαστον τοῖς θεοῖς νόμιμόν ἐστιν· τοὺς
παιᾶνας ᾄδειν ἐν ταῖς θυσίαις καὶ ἐν ταῖς πο[μ-]
παῖς καὶ ἐν ταῖς παννυχίσιν αἷς δεῖ γενέσθαι
κατὰ τὰ πάτρια καὶ εὔχεσθαι ὑπὲρ ἱερᾶς συν-
κλήτου καὶ τοῦ δήμου τοῦ Ῥωμαίων καὶ τοῦ
δήμου τοῦ Ἐφεσίων. ἄλλο μέρος·
διδόναι δὲ γέρα τὸν πρύτανιν τῷ ἱεροφάν-
τῃ παντὸς ἱερείου τοῦ τυθέντος τοῖς θε-
οῖς κεφαλὴν καὶ γλῶσσαν καὶ τὸ δέρμα διὰ τὴν
ἐνπειρίαν καὶ τὸ μέγεθος αὐτοῦ τῆς ὑπαιρεσί-
ας, τῷ δὲ ἱεροκήρυκι καὶ αὐλητῇ καὶ σαλπικτῇ
καὶ ἱεροφάντῃ δευτέρῳ καὶ τῷ ἱεροσκόπῳ
καὶ ἑβδομοκούρητι σπυρίδας κατὰ προέλευ-
σιν· εἰ δέ τι ἐνλιπὲς ὑπὸ τοῦ πρυτανεύοντος
τῶν προειρημένων καθ' ἓν ἕκαστον· γείνηται,
ὀφείλειν τὸν πρύτανιν εἰς προ<σ>κόσμημα τῆς
ἐν τῷ πρυτανείῳ ἑστώσης Δήμητρος Καρ-
ποφόρου, ἧς ἐστι ὁ νεώς, καὶ εἰς ἐπισκευὴν
τοῦ πρυτανείου στατῆρας Δαρικοὺς ι´· πράσ-
σεσθαι δὲ τοὺς κούρητας καὶ τὸν ἱεροφάν-
την ὑπὲρ τοῦ μὴ [φρ]ον[τίσαι] ἑ[νὸς] ἑκάστου
κ[αθ]ότι προ[γέγραπται - - -]
- -

For good fortune. Summary of an ancestral law: The *prytanis* is to light fire on all the altars and to offer the incense | and the cultic aromatic herbs, bringing before the gods on the customary days animal sacrifices, in number 365, 190 (of them) with their hearts drawn out and thigh bones removed, and 175 offered whole(?), (providing them) out of his private resources, | with the publicly funded hierophant giving direction and instructing him how each one is conformable to the law for the gods. They are to sing the paeans

at the sacrifices, at the processions and at the night festivals which must be held | according to the ancestral practices and at which it is necessary to pray on behalf of the sacred senate and the people of Rome and the people of Ephesos. Another part: The *prytanis* is to give as a perquisite to the hierophant, of every victim sacrificed to the gods | the head and tongue and hide on account of his expertise and the importance of his service, and to the sacred herald and flautist and trumpeter and second hierophant and to the *hieroskopos* and the *hebdomokoures*, bonuses according to (their position in) the procession(?). | If any single point of the aforementioned matters is left out by the person serving as *prytanis*, the *prytanis* is to be required to pay ten Daric staters for the adornment of the (statue), which stands in the prytaneion, of Fruitful Demeter, to whom the temple belongs, and for the repair | of the prytaneion; and the *kouretes* and the hierophant are to make exaction for the failure to mind each single point as has been written above . . .

With these provisions may be compared the declarations of *prytaneis*' duties in a speech (by a *prytanis*?) at *I.Eph.* IV.1201a (Imperial), largely restored from the text above. It appears that the sacred laws of this temple were passed down in an oral tradition, of which the chief keeper was the hierophant (*ll.*10-12; cf. *ll.*20-22). The text does not reveal the motives for this summary being made, but the nature of the regulations recorded suggests that it was aimed primarily at defining the responsibilities of the *prytanis*, and even those practices which are not explicitly stated as his responsibility may have been: the provision of incense (*ll.*4-5), of any singers and musicians needed for the paeans (*l.*13), of trappings and equipment used in processions (*l.*14). The laying down of how many victims he must provide, at his own expense, of the authority of the hierophant over the *prytanis* concerning cult practices, of the perquisites due to the cultic officers, the imposition of a fine for negligence on the part of the *prytanis* (or his delegate?), and the authority of the hierophant and *kouretes* to exact the fine, all this seems designed to strengthen the position of the cult officers, in particular the hierophant, vis-à-vis the *prytanis*, who was presumably a wealthy layman. If this was the case, this text illustrates another way in which cults could use laws to maintain their sanctity by protecting themselves from outside interference and preserving priestly prerogatives, giving a glimpse of how the idea of the sacred could be used, albeit unconsciously, as an instrument of social influence.

This text, first published in 1960, illustrates the continuing contribution of epigraphical finds to Greek vocabulary: the Supplement to LSJ cites the inscription for the rare word καρδιουργέω and for the *addenda lexicis* ἐκμηρίζω and κατατελίσκομαι. Also in the text are a number of words found in the NT and worthy of brief comment. The use of κεφάλαιον in *l.*2 is somewhat different from its meaning in Heb. 8.1 where it has the sense 'chief, main point', but a better parallel to the NT occurrence is found elsewhere in this year's reading, at *P.Köln* 114 (provenance unknown, V; *ed.pr.* — L. Koenen, *ZPE* 4 [1969] 192), of which the short, complete text reads: ἀνάγνωθι αὐτό, | σημείωσον τὰ | κεφάλαια, 'Read it, note the main points'. Both these texts may be added to the small number of documentary parallels in MM, s.v. In Mark, Luke and John ἀρώματα (cf. *l.*5 above) are said to have been prepared for Jesus' burial. MM, s.v. ἄρωμα, only cites examples which refer to uses of spices for cultic purposes such as here and provides no parallels to the NT use. On frankincense (λιβα|νωτόν, *ll.*4-5) and myrrh see **29** below. Μέγεθος in *l.*21 has been translated 'importance', but could mean 'magnitude' in the sense of 'weight, extent of the demands' of his service. The latter meaning is closer to that of the only NT use, which is found at Eph. 1.19, τὸ ὑπερβάλλον μέγεθος τῆς δυνάμεως αὐτοῦ. None of the dated examples in MM, s.v., is earlier than mid-III and all but one are titles, τὸ σὸν μέγεθος ('Your Greatness').

Guarducci in her chapter on sacred laws includes half a dozen texts regulating sacrifices. Among these is the following inscription (*EG* IV.25; Attica, I?; = *IG* II/III^2, 1364) which shows the same dependence on oral tradition and concern with prerogatives as seen above:

ἱερὸν τὸ τέμενο[ς]
τοῦ Ἀσκληπιοῦ καὶ
τῆς Ὑγιείας.
θύειν τοὺς γεωργοὺς
καὶ τοὺς προσχώρους
τοῖν θεοῖν ἧι θέμις
καὶ τὰς μοίρας νέμειν
τῶι τε εἱσαμένωι καὶ
τῶι θεηκολοῦντι·
τῶν δὲ κρεῶν μὴ
φέρεσθαι.

The precinct of Asklepios and Hygieia is sacred. Let the farmers | and their neighbours sacrifice to the two deities in the way which is right and distribute the portions to the founder and the priest. | Let them not take away any of the meat.

An inscription recording the sale of a priesthood of Zeus Nemeios for life (Theangela in Caria, III BC; *SEG* 1088; *ed.pr.* — Ç. Şahin/H. Engelmann, *ZPE* 34 [1979] 211-13; cf. *BE* 460) specifies which parts of victims the priest will receive as his due portion and interestingly stipulates that at banquets he will have an equal share with the *prytaneis* (ἰσόμ|οιρος ὤν, *ll.*13-14). Guarducci includes in her selection a text of V BC from a Thesmophorion on Thasos which specifically grants portions of the sacrifices to women (*EG* IV.12; = C. Rolley, *BCH* 89 [1965] 447 no.6 [fig.6]). Another, however, from the same century, but from Elatea in Phokis and for some local male deities, specifically prohibits women from being present (*EG* IV.13; = *IG* IX, 1 [1897] 129). The activities of cults were also laid down in calendars of which Guarducci reproduces four examples. The last (perhaps from Dardanos in the Troad or Mytilene, late Imperial: *EG* IV.44-45; = *IG* XII *Suppl.* [1939] 29) is the bottom of a record of times at which a cult celebrated its principal ceremonies: the ascent of the goddess, the water-drinking, the procession, the fallow lands, the descent of the goddess and the banquet.

At *EG* IV.20 Guarducci reprints an inscription (Lykosura in Arkadia, III BC; = *IG* V, 2 [1913] 514, a text frequently cited by LSJ) which describes the types of offerings and sacrifices acceptable to the goddess Δέσποινα. However, it opens first with prohibitions against carrying various objects or dressing in certain ways when entering the sanctuary. (Note the numerous Arkadian features, including infinitives in -ην, ᾱ for η, ο for ου or ω, apocopation of ἀνα- and παρα- , ἐν with acc., πός for πρός.)

Δεσποίνας.
[- - - - - - - - - - - - - - -] μὴ ἐξέστω
παρέρπην ἔχοντας ἐν τὸ ἱερὸν τᾶς
Δεσποίνας μὴ χρ[υ]σία ὅσα μὴ ἰν ἀνά-
θεμα μηδὲ πορφύρεον εἱματισμὸν
μηδὲ ἀνθ̣ινὸν μηδὲ [μέλ]ανα μηδὲ ὑπο-
δήματα μηδὲ δ̣ακτύλιον· εἰ δ' ἄν τις
παρένθη ἔχων τ̣ι τῶν ἁ στάλα [κ]ωλύει,
ἀναθέτω ἐν τὸ ἱερόν. μηδὲ τὰς τ̣[ρί-]
χας ἀμπεπλεγμένας, μηδὲ κεκαλυμ̣-

μένος· μηδὲ ἄνθεα παρφέρην, μηδὲ
μύεσθαι [. . . . . . .] κυένσαν μηδὲ θη-
λαζομέναν· τὸς δὲ θύοντας πὸς θύ[η-]
σιν χρέεσθαι ἐλαίαι, μύρτοι, κηρίο[ι],
ὀλοαῖς αἰρολογημέναις, ἀγάλματ[ι],
μάκωνσι λευκαῖς, λυχνίοις, θυμιά-
μασιν, ζμύρναι, ἀρώμασιν. τὸς δὲ θ[ύ-]
οντας τᾶι Δεσποίναι θύ[ην]
θήλεα λευκ[ὰ . .]ο . . . ος καὶ κ-
- - - - - - - - - - - - - - - - -

Belonging to Despoina . . . let it not be permissible for those to pass in who are bringing into the sanctuary of Despoina any gold objects which are not intended for dedication | nor purple, flower-decorated or black clothing, nor sandals nor a ring. If anyone does enter with any of the things which the stele prohibits, let him dedicate it in the sanctuary. Nor (let it be permissible to enter) for women with their hair | braided, nor for men with their heads covered. Nor (let it be permissible) to bring in flowers, nor for a woman who is pregnant or breast-feeding to become an initiate . . . And let those making sacrifices use for sacrifice olive, myrtle, honeycomb, | barley-groats cleared of darnel, a statue, white poppies, (small) lamps, (various kinds of) incense, myrrh, and aromatics. And let those making sacrifice to Despoina sacrifice a white, female . . .

The goddess here requires simplicity of dress among both men and women coming to worship her. The prohibition against black clothing is complemented by the requirement for white sacrificial victims. Sandals are also forbidden in a sacred law from the temple of Alektrona in Ialysos on Rhodes (Helbing, *AGI* 19 [III BC]; cf. *SIG*^{3} 338.20-35): μηδὲ ὑποδή|ματα ἐσφερέτω μηδὲ ὕειον μη|θέν, 'and let no one bring in sandals, nor anything made from pigs' (*ll.*7-9). The regulation concerning women's hair and men's head-covering may recall us to Paul's much-debated comments at 1 Cor. 11.4-7. For a brief discussion of clothing regulations, which cites among others the law of Despoina's cult above, see H. Mills, *ZPE* 55 (1984) 255-65. Mills argues against the view that for Greeks decoration in clothing was purely ornamental rather than symbolic and suggests that laws governing dress in both religious and secular settings show many similar characteristics: 'the particular concern with women's dress, the use of religious sanctions to encourage obedience, the amazing details regarding fabric, cost and decoration, the delineation of different classes of women (free women, *hetairai*, adulteresses), the confiscation of the offensive objects' (265).

The rest of *AGI* 19 is concerned with preventing animals from being brought into the *temenos*, and similarly, a text at Guarducci *EG* IV.11 (Thasos, V BC; = *IG* XII, 8 [1909] 358) prohibits the entry of sheep and goats. Such regulations were intended no doubt to protect shrines, temples and their grounds from damage likely to be caused by the animals.

In the text from Lykosura above the reason for the restriction on women who were pregnant or breast-feeding is not specified, but it may stem from a notion of ritual impurity caused by childbirth. G.W. Clarke has drawn my attention (*per litt.*) to a passage in the letter of Dionysios, the third-century bishop of Alexandria, to Basilides (*ad Basilid.* β; = Migne, *PG* 10.1281), in which Dionysios says that in his opinion pious women who were menstruating would not come to church or receive communion: anyone who was not clean in body and soul ought not to be allowed to come. The idea of impurity resulting from childbearing, menstruation and other activities, occurs in another sacred law from Arkadia, published by G.-J.-M.-J. Te Riele, *BCH* 102 (1978) 325-31 (pl. on p.327; = *SEG* 28 [1978] 421), which was found near Megalopolis and is dated to II init. The the text is inscribed on a stele 57B x 64H cm. in 'Doric *koine*' (with ᾱ for η, e.g., στάλα, ἁμέρας; but cf. αὐθημερί). A flaw in the stone at *l.*9 occasioned the *vacat* within the first word.

στάλα Ἴσιος Σαράπιος.
Θεός, τύχα ἀγαθά. ἱερὸν ἅγιον Ἴσιος
Σαράπιος Ἀνούβιος. *v.* εἰσπορεύεσ-
θαι εἰς τὸ ἱερὸν τὸν βουλόμενον
θύειν καθαρίζοντα ἀπὸ μὲν
λέχ[ο]υς ἐναταίαν, ἀπὸ δὲ δι-
αφθέρματος *v.* τεσσαράκοντα
καὶ τέσσαρας ἁμέρας, ἀπὸ δὲ τῶ[ν]
φ *v.* υ̣σικῶν ἑβδομαίαν, ἀπὸ φό[ν]ο̣υ
ἑπτὰ ἁμέρας, ἀπὸ δὲ αἰγέου καὶ
προβατέου τριταῖον, ἀπὸ δὲ τῶν
λοιπῶν βρωμάτων ἐκ κεφαλᾶς
λουσάμενον αὐθημερί, ἀπὸ δὲ
ἀφροδισίων αὐθημερί *v.* λουσά-
μενον, ἀπὸ ΠΑΘΙΝ[ ]ΙΑΜΕΙΙΓΑΝ
ΜΟ̣Α̣Ν̣ αὐθημερὶ λουσάμε[ν]ον Υ
[- - - - -]υεσθαι ΜΗΔΕΜ̣[- - - - - - - -]
[- - - - - -]ε̣ἰσπορεύεσθα[ι- - - - - - - - -]
[- - - - - - -]Μ̣ΕΩΝΠΟ[- - - - - - - - - - -]
[- - - - - - - - -]ΣΘΕ[- - - - - - - - - - - - - -]

Stele of Isis and Sarapis. God, good fortune. A holy sanctuary of Isis, Sarapis and Anoubis. Let anyone who wishes to sacrifice enter the sanctuary | upon purification, after childbirth on the ninth day, after an abortion for forty-four days, after menstruation on the seventh day, after bloodshed | for seven days, after (eating) goat's meat and mutton on the third day, after all other sorts of food on the same day when one has washed from the head down, after sexual intercourse on the same day when one has washed . . .

This text provides the first evidence of an official and organised cult of the Egyptian gods in Megalopolis, and disproves the view based on previously known inscriptions that devotion to Isis and Sarapis in the Peloponnese was only of a personal nature. The formula with ἀπό is found commonly in such lists of prohibitions from other parts of Greece and Te Riele notes the principal examples which include texts from mainland Greece, the Aegean, Asia Minor, Egypt and North Africa. Te Riele explains that ἀπό in these contexts must mean 'after having been in contact with' or 'after having eaten' (328-29). However, in the case of the first three interdictions in the text above — after childbirth, abortion (or miscarriage) and menstruation — the meaning is rather 'after having been involved in or affected by'; and Te Riele himself reads λέχους ('bed', i.e., childbirth) and not λεχοῦς ('woman who has just given birth') because here it is not a question of contamination from contact with a person, but from the function itself (329). The periods of purification are variously described by ordinal and cardinal numbers. This may indicate that depending on the impurity's nature purification was to be carried out either on the last day of the delay only (ordinal number) or on every day (cardinal). Possibly the actions requiring the former were regarded as continuing sources of impurity following the initial onset — continuing discharges after childbirth and the onset of menstruation, a period of digestion after the eating of a goat or sheep — which made it pointless to purify oneself until this state was considered to be over. However, abortion would presumably have produced a similar condition; so perhaps the two actions whose delays are described by cardinals (abortion, or miscarriage, and killing) were perceived to be more serious and required repeated purifications. Again, since ordinals and cardinals alternate, it may simply be that here we have alternation of expression for the sake of variety. The use of τριταῖον (*l*.11), a masculine for the general case, shows that the ordinals (which are accusative singular agreeing with the subject of εἰσπορεύεσθαι) are not used simply to mark those regulations applying only to women (cf. *ll*.6, 9). The word διάφθερμα is otherwise unknown, but the verb διάφθείρω and other cognate forms frequently refer to abortion or miscarriage, and in similar texts the delay after abortion is commonly forty days (Te Riele, 329).

A text from the island of Astypalaia (Helbing, *AGI* 20 (*c*.300 BC; = *SIG*³ 980) reads, [ἐ]ς τὸ ἱερὸν μὴ ἐσέρπεν ὅσ|τις μὴ ἁγνός ἐστι, ἢ τελεῖ | ἢ αὐτῶι ἐν νῶι ἐσσεῖται, 'let not anyone enter the sanctuary who is not pure; either he will pay or he will become aware of it' (though Helbing reads τέλει<ος>, interpreting the meaning to be ' . . . who is not pure or perfect [in body]; otherwise . . . '). Ἁγνός is likely to refer to bodily purity here, especially if τέλειος is right. What form the punishment of the impious will take is left to the deity to whom the sanctuary belongs; but retribution is promised. With the vague and understated threat used here compare the very specific punishment promised in the text which opened this entry. Cf. also the so-called Eumenian formula, ἔσται αὐτῷ πρὸς τὸν θεόν, discussed at *New Docs 1978*, **98**, pp.136-39.

Bodily impurity, however, was not the only ground on which one could be barred from a place. A first-century Rhodian inscription discussed by Guarducci at *EG* IV.31 (= F. Sokolowski, *Lois sacrées des cités grecques, Supplément* [Paris, 1962] no.108), after prescribing various regulations concerning physical purity, concludes with the elegiac couplet, ἁγνὸν χρὴ ναοῖο θ[υ]|ώδεος ἐντὸς ἰόντ[α] | ἔνμεναι· οὐ λουτροῖ | ἀλλὰ νόῳ καθαρόν, 'who enters within the temple fragrant with incense, must be holy; pure not through washing, but in mind' (*ll*.4-7). For an example of a private cult at Philadelphia in Lydia in which moral purity was the principal qualification for being admitted and remaining a member see *SIG*³ 985 (late II/I init. BC), and for discussion of this cult comparing it with early Christian churches, see S.C. Barton/ G.H.R. Horsley, *JbAC* 24 (1981) 7-41; cf. also *IG* II/III² 1369 (Athens, late II), a regulation governing admission to an association.

Entry into the temple at Jerusalem was determined principally by race, except of course in the case of proselytes. Guarducci, at the end of her chapter on boundary markers for the sacred precincts of pagan cults (*EG* IV.46-73), discusses two nearly identical and very well-known inscriptions which were discovered near the site of the temple and date from before 70 (*EG* IV.71-73, fig.28). One of these (= *OGIS* 598; for the other see *SEG* 8 [1937] 169) reads μηθένα ἀλλογενῆ εἰσπο|ρεύεσθαι ἐντὸς τοῦ πε|ρὶ τὸ ἱερὸν τρυφάκτου (*read* δρυφ-) καὶ | περιβόλου. ὃς δ' ἂν λη|φθῇ ἑαυτῶι αἴτιος ἔσ|ται διὰ τὸ ἐξακολου|θεῖν θάνατον, 'let no foreigner enter within the balustrade and enclosure around the sanctuary. Whoever is caught will have himself to blame because his death follows'. Guarducci cites passages in which Josephus mentions such a prohibition and penalty, which applied even to Roman citizens: *BJ* 5.194; 6.125; *Ant*. 12.145; 15.417.

The juxtaposition of ἱερὸν and ἅγιον in *l*.2 of Te Riele's text above raises the question of the distinction between these two words. Used substantively ἅγιον seems to mean a more holy place within a ἱερόν (e.g., *SGPI* 38.59 [Kanopos, 239/8 BC; = *OGIS* 56], and Heb. 9.1-2; cf. BAGD, s.v. ἱερόν, 2); this suggests that in others of its uses ἅγιος could have a stronger sense than ἱερός. However, the distinction should not be pressed too hard: in Rom. 1.2 Paul speaks of γραφαὶ ἅγιαι referring to the prophets, and in 2 Tim. 3.15-16 he says that Timothy has known ἱερὰ γράμματα and reminds him that πᾶσα γραφή (which must include those γράμματα) is inspired (cf. ἱεραὶ γραφαί in *1 Cl*. 43.1).

In Rom. 7.12 Paul calls the law (ὁ νόμος) ἅγιος in the sense that it is perfect or worthy of God (cf. BAGD, s.v. ἅγιος 1a, β), but in a fragmentary inscription, first published fully in Guarducci, *EG* III (Rome, 1974) 15-17 (fig.5), the law is 'holy' as being dedicated to or reserved for God's service (cf. BAGD, s.v., 1a, α):

pro salute Aug(usti)
οἰκοδόμησεν κὲ αἰπο[ί-]
ησεν ἐκ τῶν αὐτοῦ δο-
μάτων καὶ τὴν κειβωτὸν
ἀνέθηκεν νόμῳ ἁγίῳ
Μίνδις Φαῦστος με-
[- - - - -]διω[- - - - -]

For the good health of the emperor. Mindi(u)s Faustus built and had made out of his own gifts and | dedicated the ark for the holy law . . .

This inscription from Ostia was probably first inscribed in II^{2}; later (III fin.) the portion after *l.*5 containing the name of the original dedicator was erased and the name of Mindius Faustus added — presumably because he had paid for renovations. Guarducci suggests that the emperor invoked in the Latin superscription is perhaps Marcus Aurelius or Commodus, and observes that in their reigns the use of such a *pro salute* invocation by a Jew would have been only customary and certainly not very sincere. Indeed, as R. Tracey has suggested to me, the invocation was so common by this time that any necessary connection with emperor worship may have been lost and it could have been included automatically in all sorts of documents. It may be suggested that the separate fragment containing three letters in *l.*7 may belong further to the left on the line, thus allowing the restoration με|[τὰ τῶν ἰ]διω̃[ν, i.e., Faustus together with the members of his family provided a gift for the Ostian synagogue. With this use of ἅγιος to describe the Law of Moses may be compared the phrase ἱεροὺς νόμους (where νόμος has a very different meaning) in *I.Eph.* III.614A, a very fragmentary two-line text found near the temple of Artemis in which the brother of Mark Antony is honoured:

Λεύκιον Ἀντώνιον Μάρκου υἱὸν [ταμίαν κ]αὶ ἀντιστράτηγον, πάτρων[α καὶ εὐεργέτην τῆς] Ἀρτέμιδος καὶ τῆς πόλεως, τε[τηρηκότα] τῆ[ς θεᾶς τ]οὺς ἱεροὺς νόμ[ους - - - καθαρῶς κ]αὶ δ̣ικαί[ως]

(The city honoured) Lucius Antonius, son of Marcus, quaestor and propraetor, patron and benefactor of Artemis and of the city, since he has observed the sacred laws of the goddess . . . with pure motives and with uprightness.

This text dates from 49 BC, the year of his presence in Asia as propraetor. The notes to *I.Eph.*, ad loc., give references to other inscriptions which honour him (two each from Pergamon and Thyatira, one from Magnesia on the Sipylos). At *BE* 398 this Ephesian text is compared with Jos., *Ant.* 14.235, where the same Antonius confirms the right of the Jews of Sardes to hold meetings in accordance with their ancestral customs, and to have an actual place for this: σύνοδον ἔχειν ἰδίαν κατὰ τοὺς πατρίους νόμους ἀπ' ἀρχῆς καὶ τόπον ἴδιον.

(A.L. CONNOLLY)

26. The dangers of sea travel

El-Kanaïs in Egypt mid II-I fin. BC
ed. — *OGIS* 73, 74

(a) εὐλόγει τὸν θεόν.
Πτολεμαῖος
Διονυσίου
Ἰουδαῖος.

(b) Θεοῦ εὐλογία·
Θευόδοτος Δωρίωνος
Ἰουδαῖος σωθεὶς ἐκ πε-
λ<άγ>ους.

Two separate inscriptions carved into rock faces to the west of the Temple of Pan near Redesieh in the Thebaid. Both were inscribed within borders measuring 23B x 13H cm. and 40B x 32H cm. respectively.

Bib. — *A. Bernand, *Le Paneion d'El-Kanaïs: les inscriptions grecques* (Leiden, 1972) 34 (pl.34), 42, (pls.37.1, 38.2); Guarducci, *EG* III (Rome, 1974) 205-206 (fig.79).

(a) **Praise (our) God. Ptolemaios the son of Dionysios, a Jew (made this).**
(b) **Praise be to God. Theodotos the son of Dorion, a Jew, saved from the sea (made this).**

These two texts have posed several questions of interpretation. Dittenberger in his *OGIS* text and Guarducci accentuate the first word of (a) as a present indicative, εὐλογεῖ, making Ptolemaios the subject. Guarducci rejects Bernand's accentuation (as above) on two grounds: that the imperative addressed to a passer-by rather than a benediction in Ptolemaios' own mouth seems somewhat strange; and in particular that the names of divinites are elsewhere used as direct objects of εὐλογεῖν, e.g., *CIG* 3 (1877; repr. 1977) 4705b and c in the Addenda on p.1190 (Tell el-Amarna), referring to Pan and Isis respectively. These two examples from *CIG*, however, have the first person singular, εὐλογῶ, and so do not yield exact parallels to (a) above. Bernand for his part supports reading the imperative on the basis of the form of text (b) — an acclamation followed by a record of the worshipper's name — which he would adopt for (a). A sure resolution of this problem is not possible without numerous unambiguous parallels to illustrate the usual intention of such texts. The two texts printed above are dated rather earlier (III BC) in BAGD, svv. εὐλογέω, 1; εὐλογία, 1. On the word εὐλογέω see **56** below.

These two inscriptions are among ninety texts found around the Paneion at El-Kanaïs which have been published or republished by Bernand. Most of the inscriptions are addressed to Πανὶ Εὐόδῳ, Pan of the Successful Journey. In about a dozen of these the worshippers make explicit their belief in Pan's assistance of travellers by testifying that they have been saved from some peril (σωθεὶς ἐκ . . .) while in foreign parts. Most have been saved ἐκ Τρογοδυτῶν, 'from the land of the Trogodytai', a tribe living to the south of Egypt. The saving power of Pan is lauded in a graffito republished as Bernand, no.8 (provenance unknown, late III BC?; pls.23.1, 2; = E. Bernand, *Inscriptions métriques de l'Egypte gréco-romaine* [Leiden, 1969] no.164), of which the first fourteen lines are printed here arranged metrically (the remaining lines are too fragmentary to warrant inclusion). In the version below minor misprints in Bernand's text are silently corrected and some other changes introduced to follow more closely the lettering given in the diplomatic transcription in his pl.23.2.

Π̣ανὶ τόδε εὐάγρῳ καὶ ἐπ[ηκό]ω̣ι̣ | ὃς διέσωισεν
Τρωγο̣δυτῶν με [ἐκ] | γῆς, πολλὰ παθόντα πόνοις
δισσοῖς, σ̣[μυρνο]|φόρου θ' ἱερᾶς Κ̣ολοβῶν τ̣ε̣ ἀπο[. .]ροις.
σώισας τε ἐν π[ε]|λάγει πλαζο̣μένους Ἐ̣ρ̣υ̣θ̣ρ̣[ᾶ̣],
οὖρον νευσὶ με|θῆκας ἑλισσ[ομ]έναις ἐνὶ πόντωι,
συρίζων | λ̣ιγυροῖς πνεύμασιν ἐγ δονάκ[ων]
μέχ̣ρι κ̣α̣ὶ εἰ[ς | λιμ]ένα Πτολεμ̣αΐδος ἤγαγες αὐτὸς
σ̣αῖσι κ[υ|βε]ρνήσας χε̣[ρ]σ̣ὶ̣[ν ἐ]παγροτ[ά]{τα}τα̣ι̣ς̣.
ν[ῦν, | φί]λε, Ἀλεξάνδρο̣υ̣ [σ]ῶισον πόλιν ἥν πο̣[τε] | π̣ρ̣ῶτος
τε[ῦ]ξ[ε]ν̣ [ἐ]π' Αἰγύπτου, κλεινο[τάτην | π]ο̣λ̣ί̣ων,
| [α]ὐ̣δή[σω] δ̣[ὲ] τ̣ὸ σὸν κράτος, ὦ̣ [φ]ίλε [Πάν], | [δ]ι̣α̣σω̣[θ]εὶς
πρὸς Πτολεμαῖ[ον]? . . .

(I dedicate) this to Pan of the Successful Hunt, who listens to prayers, who brought me safe from the land of the Trogodytai when I suffered greatly with double toils, the . . . of the holy myrrh-bearing (land) and the Koloboi. And having saved us when we were wandering on the Red Sea, | and having sent a fair wind for the ships turning round and round on the sea, whistling with shrill breaths from your pipes, you yourself led us right up to the harbour of Ptolemaïs steering with your hands most eager for the hunt. Now, friend, save the city of Alexander which once he, first, | built near Egypt, most famous of cities. And I shall proclaim your power, O friend Pan, because I was brought safely to Ptolemy(?) . . .

With *l*.4 of this text and the traveller's texts above cf. *OGIS* 69 (Koptos, Ptolemaic), θεοῖς μεγάλοις Σαμοθρᾷξι | Ἀπολλώνιος Σωσιβίου | Θηραῖος, ἡγεμὼν τῶν | ἔξω τάξεων, σωθεὶς | ἐγ μεγάλων κινδύνων ἐκ|πλεύσας ἐκ Ἐρυθρᾶς | θαλάσσης, | εὐχήν, 'To the great Samothracian gods, Apollonios of Thera, the son of Sosibios, staff officer, (made this) because he had been saved from great dangers when he sailed out from the Red Sea, (in fulfilment of) a vow'. Theodotos the Jew in text (b) above may also have been saved from disaster on the Red Sea and while passing the Paneion made his dedication, aware that other travellers made similar dedications there. Perhaps his, too, was made in fulfilment of a vow. L. Robert in a dicussion of the maritime activities of the city of Nikomedia, *BCH* 102 (1978) 419-28 (cf. *BE* 552), cites an epitaph, *IG* II/III^2 (1913-40) 8395 (Athens, III/IV), in which a Nikomedian, who had been saved from the sea but later died at Athens, wishes sailors safe returns: σω|ζέστω ἰς πατρί|δαν πᾶς ὁ πλοϊ̣|ζόμενος, 'let everyone who sails the sea reach his native land in safety' (*ll*.8-11, with Robert's readings). For two examples, on the other hand, of curses upon grave disturbers which threaten them with impassibility of the sea, cf. **6** above. For a traveller who died at sea, cf. the metrical epitaph *IG* IX, 1 (1897) 884 (Corcyra, II): τηλόθι γὰρ πάτρης Βειθυνίδος ὤλεσα θυμὸν | ναυτιλίῃ λυγρῇ νηΐ τ' ἐμῇ πίσυνος· | κεῖμαι δ' ἐν Σχερίῃ παρὰ θεῖν' ἁλὸς ἠνεμόεσσαν | ὕστατα λυγρὸν ἐμοὶ δερκόμενος πέλαγος, 'for far from my Bithynian native land I lost my spirit, trusting in my ruin-bringing seamanship and vessel; and I lie at the end in Scheria (i.e., Corcyra) by the windy shore of the sea looking on the waters which were my ruin' (*ll*.7-10).

The Twelfth Satire of Juvenal which describes a near-shipwreck provides literary evidence for such vows and dedications: in *ll*.25-28 the poet mentions the votive tablets which adorn many temples as a result of dangers at sea (cf. Horace, *Odes* 1.5); at *l*.81 the sailors on board the lucky vessel, now safely in the harbour, shave their heads, presumably in fulfilment of vows (cf. Paul at Acts 18.18); and in *ll*.83-92 Juvenal describes the sacrificial rites he performs to celebrate the preservation of his friend. Synesius of Cyrene in his fourth letter (*c*.404) describes a sea voyage which nearly ended in disaster; upon landing safely on a beach he and his fellow travellers sang hymns of gratitude to Providence as usual upon a safe return, as well as giving special thanks for their escape. Further evidence that it was customary to render thanks upon reaching harbour safely is afforded by a (votive?) bas-relief (Rome/Ostia?, *c*.200) which shows thank-offerings being made over the altar on the stern of a trading ship in harbour (L. Casson, *Ships and Seamanship in the Ancient World* [Princeton, 1971] illustr. 144, 146, cf. p.xxiv; = M. Rostovtzeff, *The Social and Economic History of the Roman Empire* [Oxford, 1966] pl.XXVI.1, opp. p.160). In the Mishnah at Avodah Zarah 1.3 the Rabbis prohibit conducting business with gentiles on days of gentile public festivals and private celebrations (such as the day on which a boy cuts off his plait or one is released from prison) including the day on which a gentile returns from a sea voyage (יוֹם שֶׁעָלָה בּוֹ מִן־הַיָּם) because on such a day a gentile was likely to be involved in idolatrous practices. In Jonah 1.16 the sailors offer sacrifices and make vows when the storm ceases.

The evidence of such vows and thank-offerings bears testimony to the difficulties which ancient mariners faced. More specific indications of the potential dangers may be found in documents such as shipping contracts. Such a contract was briefly discussed at *New Docs 1977*, **25**. Another is published as *P.Oxy.Hels.* 37 (13 Sept., 176; pl.25). Both forbid sailing at night and in storms. For more shipping documents which have similar provisions see *P.Köln* 3 (1980) 147 (provenance unknown, time of Augustus); *P.Laur.* 1 (1976) 6 (provenance unknown, reign of Trajan); *P.Iand.* inv. 616 + 245, *edd.* P.J. Sijpesteijn/K. Worp, *ZPE* 20 (1976) 162-65 (Oxyrhynchos, 1 Sept., 221); and *P.Oxy.* 43 (1975) 3111 (15 May, 257). The prohibition against sailing at night was possibly not motivated by fear of collision or grounding in the darkness, but in accordance with ordinances laid down early in the Ptolemaic period and perhaps still in force (see *P.Hib.* 2 [1955] 198.110-22 [III]). In these ordinances the possibility of night voyages on the Nile is demonstrated by the exemption of royal messengers from the prohibition; and the actual danger of night travel, the threat of attack by pirates, is made clear. Night voyages across the sea had been possible even in Homeric times (cf. *Od.* 2.434).

The experience of Paul shows how common it was for calamity to overtake ancient sea travellers — according to his claim in 2 Cor. 11.25 Paul had already been shipwrecked three times before the shipwreck recounted in Acts 27 (though none of these others is mentioned in Acts which does not report all of Paul's journeys in detail; for a summary of his journeys and their approximate distances see E. Haenchen, *The Acts of the Apostles* [ET: Oxford, repr. 1971] 702).

In Acts 27.9-12 it is the possibility of bad weather that is made the cause for the debate whether the ship carrying Paul should chance the short voyage from Kaloi Limenes to Phoinix, the latter being a safer port in which to winter. (Phoinix is to be identified with modern Phineka and not nearby Loutro: see J. Finegan, *The Archeology of the NT* [London, 1981] 196-97). The cause of their apprehension was the lateness of the season. Vegetius says that navigation was thought safe from 27th May to 14th September, that from the latter date until 10th November sailing was uncertain and that from then until 10th March the season was closed (*De re militari* 4.39; cf. Casson, 270). Pliny the Elder, however, says that the sailing season began at the start of Spring, 8th February (*HN* 2.47). The reason for the closure of the sea lanes was not only storms, but also the reduced visibility of the sun and stars (which were essential for navigation) due to persistent cloud cover in these months (cf. Acts 27.20). In the case of Paul's voyage to Rome, the Day of Atonement (10th Tishri in the Jewish calendar) had already passed (*vs*.9). F.F. Bruce (*The Acts of the Apostles* [London, 1952[2]] 455-56) and Haenchen (700 n.1), citing W.P. Workman, *ExpT* 11 (1899-1900) 316-19 (*non vidi*), look for a late dating of the Day of Atonement to complement the evident lateness of the sailing season. The latest incidence of the Day of Atonement between 57 and 62 AD is 5th October in 59, a date settled upon by both scholars. However, Finegan (14) dates this journey to Rome in 56-57, arguing that Festus succeeded Felix as procurator of Judaea in 56 (Acts 24.27), and that Paul was sent to Rome in the summer of that year. In 56 10th Tishri probably fell on 9th October.

The earlier part of Paul's journey, from Caesarea to Knidos, would have been against the northwesterly winds which prevail in the eastern basin of the Mediterranean from June to September (*vss*.4, 7). A similar voyage by Marcus Diaconus from Caesarea to Rhodes (described in *Vita Porphyrii Gazensis* 34) is cited by Casson (289): sailing well his ship covered the 400 nautical miles at an overall speed of 1.7 knots, the normal rate for vessels working against the wind being between a figure just under 2 knots and 2.5 knots (291). Paul's voyage to Knidos would probably have been slower, since they only reached the island 'with difficulty' (μόλις, *vs*.7). The voyage from Kaloi Limenes to Phoinix, which is about 40 nautical miles by the most direct course — see the map in J. Smith, *The Voyage and Shipwreck of St. Paul* (London, 1880[4]) opposite p.97 — would have taken little more than twelve hours at most in the favourable south wind (*vs*.13), calculating from figures presented by Casson. From descriptions of voyages in antiquity the latter estimates that 'ancient vessels averaged between 4 and 6 knots over open water, and slightly less while working through islands or along coasts' (288). The hesitation among those on Paul's ship at making even such a short voyage as this, let alone trying to reach Rome, shows very clearly the limitations of sea travel in antiquity.

In *P.Oxy.Hels.* 37, one of the freight contracts cited above, those hiring the boat address themselves to one Sarapion, ναυκλήρῳ καὶ κυβερνήτῃ πλοίου θαλαμηγοῦ, 'skipper and captain of a *thalamegos* vessel' (*l*.2). *Naukleros* and *kybernetes* occur in Acts 27.11 where they are sometimes translated 'owner' and 'captain' respectively (e.g., *RSV* and *NEB*). Casson translates *kybernetes* by 'captain' and describes him as 'a hired professional who had full authority over the running of the vessel and full command of its crew' (316). A *naukleros*, however, was not necessarily the owner of a vessel; he could be a charterer of a ship, he was 'the man who had the use of a vessel, and thereby the possibility of exploiting it, whether through ownership or charter' (Casson, 315 n.67). The difficulty of translating ναύκληρος is touched upon by both E.R. Bennett (*REG* 93 [1980] 543) and T. Drew-Bear (*CP* 78 [1983] 345-46) in their short reviews of J. Vélissaropoulos, *Les naucléres grecs. Recherches sur les institutions en Grèce et dans l'Orient hellénisé* (Paris, 1980; *non vidi*), a work which traces the role of the *naukleros* in the Greek world from VI BC to III AD. This book is the subject of another more extensive review by H. Hauben in *CE* 58 (1983) 237-47. Vélissaropoulos argues (52; cf. Hauben, 240) that the *naukleros* could be a shipowner who exploited his ship personally, or an agent for the owner, or a charterer of a ship. A *naukleros* could be his own *kybernetes* (Hauben, 240; Casson, 315-16), as in *P.Oxy.Hels.* 37; see also *P.Lond.* 3 (1907) 948.1-2 (no provenance given, 236), κυβερνήτης | ἰδίου πλοίου ἀγωγῆς, 'captain of his own cargo ship', *P.Cairo* inv. 10580 + 10488.7 (= P.J. Sijpesteijn/K.A. Worp, *ZPE* 20 [1976] 157-59, no.1; Hermopolite nome, 343), ναυκληροκυβερνήτην [πλ]οίου ἰδιωτικοῦ, 'shipper-captain of his own ship'; cf. ibid., 160-61, no.3. For a list of vessels from Ptolemaic Egypt with the names of their *naukleroi*, *kybernetai* and owners see H. Hauben, *ZPE* 28 (1978) 99-107. The earliest example of a chartering *naukleros* is *P.Sorb.* inv. 2395, ed. by J. Scherer in *BASP* 15 (1978) 95-101 (Ghoran, probably 272 or 269 BC). For *naukleroi* and *kybernetai* commemorated in epitaphs at Nikomedia, see L. Robert, *BCH* 102 (1978) 419-28.

In Acts 27 it is unknown whether the *naukleros* owns or is chartering the ship, which being corn-laden (*vs*.38) and en route from Alexandria to Italy (*vs*.6) was presumably one of the ships that carried the Egyptian grain tribute. The *naukleros*' standing vis-à-vis the centurion has importance for interpretation of the debate scene (*vss*.9-12). It has frequently been assumed that in this passage Luke portrays the centurion as the one with whom lay the final decision to sail to Phoinix or not; that it was he who decided between the advice of the captain and *naukleros* and that of Paul. W.M. Ramsay, *St. Paul the Traveller and the Roman Citizen* (London, 1897^{3}) 323-26, explains the precedence of the centurion by arguing that the provisioning of Rome, essential to the survival of the emperor, was too important to be left to private enterprise, and so, the ship was not privately owned, but 'belonged to the Alexandrian fleet in the Imperial service' (324). Further, he claims that 'a legionary centurion was certainly of superior rank to the captain of the vessel of the Alexandrian corn fleet' (325). Consequently he translates *kybernetes* and *naukleros* by 'sailing-master' and 'captain'. However, Haenchen (699 n.1) cites the occasion when Claudius offered such terms to private firms of merchants as would induce them to bring grain from Egypt outside the sailing season (Suet., *Claud.* 18). He explains the centurion's authority to decide the ship's course as an invention by Luke (700, 708-11). However, K.L. McKay has suggested to me (*per litt.*) the possibility that the decision made by the centurion was not whether to sail or not, but whether he and those under his command would stay on board if the ship set sail.

Whatever the centurion's status on board may have been, there is no doubt that the grain ships plying between Alexandria and Rome did sail in a fleet, as is shown by *IG* XIV (1890) 918 (Ostia, reign of Commodus), ὑπὲρ σωτηρίας καὶ διαμονῆς | τοῦ κυρίου αὐτοκράτορος [[Κομμόδου Σεβαστοῦ]] |οἱ ναύκληροι τοῦ πορευτικοῦ 'Αλεξανδρείνου στόλου, 'For the preservation and continuance of our lord Imperator Commodus Augustus the *naukleroi* of the Alexandrian corn fleet (made this dedication)', in which the emperor's name has been erased and later reinscribed. Casson cites other texts which imply the existence of a fleet (297 n.2), in particular *P.Oxy.* 14 (1920) 1763.3-5 (III), οὔπω μέχρι σήμερον τὰ πλοῖα τῆς ἀννώνας ἐξῆλθεν, 'not until today did the ships carrying the grain tribute depart'. For details about the sailing schedule of the grain ships on this route and the timing of the voyage of Paul's vessel see Casson, 297-99.

In *P.Oxy.Hels.* 37 the hirers of the vessel allow Sarapion the *naukleros* to contravene the conditions regarding safe handling of the ship, if there should occur [ἀπὸ Διὸς βί]ας αἴτιόν τι, 'some cause resulting from a violent act of Zeus (i.e., an 'act of God'; *l.*7), namely fire from the shore, stormy weather or an attack by criminals. The restoration here is made on the basis of *P.Laur.* 1 (1976) 6.9-10, ἐὰν μή τις κ[ίνδυνος ἢ βλάβος - - -] | γένηται ἤτοι ἀπὸ Διὸς βίας αλ[, 'unless some [danger or damage - - -] occurs either resulting from a violent act of Zeus . . .'. With this compare *P.Köln* 3 (1980) 147.5-6, πλὴν ἐὰν μή τι βίαιον ἐκ θεοῦ | γ[έ]νη[τ]αι ('unless some violent act of God occurs'), and χωρὶς θεοῦ βίας ('apart from a violent act of God') in *P.Oxy.* 22 (1954) 2347.11 (a deed of surety relating to a shipper; 362). On *vis maior* in Graeco-Roman law see C.H. Brecht, *Zur Haftung der Schiffer im antiken Recht* (Munich, 1962) — *non vidi* — reviewed by L. Casson, *AJP* 86 (1965) 330-32 and B.R. Rees, *JHS* 84 (1964) 186-87; see also A. Meyer-Termeer, *Die Haftung der Schiffer im griechischen und römischen Recht* (Zutphen, 1978).

(A.L. CONNOLLY)

27. Jupiter Dolichenus and religious life in the Roman army

Rome 161-80

ed. — *CIL* VI, 4.2 (1902) 31187

M(arcus) Ulp(ius) Cresimu[s, sa]cer(dos) I[ovis Dolicheni],
natione Parth-
us et ex gener-
osis Mena, tur(ma)
Issii,
fecit pro salu-
te imp(eratorum) et sing(ularium)
Aug(ustorum) et omni-
bus amici[s]
mei[s].
Q(uintus) Mar-
cius Ar-
temido-
rus
- - - templa

Marble plaque (66B x 59H cm.) with a bas-relief featuring Apollo and Artemis, found almost certainly on the Caelian Hill; the text is in the left field, except for the last word, which is in the right field immediately below the missing upper right part of the plaque.

Bib. — *AE* (1971) 21; *Speidel, *Dolichenus* 12-14, no.15 (pl.1), with previous bib. given in the notes.

Marcus Ulpius Cresimus, priest of Jupiter Dolichenus, Parthian by race and from the clan of the Mena, in the squadron |of Issius, made this for the welfare of the emperors and of the imperial cavalry guards and for all my friends. | Quintus Marcius Artemidorus . . . temples.

Speidel's careful exegesis of this text and its associated visual images in his excellent study of Jupiter Dolichenus in the Roman army is significant in several ways. First, he elicits from its iconography something of the theology of the religion to show that it was no simple soldier's religion. Secondly, he shows that this text, as well as several others hitherto assigned to late III, belong to an earlier period (this one to 161-169 or 174-180) and thus should no longer be used to elucidate the decline of Dolichenus. Thirdly, this text almost certainly establishes that a priest of Dolichenus could simultaneously be a serving soldier. Ex-soldiers certainly were priests (Speidel, no.29). A serving soldier *candidatus* (aspirant) may have belonged to the grade of Dolichene *candidati* aspiring to the priesthood (Speidel, no.26, despite his revised inclination to see him as a *candidatus* for a military rank, *PACA* 112 [1982] 212-13). Other priests were closely associated with military units (Speidel, nos. 27, 28), but they do not call themselves soldiers. The soldier-priest Cresimus makes it more likely that they were.

The priesthood was central to the life and the success of this religion, judging from the high number of Dolichene *sacerdotes* attested in inscriptions, both as a proportion of all Dolichenic texts and in comparison with the number in other cults. The exact nature of this priesthood is obscure; a study of priesthoods in general in the Roman world of the middle empire remains a major desideratum. The Dolichene priesthood may have had both professional and status elements. Several communities are known to have had two, three or even four priests (P. Selem, *Les religions orientales dans la Pannonie romaine* [*EPRO* 85; Leiden, 1980] 242); some have semitic or theophoric names and others have neutral Graeco-Roman names (A. Mocsy, *ACD* 20 [1984] 61-69), perhaps roughly correlating with priests of different origin and function. Although not all priests came from the cult centre in Commagenian Doliche (*contra,* I. Toth, *Studium* 2 [1971] 23-28), some had links to it, by origin, contact and perhaps training. A category of professional priests linked to its eponymous centre and to each other might explain its relatively consistent iconography, its missionary activities (L. Balla, *ACD* 19 [1984] 91-98), and its fading away with the destruction of Doliche by the Persians in the 250s. Some priests were certainly prepared locally, as the presence of a *pater candidatorum* and *candidati huius loci* (aspirants of this place) in some communities affirm, and as the Parthian Cresimus exemplifies. Such a category of priest accords with the more traditional status-achieving roles of western priesthoods. A priesthood encompassing such different strengths may well underlie much of the success of the religion. So did the linking of priests of different communities, witnessed by the joint dedication of the priests of a Roman province (*CIL* III, 1 [1873] 3343).

There were several types of priests in later imperial army units, where once there were none. There were priests who coincidentally were soldiers (e.g., *CIL* VI, 4.2 [1902] 30685). The existence of serving soldiers as priests extends the potential for their cults in the army. The ancestral and personal cults of individuals had traditionally been respected and had no doubt often spread through personal contact in the small social and tactical groupings of the military units. Soldier-priests represent a new and sharper focus for such spread of religions by personal contact. How the army or the religious community coped with the potential conflict of authority in having ordinary soldiers as priests and officers as mere adherents, if this was allowed to arise, would be worth knowing. That there could never be Christian soldier-priests was one of the things on which all Christians seem to have agreed. Secondly, there were priests of military units. Although traditionally the officers of the unit were responsible for religion in the army, some units at least also had official priests by 239, when the cohort at Dura had one (*P.Dura* [1959] 89). In Egypt in 323 each of the two Phoenician legions and a cavalry unit had a priest; they joined with a high priest (presumably of the whole detachment) in a dedication to Emesene deities (SB 1 [1915] 4223; cf. *ILS* II, 2.8882). The implications of the creation of such a priesthood need study; equally, of its continuation or its disappearance under the early Christian emperors (the latter should not be taken for granted). Thirdly, there were also, attached in some unclear way to military units, priests of specific cults, not of the units as a whole. A Dolichene priest set up a dedication at Rigomagus in Lower Germany in 250 for the cavalrymen (i.e., a subgroup) of *cohors I Flavia*; another priest *ad leg*(*ionem*) *s*(*upra*) *s*(*cripta*), variously interpreted as attached to the named legion (*XIII Gemina*) or as sited at the legion, set one up at Apulum in Dacia (Speidel, nos. 27, 28). It is possible that these men were priests of exclusively military Dolichene communities, particularly if Dolichene altars were set up within military camps, as seems to have happened at the Castellum Obernburg (Speidel, no.7 with n.160 on p.50) and at Sarmizegetusa (A. Popa/I. Berciu, *Le culte de Jupiter Dolichenus dans la Dacie romaine* [*EPRO* 69; Leiden, 1978] 62). But most Dolichene communities included soldiers, ex-soldiers and civilians from the area, particularly the relatives of soldiers, including women, noted in frontier dedications; the integration of military and civilian social formations and lives is a hallmark of frontier societies from later II, and common religious experience was a major linking factor. In what capacity and when Christian priests were attached to military units are questions buried in silence, but they may have acted as military chaplains earlier than their first appearance in the fifth century led A.H.M.Jones, *HTR* 46 (1953) 239-40, to suggest.

Speidel's book, which considers many other issues and documents, stimulates a stocktaking of existing approaches and views on the religious life of the Roman army. Oddly, the religion of the soldiers is diverted to the periphery of synthetic studies of the transformation of the Roman world. The army, though always given a central role in the political aspects of that transformation, rates only passing mention in explanations of its socio-cultural aspects, whether these use the older, simple crisis-response models, such as E.R. Dodds, *Pagan and Christian in an Age of Anxiety* (Cambridge, 1965) or the newer, more complex models, such as P. Brown, *The Making of Late Antiquity* (Cambridge [Mass.], 1978). That may be the lasting legacy of M. Rostovtzeff, *The Social and Economic History of the Roman Empire* (Oxford, 1957[2]); all these authors see the basic transformation in largely urban perspectives, and though rejecting his soldier-peasant versus city model in its crudest form, they seem to accept that the soldier and the city are at separate poles. Thus the soldier and his religious life are marginalised, despite his geographic and social mobility, his spreading of his ideology into all aspects of the military and civil service (*militia*) and his orchestration of so much of that transformation at both imperial and local level. Detailed study of the soldier's religion amid his social contacts might return him to the more central position in the story he deserves.

Two seminal works from the turn of the century continue to inform the direction of most studies: for the general framework, A.von Domaszewski, 'Die Religionen des römischen Heeres', *West-deutsche Zeitschrift für Geschichte und Kunst* 14 (1895) 1-124, reprinted in *Aufsätze zur römischen Heeresgeschichte* (Darmstadt, 1972) 81-209; for Christianity, A. von Harnack, *Militia Christi. The Christian Religion and the Military in the First Three Centuries* (1905; ET: Philadelphia, 1981). Recent survey articles in *ANRW* have updated each. E. Birley, *ANRW* II,16.2 (1978) 1506-41, uses his unrivalled knowledge of military documents to support or modify Domaszewski's views. J. Helgeland, *ibid.*, 1470-1505, applies useful anthropological concepts to Roman army religion, though his documentary knowledge is outmoded and his conclusions thus unsafe. Helgeland, *ANRW* II,23.1 (1979) 724-834, L.J. Swift, *ibid.*, 835-68, and J. Helgeland/R.J. Daly/J.P. Burns, *Christians and the Military. The Early Experience* (Philadelphia, 1985), though good surveys of the essential, but now psittacine and sterile debate about Christian attitudes to war, violence and military service, reflect the general failure to use documentary material and insights on military processes to give context to the literary sources.

Progress is afoot, with the oriental cults leading the way. The series *Etudes préliminaires aux religions orientales dans l'empire romain* (=*EPRO*) has collected, categorised by cult or by region, and interpreted documents on different cults in the Roman world. Over one hundred volumes have already appeared; more are promised. Soldiers figure, more or less, in most of these studies (on Mithras, Isis, Sabazios, Cybele, Men, Sol Invictus, etc. — every cult had its chance in the Roman army; only the fittest survived). But Speidel's book on Dolichenus alone focuses primarily on the military. Two brief studies on Mithraism are methodologically suggestive in using inscriptions to relate the religious life of soldiers to the totality of their lives: R.L. Gordon, *Religio* 2 (1972) 92-121, and C.M. Daniels in J.R. Hinnells (ed.), *Mithraic Studies. Proceedings of the First Congress of Mithraic Studies, Manchester,* 1971 (Manchester, 1975) II.249-74. There is little comparable collection of documents on non-oriental cults either by cult or by region (except for Britain, e.g., E. Birley, *ANRW* II,18.1 [1986] 3-112). Though quantitatively and, for some purposes, qualitatively these 'Roman' and local cults are much more important than oriental ones, the agenda of oriental superiority set by Franz Cumont seems to have left its indirect legacy even among those most critical of his ideas and his methods (cf. **125** below). Perhaps there are just too many documents.

Christianity, contrarily, has had too few, though they are accumulating — enough for a catalogue. The most progressive studies of Christians and the Roman army have proceeded via contextual studies of literary sources, particularly hagiographies, in their local socio-cultural ambience, e.g., P. Siniscalco, *Massimiliano: un obiettore di coscienza del tardo impero. Studi sulla 'Passio S. Maximiliani'* (Turin, 1974) or, less substantially, D. van Berchem, *Stud.Clas.* 24 (1986) 156-63, on Christians in the imperial guard as evidenced by *P.Bodmer* 28 (1984). Military imagery , both literary (again) and visual, is also providing more insights. All this would gain much by the matching of developments in Roman military life both to the Christian documents, old and new, and to the partisan literary material. Both the continuities and the changes of military life are constantly being reviewed by specialist military historians, whose studies are being made accessible in a useful series called *Mavors*; already published are M.P. Speidel, *Roman Army Studies* (Leiden, 1984) and J.P. Gilliam, *Roman Army Papers* (1986) and there are more volumes awaiting publication. No-one has applied this expertise to Christians in the Roman army. Speidel's study of Dolichenus, like his adventurous *Mithras-Orion* (*EPRO* 81; Leiden, 1980) and the Mithraic studies of Gordon and of Daniels noted above, offers information, ideas and possible models and analogies for such studies.

Dolichenus can lead the way. The religion is well served by the basic collection of documents in P. Merlat, *Répertoire des inscriptions et monuments figurés du culte de Jupiter Dolichenus* (Paris, 1951) and by a number of regional collections in the *EPRO* series; a new corpus of Dolichene texts and monuments by E. Schwertheim is soon to be published. Dolichene documents are more strongly correlated with the military presence than those of any other cult. The great majority of finds associated with it occur on the British, Rhine, Danube and African military zones; many of the rest, occurring in non-military areas south of the Danube, Italy and Rome, are also explicitly military in connection. Using another index, 97 out of 254 inscriptions (on Speidel's count) mention officers, soldiers, veterans or military units explicitly; other inscriptions, either incomplete or eschewing specific professional details, would swell the numbers if such details were known. Dolichenus clearly had great appeal in a military environment, but it is simplistic to see him as a merely military god. He also appears in civilian contexts and Speidel shows the essential comparability of military and civilian Dolichenic material, most pointedly through comparison of the Dolichene shrines at Rome, the military one on the Caelian and the civilian one on the Aventine. Indeed, his distinction may be too rigid, as the presence of a veteran in the Aventine community (Merlat, no.221) alongside the purely civilian members hints. A major catalytic change in military life, particularly from mid-II, was the greater opening up of its ideally closed society to outside contacts and values. It is better to view Dolichenus as appealing to a particular segment of society in both its military and its civilian guises. Mithraism would seem to offer a paradigm, but Dolichenus does not offer the literary information which allowed Gordon to interpret the social catchment of Mithraism (which seems similar to that of Dolichenus) in terms of its theology, theodicy, ritual and social organisation. Despite all this, the appeal of Dolichenus to the military remains, and its military and quasi-military aspects may have had more impact on its distinctive spread in the army than Speidel would allow. While military dress may largely have been a continuation of a Hellenistic mode of representing an oriental deity, there were less militaristic conventions for representing such a deity, as used in Mithraism; the choice of a military option by Dolichenus was not without meaning. Cult standards, too, may have been traditional in oriental cults, but it is forced not to regard their frame of reference in military contexts as the military standards.

Again, in a military environment Victoria (whether implying mundane or cosmic victory) had a particular appeal beyond that of the Victoria who was a concomitant deity in cults and dedications outside the military context. The choice and development of a fairly simple military imagery furthered the appeal of Dolichenus to the military without alienating it from civilians. Christianity, too, eventually, developed the military imagery without which its appeal to soldiers remained limited, but it was a long process, slowed down by the ambivalence in Christian attitudes to war and military service. A study of its development in the third to the fifth century would index much of the changing values of that period.

The reasons for the success of Dolichenus are to be sought in public attitudes, in the origins and movements of its adherents, and in the nature of the cult (both in its religious aspects and as a social formation).

Public support

Speidel shows that there is no solid foundation for the widely-held view that imperial directives or support underlay the late-II/early-III surge of Dolichene material. There is no public recognition of the religion by the central organs of state or by the imperial house (no coin representations, no personal imperial dedications, no iconographic assimilation of distinctive traits by the emperors). Such support was clearly not necessary for a religion to flourish. Support or opposition, where it did exist (as did both at various times for Christianity), had some, unquantifiable impact, but more important was public recognition at the local level. From the time of Hadrian, whose governor in Africa dedicated a temple to Jupiter Optimus Maximus Dolichenus near the legionary camp at Lambaesis (Speidel, no.1), governors, military commanders down the line, municipal elites and the paramilitary urban youth groups (*iuventus*; Merlat, no.121, also Hadrianic) show public recognition of the religion. Such local actions of support were not against imperial policy. The dedications come from the ruling elite and the god is not simply Jupiter, but Jupiter Optimus Maximus, the supreme deity of the Roman state and its army. There is a formulaic similarity between some dedications and those set up to Jupiter Optimus Maximus at the annual *nuncupatio votorum* of 3rd January, when military units ritually buried the old altars to Jupiter and set up new ones. It may be that Hadrian, *explorator omnium curiositatum* (Tert., *Apol.* 5.7) and recognised innovator in military discipline, took steps to lift existing constraints on such quasi-institutional religious behaviour in the light of the current composition and needs of his military forces. The first reliably dated Mithraic document also comes from a Hadrianic governor, in Moesia Inferior (M.J. Vermaseren, *Corpus inscriptionum et monumentorum religionis Mithriacae* [2 vols; The Hague, 1956, 1960] II.2296). The local level was the context in which this initiative was worked out. Even in such a universalist institution as the Roman army, particularly when its exclusiveness was breaking down, local socio-political structures were more important in determining living practices than imperial fiat.

Adherents

All are agreed on the basic model for the spread of Dolichenus along the trading/military routes of the Roman empire. The means of that spread are seen variously: priests, traders, or soldiers in the Roman army (through the recruitment of Dolichene adherents into Roman military units and/or their transfer to new units or camps). But the initial penetration into the Roman army in the pre-Hadrianic period can hardly have been by traders (even though economic factors tended to link them to soldiers rather than to separate the two) or by priests (though their presence was necessary for the communities becoming viable and permanent); only soldiers could penetrate this still relatively closed society from the outside.

There has been significant recent re-evaluation of each of the possible mechanisms of this. Speidel cautions (7) against the easy acceptance of an earlier hypothesis that the cult was originally spread by Commagenian soldiers in the Commagenian auxiliary units distributed in various armies around the empire. There is no Dolichene monument from the sites where the seven known units originally served. For all that is known, few of these Commagenians adhered to Dolichenus, who was the patrial god of only one of the Commagenian cities and whose cult may not have been widely spread in neighbouring areas when the auxiliary units were recruited in mid-I. Yet the fact that *cohors II Flavia Commagenorum* dedicated to Dolichenus at its much later site, Micia in Dacia (Speidel, no.11), may indicate that it retained a tradition of worship of Dolichenus, though its recruits were probably now essentially the localised ones of most such *auxilia*. Speidel may underestimate the role of such units as models and repositories of adherents.

Doubts are being cast on some long-held views on the nature of Roman recruitment, with implications for the spread of religious cults. Against the conventional wisdom that most recruits in the first three centuries AD were volunteers, P.A. Brunt, *SCI* 1 (1974) 90-115, has argued persuasively that most were conscripts, except for a period in early-III. G.R. Watson, *PACA* 16 (1982) 46-50, has counterargued that the proportion of volunteers was much increased by the development of local recruiting and permanent camps, both abating the great bugbear of military service, being sent far from home. That may be true, but second- and third-century recruits from Anatolia and Asia Minor (and probably from the urbanised east in general — like Christianity, the religion of Dolichenus was not primarily a rural one) continued to be sent to distant military units in the East and on the lower and middle Danube, as recent epigraphical work by Speidel, S. Mitchell, T. Drew Bear and others has shown, much of it reported in S. Mitchell (ed.), *Acta of the 1981 Asia Minor Limes Congress* (Oxford, 1983). On Watson's reasoning, and in all probability, they were conscripts; they were also from areas where the religion of Dolichenus may be presumed to have spread. Such eastern conscription may underlie the significant presence of Dolichenes in the Danubian Roman army *c.*150-250. Though onomastic argument is fraught with insecure assumptions (and soldiers were particularly prone to change of name on enlistment), and though Dolichenes do not give their origin often enough for useful quantitative analysis, the large proportion of Greek and oriental names among Dolichene soldiers suggests that many brought their religion with them from the urbanised cities of the East. Conscription from the East, granted Christian objections to the military service and the major areas of Christian spread, also explains better the significant presence of Christian soldiers in later-II, attested by Bishop Apolinarius' second-century attribution of the miracle of the Thundering legion to their prayers (Eus., *HE* 5.5) and Tertullian's more general apologetics. The names of Christian soldiers are unavailable for this period and their origins speculative, but the career of Aurelius Gaius in later-III, recruited from Pessinus and originally sent to the lower Danube, conforms to the earlier pattern (T. Drew-Bear in *La géographie administrative et politique d'Alexandre à Mahomet* [*Université des Sciences Humaines de Strasbourg, Travaux du Centre de Recherche sur le Proche-Orient et la Grèce Antiques* 6; Leiden, 1981] 93-141; cf. *AE* [1981] 777).

The recruitment of Dolichenes into military units would not seem enough to explain by itself the spread of the religion to the far western provinces, for epigraphy shows that units west of Pannonia did not receive eastern recruits. Cross-postings may be important here. A tendency to stress the more static posture of Roman military units and strategies from the time of Hadrian has been overdone. Though permanent transfer of units had virtually ceased and local recruiting was more important, there was still much movement of individuals and, in expeditionary armies, of bodies of troops, some of them transferred to different units, central or provincial, or areas.

Centurions in particular were regularly transferred between units and these officers are frequently noted in Dolichene inscriptions. If they were largely adherents of Dolichenus, a conclusion that is not always self-evident as they often acted on behalf of their military units, that will have been a most significant factor in the spread of the religion, both within the units (at the least, the lifestyle of officers has an exemplary effect on soldiers) and across the empire. There is also a remarkably high proportion of Christian centurions among the few inscriptions of clearly Christian soldiers (see the list in J.-M. Hornus, *It Is Not Lawful For Me To Fight* (Scottdale, 1980, translation of the revised 1960 French edition) 118-122 — a partisan book, but one of the few on the subject recognising the importance of documents). The fates of the would-be centurion, Marinus, in the 260s at Antioch and of the centurion Marcellus in the 290s in Africa show the difficulties of being both an officer and a Christian: H. Musurillo, *The Acts of the Christian Martyrs* (Oxford, 1972), nos. 16, 18. If it was perhaps only from mid-III that Christian centurionates became viable (paradoxically, the creation of official priests of units may have helped here), then the presence of Christian, as of Dolichene, centurions, was central to the spread of their cults. It was not, however, only centurions who show the geographic and social mobility of Christian soldiers in later-III, for both documentary and hagiographic sources show a relatively high proportion of protectors, praetorians and soldiers in the elite field armies. The fact that so many Christians served in the military elite is indicative of the increasing accommodation of Christian and Roman and gives credence to the belief of Eusebius (*HE* 8.4) that Christian soldiers served for the glory and the material gain. But such ambitions did not prevent their becoming a means of spreading the Christian religion.

Cultic nature and social formation.

The religion of Dolichenus was suited, probably tailored, to the role of a conserving god of the Roman ruling order and those who wished to belong to it, at either imperial or local level. Its stress in the Roman world, whose rulers it had long courted, to judge from the seal of the city of Doliche with its god stretching his hands to Rome's representative, was on its Graeco-Roman rather than its oriental aspects (cf. M. Hörig, *ANRW* II,17.4 [1984] 2142). Dolichenus was an energetic, worldly god, about whom there developed a theology — extrapolated from its now somewhat opaque iconography by Speidel — which incorporated many of the traditional deities of Graeco-Roman religion: Apollo, Artemis, Sol, Luna, Castor, Polydeuces/Pollux, and above all Juno and Jupiter Optimus Maximus. The connection with Jupiter is vital, granted the surge in dedications, both official and private, to this god during II/III (cf. J.R. Fears, *ANRW* II,17.1 [1981] 100-107). Dolichenus was also a most amiable god, open to interaction with a variety of other personal cults not apparently included in its own theology; dedications and gift-offerings frequently involve deities who are Graeco-Roman (as Asclepius) or oriental (as Dea Syria) or western (as Brigantia). It is overly cynical to see this as an attempt via an 'omnium-gatherum' religion to maximise its numbers, especially in an attempt to redress falling popularity in III (the material on which this latter qualification depends are more correctly placed in their proper earlier context by Speidel). Dolichene priests were hardly responsible for Asclepius advising a veteran to make a dedication to Dolichenus (*CIL* III, 1 [1873] 1614). Dolichene openness to such a range of other cults may have been especially significant to individuals in the multicultural Roman army. It was a perfect catalyst of Romanisation (understood as the spread of the values of the dominant Graeco-Roman culture) within non-Roman military units, whether such was a conscious policy of the state (so A.S. Hoey, *TAPA* 70 [1939] 456-81) or not (so A.D. Nock, *HTR* 45 [1952] 187-252). Not only did it have no obvious conflict with the practices, ceremonial, ideology or functions of Roman army religion, but it became intricately and publicly involved in that religion. There are the many dedications by military officers on behalf of units or parts of units, the use of *Jupiter Dolichenus sanctus* as a military password at Dura (R.O. Fink, *Roman Military Records on Papyrus* [Cleveland, 1971] 50.1, 13), the attachment of priests to units. All this, together with the increasing probability that there were shrines of Dolichenus and of other oriental cults within the 'sacred space' of the camps (Speidel, 50 n.160, noting a projected new study by J.P. Gilliam) requires modification of Hoey's rigid dichotomy (see the Hoey-Nock debate mentioned above) between an exclusive official Roman army religion within the camps and private religions worshipped outside. Official Roman army religion was no more static or exclusive than the ever-changing official religion of the Roman state. Some cults fitted easily and better its unchanging functional parameters. Dolichenus was one of them.

Christianity was not, at least not before Constantine. How, and to what extent, it fitted into Roman army religion under Constantine and his successors is a complex and critical issue which seems to have engaged minimal attention. The emperor who formed a garrison on the road from Jerusalem to Jericho for the protection of travellers and manned it with a *cohors I Salutaria* (Eus., *Onomast.* 24.10; cf. *Notitia Dignitatum or.* 34.48) was ignorant neither of the NT nor of the means and importance of giving military service a Christian face; so, too, with the *labarum* and much else. He was the same emperor who not only left his barbarian units their pre-Christian emblems, but publicised them (A. Alföldi, *DOP* 13 [1959] 169-84). The way in which emperors solved such ambiguities would provide another useful index of changing cultural values. Until then, however, Christianity, in its unequivocal rejection of all other gods and in its more ambivalent, but often dissociative, attitudes to aspects of Roman army religion, offered a contrast. Christian soldiers served despite the basic thrust of their religion rather than because of it. Those who served did so despite the objections of others to the acceptance of homicide implicit in military service, though this was an objection that was clearly not normative either before or after Constantine. They also served despite the pagan cultic practices embedded in Roman army religion. Partly that was made possible because Roman army religion did not require personal participation, and even Tertullian accepts (*de Idol.*16) that pagan ceremonial did not, by itself and absolutely, rule out public service. Roman army religion was intended by and large to provide cohesion within the units, not to display their disunities. Particularities were accepted or winked at. Mithraists were allowed not to wear crowns (because they were crowned only by Mithras — an ambiguity in their dual relationship to Mithras and to Caesar that is perhaps too readily passed over). Christians might generally have availed themselves of such army concessions, tacit or explicit, to ethnic and religious sensibilities. They were not proof against the petty jealousies of other soldiers or other pressures, either local or from central directive, which at times required a more obvious conformity.

Dolichenus' communal organisation was also important to its success, particularly in frontier societies. Social formations were constantly being revamped in the Roman world. In military units life had traditionally been focussed on a number of relatively small groupings, especially the *contubernium* and the *centuria/turma*. The proliferation of *scholae* of all military status grades above the ordinary soldier from later II represented a regrouping of living patterns; but it provided nothing for the ordinary soldier and it ignored the family and other civilian attachments which increasing territorialisation of military units had provided for soldiers in the century before Septimius legitimised such family life. Traditional civilian social units were also undergoing disintegration; a *collegium* at Alburnus Maior in Dacia was being wound up in 167 for lack of interest and members, which had dropped from fifty-four to seventeen (*ILS* II, 2.7215a). Not all communal religions filled these gaps. Mithraism and Dolichenus did, but Mithraism had no place for women, who figure so prominently in the religion of Dolichenus; how exactly they were involved is obscure. In Christianity, too, communal aspects were integral to its success, but neither literary nor archaeological evidence lets us know whether there were Christian churches as distinct from individual Christians in frontier areas. If, to make a reasonable assumption, the frontiers were not a prime target for the founding of Christian communities, then their absence will have denied the religion one of its major means of spread as well as jeopardising the continued adherence of individual Christians. If, further, the existence of churches in areas of military settlement (and the general opening of the army as well as Christianity to the world) was a precondition for the increase of Christian soldiers, that would accord with two features of the geographical dispersion of Christian soldiers in the later third-century. They cluster by service in north Africa, Egypt, and the East (areas where Christianity had spread most widely, perhaps even to the rural and military fringes of society) and on the Danube (linked geographically and economically to the East and an obvious area for missionary zeal); contemporary churches are likely in these areas. Christian soldiers also cluster in the elite field units greatly increased in numbers by the third-century structural changes to the Roman army and often garrisoned in great and small cities around the Empire: Rome, Verona, Poetovio, Aquileia, Milan, Anchialus, Antioch are instances. Soldiers based in cities are notoriously less encased in their own traditions, more open to urban influences; one such in many of these cities was a strong Christian community. The close attachment of the would-be centurion Marinus to the Christian ecclesiastical hierarchy at Antioch is suggestive (Musurillo, no.16). Billetting, both of Christian soldiers in non-Christian homes and non-Christian soldiers in Christian homes, may also have effected religious change.

The religion of Dolichenus faded into insignificance in the Roman army, as elsewhere, from mid-III; its latest evidence in a military context is from 253, in a civilian context from the reign of Gallienus (Speidel, 73 no.51). Admittedly, inscriptions of all kinds drop off from this date; but this was a god who had hitherto required public recognition of his adherents, as the multitude of dedications on his specific prompting attests. Archaeology signals the violent destruction of Dolichene sanctuaries on the Rhine and Danube under Maximinus (235-238), and the failure of its adherents to recover their cult objects or to rebuild their sanctuaries. All this hints at weakening Dolichene communities in certain areas and eventually everywhere; yet the communal aspect was crucial to its continued success. The reasons for its decline should relate to the reasons for its success. The destruction of the sanctuaries, particularly if ordered or allowed by the central or local authorities, as seems agreed, signified the demise of its alliance with the Roman ruling order; also the end of any acceptable replication model. Although some Dolichene shrines were built or restored in other areas in the next twenty years and the concern of votives continued to be the well-being of the imperial house, the damage had been done. A *conservator*-god who cannot protect his own is an easily discredited scapegoat in times of crisis; it was even worse when he could not protect his cult centre at Dolichenus from destruction by the Persians in the 250s. In losing its centre, the religion also lost the focus for its professional priesthood. In the competition for religious allegiance in the cities of the East, from which so many Dolichene adherents had spread their religion, all this weighed the odds in favour of other cults, especially Christianity. When the empire was reunited under Aurelian in the 270s, it was another oriental god, Sol Invictus, who was taken up as the conserving god of the Roman army and state, in a way that Dolichenus had never been, but the future of Rome, both army and state, lay not with him, but with the God of the Christians. Although the decline of Dolichenus in the army correlates in time with the rising visibility of Christian soldiers, the two facts seem to be more coincidental than cause and effect.

(P.M. BRENNAN)

28. Giving thanks to Artemis

Ephesos — Imperial period

ed.pr. — H. Engelmann/D. Knibbe, *JÖAI* 52 (1978-80) *Hauptblatt* 50 nos.92-93

εὐχαριστῶ σοι, κυρία Ἄρτεμι,
Σέξστος Πομπήιος Εὐτύχης φιλοσέ-
βαστος νεοποιὸς αὐθαίρετος σὺν καὶ Αὔγῃ
τῇ θυγατρί μου καὶ Οὐλπίᾳ Ἀρτεμιδώρᾳ
καὶ τῷ συνμήνῳ μου Ἡλιοδώρῳ Φιλίππου
δίς.
εὐχαριστῶ σοι, κυρία Ἄρτεμι, Ἡλιόδωρος
[Φ]ιλίππου δὶς ν̣[εοποιὸς αὐθαίρετος σὺν]
[κ]αὶ Ἡλιοδώρῳ [τῷ υἱῷ μου καὶ - - - Ἀ-]
π̣ολλωνίου κ̣[αὶ - - -]
Σ̣τράτωνι .[- - -]
. πο̣ν̣ .[- - -

Inscribed on the same stone is an unrelated text, *I.Eph.* II.506 (114/5), in which a certain Capitolinus and his son signal their provision of a statue group.
Bib. — *I.Eph.* III.961.

I give thanks to you, lady Artemis, (I) Sextus Pompeius Eutyches, loyal to the emperor, voluntary *neopoios*, together with Auge my daughter and Ulpia Artemidora | and my colleague Heliodoros son of Philippos and grandson of Philippos.
I give thanks to you, lady Artemis, (I) Heliodoros son of Philippos and grandson of Philippos, [voluntary *neopoios* together with] Heliodoros [my son and - - -] | son of Apollonios - - -

In this sequential pair of inscriptions two men with members of their respective families offer public thanks to Artemis. While in origin the *neopoioi* were sacred officials, during the Imperial period their duties had broadened to include civic functions. They are attested in varying numbers in several cities of Asia Minor. At Ephesos they constituted a board of management — cf. *l.*5 in the text above — responsible for the upkeep of the temple of Artemis. Since it was usual to record public documents on temple walls, their duties included responsiblity for these (e.g., decrees awarding citizenship, gifts of land to the Artemision to aid its upkeep). On these officials see D. Magie, *Roman Rule in Asia Minor to the end of the Third Century after Christ* (2 vols; Princeton, 1950) I.60 with n.31 at II.847-48; and more briefly, A.N. Sherwin-White, *Roman Society and Roman Law in the NT* (Oxford, 1963; repr. Ann Arbor, 1978) 90-91 (on the unlikelihood that Demetrios the silversmith in Acts 19.24 was a νεοποιός; on this, see further **1**, above).

In *l.*3 of the inscription Eutyches describes himself as a νεοποιὸς αὐθαίρετος. This adjective appears in several other *I.Eph.* texts, sometimes largely or wholly restored (as here at *l.*8). In III.653 we have a fragmentary statue base inscription, perhaps of Hadrianic date, honouring Tib. Claudius Zenon, twice asiarch: αὐθαίρετον occurs in *l.*3 but virtually all the rest of the line is lost. The adjective seems especially associated at Ephesos with *neopoioi*, however: *I.Eph.* III.950 (II^1(?)), 957.12 (late II(?)), 959.4-5 (Imperial), 963.3 (Imperial; almost entirely restored),

V.1579B.3-4 (III?), VI.2926.1-2 (Imperial; almost entirely restored), VII, 1.3263 (III?). This last item is an honorific statue base for Aur. Salluvius Timotheus τὸν εὐσεβῆ καὶ αὐθαίρετον | νεοποιὸν τῆς κυρίας ἡμῶν [['Αρ]]|[[τέμιδος]], 'the pious and voluntary *neopoios* of our lady Artemis' (*ll.*6-8; for the erasure of the goddess' name here, probably by Christians at a later date, cf. **125** below). Αὐθαίρετος is used in the NT only by Paul, at 2 Cor. 8.3, 17; and this group of Ephesian documentary attestations would be useful to add to the one inscription and one late papyrus text noted in MM.

The wording at *ll.*1 and 7, εὐχαριστῶ σοι κυρία Ἄρτεμι, is clearly formulaic in thanksgiving texts to Artemis and other gods: e.g., *I.Eph.* III.960.2-3, 9-10; 962.2-3 (both Imperial period). This provides a clear parallel to certain direct-speech prayer incipits in the NT (Lk. 18.11; Jn 11.41), and to thanksgiving passages (Rom. 1.8; 7.25; 1 Cor. 1.4; 14.18, etc.). MM's useful entry for the verb is full of papyrus illustrations, but only refers to inscriptional occurrences without any quotation of examples. L. Robert, *Hellenica* 10 (1955) 55-62, comments usefully on the verb, rejecting the view of W.M. Ramsay that the formula ε. τῷ θεῷ has a semitic origin. Although grammatically not distinct, εὐχαριστέω τινί used of a human being is very much less frequent in the NT, only at Lk. 17.16 (though in this passage the reference is to Jesus who 'reveals himself as God in the miracle', BAGD, s.v., 2), and Rom. 16.4. MM provides only two papyrus instances to parallel this latter use: *P.Amh.* 2 (1901) 133.2 (early II), and *P.Oxy.* 1 (1898) 71, *col.*1.22 (303). *I.Nikaia* II, 1.1210 (Kasımlar/Gölpazar, Imperial period; pl.18) is a dedication reading: Γέννιος | Δοκιμεὺς | μετὰ τῶν κοινωνῶν (*leaf*) εὐχαριστοῦμεν | Παυλείνῃ, 'Gennios of Dokimeion with his associates gives thanks to Paulina'. Robert, ibid., 58-61, provides nearly a dozen epigraphical examples of this use, including mention of the Bithynian inscription just quoted here.

While the cliché in these texts by *neopoioi* does not allow us to be sure about personal devotion to Artemis, one inscription of Trajanic date does offer good grounds for such an inference. *I.Eph.* III.690 is an honorific text for C. Julius Celer Photeinos, who is spoken of at *ll.*8-12 as the son of parents who were 'pious towards the goddess, and zealous with regard to their state', παῖδα γο|νέων εὐσεβῶν μὲν | πρὸς τὴν θεόν, σπου|δαῖων δὲ περὶ τὴν | πατρίδα. The first of these clauses may serve as some kind of parallel to the terminology in Acts used of the 'godfearers' (σέβομαι τὸν θεόν, Acts 16.14; 18.7, 13, etc.). Similarly, the term φιλάρτεμις provides a useful analogy to φιλόχριστος in the Fathers with the meaning 'devout' (see Lampe, s.v.). The former is suprisingly sparely found in *I.Eph.*: apart from texts involving C. Vibius Salutaris (Ia.27.89, 451; 33-36d), it is attested only in one other inscription, III.695.17, an honorific for C. Laecanius Bassus, proconsul of Asia in 80/1.

Just as there are thanksgiving inscriptions to Artemis, so the inscriptions of Ephesos attest similar documents addressed to Hestia, where εὐχαριστέω is employed, e.g., *I.Eph.* IV.1065, 1070. At no.1066 (III?) a certain *prytanis* Aurelia Juliane, who comes from a distinguished family, 'gives thanks to lady Hestia and to all the gods, because they healed me (and) restored me to my parents', εὐχαριστῶ | τῇ δεσποίνῃ Ἑστίᾳ καὶ πᾶσιν τοῖς θεοῖς, ὅτι με ὑγιαίνουσαν | [τ]οῖς γονεῦσιν (*vac.*) ἀπέδωκαν (*ll.*4-6). For the wording here cf. Lk. 7.15 where Jesus raised the son of the widow of Nain and ἔδωκεν αὐτὸν τῇ μητρὶ αὐτοῦ. In one of two θεὸς ὕψιστος dedications in fulfilment of a vow, *I.Eph.* IV.1234, 1235 (both Imperial period), the latter includes the participle εὐχαριστ[ήσας]. There is no reason to assume either of these texts must be Jewish (cf. *New Docs 1976*, **5**).

Mention was made above of land owned by Artemis for the upkeep of the temple and cult. This was a common enough phenomenon: at 'Pisidian' Antioch, where the focal sanctuary for the god Men was located, there is evidence for sacred estates (see *New Docs 1978*, **7**, p.30). Boundary stones have been located indicating Artemis Ephesia as the owner of extensive tracts of land in the Kaystros valley, as far as *c.*35 km. NE (as the crow flies) from the city itself. A dozen of these stones are reprinted at *I.Eph.* VII, 2.3501-12 (ranging in date from Augustus to Trajan; cf. *SEG* 1099-1102) together with a useful map at ibid., p.296. To give force to the placement of these inscriptions the formula included an imperial authorisation. No. 3511 (dated 111/2) is a typical example:

[κατὰ τὴν τοῦ Αὐτο-]
[κράτορος Νέρουα]
[Τραιανοῦ Καίσαρος]
Σεβαστοῦ Γερμαν[ι-]
κοῦ Δακικοῦ διατα-
γὴν ὅρος ἱερὸς Ἀρτέ-
μιδος τεθεὶς ἐπὶ ἀν-
θυπάτου Φαβίου Ποσ-
τομείνου κατὰ τὸ Το-
ύλλου διάταγμα.

In accordance with the ordinance of the emperor Nerva Trajan Caesar Augustus Germanicus | Dacicus, (this) sacred boundary mark of Artemis was placed (here) in the proconsulship of Fabius Postumius, in line with the | edict of Tullius.

The noun διαταγή forms part of the standard terminology for these texts from Domitian on (3506-12), though it is fully preserved only on one other (3507). Its use here serves as a good illustration of the two NT passages where it occurs, Acts 7.53, and particularly Rom. 13.2. Similarly, διάταγμα here provides a good parallel for the sole NT use at Heb. 11.23. The index vol. to *I.Eph.* lists several other inscriptions where this noun is found. The fragmentary *I.Eph.* VII, 2.3513 provides evidence of a new survey having been made of the extent of Artemis' estates, probably under Augustus. At *l.*9 in that inscription most of the noun ἀποκατάστασις survives, referring to the restoration of boundary *stelai.* This noun appears in the NT only at Acts 3.21.

29. Frankincense and myrrh

In the treasury of a second-century BC Hellenistic palace at Ai Khanum in Baktria have been found several potsherds with Greek writing on them: M.P. Bernard, *CRAI* (1978) 421-63, especially 450 (cf. *BE* 605). Among them are two marked λιβανωτοῦ, meaning '(jars) of frankincense'. Λιβανωτός is also found in *I.Eph.* Ia.10.4-5 (probably III; repr. above at **25**). The word occurs twice in the NT at Rev. 8.3 and 5 where the context requires the meaning 'censer', which has so far been found nowhere else (cf. LSJ, MM and BAGD, s.v., and J.H. Moulton/ W.F. Howard, *A Grammar of New Testament Greek*, II [Edinburgh, 1929, repr. 1968] 372). Why the author of Revelation should alone use the noun in this way is not clear. MM, s.v., remark that at *SIG*[2] 588.156 (*c.*180 BC) — not reprinted in *SIG*[3] — the word λιβανωτίς, which usually means 'censer', is used with the meaning 'frankincense'; and they suggest that there may have been some confusion of the product and its container.

Another word for frankincense, λίβανος, occurs in Mt. 2.11 among the gifts of the Magi, χρυσὸν καὶ λίβανον καὶ σμύρναν. *Smyrna*, 'myrrh', is mentioned once more in the NT, at Jn 19.39, where it is said to have been mixed with aloes in about one hundred pounds of spices brought by Nikodemos for the burial of Jesus. The perfect participle of σμυρίζω is found at Mk. 15.23 describing water, mixed with myrrh, which was offered to Jesus just before he was put on the cross. The word ζμύρνα occurs once in this year's culling, at Guarducci, *EG* IV.20 (Lykosura, III BC; repr. above at **25**), where it is mentioned in a list of acceptable offerings for the goddess Despoina. For myrrh used in eyesalves see *New Docs 1978*, **17**, pp.56-57.

Frankincense and myrrh were very costly in antiquity because their only sources were Southern Arabia and Somaliland. Pliny, *HN* 12.65, says that the highest grade of frankincense cost six denarii a pound, the second grade five denarii and the third three. In Diocletian's edict regulating prices (301) the price (whether retail or wholesale we do not know) of the best quality frankincense was set at one hundred denarii a pound (S. Lauffer, *Diokletians Preisedikt* [Berlin, 1971] line 36.56, on p.197). The same price was set on one καστρήσιος μόδιος (i.e., probably about 17.5 litres; cf. ibid., p.54) of corn (ibid., 1.1a, p.99). As for myrrh, Pliny says (*HN* 12.70) that the price per pound of the most prized variety might reach fifty denarii, but that the highest price of cultivated myrrh was eleven denarii. On the cultivation and transportation, use and value of frankincense and myrrh see G.W. van Beek, *BA* 23 (1960) 70-95. On the mythological associations of myrrh among the Greeks see M. Detienne, *Les jardins d'Adonis. La mythologie des aromates en Grèce* (Paris, 1972).

Libanos is found once more in the NT, at Rev. 18.13 in a list of goods which also includes μύρον, 'sweet-smelling ointment, perfume'. Μύρον and the related verb μυρίζω are found in several documents from this year's culling. At *IGUR* 1245.17-19 (quoted at **18** above) the deceased tells the reader of his epitaph not to favour his tomb-stone with μύρα and στεφάνους as they are only wasted. The use of *myron* as a gift for the dead combines two associations attaching to this word which are often separate, perfumes for the burial of the dead and perfume as a sign of luxury and pleasure-taking. These two associations appear clearly in the story of the Anointing at Bethany (Mt. 26.6-12 = Mk. 14.3-8 = Jn 12.1-7; cf. Lk. 7.36-46), in which this word occurs several times. In Mark and John's accounts of this incident the μύρον is specified as being νάρδου, on which see *New Docs 1976*, **41**. In Lk. 23.56 the women followers of Jesus prepared ἀρώματα καὶ μύρα for his burial.

In two other funerary inscriptions, however, perfumes are connected only with the life of pleasure. The deceased in *IGUR* 1329 (Rome, Imperial period; pl. on p.184; *ed.* — *IG* XIV [1890] 2002), being no more than bones now that his soul has departed, advises the reader: ὡς οὖν καιρὸν ἔχεις, λοῦσαι, μύρισαι, σπατάλησον | καὶ χάρισαι, δαπάνησον ἅπερ δύνασαι· τίνι τηρεῖς; 'while, therefore, you have the opportunity, wash, anoint yourself with perfume, live in comfort and enjoy yourself, spend what you can — for whom are you keeping it?' (*ll.*6-7). In the NT the verb μυρίζω occurs only in Mk. 14.8 of anointing for burial (εἰς τὸν ἐνταφιασμόν).

Even if the deceased in the inscription just cited may have missed out on the good life, a woman who is commemorated in another text, *IGUR* 1411 (Rome, Imperial period; pl.; *ed.* — *IG* XIV [1890] 2135), but whose name is lost, was able to declare in this metrical epitaph (line divisions on the stone are marked by vertical bars):

[- ἀλ]λὰ βρότ̣ειον·
πάντες γάρ̣ [μ' ἐπό]||θουν, ἤμην γὰρ πᾶσι προσηνής,
| καὶ στεφάνους ἐφόρουν· πολλο̣ῖ[ς δὲ μύ]||ροισιν ἐχρώμην
καὶ κ̣λε[ί]ν[αισιν] | ἐκοιμώμην καὶ στρώμ̣[ασι κα]λ̣ο̣[ῖς],
| ἐνδεδύμην δὲ τὸ σῶμ[α πανειδέ]||σι χρώμασι θείοις,
| κάλλος ἔχουσα τύποισ[ι]· | ταφῆς ἔτυχον μετὰ τοῦτο
| καὶ ζῶ κοὐκ ἔθανον, τοῖον [ἔχουσα] | τάφον. (*leaf*)

. . . but it is common to all mankind. For all desired me, for I was gentle with all, and I was accustomed to wear crowns. I used many perfumes and lay on couches and fine beds, | and I put on my body every sort of divine colour, being beautiful in my features. I chanced upon the grave after this, and I live and have not died, since I have such a tomb.

Moretti mentions the views that this epitaph may have been for an actress or a prostitute (n. ad loc.).

Myron is also found in *CPR* 32 (Hermopolis Magna, II), a fragment from a pharmacist's price list. On the left side remain the prices from one column, but the products themselves are lost; on the right, in *col.*2, are products, but their prices have been broken off. The wares listed in *col.*2 all begin with μ-, but are not in alphabetical order amongst themselves. The list includes the prices of perfumes or ointments (μύρων, *l.*3), black pigment (μέλανος γραφι[κοῦ, *l.*6; μελαντηρίας, *l.*9), powder of frankincense (μάννης τοῦ [λιβάνου or λιβανωτοῦ, *l.*7), a container of perfume or ointment (μυροθήκης, *l.*11), a grinder (μύλου, *l.*11), a mortar (μάκτρας, *l.*12), ruddle (? — μίλτα in *l.*13 may be related to μίλτος), ben-nut oil (μυροβα[λάνου, *l.*15) and musk (? — μοσχ[, *l.*19). Reilly, *Slaves* (cf. **90** and **94** below), includes in her list of manumitted slaves two who were myrrh sellers (nos.4 and 984). Both of them are mentioned in an inscribed list of people dedicating *phialai* upon manumission (D.M. Lewis, *Hesperia* 37 [1968] 169-74 [Athens, *c.*330 BC]): Hippokrates, a metic living in the Peiraieus, appears as the master of the myrrh sellers Habrosyne and Hermon and of a second female slave whose name is lost. This third slave is described as a παιδίον; perhaps she may have been the daughter of Habrosyne and Hermon. On manumissions of children with their parents see **24**. For another myrrh seller see *P.Oxy.* 42 (1974) 3065.26, reprinted at **16** above.

It is worth a note in passing here that in the ruins of the palace at Ai Khanum, with which this entry began, there were found the imprints of some papyrus fragments 'fossilised' in hardened dust (Bernard, 456-58 [fig.20]). The fragments have been dated palaeographically to the first third of III BC and appear to deal with a philosophical topic. Bernard remarks that the philosopher Klearchos of Soloi is known to have travelled to Ai Khanum in *c.*300 BC. For this man see further at **13**, above.

(A.L. CONNOLLY)

30. 'The weaker sex'

At 1 Pet. 3.7 the writer admonishes husbands that in their married life they should live considerately as with a weaker vessel, namely the female one, or — since the phrasing and therefore the meaning are not certain here — render honour as to a weaker vessel (ὡς ἀσθενεστέρῳ σκεύει τῷ γυναικείῳ). The notion of women being the weaker sex occurs in a number of petitions from III-IV, one of which appears among this year's publications, but which is too fragmentary to reprint here in full. *CPR* 15 (Hermopolis, *c.*330?; pl.10) is the draft of a petition, presumably addressed to the *praeses* of the Thebaid, from a woman whose name is lost. She claims that certain officials have dealt with her illegally in the collection of some taxes (for a female petitioner with a similar problem in the same district and at about the same time cf. *CPR* 1 [1895] 19 [Hermopolis, 330]). In seeking to win the sympathy of the *praeses* she flatters him saying πά]ση εὐμενίᾳ, δέσποτα ἡγεμών, | [τὸ μεγαλεῖόν σου εὐεργ]ετεῖ τοὺς ἀδικουμένους μάλιστα | [δὲ γυναῖκας διὰ τὸ τ]ῆς φύσεως ἀσθενές, 'through all goodwill, my Lord governor, your Magnificence shows kindness to those who are wronged and especially to women on account of the weakness of their nature' (*ll*.2-4). Further on she writes that the oppressive officials set upon her κατ[α]φρο|[νοῦντες τῆ]ς ἀσθενοῦς μου γυναικ[είας φ]ύσεως, 'despising my weak nature as a woman' (*ll*.12-13). The reason why this woman looks to the *praeses* for help is — if the restoration is correct — that she is a widow, for she says ὅθεν μὴ φέρουσα γυνὴ | [χήρα] τὴν [τ]ούτων παράνομον ἀπαίτησιν καταφεύγω | [πρὸς το]ὺς σοὺς τοῦ ἐμοῦ κυρίου πόδας, 'wherefore, as I a widow woman cannot endure the unlawful demand of these men, I flee to the feet of you my lord' (*ll*.16-18).

It is clear from the manner in which the notion of woman's frailty is used in other petitions that it had become a commonplace in the rhetoric of petitions. The following is a list of some petitions which use this appeal:

— *P.Flor.* 1 (1906, repr. 1960) 58 (Hermopolis Magna, after Jan./Feb., 226), a badly damaged petition to an *epistrategos* in which Aurelia Aretous alleges that two men managed(?) land she had inherited from her father to their own advantage, [καταφρονο]ῦντές μου ὡς γυναικὸς ἀσ[θ]ε[νο]ῦς, 'despising me as a weak woman' (*l*.14).

— *P.Oxy.* 34 (1968) 2713 (297), a highly rhetorical petition to the prefect, Aristius Optatus, from Aurelia Didyme who claims that her uncles have been depriving her of her inheritance and who after explaining that she is an orphan (both her parents have died) says further, ἄμεινον δ' ἐπίστασε (*read* ἐπίστασαι), ἡγεμὼν δέσποτα, ὅτι τὸ γυναικεῖον γ[ένος] | εὐκαταφρόνητον πέφυκεν διὰ τὸ περὶ ἡμᾶς τῆς φύσεως ἀσθενές, 'and you are well aware, my Lord governor, that the female sex is by nature easily despised because of the weakness of nature on our part' (*ll*.8-9).

— *P.Oxy.* 1 (1898) 71, *col*.2 (303), an incomplete petition to a prefect from Aurelia Gl. . . who, being a widow and lacking the protection of her two sons who are soldiers away on foreign service, claims she is being robbed by her estate managers and writes, πᾶσι μὲν βοηθεῖς, ἡγεμὼν δέσποτα, καὶ πᾶσι τὰ ἴ[δ]ια ἀπονέμις (*read* -νέμεις) [μάλιστα] | δὲ γυναιξεὶν διὰ τὸ τῆς φύσεως ἀσθενές, 'you help all, my Lord governor, and you apportion to all their due, and especially to women on account of their weakness of nature' (*ll*.3-4).

— *P.Amh.* 2 (1901) 141 (Ashmunên, 350), a petition to a *praepositus* in which Aurelia Thaesis complains of an assault upon her by her brother and his wife and says, [ὅ]θ[ε]ν οὐ δυναμένη ἀφησυχάσαι γυνὴ | [ἀσθε]νὴς καὶ χήρα ἐπιδίδωμι τῇ ἐπιεικείᾳ | [σο]υ τάδε τὰ βιβλία [μο]υ, 'wherefore, since I cannot silently let it pass, I a weak woman and a widow present to your Reasonableness this petition' (*ll*.15-17).

With these five may be compared *P.Sakaon* (1978) 36 (Theadelphia, *c*.280; *ed.pr.* — *P.Ryl.* 2 [1915] 114; discussed in *New Docs 1978*, **5**), a petition from a widow with infant children who does not explicitly mention the weak nature of women, but makes much of her widowhood and begins her appeal saying that she is aware of the prefect's 'care for all, especially women and widows', περὶ πάντας κηδεμονίαν, | [μάλιστα περὶ γυ]ναῖκας καὶ χήρας (*ll*.4-5).

No doubt widows and orphans, especially female ones, could find themselves in an insecure position, particularly when they lacked other family connections to assist them; cf. **71** below. However, it is apparent that the appeal to the weak nature of women is somewhat conventional and should not be taken as evidence that the particular women who employed it were necessarily more vulnerable than others. Indeed, in the case of some of the women cited above, judging from the property troubles about which they were petitioning, and from the high stylistic quality of the documents they submitted, the women came from well-to-do families and may not have been as vulnerable as they claim. Nevertheless, the disadvantaged position of women in general (from which this conventional plea drew its plausibility) is suggested by other documentary evidence. Of the 110 women that P.J. Sijpesteijn lists as holding the right to act without a *kyrios* by reason of the *ius trium liberorum* (Appendix II in *P.Mich.* 15 [1982] pp.158-171; cf. the discussion of this right at **24**) twenty-five explicitly state that they are acting with the sponsorship of a man, usually a husband. So even where a woman could act on her own *de iure*, in practice it was often necessary for her to be seconded by a male.

P.Sakaon 36 (mentioned above), as well as using the theme of female frailty, also employs another commonplace occurring not infrequently in petitions, that of the quiet life. For the writer says that she has perceived the prefect's 'love of moderation' (τὸ μετριοφιλές, *l.*3). In a petition from a man, *P.Sakaon* 41 (Theadelphia?, 322; *ed.pr.* — *P.Ryl.* 4 [1952] 659) the petitioner, Arion Dioskoros, says that tax-collectors are unfairly setting upon him, καταφρονοῦντες τῆς μετριότητός μου καὶ | ἀπραγμοσύνης ὁμοῦ τε καὶ τοῦ γήρους καὶ τῆς ἀτεκνείας μου, 'despising my moderation and lack of worldly involvement as well as my old age and childlessness' (*ll.*7-8). This Arion who has been deprived of his wife and children provides an excellent male counterpart to the widows and orphans. In *P.Merton* 2 (1959) 91 (Karanis, 30 Jan., 316; pl.39) Aurelius Isidoros praises the prefect to whom he addresses his petition saying, πᾶσι μὲν βοη[θεῖν] εἴωθεν ἡ σὴ περὶ πάντα κηδεμονί[α], ἡγεμὼν δέσποτα, ἐξαιρέτως [δ]ὲ ἡμεῖν τοῖς μετρί[ο]ις καὶ καλῶς εὖ βιοῦντες (*read* βιοῦσι), 'your care regarding all things, my Lord master, is accustomed to come to the aid of all, and especially of us of moderate means and living rightly and well' (*l.*6). On this meaning for μέτριος, 'of moderate means, poor', see ed. n. ad loc. This connotation should perhaps also be understood in the noun as well. The petitioner in *P.Oxy.* 1 (1898) 71, *col.*1 (303) also includes himself among the μέτριοι (*l.*3) and describes his troublesome debtor as 'despising my moderation' (*l.*14); and in *col.*2 of *P.Oxy.*71, in a petition already described above, the petitioning widow claims that her estate managers act περι[φ]ρονοῦντές μου τῆς ἀπραγμ[οσύνης] (*l.*16). For another petition using this argument of the quiet life, see *New Docs 1978*, **101**, where *P.Sakaon* 41 is also more fully discussed. On rhetorical clichés in papyrus petitions of II-IV which contrast the virtues of the poor with the vices of the rich and powerful see A.B. Kovel'man, *VDI* 168 (1984) 170-84 (in Russian).

The formulaic nature of all these petitions is revealed not only by the recurrence of such commonplaces, but also by the use of certain other common expressions several of which may be mentioned here. In *CPR* 15 the widow metaphorically flies to the feet of the *praeses*. The same wording is used by the widow in *P.Oxy.* 71, *col.*2.17-18, but *P.Merton* 91 has ἠπίχθην (*read* -είχθην) οὖν τὴ[ν] καταφυγὴν ποιήσασθαι πρὸς τοὺς σοὺς τοῦ ἐμοῦ κυρίου πόδας, 'therefore I was impelled to make my flight to the feet of you my lord' (*l.*16). A number of the petitioners preface the tale of their troubles with an expression like 'the matter as it concerns me is of the following nature', τὸ δὲ κατ' ἐμὲ πρᾶγμα τοῦτον ἔχει τὸν τρόπον (*P.Merton* 91.6; *CPR* 15.4-5, where partly restored; cf. *P.Sakaon* 36.6-7). Nearly all close their appeals with promises of undying gratitude to the magistrate if he should grant their petition, the most simple form being exemplified by *P.Thead.* (1911, repr. 1974) 19 (Theadelphia, IV), καὶ τούτου τυχὸν (*read* τυχὼν) διὰ παντὸς χάριτάς σοι ὁμολογήσω, 'and obtaining this I shall ever acknowledge thanks to you' (*l.*18).

For a petition from the same period, but in less florid style see *P.Oxy.Hels.* 26 (297; reprinted above at **24**). Possibly the use of a less elevated style is to be explained by the fact that this document is addressed to the *nyktostrategoi*, officials of a lower station than the prefect or *praeses*. An earlier petition, *P.Oxy.Hels.* 23 (212), is reprinted at **23**.

(A.L. CONNOLLY)

31. Brother against brother

A lengthy decree recording an arbitration between Temnos and Klazomenai has been published by P. Herrmann, *MDAI* 29 (1979) 249-71 (pls.68-70); cf. *SEG* 1130 *bis*; *BE* (1980) 438. The text is opisthographic, written on the front and back of a single stele. Whereas dialectal features are present on side A, side B is written in *koine*. Six men from Knidos were chosen to re-establish harmonious relations between the cities after a local war. The second side preserves an agreement (συνθήκη, B.30, 42, 53) between the two cities.

Though there are many features of interest in the content and language of this text (Klazomenai?, II^1 BC), one passage only is noted here. At B.37-44 occurs a set of clauses forbidding family members to give judgement against each other.

> ο[ὕ]ς οὐ δεῖ δικάζειν· μὴ δικάζειν πατέρα παιδ[ὶ] μηδὲ παῖδα πατρὶ μ[ηδ]ὲ ἀδελφοὺς ἀδελφῶι μηδὲ ἀδελφιδοῦς μηδὲ πάτρωας μηδ[ὲ] μήτρωας μηδὲ γαμβροὺς μηδὲ πενθεροῦς μηδὲ κοινωνοὺ̣[ς τῆ]ς [δί]κ̣ης μηδὲ προξένους μηδὲ τοὺς εἰσαγωγεῖς τῶν δικῶν μηδ[ὲ τοῦς τρ]εφομένους ὑπὸ τῆς πόλεως· ἐὰν δέ τις πα<ρὰ> ταῦτα δικάσηι οὓς ἡ̣ [συνθή]κ̣η ἀπείργει, ἀποτισάτω ὁ δικάσας τῶι δικαζομένωι τὸ πέμπ̣[τον μέ]ρος τοῦ ἐπιγράμματος τῆς δίκης ἣν ἐδίκασεν καὶ τῆς δίκης ὑπ̣[όδικο]ς ἔστω. κτλ

Those who ought not to judge: a father should not act in a judicial capacity over his son, nor a son over his father, nor brothers their brother, nor nephews, nor paternal uncles nor maternal uncles nor sons-in-law nor fathers-in-law, | nor those who have an interest in the case, nor patrons, nor prosecutors of cases, nor those who are reared by the city. If anyone acts in a judicial capacity contrary to these clauses which the agreement forbids let him who so acted pay to the one judged a fifth part of the damages bill for the case which he judged, and let him be liable for trial.

This passage provides background context at a general level for the Gospel saying at Mk. 13.12 (= Mt. 10.21), καὶ παραδώσει ἀδελφὸς ἀδελφὸν εἰς θάνατον καὶ πατὴρ τέκνον, καὶ ἐπαναστήσονται τέκνα ἐπὶ γονεῖς καὶ θανατώσουσιν αὐτούς. The parallel is not exact, of course: the context of the saying in Mk, and especially in Mt., appears to be one of persecution which has reached the stage of civil litigation.

32. A question of paternity

Dodona — II BC

ed. — SIG^3 1163

> Ἐρωτῇ Λυσανίας Δία Νάϊον καὶ Δηώνα<ν>, ἦ οὐκ ἔστι ἐξ αὐτοῦ τὸ παιδάριον ὃ Ἀννύλα κύει.

Lead tablet, reflecting the Doric features expected from Dodona.

Bib. — Helbing, *AGI* 24; H.W. Parke, *The Oracles of Zeus* (Oxford, 1967) 266, no.11; *Guarducci, *EG* IV.85-86 (fig.31).

5 **Lysanias asks Zeus Naios and Dione whether | the child which Annula is carrying is not by him.**

Is this question addressed to the oracular shrine at Dodona by a husband who does not trust his wife? Or is it being put by a man who is seeking divine confirmation to back a denial that he has got Annula 'into trouble'? We cannot know, of course. But the text is of interest for the fact that a divine answer is sought on a basic issue. The most common word for an embryo is βρέφος (cf. in the NT, Lk. 1.41, 44). Here we have παιδάριον, presumably a loose usage, and perhaps occasioned by the meaning 'infant, child' which is also common for βρέφος (NT: Lk. 2.12, 16, etc.). On βρέφος see further at **12** above. In passing, this inscription provides testimony to the name Lysanias (NT: Lk. 3.1 only), which may be noted for a new MM entry. This short text is one of a number of similar items discussed by H.S. Versnel in id. (ed.), *Faith, Hope and Worship. Aspects of Religious Mentality in the Ancient World* (*Studies in Greek and Roman Religion*, 2; Leiden, 1981), 1-64, at 5-6 (cf. *SEG* 1773). The whole of this volume is well worth attention, for in addition to Versnel's contribution on the mentality which gave rise to prayers in Graeco-Roman antiquity, there are essays by F.T. von Straten, on votive offerings to the gods (65-151, including a long appendix [105-51, and many plates] on votive offerings in the Greek world which are shaped in the form of parts of the body; cf. *SEG* 1772), and by H.W. Pleket, on the religious believer as the god's slave (159-92). Also included is a contribution by J.M. Bremer on Greek hymns (193-215; cf. *SEG* 1774), and one by P.A. Meijer on the attitudes of intellectuals to religion (216-63). A considerable number of inscriptions are brought into the first three of these essays, and a few papyri are discussed in the first.

A similarly fundamental question occurs in Helbing, *AGI* 23, another oracle text on a lead tablet from Dodona (IV/III BC; = SIG^3 1161): ἱστορεῖ Νικοκράτ[ει]α, τίνι θεῶν θύουσα | λώϊον καὶ ἄμεινον πράσσοι καὶ τὰς νόσου | παύσα<ι>το, 'Nikokrateia enquires, to which of the gods she should sacrifice in order to be better and stronger and cease from her illness'. Here is a woman beyond the help of the doctors, either because of the nature of her disease or her poverty, and who seeks to discover the most efficacious divine healer of her particular malady. For this type of question see Versnel, 5, 13. K.L. McKay has drawn to my attention (*per litt.*) the close parallel at Xen. *Anab.* 3.1.5, . . . ἐπήρετο τὸν Ἀπόλλω τίνι ἂν θεῶν θύων καὶ εὐχόμενος κάλλιστα καὶ ἄριστα ἔλθοι. In both passages two synonymous adverbs are employed as well as a potential optative (though in the inscription ἄν is omitted). On potential optatives without ἄν see further at **50**, below.

In the oracle question the verb ἱστορέω in its regular sense, 'inquire', may be noted here, not the way it is employed in the NT at Gal. 1.18. The meaning 'visit', which that NT passage appears to require, does occur in documentary texts, however: in addition to the references given by BAGD, s.v., we may add Guarducci, *EG* III (Rome, 1974) 209-10 (Egyptian Thebes, I or II), a graffito recorded by a visitor from the Black Sea to the underground vault of the late New Kingdom Rameses VI: Ἑρμογένης Ἀμασ[εὺ]ς | τὰς μὲν ἄλλας | σύριγγας | ἴδων ἐθαύ|μασα, τὴν δὲ τοῦ Μέμνονος | ταύτην [[ει]] ἱστο|ρήσας ὑπερεθαύμασα, 'I, Hermogenes of Amasia have seen other chambers and was amazed, but when I visited this one of Memnon I was completely astounded'. This tomb of Rameses VI (*not* Rameses V, *pace* Guarducci, ad loc.) was identified with that of the Greek mythological hero Memnon in this and other graffiti because Rameses' *praenomen* Mimmuria provided a homonym for the name Memnon (see *Lexikon der Ägyptologie*, IV [1982] *col.*24).

Guarducci, *EG* IV.74-122 provides an extensive discussion of oracles as evidenced by epigraphical texts. One of those she reprints (117-19) is an epigram (Memphis, IV fin./III init. BC; fig.38) below which is portrayed the bull Apis and an altar: ἐνύπνια κρίνω | τοῦ θεοῦ πρόσταγ|μα ἔχων· τυχἀγα|θᾶι· Κρής ἐστιν ὁ | κρίνων τάδε, 'I interpret dreams, having God's directive. For good fortune; the one who interprets them is a Cretan'. The first word in this text appears in the NT only at Acts 2.17, quoting Joel 3.1; it thus offers a useful example of a standard word in current *koine* adopted by the LXX translators. Of more interest at a general level is the following funerary altar, reprinted at Guarducci, *EG* IV.119-20 (Thyatira in Lydia, II/III):

Ἀμμιάδι
τὰ τέκνα καὶ οἱ μύσ-
ται τῶν θεῶν ἀνέ-
στησαν τὸν βωμὸν
σὺν τῇ πυαλίδι,
τῆι ἱερείῃ τῶν
θεῶν μνείας
χάριν.
εἴ τις δὲ θέλει τὸ ἀλη-
θὲς μαθεῖν παρὰ
ἐμοῦ, ἰς τὸν βω-
μὸν ἐνευξάσθω
ὃ ἂν θέλει καὶ ἐπι-
τεύξεται, διὰ ὁ-
ράματος, νυκτὸς
καὶ ἡμέρας.

To Ammias, her children and the initiates of the gods set up the altar | with the sarcophagus for the priestess of the gods as a memorial. And if anyone wants to learn the truth | from me, let him pray at(?) the altar for whatever he wants and he will get it, via | a vision, during nightime and day.

Here we have the members of a cultic association combining with the dead woman's children to provide a memorial for their former priestess. Ammias' open invitation to anyone to invoke her at any hour (the phrase in *ll.*15-16 goes most naturally with the prayer clause in *ll.*11-12) is accompanied by a promise of an answer using the common medium of a dream-vision. She is presented here as one with semi-divine status now that in her deceased state she has full access to the truth and can impart that to the living. It is possible that τὸ ἀληθές (9-10) refers simply to enquirers wanting to know the answer to their everday questions; but in the context of a cultic association it is more likely that her invitation is addressed to seekers after truth on a metaphysical level.

33. Reciprocal affection

Φιλοστοργία and its related noun have been given due attention previously: *New Docs 1977*, **80**; and *New Docs 1978*, **11**. But a usage arises among the inscriptions of Ephesos which was not noted there: that of φιλοστοργία between cities.

In *I.Eph.* Ia.12 (II; pl.13) the athlete Aurelius Achilleus is honoured by Ephesos. The inscription, the surviving copy of which was actually recovered from Aphrodisias, begins by dwelling on the harmonious relations between the two cities, and the phrase περὶ | [τ]ὴν ἀντίδοσιν τῆς φιλοστοργίας occurs (*ll.*13-14) to explain that Aphrodisias enjoys many outstanding rights 'relating to her reciprocation of affection'. A related use appears in the very lengthy foundation document of C. Vibius Salutaris (on this see **14** above), where the noun is used twice (*I.Eph.* Ia.27.79, 380) to refer to his affection for his city.

The name Philostorgos survives on an imperial-period epitaph probably originally from the Levant: Pfuhl/Möbius II.1169. In a funerary epigram, ibid., I.940 (Kyzikos, II) a woman is said to have manifested to her husband her affectionate acts of gracious care, ἀνδρὶ φιλοστόργους δεικνυμένα χάριτας (*l.*6). On the verb φιλοστοργέω in Tibiletti, *Lettere*, no.2 see the discussion at **17**, ad fin.

In a metrically unusual epitaph for Melite — *IG* II/III^2 12067, repr. and discussed as Pircher, no.12 (Peiraieus, *c.*365-340 BC) — she is said to have loved in return her husband Onesimos who loved her: φιλοῦντα | ἀντιφιλοῦσα τὸν ἄνδρα 'Ονήσιμ|ον ἦσθα κρατίστη (*ll.*2-4).

34. A crucified donkey

The well-known graffito from the Roman Palatine showing the crucifixion of a man with a donkey's head (III) is discussed again by G.M.A. Hanfmann, in G. Kopcke/M.B. Moore (edd.), *A Tribute to P.H. von Blanckenhagen* (Locust Valley, 1979), 205-07 (pl.55.1-2). He draws attention to the punishment accorded the Seleucid pretender Achaios at Alexandria in 214 BC: τὴν κεφαλὴν ἀποτέμοντας αὐτοῦ καὶ καταρράψαντας εἰς ὄνειον ἄσκον ἀνασταυρῶσαι τὸ σῶμα (Polyb. 8.21), '. . . cutting off his head and sewing him into the hide of an ass to crucify (impale?) his body'. In the Palatine graffito a man stands beside the crucified creature and the crudely-carved text reads 'Αλε|ξάμενος | σέβετε (*read* -αι) θεόν, 'Alexamenos worships (his?) god'. Hanfmann sees a parallel here 'in the equation with the despised animal and the crucifixion of one who pretended kingship — Achaios to the Seleucid throne, Jesus allegedly to kingship over the Jews' (206). F.I. Andersen draws to my attention (*per litt.*) the connection with Jer. 22.19, but points out that this is puzzling, 'for Israel did not have our lore about the donkey as a bad animal. The ox and the ass are the two good domestic beasts, well spoken of in Is. 1.3, and making their way, via the Barbarini recension of Hab. 3, into the icongraphy of the Nativity, and all the hymns, in spite of the complete silence of the NT on this detail'.

A different type of mockery occurs in Philo, *In Flacc.* 37 — discussed most recently by J.R. Rea, *Pap.Brux.* 18, pp.34-38 — where Agrippa I is taunted by anti-Jewish Alexandrians and an idiot is dressed up as a king with βύβλος on his head ἀντὶ διαδήματος. Rea interprets the mock-crown as a papyrus book roll 'loosened far enough to allow the empty space at the axis of the roll to fit over a man's head' (35). This and a parallel passage also considered by Rea (Appian, *Mith.* 111) may serve to illustrate in a general way the mock-crowning in the Passion Narratives (Mk. 15.16-20; Mt. 27.27-31; Jn 19.1-3; cf. Lk. 23.11).

More recently, Hanfmann has discussed an ampulla found at Sardis: *HTR* 78 (1985 [1986] 421-26). This terracotta flask, dated to the early Byzantine period, shows on one side a donkey carrying a cross (ibid., fig.1) and on the other a donkey carrying a sphere above which stands a cross (fig.2). These objects were made for the pilgrim trade at holy sites. The devout purchased them to transport home holy water or relics. Hanfmann interprets the representation on this ampulla as symbolising Christ's entry into Jerusalem (Mt. 21.1-7).

35. The Rotas-Sator word-square again (cf. *New Docs 1976*, 99)

Another example of the Rotas-Sator word-square has been found, at Mamucium (Manchester, England), on an amphora sherd found in a late II AD rubbish pit. The surviving lettering yields: *rotas* | *opera* | *tene*[*t*] | [*arepo*] | [*sator*]. See M.C.W. Hassall/R.S.O. Tomlin, *Britannia* 10 (1979) 353 (pl.20B); cf. *AE* 387. Hassall/Tomlin provide a very comprehensive, yet succinct note (353 n.70) concerning previously-discovered examples. They conclude that '. . . it seems possible that the word-square was adopted by Christians during the fourth century, but it is unlikely that they devised it or were its exclusive users. It should not be seen in isolation as evidence of Christianity in second-century Manchester'.

The most comprehensive, recent survey of this word square is H. Hofmann, *PW Suppl.* 15 (1978) 478-566.

36. Galatia in recent research

In *Historia* 28 (1979) 409-38 (cf. *SEG* 1737; *BE* [1980] 531, 541) S. Mitchell discusses the cities Ikonion and Ninika, both of which he argues were 'double' communities. This signifies rather more than cities with different population groups living in particular quarters of the town. The term indicates a situation where two separate ethnic groups live in the same city, each with constitutional, administrative and judicial independence of the other. Other clues to the existence of such communities are the right to mint their own coins, and the ability to pass their own decrees. In Ikonion's case, recently published numismatic evidence proves the existence of the two separate communities, Colonia Iulia Augusta Iconium, and Klaudeikonion. The colonial status goes back at least to Augustus; these newly published coins thus cause to founder the view accepted since W.M. Ramsay that when Ikonion was spoken of as a *colonia* this was purely honorific (Mitchell, 413-14). Ikonion's situation as both a Roman *colonia* and a *polis* dates at least from the time of Claudius; under Hadrian the double community was amalgamated. Mitchell points out (412) that when the gentile inhabitants of the city are spoken of as Ἕλληνες in Acts 14.1, the writer endorses the view that 'the community had been thoroughly hellenised' by mid-I.

Ikonion was the third largest city of Galatia, after Ankyra and so-called 'Pisidian' Antioch (properly Antioch 'by Pisidia'). The lack of large cities in Galatia is dealt with by Mitchell in *ANRW* II.7.2 (1980) 1053-1081 (cf. *BE* [1981] 594) as part of his discussion of the population and land in Roman Galatia. The population of cities like Ikonion was ethnically quite mixed: its position on the borders of Phrygia and Lykaonia was a prime reason for this. Cf. Acts 14.6 where the city is by implication seen as Phrygian. Galatia was a rural province, whose main products were cereals and wool (ibid., 1069-70). Most cities were small and geographically isolated, linked only by the Roman road network. In place of cities there were numerous large family estates. One of these families was the Sergii Paulli, who had a connection with Antioch probably by virtue of the proximity of their estate to the *colonia* (ibid., 1074). The best known member of this senatorial family was L. Sergius L. *f.* Paullus, proconsul of Cyprus when Paul visited the island (Acts 13.7). Mitchell's suggestion is attractive (ibid., 1074 n.134) that it was the proconsul's family's link with Antioch which made Paul decide to head for that city next, provided no doubt with an entrée from Sergius to the upper class of the colony. The inference is that Paul did not have a pre-determined, inflexible itinerary for his missionary journey. On some mid-I AD proconsuls of Cyprus see most recently M. Christol, *Chiron* 16 (1986) 1-14.

On the formation of the province of Galatia, under Augustus, and its subsequent history down to Trajan see R.K. Sherk, *ANRW* II.7.2 (1980) 954-1052 (cf. *BE* [1981] 201). Certain geographical areas were attached or subtracted during this period. Changes were made in the administration of the province, too: whereas under Augustus the governors were either of praetorian or consular rank, from Tiberius they were praetorians. Vespasian altered the arrangement again, appointing consular legates with a praetorian assistant (ibid., 1040-46). Sherk discusses each of the known governors in the period, and follows this subject up in an article which appeared just prior to the *ANRW* survey, though no doubt written subsequently: *AJP* 100 (1979) 166-75, dealing with governors of Galatia from 112-285 (cf. *SEG* 1367).

Most recently, Mitchell argues in *Chiron* 16 (1986) 17-33 that Tiberius' principate was crucial for the development of the Imperial cult in Galatia. The Temple of Rome and Augustus at Ankyra was begun under Augustus and finished *c.*19/20 AD. Other major Galatian cities, Pessinos and Antioch, also received large-scale temples for the promotion of the provincial cult (ibid., 33). In this article there is published (23-25) a new short Latin inscription from Attaleia which throws light on the Roman policy of linking the network of colonies in Pisidia with the cities of the Pamphylian coast. From this inscription Mitchell plausibly infers (25) that the road was begun under Tiberius and finished during the time of Gaius. We may presume that this newly-built road was the route used by Paul on his journey inland to Antioch. This article also offers further comment (25-27) on the edict from Sagalassos concerning the requisitioning of local transport, first published by Mitchell in *JRS* 66 (1976) 106-31. At *New Docs 1976*, **9**, this text is reprinted and a new date (18/19) suggested by E.A. Judge. Mitchell now accepts that the inscription is Tiberian, but doubts that it can be specified so tightly to one particular year.

In his *ANRW* contribution Mitchell draws attention (1081) to the primacy of epigraphical evidence for the social history of Asia Minor, and notes the besetting problem for Galatia of the dispersed publication of this material. In order to rectify this he has now published *The Inscriptions of North Galatia* (*RECAM* 2 = *BIAA* Monograph 4 = *BAR International Series* 135; Oxford, 1982). The first volume of the *RECAM* series will be devoted to inscriptions of Ankyra (in the meantime, cf. id., *AS* 27 [1977] 63-103).

37. Kenchreai's architecture

Acts 18.18 and Rom. 16.1 constitute two of the only five literary testimonia known from Kenchreai, one of the two important ports for Corinth, about 9 km. from the ancient city. R. Scranton, et al., *Kenchreai. Eastern Port of Corinth, I. Topography and Architecture* (Leiden, 1978) publishes the detailed results. The site has yielded much less information than was anticipated. Matters treated in this volume naturally focus upon the harbour area, with its moles, quay and anchorage (13-38; considerable space is given to the *piscinae*, 'fish tanks', 25-35; cf. *CIL* III *Add.* 30, quoted below at **109**), and the shops (39-52) and sanctuaries (53-90; Isis, Aphrodite) clustered near the harbour. The common phenomenon of a sanctuary (in this case, of Isis) being converted into a Christian church, perhaps in the last quarter of IV, receives considerable attention (71, 75-78). On this see also Pallas, *Monuments paléochrétiens*, 171-72 no.80. Pallas' book notes other instances of Christian re-use of pagan sacred sites, e.g., at Philia in Thessaly a basilica was built over a sanctuary of Athena before V[2] (58-59, no.35). Similarly elsewhere: *I.Apollonia* 5-8 (with Reynolds' comment on no.5, p.297), where the temple underlying the East Church may have been dedicated to Apollo. Briefer space is allocated to the upper town area of Kenchreai (6-12). Appendix E (144-47) considers the question of the change in relative sea level since Hellenistic antiquity, taking into account seismic activity as a contributing factor.

The third volulme in the *Kenchreai* series dealt with the coins recovered; cf. *New Docs 1978*, **20**. Volume II (1976) was devoted to *opus sectile* panels made of glass.

L. Mummius, the destroyer of Corinth in 146 BC, who then instituted the political reorganisation of Achaia, is mentioned in a brief inscription from Eretria: *BE* 350; cf. *AE* 589.

38. In brief

(a) Well-preserved **apprenticeship contract** for a weaver: *P.Oxy.Hels.* 29 (Oxyrhynchos, 8 Sept., 54 AD; pl.19): a woman apprentices her grandson (whose parents are apparently dead) to her son, the boy's uncle. A document like this may offer a general illustration of the conditions under which Paul learned his trade as a tentmaker (Acts 18.3).

(b) **Avaricious doctors** criticised in *I.Eph.* IV.1386 (probably I): φιλάρ]γυροι ἰατροί occurs with the same amount of restoration at both *ll.*6 and 7. MM has one hellenistic papyrological attestation to illustrate this adjective, which appears in the NT at Lk. 16.14 and 2 Tim. 3.2. Cf. Spicq, *NLNT* II.928-29 (at I.53-56, 169 the privative ἀφιλάργυρος is treated).

(c) **'Marvellous books'** (βιβλίοις θαυμαστοῖ[ς], *l.*16) donated by T. Aelius Alkibiades, a Roman citizen of Nysa, to adorn the sanctuary at Rome of the association of Dionysiac artists: *I.Eph.* Ia.22 (Nysa, copy of decree honouring the man resolved by the Ephesos chapter of the association, time of Antoninus Pius; pl.15). On this inscription see further L. Robert in *ΣΤΗΛΗ. Τόμος εἰς μνήμην Νικολάου Κοντολέοντος* (Athens, 1980) 16-18.

(d) **Rescript of Septimius Severus designed to curb Christian proselytising**: discussion but no text in *Φιλίας Χάριν. Miscellanea di Studi classici in onore di E. Manni* (Rome, 1979?) IV.1317-28.

(e) **The consolation of culture**. *IGUR* 1311 (Rome, III[1]; pl. on p.169), epitaph for Publiana, wife of a consul (C. Arrius Calpurnius Frontinus Honoratus?), tracing her ancestry back to the Scipiones. Her husband and children predeceased her, and in her grief she 'soothed her mind only by (her devotion to) cultural pursuits', μούσαισιν μοῦνον τὴν φρένα θελγομένη (*l.*8).

(f) An **unusual proskynema formula** in a letter: *P.Oxy.Hels.* 50 (Oxyrhynchos, III; pl.36): τὸ προσ[κ]ύνημά σου | ποιῶ εὐχόμενός σοι τὰ ἐν βίῳ κάλ|λιστα ὑπαρχθῆναι (*ll.*2-4), 'I make obeisance for you, praying for your possession of the best things in life'. Cf. *New Docs 1978*, **52**.

(g) **Graffito invoking Roma**, *I.Eph.* II.599: Ῥώμα ἡ παμβασίλεια, τὸ σὸν κράτος οὔποτ' ὀλεῖται, 'Roma who rule over all, your sovereignty will never be destroyed'. For κράτος of God's power in the NT cf. BAGD, s.v., 1, 4. Cf. a fourth-century **verse invocation to Christ** (*IGM* 101) on a column at Rome, moved by Constantine to Byzantion, in which he is asked to protect 'this city your slave, and my position as ruler, and the sovereignty of Rome', τήνδε σὴν δούλην πόλιν | καὶ σκῆπτρα τᾀμὰ καὶ τὸ τῆς Ῥώμης κράτος (2-3).

(h) **Graeco-Roman Syria**: J.P. Rey-Coquais, *Actes Constantza*, 171-83, uses onomastic data to assess the success and limits of Hellenisation. On Romanisation see R. Tracey, *Romanisation in Syria-Palestine in the Late Republic and Early Empire* (Diss. Macquarie, 1986).

(i) **Romanisation of Scythia Minor**, and the contribution of Christianity to this process, is surveyed by E. Popescu, *Actes Constantza*, 273-92. Four inscriptions for martyrs are known, dated between IV-VI.

(j) The contribution of Greek epigraphy to our understanding of **indigenous and Greek cults in the Egyptian Fayum** is assessed by E. Bernand in *Hommages à la mémoire de S. Sauneron* (Cairo, 1979) II.57-76.

B. MINOR PHILOLOGICAL NOTES

39. ἀμέμπτως

Although MM lack a separate entry for this word, half their discussion under ἄμεπτος is devoted to examples of the adverb. Only one inscription is instanced to illustrate the NT occurrences at 1 Thes. 2.10 and 5.23; yet it is quite common in epigraphical texts, particularly funerary ones. For its use in an honorific inscription see, e.g., F.W. Danker, *Benefactor. Epigraphic Study of a Graeco-Roman and New Testament Semantic Field* (St. Louis, 1982) 73-74, no.10.1 (= frag. a of *MAMA* 8 [1962] 413); cf. his brief discussion at 354-55. At 387 n.178 he refers to two attestations in epitaphs. From the present year's culling comes the following list of instances in funerary texts:

SEG 1197 (Saittai in Lydia, 209/10), Ammion and her sons set up an epitaph for her husband who lived ἀ. for 48 years;

I.Nikaia I.193 (Ortapınarlar, near Nikaia, III; pl.17; cf. *SEG* 1293), epitaph for Aurelia Agathe, who lived ἀ. for 40 years;

.286 (probably III; pl.25; cf. *SEG* 1292), fragment of an epitaph for a woman in which the adverb is partially but plausibly restored;

II,2.1251 (III?; pl.6), Papianos set up a tomb for Bassa, τὴν πινυτὴν ζήσασαν ἀμένπτως, aged 60;

.1459 (probably II; pl.26), very fragmentary epitaph mentioning a woman who lived ἀ. for 70 years;

.1474 (Imperial; pl.29), epitaph for a child aged 9, who lived ἀ.;

Pfuhl/Möbius II.1184 (Nikomedia, II; cf. *BE* 12, *SEG* 1346), epitaph for a *naukleros* — on this term see **26** — who lived ἀ. for 70 years;

.1410 (Tomi, probably II/III; pl.205), tomb erected by Abaskantos for himself καὶ τῇ συνβίῳ Ζωσίμῃ | ζησάσῃ ἀμένπτως παρ' ἐμοί (*ll*.3-4);

BE 558 (Nikomedia, Imperial; cf. *SEG* 1350), Paulina, who erected a tomb for her husband, describes herself as συνζήσασα ἀμ|έμπτως (*ll*.3-4).

The adjective (mentioned briefly at *New Docs 1977*, **83**), occurs in *I.Nikaia* II, 2.1319 (Imperial; pl.8), referring to a wife who συνζησάσᾳ αὐτῷ βί|ον ἡδὺν ἄμεμπτον (*ll*.6-7). The name Amimptos (= Amemptos) appears in *I.Nikaia* I.540 (Imperial; cf. *SEG* 1319), a brief Christian epitaph.

40. ἀνακάμπτω

MM provides one example each of the literal and figurative uses of this verb, both from papyri. In a Hellenistic inscription dated *c*.290 BC, a fragmentary copy of a land agreement, *I.Eph.* Ia.3 (pl.3) the following protasis clause occurs at *ll*.8-10: καὶ ἐὰν τεῖχος δέ|μωμεν ἀπὸ τοῦ πύργου τοῦ 'Αστυάγου πάγου τὸ κατὰ τὸ Ἕρμαιον καὶ | ἀνακάμπτωμεν ἄνω, κτλ, 'and if we build the wall which is in the neighbourhood of the shrine of Hermes from the tower on the hill of Astyages, and bend it back uphill . . .'. Although there is no NT passage which employs the verb in this primary sense, the instance deserves notice for a revised MM entry to show the word's semantic range.

41. ἀνασῴζω

The 𝔓[46] text of Heb. 10.14 is the only one to preserve this verb as the reading, in place of τοὺς ἁγιαζομένους. This constitutes the only occurrence of ἀνασῴζω in the NT. Since 𝔓[46] was not published until after the appearance of MM, it is no surprise that an entry is lacking there. As merely a single instance from the year's culling — the verb is common enough — attention may be drawn to a decree of the Ephesians from the year 138, *I.Eph.* Ia.21 (= VI.2019; pl.3) concerning the celebration of Antoninus Pius' birthday. After the introductory formulae it is determined that 'since in accordance with the general prayers of the world the most divine and august imperator Titus Aelius Antoninus, having received the empire handed on to him from his deified father, saves the whole race of men . . . it is resolved to celebrate his birthday annually . . .', ἐπειδὴ κατὰ τὰς κοινὰς τῆς οἰ[κουμένης] | εὐχὰς ὁ θειότατος καὶ εὐσε[βέστατος] | αὐτοκράτωρ Τίτος Αἴλιος Ἀντ[ωνεῖνος] | τὴν παρὰ τοῦ θεοῦ πατρὸς πα[ραδοθεῖσαν] | αὐτῷ βασιλείαν παραλαβὼν π[ᾶν μὲν τὸ τῶν | ἀνθρώπων ἀνασῴζει γένος, . . . | . . . | . . . | . . . | . . . δεδόχθαι κ[ατ' ἔτος ἕκαστον] | ἑορτάζειν τὴν γενέθλιον αὐ[τοῦ, κτλ, (*ll.*16-21, 25-26). This inscription was used by MM under the lemma *OGIS* 493 to illustrate ἑορτάζω.

A fragmentary testamentary foundation document inscribed on a sarcophagus specifies that the beneficiaries, the *katoikia* of the . . . *renoi* (perhaps Almourenoi; this community appears in VII, 1.3250-3264) are to celebrate annually the emperor's birthday, τῇ γενεθλίῳ ἡμέρᾳ (*l.*16; cf. *l.*1): *I.Eph.* VII, 1.3245 (Imperial period). Acts 17.26 is the only place in the NT where κατοικία occurs, and there it denotes the general term 'habitation, territory'. The word index to *I.Eph.* signals nearly a score of instances of the noun (a few largely restored) where the word is used in a more delimited sense to refer to a particular, named community, as in the text noted here.

42. βασανίζω

The NT uses this verb in a variety of ways (see BAGD), but only once (Mt. 8.6) of physical illness, a secondary development from its primary, classical meaning, 'torture'. In the conclusion of a letter, *P.Oxy.Hels.* 46 (Oxyrhynchos, I/II), the writer explains why he has not been able to correspond: οὐ γὰρ ἠδυνήθην ἐπὶ τοῦ | παρόντος γράψαι οὐδενὶ διὰ τὸ ἀπὸ | νόσου ἀναλαμβάνειν καὶ ψυγμοῦ | μεγάλου καὶ μόγις ἠδυνήθη(ν) καὶ ταῦ|τα γράψαι βασανιζ[ό]μενος (*ll.*15-19), 'for I could not write to anyone for the present because I am recovering from an illness and serious fever; and it was (only) with difficulty that I could write even this, racked as I am'.

43. γνόφος

MM's entry notes no documentary instances of this noun, found in the NT only at Heb. 12.18 (quoting Deut. 4.11). An instance surfaces among texts read for the current volume, in Guarducci's reprinting of a gnostic magical invocation, *EG* IV.276-78 (provenance unknown in Egypt, Imperial): '(hear me . . .) lord of lightning and thunder and darkness and winds', ὁ ἀστραπ|τῶν καὶ βροντῶν κα<ὶ> | γνόφου καὶ ἀνέμω|ν κύριος (*ll*.6-9). At a more general level this ascription of mastery over the natural elements finds a resonance in the Gospel narratives of the stilling of the storm (Mk. 4.35-41; Mt. 8.23-27; Lk. 8.22-26).

44. γνωστός

MM notes that the use of this adjective applied to persons is uncommon: in the NT it appears at Lk. 2.44 (absolutely); 23.49; and Jn 18.15, 16. In such passages the notion must be 'close friend, intimate' of X. Neither MM nor BAGD, s.v., 1b, provides any documentary instances to illustrate the meaning.

P.Laur. 60 is a petition (Oxyrhynchos, III) which, although fragmentary in its surviving lines, yields enough information to indicate that the petitioner, a swineherd, lost one of his six pigs from the farm (ἔπαυλις, 6, 12, 15, 16) where he tended them. Although the papyrus is broken, at *l*.17 there is mention of a female who is γ̣ν̣ωστὴ τοῦ αὐτοῦ Θωνίου, 'a close friend of the same Thonios', the latter living on a neighbouring farm. In Imperial parlance σεβαστόγνωστος and the participle γινωσκόμενος have become semi-technical terms: see *New Docs 1978*, **75**, *ad fin*.

Worth passing mention in this text, too, is the interchangeability of χοῖρος (19) and its diminutive χοιρίον (9), both referring to the same group of pigs. On κύων/κυνάριον see **66**.

45. γογγυσμός

In a letter to his mother — Tibiletti, *Lettere*, no.1 (*ed.pr.* — *P.Ross.Georg.* 3 [1930, repr. 1966] 2 [provenance unknown, III]; pl.2) — Serenos explains that despite her recent bereavement he has not been able to send his brother Marcus to her, because their medical work has been too demanding — he has not even been able to sit down for several days (οὐκ ἦν με πρὸς ὀλίγας ἡμέρας κα|θίσαν[τα, *ll*.14-15). He says that it is not easy to leave a lot of patients μὴ καί τι[ς γ]ονγυσμὸς κ̣[α]θ' ἡμῶν γένηται, 'lest indeed there should be some murmuring against us' (*l*.11). A similar expression occurs in *PSI* 8 (1927) 895 (provenance unknown, III/IV), ἀλλ' ἵνα μ̣ὴ̣ γ̣ογ[υσ?]|μός τις π[άλι]ν γένηται [- - -]| τὸ ἴσον τοῦ λόγου παντὸς ἀπέστιλα τῷ δεσπότῃ μου, 'but in order that there may be no complaint again . . . I have sent a copy of the whole account to my lord' (*ll*.12-14). The noun γογγυσμός occurs in the LXX eleven times (five of them in Ex. 16, the story of the gift of manna) and in the NT four times, at Jn 7.12; Acts 6.1; Phil. 2.14 and 1 Pet. 4.9. MM, s.v., provides no documentary examples of this word, and BAGD, s.v., cites a late text, *P.Cair.Masp.* 2 (1913, repr. 1973) 67159, a contract of association between two carpenters (Antinoe, 16 Dec., 568) who agree to work together δίχα πάσης | ῥαδιουργίας καὶ γογγισμοῦ (*read* γογγυσ-) καὶ ὑπερθέσεως καὶ ἀναβολῆς | ἔργων διόλου, 'without any laziness or complaining or postponement or delaying of jobs at all' (*ll.*26-28).

The text with which this entry began contains a number of other words of interest. In *ll.*12-13 there is an example of μηνύω used in its non-forensic sense, as at Lk. 20.37 and 1 Cor. 10.28: Serenos writes π[άν]τως σοι ἐμήνυσεν ὁ Μᾶρκος δι' ἐπιστολῆς | τὴν ἐμὴν ἀσχολασίαν, 'certainly Marcus has informed you by letter of my lack of time'. The verb οἰκονομέω, which is found only once in the NT (Lk. 16.2) with the meaning 'be a manager', occurs in *l.*28 where Serenos tells his mother to come to him εὐθέως οἰκονομήσασα τὰ σεαυτῆς, 'as soon as you have arranged your affairs'. Cf. the discussion of οἰκονόμος at **69** below. Finally, ἀποδημία (for which BAGD, s.v., cites two occurrences in ECL) is found in *l.*24; for an example of the verb ἀποδημέω, cf. *New Docs 1976*, **20**.

(A.L. CONNOLLY)

46. δεσπότης τῆς ἐμῆς ψυχῆς

This is only one of several honorific titles used in *P.Strasb.* 3 (1963) 286, repr. in Tibiletti, *Lettere*, no.29. The phrase, or minor variants of it, occurs at *ll.*1, 16 (written by a second hand), and in the address on the back (*l.*19). *P.Grenf.* 1 (1896) 61.1 (Fayum, VI) offers an exact parallel. Tibiletti may be right to suggest that the mid-IV date suggested in *ed.pr.* for the *P.Strasb.* letter is too early. MM, s.v. ψυχή, suggests that in the *P.Grenf.* text the noun means 'soul'; while this cannot be ruled out, 'life' may be more appropriate if that letter is indeed from a slave to her master, as Grenfell suggested. For discussion of some uses of ψυχή see **11** above. Stereotyped though the phrase must be, in view of the *P.Strasb.* evidence where the writer calls the addressee 'brother' as well as using various honorific terms, it is at least possible that a spiritual oversight is to be inferred from the phrase. Whether this letter is Christian or not is uncertain, in Tibiletti's judgement (p.17). Certainly, it is not as explicit as the *P.Grenf.* text in which the same phrase occurs. But if the later dating which he suggests is followed, that may encourage us to think of a Christian milieu, though it would fall short of establishing it.

Other titles used in the letter include ἡ σὴ [τελ]ε<ι>ότης (8, in the genitive case), ἡ σὴ τιμιότης (10), σεμνολόγημα | ἐμόν (17-18). The nouns in the first two of these phrases occur in the NT, though not as titles (Col. 3.14 and Heb. 6.1; Rev. 18.19 respectively).

47. δικαιοσύνη

The sense 'justice', 'uprightness' (BAGD, s.v., 1), is commonly attested in honorific inscriptions; and though MM provides some instances of the noun with this meaning, BAGD does not. In the context of this type of inscription it is a regular element along with words like ἀρετή, εὐσέβεια, etc. *I.Eph.* Ia.6 (II BC; pl.7) provides a very clear instance. This text honours a gymnasiarch, Diodoros, and the *demos* votes to erect a statue of him in the gymnasium in recognition of 'the man's (proper) ambition and uprightness, and the enthusiasm and care which he has shown with regard to the gymnasium in all matters relating to his office', τὴν τἀνδρὸς φιλοδοξία[ν] | τε καὶ δικαιοσύνην καὶ τὴν γεγενημένην ἐξ αὐτοῦ π[ε]|ρὶ τὸ γυμνάσιον ἐν πᾶσι τοῖς κατὰ τὴν ἀρχὴν σπουδήν ṭ[ε] | [κ]ạὶ ἐπιμέλειαν, κτλ (*ll*.31-34). *IGB* 254 (Delos, II/I BC) is another such an example, inscribed on a base: ['Αθ]ηναίων οἱ κατοικοῦντες ἐν Δήλῳ | καὶ 'Ρωμαίων οἱ παρεπιδημοῦντες | 'Επιγένην Δίου Μελιτέα | ἐπιμελητὴν γενόμενον Δήλου | ἀρετῆς ἕνεκεν καὶ δικαιοσύνης | 'Απόλλωνι. | 'Ηφαιστίων Μύρωνος 'Αθηναῖος ἐποίει, 'The Athenians who live on Delos and the Romans who visit it (honoured) Epigenes son of Dios of the deme Melita, the overseer (of foreigners(?)) of Delos, because of his virtue and justice; (this statue is dedicated) to Apollo. Hephaistion son of Myron the Athenian was the sculptor'. This text should not be misread to mean that Epigenes is praised for his *dikaiosyne* shown to Apollo; for it is a quality exhibited by a superior (such as a benefactor) to an inferior, not the reverse. Similarly, in no.251 (Delos, mid-II BC) a priest of Apollo is honoured by 'the Athenians, Romans and other Greeks who live on Delos and who visit it (παρεπιδημοῦντες), for his *arete* and *dikaiosyne*, and his *eusebeia* in relation to Apollo and his temple and the other gods; (this statue is dedicated) to Apollo'. The last two qualities mentioned here are used of Julius Caesar in an honorific text from Pergamon, dated after 48 BC, εὐσεβείας ἕνεκα καὶ δικαιοσύνης, *IGRR* 4 (1927) 305; cf. Tuchelt, *Denkmäler,* 208. Honorific texts are not the only context for this noun combination: Pircher, no.17 (= Peek, *GVI* 1693) is a metrical epitaph for Archidike (Demetrias, III/II BC), of whom it is said that 'she practised piety and its consort, justice', εὐσεβίαν γὰρ | ἤσκει καὶ σύνεδρον τῆσδε δικαιοσύνην (*ll*.3-4). The latter term was used considerably less commonly of women than of men, according to Pircher (51 and n.13), simply because of the much lower public profile of most women. Pircher, no.13 (Athens, before mid-IV BC) — = *IG* II/III^2 9112; Peek, *GVI* 493 — provides a further instance, in which the nurse Malicha from Kythera has her upright character singled out: τίτθην . . . | . . . | . . . τήνδε δικαιοτάτην (*ll*.1-3). The choice of the word is all the more striking here, given that her profession implies a servile status.

A statue of *Dikaiosyne*, with this word only on the base, was set up in the Agora at Ephesos: *I.Eph.* II.503 (see the *Addenda et corrigenda* supplement to *I.Eph.* [1981], p.13 for further comment on this text). Spicq, *NLNT* III.130-31 with nn.5-7, lists several other epigraphical examples of Dikaiosyne personified and divinised. A house-born slave (ἐνδογένης) called Dikaiosyne was manumitted at Delphi in 140/139 BC: Reilly, *Slaves*, 689. No.688 in her list may attest another ex-slave with this name (Delphi, I BC init.), but much of the name is restored: [Δικαιο]σύνα.

The verb παρεπιδημέω in *IGB* 251 and 254 above may be noted in passing as two specific epigraphical attestations to parallel its use in ECL; BAGD, s.v., gives only papyrus references, and the general siglum 'inscr.'. A third occurs in *SGPI* 103c (Philai), in a letter to Ptolemy VIII (145-116 BC) and his consort Kleopatra from the priests of Isis at Abatos and Philai, mentioning οἱ παρεπι|δημοῦντες εἰς τὰς Φίλας στρατηγοὶ καὶ ἐπιστάται, κτλ (*ll*.4-5).

Pfuhl/Möbius, I.69 (Samos, IV BC init.; pl.18) deserves particular mention under this entry. It is a brief funerary epigram for a grandmother which begins by saying that 'if the practice of justice towards everyone is the best thing' she deserves to be so thought of, εἰ τὸ δικαιοσύνην ἀσκεῖν πρὸς ἅπαντα κράτι[στον], κτλ. The idiom δικαιοσύνην ἀσκέω is used in ECL by Hermas, *Man.* 8.10 (see BAGD, s.v. ἀσκέω for other non-ECL parallels). This statement is glossed in *l*.3 with the words ἐν δὲ βίωι πρὸς ἅπαντας ἀληθεύọυσα, 'during her life she spoke the truth to everyone'. MM, s.v. ἀληθεύω, was able to cite one documentary instance of this verb only, a papyrus of IV AD; and this is the only non-literary text referred to in BAGD's entry (NT: Gal. 4.16; Eph. 4.15). At one stroke this inscription, first published in 1970, takes the attestation in non-literary sources back eight centuries. Spicq, *NLNT* III.31-32 n.3, provides three further papyrus instances.

48. διοδεύω

BAGD, s.v., notes no documentary examples to illustrate the intransitive use of this verb (NT: Lk. 8.1). Yet MM had already drawn attention to *P.Amh.* 2 (1901) 36.13-14 (Gebelen, *c.*135 BC), a petition in which a man speaks of the dangers he encountered while travelling through various areas: διοδεύων κιν|δυν[εύω π]αρ' ἕκαστον. An epigraphical example may also be noted: *I.Nikaia* I.1 is a decree of Hadrian concerning the aqueduct over which bridges are to be built, δι' ὧν καὶ ἅμαξαι διοδεύειν δυνήσονται καὶ πάντα τὰ τετράποδα (7), 'by means of which both wagons will be able to pass as well as all kinds of beasts'. A fine is to be imposed on any who pass through the aqueduct itself, [διὰ τοῦ ὑδρα]|[γωγίου δι]οδεύειν τολμήσωσιν (7-8). For πᾶς in *l.*7 in the sense of 'every kind of', cf. in the NT, e.g., 1 Tim. 6.10, ῥίζα γὰρ πάντων τῶν κακῶν ἐστιν ἡ φιλαργυρία. Classical παντοῖος is used only in the *koine* by high-style Atticisers like Lucian and Plutarch (see LSJ, s.v.). Though now held in the museum at Iznik, a Nikaian provenance for this text is doubtful, according to Şahin (ed. n., ad loc.).

The simple form of this verb occurs but once in the NT, in the parable of the good Samaritan, Lk. 10.33. BAGD, s.v., adds a further papyrus reference to the single one given by MM, but omits *OGIS* 199.28 (included by MM), presumably because of its late date (VI[1]). *I.Nikaia* II, 2.1326 (III-IV) provides a metaphorical example of the verb in a metrical epitaph for Asklepios: κῖμαι γὰρ καλο|εργὸς ἀνὴρ τὸν κόσμον ὁ|δεύσας πεντήκοντα ἔτη (7-9), 'for (here) I lie, a man of good deeds, after travelling through this world for fifty years'.

49. δόγμα

This noun is well enough attested, both in inscriptions and papyri, in its technical application to imperial edicts: the NT reflects that usage at Lk. 2.1 and Acts 17.7. The flow-on from this executive sphere to the use in ECL of the commands of Jesus (see BAGD's references) is an unsurprising one. So, in the NT, the apostles' *dogmata* are implied to have great authority (Acts 16.4). A similar, secondary development appears in a verse epitaph for a woman and her daughter, who both died, apparently, while the mother was in labour. In *IGUR* 1147 (Rome, Imperial; pl. on. p.6) Sabina, aged 26, says 'I lie in this grave with my daughter who followed close on my heels (thereby) displaying affection for her mother, by the decrees of the Fates', τῇδε σορῷ κεῖμαι θυγατρὸς μέτα, | ἥ με δίωξεν, (*leaf*) | διξαμένη στοργὴν φιλομήτορα, | δόγμασι Μοιρῶν (*leaf*) (6-9). The weakened sense of δίωκω, almost 'follow', may be noted here; a poeticism, perhaps? The phrase στοργὴν φιλομήτορα is likewise a poetic rendering of the common use of φιλόστοργος in epitaphs used especially of mothers or wives: see *New Docs 1977*, **80**, especially p.102; cf. *New Docs 1978*, **11**. Just as the commands of an Emperor are not to be disobeyed, nor the precepts of Jesus and his apostles neglected, so in this epigram the demands of Fate are not to be gainsaid. It is reasonable to see these secondary uses as consciously taking their rise from the context of the imperial edict, thus ensuring that the presence of δόγμα in such places is 'loaded' with specific force.

50. ἐμπνέω

The sole example given in MM is ignored by BAGD, s.v., 1, presumably because its intransitive nature there does not illustrate the syntactical use of this verb in the NT, found only at Acts 9.1 of Saul ἔτι ἐμπνέων ἀπειλῆς καὶ φόνου . . . The highly figurative sense here is akin to English 'fume', and the wording means simply that Saul threatened the disciples with death.

The very citation included by MM comes from a text which is repr. as *IGUR* 1379 (Rome, II/III; pl. on p.226). This poem consists of five elegiac couplets, whose carving contains one interesting feature: the caesura of each pentameter is marked by an ivy leaf. Although the epigram seems to be complete, yet we appear not to have the entire funerary monument preserved, as the name of the deceased woman and her husband are not given. *Ll.*7-10 of the epigram read:

οὐ γὰρ ἀμειλίκτους κραδίης ὀδύνας ἀκέ[ο]ι̣το
ἀθάνατος, παλάμῃ (*leaf*) κρᾶτ' ἐπαφησάμεν̣[ο]ς,
ἐς δ' ὅσον ἐνπνείει βίοτόν τε ἐπὶ ἦμαρ ἐρύκει,
δύσμορος ἀντλήσει (*leaf*) πένθος ἀεξίβιον.

For no god could soothe the cruel pains in his (the husband's) heart, by laying his hand on his head. And for as long as he lives and holds on to life for a day, | the poor wretch will drink (his cup of) grief which will last throughout his life.

Here in *l.*9 we have ἐμπνέω in the poetic form ἐμπνείω. Since ἐπαφάω means to 'touch lightly' (so LSJ), we are given a picture here of a god attempting to assuage the husband's distress with a soothing hand. The participle in *l.*8 is to be taken as equivalent to εἰ ἐπαφήσαιτο. K.L. McKay points out to me (*per litt.*) that since ἄν is occasionally omitted from a potential optative construction in Homer, it is no cause for surprise to see it missing from an epic-flavoured poem. For another example see **32** above.

51. κατ' ἐπαγγελίαν

This noun is common in the NT; and indeed this particular phrase is found there on three occasions: Acts 13.23; Gal. 3.29; 2 Tim. 1.1. The phrase can occur in honorific inscriptions, referring to an undertaking by someone to pay for the erection of the monument. An example from this year's culling is *I.Nikaia* II, 1.702 (Imperial period), in which the *demos* honours Cassius Lyaios . . . κατὰ ἐπαγγελίαν | 'Επαξ[ί]ωνος λιθου[ρ]|γοῦ (6-8), 'in accordance with the promise of Epaxion the stonemason'. This text is more likely to belong to the territory of Kios, west of Nikaia, than to that of Nikaia itself: see *BE* (1982) 413. BAGD follows MM, s.v., in noting only one example of this prepositional phrase, though it, in fact, employs the genitive. The noun itself occurs probably twice in *P.Oxy.Hels.* 23.36, 42, reprinted above at **23**, but with a meaning not found in the NT, 'threats'. At *New Docs 1976*, **12**, the noun occurs in *l.*10 of a late II AD prefectural edict seeking to circumscribe the prevalence of magic; but again the sense is not really similar to any of those found in the NT.

52. ἐπιφανής

AE 618 reprints an incomplete honorific inscription for Marcus Aurelius and Commodus on a white marble altar (Ardan-Teşvikiye in Phrygia, 177-80): *ed.pr.* — C.H.E. Haspels, *The Highlands of Phrygia* (2 vols.; Princeton, 1971) I.333-34, no.93 (pl.625); cf. *BE* (1972) 462. Some of the titulature is unusual for the period, including the phrase θεῶν ἐπιφανέστατον, applied to each emperor (*ll.*3-4, 6-7). In the first century Claudius is described as ἐμφανὴς θεός after his death, *P.Oxy.* 7 (1910) 1021.2 (54 AD). The phrase is used of Trajan in the early second century, *P.Oxy.* 36 (1970) 2754.4 (111 AD). Ἐμφανής appears twice in the NT, at Acts 10.40 and Rom. 10.20. The context of the former passage implicitly attributes divinity to Jesus, since ὁ θεὸς ἤγειρεν ἐν τῇ τρίτῃ ἡμέρᾳ καὶ ἔδωκεν αὐτὸν ἐμφανῆ γενέσθαι. For the adjective used in a more general sense see *l.*6 of the text quoted at **2** above.

MM, s.v. ἐμφανής, cross-refer to their entry on ἐπιφανής; the latter adjective may carry a similar connotation. It is used in inscriptions of Hellenistic monarchs, as MM's examples illustrate, and also of the Roman emperor as *P.Oxy.* 12 (1916) 1425.2 (318) shows. From the present year's reading of texts we may note *I.Eph.* II.251, a statue base of late Republican date (48 BC) in which Julius Caesar is honoured by the *poleis*, *demoi* and *ethne* of Asia as τὸν ἀπὸ Ἄρεως καὶ Ἀφροδε[ί]|της θεὸν ἐπιφανῆ καὶ κοινὸν τοῦ | ἀνθρωπίνου βίου σωτῆρα (5-7), 'the god manifest (descended) from Ares and Aphrodite, and the general saviour of human life'. This inscription is one of those catalogued in Tuchelt, *Denkmäler*, 141. It became a cliché in the Greek East, of course, for the emperor to be called *theos*. Examples from Ephesos include *I.Eph.* II.252 (Augustus), 265 (Nerva), 266, 274 and 275 (Nerva and Trajan). It is an especially prominent feature of honorific texts for Hadrian: he is called Zeus Soter Olympios at *I.Eph.* II.267 and VII, 1.3410; cf. II.272 (Olympian *soter* and *ktistes*), 273c and 274 (Olympios). *I.Eph.* VII, 1.3271 is a dedication to Zeus Soter Olympios and Hadrian. In *I.Nikaia* I.32 he is also called Zeus Soter Olympios on a small altar dedication. Nor is the phenomenon confined to Asia Minor: from Athens *IG* II/III^2 3315 — repr. in Guarducci, *EG* III (Rome, 1974) 92-93 — provides an example of Hadrian equated with Zeus Olympios. The date of this Athenian text, 128/9, appears to be the *terminus post quem* for this terminology applied to Hadrian.

Ἐπιφανής occurs over a score of times altogether in the Ephesian inscriptions. The Tetrarchs (293-305) are referred to with the superlative on two milestones, *I.Eph.* VII, 2.3603, 3604. At VII, 2.3825, a posthumous honorific decree speaks of Theophron as priest of the most manifest Anaitis Artemis (*ll.*17-18). As merely a final example note also VI.2055, in which the Ephesians honoured the people of Kos by erecting a statue of Demos: τὸ]ν ἐπιφανέστατον | . . . | . . . | . . . τὸν | [ἀδελ]φὸν αὐτῆς Κωίων | [Δῆ]μον, κτλ (*ll.*3-8). Another way in which ἐπιφανής is used in inscriptions is to indicate that someone is deceased. Pfuhl/Möbius II.1349 provides an instance of this: ἥρως ἐπιφανὴς Σωκράτης (provenance unknown, but possibly Lampsakos or Perinthos, Imperial period?; pl.197). This text is included in P. Frisch, *Die Inschriften von Lampsakos* (*IK* 6; Bonn, 1978) as no.24; cf. *BE* 376. Spicq provides further documentary references for the adjective at *NLNT* I.287 n.2.

In the NT ἐπιφανής is found once only, at Acts 2.20, a quotation from LXX Joel 3.4, ἡμέραν κυρίου τὴν μεγάλην καὶ ἐπιφανῆ. Here the adjective approximates to a transferred epithet: what makes the 'Day of the Lord' important is his epiphany. So we may detect here, as with ἐμφανής, terminology used of Hellenistic monarchs (and subsequently in the Roman Imperial cult) being applied to God. The implication of the presence of the word in Peter's Pentecost speech is to suggest Jesus' divinity, as the following verses more explictly indicate (Acts 2.22, 36).

53. ἐπουράνιος

Used of God, this adjective is found only as a *v.l.* in the NT, at Mt. 18.35, ὁ πατήρ μου ὁ ἐπουράνιος. Two dedications to Zeus Epouranios from Aktaş/Gölpazar, in the territorium of Nikaia, provide the first testimony to the use of the word as an epithet of Zeus outside Syria and Egypt: *I.Nikaia* II, 1.1114, 1115 (IV, and probably III, respectively). See Şahin's n. ad no. 1114 for further discussion: these altar dedications to 'heavenly Zeus' (pls. 19, 20) testify to the increasing prevalence of henotheism in late antiquity, according to Şahin.

54. ἑπτάκις

This numerical adverb is not especially common in documentary texts, but LSJ know of a couple of epigraphical instances. MM's entry provides none; BAGD, one papyrus reference to a magical text. The presence of a poetical example in *IGUR* 1221 (Rome, II; pl. on p.81) may be signalled here. This text commemorates in verse the members of a family, the father of which was a sculptor from Aphrodisias aged 70, ἑ|πτάκι δέκα (15-16). He mentions that the deceased now lie ἄλαλοι (16), an adjective which occurs in the NT only in Mk., at 7.37; 9.17, 25. MM lacks an entry for this word; BAGD, however, notes this inscription from Rome under the siglum *IG* XIV.1627.

In fact ἄλαλος occurs in two other funerary epigrams encountered among the reading for this volume. In *IGUR* 1154 (Rome, Imperial period; pl. on p.13) the dead lyric poet and lyre player Ammon is addressed as 'a shadow, (now) mute to men', ἄλα|λος ἀνθρώποις σκιά (*ll.*3-4). And in Pfuhl/Möbius, I.355 (Kula in Lydia, 250/1; pl.59) the dead man says that though he was young he has died, and 'I live in the darkness; now the earth holds me as a drink from the mute fountain of silence', . . . καὶ τὸ σκότος οἰκῶ | γέά με νῦν καδέχει πηγῆς | ἀλάλου πόμα σειγῆς (*ll.*8-10). The metaphorical use of σκότος here, referring to the darkness of death, may be noted, along with σκιά in the *IGUR* inscription just quoted, as a parallel for Lk. 1.79, ἐπιφᾶναι τοῖς ἐν σκότει καὶ σκιᾷ θανάτου καθημένοις. In the Pfuhl/Möbius epigram πόμα is perhaps worth passing mention as a documentary parallel for this noun which in the NT is mainly used of the 'spiritual' drink (1 Cor. 10.4; 1 Cor. 12.13 *v.l.*, but literal at Heb. 9.10).

55. ἔσοπτρον

This word appears in a votive inscription reprinted by Guarducci at *EG* IV.215-216: Μαλθάκη Φ[ιλεί]νου ἀρχιθ[ε]ωρή|σασα τὸ ἔσο|πτρον Ἀμφι<τ>ρεί|τη ἀνέθηκε, 'Malthake, daughter of Philinos, former *architheoros*, dedicated the mirror to Amphitrite' (Tenos, Hadrianic period). The stone was found near the site of the sanctuary of Poseidon and Amphitrite, of which two deities Malthake was an hereditary priestess (cf. *IG* XII *Suppl.* 322). Other examples of dedications of mirrors are one dedicated to Persephone (Locri Epizephyrii, VI BC; Guarducci, *EG* I [Rome, 1967] 302-303, and one to Asklepios (Pergamum, time of Trajan or Hadrian[?]; *ed.pr.* — C. Habicht, *Die Inschriften des Asklepieions* [*Altertümer von Pergamon* VIII.3; Berlin, 1969] 113b; cf. *BE* [1971] 546). Malthake may have been dedicating this mirror at the time of her wedding, or perhaps for use in catoptromancy. For bibliography on the subjects of divination by mirrors and mirror imagery in general see R. Mortley, *VC* 30 (1976) 110. The various uses of mirror imagery by Classical writers have been classified as commonly symbolising three ideas, purity (from the clean surface of a mirror), self-knowledge, or indirect knowledge. On these notions see J.H. Harrop, *JEA* 48 (1962) 139-40. In the NT the mirror imagery of Jas. 1.23 belongs to the second type, while that of 1 Cor. 13.12 and 2 Cor. 3.18 is of the third kind. On NT mirror imagery see Spicq, *NLNT*, I.292-95.

A text which intertwines both the last two types is a fourth-century Christian letter of recommendation (*ed.pr.* — Harrop, *art.cit.*, 132-40; = *P.Oxy.* 31 [1966] 2603; Naldini, no.47; the text is noted briefly at **124** below) in which the writer, Paul, in a rhetorically elaborate proem, flatters his addressee with the compliments that he has self-knowledge just as a man possessing a mirror (ἔσοπτρον, *l.*1) knows his own appearance, and that ὡς δι' ἐσ[ό]πτρου κα|τῖδες τὴν πρὸς σέ μου ἔ[μ]φυτον | στοργὴν καὶ ἀγάπην τὴν ἀεὶ νέαν, 'as through a mirror you have seen my implanted affection and love for you ever fresh' (*ll.*17-19). This letter is interesting for several other reasons. This Paul, who is obviously well-educated, and his addressee (perhaps to be restored as Sarapion: see *ed.pr.*, note on *l.*1) could each be any of half a dozen fourth-century clerics known from other sources — Harrop conjectures that the recipient may have been Sarapion, the bishop of Thmouis, 'a man of undoubted learning and considerable literary activity' (138), and the author Paul of Oxyrhynchos, who like Sarapion was a strong anti-Arian (139). In *ll.*28-29 the words καὶ εἴ τι αὐτοῖς ποιεῖς ἐμο[ὶ] ἐποί|ησας, 'and if you do anything for them, you have done it for me', clearly recall Mt. 25.40. Since also we read in *ll.*3-4 of a mirror or some other such thing 'in which faces are seen in reflection', ἐν οἷς τὰ πρόσωπα ἐνοπτρίζεται, this papyrus provides another verb form with which to compare the controversial κατοπτριζόμενοι of 2 Cor. 3.18. Moreover, this text provides the only metaphorical reference to mirrors in the documentary sources, and should be added to a new MM even though it is Christian.

Mirrors are mentioned elsewhere in the papyri, but without metaphorical meaning. Nearly all the occurrences are in lists, particularly catalogues of articles taken by brides into their marital homes, e.g., *P.Mich.* 2 (1933) 121.*r* IV. i. 3 (Tebtunis, 42 AD); *P.Osl.* 2 (1931) 46.7 (provenance unknown, III). Mirrors seem to be standard equipment for brides, as are statuettes of Aphrodite (see note to *l.*6 of the *P.Osl.* text cited). The mirrors mentioned in the papyri are most commonly called κάτοπτρα, a few only are ἔσοπτρα while more are called ὄσυπτρα, e.g., *P.Oxy.* 12 (1916) 1449.16 (213-17); *P.Fuad* 1 (1949) 8.6 (provenance unknown, II?), and in a bilingual text, *osyptrum*, *P.Mich.* 7 (1947) 434.12 (provenance not given, II); cf. ὄσιπτρον, *P.Strasb.* 3 (1963) 237.16 (provenance unknown, 142); ὄσοπτρον, *CPR* 1 (1895) 27.10 (Arsinoite, 190). There is no discernible difference in meaning between these forms. The spelling ὄσυπτρον — not given in LSJ — may reflect a metathesis of vowels, from an original εἴσοπτρον; but it appears that ὄσυπτρον had become a common form. This may have been a a local Egyptian phenomenon, but if it was more wide-spread the choice of ἔσοπτρον in the NT (1 Cor. 13.12; Jas. 1.23) may then reflect what was considered appropriate for a more literary level of language. On ο for ε in this word see Gignac I.292.

(A.L. CONNOLLY)

56. εὐλογέω

Neither MM's entry nor that in BAGD (s.v., 2a) provides any documentary illustration of this verb when it is used to refer to speaking well of someone, such as occurs in the NT at Lk. 6.28 and Rom. 2.14. Pfuhl/Möbius, II.1606 republish a bilingual — Greek and Latin — inscription (Tomi, probably II; pl.234) for Cornelia Fortunata also known as Doutoros, who died at the age of thirty. The Greek epigram on the relief runs:

τὴν Σταβυλίωνος σύνβιον Κορνηλίαν
ἀνάγνωθι Φορτουνᾶταν εὐλογῶν, ξένε,
στοργὴν πρὸς ἀνδρός, κοσμίαν καὶ σώφρονα
διατελέσσαν συνπαθῆ τε δάκρυα
λιποῦσαν. εἶτα πάριθι καὶ ἐπιτύγχανε.

Praise the affection on the part of her husband, stranger, as you read of the wife of Stabulio, Cornelia Fortunata. She continued respectable, modest, and | left him sympathetic tears. Well, go on your way and prosper.

It would be possible, though more awkward, to render, 'Read about Fortunata (and) extol her love for her husband, a love which continued . . .'; and we would have an instance of accusative/genitive confusion in πρὸς ἀνδρός. But confusion between these two cases is unusual, especially after πρός. It should be noted that the NT references collected by BAGD, s.v. εὐλογέω, 2a, are not satisfactorily differentiated: some carry a religious connotation (request God's blessing on someone, etc.) while others, such as the passages from Luke and Romans noted above, do not bear this nuance. For εὐλογέω/εὐλογία of blessing God see **26** above.

The adjective κόσμιος is found only twice in the NT, both times in 1 Tim., at 2.9 (of women's dress), and at 3.2 in a list of attributes expected of an *episkopos*. MM's entry notes that epigraphical attestation of the word is common. Our text is of passing interest as a parallel for 1 Tim. 3.2, since in both places the adjective is used in close connection with σώφρων. Now, at *New Docs 1977*, **80**, p.101, it was suggested that '*sophrosyne* is essentially a feminine virtue'. But J.M. Rist has pointed out to me that this is not the case. Essentially, the word denotes 'co-operation', and is applied to males aplenty, as in the case of 1 Tim. 3.2. Some inscriptions from the present year's reading bear this out. The noun is used of the father of the emperor Theodosios at *I.Eph.* IV.1311. A victor at the festival of Artemis is praised ἀρετῆς ἕνεκα καὶ | σώφρονος ἀσκήσεως, *I.Eph.* V.1606.10 (Imperial). The noun is found in an epitaph which a man erects for his son, *IGB* 395 (Athens, VI^2 BC). The adjective is used in an epitaph for a man at *IGM* 2 (Phigalia, IV or III BC), the noun in another for a certain Aristokles, no.11 (Athens, IV BC). In Pfuhl/Möbius, II.1699 (Odessos?, II; pl.248) the deceased Dioskourides is described as ἀρτίγαμος, σώφρων, νέος (*l.*2).

Finally, returning to this short poem extolling Fortunata, she is called συμπαθής (*l.*4). This adjective is used of a man in a posthumous honorific inscription, *TAM* V, 1 (1981) 687 (Iulia Gordos in Lydia, 75/6), where Theophilos is described as being συνπαθῆ πρὸς τὴν γυναῖκα 'Απφίαν (*l.*17). This text is repr. at *New Docs 1977*, **18**, and the word receives brief comment at the end of that entry. The form συνπαθών (or adjectival -ῶν?) occurs in a fragmentary inscription mentioned at *New Docs 1978*, **80**, p.92. Further documentary attestations are given by Spicq, *NLNT* II.842-43.

I.Apollonia 84b is a brief funerary text for Euloge daughter of Loukas (Imperial period): 'the names suggest a Jewess' (Reynolds, n. ad loc.).

57. εὐπειθής

An epigraphical instance of this adjective, for which MM (followed by BAGD) provides only papyrological parallels, occurs in a newly-published ephebic decree from Athens, dated *c*.214/3 BC. This text — *ed.pr.*: S.V. Tracey, *Hesperia* 48 (1979) 174-78 (pl.59); cf. *SEG* 116; BE (1981) 217 — is incomplete, and badly worn on the left side of its inscribed surface. At *ll*.7-10 the Athenian motion in praise of the ephebes begins with the following clause: ἐπειδὴ οἱ ἔφηβοι οἱ ἐπὶ Διοκλ̣έ|[ους ἄρχοντος] διετέλεσαν εὐτακτοῦντες εἱς τ≪ὰ≫ γ[υμνά]||[σια· κατεσκεύασα]ν δ' ἑαυτοὺς εὐπειθεῖς τῶι τε κοσμ[ητεῖ καὶ] | [τοῖς καθεστῶσ]ιν αὐτοῖς διδασκάλοις, κτλ, 'since the ephebes in the year of Diokles' archonship continued to be well-disciplined in the gymnasia, and made themselves obedient to the *kosmetes* and the teachers set over them, etc.'. The sole use of the adjective in the NT occurs in a list of the qualities by which James describes ἡ ἄνωθεν σοφία, Jas. 3.17. In this passage, 'obedient' is not really the sense required, rather 'open to persuasion', *vel sim.*

58. εὐφροσύνη

Found twice in the NT — Acts 2.28 (quoting LXX Ps. 15.11), and 14.17 — this word is commonly enough attested in documentary texts. It is also employed frequently in Christian texts of the late Roman/early Byzantine period. *I.Eph.* IV.1310 is a late fourth-century epigram on a statue base, preceded by a Christian cross, recognising the contribution to the city made by the proconsul Stephanos. Vertical bars mark line divisions on the stone.

† εἰθυδίκῃ Στεφάνῳ κ|αθαρῆς μετὰ μόχθον ἀ[π]|ήνης
εἰκόνα λαϊνέην | στήσατο πᾶσα πόλις·
| ἔπρεπε Νάξον ≪ἔ≫χειν τέκος | ὄλβιον, ἥ ῥα καὶ αὐτόν
θρέψατο κισσοφόρον | Βάκχον ἐς εὐφροσύνην.

The entire city set up a stone statue for right-judging Stephanos after the toil of his pure magistracy. It was fitting that Naxos should have a successful offspring, for it also nurtured ivy-bearing Bakkhos himself for joy.

That Stephanos was a proconsul is indicated by mention of the *sella curulis* (ἀπήνη). A photo of the text is conveniently included in C. Foss, *Ephesos after Antiquity* (Cambridge, 1979) 68.

In a sepulchural inscription for Marcia and another person whose name is not entirely preserved, *I.Eph.* V.1628 (Imperial period), the epigram begins (*l*.5) with a quotation from Homer, *Od.* 3.196 which encapsulates the theme of the rest of the poem, that when you die you are fortunate if you have a child still living who will see to a proper funerary monument for you. The second half of this epigram runs:

καλὰν δ' ἐκσῴζων γενέτᾳ χάριν, οὐ βιότου φῶς
δεύτερον, ἀλλὰ κλέους ἧψ' ἱερὸν βίοτον.
αἰνῶ Μουσάων σεμνὸν γένος· εἰς ἀρετὰν γὰρ
δῶκαν ἐμοὶ τέκνου ζῶσαν εὐφροσύναν.

And he (the child) preserved good favour for his parent, not the light of life | a second time, but he did attain to the holy life of glory. I praise the revered family of the Muses, because (as a reward) for my virtue they gave me the living joy of a child.

In this poem we may pause to note the presence of ἐκσῴζω, found once in the NT as an inferior reading at Acts 27.39. The verb is not rare, but MM lack an entry and BAGD have no documentary references under their lemma.

From the Ephesos inscriptions, attention may also be given to *I.Eph.* II.555. This late II AD verse graffito was accorded a flurry of discussion after its first publication (W. Jobst, *WS* 85 [1972] 240-45 [pl.2]). For bibliography, see *I.Eph.*, ad loc. Vertical bars indicate line divisions on the stone. The final word reflects the common feature υ for ι.

ὦ Εὐλάλι χαῖρε, θεοῖς | πεποθημένον | οὔνομα σεμνόν·
ἐεὶ ζῇς, | ἐεὶ καὶ βίος αὐξανέτω·
| πᾶσιν γὰρ φιλίαν παρέχεις | ἀγαθαῖσι προνοίαις,
δῶρα | καὶ εὐφροσύνας, ἧς ἔχεις | ἀμβροσύης.

Greetings Eulalios, a revered person desired by the gods. May you live forever, and forever let your life increase. For you provide friendship to everyone, with good foresight, together with the gifts and joyous banquets of the ambrosian (plenty) which you possess.

In *l*.2 read αἰεί in both places. This poem is an extended version of those acclamations widespread especially in later antiquity; examples of these in *I.Eph.* include II.585 (partly quoted at **1** above), 587 (very fragmentary); IV.1313 (Christian), 1321; VI.2045; VII, 1.3090. For ὄνομα, 'person', cf. Acts 1.15; the usage has been noted at *New Docs 1977*, **113**, but see also the discussion in G.P. Shipp, *Modern Greek Evidence for the Ancient Greek Vocabulary* (Sydney, 1979) 416.

A II/I BC funerary stele from Knidos contains four epigrams for Atthis: Pircher, no.22c (= Peek, *GVI* 1874). In the second of these poems the husband says that whereas while she still lived Atthis gave him a joyful spirit, her death has bequeathed to him merely an occasion for weeping, Ἀτθίς, ἐμοὶ ζήσασα καὶ εἰς ἐμὲ πνεῦμα λιποῦσα, ὡς πάρος εὐφροσύνης, νῦν δακρύων πρόφασι (*ll*.6-7). The noun occurs also in *IGUR* 1159, a funerary epigram for Apollophanes which contains Epicurean sentiments: the text is quoted in part at **18** above.

Euphrosyne is a common slave name: Reilly, *Slaves*, 1209-1236 records over two dozen examples, ranging from II BC-II AD. For the newly attested noun συνευφροσύνη see **32** above.

59. ἕως

P.Ross.Georg. 3 (1930) 3 (Arsinoite nome, III; repr. Tibiletti, *Lettere*, no.12) is a long, well-preserved letter from Ammonios to his brother Apion, in which he conveys instructions concerning various financial matters. The final request informs Apion that 'if my brother Dionysios has need, give him up to 100 drachmai and get reimbursement from me, but otherwise not (i.e., don't give him any money unless he really needs it)', ἐὰν χρίαν ἔχῃ Διονύσιος ὁ ἀδελ|φός μου, ἕως δραχμῶν ἑκατὸν δός αὐτῷ καὶ λα<βὲ> | αὐτὰς παρ' ἐμοῦ, ἀλλὰ μὴ ἄλλως (*ll*.21-24). This use of ἕως parallels well such NT occurrences as Mk. 6.23, ἕως ἡμίσους τῆς βασιλείας μου, and Rom. 3.12 (quoting Ps. 13.3), οὐκ ἔστιν ὁ ποιῶν χρηστότητα, οὐκ ἔστιν ἕως ἑνός. Further examples of this conjunction used as a preposition to denote degree are given at BAGD, s.v., II.4. This papyrus example with a numeral following offers a closer parallel to these NT instances than does *P.Tebt*. I (1902) 56.7, cited by both MM and BAGD.

Is this letter from a Christian circle? Tibiletti, *Lettere*, 10, thinks not, in view of the formula θεῶν θελόντων (*l*.5; but cf. τοῦ θεοῦ {θεου} θέλοντος, 10; on this phrase and variations of it see **18** above). When Ammonios greets τὴν ἀδελφήν 'and all your (Apion's) children' (2-3), ἀδελφή is being used in the sense commonly attested in Egypt, 'wife'.

60. θεολόγος

In an Imperial letter(?) concerning St. John and Polycarp of Smyrna, *I.Eph*. Ia.45 (VI), the former is referred to as ἀγαπητὸν . . . μαθητήν (2), θεο|[λόγος τε κ]αὶ βροντῆς υἱὸς εἰκότως ἐκλήθη (6-7). The text is translated with notes in P.R. Coleman-Norton, *Roman State and Christian Church* (London, 1966) III.1014-15, no. 577. *I.Eph*. IV.1279 is a Byzantine prayer to Christ and John — name restored — ὁ θεολόγος (*l*.2). Θεολόγος occurs in several other *I.Eph*. texts: Ia.22.4, 63 (Nysa, time of Antoninus Pius), 27.295 (104 AD), 47.73 (time of Commodus; perhaps also *l*.101); III.645.6 (Imperial period; quoted below at **83**); IV.1023.4 (after 104); VII, 1.3015.2 (*c*.220), 3074 (Imperial); VII, 2.4336.12 (time of Gordian III). Further instances are listed in the index volume (VIII, 1), s.v. On the term, which appears in the NT only as *v.l*. in the title of Rev., see L. Robert, *ΣΤΗΛΗ. Τόμος εἰς μνήμην Νικολάου Κοντολέοντος* (Athens, 1980) 16-17. See further **8** and **18** above.

61. θλίβω

MM provide a useful array of examples to illustrate the range of use of this verb. From the current year's crop it occurs twice in a late letter to an abbot possibly from a nun, *P.Köln* 111 (provenance unknown, V/VI; pl.17). The body of the letter is preserved, though beginning and end are lost. The writer sends her letter to indicate troubles she is experiencing at the hands of others, and insistently to request the abbot's prayers:

ὅτι πάνυ θλίβομαι· οἱ γὰρ ὀφθαλμ̣[οὶ τῶν] κακῶν ἀνθρώπων οὐκ ἐοῦσίν τινα ἀνανεῦσεν. ὅθεν οὖν παρακαλῶ· εὐχοῦ περὶ ἐμοῦ, εἵνα λοιπὸ̣ν ὁ θεὸς καταλλαγ̣ῇ καὶ δυνηθῶ ἀπαλλαγῆ̣ν̣α̣[ι τῶν] κακῶν ἀνθρώπων τὰς ἐπιβουλάς. λέγω δέ, [ὅτι] μοι τοῦτο συνέβη, ἐπιδὴ ου . . . . . .[. ὅθ]ε̣[ν δέομαί] σου λοιπὸν κἂν νῦν· εὐχοῦ περὶ ἐμοῦ, ὅτι κακ̣[ῶς] θλίβομαι καὶ τὴν ἁγίαν προσφοράν.

| . . . because I am much oppressed; for the eyes of wicked men do not allow me to look up (to God). Accordingly, therefore, I beseech you: pray for me so that in future God may be reconciled and I may be able to be rid of the plots of wicked men. I mean that | this has happened to me, since . . . Accordingly, I beg you then now at least: pray for me because I am badly oppressed also in respect of my holy offering.

The request for help in affliction is reminiscent of the OT, but only in general terms, for the exact phraseology is naturally not paralleled. Note, however, Ps. 30 (31).9, ἐλέησόν με, κύριε, ὅτι θλίβομαι; Lam. 1.20, ἰδέ, κύριε, ὅτι θλίβομαι. In the NT, passive θλίβομαι used absolutely occurs at 2 Cor. 1.6; 4.8; 7.5; Heb. 11.37.

Of other words in this passage the following may be noted briefly: for ἀνανεύω (6) in the sense 'raise (eyes to God in supplication)' see Lampe, s.v., 2. The adverbial λοιπόν (7, 11) is common enough: but note that it is used with different force in each of its two occurrences here. For the first cf. BAGD, s.v., 3a, β (in the NT note Gal. 6.17); the second is an instance of the not uncommon vague use, imprecise in meaning, perhaps 'so, well, then'. In *l.*8 the writer uses καταλλάσσω absolutely, as at Rom. 5.10; but unlike the NT usage, here God is spoken of as being reconciled (to the penitent), not vice versa. For the sense of ἀπαλλάσσω (8) cf. Lk. 12.58, δὸς ἐργασίαν ἀπηλλάχθαι ἀπ' αὐτοῦ. For κἂν serving as a particle with the meaning 'at least' (*l.*11) see BAGD, s.v., 3, quoting NT instances like Mk. 5.28; Acts 5.15; 2 Cor. 11.16 (cf. BDF §374). The phrase τὴν ἁγίαν προσφοράν (12) is awkward grammatically; perhaps to be thought of as an accusative of respect. For the sense 'offering (of prayer)' cf. *1 Cl.* 36.1 (cited by BAGD, s.v.), where Jesus is spoken of as ὁ ἀρχιερεὺς τῶν προσφορῶν ἡμῶν.

On a request to another monastic to pray for someone who is sick see **123** below.

62. ἱερατεύω

MM's good entry for this verb (NT, only Lk. 1.8) notes only one papyrus occurrence. From this year's catch we may add *P.Köln* 81 (provenance unknown, 105/4 BC), a decree making mention of the priesthood of the cult of Alexander and of the saviour gods held by queen Kleopatra, ἱερατευούσης βασι|λίσσης Κλεοπάτρας . . . | . . . Ἀλεξάνδρου καὶ θεῶν Σωτήρων, κτλ (*ll*.3-5). Also from North Africa are *I.Apollonia* 6a.2 in a list of priests of Apollo (I BC-I AD), and 14.1 (late III/early II BC). The *I.Ephesos* volumes yield the following score of items attesting the verb:

Ia.9 (= VI.2030; 51/0-18/7 BC), priest of Roma (*l*.18).
II.293.8, honorific text for Commodus.
III.702.6-7, priest of Roma.
839.6, fragmentary context, recording someone's offices.
906.1-2, list of priests in the guild of *molpoi*.
950.4, a priestess at the beginning of a list of *neopoioi*.
980.8-9, Claudia Krateia Veriane, priestess of Artemis.
984.6, priestess Hordeonia Pulchra (verb largely restored but not in doubt).
987.9-10, Vipsania Olympias, priestess of Artemis.
988.11-12, verb heavily restored by analogy with no.987, for her sister Vipsania Polla, priestess of Artemis.
IV.1139.5, dedication to Ephesian Artemis, the emperors and the Ephesian people by the priestess Tryphosa, made in accordance with the promise of her father.
1145.5 (time of Hadrian), in a text recording that the *epheboi* sang in honour of the emperor's visit.
1213.3, dedication to Isis and Sarapis by the priest C. Sossianus.
1270.3-4 (time of Domitian -Trajan), T. Flavius Perigenes, priest for life of Dionysos Phleos.
V.1579b, *l*.6, Larkia Juliane, priestess.
1595.2, *NN*, priest for life of the *mystai* of the Demetriastai and of Dionysos Phleos, whose cult is πρὸ πόλεως (*ll*.3-4). For this phrase edd. n. ad loc. refers to Acts 14.13, ὅ τε ἱερεὺς τοῦ Διὸς τοῦ ὄντος πρὸ τῆς πόλεως, κτλ.
1872.1, fragmentary text mentioning a priestess.
VII, 1.3059.1, priestess of Artemis.
3233.5-6 (North of Büyük Kale in Kaystros valley, *c*.20 km. N.E. of Ephesos, after 212), statue of Aurelia Apollonia, priestess of Artemis.

Almost all these texts belong to the Roman Imperial period, but few can be dated more closely. The diversity of deities served by this random sample of priests underscores MM's comment that the LXX translators and Luke merely adopted the normal general word for holding a priesthood; there were no cultural connotations attached to it which made them avoid it in favour of some other verb. The same may be said of ἱερωσύνη, discussed above at **2**.

63. καθηγητής

MM, followed by BAGD, note only papyri in illustration of the NT's use of this noun at Mt. 23.10 (and as a *v.l.* in the following verse). An epigraphical attestation crops up in *IG* XIV *Suppl.* 2454 (Massilia, Imperial period), Τίτος Πομπήϊος | Ἀπολλωνίδης | Τίτῳ Φλαουΐωι | Νεικοστράτωι | τῶι καθηγητῆι | μνήμης χάριν, 'Titus Pompeius Apollonides (erected this gravestone) to Titus Flavius Nikostratos (his) teacher as a memorial'.

64. κέντρον

An epitaph for Theodoros, an elementary teacher (*grammatikos*), mentions that he achieved a great reputation for his skill as a teacher at Athens, and thereby brought renown to his native city of Byzantion: Pfuhl/Möbius I.172 (Byzantion, probably II; = Peek, *GVI* 1479). The text concludes (*ll*.7-8):

Λούκουλλος φιλίας τάδε σοι μνημήι' ἔγραψεν,
σῆς γλυκερῆς ψυχῆς κέντρον ἄπαυστον ἔχων.

Lucullus wrote this as a memorial of his friendship for you, because he has an unceasing 'sting' for your sweet soul.

MM, s.v. κέντρον, quotes this final line of the epigram as their sole documentary parallel; but the attestation was not drawn into BAGD, perhaps because of MM's rendering 'desire'. Rather, we have an elliptical example carrying a figurative meaning as it does also at 1 Cor. 15.55-56: the death of Theodoros is an unassuageable pain for his friend Lucullus. Though BAGD and NT commentaries rightly perceive in Paul's statement a reference to Hos. 13.14, this documentary attestation of κέντρον ought not to be overlooked.

65. κριτήριον

This noun may carry the meaning 'tribunal, law-court', or 'lawsuit, legal action', in the NT (Jas. 2.6 for the former, 1 Cor. 6.2, 4 for the latter). Both these are developments from the primary sense 'means/standard of judging', whence 'judgement': see LSJ, s.v., whose examples show that the basic sense had not become obsolete after the classical period. An example to illustrate this occurs at Pfuhl/Möbius I.788 (Smyrna, 41 AD; pl.116), a funerary epigram in which the exclamation, φεῦ Μοίρης | εἰκαῖα κριτήρια, 'alas for the random judgements of Fate!', occurs as an outburst against the death of the infant (νήπιος, *l*.1) Menogenes. This poem also contains the verb τεκνόω at *l*.4: ἐτέκνωσεν | δέ με Λόλους. This verb — no entry in MM — occurs in the NT only as a *v.l.*, at Heb. 11.11D. This text is included as no.541 in G. Petzl, *Die Inschriften von Smyrna*, I (*IK* 23; Bonn, 1982).

66. κυνάριον

I.Eph. II.506 is a dedication of a statue group (114/5) which depicts the mythological hunter, Aktaion, and the satyr Silenos with Pan and δυσὶ κυναρίοις (*l*.4). It is not clear from the text whether by κυναρίοις are meant simply 'dogs', or whether the diminutive form has the meaning 'puppies' or 'small dogs', or carries a hypocoristic sense. In such company one might expect hunting dogs, normally referred to as κύνες, though the presence of affectionate dogs (could this be the force of the diminutive form?) would increase the pathos surrounding the ill-fated Aktaion, who as a punishment was changed by Artemis into a stag and was torn to pieces by his *own* hounds.

Apart from this example of the word the only documentary use of it known to me occurs in *PGM* 1 (1973²) 4.2945, 2947, 2951 (Thebes, IV), where it is used of a model dog fashioned from dough or wax. Κύων is found in documentary sources referring to house dogs (Pfuhl/Möbius, II.2196 [Mytilene, II]), hunting dogs (*P.Col.* 4 [1940] 93.9 [Philadelphia; III BC]; *P.Oxy.* 34 [1968] 2707.9 [VI]), and guard-dogs (cf. *BE* [1968] 247, p.458). Κυνάριον occurs in a number of literary passages in which the contexts suggest a true diminutive sense, e.g., Pl., *Euthyd.* 298 d-e and Athen. 12.518f, 519b. Among these should also be included Plut., *Arat.* 7.3, against BAGD (s.v. κυνάριον) since, although the gardener's dogs are also called κύνες, they are said at 5.5 to be 'small, but extraordinarily fierce and savage' (μικρῶν μέν, ἐκτόπως δὲ μαχίμων καὶ ἀπαρηγορήτων); and at 8.1 their size is implicitly contrasted with that of a κύων μέγας, a θηρατικός. MM, s.v. κυνάριον, implicitly suggests that κυνάριον was an equivalent for κύων, but the context of the example cited from Epict. 4.1.111 requires a depreciatory sense for the diminutive form (cf. W.A. Oldfather's Loeb translation, 'a paltry dog').

In the NT this diminutive is found only at Mt. 15.26, 27 (= Mk. 7.27, 28) in the story of the Syro-Phoenician woman, where both she and Jesus use the word. However, there is no clear diminutive force in these passages. D.C. Swanson, *JBL* 77 (1958) 134-151, suggests that the word is an example of a diminutive form expressing, not small size, but endearment, and meaning 'pet dog', as opposed to κύων which 'has a neutral or bad sense'. BDF §111(3) contrasts κυνάριον with the κύνες of Lk. 16.21 which they take to mean 'stray dogs'. It is certain that κύων often has a pejorative meaning — in the LXX dogs are frequently mentioned in parallel with pigs and prostitutes (e.g., 3 Kgdms 22.38; cf. Mt. 7.6; 2 Pet. 2.22), or associated with the wicked (Ps.21 (22).17; cf. Phil. 3.2, Rev. 22.15), or used as a term of depreciation (1 Kgdms. 17.43; 24.15); although in Tobit the dog is a pet (AB 5.17, ℵ 6.1). For references to Rabbinic comparisons of Gentiles with dogs see W.L. Lane, *The Gospel According to Mark* (Grand Rapids, 1974) 262 n.63. Nevertheless, κύων, too, can be used of a pet dog, as in Pfuhl/Möbius II.2196, a charming epitaph for a dead pet called Parthenope ('Girl-face'), ᾗ συνάθυρεν ('with whom [her master] played'), whose case shows that ἐστ' ἆθλον στοργῆς ἄρα καὶ κυσίν, ὥς νυ καὶ ἥδε | εὔνους οὖσα τροφεῖ σῆμα λέλονχε τόδε (*ll.*3-4, 'there is, then, a reward for love even for dogs, since indeed this one, who was good-natured towards her keeper, has obtained this tomb'). This more affectionate attitude to dogs is displayed in other epitaphs for dogs: from this year's reading see Pfuhl/Möbius II.2197-2201 (Aegean and coastal Asia Minor, II-III); *IGUR* 1230 (Antonine period); *IGM* 52 (provenance unknown, III); *IGM* 51 (Thessaly, V); *IG* XIV *Suppl.* 2566 (Bonn, n.d.); and see n.2 at *IGM*, p.41 for other examples. Tombstones which depict the pet dogs of the deceased also witness to it (see Pfuhl/Möbius II, index, s.v. 'Hund'). Of particular relevance to Jesus' conversation with the Syro-Phoenician woman are scenes depicting dogs near the tables of their reclining owners, e.g., Pfuhl/Möbius II.1858, 1898, 1908, 1909 (Perinthos, Teos and Methymna, II BC-III AD).

The various evidence, then, supports Swanson's view of κύων; as for κυνάριον the few literary and documentary examples suggest that it was not simply a faded diminutive, but could take on various nuances expressed by the diminutive form. The sense of the diminutive in the NT passages has been understood as the hypocoristic 'pet dog' motivated either by a desire to soften the saying by avoiding κύων (see V. Taylor, *The Gospel According to Mark* [London, 1966] 350; cf. J.D.M. Derrett, *NovT* 15 [1973] 69 n.4) or by a necessary lexical choice when describing dogs that could be present at a home meal (Lane, *op.cit.*, 262; R.H. Gundry, *Matthew.*

A Commentary on his Literary and Theological Art [Grand Rapids, 1982] 315). Derrett, however, takes κυνάριον as a true diminutive meaning 'puppies' (169-70), making the whole scene an allusion to Ps. 17.14 and equating 'babes' with puppies.

Mark's version of this story contains three other diminutive forms (δαιμόνιον [*vss.*26, 30] is not a diminutive; see Swanson, 139-140), two of which are not in Matthew: θυγάτριον (*vs.*25; cf. Mt. 15.22 θυγάτηρ), παιδίον (*vss.*28, 30; cf. Mt. 15.26 τέκνον), and ψίχιον (*vs.*28; = Mt. 15.27). For the greater frequency of diminutives in Mark see Swanson (142-43), who discusses the methodology of comparing the frequency of diminutives in books and shows that although the other three evangelists use a wide range of diminutive words, Mark has a greater frequency of different forms for the length of his gospel and uses the diminutives in his range more often. Swanson also argues that the NT as a whole has a relatively large range of diminutives, as do Aristophanes and Herondas (who are cited as authors closer to the spoken language) compared with the LXX and Polybios. On χοῖρος/χοιρίον see **43** above.

In this discussion of dogs we may include a possible Christian epitaph (A.R.R. Sheppard, *AS* 29 [1979] 180; = *SEG* 1426; cf. *BE* 496 [western Phrygia, probably III]) in which the deceased Charidemos is described as φιλοκυνήγος, 'loving the chase' or 'fond of wild beast fights'. For another example of this word see *SEG* 1401.16-17 (near Hasanlar in N-W Phrygia, II^2/III^1). Sheppard sees the Eumenian formula, ἔσται αὐτῷ πρὸς | τὸν θεόν, in *ll.*9-10 as a sign that Charidemos was a Christian and takes this text, in view of Charidemos' predilection, as 'a further example of the relaxed attitude of the Church in this part of Phrygia' (180), which is a central theme of his article. Sheppard may be right in accepting this as a Christian text, but on the use of the Eumenian formula by Jews and pagans as well as Christians, see *New Docs 1978*, **98**, pp.136-139.

(A.L. CONNOLLY)

67. μειζότερος

This non-classical form which developed in the *koine*, no doubt because it was a simpler form morphologically than μείζων, is found in the NT only at 3 Jn 4. MM, s.v. μείζων ad fin., notes three papyrological texts, from IV and later. References may be given here baldly to several inscriptions which also employ the form. C. Roueché, *GRBS* 20 (1979) 178 no.3 reproduces in part a text from Tarsos which she argues is a building inscription, not a funerary monument, to be dated V/VI, not IV. In noting this, *BE* (1980) 544 suggests that μει]ζοτέρου should be restored at the conclusion of the text; cf. *SEG* 1530. *BE* (1981) 254 comments on an inscription re-edited by D. Feissel in *BCH* 104 (1980) 459-72, marking the grave of Euphimia τῆς μιζοτέρας — the text is repr. below at **129** — and refers to several other instances noted in previous issues of *BE*. Note also the tomb of the Christian Mauros μιζοτέρου, *SEG* 27 (1977) 570 (Chalkis, early Byzantine). In these cases of early Byzantine use the term is a title, 'steward, manager'. See also references (some overlapping with the above) given by Robert at *Dacia* 22 (1978) 325 n.6.

68. μετάνοια

MM's documentary instances of this noun are all papyrological, and Christian; BAGD's entry makes no mention of any non-literary attestations. Though it is in too fragmentary a context to be of much use, the noun may be noted as occurring in the metrical epitaph, *IGUR* 1409 (Rome, Imperial; pl. on p.243): - -] τῇ μετανοίᾳ |[- - - (*l*.3). Moretti (n. ad loc.) wonders whether the text may be Christian, though does not indicate why he is predisposed to this view.

Spicq, *NLNT* III.456 n.2, notes three papyrological texts published since MM which include either the verb or the noun. *P.Oxy*. 20 (1952) 2270 is the only one with the noun, and is worth quoting in part. Though it dates from early V this contract concerning the sale of a dining room employs the noun three times in a stock phrase: εἰ δὲ ἐμ | μετανοίᾳ γενώμεθα ἐπὶ τῇ διαπράσει ἢ αὐτὸς ἐμ μετανοίᾳ γενόμενον (*read* γενῇ) ἐπὶ τῇ ἀγορασίᾳ, | ἐπάναγκες τὸν ἐμ μετανοίᾳ γενόμενον παρασχεῖν τῷ ἐμμένοντι μέρι λόγῳ προστίμου | χρυσοῦ ο[ὐγκί]α[ν] μίαν, 'And if we change our mind over the sale, or you yourself change your mind over the purchase, it is obligatory for the one who changes his mind to provide to the party who holds to the agreement one ounce of gold as a penalty'. Clearly, no theological connotation is in view here.

69. οἰκονόμος

The *I.Nikaia* volumes include from Nikaia and its extensive territory a considerable number of examples of this noun, used always in its literal sense of steward, manager of an estate. In the NT the literal meaning occurs at Lk. 12.42; 16.1, 3, 8; and 1 Cor. 4.2. MM and BAGD, s.v., provide no epigraphical example of this particular use. Examples from *I.Nikaia* of *oikonomos* in its primary sense include (all broadly of Imperial date unless further specified):

I.192 (I/II; cf. *BE* 542; repr. at *New Docs 1978*, **10**), verse epitaph (two elegiac couplets) for a slave Italos, described as οἰκονόμον πιστόν (*l*.3); this wording offers a close parallel for Lk. 12.42.

196 (pl.18), epitaph for Philon, οἰκ. of Claudia Gallite, aged 61.

205 (pl.20), epitaph for Claudius Thallos, οἰκ. of C. Claudius Calpurnius, aged 50.

II,1.753, epitaph of Quintus Caricus, aged 40, erected by his wife.

1057 (probably III), dedication of an altar to Zeus Hosios Epekoos, made by Kosmianos the *oikonomos* ὑπὲρ τῶν δεσποτῶν (unnamed). This is best interpreted as a dedication made by Kosmianos not at his master's behest, but for their health/preservation. Cf. *I.Nikaia* II, 1.1118 (II/III), a dedication by two men of an altar to Zeus Okkonenos ὑπὲρ τῆς τῶν | δεσποτῶν | σωτηρίας (3-5). For the terms ὅσιος and ἐπήκοος as attributes of Zeus in no.1057 see Şahin's n. ad loc., with bibliographical references.

1062 (probably III; pl.14), dedication of a statue to Zeus Agathios by Graptos, *oikonomos* of Annia Astilla. The same woman is attested in a Latin text, no.1208 (pl.25), either honorific or funerary. Another dedication to Zeus Agathios appears as no.1061 (see ed. n., ad loc.).

1201, honorific inscription for Doryphoros, *oikonomos* of Claudia Eia, and for his wife, 'because of his incomparable patronage of us (viz., the village of the Okaenoi which voted the honours)', διὰ τὸ ἡμᾶς πατρω|νεῦ<σ>θαι ὑπὸ αὐ|τοῦ ἀσυνκρίτως (*ll*.13-16).

II,2.1292, funerary epigram for Ennius νέος οἰκονόμο[ς] (*l*.3) and his family, including several children who are described as οἱ φιλάδελφοι (*l*.14). This text was noted at *New Docs 1978*, **74**, under the siglum *I.Bithynia* III.8, pp.57-58. From that same entry, *I.Bithynia* III.7, pp.56-57 is now repr. in *I.Nikaia* as II, 2.1293. No.1579 includes the adjective in a fragmentary grave epigram.

1336 (pl.8), epitaph: [Κυ]ιρῖνος Εὐανγέλου | οἰκονόμος ζήσας | ἔτη (*vac.*) κα', χαῖρε. Quirinus may be the steward of Evangelos; or equally the latter name may be a patronymic. At his death at the age of 21 he already held the position; cf. no.1292 above where Ennius is described as νέος.

1413 (pl.19), epitaph for the fifty-year-old Evangelos, *oikonomos* of Antipatris.

1466 (probably II; pl.29), epitaph for Eupraxia, οἰκ|ονόμισα of C. Catillius Thrason; deceased at the age of 23. Şahin (ed. n., ad loc.) mentions another Bithynian inscription (unpublished), for Anthousa, wife of Phoibes, οἰκονόμισσα of Timotheos. A V AD epitaph from Isauria Nova — *ed.pr.*: A.M. Ramsay, *JHS* 24 (1904) 283, no.24 — reads Δόξα οἰκονόμεισσα ἡ σεμνή; the editor is undecided whether the term 'should be taken as the title of a female official in the church, or as meaning simply the wife of an οἰκονόμος'. But these two new inscriptions from Bithynia show women exercising the function in their own right. In no.1466, there is no mention of a husband, but only of the man for whom the young Eupraxia worked; and in the unpublished text from Bursa Museum (noted above) the wording is such as to put the question beyond doubt. On the subject of women's titles being honorific (because their husbands exercise the function) or reflecting actual function see **113** below.

One further example from the year's culling may be noted: Pfuhl/Möbius, II.1142 (provenance unknown within Bithynia, II; pl.172), an epitaph for the wife of Hesperos son of Hesperos, *oikonomos* of Tiberius Claudius Phaitros.

Several points of interest emerge from this brief catalogue. The position could be entrusted to relatively young people, in their early 20s (nos. 1336, 1466), and to women no less than men (no.1466). The *oikonomos* may be a slave (no.192), or a person of some influence, able to provide patronage for a local village (no.1201). The fact that several *oikonomoi* are attested whose employers are female simply reflects the well-known phenomenon in the Empire of women of wealth, who owned estates in their own right. Şahin provides a number of further references to *oikonomoi* in his n. to no.1062.

Lest it be thought that there are no pre-imperial attestations, attention may be drawn to P. Frisch, *I.Lampsakos* (*I.K.* 6; Bonn, 1978) 33.29 (Kolophon, III BC(?)), an honorific decree in which the *oikonomos* Phanodikos is assigned the task of seeing to the erection of the stele, and the inscribing of the decree. This man is thus one of the public *oikonomoi*, such as is attested for Corinth at Rom. 16.23. From the present year's texts note also the metaphorical use in Pircher, no.23 (Rheneia, II/I BC; = Peek, *GVI* 702), a funerary epigram for a woman in which she speaks of herself as ἀγαθὰ . . . βίου οἰκονόμος (6).

For οἰκονομέω cf. **45** above. The noun οἰκονομία is found at *I.Eph.* Ia.27.397 referring to the function of an administrator (104 AD); in the NT cf. Lk. 16.2-4 for this meaning. With the non-NT sense 'arrangements, plans' (cf. BAGD, s.v., 2a) it occurs at *l*.35 of *I.Eph.* Ia.8 (86/5 BC; pl.10), a decree concerning the war against Mithridates. In *I.Eph.* V.1671 (Imperial period) the deceased is described as ἐπὶ τῆς οἰκίας (*l*.2), a periphrasis for οἰκονόμος. Spicq, *NLNT* II.606-13, includes numerous references to documentary instances of οἰκονομ-words.

70. ὁλοκληρία

Found only once in the NT — Acts 3.16, ἔδωκεν αὐτῷ τὴν ὁλοκληρίαν ταύτην — this noun is a cliché in papyrus letters, as MM's examples show. It is much rarer in other documentary contexts. MM, followed by BAGD, cite as their only inscription *SIG*[3] 1142 (I/II), in which Meltine offers a dedication to fulfil a vow [ὑ]πὲρ τῆς ὁλοκληρίας [τῶν] ποδῶν. *I.Nikaia* II, 1.1131 (Çalti/Söğüt, III?), provides a further epigraphical attestation, a dedication to Zeus Soter by P. Postumius Philiskos ὑπὲρ τῆς . . . ὁλοκληρίας καὶ διαμονῆς, 'for the complete health and its continuation', of himself, his family and his *patronus*. On this text see further L. Robert, *Hellenica* 10 (1955) 96-104 (pl. 17.2), whose useful discussion is mostly devoted to the term ὁλοκληρία and related forms. He notes (98) that the provenance of *SIG*[3] 1142, usually given as Phrygia, is in fact Kula in Lydia. A further epigraphical example, discussed by Robert (99-100), is a dedication to the Nymphs of a statue of Asklepios made by a barber, consequent upon a dream, 'for his good health': Εὐτυχιανὸς ὁ κουρεὺς ἰδὼν καθ' ὕπνου ἀνέθηκεν ταῖς Νύμφαις αὐτοῦ ὁλοκληρίᾳ (on the case, and sense, see Robert, 100, n.1) Ἀσκληπ(ε)ιὸν καὶ εὐχαρίστησα (*sic*) . In all these contexts the word is an equivalent for σωτηρία, physical health and safety. This equivalence of these nouns may be seen by comparing Philiskos' dedication, above, with *I.Nikaia* II, 1.1118, (II/III), a dedication by two men 'for the *soteria* of their masters' (partly quoted at **69** above). Though σωτηρία has a wider semantic range, no spiritual dimension seems ever implied by ὁλοκληρία. A few further documentary instances of the latter noun are noted as Spicq, *NLNT*, II.616-17.

71. ὀρφανός

MM quotes a series of useful papyrus texts to illustrate this adjective, used frequently as a noun. In the NT the word occurs with its primary, literal meaning only at Jas. 1.27, where θρήσκεια is defined in part as ἐπισκέπτεσθαι ὀρφανοὺς καὶ χήρας ἐν τῇ θλίψει αὐτῶν. The D text of Mk. 12.40 adds καὶ ὀρφανῶν on to the end of the scathing comment about 'those who devour widows' houses'. This interpolation reflects how frequent is the collocation 'widows and orphans' both in the OT and in Greek literary and non-literary texts (a few instances occur in some of the examples quoted below). A non-literal use of the adjective is to be found at Jn 14.18, οὐκ ἀφήσω ὑμᾶς ὀρφανούς.

Yet the meaning of the adjective and some of its related forms deserves a little scrutiny; for the way it is employed in various texts indicates that it need not always carry the narrower, modern sense of a minor *both* of whose parents are dead. One of the texts in MM's entry, *P.Tebt.* 2 (1907) 326, illustrates this, although MM does not comment on its significance. This petition (Tebtynis, *c*.266) is presented by a woman on behalf of her daughter who is described as *orphane* and a minor: ὑπὲρ θυγατρὸς ὀραφανῆς | καὶ καταδεοῦς τὴν ἡλικίαν (2-3). Here the word must mean 'fatherless': the mother acts on her behalf because the father is dead. An inscribed decree of Eumenes I, known since late last century and most accessible as *OGIS* 266 (Pergamon, 263-241 BC), contains a clause which reads: ὑπὲρ ὀρφανικῶν, ὅπῳς ἂν | οἱ ἄγχιστα γένους λαμβάνωσιν, ἢ ὧι ἂν ἀπολίπηι, 'concerning the property of orphans, in order that his (viz., the deceased father/soldier's) next-of-kin may get it, or to whomever he bequeaths it'. Christophilopoulos, *Νομ. Ἐπιγ.* I.69-70 (cf. *BE* [1977] 389) discusses this clause and interprets its second half by analogy with the second speech against Stephanos in the Demosthenic Corpus, [Dem.] 46.24, in which a law is adduced to show that a father's will remains valid even if he has legitimate sons, provided they are deceased within two years of reaching their majority. That is to say, the father's will can override the passing of inheritance to immediate relatives in certain, tightly-defined circumstances. In this Pergamene text, what is solely in view for our understanding of τὰ ὀρφανικά is the death of the father on active service. *SEG* 82 alludes to an interesting Athenian inscription of 403 BC, published by R.S. Stroud, *Hesperia* 40 (1971) 280-301 (cf. *SEG* 28 [1978] 46, where the text is reproduced and some bibliography provided). This text of 403/2 BC concerns provisions made for the sons of Athenian men killed the preceding year under the rule of the Thirty Tyrants; ὀρφανός occurs in the extant lines at *ll.*11 and 19.

Another example again is *P.Med.Bar.* 1 (142 BC), partly published by O. Montevecchi, *Aeg.* 61 (1981) 103-15, in which one of the petitioners, Herakleides, is spoken of as ὀρφανοῦ (*l.*3) and his mother acts for him, μετὰ προστάτιδος (*l.*4); on this latter phrase see **122** below. A further instance, this time from the 1979 culling, is provided by *IG* XIV *Suppl.* 2437 (Massilia, Imperial period), a funerary epigram for a man which concludes with the couplet: . . . μητρὶ μὲν ἐν {ἐν} | γήρᾳ δάκρυ θήκατο τῇ δὲ | γυνα<ι>κὶ χηρίαν δυστήνου παιδὸ<ς> | ἅμ' ὀρφανίῃ, '(envious fortune has done you wrong and) given tears to your mother in her old age, widowhood to your wife, as well as making an orphan of your poor child' (9-12).

In contrast to these examples where the word refers to the fatherless, the metrical *CIJ* II.1510 may be considered (Tell el-Yehoudieh in Egypt, 28 Jan., 5 BC) in which the deceased says, 'I was left an orphan by my mother when I was young; and when the flower of my prime ripened me for marriage my father yoked me to Phabeis. But with the confinement of my first-born child Fate brought me to the end of my life', ὀρφανικὴ λεί|φθην γὰρ ἐγὼ{ι} μεικρά περ ἐοῦσα | μη{ι}τρός· ἐπεὶ δὲ μ' ἀκμῆς ἄνθος ἐν|υμφοκόμει, ἔζευξέν με Φαβεῖτι πα|τήρ, ὠδεῖνι δὲ Μοῖρα πρωτοτόκου | με τέκνου πρὸς τέλος ἦγε βίου. Here the adjective refers to the lack of a mother, not of a father. In passing, this text is interesting in other ways: with πρωτοτόκου . . . τέκνου we may compare Lk. 2.7 τὸν υἱὸν αὐτῆς τὸν πρωτότοκον. Another instance of the latter adjective occurs in Guarducci, *EG* IV.363-65 (Herakleia-Perinthos, III fin./IV init.; fig.105) an epitaph for a Christian family, the eldest son of whom is described as πρωτότοκος (*l.*2). For μικρός, 'young', cf. BAGD, s.v., 1, b; another example is noted in the text quoted at **17** above. Μικρός is brought into conjunction with ὀρφανός also in another, briefer epitaph from the same provenance (11 May, 1 BC), for Dosthion, son of Sabbataios, aged about three years (*CIJ* II.1524): here the adjectives used of him are ὀρφανέ, μεικρέ, τραυματία (i.e., he died from some injury which befell him).

Mention of these examples is intended to demonstrate that the usage can be more fluid than English 'orphan'; but that meaning taken strictly certainly occurs, of course. For example, Pfuhl/Möbius I.858 (Smyrna, mid-I BC; pl.126; = G. Petzl, *I.Smyrna* [*IK* 23; Bonn, 1982] 519) is an epigram for a girl whose premature death causes grief to her parents: they lament her fate as an orphan, σὸν ὀρφανίης πότμον ὀδυρόμενοι (*l.*4). Here, the noun is employed as a conceit, and verges on a figurative use, for she is deprived of her parents in the underworld since they are still alive. More straightforward is Pfuhl/Möbius II.1418 (Odessos, II[1]; pl.206) an epitaph for a young man in his late teens whose parents had predeceased him: ἐξ ἀγαθῶν γονέων παῖς ὀρφανός, ὦ παροδεῖτα, λειφθείς (*l.*2). Of rather later date is *P.Col.* 173 (Karanis, *c.*330-40(?)), a petition by Aurelia Tapaeis concerning the wrongful sale by two men of land belonging to her, one of whom appears to be her step-brother. This document is of some curiosity in that, although she is an orphan and a minor — παῖδα ἀτε|λῆ κ[αὶ ὀρ]φανὴν ο[ὖσαν (8-9; on ἀτελής, also at *l.*17, see Bagnall's n., ad loc.); cf. παῖς ὀρφανὴ δεομένη, 'an orphan child who is in need' (20) — she presents the petition herself, not through the agency of a guardian. It is true that she is illiterate, and accordingly someone writes on her behalf; yet there is no suggestion but that she is acting on her own initiative (for women acting without a *kyrios* see **24** above). In *P.Col.* 181, dated 342, she is said to be about 22 years old (*l.*3); so at the time of no.173 she is somewhere in her teens. For more on her and the family relationships see Bagnall's useful general introductory comments in *P.Col*, pp.4-8. A fragmentary verse text, *SEG* 1219 (Kyme in Aiolis, late Hellenistic) — H. Engelmann, *I.Kyme* (*IK* 5; Bonn, 1976) 51, with some restorations suggested by W. Peek, *ZPE* 33 [1979] 75; cf *BE* 386 — mentions that the children of the deceased will have the life of an orphan ahead of them, παισὶν δ' ὀρφανικὸς [βίοτος . . . (*l.*5), testifying to its readily-perceived difficulties in antiquity. A broken verse epitaph for a man (area of Tsaprani in Macedonia, Imperial period) appears to emphasise the problem of penury besetting orphans, πενίῃ λείπεις ὀρφανικὸν ΕΝ[- - - (*l.*5): D. Feissel/M. Sève, *BCH* 103 (1979) 308-09, no.52 (pl.; cf. *SEG* 647; *BE* [1980] 316).

Two inscriptions from Ephesos may also be drawn into the present discussion. *I.Eph.* Ia.4 (= V.1477), is a long law (297/6 BC; pls. 4-6 in vol. Ia) concerning the liquidation of debts in which provisions are laid down concerning orphans, to protect their χρήματα from their guardians (54); the latter are required to provide a dowry for females under their care (ταῖς ὀρφαναῖς, 63). There is nothing unusual about the provision (57) of a guardian being allocated for an orphan either by the child's father (i.e., via his will), or by the *demos* (where a will is lacking): see, for Classical Athens, W. den Boer, *Private Morality in Greece and Rome. Some Historical Aspects* (*Mnemosyne Suppl.* 57; Leiden, 1979) 40. Den Boer's monograph discusses a wide range of issues, and devotes considerable space (37-61) to the question of the treatment of orphans both in Graeco-Roman and Jewish antiquity; nothing is said of the relevant NT passages. This inscription from Ephesos has a large secondary literature, and contains numerous words of interest for the NT, including διαίρεσις (13, 14, 24-25), διασπάω (10), ἔπαυλις (13-14, 68), μερισμός (20, 23; heavily restored at *l.*18).

The second Ephesian text, *I.Eph.* VII, 2.4106 is the surviving conclusion only of an inscription on the border of a fountain in the church of St. Mary which includes the following phrase implying, perhaps, that the fountain served as a baptismal font: τὸν γλυκὺν ὀρφανοῦ κι|θωνάριον σὺ ἔνδυσαι (*ll.*3-4), 'put on your sweet orphan-robe' (i.e., which marks that you are an orphan?). The figurative application of the word here is different from that at Jn 14.18.

Finally, another context in which widows and orphans are mentioned in inscriptions is in certain curse formulas in epitaphs. L. Robert has discussed a number of examples of this motif from Phrygia, Lykaonia and elsewhere, in *CRAI* (1978) 253-69, especially 253-61 (cf. *BE* [1979] 511). A typical example is *MAMA* 7 (1956) 535 (Pillitokome, Imperial period) in which the verse imprecation runs: [εἰ δ]έ τις ὧδε κακὴν ἐπὶ σήματι χεῖρα βάλητε, ὀρφανὰ τέκνα λίποιτο, χῆρον βίον, οἶκον ἔρημον, 'if anyone lays a wicked hand on the tomb here may he leave his children orphans, a life of widowhood (to his wife) and his house abandoned'.

72. οὐθείς again (cf. *New Docs 1977*, 44)

This spelling of οὐδείς, which was common in the period III-I BC, occurs in the phrase φρο[ν]τίζων οὐθὲν ἧττον in an inscription, of which a part has been reprinted at *SIA* II, p.199 (= *SEG* 3 [1927] 101, reporting on *IG* II^2.833; Athens, late III BC). An example of the masculine nominative is found at *SEG* 1516 (Telmessos, beginning of II BC; see **77** below for text and details), a letter of a Hellenistic king about taxes, which also includes the following provision: τοῦ χόρτου κα[ὶ]| τῶν ἀχύρων παρίεμεν ὑμᾶς μηθὲν τελοῦν|τας, 'of green fodder and chaff we allow you to go on paying no contribution' (*ll.*2-4). The -θ-spelling of μηδείς also occurs in an inscription found in the Athenian agora and edited by R.L. Pounder, *Hesperia* 47 (1978) 49-57 (late III BC; cf. *BE* 158). In this inscription the Athenians honour Antioch of the Chrysaoreans (identified with Alabanda in Caria) and among other decisions make the magistrates responsible for watching over resident Antiochians ὅπως ὑπὸ μηθενὸς ἀδικῶνται (*ll.*25-26).

Gignac, observes (I.97) that οὐθείς, μηθείς, etc. 'do not represent an actual interchange of δ and θ', but 'they represent the assimilation of /d/ before a rough breathing'. He notes that sometimes both spellings are found in the same document. In the NT μηθείς occurs once (as a neuter: Acts 27.33), and οὐθείς etc. nine times, in Lk. 22.35; 23.14; Acts 15.9; 19.7; 20.33;

26.26; 1 Cor. 13.2, 3; 2 Cor. 11.9, though not all have equally strong manuscript support. These four NT works in which the -θ- forms are attested also use -δ- forms in similar contexts, so that it is not clear why the less common -θ- should occur at all. The seven occurrences in Luke-Acts are found in direct speech, but -δ- spellings are also in direct speech. Perhaps the declining -θ- forms had an old-fashioned ring or were reminiscent of the LXX (in which they are not uncommon), and may have suited Paul's poetic style in 1 Cor. 13. An emphatic reading of all ten uses of the -θ- forms is possible, though their contexts do not demand such a meaning.

The MM entry, s.v. οὐθείς, needs correction as the date for *P.Strassb.* 2 (1920) 125 of 5/4 BC (i.e., years) has been misread as V/IV BC (centuries), an error which has been carried over into BAGD, s.v. οὐδείς.

(A.L. CONNOLLY)

73. παραδίδωμι

At 1 Tim. 1.20 the writer mentions Hymenaios and Alexandros οὓς παρέδωκα τῷ σατανᾷ. Again, at 1 Cor. 5.5 Paul instructs his readers how to deal with a particular case of sexual immorality in the congregation: παραδοῦναι τὸν τοιοῦτον τῷ σατανᾶ. In general terms, these passages recall God's address to Satan at Job 2.6, παραδίδωμί σοι αὐτόν. A convenient brief bibliography on these two NT passages is provided by Spicq, *NLNT* III.512 nn.2, 3. A close parallel to this use of παραδίδωμι may be found in the extant concluding warning on an epitaph re-ed. in *I.Nikaia* I.87 (Hisaçık near Nikaia, Imperial period): ὃς ἂν δὲ εἰς τοῦτο | τὸ μνημεῖον δόλον | πονηρὸν πυήσει, πα|[ρ]αδίδωμι αὐτὸν θεο[ῖ]|[ς] καταχθονίοις (2-5), 'whoever performs any wicked treachery against this tomb, I hand him over to the infernal gods'. For δόλος πονηρός we may compare Ignatius' letter to the Ephesians 7.1 (noted by BAGD, s.v. δόλος). πονηρίαι and δόλος are included together in one of the NT vice lists, at Mk. 7.22.

74. παραθαλάσσιος

MM provides one documentary parallel for the NT's use of this adjective at Mt. 4.13, and Lk. 4.31D (Capernaum a city of Galilee τὴν παραθαλάσσιον ἐν ὁρίοις Ζαβουλων καὶ Νεφθαλιμ). In addition to that inscription (*SIG*[3] 709.20, dated 107 BC), we may note the more recently published *I.Eph.* III.680, a statue base for M. Gavius Bassus, in which the Latin text (1-7) is followed by a Greek version (8-17), the inscription concluding with a list in Latin of various officers who served with him. Under Trajan Bassus achieved military distinction in the Dacian War, and attained to the position of prefect of the sea-coast area of Pontus, [ἐπάρχω]ι ὄ̣χθης Ποντικῆς παραθαλασσίου (17; cf. *praef. orae Ponticae maritimae*, *l.*7).

75. παραμυθία again (cf. *New Docs 1978*, 56)

In the previous volume an epigraphical instance of this noun was quoted, a text already noted in BAGD. That lexicon also notes as another attestation *SIG*[3] 796B (Epidauros, *c*.40 AD), recording the bestowal by the Athenians of posthumous honours on a young man prematurely dead. A decision is made to send an embassy to console (παραμυ|θήσεται, 39-40) his parents and grandfather in order that the citizens' motion will be plain to all, 'providing efficacious honour for the dead and consolation for the living and unfortunate', τήν τε δυνατὴν τειμὴν | τοῖς τετελευτηκόσι καὶ παραμυθίαν τοῖς ζῶσι καὶ ἠτυχηκόσι παρεχομένη (*ll*.43-44). Another example of the verb παραμυθέομαι (found in the NT at Jn 11.19, 31 and 2 Thes. 2.12 and 5.14) occurs in Tibiletti, *Lettere*, no.1 (*ed.pr.* — *P.Ross.Georg.* 3 [1930, repr. 1966] 2 [provenance unknown, III]). Serenos writes to his mother, πολλὰ δὲ καὶ τὸν Μάρκον παρε|μυθησάμεθα λυπούμενον, 'but we did greatly console Marcus who was grieving' (*ll*.3-4).

A further inscriptional example of the noun turns up in the present year's reading, at *IGB* 303 (Rhodes, probably Imperial period). This honorific inscription on a statue base was inscribed by the *damos* and *boula* of the city to praise a man for his goodwill and the consolation which he provided for his parents, ε[ὐ]|ν[οία]ς ἕνε[κα καὶ πα]ραμυθίας | τᾶς εἰς τ[οὺς γον]εῖς αὐτοῦ (3-5). The word is sufficiently vague in this brief and somewhat fragmentary context to serve as a parallel to the equally generalised use of the noun at 1 Cor. 14.3, where it is perhaps to be taken as a hendiadys with παράκλησις.

For παραμύθιον see **2** above. For further documentary attestations of παραμυθ- words see Spicq, *NLNT* II.658-63.

76. παραχειμασία

One documentary instance only is noted in the lexica for this rare word. That text, *SIG*[3] 762 (Dionysopolis, near Odessos, 48 BC; MM wrongly gives the date as 48 AD), is an honorific inscription in which occurs the phrase κα]|[τὰ τὴν Γαΐου] 'Αντωνίου παραχειμασίαν, 'during the wintering of C. Antonius (at the city)'. Another example of the noun is published now in *I.Nikaia* I.60 (Nikaia, 218-22; pl.6), an honorific inscription for Fl. Severianus Asklepiodotos which refers to the occasion when Elagabalus spent the winter in the region, παραχειμασίᾳ τῇ ἐν τῇ ἐπαρχείῳ | τοῦ θειοτάτου αὐτοκράτορος 'Αντωνίνου (*ll*.18-19). Though later in date than the *SIG*[3] text, this new inscription offers a further good parallel to the sole NT occurrence, Acts 27.12, ἀνευθέτου δὲ τοῦ λιμένος ὑπάρχοντος πρὸς παραχειμασίαν.

77. παρενοχλέω

A recently-published fragmentary inscription from Telmessos in Lykia (II BC init.) may be part of a letter of Antiochos III or Eumenes II. This text, of which beginning and end are lost and most of only nine lines survive, was first edited by M. Wörrle, *Chiron* 9 (1979) 83-111 (pl.3); cf. *SEG* 1516. The document concerns the granting of certain privileges, either to Telmessos (so *ed.pr.*) or to a colony which established itself perhaps on the borders of its territory (so *BE* [1980] 484, in a very long discussion). One of the privileges granted is alleviation from billeting of soldiers: τῆς ἐπισταθμείας μέχρι μὲν ἐτῶν δέκα | οὐθεὶς ὑμᾶς παρενοχλήσει, μετὰ δὲ ταῦτα ἐπιδέξεσθε κατὰ τὰς ἀναγχαίας χρείας (*ll*.4-6), 'as for your billeting liability, for ten years no one shall trouble you, but after that you shall receive (billets) in accordance with essential duties'. The futures here amount to prescriptions, in place of imperative forms, a usage attested also in the NT, e.g., Mt. 5.43; 19.18, 19. K.L.McKay discusses this phenomenon with further references at *NovT* 27 (1985) 219-20. In the sole NT occurrence of παρενοχλέω (Acts 15.19), the verb takes a dative, a much rarer construction than the usual accusative, as here (cf. MM, s.v.).

The verb also occurs, again with the accusative, at *SGPI* 103c (Philai, 146-116 BC), in a letter from the priests of Isis to Ptolemy VIII, requesting him to write to Lochos commanding him not to harass them, μὴ παρενοχλεῖν ἡμᾶς (*l*.16). This text was already noted as *OGIS* 139 in MM's entry.

Another letter inscribed on the same obelisk, *SGPI* 103b (= *OGIS* 138), is from Ptolemy VIII and his consort Kleopatra to Lochos telling him not to ἐνοχλεῖν αὐτούς (*sc*. the priests, *l*.8). This verb is reasonably common (see MM, s.v.), and appears in the NT at Lk. 16.18 and Heb. 12.15. Whether there is any real difference in force between it and the double compound, with which this entry began, is uncertain. Another example of ἐνοχλέω from the current year's volumes is *IGUR* 1146 (Rome, Imperial period), where it is said of the dead girl that now she is dead 'neither winter nor heat cause you distress, sickness does not trouble you . . .', οὐ χείμων λυπεῖ σ', οὐ καῦμα, | οὐ νοῦσος ἐνοχλεῖ (*ll*.9-10). A further instance comes on a portion of an epitaph written on the left side of the main face of an altar: *I.Eph*. V.1627 (Imperial period). The main face (a) records that the deceased, L. Calpurnius Calpurnianus, from Kios in Bithynia, died at the age of twenty years, having been a student at Ephesos for the last five of them: ἔτη δ' ἐπὶ πέντε λόγοισιν | ἰν (*sic*) Ἐφέσωι σχολάσας εἰκοσέτης ἔθανον (*ll*.10-11). The left face (b) mentions the usual imposition of a financial penalty for anyone who disturbs the tomb: ὁ ἐνοχλήσας τούτωι | τῶι βωμῶι ἢ τῶι τόπωι | καταβαλεῖ εἰς τὸν φίσκον | ✱ (*leaf*) μύρια. In *I.Eph*. II.223, an imperial letter to the city, the left side of which is lost, the emperor concludes: γεγράφαμεν δὲ καὶ | [- - -] ὡς ἀντιλαμβάνωνταί τε ὑμῶν | [- - μὴ ἐ]νοχλεῖν ὑμᾶς, 'I have written also . . . so that they may assist you . . . not to cause you trouble'.

78. παρουσία

From this year's reading come two examples of this word which may be added to the two recorded at *New Docs 1977*, **103**. Helbing, *AGI* 7a, b (Nysa in Caria, after 88 BC; more accessible in *SIG*[3] 741.III, IV whose text is followed here) reprints two letters written by king Mithridates of Pontos to a satrap in Caria. In both Mithridates says that upon hearing of his 'coming' the rebel Chairemon fled: ν[ῦν] τε τὴ[ν] ἐ[μὴ]ν παρουσίαν ἐπιγνοὺς τούς [τε υἱ]|οὺς Πυθόδω[ρ]ον καὶ Πυθίων[α] ἐξέθετο καὶ αὐ[τὸς πέ]|φευγεν, 'and now having found out about my coming he has both removed his sons Pythodoros and Pythion to safety and himself fled' (*SIG*[3] 741.21-23); νῦν τε τὴν ἐμὴν παρουσίαν πυθό[μενος] | εἰς τὸ τῆς Ἐφεσίας Ἀρτέμιδος ἱερὸν καταπέ[φευγεν], 'and now having learnt of my coming he has escaped to the temple of Ephesian Artemis' (30-31). In this context *parousia* takes on connotations of retribution (the purpose and consequence of the king's coming) and makes a good parallel to eschatological uses of the word in the NT (e.g., Mt. 24.27, 37, 39).

A more recently published occurrence of the word in the papyri may be found at *P.Oxy*. 47 (1980) 3357 (late I), a business letter. In it Didymos says that he asked someone ἀναμεῖναι | τὴν Φανίου παρουσίαν, 'to wait for the arrival of Phanias' (*ll*.7-8). Didymos is speaking of an arrival which he sees as an event that will only affect the person waiting when it achieves actual physical fulfilment (through the presence of Phanias). In the letters of Mithridates above, however, the *parousia* is an impending arrival: Chairemon fled on hearing not of the king's actual presence, but of his imminent arrival. It is not clear who Phanias is, but it seems that he is a business associate rather than a visiting official, in which case this example parallels the use of *parousia* in the NT for the arrival of Titus (2 Cor. 7.6, 7) and Paul (Phil. 1.26; 2.12). Spicq provides several references to the noun from documentary texts at *NLNT* II.673-75.

Parousia has already been discussed at *New Docs 1976*, **11**, a copy of an official circular announcing a prefectural visit, in which the cognate verb πάρειμι is used (cf. *New Docs 1976*, **2**, p.15 for another example). This verb is also found in Helbing, *AGI* 9 (Akraiphia in Boiotia, 28 Nov., 67), a well-known edict and speech of Nero pronounced at Corinth and conferring liberty on Greece. Helbing reprints only the first 26 lines, but the whole text can be found as no.64 in E.M. Smallwood, *Documents Illustrating the Principates of Gaius, Claudius and Nero* (Cambridge, 1967), and at *SIG*[3] 814. Nero orders that from the province as many men as possible, as far as it is possible for them, should be present at Corinth on 28 November (κελεύω πλείστους καθ' ὅ[σ]ο[ν] | ἐνδέχεται ἐκ ταύτης τῆς ἐπαρχείας παρῖναι | ἰς Κόρινθον τῇ πρὸ τεσσάρων καλανδῶν Δε|κεμβρίων, *ll*.3-6). The future is found in *P.XV Congr.* 8.8 (Philadelphia, III BC; pl.7a), a fragmentary letter to Zenon, whose correspondent informs him that he will be present at a court case involving a friend, παρέσομαι δὲ καὶ αὐτός. The present participle παρόντος also appears two lines above, but in a broken context.

A number of other NT words occur in Helbing, *AGI* 7b and 9. In no.7.8 κήρυγμα is used of a proclamation of a bounty on the rebel and his sons. The phrase συνελθόντων τῶν ὄχλων ἐν ἐκκλησίᾳ found at *AGI* 9.7 does not occur in the NT, but is reminiscent of similar wordings with parts of συνάγω, συνέρχομαι and συμπορεύομαι (e.g., Mt. 13.2; Mk. 3.20; 10.1; Lk. 5.15). It is from this text (*l*.17) that MM draw one of their two documentary examples of ἀκμάζω: here it is used figuratively, but the sole NT example (Rev. 14.18) has a literal sense.

The second of Mithridates' letters (*AGI* 7b; = *SIG*[3] 741, IV) is also interesting because Chairemon is said to have taken refuge in the temple of Artemis in Ephesos, since the city was opposing Mithridates and had sided with the Romans, a stand proclaimed in a decree outlining measures to be taken in the city, *I.Eph.* Ia.8 (86/85 BC). According to Mithridates, Chairemon made the most of his sanctuary: ἐντεῦθέν τε γράμματα πρὸς τοὺς κοινοὺ[ς πολε]|μίους διαπέμπεται Ῥωμαί|ων (*read* -ους) ἔστιν δὲ ἡ [τούτου] | ἄδηα (*read* ἄδεια) τῶν γεγενημένων ἀδικημάτων ὁ[ρμη]|τήριον τῶν καθ' ἡμῶν πραττομένων, 'and from there he sends out letters to our common enemies, the Romans; and his immunity from punishment for the crimes that have been committed is an incitement to activities against us' (*ll*.6-9). Though fragmentary, *I.Eph.* V.1520 provides us with the wording of an *asylia* inscription written on the exterior wall of the Temple of Artemis: τὸ τέμενος τῆς Ἀ[ρτέμιδος ἄσυλον] | πᾶν ὅσον ἔσω π[εριβόλου· ὃς δ' ἂν] | παραβαίνῃ, αὐτὸς [αὑτὸν αἰτιάσεται], 'the *temenos* of Artemis is inviolate, the whole area inside the perimeter. Whoever transgresses (this provision) will have himself to blame'. This wall was rebuilt under Augustus, so even though the *asylia* provision predates that period this particular inscription probably belongs to late I BC/I AD init. Another inscription declaring a sanctuary of Artemis to be *asylos* is Guarducci, *EG* IV.65-66, a boundary marker for a Hellenistic santuary at Hierocaesarea in Lydia. Guarducci reprints two other sanctuary marker-stones which mention *asylia*: *EG* IV.69-70 (Corinth, V BC init.; fig. 27); and IV.70-71 (Tralles, I?), the latter threatening destruction upon anyone harming a suppliant at this sanctuary of Dionysos Bakkhos. For *asylia* at the temple of Aphrodite at Aphrodisias and at the Asklepieion at Pergamon see **19** above.

On *asylia* in temples of Ptolemaic Egypt see F. Dunand in *Hommages à la mémoire de S. Sauneron* (2 vols; Cairo, 1979) II.77-97 which draws on both epigraphic and papyrological evidence. For a synagogue in late(?) Ptolemaic Lower Egypt which was designated an *asylon* by royal decree see **110**.

(A.L. CONNOLLY)

79. πορισμός

This noun appears in the NT only at 1 Tim. 6.5, 6; neither MM nor BAGD provides any documentary illustration. An instance occurs among the inscriptions of Ephesos. About 44 AD the proconsul Paullus Fabius Persicus issued an edict concerning the financial management of the Artemision and the city. Portions of four copies of this document survive, two in Greek (*I.Eph.* Ia.17, 18) and much smaller fragments of two Latin versions (ibid., 19a, b). No.18 provides us with the fullest amount of text, but the other copies aid in restoration of lacunose portions. In no.18, block b, Fabius censures those who have sought personal financial benefit from the temple's assets: ὁσάκις τε γὰρ ἂν ἀπὸ Ῥώμης ἱλαρωτέρα ἐλθῇ | ἀγγελία, ταύτῃ πρὸς τὸν ἴδιον ἀποχρῶνται πορισ|μὸν τό τε σχῆμα τῆς θείας οἰκίας προκάλυμμα | ποιούμενοι τὰς ἱερωσύνας ὥσπερ ἐν ἀπαρτεί|ᾳ πιπράσκουσιν καὶ ἐκ παντὸς γένους ἐπὶ τὴν | ὠνὴν αὐτῶν συνκ<α>λοῦσιν ἀνθρώπους, κτλ (*ll.*11-16), 'for whenever more joyful news comes from Rome they misuse it for their own gain, and making the appearance of the divine building a cloak (for what they do) they sell priesthoods as though at an auction; and they summon people from every family for the purchase of them . . .'

This short extract illustrates the wealth of lexical parallels for the NT which the inscriptions from Ephesos yield: ὁσάκις, ἱλαρός, σχῆμα, and πιπράσκω, as well as πορισμός and a number of other words. The present Review cannot do more than provide a sampling, to underline the danger of neglecting epigraphical evidence for such research.

80. πραΰτης

The ideal of 'gentleness' may be used to trace a number of interconnected themes in Greek culture. This has been done comprehensively for the first time by J. de Romilly, *La douceur dans la pensée grecque* (Paris, 1979; cf. *SEG* 1794). Even the harsh world of epic and tragedy admired the powerful figure who could become ἤπιος ('mild'). The democratic passion for justice, however, did not leave much room for gentleness. With the decline of the *polis* in IV BC, πρᾶος takes the place once held in literature by ἤπιος, and is joined by φιλάνθρωπος and ἐπιεικής ('fair'). The theatre of Menander celebrates the gentle man, and Hellenistic civilisation carried this emphasis through to its apogee in Roman times in the work of Plutarch. Although πραότης is first known from Thucydides, the ideal has no early epigraphic attestation. The inscriptions amply document the diplomatic philanthropy of the Hellenistic royal houses, but progressively, and especially in Roman times, they also show how a great variety of affective terms for gentle behaviour came to expression in the monuments of more ordinary people (de Romilly, 227-30, 268-74).

Nevertheless, de Romilly claims there was 'une complète révolution morale' (312) between classical gentleness and Christian goodness. The one stems from a principle of restraint (σωφροσύνη) or self-respect (αἰδώς) which moderates one's own behaviour, the other from a more active concern (ἀγάπη) for the need of the weaker party to whom one inclines. Behind this lies the unexpectedly frequent use of πρᾶος/πραΰς in the LXX for the 'poor'. The word appears to have crossed a social boundary, from denoting the character suitable to those with power, to denoting those who need their favour. But πρᾶος had never indicated a social category, nor would poverty, humility or suffering ever have been morally recommended in classical culture. In fact, the biblical 'poor' are an eschatological category, their virtue lying in their expectation of the Kingdom. So in Mt. 5.5 ('the meek shall inherit the earth') the righteous poor of Ps.36(37).11 are seen in terms of their moral stance, while Mt. 21.5 recalls the fact that in Zach. 9.9 πραότης could be posited of the humble king (mounted on a donkey). Biblical humility was perhaps from the beginning coloured by Hellenistic gentleness (de Romilly, 315, following earlier work by Spicq, whose most recent discussion of πραΰτης and related words occurs in *NLNT* III.570-82). The Greek Fathers gradually reasserted the values of classical humanism, competing in IV AD with Julian, Libanios, and Themistios in what had become a no-man's-land of morality claimed by the rival world-views.

Both the contradictions and the congruence of the two traditions can be seen in the word-groupings of the NT. The coupling of gentleness with humility in the self-description of Jesus (Mt. 11.29) entailed for Paul the paradox of self-abasement (Phil. 2.8) which proved incredible in his own case (2 Cor. 10.1). Ταπεινοφροσύνη and μακροθυμία (tolerance towards others) became regular partners of the more traditional πραΰτης (Gal. 5.23; Eph. 4.2; Col. 3.12). But πραΰτης is plainly still an attribute of those with authority (1 Cor. 4.21; Gal. 6.1; 2 Tim. 2.25), while ἐπιείκεια (Acts 24.4; 2 Cor. 10.1) and φιλανθρωπία (Acts 27.3; 28.2; Tit. 3.4) are limited to condescension, human or divine — for ordinary human relations they are displaced by ἀγάπη. Some epithets prominent in the field studied by de Romilly that do not feature in the NT are ἀνθρώπινος (only of being a human being, 1 Cor. 2.13; Jas. 3.7), ἥμερος (though ἤπιος occurs in 1 Thes. 2.7; 2 Tim. 2.24), κοινωνικός (only in 1 Tim. 6.18), μειλίχιος, and φιλόστοργος (only Rom. 12.10; see *New Docs 1977*, **80**; *New Docs 1978*, **11**). The noun εὐεργεσία occurs only of the service performed by slaves (at 1 Tim. 6.2), but χρηστότης is found several times (2 Cor. 6.6; Gal. 5.22; Col. 3.12).

(E.A. JUDGE)

81. πρίζω

A well-preserved edict from Ephesos of the proconsul L. Antonius Albus, concerning the need to keep the harbour area clear, includes this uncommonly attested verb: *I.Eph.* Ia.23 (146/7; pl.21): παραγγέλλω [οὖ]ν καὶ τοῖς τὰ ξύλα καὶ τοῖς | τοὺς λίθους ἐνπορευομένοις μήτε τὰ ξύλα | παρὰ τῇ ὀχθῇ τιθέναι μήτε τοὺς λίθους | πρίζειν (*ll.*13-16), 'therefore I give instructions both to those who trade in timber and to those who trade in stone not to place the timber beside the wharf nor to saw the stone (there)'. The NT employs πρίζω only at Heb. 11.37 where it appears to be intended literally of people being 'sawn asunder'; but a hyperbole may be involved. MM provides one papyrus example of the verb, taken over by BAGD under another *siglum* (*C.P.Herm.* in MM = *P.Hermopol.* in BAGD = *SPP* 5 [1905]).

82. προκυρόω

MM lacks an entry for this verb, found in the NT only at Gal. 3.17, διαθήκην προκεκυρωμένην ὑπὸ τοῦ θεοῦ. A good parallel to this may be found in a fragmentary decree of the Ephesians concerning the distribution of water, *I.Eph.* VI.2018. The end of *l.*8 reads: π]ροκεκυρω[μέν]α ψηφίσματα ὑπὸ τοῦ δή||[μου - - -], 'decrees which have been ratified previously by the people'. The text is to be dated between 4-14 AD. Earlier in date than this instance is an inscription from Rhodes (II BC), noted by BAGD, s.v., in which mention is made of matters laid down 'in the previously ratified decree', ἐν τῷ προκεκυρωμένῳ ψαφίσματι: *SEG* 3 (1929) 674.28 (the same phrase also at *l.*30).

Similar wording involving the simple verb κυρόω (cf. Gal. 3.15) appears at *I.Eph.* VI.2054 (after 211). Here the Ephesians set up a statue of the *demos* of Knidos to mark their sister-city relationship: . . . κατὰ τὸ κυ[ρω]|θὲν ψήφισμα ἐτείμησεν | τὴν λαμπροτάτην Κνιδίων | πόλιν τὴν ἀδελφήν, (*ll.*3-6), 'in accordance with the decree that was formally ratified, (the city of Ephesos) honoured the most illustrious city of the Knidians, their sister (city)'. The word-index volume to *I.Eph.* lists over a dozen further instances of the verb. The Hellenistic inscription from Rhodes noted above employs the wording κυρωθέντος τοῦδε τοῦ ψαφίσματος twice (*ll.*7-8, 26).

83. προσφιλής

The sole epigraphical reference provided by BAGD for this adjective, *OGIS* 331.9, is in fact an attestation of the adverb (the relevant wording is quoted by MM, s.v.). MM notes that the adjective is common in epitaphs, citing one example.

In the NT the word occurs only at Phil. 4.8, as a neuter plural in a list of qualities recommended to be given contemplative attention. This absolute use occurs in *SEG* 787 (Thasos, Imperial period?), consisting of brief epitaphs for two men: Διομήδης [Φιλό]|φρονος προσ[φι]|λὴς χαῖρε. | Λ. Ἄρριος Σενέ|κας προσφιλὴς | χαῖρε. In *SEG* 784 (Thasos, Imperial period(?)) a funerary base has the word largely restored twice: [προσ]φιλὴς χαῖρε | [- - -]τα Διοτίμου | [- - -]μος Διονυσίου | [προσφι]λὴς χẽρε. The restorations are justified by the formulaic use apparently being employed in funerary texts on Thasos. That its use was conventional there is confirmed by *CIL III Add.* 248, a sarcophagus from Thasos (Imperial period(?); = *IG* XII, 8.506) with inscriptions recording the burying there of several people. On this monument the adjective occurs six times.

Two further instances may be mentioned here (a third occurs in the text printed at **129** below). Pfuhl/Möbius II.1187b — on pp.481-82 — is an epitaph for Dionysodoros (provenance and date not given [Imperial?]; pl.179) which concludes by saying that he was πᾶσι προσφιλ[ῆ] (*l.*5). *I.Eph.* III.645 is an Imperial-period text in which the *hymnodoi* of Artemis honour one of their number: [τ]ὸ προσφιλέ|[στ]ατον τ[ῆ] ἁγιωτάτῃ | [θ]εῷ Ἀρτέμιδι | συνέδριον | [τ]ῶν ὑμνῳδῶν | [κ]αὶ θεολόγων | [κ]αὶ θεσμῳδῶν | [Τι]β. Κλ. Μοσχᾶν, κτλ (*ll.*1-8). On ἅγιος used of Artemis here cf. BAGD, s.v., 1b, δ, for NT examples where this adjective is used of God. For θεολόγος see **60** above.

84. πρωτεύω again (cf. *New Docs 1977*, 72)

MM's entry quotes three papyrus instances, ranging from IV-VI, and refers to one inscribed epigram (IV BC) where the verb occurs. At *New Docs 1977*, **72** a further, late papyrus witness was mentioned. Since then two inscriptions have come to attention. From the present year's culling *I.Eph.* VII, 1.3071 (mid-III) honours M. Aurelius *NN* for the offices he has undertaken and his benefactions to the city, speaking of him as one who 'oversaw the most important tasks of the state', ἐπιστάντα ἔργοις | τῆς πατρίδος τοῖς πρωτεύουσιν, κτλ (*ll.*13-14). Also to be noted is T. Ihnken (ed.), *Die Inschriften von Magnesia am Sipylos* (*IK* 8; Bonn, 1978) 32 (Imperial period), another honorific inscription for a 'very fine man, of first rank in the state', ἄνδρα ἄριστον, πρωτεύον|τα ἔν τε τῇ πατρίδι, κτλ (*ll.*3-4). The Ephesian text illustrates a usage of ἐφίστημι found in ECL but not in the NT (BAGD, s.v., 2c); but it parallels less closely than does the Magnesian example the use of πρωτεύω at its sole NT occurrence, Col. 1.18.

85. σκήνωμα

MM supplies no documentary parallel for this noun, while BAGD notes a reference in *PGM*. An instance appears in Tsigaridas, *Κατάλογος*, 8 (Thessalonike, VI; = *IG* X 2, 1 [1972] 397), an epitaph of Eutychios διδασκάλου χρη|στιανοῦ (*ll.*2-3), which includes the warning ὅπου | μή τις τολμήσῃ | ἀνύξας ἄλλο σκήνω|μα ἀπόθητε (*ll.*4-7), 'see to it that no-one dares open (the grave) and deposit another body'. This figurative notion of the body as the 'tent' in which the soul resides offers a useful parallel to 2 Pet. 1.13, 14, ἐφ' ὅσον εἰμὶ ἐν τούτῳ τῷ σκηνώματι . . . εἰδὼς ὅτι ταχινή ἐστιν ἡ ἀπόθεσις τοῦ σκηνώματός μου, κτλ. The NT passage is more self-conscious in its use of the word metaphorically, however. By the time of this Byzantine inscription σκήνωμα has come to mean merely 'body'. In this epitaph Eutychios is spoken of as νεοφώτιστος, 'newly baptised' (*l.*4; cf. *New Docs 1976*, **88**); and since he is no recent convert — in view of his function as a Christian teacher — the word is probably indicative of the practice of delaying baptism until death was imminent.

An uncertain epigraphical attestation occurs in *I.Nikaia* I.340 (pl.26; = *SEG* 1343), a fragmentary text whose full preserved wording is]τοπον σκη||[? ν]ώματος δο|[ ] ης σου. Şahin appears to see this as a gravestone; no date is suggested by him, but it is presumably from the Imperial period. The reading cannot be accepted as beyond doubt here, for it is unclear how much is lost on the left side of the stone.

86. συμμερίζω

MM (s.v. συνμ-) has no documentary instances of this verb, found in the NT only at 1 Cor. 9.13, οἱ τῷ θυσιαστηρίῳ παρεδρεύοντες τῷ θυσιαστηρίῳ συμμερίζονται. The verb now appears in abbreviated form in a fragmentary set of agricultural accounts, *P.Strasb.* 686.20 (Arsinoite nome, II^2): . . . συμμεριζ(οντ) καλάμου. The participle which appears to be required could equally be resolved as a middle here, 'having a share of the reeds' (for κάλαμος as a collective see LSJ, s.v., III,1).

87. Ταρσεύς

Neither MM nor BAGD offers any documentary attestations of this noun — NT: Acts 9.11; 21.39 — in their respective entries. From this year's publications we may note three. Pfuhl/Möbius, II.1756 (pl.255) is a funerary relief (Xanthos(?) in Lykia, *c*.200 BC) which carries the wording Ἑλλανίων Ταρσεύς. Equally brief is a signature on a strigil, *SEG* 1058 (Vajta in Pannonia, mid-II/early III), Ῥοῦφος Ταρσεύς ἐποίει (cf. *BE* [1980] 336 where the definite article is read in front of the name). Ταρ|[σέ]α is a reasonable restoration in *I.Nikaia* I.277 (repr. above at **4**).

Paul is less specifically identified as Κίλιξ in the Western version of Acts 23.34, ἀναγνοὺς δὲ τὴν ἐπιστολὴν ἐπηρώτησε τὸν Παῦλον· Ἐκ ποίας ἐπαρχίας εἶ; ἔφη· Κίλιξ. καὶ πυθόμενος ἔφη· Ἀκούσομαί σου. Attested as far back as Homer (see LSJ, s.v.), this word appears twice in inscriptions from Rome of this year's culling: an inscription for Numenius, *IGUR* 1286.1 (Imperial period?) begins τίς ἦν σε ὁ θρέψας; — ἦν Κίλιξ Ἀθήναιος, ' "Who was the one who reared you?" "He was a Cilician, Athenaios." ' The second text, *IGUR* 1361, is a single iambic line (Imperial), Χρύσιππος Αὐγουστανὸς πρεσβευτὴς Κίλιξ, an epitaph for a man from Augusta, a city in Cilicia founded in honour of Livia Augusta (so Moretti, ad loc.), who died at Rome while on an embassy there. The word received no entry in MM. Though not from a 1979 publication Κίλιξ also occurs in an epitaph for a gladiator, published by L. Robert, *Hellenica* 8 (1950) 40 (Ankyra, Imperial?; pl.15.1): Δα[ναὸς] Θρᾶιξ | πάλος πρῶ|τος Κίλιξ Ἀν|αζαρβεύς. | Τυχάριν Δ|αναῷ ἰδ[ιῷ] | ἀνδρὶ [μνή]|μης χ[άριν], 'Danaos, a member of the first Thracian squad, from Anazarbos in Cilicia. Tycharion (erected this) for her own husband Danaos as a memorial'. On gladiators see **4** above.

88. καθ' υἱοθεσίαν

Paul is the only NT writer to use this noun (Rom 8.15, 23; 9.4; Gal. 4.5; Eph. 1.5), though he does not employ this particular prepositional phrase which was noted as commonly attested in inscriptions by Deissmann (*Bible Studies*, 239), MM, BAGD, et al. Nine instances turn up in *IGB*, all of which follow the standard form A son of B, καθ' υἱοθεσίαν δὲ of C. These items are: *IGB* 174.2 (Lindos, III/II BC), 185.10 (Rhodes, II BC init.), 188.4 (Rhodes, II BC?), 189.4 (Rhodes, II BC?), 191.3 (Lindos, II BC?), 198.2 (Lindos, II BC?), 214.3 (Delos, II BC), 300a.3 (Halikarnassos, II/I BC; phrase partly restored), 305.1-2 (Halikarnassos, II/I BC).

89. ὑψόω

In *I.Nikaia* II.1, pp.301-09, Şahin reprints as no.89 the text of five sepulchral epigrams written on an obelisk set up to commemorate Sacerdos and his wife Severa (cf. *BE* [1982] 408). This funerary monument (perhaps of Hadrianic date, or later) — its style was not unique in Nikaia: *I.Nikaia* I.85 preserves a much briefer prose epitaph for C. Cassius Philiskos on an obelisk

(II init.) — was erected just near Lake Ascanius, the modern Iznik Gölü, which borders Nikaia on the west. Sacerdos is praised for numerous achievements, among them that he 'raised from the ground his homeland when it was cast down', τὸν πάτραν ἐριποῦσαν ἀπὸ χθονὸς ὑψώσαντα (*l*.11). Although the force of the verb here is primarily literal, referring to restoration work in the city funded by him after an earthquake, yet the figurative sense 'enhance' may be present too. In the NT the figurative sense is far more common; but the literal meaning occurs at Jn 3.14a; in 3.14b both literal and figurative senses come together.

90. Φρύγιος

In *JTS* 27 (1976) 122-26 and 28 (1977) 99-101 C.J. Hemer drew attention to the neglected but plentiful examples of triple-termination Φρύγιος, both in literary and epigraphical texts, to parallel the adjectival use of the word in the phrase at Acts 16.6, τὴν Φρυγίαν καὶ Γαλατικὴν χώραν (cf. 18.23, which varies this word order). Hemer's no.18 (in his second article) is a manumission text (Delphi, 155/4 BC) for a certain Diodora, τὸ γένος Φρυγίαν. This inscription figures as no.696 in the catalogue of servile names extrapolated from manumission texts in Reilly, *Slaves*. In the same catalogue, no.1875 refers to Menias, τὸ γένος Φρυγίαν (Naupaktos, mid-II BC); while no.1852 is a text where the male slave being freed is τὸ γένος Φρύγα (i.e., acc. of Φρύξ).

The computerised listing assembled by Reilly throws up a number of other ethnics which also appear in the NT. A near parallel to the word above occurs in no.3247, where a manumitted male slave is described as τὸ γένος Πισίδαν (Delphi, 138/7): should this be resolved as Πισίδ<ι>≪ο≫ν, to agree either with his name (in the accusative) or with the neuter γένος, both formulas being commonly employed? If so, we would have an attestation of this word used adjectivally to parallel Acts 13.14, εἰς Ἀντιόχειαν τὴν Πισιδίαν. But the example should not be pressed.

The following other adjectival forms which indicate ethnic origin may be noted from Reilly as parallels for NT words: Αἰγύπτιος (730, 766) Ἀλεξανδρεύς (2681), Ἀντιοχεύς (687), Ἄραψ (1753, 1797, 2340, 2375, 2386), Ἐφέσιος (1249; the name index to *I.Eph*., vol. VIII, 2, p.74, lists four people who bear the name Ephesios), Σιδώνιος (2387), Σύρος (366, 408, 412, 468, 477, 480, 508, 566, 660, 819, 837, 850, 1014, 1022, 1050, 1093, 1190, 1295, 1316, 1342, 1530, 1610-12, 1682, 1713, 1754, 2073, 2075, 2123, 2210, 2271, 2275, 2419, 2458, 2480, 2732, 2736, 2783, 2796, 3214 — this last person being further defined as being from Beirut, Βηρύτιον). The large number of attestations here of ex-slaves of Syrian origin — cf. **94** below, where a dozen women named Syra are noted, another indication of their ethnic background — is paralleled only by Thracians in Reilly's collection of over 3000 slave names.

It is perhaps worth passing mention that these and other indications of ethnic origin for slaves released at Delphi, various locations in Thessaly, and elsewhere on the Greek mainland or the Aegean islands — this constitutes the geographical scope of Reilly's catalogue — illustrate quite incidentally the great mobility of people in Graeco-Roman antiquity. For further comment on this question in relation to Rome see **114** below.

91. χολάω

This verb, which is a NT *hapax legomenon* at Jn 7.23, and its compounds are attested by no documentary example. W.M. Ramsay, *Cities and Bishoprics of Phrygia* I, ii (Oxford, 1897) 471 no.312 (Apamea in Phrygia, 247/8), actually uses the verb χολόομαι; this reference should therefore be deleted from BAGD, s.v. χολάω. Similarly, MM's only documentary example attests χολόομαι, *SB* 1 (1915) 4531 (an inscription found at Gebel Tukh near Ptolemais, n.d.). Χολόομαι has a restricted use which does not elucidate the meaning of χολάω, as two examples from this year's culling illustrate. These two texts from Ephesos warn against defiling (holy?) places: *I.Eph.* II.567 (n.d.), εἴ | τις ἂν ὧδε | οὐρήσῃ, ἡ Ἑκά|τη αὐτῷ κε|χώλωται (*read* -χολ-), 'if anyone urinates here, Hekate is filled with wrath against him'; ibid., 569 (n.d.), ὧδε οὐρήσαντι ἡ Ἄρτεμ[ις] | [κ]εχόλωται, 'Artemis is filled with wrath against anyone urinating here'. For similar warnings see *I.Eph.* II.568; *SB* I.4531, 4532; and for ones in which the divine threat is only implied, see the two inscriptions listed under *I.Eph.* II.568A (n.d.), which are identical texts found in different buildings of the city with an injunction given via a dream (κατ' ὄναρ) against urinating ἰς τὴν καμάραν, 'in the vaulted room'. The participle κεχολωμένος, used always of divine powers and combined usually with a part of ἔχω, is found not uncommonly in imprecations against disturbers of graves, e.g., *I. Magnesia am Sipylos* (*IK* 8; Bonn, 1978) 28.11-13 (= Guarducci, *EG* III [1974] 181-82; II), τοὺς ἐπουρανί|ους καὶ καταχθονίους θεοὺς | κεχολωμένους (cf. Guarducci -χωλο-) ἔχοισαν, 'may they have to deal with the gods above and below in their wrath'. For other examples, both Christian and pagan, see *SIG*^{3} 1241.5-8 (Lyttos, III) and the note to *l*.2 there, and L. Robert, *Hellenica* 11/12 (1960) 406 n.10, 407 nn.8, 9. Also from this year's publications comes *CIL III Add.* 128, a bilingual epitaph from Eleusis. For optatives like ἔχοισαν see BDF §84(4).

All the known documentary examples of χολόομαι (there are no occurrences attested so far in the papyri) are forms of the perfect tense, and all refer to divine retributive anger. For a literary parallel note Plut., *Fab*. 22.5. It seems that the word, common in epic poetry, had become restricted to this use and probably had an antique ring.

It is clear from Jn 7.23 that χολάω was not restricted in the same way, as there the reference is to the Jews' anger against Jesus. Nevertheless one must wonder if the word does have a special sense or belong to a higher level of language since other words for 'being angry' (cf. ὀργίζομαι, ἀγανακτέω, θυμόομαι) are common enough in the NT, LXX and papyri (cf. also δυσφορέω, δυσχεραίνω and μηνίω). Not only is χολάω absent from documentary sources, but it is also uncommon in literature. It is not listed in Lampe, although see χολέω and χολαίνω s.vv. Why is it so rare? The authors cited in LSJ and BAGD, s.v., include several comic poets of V-III BC, a bucolic and epic poet of II BC, and the Atticistic 3 Maccabees.

The context of 3 Macc. 3.1, which has the compound ἐκχολάω in the A text and the uncompounded form in others (the only example of either verb in the LXX), implies that strong anger is being described. At 1.4 in the *Oneirocritica* of Artemidoros Daldianos (II AD), χολάω is used to describe the anger of a man in a dream who has lost at draughts and chases the man who is dreaming because the latter helped his opponent. The dreamer sees himself running away and shutting himself behind the doors of a building. Again, the context suggests that χολάω has a strong meaning. In D.L. 9.66, however, the philosopher Pyrrho, who was famed for his indifference to physical existence but did on rare occasions fail to remain unmoved, is described as χολήσας τι ὑπὲρ τῆς ἀδελφῆς, 'somewhat angered on behalf of his sister': the τι makes a strong sense unlikely here because 'somewhat enraged' would only be appropriate in an ironical context; and further, in the following context it is said that Pyrrho was once 'scared away' (διασοβηθέντα, διασοβέω being a verb with a weak sense) by a rushing dog. It seems that Diogenes' intention here was to minimise the force of his exceptions.

It is beyond the scope of this entry to resolve this problem fully, but two possible understandings of χολάω in Jn 7.23 ought to be kept in mind. First, it may have the stronger sense of 'being enraged', which would fit in well with the murderous intentions of the Jews in Jn 7.14-26. Second, it may be another example of an elevated word used of Jesus or by him, for which see J.A.L. Lee, *NovT* 27 (1985) 1-26, discussing this feature in Mark though referring to its existence in other books (25).

It is worth mentioning here that in D.L. 9.66 we read of Pyrrho's aim to ἐκδῦναι τὸν ἄνθρωπον, 'to strip off one's human nature'; this affords an interesting literary parallel (not noted in BAGD, s.v. ἀπεκδύομαι) to Col.3.9, ἀπεκδυσάμενοι τὸν παλαιὸν ἄνθρωπον (cf. Eph. 4.22 and 2 Cor. 5.4). MM has no entry for this verb, but discusses it briefly under ἀπέκδυσις and follows Lightfoot in accepting both words as Pauline neologisms, there being no examples earlier than the occurrences in Paul.

(A.L. CONNOLLY)

92. χρηματισμός

In the NT this noun occurs only once, at Rom. 11.4, ἀλλὰ τί λέγει αὐτῷ ὁ χρηματισμός; The OT quotation which follows helps us interpret the word in a general sense as 'divine utterance', rather than as 'oracle', specifically. MM notes a further generalised use illustrated by two papyri, but their discussion needs correction; see E.A. Judge in *New Docs 1976*, **26**, p.77. Their entry includes no epigraphical attestations; BAGD merely states 'inscr.'. *I.Nikaia* II, 1.1071 (Gölpazar, I or II; cf. *BE* [1982] 414) is a dedication to Zeus Archagathos: on the altar there is both a verse section (2-9, consisting of two couplets) and a prose portion (19-17). M. Cassius Puplianus Nikadas has held various public offices, including ἐπιμελητὴς τοῦ νεοκτίστου ναοῦ (14-15), and dedicates a statue of an eagle with an altar in accordance with a divine utterance in a dream, κατὰ χρηματισμὸν ὀνίρου τὸν αἰετὸν | σὺν τῷ βωμῷ ἀνέθηκα (16-17). Here we have a general use of the noun which exactly parallels the NT passage. The equivalent of this phrase in the verse text is σαῖσι ταγαῖς πεισθείς, 'obeying your commands'. The noun ταγή is noted in BAGD as occurring in ECL only at *1 Cl.* 20.8. At the end of the epigram the optative δοῖς occurs (*l*.8), which Şahin (n. ad loc.) notes as equivalent to δοίης (cf. BDF §95(2), BDR[15] §95 n.2, referring to ἀποδοῖς at Lk. 12.59D).

Χρηματισμός also appears in the Ptolemaic inscriptions collected in *SGPI*. The long, trilingual (Greek, Hieroglyph, Demotic) Kanopos decree, no.38 (= *OGIS* 56), uses the word at *l*.23 (239/8 BC). It is found also in *l*.55 of the even more famous trilingual Rosetta stone, *SGPI* 69 (time of Ptolemy V; = *OGIS* 90). *SGPI* 103 (= *OGIS* 137-39) records on the bottom of an obelisk at Philai the text of royal letters from and to Ptolemy VIII (145-116 BC) and his consort Kleopatra; in text C (*OGIS* 139) on this monument the noun appears at *l*.18. In all of these instances the word has its common meaning 'report'.

The related verb χρηματίζω is found at *SGPI* 93.7 (near Ghazi in Egypt, time of Ptolemy VI, 180-145 BC; = *OGIS* 106), in the frequently-attested sense, 'do business', a meaning not employed in the NT.

93. A collection of NT lexicographical notes

The first two volumes of Spicq, *NLNT* were published in 1978, but did not come to my attention in time to be treated in *New Docs 1978*. A third, supplementary volume has also appeared (1982). This large work comes at the end of a long career: Spicq's publications extend back over more than half a century, in the area of NT exegesis and theology. In view of this great productivity the mere collecting together — if that were all it was! — of this series of lexicographical studies from his earlier books and articles would be in itself a great service. About 670 Greek words (including a small number of phrases) are dealt with in just over 400 entries (Greek head-words), spanning *c.*1700pp.

A theological orientation is primary in these books, as Spicq makes clear (*NLNT* I.7); yet it does not interfere with his philological judgements. The theological treatment is allowed to become more discursive in vol.III, which contains considerably fewer entries though more pages than either of the two preceding volumes. Spicq seems thoroughly aware of the latest secondary literature relevant to the words he chooses to study. What makes his contribution so admirable, and the reason for noting it here, is his thorough-going collection of documentary attestations — not that literary ones are excluded — coupled with cautious discussion. Spicq has undoubtedly kept in touch with recent papyrological and epigraphical publications. Yet while his assembling of evidence is impressive it must be stated that users of these volumes need to be on their guard about the state of the texts which are quoted. As is the way with written survivals on stone or papyrus or ostracon, most texts are partly or very lacunose, sometimes hopelessly so. It must be presumed that Spicq has removed brackets indicating editorial restorations, subscript dots, etc., for the ease of his printer and for theological readers. As merely one instance of the false impression this creates, his quotation at *NLNT* III.432 of *SB* 6293.10 does not indicate that the very words which provide the *raison d'être* for the quotation, ὑπὲρ λύτρων, are entirely restored. Further, the date he gives for this text (III) is too loose: in fact it belongs to 195/6 AD. On this document see *New Docs 1978*, **46**, p.75.

In his approach to the vocabulary of the NT Spicq is heir to that tradition with which the names of Deissmann and Moulton are particularly linked. The former's *Bible Studies* provides the closest analogy to Spicq's *NLNT.* The *New Docs* volumes are likewise set firmly in this tradition, and thus have close affinities with Spicq's work, except for the intentional lack of any explicit theological thrust. Both works call attention independently to the neglect of Greek documentary sources for illustration of the language, and especially of the vocabulary of the NT.

It is a great misfortune that the first two volumes, published in 1978, are already out of print and unobtainable. Words treated in Spicq, *NLNT* which are also discussed in the present Review are noted at the relevant entry.

94. Dorkas

In the Joppa incident recorded at Acts 9.36-42, the writer indicates (9.36) that Dorkas is the translation name of Tabitha, the woman restored to life by Peter. Each name is employed separately in the passage, at 9.39 and 40, the latter reflecting Peter's address to her in Aramaic.

MM rightly notes (s.v.) that this name is used by both Greeks and Jews. The single epigraphical attestaton given there is also noted by BAGD. That text, *SIG*^{2} 854 (not included in *SIG*^{3}), occurs also as *Sammlung der griechischen Dialektinschriften* (= *GDI*) II, i (repr.

Nedeln, 1978) 1884 (Delphi, 170-157/6 BC). Two other manumission texts from Delphi mention a Dorkas: *GDI* 1866 and 2062. This latter pair is catalogued in Reilly, *Slaves* as nos.780 (175/4 BC) and 781 (180/79 or 179/8 BC). The latter is a woman of Thracian origin.

Reilly's catalogue lists nearly 3,250 instances of slave names; about their status there can be no question, for she has only included the evidence of manumission texts from mainland Greece and the Aegean islands within the eight centuries from V BC-III AD. Delphi is by far the most common single provenance for these texts: over 1,300 of the items in Reilly's list come from there. Several names from the NT onomasticon crop up. Those not discussed elsewhere in the present Review include: Demetrios (Reilly, 658-70), Eutychos (1175-91), Jason (1490-93), Philippos (3095-99), Rhode (2412-16), Rufus (2441), Simon (2497-98), Stephanos (2542-46), Sosthenes (2655), Tertia (2986), Theophilos (1453-55, 1468), Timotheos (2979, 2995-96), Trophimos (3011-12; cf. *New Docs 1978*, **80**), Tryphaina (3014-15; cf. *New Docs 1978*, **81**). The presence of a Scipio (Reilly, 2503) warns us against assuming that all these names in her catalogue are customary slave names. Thus, the presence of several ex-slaves called Theophilos should not lead to rash inferences about the status of the man to whom Lk./Acts is addressed.

A small number of Jews can be identified in these manumission texts listed by Reilly. No.199 (Delphi, 158/7 BC) names Antigona, τὸ γένος Ἰουδαίαν. No.1507 provides a clearcut example of ethnic background determining the name accorded to the slave by his master: Ioudaios τὸ γένος Ἰουδαῖον (Delphi, 163/2 BC). No.2451 (Doliche in Thessaly, II) is for a Samba[t]ion, who may be Jewish, given the name and date; but see further **116** below where some non-Jewish instances are noted. No.2500 (Larisa in Thessaly, n.d.) mentions a Sirakos: an attempt, perhaps, to render Sirach by adding a Greek termination? T. Muraoka points out to me (*per litt.*), however, that Sirach, if the same as Ben Sirach, is often considered to be a Graecised form of Semitic Sira. The name Ἰόππα is attested in no.1506 (Delphi, 124-116 BC); we may infer that this slave originated from that coastal city in Palestine. The same phenomenon is at work in those ex-slaves who were called Zmyrna or Smyrna by their masters (Reilly, 1255-56 and 2510-12, respectively). On this orthographical difference cf. the entries in BAGD. The adjective Ζμυρναῖος occurs in Pfuhl/Möbius II.2178 (Samos, II[1]; pl.311): the NT has Σμυρ- only, in the *t.r.* of Rev. 2.8. Similarly, Reilly nos. 2602-13 attest a dozen women called Syra, and 2614 has a Syrion. On the use of this adjective as an ethnic rather than as a name see the example cited at **90** above.

Helbing, *AGI* 34, reprints and comments on a text from Steiris in Phokis (*IG* IX, 1 [1897] 42) in which a man frees a female slave καὶ τὸ ἐξ αὐτᾶς παιδάριον, perhaps his own child by her. This text — repr. above at **24** — is catalogued as no.1117 in Reilly, *Slaves*, where the date given is II BC init.

95. Euodia

By oversight, BAGD, s.v., does not include its usual indication that MM has an entry with documentary attestations of this name (NT, only at Phil. 4.2). Yet some of the specific texts noted by BAGD have clearly been drawn from MM. A woman with this name appears among the current crop of texts, in Pfuhl/Möbius, II.2199 (Pergamon, II; pl.313), Ἐλπὶς Εὐοδίᾳ (*leaf*) | τῇ θρεψάσ(η) | μνείας (*leaf*) χάριν, 'Elpis (erected this monument) as a memorial to Euodia who reared her'. A dog is carved in relief on the stone, causing the word θρεψάσῃ to be split in two, after the *psi*. Another Euodia is an ex-slave: Reilly, *Slaves*, no.1079 (Kalymna, II). In another manumission text, *IG* V, 2 (1913) 277 (repr. at Guarducci, *EG* III [Rome, 1974] 292-93; cf. Reilly, no.876), Euodia manumits Elpis, her own daughter and slave, τὴν | ἰδίαν θυγατέρα καὶ δού|λην ἠλευθέρωσεν (*ll*.4-6; Mantinea, II). *CIJ* I.391 (Rome, Imperial period) is a family epitaph, including mention of the wife Euodia (discussed briefly below at **114**, list 1b).

96. Onesimos

From this year's reading come around sixty examples — all in inscriptions — of the name Ὀνήσιμος/Ὀνάσιμος which is found in the NT at Col. 4.1 and Philemon 10. They are listed here in summary form, including doubtful cases (which are marked by an asterisk):

CIL III Add. 250
I.Eph. Ia.20, 47
II.572
III.668a (not 688a as in Index), 898a*, 970
IV.1030-1044
V.1600, 1662, 1936
VI.2900, 2948c
VII, 1.3017, 3458b, 3472
VII, 2.3709, 3804, 3825a*, 4361*
I.Nikaia I.61
Pfuhl/Möbius, I.154, 1070* (= *I.Eph.* VII, 2.3825a)
II.1138 (= *SEG* 1425), 1149, 1284, 1491, 1632 (= *SEG* 1254), 1724, 2134, 2209, 2293
Pircher, no.12 (cf. **33** above)
Reilly, *Slaves*, nos.2121-26 (Ὀνάσιμος), 2161-70 (Ὀνήσιμος)
SEG 127, 152, 1204.

The index to *I.Eph.* mistakenly records a further occurrence as being found at text 2200a. On *I.Eph.* I.20 see *New Docs 1978*, **4**, pp.18-19. Occurrences of the name at Rome collected by Solin (*GPR* II.913-19, III.1366; cf. III.1348) number about 450, which makes it the fourth most common name found there. More epigraphical examples can be found in *BE* in the following entries: (1932) p.210; (1955) 181; (1963) 230; (1964) 236; (1966) 329, 508; (1967) 337; (1968) 603; (1970) 677; (1971) 753; (1972) 520; (1973) 406. For two other examples see *New Docs 1976*, **54**.

About one third of the attestations from this year's culling come from Ephesos or close by it. Others come from Athens (9, from 4 inscriptions), Phrygia (4), Bithynia (3), Lydia (2, or one from each of Lydia and Mysia), Odessos in Moesia (1), the Propontic area (1) and Samothrace (1; though the man belongs to the retinue of a Roman proconsul). Examples collected from *BE* have provenances in the Aegean, Caria, Lydia, Cilicia, Illyria and Locri in Italy. Robert expresses surprise over the example from Cilicia (there being no others from the southern coast of Asia Minor) and reinterprets the words Ὀνήσιμος Τοκιμεὺς ἐποίει to mean 'Onesimos from Dokimeion made it' (*BE* [1972] 520, p.498), thereby giving this Onesimos a

Phrygian origin. For Egyptian examples see *NB* and Foraboschi, s.v. Balancing the predominantly eastern origin of these attestations is Reilly's collection which includes ten occurrences from Thessaly and five from Central and Western Greece (though it should be remembered that manumission texts are found in the place of manumission which may not have been the place of residence). It is interesting to observe, however, that none of Reilly's instances from mainland Greece is later than I, whereas the majority of occurrences found elsewhere (excluding Rome) are later than I. The geographical distribution of the name in the time of the Empire, therefore, seems to have been the islands and coast of the Aegean and Black Sea, N-W Asia Minor and Egypt.

The archives of the Temple of Zeus in Locri provide the earliest documentary examples of the name dating from late fourth or early third century BC (cf. *BE* [1965] 494). Another early example is the slave Onesimos mentioned in letters to Zenon, *P.Cair.Zen.* 2 (1926) 59148 (Philadelphia, 23 August, 256 BC) and 59285 (Philadelphia, 2 March, 250 BC). Reilly lists four occurrences from III BC. The chronological range of examples from Rome is I BC to IV/V; but at least four-fifths of the instances date from I BC-II AD). This distribution is not reflected in the datable occurrences from this year later than II BC: thirteen from I BC-II AD, eleven from II-II/III, ten from III-III/IV.

Among the texts published in 1979 are some more nearly contemporary parallels for the NT Onesimos than those in MM, s.v. From I AD come: *I.Eph.* I.20 (a list of contributors to a building project, 54-59) with mention of three men called Onesimos; Pfuhl/Möbius, II.1284 (near Miletopolis, *c.*100) an epitaph for Ὀνησίμῳ Περγανηνῷ | ἥρωι; and II.1632 (Propontis?, I) a memorial for an Onesimos son of Asklepiades.

According to Solin, in at least half of the cases from Rome from I BC-II AD the persons were or were probably of servile status, and of the attestations from the same period in this year's reading at least half were slaves. The frequent application of the name to slaves is made clear by Solin's data for Rome taken as a whole which shows that of the large number of persons attested only two are certainly free, but just over two hundred are certainly or probably of servile status (the remainder — more than half — being of uncertain status). However, a number of those called Onesimos from this year's culling are certainly free men:

I.Eph. III.668a (Smyrna [*sic*], II) an inscription set up by an Onesimos honouring his *syngenes* T. Flavius Apollon who had held several high offices, probably including that of *advocatus fisci*.

VII, 1.3017 (II/III?) an honorific inscription for Ulpius Lollianos Onesimos with mention of numerous of his relatives who had held high offices (priests, or priestesses, a procurator, an asiarch and two persons of consular rank).

VII, 2.3804 (Hypaipa, late Imperial) a land-registry list recording an Onesimos as the three-year-old son of Aurelios Kalachrotios son of Abaskantos.

I.Nikaia I.61 (III) a declaration of honours conferred by the gerousia on Onesimos the son of Onesimos.

SEG 152 (Athens, inscribed 175/76) two ephebic catalogues inscribed together including four epheboi called Onesimos (twice with patronymic: son of Ialysos and son of Soter; and twice without).

These examples show that the name Onesimos could be borne by free persons of no insignificant status and that it is far from being a sure indication of servile status. Consequently the editor's suggestion at *I.Eph.* IV.1040, note to *l.*30, that the Onesimos mentioned in this and several other lists of *kouretes* (*I.Eph.* IV.1030-1044) was a freedman, is by no means certain.

A number of the others listed above are likely to have been free, but cannot be proved so. None, however, can be shown to have been a slave or freedman. Nevertheless the occurrences collected here fail to provide examples of persons who bore this name and were certainly not of servile origin.

The clear assocation of the name with servile status gives rise to important consequences for the interpretation of Pfuhl/Möbius, I.154 (Dokimeion?, III), a funerary door-stele which commemorates several people, including 'Ονήσιμος | θεοῦ δοῦ|λος. The first editors of this text (*ed.pr.* — *MAMA* 4 [1933] 32; pl.16) were confident that it was of Christian origin and saw θεοῦ δοῦλος as a play on the possibility of θεοῦ referring to God or to Caesar, calling this 'a good example of the studied ambiguity of crypto-Christian epitaphs in Phrygia in the third century' (*MAMA* 4, p.x). Pfuhl/Möbius do not mention Christian interpretation of the text. In their comments on the relief which the inscription accompanies they seem to imply that it is not Christian when they say that round objects on a flat dish in the scene are fruits rather than loaves of bread. More recently, however, M. Waelkens has republished this text (*Die kleinasiatischen Türsteine* [Mainz, 1986] 486 [pl.75]) which he dates more closely to 'probably the third quarter of III'. Interpreting the round shapes as eucharistic loaves he says that Onesimos was probably a Christian priest. Waelkens also observes that the upsilon of θεοῦ has a horizontal bar, probably to make a cross. Do we have here, therefore, a Christian priest who was a descendant of a slave, or was himself a freedman or even a slave? The last is unlikely, given the elaborate nature of the memorial; but the possibility that Onesimos was a freedman must be considered. H. Gülzow, *Christentum und Sklaverei in den ersten drei Jahrhunderten* (Bonn, 1969), argues (176) that at the end of II the path to the highest Church offices lay open for persons of servile status, illustrating this with a discussion of the career of Callistus (died *c*.223) who rose from being a slave to the position of Bishop of Rome. For the deacon Nikostratos, who was a fredman, mentioned in Cyp., *Ep*. 50.1.2, see G.W. Clarke, *The Letters of St. Cyprian of Carthage* (*Ancient Christian Writers* 44; New York, 1984) II.279-80. The name Θεόδουλος occurs in *P.Köln* 110 (provenance unknown, V/VI), a letter to a church official, and in Tsigaridas, *Κατάλογος* 1 (Thessalonike, V; = *IG* X, 2.1 [1972] 790), an epitaph. On eucharistic loaves in grave reliefs see **121** below.

(A.L. CONNOLLY)

97. Onesiphoros

The name Onesiphoros, which occurs in 2 Tim. 1.16 and 4.9, is found among this year's texts six times:

I.Eph. VI.2948a, (Byzantine?) a list (of athletes?) mentions 'Ον]ησίφορος νεώτερος, implying the existence also of an elder Onesiphoros.

VII, 1.3457a, (Chondria, after 212) in which Aurelius Onesiphoros allows Aurelius Glykon to share his grave.

Pfuhl/Möbius I.139 (provenance unknown, after end of I BC), an epitaph for 'Ονησίφορος Γλαύκου, thought by the editors to have been inscribed later than the carving of the original monument at the end of I BC.

I.1011 (Rhodes, late Hellenistic), epitaph of Ζωσαρίου | 'Ονησιφόρου Βυβασίου.

II.1177 (Magnesia on the Sipylos, II) a monument set up by Julia Elpis for her husband Julius Onesiphoros.

II.1392 (Telmessos, Imperial period) a monument set up by Philetairos son of Onesiphoros.

In addition to these are the occurrences in manumission texts from Greece listed by Reilly, *Slaves* (cf. **90** and **94**), which contains only one attestation of 'Ονησίφορος (no. 2174), but of the neuter forms 'Ονασίφορον and 'Ονησίφορον, which refer to females, a total of 25 (nos.

2129-50 and 2171-73 respectively). Of these 26 instances 23 come from Delphi and one from each of Tithora in Phokis, Hypata and Mantinea (though of course these are not necessarily the places of residence of these ex-slaves). Except for one from II BC, the rest are dated I BC or I AD. Both these and the texts cited above provide useful parallels for the Onesiphoros from Ephesos in the NT considering both their provenance and their date, as MM, s.v., offers no literary or documentary examples of this name.

Only one papyrus example is known to me, *SB* 5.2 (1938) 7872 (exact provenance unknown, time of Constantine; on this text see **16** above), a fragmentary Christian letter which quotes verbatim from 2 Tim. 1.16 and may, therefore, not be testimony of a contemporary Egyptian Onesiphoros. Solin, *GPR* I.126, records only thirty finds at Rome, which are spread more or less evenly between the first five centuries AD with a slight preponderance in I-II. Eleven of the thirty are classified as servile or probably freed, one as a *peregrinus*, and the rest as being of uncertain status. Other epigraphical examples may be found in *BE*: (1953) 66 (Attika, late Imperial period); (1965) 177 (Thelphousa in Arkadia, n.d.); (1970) 286 (Messene, 192); 676 (Brindisium, Imperial period); (1972) 321 (Rhodes, n.d.); (1973) 190 (Epidauros, II[1]). It is noteworthy that half of these examples come from the Peloponnese, especially in view of the preponderance of attestations from Delphi collected by Reilly.

(A.L. CONNOLLY)

98. Quirinius

MM lacks an entry for this name (NT: Lk. 2.2), while BAGD, s.v. Κυρήνιος, notes one documentary attestation. Yet it cannot be excluded that this spelling may stand for Cyrenius no less than Quirinius. Another example of this name is found at *I.Nikaia* II, 2.1594 (= Pfuhl/ Möbius, II.2310 [pl.325]; probably II), an epitaph for L. Antoninus Κυρήνιος who died at the age of 22. *I.Nikaia* II, 2.1336 (I-II) yields another name which closely resembles it: [Κυ]ιρῖνος, an *oikonomos*, aged 21. On οἰκονόμος see **69** above. Quirinius is attested both as a *nomen* and as a *cognomen*.

99. Salome

MM has no entry for this name, used of one of Jesus' followers at Mk. 15.40 and 16.1. BAGD provides one epigraphical reference, from I AD Jerusalem. To this may be added an item from the present year's reading, *IGUR* 1323 (Rome, Imperial period), an epitaph for an eleven-month infant with this name, partly restored as [Σα]λώμη. Though the country of origin is not stated, it may be inferred from *l*.6 of the text that she and her mother were not native to Italy, since the mother states on the epitaph her intention to send her child's ashes to her homeland.

100. Sousanna

This name is attested very rarely indeed in documentary texts. *CIJ* records two examples: I.627, Σοσάνα (Rome, III), and 637, Σωσάνη (Rome, Imperial; Latin text written with Greek letters). All the examples listed in *NB* and Foraboschi prove to be late and Christian: for inscriptions note G. Lefebvre, *Recueil des inscriptions grecques-chrétiennes d'Egypte* (Cairo, 1907; repr. Chicago, 1978, under the title *Inscriptiones Graecae Aegypti* V. *Inscriptiones Christianae Aegypti*) 363 (Lepidotonpolis), S. daughter of Anna, originally from Isauria; 571 — Sousana (*sic*) — and 577 (both from Aswan; the latter is quoted in part at *New Docs 1978*, **80**, p.93). As for papyrus occurrences, these may merely be listed with the spelling of the form noted only if it varies from Σουσάννα: *P.Flor.* 1 (1906) 78.27 (Hermopolis Magna, V/VI(?)), the only item specified in MM); *P.Monac.* 1 (1914) 5 *front*, *l*.2 — *P.Lond.* 5 (1917) 1726, where the name is restored at *l*.10, joins this as part of the same text — dated 581; *P.Oxy.* 16 (1924) 1895.3 (554), Sosanna, a widow; *P.Oxy.* 16.1917.34 (VI); *P.Oxy.* 16.1976.10 (582), Sosanna; *P.Edfou* 1 (1937) pap. 3.7, 19, 26 (Edfu, 618); *P.Cair.Masp.* 3 (1916) 67330, *col*.3, *l*.10 (Aphrodito, Byzantine), Sosana. There are no examples listed in *CPJ*. From Rome, a Sousanna is mentioned on a fragmentary inscription from a Christian catacomb: cf. *BE* (1973) 547a.

From the current year's reading one more woman may be mentioned: Pfuhl/Möbius I.1044 (Nikomedeia, Imperial period), a funerary monument containing as its inscription merely the three names Apollas, Sousanne, and Trophides. There is nothing to suggest whether we are dealing with Christians or Jews here. BAGD, s.v., notes no documentary attestations to illustrate the sole NT use at Lk. 8.3.

101. Theudas

The sole person with this name in the NT (Acts 5.36) is an insurrectionist, like the Theudas alluded to in Jos., *Ant.* 20.97-98 who came to prominence in Judaea and met his death probably in 44 AD during the procuratorship of Cuspius Fadus. Whether the two are to be identified is problematical on chronological grounds — see Haenchen's *Comm.*, ad loc.; more recently, P.W. Barnett, *NTS* 27 (1981) 680-81, 694 n.2 — but perhaps ought not to be ruled out entirely.

Here, though, our concern is with the attestation of the name, by no means common, but certainly better attested than the entries in MM and BAGD suggest. One cause of confusion in identifying people of this name is the presence of orthographical variations, and abbreviated forms in the papyri. The list attached provides all attestations from this year's culling, plus a selection of other items which came to notice.

1. Θευδᾶς

I.Eph.

— Ia.20a.27 (54-59 AD), Didymos son of Th., one of many fishermen in a building inscription.
— III.905a, *col*.iii.14 (probably I BC), Th. son of Theodotos in a list of names (probably ephebes).
— III.908a.3 (n.d.), [Th]eudas in a fragmentary list of names.
— IV.1001 (time of Tiberius), Neikomachos Th., son of [Theo]klytos, *prytanis*.
— IV.1015.7 (95-98 AD), Th. ἱεροκῆρυξ in a list of *kouretai*; cf. the table on pp.56-57 of *I.Eph.* IV.
— IV.1016.12 (96-99 AD), same man (name heavily restored on the basis of 1015).

— VII, 2.4103, *col.*ii.20 (early II BC(?)), Sotas son of Th. in a list of names of *molpoi* or *gerousiastai.*

I.Iasos (ed. W. Blümel; *I.K.* 28.1, 2; Bonn, 1985)

— I.113 (n.d.), honours voted for the ephebarch Atilius son of Th.

— I.122.1, 4 (n.d.), posthumous honorific inscription for the gymnasiarch Th.

— I.123.1, 3 (n.d.; = *BCH* 11 [1887] 13-15, noted by BAGD, s.v., init.), posthumous honorific inscription for the gymnasiarch Th. son of Th. (i.e., son of the man in no.122).

— II.284.8, 9 (n.d.), Artemisias son of Th., and Aretaios son of Th. (brothers?), in a list of ephebes.

— II.343.1 (n.d.), very fragmentary victory inscription, name Th. fully preserved.

— II.346.2 (n.d.), name Th. in a brief victory inscription.

— II.405 (n.d.), grave of Th. son of Arteme[i]sios (= *CIG* II.2684, noted in BAGD, s.v. Θευδᾶς).

CIG

— II.3563 (Pergamon, n.d.), Θευδᾶ[ς] καὶ Μένα[νδρος (?); nature of this text not clear.

— II.3920 (= *SIG*[3] 1229; Hierapolis, late I/early II), epitaph for Flavius Zeuxis, one of whose sons is Flavius Th.

— III.5698 (Katana, n.d.), tomb of Aphrodisia, Theudas and Marulla set up by their children: presumably Th. married twice. (Note that the *CIG* reference is misprinted in BAGD, s.v. Θευδᾶς.)

SB

— I (1915, repr. 1974) 5025 (Alexandria(?), n.d.), epitaph for Th. son of Peteaus, aged 14, described with a series of epithets including νύμφιος and ἄγαμος (on this question of marital age see **114** below); = E. Breccia, *Inscriptiones Graecae Aegypti*, II (Cairo, 1911; repr. Chicago, 1978) 353 (cf. *New Docs 1978*, **11**, p.43).

— I.5026 (Alexandria, n.d.), epitaph for Θευδᾶς (= Breccia, *IGA* II.354).

Other

— *BE* (1960) 417, the name Th. at Djebel Harazeh-Tatamah in Transjordan (n.d.).

— Pfuhl/Möbius I.702 (Samos, probably I BC). The relief (pl.105) shows two women, yet the text appears to name four couples: 'Aristion, Rhodokleia, | Pisistratos, Zois, | Andromenes, Artemisio[s] (female?), | Theudas, | Antiochis, | *heroes*, greetings!'

— *P.Lond.* 2 (1898, repr. 1973) 194.23 (provenance unknown, I AD), Th. in a register concerning land and taxation.

— *P.Mich.* 5 (1944) 318.4 (Tebtynis, 40 AD), Th. as one of three individuals receiving a share of property. Nos. 319 and 320 are copies of this text with slight orthographical variations.

2. Θεοδᾶς

I.Eph.

— III.901.27 (*c.*100 BC), Th. son of Theodoros, in a list of *molpoi.*

— Note that the Index vol., VIII.2, s.vv. Θευδᾶς and Κάσσανδρος, mention a Theodas son of Kas[sandros] at 902a.2. The reference is incorrect, but I cannot find the correct number for this text in *I.Eph.*

Other

— *Chrest.* I.2 (1912, repr. 1963) 155.9 (Memphis, III init.), [Θε]οδᾶ (genitive) in a catalogue of books and authors.

— *P.Iand.* 6 (1934) 104.4 (provenance unknown, time of Tiberius), genitive Θεοδᾶ in a letter.

— Note that the form Θεοδα. .[α] at *P.Lond.* 4 (1910, repr. 1973) 1435.160 (Aphrodito, 715-16) is unlikely to be the name Theodas.

— Note that *P.Ross.Georg.* 3 (1930, repr. 1966) 26.4 (Memphis, 233/4) has the name Theodotos, not Theodas in a certificate; the wrong name is given in the index to that volume, whence included in Foraboschi, II, p.134, s.v. Θεοδᾶς.

3. Θεύδης

— *P.Oxy.* 10 (1914) 1242, *col.*i.14 (early III), Theudes as one of several Jewish ambassadors at a meeting with Trajan.

— *I.Eph.* VII, 1.3312 (Tire in the Kaystros valley, n.d.), Theudes in an epitaph. In passing we may note in this text that space is designated for the deceased by the use of the phrases: πρὸς δυ[σ]|μὴν κλισία (*ll.*1-2), ἡ δὲ πρὸς ἀ|νατολὴν κλισία (*ll.*4-5), and ἡ δὲ μέση κλισία (*l.*8). Although κλισία is plural in its sole NT occurrence (Lk. 9.14), this example may usefully illustrate another sense of the primary meaning 'lying (down)'. Cf. the comparable use of κλίνη in a sepulchral context in the phrase ἡ ἐν δεξιοῖς κλείνη at *I.Eph.* VII, 1.3460 (Metropolis, II); this noun again at no.3469.

— *BGU* 9 (1937, repr. 1972) 1898 (Theadelphia, 172), the genitive(?) form abbreviated as Θευδο: in a list.

4. Θεύδις

— *SB* 6.3 (1961) 9325.4 (Bakchias, 28 August, 209).

5. Θευδοῦς

— *CPJ* 2 (1960) 421, *col*.xii.188, Theudous (a woman), in a document listing Jewish tax (Arsinoe, 16 May 73).

Of these five names, no.2 is an orthographical variant of no.1. Probably nos. 3 and 4, and certainly no.5 attest other, related names; hence BAGD, s.v. Θευδᾶς, was right to exclude reference to the Theudes in *P.Oxy.* 10.1242, quoted by MM. There is certainly no reason to see the name as distinctively used by Jews; the NT and Josephus' references to one (or two) Jews with this name should not be allowed to mislead us into thinking that it was distinctively used by them. There are no attestations of the name in *CPJ*, and the two possible items in *CIJ* are problematic. *CIJ* II.1255 and 1265 are ossuary inscriptions found on the Mount of Olives (n.d.). The first consists of a line of Hebrew (יהודה בן תודוס) followed by a corresponding Aramaic version (בר for בן). Frey takes this to mean 'Judas son of Theudas', though a more careful rendering would be 'Judah son of T(h)udos (or T(h)odos)'. Again, in II.1265 we have an Aramaic text mentioning Shalamasion, בת תדיון, 'daughter of T(h)adion' (Frey suggests Theudion). G.J. Cowling points out to me that these inscriptions reflect an attempt to put Greek names into a Semitic script. It is possible that in II.1255 we have an approximation of Theudas, and in II.1265 its diminutive; but the identification is not certain. Are the names in these two inscriptions versions of Todah, said to be the name of one of Jesus' disciples according to a passage in the Talmud (*Sanhedrin* 43a)? On this name, cf. G. Dalman, *Jesus Christ in the Talmud* (ET: Cambridge, 1893; repr. New York, 1973) 76.

Even allowing for the fact that this list is not an exhaustive one — from Rome, e.g., Solin, *GPR* I.407, lists one Theodas, a soldier (dated 210) and eleven males called Theuda, one of whom is Jewish — the geographical spread is of some small interest. For while Asia Minor and Rome are well-represented, Egypt is considerably less so, and Palestine possibly not at all.

MM, s.v. (followed by BAGD), suggested on the basis of *CIG* II.3920 (= *SIG*^{3} 1229) that Theudas is not a hypocoristic form of Theodoros, since in that epitaph two brothers are mentioned, who each have one of these names. This argument is an instance of 'one swallow not making a summer', by no means proving that Theudas was *never* thought of as a shortened form of Theodoros. (However, two close analogies may be noted: first, a sculptor's signature from Phrygia — quoted in E. Gibson, *The 'Christians for Christians' Inscriptions from Phrygia* [Missoula, 1978] 69 no.14 — mentions two brothers, Asklas and Asklepas, sons of Asklepas. Second, Gibson, *ZPE* 28 [1978] 11-13 no.1 [Altıntaş plain in N. Phrygia, 232/3] is an inscription mentioning brothers, Zosimos and Zosas.) *Per contra*, in his note to *CIJ* II.1255 Frey assumes without any basis that the name is hypocoristic for Theodoros. MM's opinion, that Theudas may be a short form of Theodotos is merely a guess; but it may receive some support from *I.Eph.* III.905a (listed above), in which we have a Theudas son of Theodotos — named after his father, perhaps, but given a shorter form to differentiate him? Yet if Theudas were an apocopation of either of these nouns — or both, in different contexts — we should expect the most common form to be Theodas, which in fact is sufficiently less often attested as to be seen properly as an orthographic variant of Theudas. Although there may have been instances where Theudas was consciously considered an hypocorism, on balance, we should view Theudas as a name in itself, and not primarily a 'mere' hypocorism, even though there may have been instances (no conclusive examples of which are attested) where it was so employed. Even if it is in origin an apocopated form of Theodoros or Theodotos (*vel sim.*), this awareness had been largely lost from sight by the Roman period. For further comment on hypocoristic forms see **5**, above.

102. In brief

(a) **Ἀγωνίζομαι ἀγῶνας** in *I.Eph.* V.1604.7 (*c*.170), of a victor at the Epheseia festival; cf. 1 Tim. 6.12; 2 Tim. 4.7.

(b) **Ἀθροίζω** in a fragmentary imperial letter concerning deliveries of corn from Egypt, *I.Eph.* II.211, including the phrase τὸν . . . | . . . ἀθροιζόμενον πανταχό|θεν πυρόν (*ll*.9-11), 'the corn collected from everywhere'. This verb occurs once only in the NT, at Lk. 24.33.

(c) **Ἄκακος** in an Imperial-period grave epigram for a twelve-year-old child, *I.Eph.* VI.2102, which speaks of the dead Eucharistos as παῖς νέος ὢν ἄκακος. No instances of this adjective are quoted by MM which parallel the NT sense, 'simple, without guile', at Rom. 16.18 and Heb. 7.26. BAGD, s.v., lists no documentary references.

(d) Dedication to the emperor Claudius **κατὰ τὴν | διαθήκην** of Tiberius Claudius Damonikos: *I.Eph.* II.259B (mid-I). The man's heirs were responsible for erecting the monument. In view of his name Damonikos may have been an Imperial freedman of Rhodian origin (the cognomen is given in Doric form). The parallel Latin phrase, *ex testamento*, occurs on *I.Eph.* II.262, a dedication to Titus.

(e) **Διόρθωσις** in a fragmentary governor's letter: *I.Eph.* II.217 (Imperial period), ἵνα τῆς τε προσηκούσης διορθώσε[ως τύχητε - - -], 'in order that you may meet with suitable improvement(?) . . .' (*l*.2). No epigraphical instances are given by MM or BAGD. This passage is not sufficiently complete to establish firmly an exact parallel for Heb. 9.10.

(f) **Λαός** discussed by O. Montevecchi, *Pap.Brux.* 19, pp.51-67, from Mycenaean to Patristic usage (pp.62-67, the term in the Greek Bible).

(g) **Τὸ λῖμμα** *I.Eph.* Ia.13, *col*.i.35 (Flavian period). It is unclear whether this stands for τὸ λεῖμμα, 'remnant' (only at Rom. 11.5 in the NT), or τὸ λῆμμα, 'receipt, gain, profit' (ECL, not NT). In the *ed.pr.* at *JRS* 65 (1975) 88 n.216, C. Habicht regards the word here as enigmatic in meaning, but thinks the former makes no sense in the context of the document, which lists communities in *provincia* Asia arranged by assize districts (διοικήσεις = *conventus iuridici*).

(h) **Παραχρῆμα** in a fragmentary context at the conclusion of a civic resolution, *I.Eph.* IV.1382.8 (Imperial period): τὸ δὲ ἀνάλωμα προχρῆσαι παραχρῆμα τοὺ[ς ἀργυροταμίας(?), 'the treasurers(?) are to advance the cost forthwith'. No epigraphical examples in MM, s.v., for this adverb which is common in Lk./Acts but elsewhere in the NT is confined to Mt. 21.19-20.

(i) **Παρεμβολή** occurs as Latin *parimbola* in a fragment from a building inscription: *RIS* 1.56 (Vidy in W. Switzerland, n.d.). Ed. n. ad loc. notes this as a technical building term probably referring to wall-panelling; the NT uses are rather different (see BAGD, s.v.).

(j) **[K]eiphas** may occur as the name of a Christian in an early Byzantine inscription, *I.Eph.* VII, 2.4284; but the reading is not secure.

(k) The name **Tyrannos at Ephesos**: *I.Eph.* IV.1012 (92/3), and 1029.6-7 (perhaps 30 or so years later). L. Tarutilius Tyrannos figures in both these lists of *kouretes*. Cf. the Tyrannos at Ephesos mentioned at Acts 19.9.

C. BIBLICAL AND RELATED CITATIONS

103. New fragments from Sirach

P.Laur. 55 (provenance unknown, IV/V; pl.52; cf. K. Treu, *APF* 28 [1982] 93), comprising two fragments from a parchment codex, preserves Sir. 26.1-2, 5-7; 27.29-30 and 28.1-8. These may be added to the half-dozen other finds containing portions of this book. The other texts are listed by J. O'Callaghan at *Stud.Pap.* 14 (1975) 40 and itemised in van Haelst:

— *P.Ant.* 1 (1950) 8 (Antinoopolis, III) containing Sir. 45.14, 19, 20-22 in two fragments from a papyrus codex-leaf; van Haelst, 254; not in Turner, *Typology*.

— *Ist. Pap. 'G. Vitelli'* inv. 531 (provenance unknown, III-IV); *ed.pr.* — A. Dianich, *ASNP* 26 (1957) 178-79, Sir. 29.15-18, 25-27, from a papyrus codex-leaf; van Haelst, 281; Turner, *Typology*, no. OT180A.

— *P.Chester Beatty* XI (Fasc. VI [1937]; provenance unknown, IV), Sir. 36.28-37.22; 46.6-11, 16-47.2 preserved on one and a half papyrus codex-leaves; van Haelst, 282; Turner, *Typology*, no. OT181.

— *MPER* 4 (1946) 28 (= *P.Vindob.Gr.* 26782; Hermopolis Magna, V), Sir. 42.17-19 in a fragment from a papyrus codex-leaf; van Haelst, 283; Turner, *Typology*, no. OT182.

— *P.Oxy.* 13 (1919) 1595 (VI), Sir. 1.1-6, 8-9, from a papyrus codex-leaf; van Haelst, 279; Turner, *Typology*, no. OT180.

— an unedited fragment from a parchment codex (provenance unknown, n.d.) containing Sir. 1.25-2.11a, thought by W. Baars (*apud* K. Treu) to be from the Chester Beatty papyri, but certainly not part of the Chester Beatty Sirach which is from a papyrus codex; described by Treu, *APF* 22/23 (1974) 370; van Haelst, 280; not in Turner, *Typology*.

The fact that these six and the new pieces are all fragments from codices suggests, as one would expect from the contents of Sirach, that the book was only read and copied as a whole and was not found useful as a source for extracts to adorn buildings and utensils. On the popularity of different biblical books as such sources see **104** below. *P.Ant.* 1.8 illustrates this well as its Sirach fragments have come from a single-quire codex containing other Wisdom literature, certainly at least Proverbs and the Wisdom of Solomon (*ed.pr.*, 2-3). The *P.Laur.* codex was a miniature, since from the remains it can be estimated that each page held an average of twenty lines making the page height approximately 11 cm. (*ed.pr.*, 29). On miniature codices see Turner, *Typology*, 29-31.

The new fragments show one variant at 28.1. Here Rahlfs and Ziegler both print in their editions διατηρῶν διατηρήσει (the reading of a considerable number of minuscules); but the editor of *P.Laur.* 55, R. Pintaudi, has restored διαστηριῶ]ν διαστ̣ηρίσ[ει on the basis of the oldest codices, A, B, א. Rahlfs rejected the latter reading on the grounds that διατηρεῖ appears in *vs.*5 and the LXX writers no longer used the future participle, which is found in the LXX only in this variant reading and at Judg. 4.9A (H. St. J. Thackeray, *Grammar of the OT in Greek*, I [Cambridge, 1909] 49). In the NT the future participle is rare outside Luke-Acts, nor is it common there (BDF §§65(1c), 315). The strengthening of a finite verb with the cognate participle is found in the NT only in quotations from the OT (BDF §422). On the similar construction with the cognate noun see Thackeray, 48-49 for the LXX, and BDF §198(6) for the NT. Διατηρέω is found in the NT only at Lk. 2.51 and Acts 15.29 (cf. *New Docs 1978*, **31** and **32**).

The plate of the flesh side of the smaller fragment (frag.I, side B) clearly shows two vertical lines on the left-hand side of the page drawn with a dry point (*ed.pr.*, 29). These were guide lines so that the scribe could indent every second line by about 2-3 letters. In the plate of the hair side of frag.I (side A) there are no guide-lines visible for regulating the length of lines in the right margin. In frag.I side B each *stichos* begins on the far left and is completed by the following indented line. However, this arrangement cannot be reconstructed on the other three sides (IA, IIC, IID): on side IA the first word of chapter 26.2 appears to end *l*.3; in all other cases verses can be made to start lines, but not always from the far left margin. For discussion of the use of two left-hand margins in biblical texts see *New Docs 1977*, **87**, pp.115-16.

Another fragment of Sirach was published at *P.Rainer Cent.* (1983) 27 (provenance not given, probably IV/V; pl.48; cf. K. Treu, *APF* 31 [1985] 60). The *front* and *back* of two non-contiguous pieces from a leaf of a parchment codex preserve Sir. 29.13-26a. Each page contained 21 lines written in small uncials and, with original margins of between 1 and 2 cm., would have measured *c*.9B x 11H cm., making the codex a miniature one for private use. As in *P.Laur.* 55 there are two guides on the left: each *stichos* begins on the left-hand line and any words running over are indented from the right-hand line. However, the pairs of *stichoi* making up *vss*.15, 21 and 22 are each crammed into three lines (one long and two indented), with no regard for the *stichos* divisions. Since other long pairs take up four lines, these three pairs must have been thought of as sense units requiring enjambment. Two noteworthy readings are preserved: *vs*.23b is omitted as in א*, A and B; and *vs*.24 supports the poorly attested reading τὸ στόμα (found in 307 and 443) instead of simply στόμα. Other readings which may have been of interest have been lost, but are commented on by the editor, K. Niederwimmer; in *vs*.19a, however, ἐ[μπεσεῖται (*v.l.* ἐμπεσών) is restored without comment.

(A.L. CONNOLLY)

104. Miscellaneous OT quotations

A number of OT verses, mainly from Psalms, appear in various types of inscriptions and papyri from this year's culling. *P.Köln* 79 preserves Ps. 14.1-3 on a parchment fragment (provenance unknown, V; *ed.pr.* — *ZPE* 1 [1967] 74; cf. K. Treu, *APF* 19 [1969] 176) which is blank on the back, and so probably not from a codex. If *ll*.2-3 have rightly been understood as an introductory comment and restored as [εἴρηται δ' εἰ]ς̣ τὸν αἰῶνα [ὑ]||[πὸ τοῦ αὐτο]ῦ ('but "forever" was said by the same one'), then this fragment may have been part of a collection of verses dealing with eternity, since Ps. 14 ends in *vs*.5 with the words εἰς τὸν αἰῶνα.

At *EG* IV.510-12 Guarducci reprints three inscriptions from what was perhaps a ciborium dedicated by a high-ranking military officer (near Iulia Concordia, N. Italy, VI-VII init.). The first names Stephanos who made the dedication; the second, [ἔ]κραξα πρός (σ)ε, ὁ Θ(εός) μου, καὶ ἐπίκουσάς (*read* ἐπήκ-) μου πληρόσας μου τὴν ἐπιθυμί[αν] ('I cried to you, my God, and you heard me, fulfilling my desire'), seems to be based on the wording of Ps. 21.25; 29.3 and 140.1

for the first half and 126.5 for the second; the third reads [ὁ ἐ]γίρας (*read* ἐγείρας) ἀπὸ γῆς πτοχὼν καὶ ἀνυψῶν ἀπὸ κοπρέας πένιτα (*read* κοπρίας, πένητα) Κ(ύρι)ε ΛΩΞ (= δόξ[α]?), 'You who have raised from the earth the beggar and lifted up from the dung the pauper, Lord, . . .', and is a quotation from Ps. 112.7. These references to the psalms presumably express the nature of the experience which caused Stephanos to make his dedication. Ps. 112.7 may be behind *IMS* 114 (Bregovina, VI), † *Qui pauperem ae stercore* [*elevas*?] | *d*(*omi*)*ne nos umiles servos* [*adiuva*?], 'You, Lord, who raise(?) the pauper from the dung, help(?) us your lowly servants', though the editor may be right to see 1 Kgdms 2.8 as the model. The purpose of this inscription is unknown.

Verses 3-15 of the penitential Ps. 50 are preserved on a papyrus leaf broken on all sides (*P.Laur.* 54, provenance unknown, IV init.). Since the *back* is blank, this may have been a text for private devotional use. *Nomina sacra* appear in *l.*11 and other abbreviations are numerous. It seems that each line contained two stichoi, so that each verse took up one line, except *vs.*6 which has four stichoi; *vs.*13, though having two stichoi, perhaps took up two lines, but the text is broken in this place. The omission of μου after ἁμαρτ(ιῶν) in *vs.*11 is probably accidental rather than being a textual variant.

Ps. 79.2-16 have been found written on one side of a rolled sheet of lead (12B x 16H cm.) republished by Guarducci at *EG* IV.365-68 (island of Rhodes, III?; *ed. pr.* — F. Hiller von Gaertringen, *Sitzungsber. Akad. Berlin* [1898], 2, pp.582-88). Guarducci follows the first editor in believing the use of a lead sheet to be an indication that the text had an apotropaic purpose (for other apotropaic texts in this year's culling see **134** below). On the basis of the psalm's content, which in *vss.*9-16 deals with the metaphor of Israel as a vine planted by God, Guarducci suggests that this talisman could have been used to protect a vineyard and observes that the text stops before *vs.*17 where there is mention of the vine's destruction. However, there is no other evidence to support this suggestion. The text contains *nomina sacra* wherever God is mentioned (*vss.*4, 5, 8, 11 and 15), which indicates that the talisman was probably made by a Christian; but on the use of *nomina sacra* in Jewish texts see *New Docs 1976*, **69**, pp.108, 110, *New Docs 1977*, **87**, p.112, and *New Docs 1978*, **82**, p.96. The likelihood of this text having a Christian origin is increased by the omission in *l.*30 (= *vs.*16b) of ἀνθρώπου to read, κα]ὶ ἐπὶ υἱὸν ᾧ (*read* ὃν) ἐκρατέωσ[ας σεαυτῷ], 'and (look) upon the son whom you have strengthened for yourself'. Guarducci dates the text on palaeographical grounds to the third century 'with great probability' (van Haelst, no.177, suggests I-III or at the latest IV). If her dating is correct, this may be, as she says (368), the oldest documentary testimony to Christianity on Rhodes and in the Aegean islands (cf. *IG* XII, 1 [1895] 671, 674 and 675 — all undated — for other inscriptions from Rhodes which may be Christian). However, D. Feissel, in C. Mondésert (ed.), *Le monde grec ancien et la Bible* (Paris, 1984), 223-31, concurs with the view that this text,'the antiquity of which has sometimes been exaggerated', should be dated V-VI (230).

Ps. 90.1-3a are quoted on a bronze bracelet bearing a medallion (district of Bethlehem?, IV-VI; *ed. pr.* — M. Piccirillo, *SBF* 29 [1979] 244-52, pls. 25-27; cf. *SEG* 1606). The verses, which are written in three lines on the band of the bracelet, do not differ from the LXX text except in spelling and the omission of the second μου in *vs.*2. This quotation is followed by the words, τὸ ἕμα (*read* αἷμα) τοῦ Χριστοῦ παῦσε (*read* -σαι) ἀπὸ υ . . . . . ιας, an invocation of the blood of Christ presumably for apotropaic purposes (cf. *P.Lit.Lond.* [1927] 231.5, and *B.K.T.* 6 [1910] VII.1.21-23). The medallion was also clearly worn as a phylactery, since it depicts a rider piercing with a lance a half-naked woman who is lying on the ground; a seven-pointed star appears near the rider's head. Around this scene is written εἷς θεὸς ὁ νικῶν τὰ κακά. Other medallions bearing similar scenes name the rider as Solomon, who according to the *Testament of Solomon* was given power to 'seal demons' (Piccirillo, 251). Where the band meets the medallion, on one side is a lion, on the other a cross with the inscription Ἰ(ησοῦ)ς Χ(ριστό)ς Α Ω. On lion imagery see *New Docs 1978*, **16**, and for another medallion bearing Ps. 90 see *New Docs 1977*, **88**. On the great popularity of this psalm see *New Docs 1978*, **93**, pp.113-14.

Hagg. 2.9 is found in an abbreviated form on an architrave of a church republished by Guarducci at *EG* IV.424-25 (Eski Kale, in the Lamos Valley, Cilicia, IV-V), where it is used to equate this small church with the Temple in Jerusalem: † τάδε λέγει Κ(ύριο)ς παντω|κράτωρ· μεγάλη ἔσται ἡ δό|ξα τοῦ οἴκου τούτου καὶ ἐν τῷ | τόπῳ τούτῳ δώσω εἰρήνην | εἰς περιποίησιν παντὶ τῷ κτί|ζοντι τοῦ ἀναστῆναι τὸν | ναὸν τοῦτον. ἀμήν †, 'Thus says the Lord almighty: "Great is the glory of this house and in this place I shall give peace as a possession to everyone who acts as a founder for the raising up of this temple". Amen'.

Another inscription on an architrave of which six fragments survive comes from the Church of St John in Ephesos (*I.Eph.* VII, 2.4301; n.d.). The content of the remaining words on the inner side is too fragmentary to be reconstructed, but the words on the outer side clearly formed part of Ps. 131.15-16 in which the mention of God feeding the poor with bread is particularly apt for a church. For another possible quotation of these verses see *New Docs 1976*, **56** (cf. *New Docs 1977*, **88**).

I.Nikaia I.493-495 (Byzantine) are three of ten mosaic inscriptions from the Koimesis Church. They contain respectively Ps. 92.5, Ps. 109.3, and part of Deut. 32.43 (καὶ προσκυνησάτωσαν αὐτῷ πάντες ἄγγελοι, in which υἱοὶ θεοῦ has been replaced by ἄγγελοι, standing as it does beneath a representation of angels; cf. the textual variation at Gen. 6.2 where A^{r} and VL have 'angels' against the reading 'sons' found in MT, other Greek texts and the Vulgate). *I.Nikaia* I.615 (inscribed on the narrow side of the same stone as no.472, which is dated to IX) records an adaptation of Ps. 135.25 below a menorah. *I.Eph.* VII, 2.3822 (Hypaipa, n.d.) is another Jewish text: the words Ἰουδαί|ων νε|ωτέ|ρων, which constitute the whole inscription, are thought by the editors to be an allusion to the story of Susanna in which the young Jews are shown to be more pious than their elders (Sus. 63).

The popularity of particular verses for inscriptions and the types of structures they adorned are discussed by Feissel (*art. cit.*). He observes that nearly all biblical citations are of Christian origin and were inscribed on church buildings or equipment, the lintels of houses or funerary monuments. Almost half the citations that Feissel found in his survey were from the doorways and windows of simple houses, whereas from among the large numbers of surviving epitaphs came only several dozen, a small proportion of all citations. In churches the most common verse is Ps. 117.20, with few others enjoying wide popularity, though Ps. 28.3 occurs not a few times. The most frequently found in private houses is Ps. 120.8, and Ps. 90.1 is also popular; Lk. 2.4 is used a number of times in Syria. On funerary monuments citations from Psalms are again dominant, but no one verse is especially favoured. The popularity of texts varied from place to place; for example, Ps. 120.8 is found chiefly in Syria. Overall only about twenty inscriptions cite verses from OT books other than Psalms, Isaiah being the best represented of these. There are three times as many OT citations as NT ones. Feissel concludes his article pointing out that despite the limitations on the usefulness of such inscriptions for textual criticism these citations can offer some clues about the nature of the biblical texts read in various regions.

(A.L. CONNOLLY)

105. Miscellaneous NT quotations

P.Köln 80 (*ed.pr.* — Ch. Charalambakis et. al., *ZPE* 14 [1974] 37-40; = 𝔓[86]; cf. K. Treu, *APF* 26 [1978] 154; id., *APF* 27 [1980] 252) republishes a fragment from a papyrus codex preserving Mt. 5.13-16, 22-25 (provenance unknown, IV init.). The text-type shows an affiliation with ℵ and B in three places. On the front at *ll.*2-3 the words β[λη]|θὲν ἔξω καταπατεῖσθαι, written by *m.*1 and following the 'Egyptian' reading of ℵBC (*ed.pr.*, 40), have been half-corrected by *m.*2 to βληθὲν ἔξω `καὶ´ καταπατεῖσθαι under the influence of the other codices which read βληθῆναι ἔξω καὶ καταπατεῖσθαι. At *back l.*2 the papyrus follows ℵ and B in reading ὃς δ' ἂν εἴπῃ, Μωρέ (Mt. 5.22) against LΘ, ὃς δ' ἂν εἰπῇ τῷ ἀδελφῷ, Μωρέ. In 5.23 the papyrus also follows ℵ and B at *back l.*5 in reading [κ]ἀκεῖ μνησθῇς and not καὶ ἐκεῖ with some other codices and minuscules.

Most interesting in the light of this agreement with ℵ and B is the papyrus' reading in *front l.*1 of τὸ ἅλας μαρανθῇ instead of μωρανθῇ. The latter is the reading of all other Greek MSS here, though the former reading is supported by the Old Latin, the Vulgate and the Georgian and Bohairic versions (*ed.pr.*, 30). Μαρανθῇ is read for μωρανθῇ in the Minuscules 56, 58 and 69 in the parallel passage at Lk. 14.34 (*ed.pr.*, 39). The word μαραίνω occurs in two other texts from this year: once in the perfect in a fragmentary funerary epigram (Porto, in Italy, undated; *ed.pr.* — G. Sacco, *ArchClass* 31 [1979] 246-48 [pl.], cf. *SEG* 979); and once in a funerary epigram for a child reprinted at *SEG* 1190 (Saittai in Lydia, 182-83; *ed.pr.* — S.Bakır-Barthel/H.Müller, *ZPE* 36 [1979] 188-90) which concludes, ὦ Φθόνε καὶ Μοῖραι | μερόπων ἐμαράνατε κάλλος, 'You, O Envy and Fates of mortals, make beauty wither' (*ll.* 16-17; the verb here is a gnomic aorist). Müller concurs with the view that in epitaphs μαραίνω usually refers to a premature and unexpected death. The latter text provides a parallel to the use of this word in Jas. 1.11 where the demise of the wealthy man is likened to the perishing of a flower's beauty.

The text of *P.Köln* 80 displays a number of minor errors: at *front l.*2, εἰς οὐδενὶ εἰσχύει (or εἰς οὐδὲν {ι}εἰσχύει) for οὐδὲν ἰσχύει; *front l.*7, τὸ μό[δ]ιον (perhaps through pronunciation as τὸμ μόδιον) for τόν; *back ll.*3-4, προσ]|φέρῃ for προσφέρῃς; *back l.*6, ἄφες corrected from οφες. A *nomen sacrum* is restored at *front l.*3: ὑπὸ τῶν [ανων] for ἀνθρώπων. High stops for punctuation are preserved at *back ll.*2, 7, 8 and 9, all at sense breaks, though a break after μόδιον is somewhat unexpected, especially when this is compared with the lack of a stop at the major break after κόσμου.

A fragment of a *Pater noster* has been republished by Guarducci at *EG* IV.336-38 (Megara, V; fig.97; = *PGM* 2 [1931/1941; repr. 1974] *O.* 4; van Haelst, 348). The fragment is the bottom right-hand corner of a clay tablet and bears the text of Mt. 6.11-13. The text was incised in the tablet while the clay was soft, indicating that the tablet was made for the express purpose of bearing this text. Guarducci suggests that this purpose was prophylactic and that the tablet may have been intended to be kept in a home. For examples of the *Pater noster* used as an amulet see *New Docs 1978*, **88**, where this item is noted in the list at p.104 as no.3. The likelihood of this text having been an amulet is strengthened by the fact that this short form of the Lord's Prayer, which ends ἀλλὰ ῥῦσε εἰ|[μᾶς ἀ]πὸ τοῦ πονηροῦ (*ll.*7-8 on the tablet; *read* ῥῦσαι ἡμᾶς), is followed (*l.*9) by Κ]ύριε with room for half a dozen letters before the *kappa*. Guarducci wonders if a phrase such as σῶσόν με or ῥῦσέ με stood before Κύριε (338). The only variant reading is in *l.*10 where the tablet has ἀφίομεν (as does D) and not ἀφήκαμεν (cf. Lk. 11.4).

It is appropriate to correct briefly here information given in a previous volume about *P.Macquarie* inv. 360, a papyrus fragment preserving parts of Acts 2.30-37, and 2.46-3.2. At *New Docs 1978*, **92**, p.113 (cf. *New Docs 1977*, **91**, p.140) it was stated that the text of this fragment overlapped with that of *P.Mil.Vogl.* inv.1224 and that therefore the two fragments could not be from the same codex. In fact there is no overlap and the two pieces align showing that they are remains of a single page. Details can be found in the *editio princeps* by S.R. Pickering, *ZPE* 65 (1986) 76-78 (pl.I b, c); cf. K. Treu, *APF* 32 (1986) 88.

A unique item is described, though not published, by A. Wouters in *Pap.Brux.* 18, pp.97-107. It is a codex in the Chester Beatty Collection, having 104 pages (of which only 23 are written on, the rest being blank) which contain extensive conjugation tables of Greek verbs (13pp.), and a Graeco-Latin lexicon (10pp.) — of sorts — on portions of Rom., 2 Cor., Gal. and Eph. This same codex is described by E.A. Lowe, *Codices Latini Antiquiores. Supplement* (Oxford, 1971) no.1683, but without mention of the Pauline lexicon. Wouters believes the codex is to be dated mid-IV (Lowe: V^2). The codex was clearly devised by someone more at home with Greek than with Latin, perhaps a person keen to improve his grasp of the latter. Of greatest interest for the present context, however, is Wouters' observation that this 'lexicon' provides a number of new readings for the Greek text of these epistles and also a good many readings in the Latin which are consonant with the Vetus Latina, not with the Vulgate. Nevertheless, he cautions (105) that 'the value of these readings is of course reduced somewhat by the fact that we have only lemmata, not a full text'.

A Christian epitaph (IV or V) found on the island of Salamis concludes with a quotation from 1 Cor. 16.21: if anyone buries others in our grave, 'let him give account to God and let him be "anathema". Maran atha', λόγον δῴ|η τῷ θεῷ καὶ ἀ|νάθεμα ἤτω. | Μαρὰν ἀθάν. This text is reprinted twice in *SIA* III, at p.30 (= *IG* III, 2.x.3509), and at p.161 (= C. Bayet, *de titulis Atticae Christianis antiquissimis* [Paris, 1878], no.107). For the 'give account' formula see *New Docs 1978*, **98**, p.136. The deceased man in this tomb was a lector, ἀνα|γν`ώ΄(στου), *ll.*2-3). For another lector who apparently earned his living as a cutler (μαχαιρᾶς), see J.S. Creaghan/A.E. Raubitschek, *Hesperia* 16 (1947) 31-32, no.XV (repr. in *SIA* III, pp.215-16; text also in Guarducci, *EG* IV.323-24 [fig.90]). See ibid., 32 n.167 for instances of other individuals whose profession and church office are given (e.g., doctor/deacon, doctor/elder, painter/elder).

I.Nikaia I.497 (n.d.) records an inscription which is written over the heads of angels depicted in a mosaic in the Koimesis Church:

ἀρχέ	δυνάμις
κυριότιτες	ἐξουσίε

(read ἀρχαί, δυνάμεις, κυριότητες, ἐξουσίαι, 'principalities, powers, dominions, authorities'). The exact significance of these words standing over the angels is not clear, but they are surely drawn from the numerous places in the Pauline epistles where two or more of these words are linked in references to spiritual and sometimes temporal powers (e.g., 1 Cor. 15.24; Eph. 3.10; Col. 1.16; 2.15; Tit. 3.1). All four appear together, though in the genitive singular not nominative plural, in Eph. 1.21. The meaning of these words in Pauline theology has been treated by G.B. Caird in *Principalities and Powers* (Oxford, 1956). Caird discusses OT evidence for Jewish belief in spiritual powers (1-11), and the development of corresponding Greek terminology in the LXX (11-15). He argues that Paul 'was imbued with the Jewish idea of angelic powers behind the world order' (16), that a clear distinction in Paul's understanding between spiritual and temporal rulers ought not to be made (22-23) and that the Jewish Law was for Paul a 'demonic agency' which was one of the 'powers' (43). In a more recent study, *Angels and Principalities* (*SNTSMS*

42; Cambridge, 1981), W. Carr rejects these views and argues that Paul did not apply the terms used for powers to demons, but to forces both spiritual and temporal serving God's purposes (122-23), and that the understanding of the powers as demonic is post-Pauline (152, 176-77).

I.Eph. VII, 2.4138 (found near the church of St John) comprises ten Byzantine graffiti most of which are elaborations upon the theme κ(ύρι)ε βοήθη (*read* -θει) τὸν δοῦλον, 'Lord, help your servant'. Text (b), however, is a longer one (though very fragmentary) and contains the clause κ(ὲ) κερδάνε ἐλπήζετ[ο] | πάντα τὸν κόσμον 'and he/she hoped to gain the whole world' (*ll.*3-4), words which are reminiscent of Mt. 16.26, Mk. 8.36 and Lk. 9.25. On a column belonging to the portico of the Kuretenstrasse in Ephesos (*I.Eph.* IV.1365 (1); n.d.) are found the words ὁ θεὸς τῆς δόξης from Ps. 28.3 or Acts 7.2, and ὁ πατὴρ τῶν οἰκτιρμῶν from 2 Cor. 1.3. An undated plaque, *I.Eph.* IV.1365 (2), reads]ων | [- - -] δόξης and may be the remains of similar citations. Their purpose is unknown. Equally obscure are fragments from an undated marble plaque (*I.Eph.* IV.1334) bearing the tenuously restored word χειροπ[οιητ- which, although not a NT word, the editors find reminiscent of Acts 19.26. However, if the restoration is correct another possible source for the fragment's content may be one of the fifteen LXX passages where the word itself is found.

The slippery nature of the evidence when attempting to discern echoes of biblical language in documentary texts is illustrated by *P.Oxy.* 12 (1916) 1494 (IV) which though already known for a long time has been reprinted by Tibiletti, *Lettere*, 169-70, no.21. The letter is almost certainly Christian, in view of the names Boethos (the writer) and Makaria (one of those greeted; on the masculine form of this name see *New Docs 1978*, **104**), and the greeting accorded equally to a slave and her owner (cf. **124** below), in addition to the general tenor of the letter. The section requesting prayer exemplifies this:

μά[[λ-]]
λειστα μὲν δεήσει καὶ ὑμᾶς εὔ-
χεσθαι περεὶ ἡμῶν, εἵν' οὕτως
ἐπακούσῃ ὁ θαιὸς τῶν εὐχῶν
ὑμῶν καὶ γένηται ἡμεῖν ὁδὸς
εὐθεῖα.

5 | **Especially you ought to pray for us, in order that in this way God may hear your prayers and our way become straight.**

Do we have a biblical echo here? Tibiletti notes for comparison LXX Hosea 14.10, διότι εὐθεῖαι αἱ ὁδοὶ τοῦ κυρίου, καὶ δίκαιοι πορεύσονται ἐν αὐταῖς, οἱ δὲ ἀσεβεῖς ἀσθενήσουσιν ἐν αὐταῖς. But there is no real common sentiment here, nor indeed any clear verbal similarity for a definite link to be established. The papyrus letter uses the words metaphorically of a person's own way. Boethos is merely asking in pious language that he may have a trouble-free business trip. Similarly, it is doubtful that we have a reminiscence of NT passages like Acts 13.10 or 2 Pet. 2.15. In fact the wording has a classical pedigree: see D.L. Page's n. on *l.*384 in his edition of Eur. *Medea* (Oxford, 1938; repr.), a reference drawn to my attention by K.L. McKay.

On the popularity of certain NT verses for use in inscriptions see **104**.

(A.L. CONNOLLY)

106. Patristic texts on papyrus

From this year's reading come two texts which are certainly patristic and a third which is probably so. The most important of these is a papyrus fragment (provenance unknown, late III-IV; *ed.pr.* — K. Treu, *ZPE* 35 [1979] 43-48, pl.3; cf. id., *APF* 27 [1980] 256) containing sections 3.1.6-8 of Origen's Περὶ ἀρχῶν, better known under its Latin title *de Principiis*. This text has now been re-edited as *P.Amst.* 1 (1980) 25 (pl.12; cf. Treu, *APF* 30 [1984] 125). Above the wide bottom margins the *front* preserves portions of 17 lines and the *back* parts of 19. An estimated 33 lines are lost from the top of the *back* and a similar number from the *front*, giving a writing area of 13B x 28H cm. which Treu thinks extremely narrow, although he doubts (43) that there were two columns to a page.

Treu judges that the piece was part of a codex rather than a single sheet because, although the text on the *back* can be made to finish at the end of 3.1.8, a natural sense-break, the start of the text on the *front* would fall in the middle of a section (44). He suggests, therefore, three possible contexts for this fragment: either it was part of the extract from Περὶ ἀρχῶν (namely Books 3-4) which Basil and Gregory of Nazianzos included in their anthology of Origen's work, the *Philocalia*, compiled in 358; or it was an extract incorporated in a similar work now lost, but perhaps earlier than the *Philocalia*; or this may even be a fragment from a continuous text of the Περὶ ἀρχῶν itself (46-47). In view of the loss in its Greek form of this major work of Origen, existing now only in its Latin translation except for the passage in the *Philocalia*, this fragment is important as an early witness to the Greek text. Indeed early texts of any of Origen's works are few: the earliest MSS of the *Philocalia* are tenth-century; the Tura papyri (VI fin./VII), which in two codices preserve 182 pages of works by Origen, are much later than this new piece; and among other possibly Origenic fragments only *P.Bon.* 1 (1953) 1 (provenance unknown, III) is certain and early (47). The new fragment has no major variants from the medieval texts of the *Philocalia*, and so witnesses to the reliability of those later texts.

A fragment of Sermon 22 on the Calming of the Storm by the fifth-century bishop, Basil of Seleucia, is published at *PSI* 1453 (Oxyrhynchos, late V/early VI; *ed.pr.* — M. Naldini, *Aeg.* 38 [1958] 139-46 [pl.]; cf. van Haelst, 630; K. Treu, *APF* 19 [1969] 188). The twenty-two fragmentary lines are written across the fibres of a piece from a papyrus roll; the other side is blank. Because this text shares date, provenance and palaeographical characteristics with another Christian text, *PSI* 1 (1912) 27 (written on the back of *PSI* 1.26 [V] — both are hagiographical in content), the editor suggests that the two may have belonged to the same Christian library in Oxyrhynchos. The surviving passage (which is heavily restored from Migne, *PG* 85.268) is a retelling of the story following mainly Matthew's version (8.23-37), but with elements from the other synoptic accounts (Mk. 4.36-41; Lk. 8.23-25). Basil's choice of elements for his own version seems to be influenced by a desire to increase suspense by delaying the miraculous calming, and to contrast Jesus' self-possession and the disciples' fear. Consequently Basil uses Matthew's order of events in which Jesus' upbraiding of the disciples comes before the calming of the storm, not after it as in Mark and Luke. The disciples' plea in *l.*3, [σῶσ]ọṿ ἡ̣μ̣ᾶ̣ς, [ἀ]πολλ[ύ]μεθα̣, is an echo of Mt. 8.25 (cf. Mk. 4.38; Lk. 8.24), as is Jesus' reproach that they are ὀλιγόπ̣ιστοι (*l.*12; cf. Mt. 8.26; Mk. 4.40; Lk. 8.25). However, σιώπα, λέγ]ω̣ṿ, π̣εφ[ί]μ̣ωσ[ο] (*l.*19) is from Mk. 4.39, and κλύδων (*l.*5) is only found in Luke's account (8.24).

Basil draws out the theme of Jesus as saviour by expanding the speeches: the disciples implore Jesus at length to help them, as he is their only hope of salvation; Jesus lectures them, also at length, on their lack of faith. As a result Basil's story is about five times as long as any of the gospel versions. Basil employs vocabulary which does not appear in the NT (e.g., [πλα]σιάζει, *l.*2; ἀτονίαν, *l.*5; τυραννουμένου[ς], *l.*8) and he uses literary spellings (e.g., θαλάττης, *l.*15, but cf. θαλάσσης, *l.*8; and ταραττομένων, *l.*13). All these differences are only to be expected when we consider that this is a sermon written in elevated fourth-century language; but they serve to draw attention to the possibility of treating gospel stories in a variety of ways, and to the question of what purposes the evangelists had in mind when they wrote their own versions.

PSI 1453 presents only one reading varying from the text of the two codices with which Naldini collated it: at *l.*7 the papyrus reads διαλέχθητι εἰ[ρήνην against διαλέχθητι περὶ εἰρήνης found in *codd. Laur. Plut.* 7-1 (XI AD) and *Vat. gr.* 1494 (XVI AD). The papyrus agrees at this point with the text of Migne, whose ultimate manuscript source, however, is unknown (*ed.pr.*, 140, 141 n.1). The substantial agreement of *PSI* 1453 with the codices indicates a reliable transmission of this text in the intervening centuries.

A third text from this year is probably patristic. *P.XV Congr.* 4 (= *P.Palau Rib.* inv. 31; provenance unknown, IV^2/early V; cf. K. Treu, *APF* 28 [1982] 96) consists of two fragments from a papyrus codex (A and B), possibly from the same page, although they cannot be made to join. Since they look as though they may join, perhaps they came from different pages which suffered in the same accident and broke in very similar ways. The content, though obscure, may support this view as the front and back of each fragment appear more related in vocabulary to themselves than to the other fragment. J. O'Callaghan, who edited this text, has observed that these fragments come from the same scriptorium, perhaps even the same codex, as three patristic texts, *P.Palau Rib.* inv. 4, 68 and 72 (on the last two of these see *New Docs 1978*, **92**). The work has not been identified and the text's lacunae cannot be fully restored; but its theological or philosophical nature seems certain from repeated mentions of σῶμα and ψυχή (A *front* 4, *back* 9) and ἀνάγκη (A *front* 9, *back* 4), and from phrases such as κατὰ τὸ θέλον (= θέλημα?, A *front* 11), κατὰ πάντα τρόπον τοῦ ἀνθρώ[που (A *front* 12) and δ]ίκαιον(?) βούλημα (A *back* 10). Most telling, however, are B *back* 4-5, ἀμιγὲς κακίᾳ μονότροπον μον[ο]||ούσιον ἀδιαίρετον ἀλώβετον ἀχείρωτον, 'unmixed with evil, of one kind and one substance, undivided, unblemished, unconquered'. These last lines may form part of a discussion of the Trinity; the negative theology is prominent. Nevertheless there is no specifically Christian reference in the text, nor is ἀνθρώ[που(?) written as a *nomen sacrum*, the only word in the surviving fragments which might be a candidate for such abbreviation.

The remains of a work which shares some similar features have been published as *P.XV Congr.* 2 (provenance unknown, V). Despite the mention of ἡ οἰκουμένη (*back* 27) and the 'generally moralising tone' (*ed.pr.*, 17), again there are no specifically Christian elements, and ἄνθρωπος is written in full (*back* 4, 24). The mention of τὰ Πλούτωνος καὶ Μουσῶ[ν] (*back* 22) may simply be a conventional reference to wealth and the arts and need not rule out Christian authorship. There are, however, various signs that this work may be a defence speech and the editor, K. Treu, wonders if it originated from the milieu of the Second Sophistic: there are numerous rhetorical elements; at *front* 13-18 the writer seems to be justifying his failure to do something on the ground of illness; and on the back he seems to be finding fault with another man.

For recent work on the biblical commentaries of Didymos 'the Blind' see **107**.

(A.L. CONNOLLY)

107. The insights of Didymos 'the Blind'

Perhaps the single most important — and undoubtedly the largest — papyrus find ever made of patristic material was discovered in August 1941 in a cave at Tura, about 12 km. south of Cairo. The more than 2000 sheets of papyrus, including eight codices, had probably been hidden at some time after VI/VII init., the latest date of writing of the texts. Not far away was the monastery of St. Arsenios, which was the likely owner of the documents.

Apart from some extended fragments (all but one of more than thirty pages) of works by Origen — for details see van Haelst, 683-687; no. 684, there cited as ined., has been published subsequently as O. Guéraud/P. Nautin (edd.), *Origène. Sur la Pâque* (*Christianisme antique* 2; Paris, 1979); cf. K. Treu, *APF* 28 (1982) 94-95 — the cache consisted mostly of works by Didymos 'the Blind' (313-98), bishop of Alexandria, a one-time student of Origen, and himself the teacher of men like Jerome, Rufinus and Palladius. His influence waned from mid-VI when his works came to be regarded as heretical. What survived of Didymos' 'writings' via a MS tradition is included in Migne, *PG* vol.39. His works fall into two main types: exegetical commentaries on various books of the Bible, and treatises of dogmatic theology. Five of the former of these are well represented in the Tura material: his commentaries on Genesis, Job, Psalms, Ecclesiastes and Zachariah. The first and last have been published in the *Sources Chrétiennes* series:

— P. Nautin/L. Doutreleau (edd.), *Didyme l'Aveugle, Sur la Genèse* (2. vols., *SC* 233, 244; Paris 1976, 1978); cf. K. Treu, *APF* 27 (1980) 253-55; van Haelst, 643;

— L. Doutreleau (ed.), *Didyme l'Aveugle, Sur Zacharie* (3 vols, *SC* 83-85; Paris, 1962); cf. L. Koenen, *APF* 17 (1962) 61-105; cf. K. Treu, *APF* 19 (1969) 189; van Haelst, 647.

The commentaries on Job 1-16.8, Ps. 20-44.4, and Eccl. 1-12 (with lacunae in each) have been published in a multitude of volumes in the series *Papyrologische Texte und Abhandlungen* (Bonn). As these publications have almost reached finality, apparently, it may be useful to list them here. Two of the volumes from the set comprising Didymos' commentary on Ecclesiastes appeared in 1979.

A. *Commentary on Job* (van Haelst, 646)

vol.I, ed. A. Henrichs (*PTA* 1; 1968), ch.1-4;
II, ed. id. (*PTA* 2; 1968), ch.5.1-6.29; on vols. I and II cf. Treu, *APF* 20 (1970) 145-47;
III, edd. U. and D. Hagedorn/L. Koenen (*PTA* 3; 1968), ch. 7.20c-11.20; cf. Treu, *APF* 20 (1970) 147-49;
IV, 1, edd. iid. (*PTA* 33.1; 1985), ch.12.1-16.8a; cf. Treu, *APF* 32 (1986) 88-89;
IV, 2, edd. iid. (*PTA* 33.2; forthcoming); this volume will contain the notes on vol.IV, 1 and an index to the whole *Commentary*.

B. *Commentary on Psalms* (van Haelst, 644)

vol.I, edd. L. Doutreleau/A. Gesché/M. Gronewald (*PTA* 7; 1969), Ps. 20-21; cf. Treu, *APF* 22 (1973) 373-77;
II, ed. M. Gronewald (*PTA* 4; 1968); Ps. 22-26.10; cf. Treu, *APF* 20 (1970) 149-50;
III, ed. id. (*PTA* 8; 1969), Ps. 29-34; cf. Treu, *APF* 23 (1973) 373-77;
IV, ed. id. (*PTA* 6; 1969), Ps. 35-39; cf. Treu, *APF* 21 (1971) 207-09;
V, ed. id. (*PTA* 12; 1970), Ps. 40-44.4; cf. Treu, *APF* 24/25 (1976) 254-56.

* Note also *Pap.Colon.* 1: *Der Psalmenkommentar von Tura Quaternio IX* (*Pap.Colon.Theol.* 1), ed. A. Kehl (Köln, 1964); cf. Treu, *APF* 19 (1969) 189.
* T. Muraoka informs me that this work of Didymos has also appeared in E. Mühlenberg, *Psalmenkommentare aus der Katenenüberlieferung* (3 vols.; Berlin, 1975-78) — *non vidi.*
* T.W. Mackay/C.W. Griggs, *BASP* 20 (1983 [1985]) 59-60, have signalled the rediscovery of ten leaves of the Psalms Comm., comprising the missing pages between Ps. 26.10-29.2; i.e., between the *PTA* series' vols II and III. This section will be included in a forthcoming vol. of *PTA*.
* See also below, under D.

C. *Commentary on Ecclesiastes* (van Haelst, 645)

vol.I, 1, edd. G. Binder/L. Liesenborghs (*PTA* 25; 1979), ch. 1.1-2.14; cf. Treu *APF* 30 (1984) 124-25;

I, 2, by G. Binder (*PTA* 26; 1983), notes on I, 1;

II, ed. M. Gronewald (*PTA* 22; 1977), ch.3-4.12; cf. Treu, *APF* 27 (1980) 255;

III, ed. J. Kramer (*PTA* 13; 1970), ch.5-6;

IV, edd. J. Kramer/B. Krebber (*PTA* 16; 1972), ch.7-8.8; on vols. III and IV cf. Treu, *APF* 24/25 (1976) 256-59;

V, ed. M. Gronewald (*PTA* 24; 1979), ch.9.8-10.20; cf. Treu, *APF* 29 (1983) 107-08;

VI, edd. G. Binder/L. Liesenborghs (*PTA* 9; 1969), ch.11-12; cf. Treu, *APF* 23 (1973) 377-78.

D. *Miscellaneous smaller items*

B. Kramer (ed.), *Kleine Texte aus dem Tura-Fund* (*PTA* 34; 1985). This volume includes four texts, three of which have already been published:

i. Psalms Homily; = *ZPE* 16 (1975) 164-213; cf. Treu, *APF* 26 (1978) 157;
ii. Didymos, *Commentary on John*, covering ch.6.3-33;
iii. Protocol of a dialogue between Didymos and a heretic; = *ZPE* 32 (1978) 202-12; cf. Treu, *APF* 27 (1980) 257;
iv. Didymos, *Commentary on the Psalms*, ed. M. Gronewald, providing two further pages to add to the previously published set for Psalms; = *ZPE* 46 (1982) 97-111; cf. Treu, *APF* 30 (1984) 124.

Naturally, this wealth of material has been given widespread attention in journals and books. Four earlier articles may be singled out as being still of considerable interest for their laying out of the immensity of the find, and the milieu in which these texts were felt worthy of recopying and preservation: H.-C. Puech, *RHPhR* 31 (1951) 293-329; L. Doutreleau, *RSR* 43 (1955) 161-93; L. Koenen/L. Doutreleau, *RSR* 55 (1967) 547-64; L. Koenen/W. Müller-Wiener, *ZPE* 2 (1968) 41-63. More recently, B. Kramer has provided a useful brief survey article of Didymos with a good bibliography in *TRE* VIII.4/5 (1981(?)) 741-46.

The discovery of so much of Didymos' output has done much to help us appreciate why his standing as an exegete in the Church was so high. We know from writers like Jerome that his range of commentaries was very extensive. The one fragment from the *Commentary on John* (Kramer, 1985) is the only surviving evidence of his contribution to NT exegesis; but he delivered lectures as well on Mt., Acts, 1 and 2 Cor., Gal., Eph., the Catholic epistles, and Rev. His dogmatic works were often directed against those of other theological persuasions, such as the Arians or Manichaeans. The debate recorded between Didymos and a 'heretic' (perhaps an Apollinarist) — repr. in Kramer, 1985 — is the closest we come to this feature of his work in the Tura cache. The *Commentaries*, which take the form of his lectures copied down by an amanuensis complete with the interjections and questions from Didymos' auditors, reveal very clearly the Alexandrian exegetical method: a literal interpretation of the Biblical text is followed by exposition of its allegorical significance. Scattered through these lectures is plenty of theological polemic, which provides insight into the liveliness of the theological disputes current in the fourth century.

It is not only Christian texts to which Didymos alludes; as we should expect of someone whose home was the Alexandria of Origen, Didymos shows his easy familiarity with classical texts, especially with those of the philosophers. On this see G. Binder, *RBPh* 57 (1979) 51-56, who notes quotations from/allusions to Leukippos, Prodikos, Epikouros, Solon, and Sokrates in the *Comm. on Eccl.* One bonus as a result is the recovery of some new fragments of certain classical authors, e.g., a new fragment of Epikouros (Binder, et al., *ZPE* 1 [1967] 33-44).

A great advance in our knowledge of Didymos has been gained as a result of the discovery and publication of this massive corpus. The evidence it betrays of Greek orthography is occasionally interesting, since these do not attempt to be polished, 'literary' works, but copies of transcriptions based on oral delivery in a less than fully formal context. Where quotations from the Bible differ from the text as it has been otherwise transmitted, this may largely be due to paraphrasing, or lapse of memory. But detailed study of these divergences may yet prove to throw up further clues to which Greek text of the OT was in use, and whether there were in fact readings unique to the text of the NT in use in Egypt's metropolis in the fourth century.

108. Variations on the Trishagion

Five late texts republished in Lodi, *Enchiridion* — on this work in general see **109** — demonstrate both the influence of liturgical language on other genres and the various adaptations of the original Trishagion from Is. 6.3. Lodi, *Enchiridion*, no.777 is a preface to the Latin Mass (from *cod. Vat. lat.* 4770; V) which ends with the acclamation of the angels, cherubim and seraphim, *sanctus, sanctus, sanctus dominus deus sabaoth*. No.917 (Egypt, VI; *ed.pr.*— H.R. Hall, *Coptic and Greek Texts . . . in the British Museum* [London, 1905] 17 — *non vidi*) is a Coptic hymn elaborated from the form of the Trishagion which, in fact, ends the hymn: ἅγιος ὁ θεὸς ἅγι<ο>ς εἰσχυρὸς ἅγιος ἀνδα̣ νατος (*read* ἀθάνατος?). No.769 is the opening of an epitaph for Amachis (*ll.*1-13; provenance not given, V; *ed.pr.* — G. Millet, *OC* 29 [1932] 303-16; *non vidi*) in which an address from the tomb to the living by the deceased is prefaced by ἅγιος, ἅγιος, ἅγιος. Interestingly, by a play on the ancient cliché which equated life with seeing the light of day, the living addressed here are perhaps the spiritually enlightened, οἱ τὸ γλυ|κὺ φῶς βλέπον|τες τοῦ πατρὸς | ἡμῶν τοῦ ἐν τοῖς | οὐρανοῖς ('you who see the sweet light of our Father in heaven'). This particular light metaphor is not found in the NT. Lodi no.771 is another sepulchral inscription (Egypt, V; *ed.pr.* — S. de Ricci, *CRAI* (1934) 256-61; *non vidi*) in which the elaborate Sanctus, ἅγιος | ἅγιος ἅγιος κύριος | σαβάωθ, πλήρ(ης) ὁ | οὐρανὸς καὶ ἡ γῆ τῆς | ἁγίας σου δόξης, is added to a prayer on the tomb that the deceased may be given rest in paradise. De Ricci (cited at *DACL* 14.2 [1948] *col.*1769, *s.v.* 'Prière') observes that in this inscription the phrase μετ' ὁσ[ί]ων καὶ δικαίων ('with the pious and the just', *l.*4) has been borrowed from Jewish formulae. No.775 (near Antioch, V; cf. K.M. Kaufmann, *Handbuch der altchristlichen Epigraphik* [Freiburg, 1917] 162) is a Trishagion in the post-470 form: ἅγιος ὁ θεός, ἅγιος ἰ[σ](χ)υρός, ἅγιος ἀθάνατος, (σ)τα(υ)ροθ(εὶ)ς δι' ἡμᾶς ἠλ[έ]ησον ἡμᾶς (cf. *New Docs 1977*, **95**).

Four other inscriptions from this year's culling, all of uncertain though probably late date, are less well preserved but show similarities of form. Two from Ephesos are fragmentary: *I.Eph.* IV.1359 (where bibliographical information on the Trishagion is given) reads [ἅγιο]ς ἰσχυρὸς (Χρ.) ἅγ[ιος ἀθάνατος - - -]; IV.1369, a moulding (from a doorway?) whose text reads vertically from the top a letter to a line, [ἅ][γ][ι]ος [ἀ][θ]άνατος. A text in the Koimesis Church in Nikaia (*I.Nikaia* I.492) is written above a mosaic representation of the Virgin at prayer and reads ἅγιος | ἅγιος | ἅγιος. The fourth, from the basilica of Thyrsos in Tegea (Pallas, *Monuments paléochrétiens*, 181-83 no.89D) is found between two decorative mosaic panels in the church's annex: † ἅγιος, ἅγιος, ἅγ[ιος κύριος ὁ θεὸς?] σὺν υἱῷ κ[αὶ] πνεύμ[ατι ἁγί]ῳ ΙΗ(?). Pallas, *ad. loc.*, sees this as possibly influenced by disputes concerning the Trinity. For other Trishagia and further discussion see **7** above; and previously in *New Docs 1978*, **88**, p.104 no.7, and **91**.

(A.L. CONNOLLY)

109. Liturgical prayers

Lodi, *Enchiridion*, is a massive collection of prayer texts from liturgical sources. Into one volume of nearly 2000pp. and *c.*3500 items Lodi brings together a vast range of material, ranging from V BC Greek literature to Cranmer in the XVIth. Naturally, Christian sources (Eastern and Western) heavily predominate; and this material is catalogued chronologically. The following very brief breakdown of the coverage down to the early Byzantine period may be noted (Lodi's item numbers are given):

1-31 — Greek/Roman literature
32-95 — Jewish material, printed only in Latin translation
96-131 — Jewish-Christian literature (*Didache*, Odes of Solomon, Hermas, etc.)
132-38 — OT
139-50, 832 — NT
151-77 — Subapostolic (Clement of Rome, Ignatius, Polycarp)
178-273 — II AD patristic material; items 254-73 are funerary inscriptions from II-VI, all but two in Latin
274-369 — III AD patristic material; 306-12, inscriptions and papyri
370-685 — IV AD patristic and other material; 641-48, inscriptions and papyri
686-831 — V AD patristic and other material; items 765-767a are papyri, 769-777 are inscriptions
832-851 — texts which narrate the institution of the Eucharist (biblical and post-biblical)
852-922 — VI AD patristic and other material; 910-920, inscriptions and papyri.

Though well indexed, the book is nevertheless frustrating to use, at least for those whose interest may be historical, or whose concern is with documentary texts. No notes are provided ad loc. on any of the items, nor cross-references to comparable items in other sections. However, in a companion volume, subtitled *Clavis methodologica cum commentariis selectis* (Bologna, 1979), Lodi provides concise notes on various features in certain of the texts. The inscriptions and papyri are often referred to in ways which make their identification difficult except (no doubt) to specialists on Christian liturgical texts which survive on stone, ostrakon or papyrus. How, for example, is no.767a, a communion hymn, to be quickly identified if it is called simply '*Pap.* 7561'? In fact, this is *P.Berl.* inv. 7561 (van Haelst, 724). This may well be just a printing omission, but some other references are merely too vague. Another communion hymn, no.912, is described simply as *ll.*1-9 from an ancient Coptic ostrakon. Again, Lodi, no.648 is a short prayer to God, 'named above every rule and authority and dominion and name . . .', which is indicated to be an excerpt from 'pap. Arsinoe', too unclear an allusion to be quickly traceable. It is true that further references are given for these documentary texts, e.g., to a discussion in *DACL*; but that does not aid rapid identification of the item. Additionally, these texts are not presented in a useful manner since no indication is provided of lacunae in the document; nor is there consistency in questions of orthographical treatment, whether these documentary items should be given accents and other diacritics and whether the spelling should be normalised. Contrast nos. 913 and 914 in this regard, for example.

It should be stressed that the inscriptions and papyri included are only a selection of those relevant for such an anthology. So, too, the items from Classical literature, and no doubt the Jewish passages too, serve only as representative pieces. All the documentary texts included are specifically Christian; one possible exception is no.766, *P.Lond.Christ.* (1935) 4, for which van Haelst, 921 cites a bibliographical item which argues that it may be Jewish. Certainly, it would have been a help were the appropriate van Haelst numbers appended to each papyrus in Lodi's collection. For that would have provided users of his book whose main interest was liturgical with information about the surviving text, including later bibliography. A case in point is provided by Lodi, no.308 = *P.Oxy* 15 (1922) 1786 (III), the earliest known Christian hymn with surviving musical notation. This text — van Haelst, 962 — has attracted a considerable bibliography in the years since it was first published. As another example, the so-called 'Psalmus Responsorius' is included as Lodi, no.679. This long, fourth-century Latin hymn, which has been thought to be addressed to the Virgin, has been the subject of numerous articles since it was first published; it is reprinted with discussion at *New Docs 1977*, **92**.

While most of the Latin translations of the Greek texts are clear enough, one defect involving a Christian inscription may be noted. No.263 (= Diehls, *ILCV* I.2328) is written in Greek, but is a mixture of Greek and Latin: Δημήτρις ἐτ Λεοντία | Σειρικε φειλιε βενεμερεν|τι, μνησθῇς, Ἰησοῦς ὁ κύριος, τέκνον, 'Demetrios and Leontia for Serikia their daughter who merits well. Remember, Lord Jesus, our child'. Lodi's error here is to fail to perceive φειλιε as an attempt to write Latin *filiae*; he renders it as *amatae*. The same phenomenon recurs in *IGUR* 1306 (Rome, Imperial period), where one of the three people responsible for erecting a tomb for Polymnestos was 'his most revered daughter, Eustorgos', σεμνοτάτη φιλια Εὔστοργος. For another instance note *CIJ* I.637 (Ferrara, Imperial period), a Latin text written in Greek which includes the word φιλιη (for *filiae*).

The question of bilingual interference having come up, the opportunity may be taken to note here briefly one other short text from the year's culling which is of interest solely for this reason. *CIL III Add.* 30 (Andros, I BC init.) is a short building inscription in Latin by someone who has not fully mastered the language: *DIOGENHS PISCINAM* | *BETEREM NOBAM* | *[F]HCIT · TOTAM*, 'Diogenes entirely renovated the old fish tank'. It cannot be ascertained whether the mason or the commissioner of the inscription was responsible for the Greek *eta* in the first and fifth words. As for the words in the second line the orthography is a carry-over from the common phenomenon of *beta* being used for Latin *V* (cf. Λείβιος for *Livius* in *CIL III Add.* 39). In this text we witness interference between two orthographies. On *piscinae* at Kenchreai cf. **37** above.

A fragment from the end of the Niceno-Constantinopolitan creed is preserved on an inscription dated 938: *I.Eph.* IV.1278. For this creed noted previously see *New Docs 1976*, **66**; *New Docs 1977*, **110** (*ad fin.*); *New Docs 1978*, **93**, p.116. An equally brief remnant of the Nicene creed survives as *I.Eph.* V.1675 (Byzantine?). See previous mentions of this creed at *New Docs 1976*, **66**; *New Docs 1978*, **88** (*ad fin.*).

D. JUDAICA

110. Ptolemaic synagogues again (cf. *New Docs 1978,* 94)

In the previous volume's entry four Hellenistic inscriptions from Egypt were noted in which προσευχή is used for 'synagogue'. Those items have been reprinted in various places over the years. So, too, have the following additional examples noted from the present year's culling. Where there are different readings the text followed is that given in B. Lifshitz, *Donateurs et fondateurs dans les synagogues juives* (*Cahiers de la Revue Biblique* 7; Paris, 1967).

1. *SGPI* 166 (Athribis in Egypt, 181-145 BC; = *OGIS* 101; *CIJ* II.1444; Lifshitz, no.96), ὑπὲρ βασιλέως Πτολεμαίου | καὶ βασιλίσσης Κλεοπάτρας | καὶ τῶν τέκνων | Ἑρμίας καὶ Φιλοτέρα ἡ γυνὴ | καὶ τὰ παιδία τήνδε ἐξέδραν, | τῆι προσευχῆ, 'For King Ptolemy and Queen Kleopatra and their children, Hermias and Philotera his wife and their children dedicated this portico for the synagogue'.
2. *SGPI* 167 (Athribis in Egypt, 181-145 BC; = *OGIS* 96; *CIJ* II.1443; Lifshitz, no.95), ὑπὲρ βασιλέως Πτολεμαίου | καὶ βασιλίσσης Κλεοπάτρας | Πτολεμαῖος Ἐπικύδου, | ὁ ἐπιστάτης τῶν φυλακιτῶν | καὶ οἱ ἐν Ἀθρίβει Ἰουδαῖοι | τὴν προσευχὴν | θεῷ ὑψιστῷ, 'For King Ptolemy and Queen Kleopatra, Ptolemaios son of Epikydes, superintendent of the police, and the Jews at Athribis dedicated the synagogue to the highest God'. For the non-Jewish benefactor here cf. the centurion at Capernaum who τὴν συναγωγὴν αὐτὸς ᾠκοδόμησεν ἡμῖν (Lk. 7.5).
3. Helbing, *AGI* 18 (Lower Egypt; = *OGIS* 129; *CIJ* 1449; not in Lifshitz), βασιλίσσης καὶ βασιλέως προσταξάντων | ἀντὶ τῆς προανακει|μένης περὶ τῆς ἀναθέ|σεως τῆς προσευχῆς πλα|κὸς ἡ ὑπογεγραμμένη | ἐπιγραφήτω· | βασιλεὺς Πτολεμαῖος Εὐ|εργέτης τὴν προσευχὴν | ἄσυλον. | *Regina et* | *rex iusserunt*, 'On the orders of the queen and the king: in place of the plaque which was previously situated here concerning the erection of the synagogue, the text given below is to be inscribed: "King Ptolemy Euergetes (has made) the synagogue an asylum. The queen and the king have ordered it" '. This text has been most recently discussed by J. Bingen in J. Quaegebeur (ed.), *Studia P. Naster oblata,* II. *Orientalia Antiqua* (*Orientalia Lovaniensia Analecta* 13; Leuven, 1982) 11-16. He argues that Mommsen's proposed date of *c.*270-72 AD is wrong, and that the text belongs to *c.*47-30 BC, the royal figures mentioned being Kleopatra and Ptolemy XIV Caesarion. On *asylia* see **78**.

To round out these examples we may note the presence of προσευχή, 'synagogue', in *CIJ* II.1441, 1442, both from Egypt and dated 143-116 BC (the former is from Xenephyris, the latter from Nitria). These items are included in Lifshitz' monograph as nos. 93 and 94. The four inscriptions noted at *New Docs 1978*, **94**, are also all in Lifshitz: *CIJ* II.1432, 1433, 1440 and *CPJ* III, App.1, no.1532a are respectively Lifshitz, nos. 86, 87, 92 and 99. Thus between mid-III BC and I^2 BC Egypt yields nine examples of προσευχή meaning 'synagogue'.

In *I.Berenike* 16, dated to 3 Dec. 55, the second year of Nero's administration, the Jewish synagogue in the city erected an inscription to list those who had contributed to the building's repair. Here both the building (*l.*5) and the members meeting there (*l.*3) are called a συναγωγή, thus offering a good parallel for the development of the use of the ἐκκλησία among Christians. Reynolds' comments on this text (ad loc.) are brief but useful. Of the surviving names of the donors ten are ἄρχοντες and one a ἱερεύς. See further the discussion in S. Applebaum, *Jews and Greeks in Ancient Cyrene* (*Studies in Judaism in Late Antiquity* 28; Leiden, 1979) 161-64; cf. *BE* 658.

For discussion of the term ἀρχισυνάγωγος, taken over into Jewish circles at a time when συναγωγή was superseding προσευχή as the standard word for 'synagogue' see **113**, section (h), below.

For a non-Jewish use of συναγωγή note from the current crop of texts *I.Eph.* II.419A (92/3), which records the building of an aqueduct during the proconsulship of P. Calvisius Ruso, the work being supervised by the council of the *neopoioi*, ἐργεπιστ[ατούν]|των τῆς συνα[γωγῆς] | τῶν νεοποι[ῶν] (*ll.*7-9; the participle is strictly ungrammatical, but has been made plural in an *ad sensum* agreement with the last noun). The editors' n. ad loc. glosses συναγωγή as equivalent in meaning here to συνέδριον. For the *neopoioi* see **28** above.

111. Jewish renovation of an amphitheatre

Berenike (Benghazi) I BC fin./I AD init.
ed.. — J. and G. Roux, *REG* 62 (1949) 281-96 (pl.3)

(ἔτους) [ ]γ΄. Φ[αμ]ένωθ ε΄ ἐπὶ ἀρχόντων Ἀρίμμα τοῦ
[*7 letters*]ος Δωρίωνος τοῦ Πτολεμαίου
Ζελαιου τοῦ [Γ]ναίου Ἀρίστωνος τοῦ Ἀραξα-
[ ]ντος Σαρα[πί]ωνος τοῦ Ἀνδρομάχου Νικία
τ[οῦ *9-10 letters*]Α[ ]ΣΑ[ ] τοῦ Σίμωνος. *v.* ἐπεὶ
[Δέκ]μος Ο[ὐαλέριος Γ]αίο[υ Διον]ύσιος ΠΡΗΠΟΤΗΣ
[*±9*] ΩΓΗΣ ἀνὴρ καλὸς καὶ ἀγαθὸς ὢν δια-
τελε[ῖ ?λόγῳ καὶ ἔργῳ καὶ αἱρ]έσει καὶ ποιῶν ἀγαθὸν
[ὅτι] ἄ[ν] δ[ύνηται καὶ κοι]νᾶι καὶ ἰδίαι ἑκάστωι τῶν
π[ο]λιτ[ων] καὶ δ[ὴ καὶ] ἐκονίασεν τοῦ ἀνφιθεάτρου
τ[ὸ ἔδ]αφος καὶ τοὺ[ς] τοίχους ἐζωγράφησεν
ἔ[δοξε τοῖς ἄ]ρχουσι καὶ τῶι πολιτεύματι
τ[ῶν] ἐν Βερνικίδι Ἰουδαίων καταγράψαι αὐτὸν εἰς
τὸ τῶν τ[*±6*]ΕΥΕΙΣΥΔΙΟΥ καὶ εἶεν ἀλειτούρ-
γητο[ν πά]σης [λε]ιτουρ[γί]ας [ὁ]μοίως δὲ καὶ στε-
φα[νοῦν α]ὐτὸν καθ' ἑκάστην σύνοδον καὶ νουμη-
νίαν στε[φ]άνωι [ἐλ]αίνωι καὶ λημνίσκωι ὀνομαστί
τὸ [δ]ὲ ψήφισμα τόδε ἀναγράψαντες οἱ ἄρχον[τες]
[εἰ]ς στήλην λίθου Παρίου θέτωσαν εἰς τὸν ἐ[πι-]

[σημ]ὀ̣τατον [τόπ]ον τοῦ ἀμφιθεάτρου.
λευκαὶ πᾶσαι
vac.
Δέκμος Οὐαλέριος Γαΐου Διονύσιος
τὸ ἔ̣[δ]α̣[φ]ος ἐκονίασεν καὶ τὸ ἀμφι-
θέατρον καὶ ἐζωγράφησεν τοῖς
ἰδίοις δαπανήμασιν ἐπίδομα
τῶι πολιτεύματι.

Badly worn inscription on a marble stele tapering towards the top, with a moulded gable and akroteria and a moulded base (37-39B x 77H x 11D cm.). Letter size varies from .012-.017m. Date based on letter shape and use of iota adscript.

Bib. — *CIG* III (1843; repr. 1977) 5362 and p.1241 (contains only the final five lines, so the Roux text is here treated as *ed.pr.*); **I.Berenike* 18 (further bib. listed there); G. Lüderitz, *Corpus jüdischer Zeugnisse aus der Cyrenaika* (Wiesbaden, 1983) 148-51 no.70.

In the year ̣ 3, on the 5th Phamenoth, in the archonship of Arimmas son of . . ., Dorion son of Ptolemaios, Zelaios son of Gnaius, Ariston son of Araxa. . ., Sarapion son of Andromachos, Nikias | son of . . ., *N.* son of Simon. Whereas Dec(i)mus Valerius Dionysios son of Gaius . . . remains an honourable and good man in word and deed and by inclination, doing whatever good he can, both in a public capacity and as a private individual to each one of the | citizens, and in particular plastered the floor of the amphitheatre and painted its walls, the archons and the *politeuma* of the Jews at Berenike resolved to register him in the . . . of the . . . and (resolved) that he be exempted from liturgies | of every kind; and likewise (they resolved) to crown him with an olive crown and a woollen fillet, naming him at each synod and at the new moon. After engraving this resolution on a stele of Parian marble the archons are to set it in the most visible | place in the amphitheatre. (Votes:) all white. Dec(i)mus Valerius Dionysios son of Gaius plastered the floor and the amphitheatre and painted (it) at his | own expense as a contribution to the *politeuma*.

In this inscription we see a Roman citizen who is probably a Jew being honoured unanimously (*l.*21) by the Jewish community of Berenike in Cyrenaica for his patronage. Singled out for special mention is his plastering of the floor and adorning with paintings (ἐζωγράφησεν, 11, 24) the walls of the amphitheatre. This text thus adds to the growing body of material evidence for the rapprochement between the Jewish communities and their neighbours both in Palestine and in the Diaspora, and the breakdown of the old concept of a rigid, 'normative' Jewry observing the strictest interpretation of the Law. For earlier summaries of the problem see, e.g., M. Avi-Yonah, *Oriental Art in Roman Palestine* (Rome, 1961) 29-42 (now subject to some modification in the light of more recent, detailed archaeological publications); A.T. Kraabel, *ANRW* II.19.1 (1979) 477-510; cf. J. Pelikan's foreword (xix-xxi) to the augmented re-issue of C.H. Kraeling et al., *The Excavations at Dura-Europos. Final Report*, VIII.1. *The Synagogue* (New York, 1979); E.M. Meyers, *BA* (1980) 97-108; and especially N. Avigad, *Beth She'arim* III, *Catacombs 12-23* (New Brunswick, 1976) 2, 275-87. For a more popular, but eminently readable account, see H. Shanks, *Judaism in Stone* (New York, 1979) 151-161.

The debate has tended to focus on the use or otherwise of representations of living things, especially humans. The older view is as well known as it was seemingly well documented: based on the embargo on graven images in Ex. 20.4-5 and Deut. 5.8-9, the existence was accepted of a 'normative' Judaism which eschewed all such imagery along with other cultural importations which seemed to bear on the matter. This view is amply supported not only in Rabbinic literature but, for the earlier Imperial period, by Josephus: when Herod instituted gladiatorial games at Jerusalem it was not the games themselves which produced the main outcry (though Josephus does state that the taking of human life for sport was abhorrent), but rather the trophies around the arena, erroneously taken to be disguised 'images of men' (*Ant.* XV.272-81). The Golden Eagle which Herod placed over the main gate of the Temple complex was assaulted with axes (*BJ* I.648-55; *Ant.* XVII.151-64). Similarly, later, it was the busts on the standards of Pilate's troops rather than the troops themselves which provoked the wrath of the population (*BJ* III.169-74; *Ant.* XVIII.55-59). The classicising palace of Herod's descendants at Tiberias was burned during the First Revolt on the grounds that it contained representations of animals (*Vita* 65-66). And the reaction to Caligula's attempt to place his own statue in the Temple was predictable (e.g., *BJ* II.184-203; *Ant.* XVIII.261-309).

It should be noted that this view of 'normative' Judaism was based almost exclusively on the foundation of literary evidence, epigraphical and archaeological testimony being interpreted in the light of such passages. Perhaps the best known instance of such 'explanation' is that of E.R. Goodenough, *Jewish Symbols in the Graeco-Roman World* (12 vols; New York, 1953-64), who postulated an esoteric Hellenising Jewish sect in the Diaspora to account for the depiction of Biblical scences such as those in the synagogue at Dura Europos.

Half a century ago E.L. Sukenik, *Ancient Synagogues in Palestine and Greece* (London, 1934) 63-64, mooted the idea that throughout the history of Judaism there were always some who interpreted the Law more rigorously and others who took a more 'latitudinarian' attitude. In times of crisis, when the Jews felt themselves threatened, the more stringent view gained general acceptance; in better times a more liberal attitude could prevail. His thesis was prompted by the representations of living (and semi-divine pagan) creatures in the decoration of the synagogues he examined, most spectacularly that of Capernaum, with Erotes and an *eagle* over the main gate which were otherwise 'explained away' by various ingenious hypotheses. In point of fact, animal, human or quasi-divine representations are attested for approximately thirty of the synagogues dealt with by Chiat, *Synagogue Art*: Ahmadiyya (Chiat, 615), 'Ammudim (153), Beth Alpha (275-77), Beth Shan B (290-91), Beth She'arim (159), Capernaum (206-07), Chorazin (217), Daburah (621-22), En-Gedi (514), En-Natosh (627), Er-Ramah (106), Gaza A (416), Gerasa (Jerash) A (741-42), Hammat Gadara (721), Hammath Tiberias B (231-32), Husifah (379-80), Japhia/Yaffa (164), Kafr Bar'am A (73-74), Kafr Danna (308), Kefar Qarnan (294-95), Khirbet Semâka (383), Khirbet Susiva (527), Khirbet Zamimra (629), Ma'on (556), Ma'oz Hayyim (298), Na'aran (586-87), Nabratein A (96), Qusbiyah (631), Salokia (632). As well, there is figured decoration in the doubtful synagogue at Khirbet Tieba (129). All this cannot be explained away as the result of well-intentioned but ignorant Gentile patrons or Gentile craftsmen whose work was unaccountably tolerated: Chiat argues from the inscriptions that Jewish artists participated in the decoration of the synagogues at Beth Alpha and possibly Khirbet Susiva, as well as in the non-figurative decoration of 'Alma and Kafr Bar'am B (respectively, 278, 528, 100, 112; for an indication of the problem whether 'made' refers to the donor or manufacturer, cf., e.g., 209).

While the indifferent quality of the plates in vol.4 of the microfilm copy of Chiat makes it difficult to determine whether the outside influence goes beyond the fact of figured representations (as it does, for example, in the famous Beth Alpha zodiac) in the case of the less widely published sites, it is patent that the relaxation of the embargo on 'graven images' was no mere aberration of a 'contaminated' Diaspora. For the synagogues do not stand alone: since Avigad's publication of the material from catacomb 20 at Beth She'arim (*Beth She'arim*, III) it has become apparent that in the Roman/Byzantine period a wide degree of latitude in such matters prevailed. At the end of II the 'latitudinarian' rabbi Judah Ha-Nassi, editor of the Mishnah, moved the Sanhedrin to Beth She'arim, which he adorned with columnar (i.e., in this time and place, classicising) architecture celebrated in Rabbinic literature. After his death, if not before, the city became the burial centre for wealthy Jews of Palestine and the Diaspora, buried for the most part in sarcophagi in over twenty catacombs. In catacomb 20, rabbis designated as 'the holy ones' lay in plain sarcophagi side by side with other Jews in sarcophagi bearing representations, as in the synagogues, of animals, humans and pagan quasi-divinities.

There is no question of these figured sarcophagi belonging to members of an esoteric, Hellenised sect outside the Jewish Establishment. Beth She'arim *was* the Jewish Establishment. It is clear that by this time 'normative' Judaism was pluralistic, encompassing alike both those who favoured a stringent interpretation of the Scriptures such as would preclude Classical influence, and those who took a more liberal attitude. Goodenough's hypothesis and similar 'explanations' are no longer necessary to account for these 'anomalies', since the 'anomalies' may now be seen to be part of the norm.

Although the relaxation of the embargo on figured decoration is the most striking instance of the rapprochement between the Jews and their neighbours in the Late Roman period, and enabled the admission of further influence, it is by no means the only manifestation. It has long been recognised that synagogue architecture owed much to contemporary Roman architecture, both in type (the so-called 'basilica' synagogues) and in detail — indeed, recent evidence suggests that more influence in this respect has been postulated than was actually present. Considerably more non-basilican, 'broadhouse' synagogues have now been recorded in Palestine and adjacent areas (Chiat, *passim*; for the distinction in synagogue types see, e.g., E.M. Meyers/J.F. Strange, *Archaeology, the Rabbis and Early Christianity* [London, 1981] 142-52). More generally, Kraabel (501) has cogently challenged the whole notion of applying such categorisation to Diaspora synagogues, though he does allow something of the kind for 'the Holy Land'. Even for the latter Meyers (*art.cit.*, 97-108) is similarly sceptical of the idea of a rigid stylistic development. But the concept does still seem valid for the Palestine area: Chiat includes over a score of synagogues which appear to fit the 'basilica' category, in addition to the well-known Galilee examples at Capernaum, Chorazin and Kafr Bar'am (see Chiat, 60-69, 86-98, 108-10, 118-20, 150-54, 157-66, 222-27, 271-75, 281-85, 296-302, 353-55, 377-79, 382-84, 583-85, 714-15, 717, 759; doubtful examples: 37, 326, 414, 636, 774). This evidence is sufficient to indicate a deliberate preference for the form, that is to say, a true architectural type, as opposed to the possibly fortuitous instances involving re-used buildings in the Diaspora. In detail, too, these synagogues reflect the influence of the Roman world: for example, Avigad argues (*Beth She'arim* III, 51-52) that the characteristic triple-façade, with three entrances, found in catacombs 14 and 20 as well as in many of the synagogues in Palestine, is a modification of Roman structures such as triple-arched gates and triumphal arches. Idiosyncratic details of individual synagogues also attest the impact of Classical influence in various forms.

In toto, the non-literary evidence suggests a picture very different from that previously envisaged.

The date at which this new hybrid Judaeo-Roman art began to flourish cannot be determined with precision. It is tempting to see the activities of Judah Ha-Nassi as the floodgate, giving official endorsement to earlier tendencies which may have been regarded as suspect. Avigad dates the two most classicising catacombs (14 and 20) late II/early III. However, as he himself points out, none of the evidence is conclusive. The strongest argument for the II/III date was the manifest architectural similarity to the 'early Galilean' group of synagogues, previously dated Late Antonine/Early Severan. However, the new excavations at the synagogue at Capernaum in the early 1970s have thrown the whole chronology of the development of synagogues into confusion, the excavators dating the relevant building phase at Capernaum to the fourth century, though this is still controversial. For the debate see, e.g., Chiat, 75, 96-97, 209-10 and nn. 211-12, 838-39. (An abstract of a paper by Chiat, *AJA* 88 [1984] 240, indicates that she has devised a new chronological scheme for the synagogues, but gives no details.) To my knowledge, the earliest independent dates from finds for any of the other similar synagogues are later III. If the synagogues must be dated late III, there is no insuperable barrier to Beth She'arim catacombs 14 and 20 being relocated to this period.

There are indications, however, that the prohibition on 'graven images' was already breaking down in early II AD Palestine. In later times, rules are attested for 'cancelling' such images to make it permissible to use the articles, metal vessels and so forth, which bore them (see Y. Yadin, *The Finds from the Bar Kokhba Period in the Cave of Letters* [Jerusalem, 1963] 121 and n.22; cf. 119 n.20; note also Avigad, *Beth She'arim* III, 278). What appear to be examples of such 'cancelled' images have been found on metal vessels (Yadin, 58-60, 59 fig. 16 and pl.17) in the Cave of Letters, the headquarters of the Jewish leader of the Second Revolt, Simon Bar-Kokhba, together with a seal with an unusual scene, apparently of Herakles and the Nemean Lion, which Yadin ingeniously suggests was specially designed for Bar Kokhba in a 'pre-cancelled' form: Herakles lacks his definitive attribute, the club (ibid., 119, 121 and 118 fig. 44). There is also the somewhat dubious evidence of rabbinic literature for the existence of more liberal rabbis in this period. For instance, Sukenik cites (63-64) a very interesting statement attributed to a son of Gamaliel to the effect that 'our family used a seal with faces engraved on it'. See further, e.g., S.S. Lieberman, *Greek in Jewish Palestine* (New York, 1965) 20; T. Rajak, *Josephus. The Historian and his Society* (London, 1983) 59 and n.38.

The roots of the Judaeo-Roman architecture characteristic of the 'early' synagogues and Beth She'arim catacombs 14 and 20 can be followed back even further. There is an exceptional tomb in the Jerusalem necropolis in the Valley of Hinnom with a triple-entrance façade, the middle door surmounted by an arch, as in many of the synagogues, with other possible indications of Roman influence (Avigad, *IEJ* 1 [1950/1] 104-06 and 105 fig.9; *Beth She'arim*, III.94, 133 n.27). Avigad dates it just prior to the First Revolt, though there seems no obstacle to assigning it a slightly later date, between the First and Second Revolts, since Jews were not at that time excluded from Jerusalem.

For first-century Judaea generally, matters are more problematic. Judaea was, as Kraabel concedes, a smaller, more homogeneous area than the Diaspora, and it was also at this time and in this place that there obtained the conditions which, following Sukenik's hypothesis, should promote the predominance of a more rigid stance. The memory of the policies of Antiochus IV Epiphanes had been re-awakened by the more extreme efforts of Herod I and his descendants to promote Graeco-Roman culture, and was reinforced by the less tactful gestures of Romans such as Pompey, Pilate, Caligula and Gessius Florus. The predictable result was a hostile awareness of the phenomenon of acculturation on the part of the Jews, and the tendency to regard any Classical influence as a threat to their national identity and especially to their religion. The passages relating to the period from the reign of Herod to the First Revolt already cited from Josephus demonstrate this; numerous others could be mentioned. The causes of the Revolt were doubtless many and varied, but the religio-cultural element is hardly to be disputed. The actual trigger was a disagreement over the propriety of sacrifices on behalf of the reigning emperor in the Temple (Jos., *BJ* II.409).

Yet even here there are indications of a diversity of attitudes. In Josephus' account of the trophies incident, when Herod undresses the trophies and shows them to be merely wooden stands (*Ant.* XV.279) this causes much laughter, and most of the people change their minds about their disapproval of the games — only some persist in their opposition. While the ornamentation of Herod's buildings may have been abominated, classicising architecture *per se* was in a more ambiguous position. Herod's Temple was admired — see Mk. 13.1-2 and the less explicit parallel passage in Mt. 24.1-2 — but translating admiration into imitation was a different matter. The main body of evidence for the private architecture of the wealthier classes, where one would expect to see such imitation, is the Jerusalem necropolis (e.g. Avi-Yonah, *Oriental Art*, ch.1; Avigad, *IEJ* 1 [1950/1] 96-106). Herod's architecture comprised two varieties of classicising style: old local Hellenistic forms, and new, 'state-of-the-art' Roman innovations, almost certainly produced with the aid of Roman experts, the latter best attested in the more recent excavations. On this question see most recently E. Netzer, *Greater Herodium* (*Qedem* 13; Jerusalem, 1981) *passim*, which provides earlier bibliography. The architecture of the tombs is classicising, but entirely in an Eastern Hellenistic manner, and with a repertoire of scrupulously aniconic decorative motifs, such as garlands, vine leaves and bunches of grapes; from this point of view the tombs are stylistically undifferentiated, though the presumed timespan covers the Hellenistic and Roman periods to the First Revolt. The only real exception is the tomb with the triple façade in the Valley of Hinnom, mentioned above. In other words, there was an established class of people who were prepared to admit some degree of Classical influence, provided it did not, in their opinion, conflict with the Law; they were ready to use well-established forms, but were suspicious of the new.

Exactly who these more tolerant people were is uncertain. Avi-Yonah identifies them as the Sadducees, very much in contrast to the Pharisees. However, since the Sadducees were effectively wiped out by the First Revolt, but the art characteristic of these tombs survived to become the basis of the later Judaeo-Roman synagogue art with the addition of figured representations, he is left with the uncomfortable conclusion that these people perished but their artistic tradition survived among their former opponents, the Pharisees. There is also the problem of Josephus himself, almost certainly a Pharisee (see Rajak, *Josephus*, 44, 224), but with a lively appreciation of Classical architecture and sculpture: see, e.g., his description (*BJ* VII.158-62) of Vespasian's Temple of Peace, with its art treasures. (For a good evaluation of the artificial problem of Thackeray's much-vaunted amanuenses, which bears on Josephus' own classicism, see now Rajak, ibid., 47-48, 50, 62-63, 232-36.) It may be that the distinction was not sectarian but economic. At this time there was a substantial upper class faction which supported Roman rule politically, and ultimately fought on the Roman side during the First Revolt, Josephus' famous pro-Roman 'moderates', whose method of responding to provocation was not revolt but deputations, conferences and 'passive resistance' (see, e.g., *BJ* I.11; II.72-75, 80-92, 192-98, 236-40, 280, 316, 321-25, 345-401, 411-20, 422, 529, 556; IV.97, 128, 134, 151, 163-92; V.362-419). Their existence is confirmed by Jn 11.47-52 and 16.13-14: compare the arguments ascribed to Caiaphas the high-priest with those attributed to the magistrates in *BJ* II.237. In accordance with the apologetic purpose of his work, Josephus represents them as the solid majority as opposed to a few scurrilous brigands who happened to get into power at the time of the First Revolt; but he also refers to them in ways which show them to be members of the Herodian family and other upper and priestly class families, i.e., 'the Establishment' (cf. Rajak, *CQ* 23

[1973] 351). One would expect some concordance between this group and the owners of the tombs. But the correspondence is not exact: one of the tomb façades is identified as the property of the proselyte kings and queens of Adiabene, who fought with the revolutionaries in the First Revolt.

There are even slight indications of the existence of people who did not cavil at representations of living things. Josephus, clearly, did not avert his gaze from such objects, but given the time, place and circumstances of the composition of the *Jewish War*, Josephus may have been atypical. However, Sukenik notes (64) a quotation attributed to R. Eleazar b. R. Zadok (who would have known Jerusalem in the period before its destruction in the First Revolt): 'In Jerusalem there were the faces of all creatures except men'. Unfortunately, even if the quotation is correctly attributed, there is no way of knowing who was responsible for these images.

The evidence, manifestly inadequate as it is, therefore seems to point in different directions: little or no fresh Classical influence; only forms established in Maccabaean times; Classical influence provided it did not conflict with the strict interpretation of the Second Commandment; images, other than those of men. Insofar as any conclusion may be drawn, it would seem that Sukenik was right: there was always a broad spectrum of views, and the prevailing one varied depending on the time, place and circumstances. We have been listening to only one voice, when in fact there were always several.

Against this background much of the dispute surrounding the present inscription seems unnecessary. The argument of J. and G. Roux (290-93, supported by *BE* [1951] 246) is that ἀμφιθέατρον (10) cannot carry its normal meaning of a structure designed for gladiatorial combat. Rather, it must represent a new meaning for the word which makes its reference to shape rather than function and here designates a structure belonging to the Jewish *politeuma*, used for meetings and so forth.

The principal arguments are that the Jewish community would have used the city amphitheatre for its meetings only occasionally at most and by special permission. Yet the Jews must have been under some obligation to contribute to its upkeep, since Valerius Dionysios' benefaction could only be an ἐπίδομα | τῶι πολιτεύματι (*ll.*25-26) if he relieved the Jewish community of a civic obligation by paying the whole amount himself. It is also claimed in *ed.pr.* that the plastering of the floor precludes an amphitheatre in the normal sense, because sand was used for the floor of an arena. Reynolds (247) defends the more straightforward interpretation, answering these arguments in their own terms. Noting that no 'civic amphitheatre' of the type postulated by *ed.pr.* has been found at Benghazi, she points out that the existence of such a structure there at this time would place Berenike ahead of Campania — one of the earliest areas in Italy to develop amphitheatres — with which it was certainly in contact. Reynolds also notes E. Gabba's argument that at the likely date of this text the word ἀμφιθέατρον was too new to have acquired a metaphorical sense. For painting in an amphitheatre she cites the painted corridor walls in the amphitheatre at Ptolemais, but is reliant on parallels with theatres for plastered floors and for Jewish usage of such facilities. Jewish usage is attested by the passage already cited from *Ant.* XV.272-81: the trophies incident from near-contemporary Judaea clearly indicates that the majority of the population withdrew its objections to the contests once the matter of forbidden images had been settled. As for the matter of plastered flooring, this need not have been in the arena since there was more to a formally built amphitheatre than an arena: the decision that the stele should be placed in the ἐ[πισημ]ότατον [τόπ]ον τοῦ ἀμφιθεάτρου (*l.*20) implies as much, since it would be difficult to determine what part of the periphery of an arena was ἐπισημότατος, and it is hardly likely that it was placed within the arena itself.

More importantly, the whole debate can now be seen to be somewhat superfluous: the objections to the most straightforward interpretation of the text were engendered by the presupposition that there was something extraordinary about the idea of a Jewish community patronising the amphitheatre of the city, being therefore subject, like other members of the city, to contributions to its upkeep and adornment, and conferring typically Graeco-Roman honours on a co-religionist who relieved the Jewish *politeuma* of its obligations by undertaking the work at his own expense. There need be nothing untoward about such a state of affairs in Berenike around the turn of the era, and no barrier to the most straightforward interpretation.

The inscription gives us no information about the form of the decoration which Valerius Dionysios commissioned. It is possible that the figured wall-painting from the Dura-Europos synagogue provides an analogy (so *ed.pr.*, 293); but this is not conclusive at all, for ζωγραφέω (11, 24) is too non-specific. There are alternatives. If it were deemed desirable to give the decoration a particularly Jewish flavour, the aniconic repertoire from the Jerusalem tombs, Jewish coins and ossuaries could have provided suitable motifs. Again, we may think of the architectural perspectives of contemporary Pompeian wall-paintings (e.g., the widely-illustrated *cubiculum* of the House of the Silver Wedding, or that of the Villa of the Mysteries) which, shorn of their figured inserts, could easily have provided a model that did not violate the letter of the Law — were that deemed of importance. The effect may have been similar to the non-figured wall-painting in Herod's Palace at Masada. A better indication of the boundaries of assimilation at this time and in this place may be that Valerius Dionysios was *not* voted a statue: no mention of a statue is made in the decree (*ll.*1-21), the form of the *titulus* (*ll.*22-26) with Valerius Dionysios' name in the nominative, would be unusual for a statue, and the stele, with a depth of only 11cm. is patently unsuitable either for the base of a statue or for a support for such a base. Clearly the monument was the stele itself. But the mere refurbishing of part of the amphitheatre may not in any case have merited a statue.

The problem of the honorand's exact status is also incapable of complete resolution. D. Valerius Dionysios appears to be a Roman citizen. The lack of tribal affiliation does not prove freedman status (so Reynolds, 246-47). But it is likely that he was a Jew in view of his exemption from future liturgies by the Jewish *politeuma* which is honouring him (ibid.).

Approached without the presupposition of a rigid, 'normative' Judaism, this inscription can go some way towards helping us to determine what the Jewish norm was at this time and in this particular place. Even on the most conservative interpretation it indicates a strong degree of assimiliation, and amicable interaction with the community of Berenike at large. The same is true of many recently published or re-published inscriptions. For example, *I.Berenike* 17 (= Lüderitz, no.17), dated 24/5, was likewise set up in the amphitheatre. It provides honours for a Roman official, acclaimed for his services to the city in general and to the Jewish *politeuma* in particular. Again, the most natural interpretation yields a picture of a Jewish community which retained its identity within the city as a whole, but viewed itself as part of that city, participating in the common concerns.

Finally, a brief comment is pertinent on the registration of the unanimous vote in favour of the resolution in the text with which we began. The phrase λευκαὶ πᾶσαι at *l.*21 — *I.Berenike* 17 carries the identical wording in *l.*28 — has already been noted at *New Docs 1976*, **39**, where some other instances of λευκός, 'favourable vote', are noted. Whether this usage helps to elucidate the variously interpreted wording at Rev. 2.17, δώσω αὐτῷ ψῆφον λευκήν, is uncertain. On the interpretation of this wording see most recently C.J. Hemer, *The Letters to the Seven Churches of Asia in Their Local Setting* (*JSNT* Suppl. 11; Sheffield, 1986) 96-102.

(R. TRACEY)

112. Forfeiture of Jewish property

P.Köln 97 (provenance unknown within Egypt, II [earlier rather than later]; pl. 11) is the left upper portion of a papyrus sheet concerning the arrangement for collection of taxes from land estates. Although too fragmentary to be worth reprinting, it does deserve brief notice; for the phrase Ἰουδαικοῦ λόγου occurs twice (*ll.*8, 15). This phrase has been certainly attested once previously, at *SB* 12.1 (1976) 10893 (provenance unknown, II): *ed.pr.* — A. Świderek, *JJP* 16/17 (1971) 61-62. In the introduction to the *P.Köln* text D. Hagedorn plausibly restores [λόγου] in *CPJ* III.458.1 (Fayum, II) to reveal the presence of the phrase in that text as well.

These three texts belong to a period of up to three generations after the Jewish revolt under Trajan (115-17), whose repercussions were to affect permanently the profile adopted by the Jewish community in Egypt. It has sometimes been said that those Jews whose property was confiscated by the state after the revolt had actually participated in it, whether surviving or not, e.g., E.M. Smallwood, *The Jews Under Roman Rule* (*Studies in Judaism in Late Antiquity* 20; Leiden, 1976) 405. Smallwood was apparently unaware of Świderek's discussion, and based her observation upon several papyri reprinted in *CPJ*. *CPJ* II.445 (Oxyrhynchos, 117/8?; = *P.Oxy.* 9 [1912] 1189) is a letter 'concerning the schedule of property formerly owned by the Jews', περὶ γραφῆς τῶν τοῖς [Ἰ]ουδαί|οις ὑπαρξάντων (*ll.*9-10). *CPJ* II.448 (Oxyrhynchos, 130; = *P.Oxy.* 3 [1903] 500) appears to refer to land forfeited to state control which had been owned by Jews killed (in the revolt) and by Greeks who died without heirs, . . . | ἀ[π' Ἰ]ουδαίων ἀνειρη[μ]ένων καὶ | Ἑλλήνων ἀ[κλ]ηρονομήτων (*ll.*10-12). Świderek (60 n.23) has suggested emending the first participle here — itself an emendation adopted by Fuks in *CPJ*, n. ad loc. — to ἀφειρη[μ]ένων, 'whose goods were forfeit', thus bringing it into line more closely with what is said in *CPJ* 448. *CPJ* III.468 (Hermopolis, late II or III; = *P.Amh.* 2 [1901] 98.6-11) may provide indirect testimony to the transfer of Jewish property into the hands of others; for this document is a summary of a sale contract for property 'in the Jewish lane', ἐπὶ τῆ[ς] | Ἰουδ(αϊκῆς) λαύρας (*ll.*9-10).

Another, much longer papyrus (Fayum, after 188) also published by Świderek in the same article (45-61; = *SB* 12.1 [1976] 10892), refers in several places in abbreviated form to rent for land that was (πρότερον) Ἰουδ(αίων). The phrase may have occurred as many as 16 times in the surviving 100 lines. As Świderek concludes, the very existence of a special category of land, the 'formerly Jewish category', implies that 'these confiscations had been effected on a vast scale' (62). While not ruling out the possibility that these forfeitures were confined to those who participated in the revolt, she thinks it probable that these confiscations affected all Jews (60). If so, and if this remained the position, it *may* explain why in *P.Oxy.* 44 (1976) 3203 (June/July 400) — repr. at *New Docs 1976*, **82** — a Jew is leasing part of a house from two nuns. It may also encourage the view that the landholder Sambathion who is mentioned in his advocate's memoranda was not Jewish: *P.Col.* 174 (noted at **116** below).

It was not only property that was affected. The decimation of their numbers in the revolt resulted in Jews adopting a less public visibility in Egypt. After the revolt references to Jews in the papyri are much less frequent, and more passing (such as the *CPJ* III.468 reference to the 'Jewish lane', noted above) than before. More striking is the near dearth of documents written by Jews, especially private letters. This point has already been made at *New Docs 1978*, **100**, p.142. That entry included discussion (146-47) of the question whether by the fourth century we should expect those bearing OT names to be Jews, or Christians in the main. An article forthcoming in *Numen* deals with this subject more generally, in the wider context of name-change as an indication of religious conversion, a phenomenon by no means confined to antiquity.

CPJ III covers the period from early III-VII AD; a considerable number of the texts included belong to late III or IV. Of these, several are included solely because of the presence of a Bible name or one which appears to have affinity with such. The implication of their inclusion is that these individuals are to be interpreted as Jews. Yet if R. Bagnall's argument is sound, *BASP* 19 (1982) 105-24, that the pace of conversion to Christianity after early IV was very rapid, then several texts included in *CPJ* III *on the ground of Jewish nomenclature* may well be referring rather to Christians.

Now, at p.4 of *CPJ* III Tcherikover acknowledged that some of his inclusions were at least open to doubt as Judaica. These items are: 469 (cf. his comment at the end of p.3), 470, 472a, 472b, 473, 474, 475 (yet cf. his commentary on this text, ad loc.), 476, 477, 478a, 479, 480. The reason why he inclines to accept all these Isaacs, Johannes, etc., as Jews rather than as Christians is because of their social class: '. . . almost all of them are men of the lower classes of society (field-hands, and the like) and it would seem that Christianity, by the end of the third and the beginning of the fourth centuries, had not yet made great progress in its penetration from urban centres like Alexandria into the Egyptian villages' (*CPJ* III, p.4). It is true that the view popularised by Deissmann (*LAE* 6 n.1, 7, 8, 9, 55, 62, 144, etc.), that the Christians were from the lower and middle classes, has been brought under serious challenge. See W.A. Meeks, *The First Urban Christians* (New Haven, 1983) 51-53; and the references cited in G.H.R. Horsley, *Biblica* 65 (1984) 395 n.9. But as a blanket criterion for deciding whether a text is Jewish or Christian Tcherikover's position will not do.

Accordingly, listed below are all *CPJ* III texts claimed by their inclusion as Jewish (as distinct from those included because they refer to Jews or to Judaism), about which there *may* be some legitimate doubt now in the light of Bagnall's hypothesis. The tabulation below is *deliberately maximal* in the hope of stimulating further scrutiny of the question. Only the briefest of annotations are added, and the commentaries in *CPJ* are assumed.

455 (Theadelphia, 137) — Isakous
459 col.IX (Fayum, 149) — Somoeilos
[These two may be too early to be Christian; but is the identification of each name with a Bible name (Isaac, Samuel) really strong enough to suggest Judaism?]
469 (provenance unknown, III) — Eissak
470 (provenance unknown, Roman period) — Josepos
471 (Sebennytos in the Fayum, III) — Abramos
472a, b (Euhemereia, III) — Aurelius Johannes
474a (Karanis, 13/11/304) — Johannes (see ed. n. to *l*.2)
474b (Karanis 17/11/306) — the same Johannes
475 (Oxyrhynchos, *c*.295) — Jacob
476 (Oxyrhynchos, late III/early IV) — Isak
477 (Oxyrhynchos, 300) — Aurelius Isak
478a (Karanis, III) — Enoch
479 (provenance unknown, III or IV) — Josep
480 (Karanis, early IV) — Isak
501 (provenance unknown, IV) — Judas, Isak son of Eirene, Nathan, Nahum
502 (provenance unknown, IV) — Isak
517 (Antinoopolis, early IV) — Isak ('Since writing and phraseology indicate the first half of the fourth century, Isak may well have been a Jew', ed. comm., ad loc.).

By VI AD it was quite usual for Jews to be so designated explicitly, e.g.:

508 (Antinoopolis, 542) — Aurelius Josephios, Ἰουδαίῳ τὴν θρησκείαν
509 (Oxyrhynchos, VI) — Enoch, Ἰουδαίου
511 (Antinoopolis, *c*.570) — Peret, Ἑβ[ρα]ίου τῷ ἔθνει
512 (Fayum, VI or VII) — Abraham, Ἑβρείῳ.

Such explicit identifications occur earlier, but are by no means the norm, e.g.:

515 (provenance unknown, II) — Noumenios Ἰουδ( )
P.Oxy. 44 (1976) 3203 (June/July 400) — Aurelius Jose son of Judas, Ἰουδαῖως; repr. at *New Docs 1976*, **82**.

It should be noted that E. Wipszycka, *ZPE* 62 (1986) 173-81, has argued that Bagnall's hypothesis is misguided. Her views have some cogency, especially the point that Christianity did not spread at a uniform rate in Egypt; it was probably slower to be accepted in rural areas than in urban centres, and even in the *chora* itself the process of Christianisation did not proceed consistently smoothly. Yet the issue raised above concerns only Jews and Christians; and in this regard the weight which Bagnall has rightly placed on the minuscule size of the visible Jewish population in Egypt still makes valid the questioning here of the attribution of these documents on onomastic grounds alone to a Jewish milieu.

On the revolt in Cyrenaica, attention may be drawn to what is now 'the major piece of evidence for the history of Cyrenaica in the mid-second century' (J.M. Reynolds, *JRS* 68 [1978] 111-21, at 121). In this article Reynolds has presented additional portions of an important inscription from Cyrene which contains a dossier of imperial letters and edicts issued under Hadrian and Antoninus Pius. The earliest dates to 135, the latest is 154. A considerable portion of the text was first published by P.M. Fraser, *JRS* 40 (1950) 77-90. A portion of this inscription is also discussed by J.H. Oliver, *GRBS* 20 (1979) 157-59 (cf. *AE* 636; further bibliography at Reynolds, 111 n.1; the earlier bibliographical notice in Tod, *PGE* 224 [= *JHS* 74 (1954) 84] is now superseded). It is clear that Hadrian personally intervened (see Reynolds, 118) to ensure restoration of buildings damaged during the course of the Jewish revolt at Cyrene — cf. E.M. Smallwood, *JRS* 42 (1952) 37-38 — and elsewhere in the province (Reynolds, 120). It is the date of the destruction of these buildings that makes the link with the revolt certain. Nowhere in the extant portion of the inscription are the Jews explicitly mentioned, though Reynolds (118) offers a restoration *exempli gratia* for *l*.31 which would allude to the revolt. This inscription is referred to (without the opportunity to take account of Reynolds' article) by S.A. Applebaum, *Jews and Greeks in Ancient Cyrene* (*Studies in Judaism in Late Antiquity*, 28; Leiden, 1979) 273, 292-94. (The title of this monograph is consistently wrongly printed in *SEG* 1670-74 as *Jews and Christians* . . ..) Applebaum's treatment of the revolt in Cyrenaica (much briefer attention is given to its effects elsewhere, such as in Egypt and Cyprus) is very full, and usefully balances the greater attention generally accorded to the revolt in Egypt on which papyrus texts have thrown considerable light. In the case of Cyrene itself archaeological excavation has served to expose particular buildings damaged at this period and subsequently restored, as well as inscriptions which testify explicitly to the *tumultu Iudaico*. This actual phrase occurs in *ll*.6-7 of a Hadrianic milestone dated 118/19, set up between Cyrene and the port of Apollonia: *SEG* 9 (1944) 252, cf. Applebaum, 272-73.

Better relations between Jews and their Roman neighbours in Cyrenaica are attested for an earlier date in *I.Berenike* 17 (24 Oct., 24/5 AD). This well-preserved inscription — cf. *BE* (1979) 658, and Applebaum, 161 — records the decision of the Jewish community (πολίτευμα, *ll*.17-18, 21-22) to honour a Roman citizen for his προστασία towards them (12, 19). On this term see

122 below. Not quite so completely legible is *I.Berenike* 18 (I BC fin./I AD init.), in which the Jewish *politeuma* again votes honours for a Roman citizen who is also probably a Jew. This text is reprinted and discussed at **111** above. *I.Berenike* 16 provides a list of benefactors who contributed to the renovation of the synagogue (55/6). If *I.Berenike* 23 is indeed to be dated by letter-shape to I AD (so Reynolds, ad loc.) then this tombstone, which bears only the name Εἰρήνα, may have been for a Jewish woman. Several of the funerary inscriptions from Apollonia, Cyrene's port city, also provide evidence of the presence of Jews, especially before early II: *I.Apollonia* 48 (I^2), 67 (probably I), perhaps also 77 (I) and 84b (Imperial). All these inscriptions are now reproduced with bibliography and brief commentary in G. Lüderitz, *Corpus jüdischer Zeugnisse aus der Cyrenaika* (Wiesbaden, 1983), respectively nos. 71, 70, 72, 73 (all Berenike), 2, 1, 4, 3 (all Apollonia). In an appendix to Lüderitz's useful collection, J.M. Reynolds publishes 25 further texts, several of which contain numerous related inscribed funerary panels.

113. An *archisynagogos* of Corinth?

Corinth — Imperial period

ed.pr. — D.I. Pallas/S.P. Dantes, *Ath. Eph.* (1977 [1979]) 81-82 no. 30 (pl.)

[- - - - - -]
διδάσ̣[καλος]
καὶ ἀρχ̣[ισυνάγωγ-]
ος τῆ[ς συναγω-]
[γῆς Κορίνθου?]

Very fragmentary portion of a marble plaque found on the Acrocorinth.
Bib. — **SEG* 300.

. . . teacher and *arch[isynagog]os* of the [synagogue of Corinth?].

Little can be made of this text on the basis of what is extant. The length of each line is quite uncertain. The only word which can be restored with confidence is διδάσ̣[καλος]; and this is by no means enough to establish a Jewish context for the inscription. Even if we were to accept as possible most of the editors' restorations, the final word suggested by them ought to be ruled out, at least. For, given the size of Corinth in the Roman period, it is certain to have had more than the one synagogue which Κορίνθου might imply, even were it not too unparalleled a word to include to serve as a suitable supplement. We have no inscriptions from Rome, for example, which mention 'the synagogue of Rome'. The fact that *CIJ* has only one

Jewish inscription from Corinth (I.718), possibly reading συν]ạγωγὴ Ἑβρ[αίων], does not prove there was only one in that city. Similarly, Acts 18.4, 7 should not be pressed to mean that there was only one synagogue to serve all the Jews in the city. Tantalising as it is to consider that we may have in this text epigraphical attestation of the position of *archisynagogos* at Corinth, thus paralleling the two instances at Acts 18.8, 17, it is only wishful thinking. In particular, it should be noted that since words with the prefix ἀρχ- are very common (cf. *New Docs 1977*, **2**, p.18), there is no basis for restoring ἀρχισυνάγωγος here in preference to numerous other words starting with that letter combination (e.g., ἀρχίβακχος, ἀρχιγερουσιάρχης [cf. *New Docs 1976*, **73**], ἀρχιδενδροφόρος ἀρχιδιάκονος). An equally debatable instance from the present year's culling is *SEG* 981 (Porto, n.d.), an undoubtedly Jewish inscription in view of the presence of the name Ellel (on this cf. **115**, below ad fin.); in the fragmentary first extant line *ed.pr.* (*non vidi*) suggests the surviving letters ΣΥΝ may be restored as συν|[αγωγῆς], or as [ἀρχι]συν|[αγώγου].

Yet there are numerous inscriptions from Greece and elsewhere in which the word *archisynagogos* occurs. A recent monograph has drawn attention to Jewish epigraphical attestations: B.J. Brooten, *Women Leaders in the Ancient Synagogue* (*Brown Judaic Studies* 36; Chico, 1982) 23. Several of these inscriptions are reprinted and discussed in B. Lifshitz, *Donateurs et fondateurs dans les synagogues juives* (*Cahiers de la Revue Biblique* 7; Paris, 1967). Unfortunately, he does not include items from Italy. For our purposes, however, Jewish usage is not the only focus of interest. The following list catalogues both certain documentary attestations of the noun, and ones which are subject to some doubt. All texts are of Imperial date unless otherwise specified. Items which attest the related feminine noun are included, as are texts which include the word in an orthographically different form.

I. Certain/very probable examples

Italy

1. *CIJ* I.265 (Rome), Latin epitaph (with Greek tag at the end) for Stafylus, *arconti* | *et archisynagogo*, set up by his wife.

2. I.282 (Rome), epitaph for Isak - - - | [ἀρχισυν]άγωγος - - - | - - - συναγωγῆ[ς]. Line length is quite uncertain, as only the bottom edge of the stone survives. The restoration of the noun is very likely in the context of the combined mention of a *synagogue*, and the name Isaac. Yet see no.21 below.

3. I.336 (Rome), Euphrasis ἀρχισυναγώ|γης (*sic*) commemorated in an epitaph.

4. I.383 (Rome), epitaph for Poly[m]nis ἀρχισυν<ά>γωγος of the synagogue of the Vernaculi.

5. I.504 (Rome), epitaph for Julianus, the *gerousiarch*, son of Julianus the *archisynagogos*.

6. I.553 (Capua), Latin epitaph for Alfius Iuda, *arcon arcosy*|*nagogus* (*sic*), erected by his wife.

7, 8. I.584 (Venosa), τάφως | Ἰωσὴφ ἀρχησυ|νάγωγως (*read* -γου) υἱὼς (*read* υἱοῦ) | Ἰωσὴφ ἀρχησυ-|ναγώγου. | [שָׁ]לוֹם עַל [מִשְׁכָּבוֹ], 'tomb of Joseph *archisynagogos*, son of Joseph *archisynagogos*. Peace be upon his grave'.

9. I.587 (Venosa), epitaph of the infant (νιπίου, *sic*) Kallistos, ἀρχουσιναγώ|γου (*sic*), aged 3 years 3 months. Is a child's possession of the title a further indication that it is hereditary (cf. no.584 above)? Or may it be merely honorific to signal the active service of a parent exercising functions under that title? *CIJ* I.120 (Rome) provides a close parallel, an epitaph for Iokathinos described as ἄρχων νήπιος (age not given). For analogous instances of children being accorded titles see *New Docs 1976*, **74,** p.116.

10. I.596 (Venosa), epitaph of Silvanus(?) ἀρχοσηνω|γόγου (*sic*).

11. I.638 (Brescia; = *IG* XIV.2304), fragmentary text with the lettering ἀρ]χισυνά|γωγο[ς, *or* -γώγο[υ.

12. M.F. Squarciapino, *La Rassegna Mensile di Israel* 36 (1970) 188 (Ostia, I?), Latin epitaph reading: *Plotio Fortunato* | *archisyn*(*agogo*) *fec*(*erunt*) *Plotius* | *Ampliatus Secundinus* | *Secunda. p*(*osuit*) *t*(*itulum*) ≪m≫(*emoriae*) *et Ofilia Basilia co*<*n*>*iugi b*(*ene*) *m*(*erenti*), 'For Plotius Fortunatus *archisynagogos*, Plotius Ampliatus, (Plotius?) Secundinus and (Plotia?) Secunda made it. Ofilia Basilia also erected the tombstone as a memorial for her well-deserving husband'.

Greece

13. *CIJ* I.731c (Kisamos in Crete, IV or V; text repr. with discussion in Brooten, 11-12, 41, whose pl.2 is very clear), epitaph commemorating Sophia of Gortyn πρεσβυτέρα | κὲ ἀρχισυναγώ|γισσα Κισάμου, 'elder and leader of the synagogue of Kisamos'. This feminine formation is analogous to words like διακόνισσα and πρεσβυτέρισσα. Note also the curious *pateressa* in *CIJ* I.606 (Venosa, III-VI; Brooten, 61-62). This text from Crete is repr. with a pl. in A.C. Bandy, *The Greek Christian Inscriptions of Crete* (*Χριστιανικαὶ Ἐπιγραφαὶ τῆς Ἑλλάδος* I; Athens, 1970) 142-43, Appendix, no.3. It is also noted in K. Mentzu-Meimare's list of titles for women in Greek inscriptions from IV-X: *JÖB* 32.2 (1982) 433-43 (= *XVI. internationaler Byzantinisten-kongress, Wien, Oktober 1981, Akten* II.2 [Vienna, 1982]) at 439, no.116; cf. *SEG* 32 (1982 [1985]) 1702. Another feature of this inscription is given brief attention at **5**, above. On women elders in Jewish communities see Brooten, 41-55, and add a IV/V epitaph from Malta for Eulogia πρεσβυτήρα, discussed by R.S. Kraemer, *HTR* 78 (1985 [1986]) 431-38.
14. *CIG* II (1843, repr. 1977) 2007f (Olynthos, date uncertain), Ailianos Neikon ὁ ἀρχισυνάγωγος θεοῦ ἥρωος and the college (τὸ κολλήγιον) set up the altar to Vibius Antonius.

Macedonia

15,16. *IG* X 2, 1 [1972] 288 (Thessalonike, 154), an epitaph erected by οἱ συνήθε[ις] τοῦ Ἡρακλέ|ος (*sic*) to a member of their association; the dating formula which follows speaks of the president (ἄρχισυν|αγωγοῦντος), secretary and financial officer of the group. In no.289 (dated 155) another, more fragmentary text relating to the same association, the participle is largely restored by analogy: [ἀρχισυνα]γωγοῦντος.

17. *BE* (1972) 263 (Thessalonike, 160; *ed.pr.* — P. Petsas, *AD* 244 [1969] *Chron.* 300-02 [pl.311γ]), funerary inscription set up by an association for a colleague: ἡ συνήθια Ἥρωνος | Αὐλωνίτου Γ. Ἰουλίῳ | Κρήσκεντι· οἱ περὶ ἀρχ(ι)|συνάγωγον Ἀρτέμωνα | ζυγοποιόν, ἱερῆ | Τρύφωνα, τὰ ἐκ τοῦ | γλωσσοκόμου γινό|μενα αὐτῷ μνίας | χάριν, 'the association of Heron Aulonites for Gaius Julius Crescens. The colleagues of the president Artemon the yoke-maker (and) the priest Tryphon (paid for) the costs arising from the sarcophagus for him as a memorial'.

18. J.M.R. Cormack in *Mélanges helléniques offerts à G. Daux* (Paris, 1974) 51-55 (Pydna, 250; pl; cf. *BE* [1976] 351; text repr. and discussed briefly at *New Docs 1976*, **5**, pp.26-27), dedication to Zeus Hypsistos by a guild of worshippers (θρησκευταί, *ll.*6, 17-18); one of the five titles of officials in this almost certainly non-Jewish text is *archisynagogos* (*ll.*12-13).

19. *SEG* 27 (1977) 267 (Beroia, Imperial period; *ed.pr.* — A. Romiopoulou, *AD* 28 [1973] *Chron.* 439 [pl. 392γ]; cf. *BE* 257; brief notice of the text in *BCH* 102 [1978] 706, with fig. 145 on 707), Ἀμμία ἡ γυνὴ καὶ Κουαρτίων | ὁ ὑὸς | Γεμέλλῳ μνήμης χάριν | καὶ οἱ συνήθεις οἱ περὶ | Ποσιδῶνιν τὸν ἀρ|χισυνάγωγον, 'Ammia his wife and Quartion his son, and the associates in the circle of Poseidonios the *archisynagogos*, for Gemellus as a memorial'. This text is by no means certainly Jewish (*pace* Brooten, 23): Gemellus was a member of the συνήθεια, whose president was Poseidonios. Cf. the entirely analogous wording in no.17. above.

Moesia Inferior

20. *CIJ* I.681 (Sofia), Latin funerary monument commemorating Joses *arcisina*(*vac.*)γος | *et principales* (*sic*). The curiosity here is that the word begins in Latin and concludes in Greek, with an intervening *vacat* (the syllable which should be there has been omitted). Brooten (36) reprints the text but omits the Greek syllable. This item is thus testimony to a very shaky bilingual ability by the letter-cutter. But we should not doubt the presence of the intended word *archisynagogos*.

Thrace

21. *IGRR* I.782, mention of C. Julius Valens as *archisynag*[*og*]*os* of the barbers' guild, τῇ συναγώ[γ]ῇ τῶν κουρέω[ν].

Asia Minor

22. *I.Smyrna* I (*I.K.* 23; Bonn, 1982) 295 (III or later; = *CIJ* II.741; text repr. and discussed by Brooten, 5-7, 10-11, and pl.1), Rufina the *archisynagogos* built a tomb for her freedmen and *threptoi*. She explicitly calls herself Ἰουδαία (*l.*1). See, very briefly, *New Docs 1978*, **17**, p.52, where C.J. Hemer suggests that she was head of her household.

23. *I.Eph.* IV.1251 (Imperial?), expression of good wishes for *archisynagogoi* and elders: τῶν ἀρ|χι≪σ≫υνα-|γωγ≪ῶ≫ν | καὶ τῶν πρεσβ(υτέρων) | πολλὰ | τὰ {τὰ} ἔτη. Almost certainly Jewish; not known to Brooten.

24. Lifshitz, no.16 (Teos, III; text supersedes the version in *CIJ* II.744; text repr. in Brooten, 161 no.24), P. Rutilius Joses ὁ διὰ βίου ἀρχισυνάγω[γος] funded with his wife the erection of a building, which Lifshitz assumes was a synagogue.
25. Lifshitz, no.29 (Myndos in Caria, at least IV/V, not altogether superseding the text in *CIJ* II.756; text repr. and discussed by Brooten, 13-14, and 157 no.4, whose pl.3 is very clear), perhaps a dedication to fulfil a vow of [Th]eopempte and her son Eusebios. In *l*.2 occurs the lettering [. .]χισυνς. The last symbol is an abbreviation mark, not *sigma*; elsewhere the text uses lunate *sigmas*. The word has been resolved as [ἀρ]χισυν(αγώγου) or [ἀρ]χισυν(αγωγίσσης). In view of the names, this text is likely to be Jewish.
26,27. Lifshitz, no.33 (Akmonia in Phrygia, I fin.; text supersedes the version in *CIJ* II.766; text repr. in Brooten, 158 no.6), G. Turronius Klados ὁ διὰ βίου ἀρχισυνάγωγος and Lucius *archisynagogos* helped restore a building, along with Publius Zotikos *archon*.
28,29. Lifshitz, no.38 (Apamea, 391; = *IGLS* IV.1319, which supersedes text in *CIJ* II.803; text repr. in Brooten, 26, 27), dedication dated by three *archisynag*[*og*]*oi* as well as by various other office-holders, mentioning that Ilasios (or Hilasios? — see Lifshitz, 40 n.2), *archisynagogos* of the Antiochenes, donated a mosaic.
30. Lifshitz, no.39 (Apamea, 391; = *IGLS* IV.1320, which supersedes text in *CIJ* II.804; text repr. in Brooten, 164 no.39; also in Guarducci, *EG* IV.219-21 [fig.65]), the same (H)ilasios, *archisynagogos* of Antioch, dedicates a mosaic in memory of his relatives.

Palestine

31-33. Lifshitz, no.74 (Sepphoris/Diocaesarea, V[1]; supersedes text in *CIJ* II.991 which, however, has a plate with a transcription of the stone; text repr. in Brooten, 229 n.93). This text is difficult because of the numerous abbreviations and errors. Lifshitz reads:

ἐ̣≪π≫<ὶ> Ὑελασίου σχο(λαστικοῦ) κώ(μητος) λαμ(προτάτου) υείοῦ Ἀετίου το-
ῦ κό(μητος) Εἰούδα (ἀ)ρχισυναγώγου Σιδονίου {ἀρχισυναγ-}
{ώγου} ΠΕΡΙΕΡΘΟΝΤΑΔ Συβεριανο(ῦ) Ἄφρο(υ) ἀρχισυναγ-
ώγο(υ) Τύρου λαμπρ(οτάτου).

(In *l*.2 I suggest the following alternative: Εἰουδ(αίου) ἀρχισυναγώγου. The first four letters in *l*.4 correct Lifshitz' text in the light of the transcription in *CIJ*.)

In the time of Gelasios *advocatus*, the most illustrious count, son of count Aetios, Jew, leader of the synagogue of Sidon . . . Severianus Afer, most illustrious leader of the synagogue of Tyre.

In *ll*.2-3 the word of interest to us has been repeated, apparently by mistake. On the spelling of the first name see Lifshitz' n., ad loc.

34-36. Lifshitz, no.79 (Jerusalem, before 70 AD; = *CIJ* II.1404; repr. with discussion in Brooten, 24-25), Theodotos, priest and *archisynagogos*, built a synagogue and guest-room (ξενών). His father and grandfather are both said to have been *archisynagogoi*.
37. M. Schwabe/B. Lifshitz, *Beth She'arim*, II. *The Greek Inscriptions* (New Brunswick, 1974) no.164, painted epitaph for Eusebios, ἀρ|χισυνάγωγο|ς <τ>ῶν Βηριτῶ̣[ν], '*archisynagogos* of the people of Beirut'. Text quoted in Brooten, 231 n.114.
38. *Beth She'arim*, II.203, epitaph for Jacob from Caesarea, *archisynagogos*, originally from Pamphylia.

Africa

39. *CIL* VIII Suppl. 1.12457 (Ḥammam Lif in Provincia Tripolitana; text repr. in Brooten, 164 no.38), Latin mosaic inscription recording the provision of part of a portico floor by Asterius son of Rusticus *arcosinogogi* (*sic*). This text is included as item no.14 in Y. Le Bohec's inventory of epigraphical attestations of Jews/Judaisers in Africa, *Ant.Afr.* 17 (1981) 165-207, at 178.

Egypt

40. *SB* 5.3 (1950) 8787 (Alexandria, 3/4 AD; largely identical text at *SB* 1 [1915] 5959; repr. as E. Breccia, *Inscriptiones Graecae Aegyptae,* II. *Inscriptiones nunc Alexandriae in Museo* [Cairo, 1911; repr. Chicago, 1978] 47); very fragmentary honorific inscription which includes the words . . . [τ]ῶν ἀρχισυναγώ[γων] . . . (*l*.3).

II. Uncertain/ghost examples

Italy

41. *CIJ* I.548 (Porto; text repr. in Brooten, 229 n.93), very fragmentary dedication with the lettering ΝΑΓΩΓΩ in *l*.4, which Frey suggests may be restored as [ἀρχισυ]ναγώγῳ. Equally, we may have συ]ναγωγῷ (see LSJ, s.v.). In fact, there is nothing in this text to establish it conclusively as Jewish.

42. *SEG* 981 (Porto, n.d.), a very doubtful instance, given that only the letters ΣΥΝ survive from what may have been the word in this certainly Jewish fragment; see the brief discussion in the first paragraph of the present entry.

Greece

43. Lifshitz, no.1 (Aigina; supersedes text of *CIJ* I.722; text repr. in Brooten, 229 n.93), building inscription recording that Theodoros ἀρχ[ισυνάγωγ(ος)] erected the synagogue. Equally possible may be ἄρχ[ων . . . See further on no.51 below.

44. *SEG* 300, the item at the beginning of this entry.

45. *CIG* II (1843, repr. 1977) 2221c (Chios), [ἀρχισυν]άγωγοι οἱ ἄρξαντες | [ἐπ]ὶ Πυρ≪σ≫άνδρου . . . | . . . | . . . | . . . |[7] . . . στεφανοῦσι τὸν συν|άρξαντα ἑαυτοῖς . . ., 'the presidents who were in charge in the year of Pyrsander (i.e., when he was the city's eponymous magistrate) . . . crown their colleague . . .' (1-8). The group also has a *grammateus* (*l*.6). If our word is to be restored here — it is not the only possibility, though a plausible one — we are probably witness to a private cultic association, rather than a Jewish community. E. Ziebarth, *Das grieschische Vereinswesen* (Stuttgart, 1896; repr. Wiesbaden, 1969) 65 no.25, leaves open both possibilities.

Asia Minor

46. *CIJ* I.731g (provenance not stated, after V; text repr. and discussed in Brooten, 35-36), a gold medallion with Jewish symbols and a text reading ὑπὲρ εὐχῆς 'Ι|ακὼβ ἀρχιγοῦ | πιννωνᾶ, 'in fulfilment of the dedication of Jacob, leader (of the congregation?), the pearl-setter'. Brooten wrongly lists this item (229 n.87), as though it included an example of the word ἀρχισυνάγωγος, perhaps taking her lead from the comment in *ed.pr.* (R.D. Barnett, *JHS* 58 [1938] 255) that 'ἀρχηγός may perhaps be used in the sense of ἀρχισυνάγωγος . . . but such a use is unfamiliar'. On ἀρχηγός see Brooten, 35-39.

47. *CIJ* II.759 (Synnada in Lykia, I or II), ἀ]ρχισυν[in a very fragmentary text; not certainly Jewish.

48. Lifshitz, no.37 (Side, V; text repr. in Brooten, 229 n.93), inscription recording the installation of a fountain in the time of the *presb(yter)* Leontios, son of Jacob the ἀρχ(ισυναγώγου), or ἄρχ(οντος). Brooten acknowledges (*ad loc.*) that this does not provide a certain attestation of the noun. Though Lifshitz resolves the abbreviation in the former way his translation and commentary assume the resolution ἄρχ(οντος).

Cyprus

49. Lifshitz, no.85 (Constantia-Salamis, III; text repr. in Brooten, 230 n.93), fragmentary text (whether dedication or epitaph is uncertain) mentioning NN . . . | ΠΕΝΤΑΡΧΙ, son of Ananias who was twice *archon*. The first editor — T.B. Mitford, *Byzantion* 20 (1950) 110-12, no.3 — resolved these letters as πέντ' 'Αρχί(α), '(they erected) five (columns) of Archias' (i.e., provided by him). Lifshitz prefers πεντ(άκις) ἀρχι(συναγώγου), 'NN who held the position of *archisynagogos* five times'.

Palestine

50. *CIJ* II.1414 (Jerusalem), epitaph for Rabbi Samu[el] | ΑΡΧΗΣ[- - -], perhaps from Phrygian Dorylaion or Dokimeion. Frey resolves the letters in *l*.2 as ἀρχ(ι)σ[υνάγωγος; but other restorations may be possible.

51. Lifshitz, no.66 (Caesarea, VI; text repr. in Brooten, 229 n.93), inscription naming Beryllos ἀρχισ(υνάγωγος) | καὶ φροντιστής as the one who provided the mosaic of a dining room. Lifshitz' resolution is certainly possible, but he argues for it partly on the basis of the restoration of no.43 above, and vice versa.

52. *Beth She'arim* II.212, very fragmentary text with ἀρχ[ισυνάγωγος] restored in *l*.2; the editors acknowledge the uncertainty of this supplement.

53. *SEG* 26 (1976/7) 1687 (Tiberias), very fragmentary text, probably an epitaph, for Leontina, wife(?) of Thaumasios [ἀρχισυναγώγ(ου)?] 'Αντιοχ(έων) (*l*.4).

Egypt

54. *SB* 1 (1915; repr. 1974) 623 (Fayum, 80-69 BC), dedication on behalf of Ptolemy XII Auletes and Kleopatra by the *hippeis* in the Arsinoite nome [ὢν ἀρχισυνά]γωγος καὶ ἀρχιερεὺς | [NN . . . (6-7); other restorations are equally possible.

There are numerous issues arising from this assemblage of attestations; and it is a virtue of Brooten's monograph that she has addressed so many of them, methodological, textual and historical. Since it is beyond the scope of the present discussion to treat these at any length several observations may be offered, related to the NT evidence where appropriate. It should be noted that there are no attestations in the papyri.

a. Variant forms of ἀρχισυνάγωγος

Most of these are orthographically insignificant: ἀρχη- (7, 8), ἀρχοση- (10; cf. the Latin *arco-*, 39). No. 20 *arcisina*(*vac.*)γος is a bilingual curiosity. The morphologically distinct nouns ἀρχισυναγώγης (3) and ἀρχισυναγώγισσα (13) are quite normal formations and, apart from the distinction in gender for the latter, are to be seen as entirely synonymous in meaning. In the case of abbreviated forms (especially 25) it is not possible to say what the fully resolved word was.

b. Were the terms *archon/archisynagogos* interchangeable in such texts?

It may seem clear from nos.1, 6, and 26/27 that they were distinct titles within the Jewish communities. It is conceivable that there was a rotating president amongst a panel of rulers. But the possibility of loose usage cannot be excluded, as is clear from the Synoptics where Jairos is spoken of both as *archisynagogos* (Mk. 5.22, 35, 36, 38; Lk. 8.49) and as *archon* (Mt. 9.18, 23; Lk. 8.41). Some of Lifshitz' discussions cause confusion in this regard (see especially the comment on no.48 in the list above). While it is true that the abbreviation ἀρχ can be resolved to give either word, that does not mean that the words were interchangeable. In the NT Acts 14.2D clearly differentiates the two terms: at Ikonion, οἱ δὲ ἀρχισυνάγωγοι τῶν Ἰουδαίων καὶ οἱ ἄρχοντες τῆς συναγωγῆς ἐπήγαγον αὐτοῖς δίωγμον κατὰ τῶν δικαίων. If no.45 is indeed to be restored with our noun, this inscription, which is unlikely to be reflecting the presence of a Jewish community, also uses the participle (συν)άρχων to describe the presidents. *Archisynagogos* is also to be distinguished from ἀρχηγός (46), whose Latin equivalent is *principalis* (20).

c. Was the position hereditary?

The need to recognise fluidity of practice surfaces here. In 7/8 a father and son possess the title. But that does not prove it was hereditary, simply that this particular son attained to the same position as his father. On the other hand, no.5 cannot be pressed to show that it was *not* hereditary; the son may have died before he had graduated sufficiently through the 'cursus' to 'fill his father's shoes'. No.9 sharpens the evidential problem further: the fact that a three-year-old child had the title may suggest it could be passed to descendants. Alternatively, it may be merely an honorific bestowal to give recognition to the active service of a parent exercising functions in the community under that title. In sum, though we may not find it difficult to believe that certain families may have dominated tenure of the senior positions (cf. I. Muñoz Valle, *CFC* 4 [1972] 151-63, dealing with the Jewish commmunities at Rome), evidence to prove hereditary transmission is wanting.

d. Functional or honorific?

Mostly we should think of the former. Non-documentary sources sufficiently indicate the functions exercised by the *archisynagogos*: see the concise discussion in the new English version by G. Vermes *et al.* of E. Schürer, *The History of the Jewish People in the Age of Jesus Christ* (*175 BC -AD 135*), II (Edinburgh, 1979) 434-36. In the inscriptions listed above, the position is eponymous (28). But the term could undoubtedly serve as an honorary title as well, as the phrase '*archisynagogos* for life' (24, 26) shows.

e. How many per community?

We ought to expect variety here, too, according to the size of the group. In no.28 the dating formula suggests that at Apamea there were three eponymous *archisynagogoi*; but the president of the Antiochenes (29, 30) may also have headed a smaller group of Jews from Antioch now resident in Apamea. The NT reflects this same variety: in 'the synagogue' at Pisidian Antioch there was more than one (Acts 13.15), as also apparently at Corinth (Acts 18.8, 17), unless there was more than one synagogue there (which is not unlikely, as noted at the beginning of this entry).

f. Could the position be held more than once?

There is insufficient evidence to establish this either way; Lifshitz' resolution of the lettering in no.49 is not compelling (though neither is Mitford's), and no weight should be accorded to it (*pace* Brooten, 25, 28).

g. Female *archisynagogoi*

Their existence, though relatively rare, is beyond dispute (13, 22, and probably 25); the question is whether their title reflects an honorific status or the exercising of actual function. The burden of Brooten's discussion (especially 30-33) is that, as with other titles held by women in synagogues, function is no more to be denied for them than it is for males. In this she is surely right; but the fact that she has to argue against many *illuminati* from the past makes her over-defensive. The methodologically inadequate treatment of this question previously is brought out well in her discussion. It may be noted that if the title were merely honorific for women we should expect a considerably greater number to be attested. The same problem has been observed by others studying various aspects of the role of women in the Graeco-Roman world, e.g., female asiarchs at Ephesos (cf. **14** above, and R. Kearsley, *GRBS* 27 [1986] 182-92), female *oikonomoi* (see **69** above), female *prostatai* (cf. **122** below). These instances should not be ignored when consideration is given to women office-holders in the Church, for they provide a context in which such appointments are quite explicable. On '*episcopae*' and '*presbyterae*' as titles of the wives of bishops and priests in VI AD Gaul see B. Brennan, *Church History* 54 (1985) 311-23.

h. Non-Jewish instances

Brooten's discussion is somewhat weakened by her near total failure to take the non-Jewish evidence into account; for the latter allows the Jewish examples to be seen against a wider canvas. There are no Christian examples. The following are the non-Jewish instances: 14-19, 21, 40(?), to which may be added from the doubtful cases 41(?), 44(?), 45, 47(?), 48 (could this text possibly be Christian?), and 54(?). It is instructive to compare the terms used in no.2 with those in no.21, the former Jewish, the latter not. Both describe the community as a συναγωγή; if the restoration in 2 is accepted, both communities had an *archisynagogos*. Fragmentary as no.2 is, we see here the parallelism between the language of Jewish and non-Jewish socio-religious groups. The only feature which suggests a Jewish milieu for no.2 is the name Isaac. Brooten sees the term *archisynagogos* as a borrowing by other associations from Judaism (5, 23 with 228 n.81). But this is quite unlikely, and overestimates the influence which Judaism exercised upon *koine*. It is far more natural, with so many terms in use in the Hellenistic world to describe private associations and their office-holders (on which see Ziebarth, *passim*), to see it as a process of certain terms gaining currency within Jewish circles. M. Hengel is right to draw attention to Jewish imitation of the form of the Hellenistic private associations for the formation of the synagogue communities: *Judaism and Hellenism* (ET: London, 1974) I.244. But they took over selected elements of the terminology as well. Thus, it is not only συναγωγή but also προσευχή which acquires the specialised sense of a *Jewish* meeting house. It appears from the inscriptions that προσευχή gained this meaning first, in the Hellenistic period. See *New Docs 1978*, **94**, for a number of instances; and see further **110** above in the present

Review. It appears that by I BC/I AD συναγωγή was ousting προσευχή as the Jewish technical term; when the latter word is used in Acts 16.13, 16 it is unclear whether a synagogue is actually in view. And because συναγωγή became *the* term for the Jewish synagogue, use of the word to refer to non-Jewish associations apparently diminishes considerably. Concerning these two words, reference may be made to M. Hengel's essay in G. Jeremias et al. (edd.), *Tradition und Glaube. Das frühe Christentum in seiner Umwelt. Festgabe für K.G. Kuhn* (Göttingen, 1971), 157-84. The rise to prominence within Jewish circles of the term *archisynagogos* is to be understood in the light of this development of συναγωγή as the standard word for a Jewish meeting place. The lack of attestation of ἀρχισυνάγωγος in Hellenistic-period Jewish texts thus becomes comprehensible in the light of this observation that συναγωγή began superseding προσευχή about the turn of the era. While *archisynagogos* continues to be attested in non-Jewish private associations, this reflects not influence from Judaism but simply the survival of a term already in use in non-Jewish circles before the latter specially appropriated it. The Hebrew term רֹאשׁ הַכְּנֶסֶת (Schürer, II.434) is thus to be seen as a back-formation coined in the light of Jewish adoption of the Greek word from their contemporaries. The presence of the word in Palestine as attested both by the Synoptic Gospels and epigraphically (nos.31-38 above) thus serves as a further small pebble in the mosaic forming a picture of the hellenisation of Judaism in Palestine.

i. Christian use of the term

In the fourth century Epiphanius mentions that the Ebionites used the title *archisynagogoi*: πρεσβυτέρους γὰρ οὗτοι ἔχουσι καὶ ἀρχισυναγώγους. συναγωγὴν δὲ οὗτοι καλοῦσι τὴν ἑαυτῶν ἐκκλησίαν, καὶ οὐχὶ ἐκκλησίαν . . ., 'For they have elders, namely *archisynagogoi*. And they call their church an assembly, not a meeting . . .' (Migne, *PG* 41.436A, quoted by Brooten, 22). The Ebionites attested their origin in the period when believers in Christ did not see themselves as marked out from Judaism (cf. Jas. 2.2). This underlines the point made above under (h), that ἀρχισυνάγωγος was the natural term to use if the community was to be called a *synagoge*. A very different use has been drawn to my attention by G.W. Clarke. Dionysios, Bishop of Alexandria and a pupil of Origen, is quoted at Eus., *HE* 7.10.4 in a passage where the word refers to the pagan persecutor Makrianos: ἀποσκεύσασθαι δὲ παρέπεισεν αὐτὸν ὁ διδάσκαλος καὶ τῶν ἀπ' Αἰγύπτου μάγων ἀρχισυνάγωγος, 'the teacher and president of the Egyptian magicians persuaded him (i.e., Valerian) to get rid of them (viz., the Christians)'.

Finally, users of Brooten's monograph should be alert to an awkward overlap in her way of referring to various inscriptions. Even where the version of a text in Lifshitz, *Donateurs*, supersedes that printed in *CIJ*, reference is frequently given to the latter only. For example, Lifshitz no.33 is a superior version of *CIJ* 766, but the latter is the way in which the inscription is mentioned by Brooten on pp.24, 25, 26, etc. The index lists this inscription under their two separate editions, as though they were distinct items. On p.274 a series of page references in the book is provided for *CIJ* 766; only one of these is common with the two references given on p.276 for Lifshitz no.33. Again, the index gives five references to *CIJ* 804, only two of which are noted under Lifshitz, no.39. Yet here, too, the latter gives a version of the inscription which makes the text printed in *CIJ* obsolete. The same flaw is to be found in Schürer; in the discussion of *archisynagogoi* (II.434-36) the references are almost entirely to *CIJ* texts even though the existence of Lifshitz' book is known. The point of this observation is not to cast stones, but to draw attention to one of the besetting problems of epigraphical research, the difficulty of creating an orderly and consistent set of references to inscriptions for which several editions may be current.

114. A Jewish family from Egypt in Rome

Rome Imperial period

ed. — *IG* XIV (1890) 1648

[ἐτῶν δ]εχοκτὼ μονογενῆ καὶ παρθένον
[Θεοδο]σίαν ἔθαψε Δωρόθεος πατήρ,
[ἣν μ]ελλόνυμφον Τυβὶ μηνὸς εἰκάδι
[εἷλες, π]ονηρὲ δαῖμον, ὃς τὸν ἔμπαλιν
[οἷ νόσ]τον οὐκ ἔκλωσας, ὥσπερ ἤλπισε.

[ὀκτω]καιδεχέτης, ἔτι παρθένος οἰογένεια
[Θεο]δοσία κεῖται, Δωροθέου θυγάτηρ.
[ἀλλ' ὦ ν]ηλεόθυμε Χάρον, τί σε τόσσον ἐνηὴς
[τέ]<ρ>ψε λιποῦσα πατρὶ πένθος ἀπειρέσιον;

[*Theodosia quae et*] *Kalypso ann. XVIII.*

Metrical epitaph (now lost) consisting of iambics (*ll.*1-5) and elegiacs (*ll.*6-9), completed by a prose line of Latin.

Bib. — Peek, *GVI* 1976; **IGUR* 1231 (pl. of hand-written copy on p.91).

Dorotheos her father buried Theodosia, aged eighteen, his only child and a virgin. She was about to be married (but) on the twentieth day of the month Tybi you took her, evil spirit, you who | did not fatefully spin for her a return back (home), as she expected. Eighteen years old, still a virgin, the only child Theodosia lies (here), daughter of Dorotheos. But hard-hearted Charon, why did the kind girl delight you so much as to leave infinite grief to her father?
| [Theodosia also called] Kalypso, aged 18.

It is not only the change in metre that indicates two separate epigrams here. The contents of the two poems overlap too considerably for them to be thought of as following on from one to the other. Not only in ideas but in the wording *ll.*1-2 are closely paralleled by *ll.*6-7, while the address to Charon in *l.*8 balances the address to fate in *l.*4. That two epigrams may appear on the same funerary monument is not unheard of; note, for example, the pair of epigrams for the doctor Epaphroditos, repr. above at **5**, or the much more imposing *IGUR* 1336 (Rome, shortly after 94 AD), an altar set up to mark the poetic accomplishments of a twelve-year-old boy. But it is peculiar that two such similar poems as these for Theodosia should have been conjoined.

The names of the father and the deceased (provided the restorations in *ll.*2 and 7 are right) are a fairly sure indication that we are dealing with a Jewish family. It is true that the daughter's name is nowhere fully preserved, but [Theo]dosia (or [Theu]dosia) is the only credible option in *l.*7; see F. Dornseiff/B. Hansen, *Rückläufiges Wörterbuch der griechischen Eigennamen* (Berlin, 1957; repr. Chicago, 1978) 24. That being so, Moretti's restoration in *l.*10 so as to make the name Kalypso a by-name of Theodosia makes good sense. The use of a distinctively

Jewish name with a Greek or Roman name by Jews is well attested, in the NT pre-eminently in the case of Saul ὁ καί Paul (cf. *New Docs 1976*, **55**). Despite these names, the inscription was not included in *CIJ* (nor even in Lifshitz's supplementary Prolegomenon to vol.I), and one may speculate that the reason for this was the reference to Charon, the underworld boatman of Greek myth, as well as the thoroughly hellenic notion conjured up by ἔκλωσας (5) of the Fates spinning a person's life-span. On this cliché see **6** above. But the allusion should merely be viewed as a literary/cultural one, and is certainly not sufficient to cause this text to be rejected as not referring to Jews. Cf. *CIJ* 1.690 (Gorgippa in the Cimmerian Bosphoros, 41 AD), almost certainly Jewish despite the concluding oath by Zeus, Gē and Helios (*l.*14).

That the permanent home of Dorotheos and his daughter was in Egypt may be inferred from the inclusion of the Egyptian month-name (*l.*3). It is a credible reconstruction to think of the family (or merely the two named, the mother being perhaps already deceased) as having very recently arrived from their native Egypt, so recently that the Egyptian word slips in naturally. They appear to be in Rome for a brief visit (for the father's business?). Although not much weight should be placed on the largely restored [νόσ]τον (5), ἔμπαλιν in the previous line supports the most natural suggestion that the daughter was to be married upon her return to Egypt. Given the difficulties of sea-travel (cf. **26** above) from Italy back to Egypt in winter, we may infer that her death in mid-January occurred some months prior to the date set for her marriage. It is straining the text somewhat to see in *ll.*4-5 a reference to Jewish belief in bodily resurrection (cf. Moretti's n. in *IGUR*, referring to *CIJ* I, pp.cxxxi-ii).

Theodosia is called a *parthenos* at the age of 18, and is about to be married. This example confirms nicely the notion of *parthenos* as a girl of marriageable age (cf. *LSJ*, s.v., 2). The discussion of the word in Spicq, *NLNT* III.516-25 provides a number of documentary references. While virginity may have been expected, the word does not require that connotation wherever it is used. Now, this age seems rather late for a female to be married in the Roman period, and it is perhaps worth raising the question whether the Jewish age for females to marry was rather higher than that for Greeks and Romans. To take mainly the *IGUR* and *CIJ* volumes as a yardstick (a small number of other items from the year's culling are also included) the following relevant instances may be listed, with age at death given where known. Unless otherwise noted, all are epitaphs from Rome and undated by the ed.; but almost all will belong to the Imperial period. The inclusion of age details in epitaphs is much more common in Rome and Egypt than elsewhere, as the *CIJ* material shows (on this question see I. Kajanto, *A Study of the Greek Epitaphs of Rome* [Helsinki, 1963] 12-16).

1a. Age at marriage can be determined

IGUR II.1 (1972)

323 — Rode aged 30, married 17 years.

463 — Grania Hygeia aged 26, and her daughter aged 12; the former therefore married *c.*13 years.

673 — Sarapias aged 13 and married (presumably not for long).

II.2 (1973)

871 — Papiria Pantheia aged 21, married 9 years.

III (1979)

1265 — epitaph for Margaris, married (at age 13) for 50 years. For the notion of being married to one man (*monandros*) cf. *IGUR* 462, 579, 1205, 1311.2. Cf. the Christian Eupraxia (Guarducci, *EG* IV.332-33; = *IG* V, 2.359) who died at age 40 after 22 years of marriage, μὴ ἔχουσα ἕτερον ἄν|δρα (*ll.*10-11; Arkadia, IV). The husband in this text is scarcely mentioned, and may be presumed already deceased: in which case we have attestation of adherence to the NT injunction that widows ought not to remarry (1 Cor. 7.8-9; 1 Tim. 5.9, ἑνὸς ἀνδρὸς γυνή; though contrast 1 Tim. 5.14). Note also *CIJ* 81 in list 1b below.

For the other side of the coin note the inscription for the Christian Akakios (North Phrygia, *c*.325-50; *ed.pr.* — W.M. Calder, *AS* 5 [1955] 31-33 no.1 [pl.1a]; Guarducci, *EG* IV.392-94 [fig.113], quotes only the last seven lines of the text) which speaks of him τριάκοντα ἔτη ἐν χηροσύνῃ ὑπομίνας | μουνόγαμος, κτλ (4-5).

1267 — Markella, just married (ἀρτίγαμος κούρη, 2) at age 20.

1268 — Markia Helike aged 20, married; died 11 days after birth of third child; probably Jewish.

1279 — Myronis aged 20, married 7 years, mother of 2 children.

Pfuhl/Möbius, II.1142 (provenance unknown within Bithynia, II; pl.172) — Soteris, aged 20, married 7 years (συνζησάσῃ αὐτῷ), 3 children.

CIJ I

105 — Domitia aged 19, married 7 years (μετὰ τοῦ συ[μβ]ίου . . .).

136 — Margarita aged 19, married 4 years (μετὰ τοῦ συ<μβ>ίου . . .).

242 — Junia Sabina aged 18, married 3 years (*cum virgini<o> su<o> <q>u<a>e vixit annis III, dies III*); cf. *CIJ* 81, 319, and *I. Eph.* 3861, all in list 1b below.

268 — Venerosa aged 17, married 15 months.

302 — epitaph for Aemilius(?) Anteros aged 22, married 5 years. *Pace* Frey, this may possibly be an epitaph for a woman (name lost) set up by her husband, since it is at best uncommon for a male to marry aged 17. Yet cf. II.1502 (Tell el-Yehoudeh, n.d.), epitaph for Dosas aged about 18, set up by his *gyne* Theophila. Even more striking is the epitaph repr. as *SB* I (1915, repr. 1974) 5025 (Alexandria, n.d.; = *IGA* 2.353, noted at *New Docs 1978*, **11**, p.43), in which Theudas, who died at age 14, is said to be both νυμφίος (*l*.2) and ἄγα|μος (*ll*.6-7) — betrothed but not yet living with his bride? Cf. *CIJ* II.1468 (Tell el-Yehoudeh in Lower Egypt, n.d.), epitaph for Johannes νυμφίος, aged about 30.

527 — Probina aged nearly 18, married 3 months (*cum marito vixit*).

55*— Harnes (female?) aged 20, married 8 years (Urbino, n.d.; not Jewish).

AE 60 — Severa Seleukiane, aged 42, married 17 years; Christian (279; text repr. and discussed at **120** below).

1b. Age at marriage cannot be determined

CIJ I

81 — Agenti[a Iouli(?)]ane, μόνανδρ[ος], who lived μετὰ παρθεν[ικοῦ αὐ]|[τ]ης ἔτη θ', 'with the man of her maidenhood (i.e., her first husband) for 9 years'; for this phrase cf. *CIJ* 242 (see list 1a above), 319 and *I. Eph.* 3861 below. Note also *CIJ* II.772 (Apollonia in Phrygia, II fin./III init.), epitaph for Debbora — originally from Pisidian Antioch — who received the monument from her husband for the sake of the marriage they had shared from their virginity, παρθεν[ικῶν] | λέκτρων [ἀν]|τιλαβοῦσ[α] | χάριν (*ll*.12-15). For *monandros* cf. 392 (Rebekka μ., aged 44), 541 (Rufina μ., age not given), and the other examples noted above (list 1a) at *IGUR* III.1265.

237 — Gargilia Eufraxia aged 19; erected by her husband.

247 — Lucretia Faustina aged 23; erected by her husband.

262 — Rufilla Pietas, age not stated, married 3(?) years.

299 — husband of Flavia Flaviana, married nearly 7 years.

311 — Varia Zotike aged 26, husband's name not given so probably deceased.

314 — Gaudentia aged 19; erected by her husband.

319 — Eirene, age not given, παρθενικὴ σύμβιος of Clodius; cf. *CIJ* 81 and 242 above, and *I. Eph.* 3861 below.

391 — family grave for Proculus, his wife Euodia and their three children aged 9¾, 9 and 2¾. A useful testimony to the rapidity with which a woman may have become pregnant again following parturition, and so an implicit witness to the length of the marriage: say 10 years, in which case the mother was perhaps in her mid-late 20s. For other similar examples in *CIJ* see I.609 (epitaph for two children aged 19 months and 11 months), 94* (epitaph for three children aged 7, 4 and 3; rejected as Jewish by Frey), II.1169 (near Nablus in Palestine, n.d.; epitaph for mother and three daughters, aged 18, 14 and 13; see below), 1527 (Tell el-Yehoudeh, 37 AD; epitaph for three children aged 4, 2 and 1).

468 — Pticia Aster, aged 48, erected by her husband.

650 — Lasiferina aged 22, erected by her husband (Catania in Sicily, 383).

26*— Domitia Auge aged 25, erected by her husband (non-Jewish text).

62*— Aurelia Callistes aged 24, erected by her husband and parents (Lyon, n.d.; not Jewish).

64*— Claudia Maximilla aged 25, her husband aged 37 (Pannonia, n.d.; not Jewish). By no means certain that they died at the same time (cf. no.608 in list 2a below).

CIJ II

891 — Zoila aged 30, married in view of the epithet φίλανδρος (Apollonias in Palestine, 79 BC or 176 AD).

1481 — A. . .this daughter/wife(?) of Sabbataios, and *c*.35, died in child-birth, ἄωρος λόχω<ι> (Tell el-Yehoudeh, perhaps 25 BC); for other instances of death in childbirth note 1510 (Tell el-Yehoudeh, 28 January 5 BC), epitaph for Arsinoe (age not given) who died while bearing her first child: ὠδεῖνι δὲ Μοῖρα | προτοτόκου με τέκνου πρὸς τέλος ἦγε βίου (5-6), 'but Fate brought me to the end of my life when I was in labour with my firstborn child'. Other wording in this text is considered at **71** above. Cf. also 1515 (Tell el-Yehoudeh, 5/6 November 25 BC?), epitaph for Dosarin aged *c*.25, λοχοῦς.

1500 — Sambathi(o)n aged *c*.19, presumably married in view of the epithet ἄτεκνε as it would be pointless to include it if she were still single (Tell el-Yehoudeh, 24 December 4 BC). Cf. 1530 (Tell el-Yehoudeh, 15 June 14 BC?) where Arsinoe, aged 20, is ἄτεκνος (*l*.8) and explicit in mentioning her marriage (*l*.7, though her parents but not her husband are named — perhaps he predeceased her).

I.Eph. VII, 2

3861 — A man erects a tombstone for himself, for his wife Apollonia πα[ρ]θε|[νι]κῇ γυνηκί (*ll*.5-6; for this phrase cf. *CIJ* 81, 242 and 319 above), for her mother, their children and descendants and their descendants πιστοῖς (11). This last word suggests that the family is Christian; L. Robert, *Hellenica* 11-12 (Paris, 1960) 425 n.5, thinks that this text from Dideiphyta in the Kaystros Valley is to be dated prior to 212 on onomastic grounds.

2a. Unmarried, attested by παρθένος, *vel. sim.*

IGUR III (1979)

1203 — Elpis, age not stated, but unmarried in view of *l*.3, παρθενικὴν ζώνην οὔτις ἔλυσε βροτῶν.

1231 — Theodosia — text repr. at beginning of this entry.

1287 — Olympia aged 22, *parthenon* (*l*.7); epitaph set up by her brother: the epigram speaks of the στοργὴ . . . μεγάλη τῶν ἀμφοτέρων (8); this text is considered further above at **10**.

1318 — Prokla aged 5, *parthenos*.

1395 — Nymph. . . *parthenos*, age not stated.

1463 — fragmentary epitaph with παρθένε apparently referring to a female.

1465 — fragmentary epitaph with παρθενίῃ in *l*.6 and ἄγαμον in the following line.

1485 — fragmentary epitaph(?) with παρ]θενίης.

CIJ I

45 — Markiana [π]αρθένος, aged 15.

106 — For Doul[ki]tia παρθένῳ | μελλ[ο]νύμφῃ, no age given; erected by her father. *Mellonymphios* is used at *CIJ* I.148 of the *grammateus* Ursus; the text is orthographically poor, and it is uncertain whether his age at death was 22 or 24 (ἔζησεν κβ κ≪α≫ὶ | δύο ἔτη, 2-3). With *CIJ* 106 we may compare *BE* 292, an epitaph for a family from Nikopolis on the Ister (*ed.pr.* — G. Mihailov, in *Studia in honorem G. Beševliev* [Sofia 1978], 161-62 — *non vidi*), in which a daughter Thekla died just before her marriage, ἀκήρατος εἰς θεὸν ἦλθεν. *BE* reports *ed.pr.*'s view that the family was probably Christian, in view of this wording. For a phrase similar to this last item cf. Guarducci, *EG* IV.505-08 (fig.154), a metrical epitaph (Mediolanum, IV^2/V init.) for a Christian doctor originally from Egypt who ἐνθάδε σῶμα λιπὼν εἰς παράδισον ἔβη (*l*.6); see too the closely-related wording in the metrical epitaph for Akakios (Kotiaion, 325-50), only the last seven lines of which are quoted by Guarducci, *EG* IV.392-94 (fig.113), παραδίζοισι κατοικῶ (24); for the full wording of this Christian inscription, which includes numerous examples of alliteration (*ll*.18, 21) and other stylistic devices (*l*.23, play on words), see W.M. Calder, *AS* 5 (1955) 31-33 no.1. For a good non-Christian parallel we may note *IGUR* III.1163.9 (Rome, II^2 or III init.), σέμνον ἔβη Διὸς οἶκον, an inscription marked by Pythagorean views.

168 — Sirika παρθ[έ]νος, aged 18.

320 — Eirene, age not given, *parthenos*.

381 — Nometora aged 18, παρθαίνος.

386 — Prokla aged 19, *parthenos*.

588 — Kasta aged 14, *parthenos*.

608 — Epitaph for two sisters: Sara aged *c.*70 and married, Asella aged *c.*14, a *virgo* (Venosa, n.d.). Presumably Sara had mention of her sister included on her own epitaph although Asella had predeceased her by many years.

733 — Asther (= Esther) aged 22, παρθένος ὅσια.

CIJ II

1169 — Sarra aged 50 and her three daughters (cf. I.391 in list 1b above), of whom the second, aged 14, is Sarra θυ(γάτηρ) παρθ(ένος), perhaps so called to distinguish her from her mother (Nablus in Palestine).

I. Eph. VI

2231 — Bassa *parthenos*, age not stated (= Pfuhl/Möbius, II.2032, where dated early or middle Imperial period).

2480 — fragmentary bilingual text referring to *virgini fil*[*iae*]/παρ[θένῳ θυγατρί] (*ll.*1-3); name not preserved, nor is it certainly an epitaph (Byzantine date?).

Pircher, no.16 — Antibia *parthenos* in a funerary epigram surviving only via a literary tradition (*Anth.Pal.* VII.490), perhaps to be dated IV-III BC; clearly of marriageable age as the text speaks of many νυμφίοι coming to her father's home to seek her hand.

Guarducci, *EG* IV.363-65 (Herakleia-Perinthos, III fin./IV init.; fig. 105) — Theodoule aged 15, *parthenos* who with her five brothers and sisters all predeceased the parents. Next, the mother died, and the father arranged the stele for the family tomb, adding at the end χρειστιανοὶ δὲ πάντες ἔν|σμεν (*ll.*15-16).

Tsigaridas, *Κατάλογος*, 45 — tomb of the Christian Anna(?), *parthenos*, age not stated (Thessalonike, V-VI). Ed. n., ad loc. suggests that she may have been a nun; but there is nothing about the text which makes this view preferable.

2b. Unmarried, attested by other wording

CIJ I

30 — Theodosia also called Gorgoneis aged 26, daughter of Eli, sister of . . .; apparently unmarried.

159 — Sabina aged 16, apparently unmarried; erected by her father.

389 — Prokleina aged 18, apparently unmarried; erected by her mother.

611 — Faustina aged 14, an only child (*unica*) (Venosa, n.d.).

661 — Meliosa aged 24, erected by her parents, therefore apparently unmarried (yet cf. 1530, dealt with under no.1500 in list 1b above).

678 — Septima Marion aged 18, erected by her mother (Soklos in Pannonia, n.d.).

CIJ II

1509 — Tomb erected by Horaia for herself (age not stated), her husband, and their daughter Eirene ᾗ γάμος οὐκ ἐδόθη (6); all three died within five days of each other (Tell el-Yehoudeh, 20 BC?). It would be reasonable to infer from the comment in *l.*6 that she was not a very young child. It may be relevant to draw attention here to II.1512 (Tell el-Yehoudeh, 23 June 14 BC?), epitaph for an unmarried male apparently also about to marry: ἄρτι γὰρ οὐδὲ γάμου | μέτ<οχ>ος κῖμαι ἐν θύ<μ>βωι (4-5). Frey's resolved text in *ll.*3-4 reads σαῖς χερσὶν κόψαι | πεντάκι (πενταέτην), 'clap your hands five times — an apotropaic act — (and weep) for the five-year-old'. It would be better to read: ΠΕΝΤΑΚΙC L, replacing the second rounded E in the diplomatic transcription with a lunate *sigma*. The following symbol, often standing for ἐτῶν, may have some other function here, since (a) the symbol is unlikely to have been employed in a metrical text, even one as metrically irregular as this; (b) when it is used the symbol normally precedes the numeral (for an exception note *CIJ* II.1447 [Alexandria?, n.d.], probably but not certainly Jewish); and (c) an epitaph for a young child is at odds with the sentiment in *ll.*4-5.

1516 — Sabbathin aged *c.*16, μικρὰ φιλάδελφε (Tell el-Yehoudeh, April-June, probably 5 AD), apparently unmarried. For μικρός in such contexts note 1522 (below), 1524 (an orphan aged 3), 1528 (a male aged 28); two further instances are mentioned at **71**, above. On φιλάδελφος see *New Docs 1978*, **74**. From the current year's reading we may add *I.Nikaia* II, 2.1292.14 and 1293.13-14 (both Imperial period), the latter mentioning a man who φι|λάδελφον ἔχων γνώμην; the word also occurs in a fragmentary grave epigram in ibid., 1579 (n.d.). In *IGUR* III it occurs at 1244, 1448 and 1468 (context of the last two is fragmentary).

1522 — Pappion aged 25, μεικρόν (see on 1516 just above), apparently unmarried as there is mention only of her mother, who is 'burned up' (with grief) for her, ἡ π[επυ]ρωμένη (Tell el-Yehoudeh, n.d.). This figurative use offers a neat parallel to 2 Cor. 11.29, as also do the similar occurrences at *CIJ* 1507 and 1509 (same provenance, the latter dated perhaps 20 BC). BAGD, s.v. πυρόω, 1b, refers only to these last two in a way which shows how dependent it has been on MM. For MM refers to Lietzmann's discussion of those two inscriptions, and makes no mention of the Pappion epitaph. The updated references to *CIJ* would have been more appropriate in BAGD.

3. Marital status cannot be determined

CIJ I

257 — Ulpia Marina aged 22.
369 — Leontia aged 20.
460 — Vesula aged 25.
650a— Kalliope aged 17 (Monastero, n.d.; text in *Proleg.* to *CIJ*).
733a— Benedicta aged 22 (text in *Proleg.* to *CIJ*).

CIJ II

1472 — Nike aged 30 (Tell el-Yehoudeh, n.d.).
1475 — female (name lost) aged *c.*32 (Tell el-Yehoudeh, n.d.).
1498 — Marion aged *c.*23 (Tell el-Yehoudeh, 24 June 5 BC).
1526 — Sabbation aged *c.*22 (Tell el-Yehoudeh, 27 BC?).
1535 — Maria aged 35 (Antinoopolis, n.d.); on this text see **115**.

The significant groups for our purposes are 1a, 2a, 2b. In 1a the ages at marriage of all those in *IGUR* and Pfuhl/Möbius (plus the non-Jewish *CIJ* 55*) is 12 or 13, with the exception of *IGUR* 1267. We can infer a marital age of 12-13 for the probably Jewish Markia Helike, at *IGUR* 1268. Contrast the *CIJ* material where there is only one girl aged 12 (I.105), the remainder being 15-17. In *AE* 60 — see **120** below — the woman was married at 25 but did not become a Christian until seven years later. In group 2a where age can be determined the oldest are 22 (*IGUR* 1287; *CIJ* 733), with three Jewish girls in their late teens (*CIJ* 168, 381, 386, and *IGUR* 1231, the Theodosia text with which we began). Group 2b is composed only of Jewish texts, and the determinable age range spreads from 14 to 26. These figures should not be pressed too far, but such as they are they appear to indicate the favouring of a higher marriage age for Jewish girls. K. Hopkins, *Population Studies* 18 (1965) 309-27, shows that the average age at marriage of Christians (male and female) was higher than for their 'pagan' counterparts (319-21, 325), and suggests that this difference may be explained in part as a 'by-product of Christian asceticism' (320). But Jewish evidence is not considered by him; and the apparent Jewish preference for higher age at marriage which has been observed above may be another factor to take into account as influencing Christians towards a higher age.

Yet even if there is substance to this hypothesis most of our evidence comes from Rome; and such social *mores* as age of betrothal cannot necessarily be expected to be consistent for highly urbanised Jews in Rome and for rural Jewish families in Galilee and Judaea. Nevertheless, these figures, and the general hypothesis, are worth bearing in mind when consideration is given to the NT Birth Narratives. If there is perceptible in the Roman period some slight indication that Jewish girls were married at an older age than their Greek/Roman counterparts, then the possibility that Mary was in her later teens should not be excluded. J. Jeremias, *Jerusalem in the Time of Jesus* (ET: London, 1969) 364-68, discusses the (largely Rabbinic) evidence for Jewish matrimonial procedure: betrothal of the girl at about age 12, followed about a year later by her going to live with her husband's family. Though the father still exercised responsibility for the girl in that intervening period, the bethrothal and subsequent year can properly be called 'marriage' (ibid., 367). R.E. Brown, *The Birth of the Messiah* (New York, 1977) 123-24, points out that the Infancy Narratives present Joseph and Mary beyond the first stage but not yet at the second stage of the marriage process. Do any of the inscriptions noted above provide evidence for these two stages? It is just possible that *CIJ* II.1509 (in list 2b) may suggest that the daughter died only a little before the age when betrothal may have been expected. So also, perhaps, with II.1512 in the case of a male (though that inscription is textually problematic). *CIJ* I.106 (in list 2a) may represent the intervening period between betrothal and cohabitation, as may also the Theodosia text with which this entry began. It is conceivable, too, that *SB* 1.5025 (noted in connection with *CIJ* I.302 in list 1a above) bears witness to this same stage, since the 14 year-old Theudas is called both *nymphios* and *agamos*. *CIJ* II.1468 may reflect a similar situation, where the deceased Johannes is spoken of as a *nymphios* and a patronymic is given, but no mention is made of his wife. Although not a Jewish text, we may note also here *IGUR* 1234, which memorialises Igorios who had a bride promised to him but died before marriage (*ll.*7-10). That the beginning of the second stage, cohabitation, is the point from which the duration of the marriage is calculated may be inferred from *CIJ* I.105, 136 and 527 (all in list 1a) where in each case it is said that the deceased lived *N* years/months 'with her husband'. The phraseology in *CIJ* I.81, 242, 319 and 772 (all in list 1b, except 242 which occurs in 1a) implies a similar notion. Yet none of these texts can be taken as certain evidence for the two stages of Jewish marriage, precisely because similar wording occurs in non-Jewish texts; and the Jews may simply be following the conventional formulae (μετὰ τοῦ συνβίου, etc.). These particular texts, however, lead us naturally to think of the NT *prophetis* Anna, who in Lk. 2.36-37 is said to have been widowed 84 years, ζήσασα μετὰ ἀνδρὸς ἔτη ἕπτα ἀπὸ τῆς παρθενίας αὐτῆς (the noun *parthenia* only here in the NT). With the exception of BAGD, s.v. παρθενία, where one Latin inscription is quoted, the relevance of these documentary parallels to Luke's wording has never been noted by NT commentators, to my knowledge. For a useful discussion of the OT and women (marriage, professional roles, etc.) see G.J. Cowling, *Interchange* 21 (1977) 23-47; 22 (1977) 105-14 (largely repr. and partially revised, though lacking many of the notes, in *Ancient Society: Resources for Teachers* 9 [1979] 96-115, 158-75).

The sheer bulk and informativeness of inscriptions from Rome make them a worthwhile corpus for demographic and sociological research. There are many questions for which the epigraphical material is likely to yield useful information. As examples of what has been done note L. Moretti's study of average life expectancy in the Empire, *Epigraphica* 21 (1959) 60-78; K. Hopkins' recent *Death and Renewal* (Cambridge, 1983) 201-56; B. Rawson (ed.), *The Family in Ancient Rome. New Perspectives*, (London, 1986), especially Rawson's chapters on 'The Roman Family' (1-58) and 'Children in the Roman *familia*' (170-200), and P.R.C. Weaver's essay on 'The status of children in mixed marriages' (ibid., 145-69). However, epigraphy cannot be expected to yield useful answers to all such sociological questions: for an interesting recent discussion of this methodological issue see F. Millar in M. Crawford (ed.), *Sources for Ancient History* (Cambridge, 1983), 80-136. As two examples, note D. Engels, *CQ* 34 (1984) 386-93, questioning the hypothesis of a 10% rate of infanticide for healthy children in the Graeco-Roman world; and A.M. Devine's recent argument, *RhM* 128 (1985) 113-18, that a significant contributory factor to the low birth-rate among Romans was their practice of taking frequent very hot baths. For a discussion of the relative worth of Jewish inscriptions at Rome for demographic questions see B. Blumenkranz, *Studia Patristica* 4 (1961) 341-47; his notes provide useful references to several studies of ancient demographic issues. One further inscription from the present culling, *IGUR* 1304 (Rome, Imperial period) may be mentioned, too, for it gives evidence of a child-bearing span of 20 years for a woman. This epitaph is for a clearly unmarried son aged 27 and a daughter aged seven. There is nothing to indicate that they are other than full siblings.

Returning to the Theodosia epigrams, the inscription draws to our attention another feature of the ancient world well enough known in NT research but not often documented: the mobility of individuals. While other metropoleis attracted large numbers, it was Rome above all which acted as a particular magnet, for citizen and non-citizen alike. Inevitably, those who came brought their local customs and sensibilities which gave rise to the scorn of Tacitus and Juvenal. Some will have made the journey for reasons of job ambition (e.g., *P.Oxy.* 46 [1978] 3312 [II AD], discussed at *New Docs 1978*, **1**). We can never know what motivated the majority to come, of course. The epitaphs in *IGUR* III serve as a useful indicator of the melting pot which was Rome: nearly one in seven of the inscriptions in that volume provides evidence of the presence of foreigners in the city. Kajanto's study (op.cit., 1-6) treats this question of the origin of those recorded on Greek epitaphs; but as he deals exclusively with prose epitaphs, the following list of material from *IGUR* III (all verse texts) may serve to complement his discussion.

1151 — an example in reverse, for the young man from Rome died and was buried at Antioch in Mygdonia *c.*114-17 AD, but later his remains were moved back to Rome from Mesopotamia.
1166 — a woman whose mother was born at Tarsos, and whose family seems to have been provincial (see Moretti's n., ad loc.).
1175 — a *neos* from Amastris.
1176 — a *kouros* from Nikaia.
1186 — Cappadocia.
1187 — aged 25, from Cyprus.
1191 — Alexandria.
1200 — Tralles.
1202 — aged 18, from Laodicea.
1204 — Termessos.
1205 — Nikomedia.
1206 — Tarsos.
1210 — Corinth.
1222 — aged 70, from Aphrodisias.
1231 — aged 18, from Egypt (the text at the beginning of this entry).
1239 — Same (on the island of Kephallenia).
1243 — aged 11, from Syria; text repr. and discussed at **9** above.
1244 — Pergamon.
1257 — native of M. . .; had travelled to many cities.
1260 — Smyrna.
1262 — Crete.
1263 — aged 22, from Nikomedia.
1274 — Asia.
1278 — Tarsos.
1283 — Smyrna (if this is the same man recorded at *IGUR* 1 [1972] 102).
1286 — Cilicia the origin of the person who raised (ὁ θρέψας) the deceased; not certain whether the latter was also from there.
1287 — aged 22, Phrygian Apamea; discussed further at **10** above.
1288 — Laodicea.
1293 — husband from Keramos in Caria; wife an Athenian.
1294 — native of Sardis, worked at Tarsos.
1303e— birthplace unclear (lacuna), but evidently not Rome.
1312 — aged 35, from Macedonia.
1314 — Argos(?).
1317 — girl aged 19 months, born at Rome; father from Syria.

1321 — born at Rome, went to Egypt, dying perhaps at Alexandria (Νείλου πόλιν, 2); his wife brought his remains (σῶμα, 12) back to Rome where he was buried; this text is repr. and discussed at **10** above.
1323 — girl aged 11 months died at Rome; mother from elsewhere (specific origin unclear). On this text see briefly **99** above.
1334 — a person called both ἀνήρ and νέος; dies at Rome, with implication that his birthplace was elsewhere; travelled widely (a merchant?).
1351 — Limyra in Lykia; this text is repr. and discussed at **8** above.
1354 — aged 16, from Myrine in Aiolis.
1355 — aged 40, from Ephesos.
1357 — son sets up cenotaph (ἀγγελίης τόδε σῆμα, *l*.1, 'this tomb announces the death . . .') in Rome for his mother who died in Egypt; presumably he was a native of Egypt himself.
1358 — husband who sets up inscription is a citizen of Alexandria.
1361 — Augusta in Cilicia.
1373 — deceased died in a foreign land (i.e., Rome), but birthplace not stated.
1383 — Pontus.
1395 — a *parthenos*, from Meandria.
1457 — probably the person in this very fragmentary text is from elsewhere, as he is a *presbys*, and his parents were not present for the burial.

This list is remarkable for the absence of foreigners from the West. Whether this lack can be accounted for in terms of language use — *IGUR* has no Latin texts, of course, and we might expect Gauls, Spaniards and others to use Latin — would need much fuller investigation. For the manumission of slaves far from their country of birth as another indication of mobility see **90** above.

115. '. . . a problem like Maria'

Is this name sufficiently distinctive ethnically to allow us to identify its bearers always as Jews, or in the late Imperial period as Christians since it was taken over as a Biblical name from Jews in the NT? MM, s.v., provides two documentary examples which BAGD's entry includes, together with an extra couple. Though still not commonly attested in non-literary sources, this number can be expanded considerably.

First, *P.Meyer* (1916) *O*.33 (noted in MM), is reproduced as *CPJ* II.227; it records the payment of Jewish tax by Maria, daughter of Abietos (31 March, 116; this ostrakon was reproduced on the cover of *New Docs 1978*). Maria the daughter of Demas pays this same special impost in *CPJ* II.223, another ostrakon (Edfu, 28 Feb., 114). These are the only indubitable Jewish examples; but as Sebaste/Samaria is the provenance of a vase bearing the name — *SEG* 8 (1937) 110 (I BC/I AD); noted by BAGD — it is very likely to be Jewish (Samaritan, presumably), too.

A binding charm written on another potsherd, and conveniently reprinted in Deissmann, *LAE* 305-06, mentions another Maria, the mother of Hor against whom the magical document is directed (Ashmunen, not dated). One of the phrases in this text, κατὰ τοῦ δακτύ|λου τοῦ θεοῦ (*ll*.6-7; the lines of the text as printed in Deissmann do not appear to align with those visible in the photo given as his fig.56), has a distinctively Jewish ring to it: in the NT cf. Lk. 11.20. But since Jewish words and notions are commonly embraced in magical texts, its presence here does nothing to prove Jewish authorship for the incantation; nor does the presence of a Maria serve as a cumulative factor in such an argument.

At *New Docs 1977*, **109**, an epitaph for a Christian Maria, a *diakonos*, was reprinted (Archelais in Cappadocia, VI). In the case of *CIJ* II.1535 (repr. as *CPJ* III, inscr. 1535), an epitaph for Maria, daughter of Phamsothis (Antinoopolis, Imperial) it is at best uncertain whether this 35-year-old woman — unmarried apparently, as no husband or children are mentioned — was Christian or Jewish. The text was found in a Christian cemetery, but so also was the definitely Jewish *CIJ* 1534, as Frey points out: that is, the monument was moved there for reuse by Christians. Similarly problematical is *IGUR* 1266 from the present year's culling (Rome, Imperial), an epitaph for a soldier called Mareinos set up by his wife Maria. It is partly on the ground of this woman's name that his text has been claimed as Christian (see Moretti's n. ad loc.); but Moretti himself doubts it and appears to regard it as Jewish (his statement is not very clear: '*ipse ethnicam* [sc. *lapidis et litterarum formam*] *crediderim*'). Maria is the wife of Judas in *P.Oxy*. 46 (1978) 3314 — reprinted at *New Docs 1978*, **100** — but there is debate whether this family was Jewish or Christian.

The second of the attestations given by MM, *P.Meyer O*.56, (repr. as *SB* 1 [1915] 4252 and as *CPJ* III.462a), is one of a group of eight ostraka from Thebes in Egypt — *CPJ* 462a-h — ranging in date from 150-61, which mention Pollia Maria the younger. The fact that she is so called implies she was given her mother's name. As the woman who figures in our texts is clearly an adult, her mother at least must have been alive at the time of the Second Jewish Revolt in Egypt (115-17). Yet the daughter is making cash payments for taxes that were in arrears (462b, c), and amounts of grain held in the public granaries are being credited to her account by others (462d-h; in 462a an amount of wheat is credited to another woman from her own holding). These texts suggest that Pollia Maria is a landowner, with tenants leasing her arable land. For this woman to be Jewish may not be consistent with the very widespread confiscations of Jewish property after the Revolt, very possibly affecting all Jews, not merely those who actually participated in the Revolt; on this see **112**. It cannot be ruled out absolutely that Pollia Maria was a Jew, but at least doubt may be recorded concerning her ethnic status. Since mid-II (and early II, in the case of her mother) is likely to be too early for the presence of the name to indicate a Christian, if she is not Jewish the alternative — that she was pagan — has implications for those other texts noted above which are not clearly Jewish or Christian.

It is when we turn to *CIL* VI 6, 1 (1920), M. Bang's index of names to *CIL* VI, that we discover many examples of Maria, women from the *gens* Maria. Those few who possess a double *nomen* (like Pollia Maria) appear to be of the senatorial class (Vibia Maria Maxima, no.1636; Accia Maria Tulliana, no.31934). Latin and Greek texts will normally use the forms Maria/Μαρία even when referring to a Jew called Mariam because the latter is awkward morphologically. Thus, whether the Maria greeted at Rom. 16.6 was a Jew or a Roman cannot be determined with certainty, at least on the basis of onomastics.

Two indubitably Jewish names are attested among the year's publications. Anna[s] occurs in *l*.3 of a funerary text (Corinth, Imperial period?), *l*.4 of which is in Hebrew: *ed.pr.* — D.I. Pallas/S.P. Dantes, *Arch.Eph.* (1977 [1979]) 80-81 no.29 (pl.; cf. *SEG* 309). Ellel occurs in a very fragmentary Jewish inscription noted at *SEG* 981 (Porto in Italy, n.d.); for this name cf. the B text of Judges 12.13, 15.

116. Jews at Ephesos

There is suprisingly little epigraphical evidence for a Jewish presence at Ephesos. *I.Eph.* VII, 2.4130 allows us to infer the existence of a synagogue: the inscription contains simply τὸ θυσιαστήριον followed by a menorah. For Christian use of the noun in a mosaic inscription from a Byzantine church in Palestine note *SEG* 1610 (Hesban, VI), . . . τὸ ἅγ(ιον) θυσιαστ(ήριον) . . . (*l*.1). On archaeological remains attesting Jews at Ephesos in late Imperial times see C. Foss, *Ephesus after Antiquity* (Cambridge, 1979) 45. Additional evidence for a synagogue is provided by *I.Eph.* IV.1251, which refers to *archisynagogoi* and *presbyteroi*: see **113**, no.23, where the text is reprinted.

Apart from this evidence we have two inscriptions already included in *CIJ* II as nos.745 and 746: respectively, *I.Eph.* V.1677 and 1676. The latter is an epitaph (late II?) for a priest (ἱαιρέος *l*.3, genitive), Marcus Mussios, responsibility for whose burial was taken by οἱ Ἰουδαῖοι. No.1677 is an Imperial-period family epitaph set up by the Jewish community of the city, [- - οἱ ἐν Ἐφέ]σῳ Ἰουδε̃οι (*l*.7). The husband was an *archiatros* (*l*.2); for this term cf. *New Docs 1977*, **2**. Several other *archiatroi* are attested in *I.Eph.*: III.622 (*c*.160); V.1162.4, 6, 7 (time of Antoninus Pius), 1164 (mid-II?); VII, 1.3055.16 (late Imperial?); VII, 2.4350 (late III or IV).

It is unclear whether the three monograms of the name Johannes included at *I.Eph.* II.581 are Jewish or Christian. Equally ambivalent is *I.Eph.* VI.2306k, a grave inscription for a [Sa]mbathios: at the head of this text is a cross, yet the name is most commonly associated with a Jewish milieu. The name occurs also at VII, 1.3307, where an Aurelius Sambathios purchases a burial plot. Sambathios figures more than once in *CPR* 2 (Oxyrhynchos, I), a list of names including at least several Jews. From the year 80 AD an inspection schedule from the record office of the village of Karanis, *P.XV Congr.* 15, likewise mentions a Sambathion (*l*.31), as well as a Sambas (*l*.20); a father and son both called Dositheos (*l*.38) provide further testimony to a Jewish presence there in mid-late I AD. Over two centuries later comes *P.Col.* 174 (Karanis, *c*.325-50), which preserves the notes made by a court advocate (*rhetor*) as a basis for his oral delivery on behalf of his clients, one of whom is called Sambathion. It is at least open to question whether this man was a Jew, given that he owns property in that period (cf. **112**). Yet an unequivocally Christian Sambatis turns up on an epitaph reprinted at Guarducci, *EG* IV.319-21, no.2 (fig. 88): Σαμβάτις ἐν|θάδε κῖται | κὲ Δημάρχη | Χριστιανοί | ☧ ω ☧ α ☧, 'Sambatis lies here and Demarche, Christians (*crosses*)'. This inscription from Athens — = *IG* III.3525; repr. also in *SIA* III, p.37 and p.148 (the latter = C. Bayet, *De titulis Atticae Christianis antiquissimis* [Paris 1878], no.78) — is dated III or IV by Guarducci. Others with this name who are also undoubtedly Christian appear at *SIA* III, pp.220-21 no.xxiii, and p.226 no.13 (= J.S. Creaghan/A.E. Raubitschek, *Hesperia* 16 [1947] 1-54, at 36-37, 42; their n. 186 provides further references to documentary examples). The Christian instances are likely to be post-Constantinian or later. A Christian family including a wife called Sambatis made a dedication of a τράπεζα on the island of Karpathos in IV or V: Guarducci, *EG* IV.370-71 (fig.107). In another family epitaph the wife's name is given as Sabbatis: Tsigaridas, *Κατάλογος*, 9 (Thessalonike, IV; = *IG* X 2, 1 [1972] 785). As related examples note Sambation, a woman of Miletos, *SEG* 235 (Athens, n.d.), and perhaps Sambathion in ibid., 608 (Lete in Macedonia, n.d.). A woman called Sabbous is attested from Seleukeia on the Euphrates: *SEG* 1582 (mid-II). It should be pointed out generally in relation to all these Sabb-/Samb- names that from the evidence of *P.Oxy.* 34 (1968) 2728.33 (III/IV) and 2729.9 (IV), where the word σάμβαθον must refer to a container, the connection with the Sabbath and thereby the previously near-automatic association of these names with Jews comes into question.

Though *I.Eph.* VI.2209 is stated to be Jewish (edd. n. ad loc.), this view has been retracted in the *Addenda et Corrigenda* supplement to VII, 1 (1981), at p.28. In fact no.2209 proves to have been misread, and is to be equated with VI.2281B, a four-word epitaph for a woman. For a possible allusion in an Ephesian inscription to the LXX book of Sousanna, see **104**.

117. Divine names

An intaglio inscription on an oval agate, *IGLS* 1 (1929) 224 (near Aleppo, n.d.), has been interpreted by M. Philonenko as being three forms of the divine name: *CRAI* (1979) 297-304 (6 figs.; cf. *SEG* 1588). Incised on one side of the stone within an *ouroboros* (i.e., a snake eating its tail, and so, making a circle) are the three lines ΙΑΩ | ƵƵX | ΠΙΠ; on the other side can be read Σαβαωθ | Μιχαηλ 'Α|δωναι ἀ|βρασας. The word Ιαω is a well known Greek equivalent in magical papyri for the Hebrew divine name, יהוה, e.g., *PGM* IV (1928 [repr. 1974]) 593, 1983 (cf. Deissmann, *Bible Studies*, 324). Philonenko takes ΠΙΠ to be a shortened form of ΠΙΠΙ, the common visual imitation in Greek letters of יהוה, for which see *New Docs 1977*, **87**, p.112; and he reads ƵƵX as two *yods* in palaeo-hebraic script and a star, whose six branches have balls on their ends. The two *yods* are an abbreviation for יהוה and the star may be 'a confused memory of cuneiform writing in which a determinative, precisely in the form of a star, precedes the divine name' (302). Perhaps this star is related to the similar shapes, sometimes with four or eight branches, commonly found in magical papyri (for an example see two Coptic amulets published by P.J. Sijpesteijn, *CE* 57 [1982] 377-81 [figs.1, 2]; cf. also the intaglio discussed below). The reading of ƵƵ as an abbreviation for the divine name is supported by the reading ƵƵ at *ll.*4 and 14 of *P.Oxy.* 7 (1910) 1007 (late III; van Haelst, 5), a vellum leaf containing parts of Gen. 2-3. The double *yod* abbreviation was current in Rabbinic literature (Philonenko, 302-303).

A similar intaglio, perhaps from the same school, has been published by Philonenko (*Semitica* 30 [1980] 57-60, pl. IIIa; cf. *SEG* 30 [1980] 1682), which he explains as also bearing three forms of the divine name, again within an *ouroboros*. Line one has a star with eight branches terminating in balls followed by Ƶ, presumably for יהוה. The second line contains *yod* and *aleph* followed by a monogram which Philonenko interprets as *waw* plus *he*, יאוה. Philonenko suggests (58-59) that this is a form of יהוה with the first ה changed to א to avoid the prohibition against pronouncing the divine name according to its letters (cf. *Sanhedrin* 10, 1 of the Mishnah), and with ו and ה written as a monogram so as to give an equivalent to the trigram 'Ιαω. In *ll.*3-4 'Ενμανουηλ is another divine name, drawn from Is. 7.14. The piece is thought by Philonenko (60) to be of Jewish origin and, from the similarity of the monogram here to others on coins of the Seleucid period, to be dated to that time.

An inscribed octagonal, jasper ring-stone (12B x 11H mm.), published by A.T. Kraabel, *JJS* 30 (1979) 41-58, no.4 (provenance unknown, III?; pl.III; cf. *SEG* 991), bears the inscription (incised retrograde as for a seal), ΙΑω | ΣΑω | ΑΔωΝΙ. Kraabel interprets 'Αδωνι as a rare variant of 'Αδωναι and Σαω as an abbreviation for Σαβαω (i.e., Sabaoth). Kraabel compares this divine name with an identical text, though not retrograde, on a bronze ring, published by N. Galeotti in 1757 but now lost. He argues that one was a copy of the other or that they both came from the same source, and he suggests that they were probably Jewish amulets.

Two inscriptions from Ephesos may be noted in the present context. *I.Eph.* VII, 1.3100 is an acclamation made in response to a dream: μέγα τὸ ὄνομα τοῦ θεοῦ | μέγα τὸ ὅσιον | μέγα (*vac.*) τὸ ἀγαθὸν | κατ' ὄναρ. Similarly, IV.1247B begins μέγα τὸ ὄν[ο]μα | τοῦ θεοῦ, and proceeds to honour a man who restored a cult meeting place (τὸ συνέδρ[ιον], *l.*7). See further **19** ad fin. above, where the phrase τὸ θεῖον ὄνομα in *I.Eph.* Ia.24, frag. B.24-25 is noted. L. Robert, *Hellenica* 10 (1955) 86-89, 299 discusses other instances of such invocations of the Name of God; these texts are associated with Sarapis (so, perhaps no.1247B), sometimes with other divinities.

(A.L. CONNOLLY)

118. Hellenic influence in Palestine

That Greek influence was endemic in Hellenistic Palestine is now sufficiently recognised. Some recent evidence of various dates serves merely to indicate how deeply rooted it was. For these new items reflect day-to-day acquaintance with Greek language and culture.

F. Manns, *SBF* 29 (1979) 238-43 (pls. 1-5) publishes several items. The first pair are gold leaves, used as wreaths for crowning a bridal couple. This is to be inferred from their inscribed text, 'Good luck to the newly-weds!', εὐτυ|χῶς | τοῖς νυ|μφίοις (cf. *SEG* 1607). These wreaths are to be dated between II BC-II AD. Their function may have been faintly apotropaic. A gold tablet is also published by him: though the fourth-century text is legible its sense is not at all clear. Manns suggests that it may have affinities with the better known Orphic gold leaves from Italy; alternatively, they may have had a magical significance of some kind (cf. *SEG* 1615). Finally, Manns publishes a Roman period weighing-scale of 'late' date, which includes an inscription in Greek (cf. *SEG* 1616).

Greek culture is also in evidence in a mosaic unearthed at Neapolis (Nablus) in Palestine: *ed.pr.* — C.M. Dauphin, *IEJ* 29 (1979) 11-33 (pls. 1-8; cf. *SEG* 1612). This mid-III floor is decorated with classical motifs, including scenes from the life of Achilles. While on the subject of Achilles, a bronze urn perhaps of Egyptian origin now in Jerusalem and dated *c.*550-650 has been published with a full discussion by M. Hengel, *Achilleus in Jerusalem* (*Sitz. der Heidelberger Akad. der Wiss., phil.-hist. Kl.* 1982.1; Heidelberg, 1982). The pitcher contains scenes depicting Achilles pursuing and killing Hektor, the ransoming of Hektor's corpse where the body is weighed on scales against the ransom items, and Achilles standing listening to Briseis playing the lyre. One distinctive feature about the portrayal of the figures is that the craftsman has imitated much earlier models on the vessel, not portrayed them in a contemporary Byzantine style. It is the 'weighing of the dead' which is perhaps most suggestive of an Egyptian origin for the pitcher.

119. In brief

(a) Honorific inscription for a **former *propraetor of Judaea*** currently proconsul of Asia, Q. Ruscius Murena Coelius Pompeius Falco (his full name had 13 elements!): *I.Eph.* III.713 (123/4). Pomponia Triaria, wife of C. Erucius Clarus, a former consular prefect of Judaea and later consul in 170, is honoured at *I.Eph.* III.665.

(b) **'Christianisation' of Jewish texts** was noted at *New Docs 1976*, **69**, p.108. For a further instance, the use of the distinctively Christian κοιμητήριον on Jewish epitaphs from Athens see *IG* III, 2.x.3545, 3546 (= *CIJ* I.712, 713), repr. in *SIA* III, pp.45-46 (cf. ibid., 190).

(c) **Jewish/Christian relations** in Imperial-period Western Phrygia as revealed by inscriptions: *SEG* 1400. The article which this item signals, A.R.R. Sheppard, *AS* 29 (1979) 169-80, was noted at *New Docs 1978*, **98**, p.137; cf. also **66** above, ad fin.

(d) **'The highest God'** mentioned in an unusually worded amulet, *IG* XIV *Suppl.* 2580.1 (Valentia, not dated): τὸν θεόν σοι τὸν ὕψιστον, μή με ἀδικήσ[η]ς '(I adjure you) by your god, the highest one, do not harm me'. Note also an invocation to the highest God, 'the lord of spirits and of all flesh', τὸν κύριον τῶν πνευμάτων | καὶ πάσης σαρκός (*ll.*2-3), for vengeance on the killers of a girl, Herakleia: Guarducci, *EG* IV.236-38 (Rheneia on Delos, II^2 BC; fig.67). This well-known Jewish text is discussed at Deissmann, *LAE*, 413-24; cf. *New Docs 1976*, **5**, *ad fin.*

E. ECCLESIASTICA

120. 'In the world but not of it . . .'

Rome 279
ed. — Diehl, *ILCV* I (1925, repr. 1961) 645

cum cumvixit · Severa · Seleuci-
ane · cum Aurelio · Sabutio · annis ·
dece<m> · et septe<m> imp(eratore) Probo Aug(usto) · III · et Nonio
Paterno bis cons(ulibus). Quot vixit in seculo?
annis tricinta et duo et menses duo · imp(eratore) ·
Claudio Aug(usto) et Patern(o) con{e}s(ulibus).

Marble tablet (72.5B x 31.3H x 4D cm.) found originally in a cemetery. To the right of the text is depicted a loom and shuttle, apparently.
Bib. — A.E. and J.S. Gordon, *Album of Dated Latin Inscriptions*, III (Berkeley, 1965) 96-97 no.302 (squeeze shown as pl. 144c in the accompanying vol. of plates); *J.H. Oliver, *ZPE* 33 (1979) 116; *AE* 60.

When Severa Seleukiane had lived with Aurelius Sabutius for seventeen years the consuls were Imperator Probus Augustus for the third time and Nonius Paternus for the second. How many (years) did she live in the world? | Thirty-two years and two months, in the consulship of Imperator Claudius Augustus and Paternus.

If the picture carved on this stone is correctly interpreted, the husband and wife may both have been weavers. Since this epitaph is for Seleuciane alone it would be strange to include this allusion to the husband's trade if it were his alone. Other couples are known who followed the same vocation, e.g., doctors (see *New Docs 1977*, **2**, p.17), purple sellers (*New Docs 1977*, **3**, p.27), tent makers (Aquila and Priscilla in Acts 18.2-3).

The consulship of Probus and Paternus dates to the year 279, the consulship of Claudius Augustus and Paternus a decade earlier, 269. It is possible then to work out that Severa was married at the age of 25 and died 17 years later, aged 42. The question at the end of *l*.4 provides the only clue — apart from the find spot: in a Christian cemetery (see Gordon, 96) — that the woman (and therefore her husband?) was a Christian. It is a curiosity that on a reasonably unpretentious epitaph there should be such concern to specify the date of conversion and death by the current consulship. This was done presumably to allow the reader to calculate the 'real' age of Severa, in spite of the text otherwise wishing to avoid altogether the conclusion that life has ended. For whereas it is common on funerary texts to measure the total life-span, this epitaph provides two other spans, married life and life in the world. 'Severa's new life in Christ, though not explicitly alluded to, is thus conceived as going on beyond the old terminus of death, also not alluded to' (E.A. Judge, in a note to me).

By speaking of 'living in the world' for 32 years but actually dying a decade later she is alluding to the motif found commonly in the Fourth Gospel (Jn 8.23; 13.1; 15.19; 17.6, 15, etc.) and 1 Jn (2.15; 3.1, etc.), and occasionally elsewhere in the NT, that the believer is a stranger in this world, since it is alienated from God. Jerome's Vulgate, translated a century after the date of this inscription, uses *mundus* consistently for this pejorative sense of κόσμος (for an epigraphical example of the latter see **126** below). However, αἰών is also used with the same connotation (e.g., Rom. 12.2; 2 Tim. 4.10); and it is usually rendered by *saeculum*. G.W. Clarke tells me that the pejorative sense of the noun is frequent in Cyprian; he draws attention also to A.P. Orbán, *Les denominations du monde chez les premiers auteurs chrétiens* (Nijmegen, 1970) — *non vidi*. For further examples in Christian writers of *saeculum* in this sense see A. Blaise/H. Chirat, *Dictionnaire latin-français des auteurs chrétiens* (Turnhout, 1954), s.v., 5. Until official recognition of the Church came in the early fourth century this theme, of the Christian as an outsider to the world in which he lived, can be expected to have struck a chord at a general level with many believers.

So this text provides us with evidence of the Christian conversion of a woman at Rome between the Decian and Diocletianic persecutions (on the effect of the former see *New Docs 1977*, **105**). Another point of interest is her age at marriage: though not unparalleled, 25 seems surprisingly high. At **114** above, where female marital age is considered, particularly among Jews, one instance was noted of a woman marrying at the age of 26 (*CIJ* I.30). There is insufficient indication in our epitaph for Severa to allow us to say whether she was a convert from Judaism, seven years after her marriage. The silence of the epitaph about children allows the inference that they were childless.

121. A crypto-Christian epitaph?

Upper Tembris Valley, N. Phrygia — IV init.
ed. pr. — Pfuhl/Möbius I.783 (pl. 115)

ἀδε-		+ά-
λφῷ	(*legs*)	ριν
μνή-		
μη-		
ς		

Αὐρ(ήλιος) Τροφίμων
Κρευρηνὸς κ(αὶ)
Βερονίκης τέκ-
νῳ Τροφίμῳ κ(αὶ)
Τρόφιμος κ(αὶ) Τρ[ο-]
φιμιάνης κ(αὶ) Εὐ[τυ-]
χιανὸς

Well-preserved stele, 34B x 75H cm., dominated by a full-length male figure standing within a niche, holding a bird in his right hand and a bunch of grapes in his left. In a panel on either side of him is a vine branch with bunches of grapes. Two circles, each segmented into

four parts, are carved in the niche on either side of the figure's neck. Below the figure and to the left of the main portion of text are carved two oxen.
Bib. — *SEG* 27 (1977) 1238; cf. *New Docs 1977*, **103**, p.176 (last para.).

Aurelius Trophimon Kreurenos and Beronikes (*sic*) to their child Trophimos, and | Trophimos and Trophimianes and Eutychianos to their brother, as a memorial.

Pfuhl/Möbius accept the opinion (*per litt.*) of L. Robert that this epitaph is crypto-Christian, coming from N. Phrygia or Bithynia. Uncharacteristically, they suggest no date for the monument. Although the bird, the grapes and the oxen may all be specifically Christian symbols in some contexts, the decisive features are taken to be the two segmented circles near the figure's head, and the *chi* carved as a cross in the word χάριν. While this appears to amount to a strong cumulative argument in favour of a crypto-Christian identification for the family members who are mentioned, the question should not be thought foreclosed. In his note at *SEG* 27.1238 H.W. Pleket appears to doubt Robert's interpretation of the monument as Christian; but the stele warrants further attention, for I think we can settle the question of its date and more narrowly delimit its provenance.

First, it should be pointed out that the position of the text shows that the design was all carved before it was selected to receive the wording. Not only is most of the wording in the one blank area, the bottom right corner, but the mason was unable to fit all the text there; acordingly, he completed it higher up on the stone, on either side of the figure's legs. It follows that the designs cannot be used to interpret the lettering of +άριν, and vice versa. Furthermore, though the lettering of *chi* carved as a cross is often accepted as an indicator of a monument's Christian character (so Guarducci, *EG* IV.313 n.1), there are examples of definitely non-Christian inscriptions containing this tilted *chi.* One recently published instance is E. Gibson, *The 'Christians for Christians' Inscriptions of Phrygia* (*Harvard Theological Studies* 32; Missoula, 1978) no.16 (N. Phrygia, precise provenance unknown, 304/5); see especially her discussion on p.39 referring to other unpublished texts bearing this same feature (cf. *New Docs 1978*, **98**, p.134). Even W.M. Calder, who published a number of texts with +άριν, *vel sim.*, which he interpreted as Christian — e.g., *JRS* 14 (1924) 88-92, nos.1-5, 10; *AS* 5 (1955) 35-36, nos.3, 4 — occasionally recognised that the presence of the tilted *chi* was inadequate to prove a Christian affiliation: of inscription no.6 in the *JRS* article just cited he says, 'In this carelessly engraved text, the cross may be an engraver's error; its Christian character is very doubtful'.

An analogy may be mentioned here. *I.Eph.* VI.2277 is a funerary text for Tib. Julius Zosimos Eutyches (n.d.). The letters are cut without great care (the Z is carved back to front), and following this name (which constitutes the full wording) is a crudely incised fish. If the text is Christian, as is suggested by the editors, then the only indication is the fish. But equally, it may be a representation of a dolphin, of which there are several on *I.Eph.* funerary inscriptions (see VI.2577 and the further references noted there). Dolphins were a common funerary motif, employed on both non-Christian and Christian monuments. For an example of each see E. Gibson, *ZPE* 28 (1978) 1-34, nos. 2 and 11 respectively (pls.2b, 6b; no.11 = Gibson, '*Christians for Christians*' *Inscriptions*, no.17, pp.46-49 [pl.18]), and her discussion (3-4) with reference to other instances. The *upsilon* in the word ΕΙΟΥΛΙΟΣ in *I.Eph.* 2277 has a horizontal bar through it, which does not feature on either *upsilon* in the name ΕΥΤΥΧΗΣ. There is no special reason to perceive it as a Christian cross.

Second, the two circles with crosses ('Radkreuze', Pfuhl/Möbius) may be further examples of eucharistic bread, or even the communion paten. The interpretative parallel to which Pfuhl/Möbius (ad loc.) draw attention, Calder, *AS* 5 (1955) 33-35 no.2 (pl.2b), is not the most germane analogy. On that stele (near Kadoi in Phrygia, 179/80) the figure holds the *panis quadratus* in his right hand; as *BE* (1956) 292 points out, why should the deceased be depicted holding a loaf of bread unless it had some significance? In the figure's left hand Calder interpreted the carved feature half-hidden by the fingers as a *tau* cross, from which hang a bunch of grapes. While there are undoubted epigraphical depictions of this early form of Christian cross — e.g., *MAMA* 7 (1956) 277, 279, 297, 298; cf. *New Docs 1976*, **90** — its presence on Calder's stele is less than certain. If that monument possesses a Christian character, it would be due to the fact of the man holding the two eucharistic elements in his hands. A date at least in the third century would be more appropriate for this stele (cf. M. Gough, *The Early Christians* [London, 1961] 66-67 with fig.2). On the use of a cross as a stamp on eucharistic bread see G. Galavaris, *Bread and the Liturgy. The Symbolism of the Early Christian and Byzantine Bread Stamps* (Madison, 1970) 84, 85, 87, 169. For discussion of Pfuhl/Möbius I.154, in which eucharistic loaves may be represented, see **96** above. A closer parallel to the circles on the gravestone for Trophimos may appear to be the series of stelai published by E. Gibson, *GRBS* 16 (1975) 433-39, nos.1-3 (pls.3-5; cf. pls.6-7). She interprets these stones from Phrygia as pre-Constantinian, Montanist monuments. Her no.3 is republished with a better text by T. Drew-Bear, *Chiron* 9 (1979) 301-02 (cf. *SEG* 1418), and dated by him 'not too long after the Constitutio Antoniniana'. The series has in common a design which I. Ševčenko interprets as a communion paten surrounded by a wreath, above a communion table. The significance of the motif is taken to be that 'the deceased was a member of the clergy authorized to celebrate the Eucharist' (Gibson, 437). Yet when this design is compared with what occurs twice on the Trophimos monument, it is clear that we have something considerably simpler and more equivocal.

In sum, while a Christian milieu cannot be excluded for the stele, it possesses insufficient features to impel us towards such a conclusion. However, Gibson, '*Christians for Christians' Inscriptions*, advances the suggestive idea (42) that monument nos.3-16 have sufficient stylistic design motifs to make likely a provenance from the same workshop. All but nos.15 and 16 are Christian monuments, and no.15 appears to have had a cross carefully erased (ibid., 36). If so, this workshop 'may well have been phanero-Christian owned and operated' (ibid., 42). Stylistic comparison with the motifs on Pfuhl/Möbius 783 suggests to me that we may have another stele from the same factory: its affinities with Gibson no.16 (dated 304/5) are particularly marked (see her pl.17), although in dimensions it is considerably smaller. (M. Waelkens, *Die kleinasiatischen Türsteine* [Mainz am Rhein, 1986] 87 n.158 also connects in passing these two monuments along with others, though he does not draw the inferences advanced here.) If that is so, it follows that the provenance of this gravestone for Trophimos can be specified considerably more closely, and also a date suggested: upper Tembris Valley in North Phrygia, IV init.

On stonemasons' workshops in Phrygia see also M. Waelkens, *Actes Constantza*, 105-28 (pls.1-6). This article deals with a number of unpublished texts, including some Christian ones. On the basis of the sculptural style of the monument Waelkens (127-28) dates *MAMA* 7 (1956) 96 considerably earlier than *c*.375, proposed originally by Calder. This text from Kindyria near Laodicea Combusta reflects the milieu of the Christian Encratite sect, which is attested in parts of Asia Minor from II^2. That text carries the curse εἴσχι πρὸς τὸν | θ(εὸ)ν καὶ Ἰη(σο)ῦ(ν) Χ(ριστό)ν (*ll*.6-7). The monument is now included in Waelkens, *Türsteine*, as no.666 (pl.84), where he suggests as its date III^2, or at the latest early IV.

122. Sophia, 'the second Phoibe'

Jerusalem (mount of Olives) IV[2]

ed.pr. — L. Cré, *Rev.Bib.* 13 (1904) 260-62 (pl.)

† ἐνθάδε κῖται ἡ δούλη
καὶ νύμφη τοῦ Χριστοῦ
Σοφία, ἡ διάκονος, ἡ δευ-
τέρα Φοίβη, κοιμηθῖσα
ἐν ἰρήνῃ τῇ κα´ τοῦ Μαρ-
τίου μηνὸς Ἰνδ(ικτιῶνος) ια´
[. . .]θίτω κύριος ὁ θεὸς
[- - - - -]ισων πρεσ-
- - - - - - - - - - - - - -

Upper portion of a stele. At end of *l.*2 -ου ligatured as Ὀ̆.
Bib. — *Guarducci, *EG* IV.445 (fig. 132).

(*Cross*) Here lies the slave and bride of Christ, Sophia, deacon, the second Phoibe, who fell asleep | in peace on the 21st of the month of March during the 11th indiction . . . the Lord God . . .

The deceased is described in four ways here. 'Slave' and 'bride' of Christ are common enough, the first taking its rise from Paul's frequent self-description in the Epistles — from this year's publications note Pfuhl/Möbius I.154, epitaph erected by Onesimos, θεοῦ δοῦλος, for a grave-digger [East Phrygia, III], discussed further at **96** above; for a guild of grave-diggers see *New Docs 1977*, **113** — the second being a development which is given currency among the fourth-century Fathers. Whereas in the NT the Church (cf. Eph. 5.22-33) and the New Jerusalem (Rev. 21.2, 9; 22.17) are the bride of Christ, with the development of monasticism Chrysostom and others (see references in Lampe, s.v. νύμφη, B) begin applying the notion to individual *parthenoi.* It need not be otiose that the deceased is here described as both a virgin and a *diakonos*. While it is not common to find reference to female office-holders in the Church being married, we may at least note the epitaph (repr. at *New Docs 1977*, **109**) for Maria the *diakonos* who is said to have reared children; though in that case she may have been widowed before taking on the position. At *New Docs 1976*, **79**, mention was made of a Latin Christian epitaph for a married couple in which the word *exorcista* is probably used of the wife. Pliny, *Ep*. 10.96.8 records that in Bithynia under Trajan there were female deacons; Pliny has two *ancillae* tortured, *quae ministrae dicebantur.* From the current year's culling we may note the following other female deacons and office-holders:

1. *IG* III, 2.x.3527, repr. in *SIA* III at pp.38 and 159 (the latter = Bayet, no.105), Νεικαγόρη | διακόνισ|σα ἐνθάδε κεῖμαι (Mt Hymettos in Attika, n.d.).
2. *SEG* 425 (Patrai in Achaia, 'early Christian' period; *ed.pr.* — P. Petsas, *AD* 26 [1971] 161-63), ἡ θεοφιλεστάτη | διάκονος Ἀγριππια|νὴ ὑπὲρ εὐχῆς αὐ|τῆς ἐποίησεν (*leaf*) | τὴν μούσωσιν, 'the most God-beloved deacon Agrippiane made the mosaic to fulfil her vow'. This text was noted previously at *New Docs 1976*, **79**. For θεοφιλεστάτη of Church officals cf. *SEG* 643 (Thessalonike, 525 or 532); and *New Docs 1977*, **115**, p.205 (= *SEG* 27 [1977] 882). Another brief Christian votive inscription appears as *SEG* 589 (Fourka in Macedonia, n.d.).

3. Guarducci, *EG* IV.345-47 (Delphi, V[1]; fig.99), a well-known, lengthy epitaph for *diakonissa* Athanasia, ordained deaconess by the most holy bishop Pantamianos, κατασταθῖσα | δὲ διακόνισα παρὰ τοῦ | ἁγιωτάτου ἐπισκόπου | Παντ[α]μιανοῦ, κτλ (4-7). The noun occurs three times in this text (*ll.*2, 5, 11), which includes a version of the 'curse of Judas' formula: if anyone dares open this tomb where the deaconess is buried, [ἔχοι τ]ὴν μερίδα τοῦ Εἰού|δα τοῦ [προδότου] τοῦ δεσπότου ἡ|μῶν Ἰη[σοῦ Χριστ]οῦ (*ll.*12-14). For this expression cf. discussions at *New Docs 1976*, **61**; *New Docs 1978*, **64**, and **100**, p.146. The text is mentioned at Deissmann, *LAE* 227 n.1, and quoted by MM, s.v. προδότης, as their sole documentary illustration of that noun, even though the word is entirely restored. For the most recent discussion, with improvements to the text, see D. Feissel, *BCH* 104 (1980) 469-70.
4. Guarducci, *EG* IV.368-70 (Melos, IV init.), a family tombstone for a mother and her children; all the latter hold offical Church titles: Asklepis (female?), Elpizon and Asklepiodotos are *presbyteroi* (*ll.*2-3), Agaliasis (female) is a *diakonos* (3-4), Eutychia and Klaudiane are each specified as παρθενεύσασα (4-5). This text is of some interest for two further reasons: first, it is unlikely to be coincidental that these family members are listed in order of their ecclesiastical status, with their mother added last (5). Second, the text concludes with a wording not to add further bodies: ἐνορκίζω ὑμᾶς τὸν ὧδε ἐφεστῶτα ἄνγελον | μή τίς ποτε τολμῇ ἐνθάδε τινὰ κατάθεσθε (7-8), 'I adjure you by the angel who stands over (the tomb) here, let no one ever dare to add any (body) here'. For ἐνορκίζω here cf. 1 Thes. 5.27. The *angelos* mentioned here is clearly thought of as a divinely appointed guardian, and in this Christian text offers a continuity of outlook with the *angeloi* mentioned in the less certainly Christian epitaphs from Thera, *IG* XII, 3 (1898) 455, 933-74, and XII, 3 Suppl. (1904) 1636, 1637 (II/III AD). For *angelos* in quite another context note the dedication by a priestess of Hera of a sundial, described as ἄγγελον ὡρῶν, 'messenger of the hours', repr. at Guarducci, *EG* IV.210 (near Argos, II).
5. Tibiletti, *Lettere*, no.32 (*P.Strasb.* inv.1900; *ed.pr.* — M. Nagel, *ZPE* 18 [1975] 317-23) preserves the lower left portion of a Christian letter (provenance unknown, IV), in which mention is twice made of Kyria τὴν διδάσκαλον (*l.*5, and along the left edge of the papyrus), as also of a male teacher, Philoxenos (the recipient of the letter). The letter is confirmed as Christian by the closing salutation, ἡ χάρις τοῦ κ(υρίο)υ ἡμῶν Ἰη(σοῦ) [Χρ(ιστοῦ) μετὰ πάντων ὑμῶν] (*l.*11). For this and closely similar wordings in the NT note Rom. 16.20, 24; 1 Cor. 16.23; 2 Cor. 13.13; 1 Thes. 5.28; 2 Thes. 3.18; cf. Gal. 6.18; Eph. 6.24; Phil. 4.23; Philem. 25; Rev. 22.21. Nagel finds the mention of a female teacher in an orthodox Christian context problematical and suggests that the letter emanates from a sectarian milieu. This text was noted previously at *New Docs 1976*, **79**, where a date during the reign of Licinius was suggested (by E.A. Judge).
6. F. Barratte/B. Boyaval, 'Catalogue des étiquettes de momies du Musée du Louvre, IV', *CRIPEL* 5 (1979) 264 no.1115, Ἀρτεμιδώρας | Μικκάλου μη`τ΄(ρὸς) Πα|νισκιαίνης πρεσ`β΄(υτέρας) | ἐκοιμήθη ἐν κ(υρί)ῳ, '(mummy) of Artemidora daughter of Mikkalos, her mother (being) Paniskiane, *presbytera*; she fell asleep in the Lord' (provenance in Egypt not stated; II/III). The editors take πρεσ`β΄ as an abbreviation for 'older (in age)' — 'l'ainée' — but it is much more plausible that we have here an example of a female elder in the Church, given the *nomen sacrum* as another explicit allusion to Christianity in the text. While the word could refer to the mother, it is more likely that Artemidora is being so designated, as it is the deceased and her status that is in focus. The same issue arises for a Jewish epitaph, *CIJ* I.400 (Rome, Imperial?), ἐνθ<ά>δε | κῖται Σά|ρα Οὖρα π|ρεσβύτ≪ι≫ς (or, -τ≪η≫ς). She is more plausibly to be seen as an elder in a Jewish community. For women with this function see B.J. Brooten, *Women Leaders in the Ancient Synagogue* (*Brown Judaic Studies* 36; Chico, 1982) 41-55.

Though not part of the 1979 culling we may also note:

7. *Inscriptiones Bureschianae*, ed. A. Körte (Greifswald, 1902) no.55, repr. and discussed by E. Gibson, *GRBS* 16 (1975) 437-38: Διογᾶς ἐβίσκο|πος Ἀμμίῳ πρεσ|βυτέρᾳ μνήμης | χάριν (at or near Uşak in Phrygia, pre-Constantinian date). Gibson identifies Ammion the presbyter as belonging to a Montanist milieu 'for only the Montanists had female presbyters' (ibid., 438). This text is repr. at M. Waelkens, *Die kleinasiatischen Türsteine* (Mainz, 1986) no. 367, where dated second quarter, III AD. For a female πρε(σ)β(ῦτις) from Sicily, and perhaps another from Thera, see *New Docs 1976*, **79**. G.W. Clarke has drawn my attention to a woman acting as presbyter in Cappadocia in the mid-230s: Cyprian, *Ep.* 75.10, especially 75.10.5. For an *oikonomissa* who may possibly be a church official see **69** above.

By way of illustrating the continuity from non-Christian to Christian cultic organisation mention may be made here of *I.Eph.* VII, 1.3418 (Metropolis, n.d.), a list of male and female priests and *diakonoi* in the cult of the Twelve gods. The women mentioned are an εἰέρηạ Anatole (*l*.3), a *diakonos* Elpis (4), a ἱέρεια Elpis (11-12), and a *diakonos* Tyche (12-13). We may suspect some differentiation between the words διάκων and διάκονος at *I.Eph.* VII, 1.3414 and 3415 (Metropolis, n.d.): in both these inscriptions listing priests and other cultic officials of Zeus Kresimos two different women are spoken of as *diakon* (*ll*.7-8 and 8-9 respectively), followed immediately by a list of male *diakonoi* (*ll*.8-11 and 9-13 respectively). These are the only two instances of διάκων in *I.Eph.*, but for numerous other examples of διάκονος see the references listed in the index vol., *I.Eph.* VIII.1, s.v. For another *diakonos* in a very fragmentary text concerning an association (Thyrreion in Akarnania, n.d.) see *SEG* 478.

Returning to the epitaph for Sophia, the most arresting phrase used to describe her is 'the second Phoibe'. This is an allusion to Phoibe, 'deacon of the congregation at Kenchreai' (Rom. 16.1). But since numerous other women held the position of *diakonos* this is unlikely to be the reason for the connection between the fourth-century Sophia and Paul's associate. There are several analogies to this wording in other inscriptions, where people are titled by such phrases as:

1. 'The new Homer' — G.E. Bean, *Side kitabeleri: The Inscriptions of Side* (Ankara, 1965) 107.11, making mention of Aelius Paion φιλοκαίσαρος νέου Ὁμήρο[υ; text recently discussed by L. Robert in *ΣΤΗΛΗ. Τόμος εἰς μνήμην Ν. Κοντολέοντος* (Athens, 1980) 10-20, especially 13-16.
2. 'New Homer and new Themistokles' — Julius Nikanor in several inscriptions: *IG* II^2 1069.6, 1723.4 (with an additional fragment published by M. Mitsos, *AE* [1972] 55-57; cf. *BE* [1973] 148), 3786-89 (of these last four the title is deleted on all but 3787). On this man from Syrian Hierapolis, honoured by the Athenians in the time of Augustus, see C.P. Jones, *Phoenix* 32 (1978) 222-28; cf. *BE* 168; and Robert, *ΣΤΗΛΗ*, 15-16.
3. 'New Theophanes' — R. Hodot, *ZPE* 34 (1979) 221-37 (pl.13), inscription for M. Pompeius Macrinus (Mytilene, time of Antoninus Pius), in which he is called [νέος] | Θεοφάνης (1-2; the restoration is very likely on various grounds); cf. *BE* 315.
4. 'New Dionysos' — title for emperor Commodus accorded in an honorific inscription set up by the initiates of Dionysos, *I.Eph.* II.293.4. Also from the time of Commodus is *I.Eph.* VI.1600, a list of priests, probably members of a mysteries association, in which Evadnes Antiochos is called νέου Διον(ύσου) θρέπτ[ος?] (*l*.46). At *P.Oxy.Hels.* 25.15 (Oxyrhynchos, Feb./March 264) the words νέον Διόνυσον as a title for Gallienus are entirely restored in a papyrus which includes several documents relating to the granting of privileges to members of an association of Dionysiac artists. A similar notion of 'New Dionysos' is implied in *I.Eph.* II.275 where οἱ πρὸ πόλεως honour Hadrian σύ[ν]|θρονον τῷ Διονύσῳ (*ll*.7-8), 'ruling jointly with Dionysos'.

These people are apparently in every case major benefactors of their own or their adoptive city. As Jones points out (223-24), 'these titles . . . probably began as a shouted acclamation of the people, designed to flatter a wealthy citizen: these cries often compared someone to one of his great forerunners, "New Socrates", "New Theophanes". Thereafter a motion might be passed for these acclamations to be made official . . . and henceforth it would regularly follow the person's name almost as if it were part of it'. The situation in Acts 14.12, where Paul and Barnabas are called Hermes and Zeus by the people of Lystra, is not an exact parallel to these acclamations; but the latter provide a context at a more general level within which that incident may be viewed.

The link with Sophia should be clear: as with the similar honorific titles bestowed by a grateful citizenry, she has presumably been accorded the title 'Second Phoibe' because of benefactions provided (to her church?). The point of the allusion to Phoibe is that at Rom. 16.2 she is said by Paul to have been προστάτις πολλῶν . . . καὶ ἐμοῦ αὐτοῦ. This noun used of a woman has caused difficulty to some NT commentators; and even in late antiquity the far inferior reading παραστάτις appears in some IXth century MSS (F and G), presumably in recognition of the discomfort which προστάτις caused, and perhaps under the influence of the Vulgate's *adstitit*. For a documentary parallel to this weaker reading we may note the use of the word in an epigram probably to be associated with a statue group of Homer flanked by personified statues of the *Iliad* and the *Odyssey* in which 'Ilias' says she was set up to stand beside (πάρστατις ἵδρυμαι) the poet. This text, repr. as *SEG* 192 (Athens, time of Augustus; cf. *BE* 168) has received considerable attention in the last few years, most recently by C.P. Jones, *Phoenix* 39 (1985) 30-35.

As for προστάτης and related words we may note the following attestations from this year's culling of documentary texts.

1. *I.Berenike* 17 (24 Oct., 24/5), honorific decree by the Jewish *politeuma* for a Roman whose patronage has been distinguished: τήν | τε προστασίαν αὐτῶν ἐποιήσατο φιλανθρώ|πως καὶ καλῶς (*ll.*11-13); καὶ κατ' ἰδίαν | εὔχρηστον προσστασίαν (*sic*) ποιούμενος οὐ δια|λείπει (*ll.*18-20). This inscription is now reprinted and discussed in G. Lüderitz, *Corpus jüdischer Zeugnisse aus der Cyrenaika* (Wiesbaden, 1983) 151-55, no.71.
2. *SEG* 537 (Larisa, I) epitaph of a Jew, Alexander, σχολαστικοῦ | καὶ προστάτου, 'advocate and patron.'
3. *I.Eph.* III.614c, posthumous honorific inscription (mid-I(?)) for M. Antonius Albus, προστάτην γεγονότα τοῦ τε ἱεροῦ τῆς 'Αρτέμιδος | καὶ τῆς πόλεως (22-23), 'he was a patron of the temple of Artemis and of the city'.
4. *O.Tebt.Pad.* 67 (provenance unknown, II), list of four members of an association, preceded by the word π., 'president' (trans., *ed.pr.*).
5. *I.Eph.* V.1539, honorific inscription (II^2) for Cn. Claudius Severus, erected with a statue of him. The lacunose prose section of the text calls him προστ[άτην] (*l.*8), while in the epigram he is said to have been honoured with a statue οὕνεκα προστασίης (14).
6. *I.Eph.* III.691, the *eques* Cassius Eubiotos honours τὸν ἴδιον προστάτην (*l.*6) Julius [*NN*], legionary tribune (209-11).
7. *I.Eph.* III.636.11, Claudius Acilius Julius, π. of the guild of silversmiths (III^1(?)); on the silversmiths' guild at Ephesos see **1** above.
8. *SEG* 969, epitaph for Benjamin, ὁ προστάτη<ς> | ὁ Κεσαρεύς (area of Naples, IV/V; *ed.pr.* — E. Miranda, *Riv.Ant.Crist.* 55 [1979] 340-41 no.2 [pl.]; cf. *BE* [1980] 585); here the noun means either patron of a Jewish community, or it is an equivalent for gerousiarch. For π. used of other Jews note, in addition to the first two items in this present list, *CIJ* I.100, epitaph for Gaius π. ὅσιος (Rome, n.d.); and I.365 (n.d.), Caelius π. 'Αγριππησίων; for this community at Rome see Frey's introduction to *CIJ* I, pp.lxxi-ii.
9. *I.Eph.* V.1879, fragmentary inscription making mention of [Eut]ychios προστάτου (n.d.).
10. *I.Eph.* VII, 1.3054, honorific inscription for Caecilius Arellianus, designated as προ[στάτην] (n.d.).
11. *I.Eph.* VII, 1.3055, honorific inscription for an asiarch (name lost) designated as τὸν ἴδιον προστάτην (*l.*13) by the person who erected the monument. This text is dated II fin./early III by L. Robert, *Les gladiateurs dans l'Orient grec* (Paris, 1940; repr. Amsterdam, 1971) 196 no.201.
12. *I.Eph.* III.668a, T. Flavius Apollonius is honoured by an Antonine emperor 'for his presidency (superintendence?) of the activity of the imperial (fiscus?)', τῇ προστασίᾳ | [τῆς] πράξεως τῶν ἱερῶν | [±3]ων (*ll.*8-10).
13. *I.Eph.* IV.1063, metrical prayer for the *prytanis* Tullia that the gods may give her children 'as she accomplished her *prostasia* immaculately in your house' (4-5), ὡς ἄχραντος ἐν ὑμετέροισι δόμοισιν | ἤνυσε προστασίην (n.d.). Cf. the contemporary no.1064, another prayer for the same woman, that Hestia and Artemis would help Tullia since she served as *prytanis* with enthusiasm, 'spending her wealth on every matter bountifully' (*l.*6), τὸν πλοῦτον εἰς πᾶν πρᾶγμα ἀναλοῦσ' ἀφθόνως. (Incidentally, in this text Hestia is addressed at *l.*2 as ἀειπάρθενε; for this adjective see *New Docs 1978*, **93**, p.116. Elsewhere in *I.Eph.* it occurs only once, of Mary, in a pastoral letter or archbishop Hypatios, VII, 2.4135.19-20 [*c.*531-37; repr. at Guarducci, *EG* IV.401-04].).

— Note also M. Tačeva-Hitova, *Bulgarian Historical Review* 3 (1978) 52-65 (cf. *SEG* 686), who discusses divine epithets in Greek inscriptions from Moesia Inferior and Thrace. One of the rarest is προστάτης, occurring only once, at *IGBulg.* 4 (1966) 1934 (Serdica, n.d.), in a dedication to Asklepios Koulkoussenos. Tačeva-Hitova takes the word here to mean 'deliverer, saviour' (59).

In this list no.5 shows clearly that προστασία is the abstract noun to denote the position/office (whether formalised as president of an association, like no.4, or connoting the status of patron, as in no.3) held by a person designated as προστάτης. It is therefore a legitimate inference, in my judgement, to say that Tullia (no.13) is clearly thought of as a *prostatis*. The combination of the two inscriptions for her indicates that she is a woman of wealth, well able to provide patronage for the city while holding her civil position of *prytanis*. Lest it be felt that — the Phoibe of Romans aside (to include her would merely create a circular argument) — a woman could not possess such a status-loaded designation, attention may be drawn to the following recent discussions.

In *Aeg.* 61 (1981) 103-15 O. Montevecchi draws attention to the as yet not fully published *P.Med.Bar.* 1, a petition of 142 BC which is part of an archive. One of the two petitioners, Herakleides, is described as 'fatherless' (ὀρφανοῦ, 4); the word can only mean this — see further **71** above — since the text proceeds to say that he is acting with (the consent of) his mother, who is described as his *prostatis*: μετὰ προστάτιδος | . . . | . . . τῆς αὐ|τοῦ μητρὸς Θαΐδος, κτλ (*ll.*4-6). This is almost the first time the word has appeared in papyri, the only other instance known to me is *PGM*[2] II (1974) 36.338 (cited by both LSJ and BAGD, s.v. προστάτις) where Zmyrna (Myrrh) is invoked as the π. of the god Anoubis. Montevecchi, who discusses papyrus attestations and meanings of προστάτης, προστατεύω and προστασία (104-05), argues (107) that Thais is to be understood as her son's guardian (ἐπίτροπος). E.A. Judge, *TynB* 35 (1984) 21, suggests that the more specific word is avoided 'because of the anomaly of a woman's being in this position'. Even though the meaning of προστάτις here is not identical with the way it is used of Phoibe in Rom. 16.2, the fact that a woman fulfils such a role in relation to other (male) individuals/groups is the common link of significance. The feminine form in -ις is to be equated with the masculine form in -ης by analogy with words like μύστης/μύστις, εὐεργέτης/εὐεργέτις, etc. A useful example of the former pair occurs in this year's publications at *I.Eph.* IV.1202 (n.d.), recording the dedication of a statue of Eros and a bronze lamp to Aphrodite Daitis by a brother and sister who describe themselves as μύστης καὶ μύστις.

More recently still N.G.L. Hammond, *JHS* 105 (1985) 156-60, has examined a number of Macedonian terms for office in the period 336-309 BC. He demonstrates that *prostates* was the name for the senior civic offical beside the king both in Macedonia and various Epirot tribal states (the Molossoi and Chaonians). In Macedonia itself after Alexander's death Krateros was entrusted with the *prostasia* of the kingship of Arridaios in 323, while the latter was abroad in Asia; he was responsible for civic duties in the maintenance of the monarchy (Hammond, 156-58). Hammond then proceeds to enquire (158) whether anyone held this first-ranking office of *prostates* before 323 BC. 'Of the adult members of the royal house resident in Macedonia in 334 BC there was only one person available, Olympias, widow of Philip II and mother of the absent king, Alexander.' Hammond shows that Olympias was well-qualified to perform the various functions associated with the position. He draws in also the situation of her daughter Kleopatra, widow of the Molossian king Alexander, who from 331-326 BC acted in a way consonant with the holding of the *prostasia* there. Finally, Hammond points out that though the office of *prostates* lapsed after Krateros' departure from Macedonia and death in Asia in 321, '. . . when the office went out of use, the high honours associated with it were perpetuated in the use of its title, προστασία' (159-60).

Although *prostates* is employed by Classical Attic writers in the sense of 'patron' (see LSJ, s.v., III.2), it is not unlikely that its widespread use in this way in Roman times took its cue partly from this Macedonian context. Whether or no, at least we can say that there is an entirely reasonable case for considering that the word could be used of women no less than men. At a far remove from the time of the NT the epitaph for Sophia provides some small confirmatory evidence of the reading at Rom. 16.2, since it is hard to conceive why the wording 'the second Phoibe' would have occurred to anyone to include unless προστάτις were the word known at Rom 16.2. The common link must have been perceived to be their provision of patronage. For a useful recent study of women and wealth in the Hellenistic and Roman world note the essay by R. van Bremen in *Images of Women in Antiquity*, edd. A. Cameron/A. Kuhrt (London, 1983), 223-42. For posthumous honours accorded a woman in virtue of her munificence to her city see **2**, above.

In Hadrianic Athens a very wealthy woman (name unknown) donated the cost of a monumental shrine (*naiskos*) of Isis, built on the south slope of the Akropolis. It was probably in recognition of her benefaction that she was accorded the cult office of 'Lamp-bearer' (λυχανάπτρια) and 'Dream interpreter' (ὀνειροκρίτις). On the reconstruction of the building, and discussion of the cult of Isis in Roman Athens as attested by several inscriptions, see S. Walker, *ABSA* 74 (1979) 243-57; cf. *SEG* 190, 191, 291.

A further possible instance of a female *prostates may* occur in the Aphrodisias inscription (to be published by J.M. Reynolds) which mentions Jews, proselytes and 'godfearers' (cf. *New Docs 1978*, **96**, p.125). At one point . .|ΑΗΛ is called a *prostates*. Whether this is a woman's name, Jael, must await Reynolds' publication (cf. Brooten, op.cit., 151).

As a final comment on *prostates* here brief mention may be accorded to *CIJ* II.1447. This inscription may or may not come from Alexandria, and it is probable — though not certain — that it refers to a Jewish synagogue (see Frey's commentary on both these questions). In this text, Artemon son of Nikon is said to have been *prostates* for the *synagoge* during the 11th year. In *l.*2 the symbol is resolved in *CIJ* as πρ(οστατήσας); B. Lifshitz, *Donateurs et fondateurs dans les synagogues juives* (Paris, 1967), no.98, resolves it as πρ(οστάτης), however. Though either form makes an appropriate resolution for the context, neither can be taken as certain, for the προστατ- word group is not so common that the severe abbreviation ΠΡ would be readily understood by any ancient reader of this text.

Treatment of *prostates* here provides an opportunity to deal with another noun, πρωτοστάτης. MM (as also BAGD) offer no documentary attestations of this NT *hapax* at Acts 24.5, where Paul is described as πρωτοστάτην τε τῆς τῶν Ναζωραίων αἱρέσεως. The word occurs as the title of a short-lived office in Egypt during the years 296-*c*.298. According to A.K. Bowman, the position of *protostates* was 'designed to replace, partially or wholly, the *strategos* of the nome with a larger number of officials each serving a smaller area' (*Akten des XIII. internationalen Papyruskongresses, Marburg/Lahn, August 1971* [Munich, 1974] 48-51, at 50). For further discussion see J. Schwartz, *ZPE* 16 (1975) 235-37. Most recently, J.E.G. Whitehorne, *ZPE* 62 (1986) 159-72, has challenged Bowman's view, arguing that this new office was not instituted to replace the *strategeia*, even partially. The five attestations are:

- *P.Oxy.* 38 (1971) 2849 (21 May 296), instructions to a *hyperetes* concerning the land economy from τὸ κοινὸν τῶν πρωτοστ̣ά̣τ̣ων of Oxyrhynchos (*ll.*1, 10).
- *SB* 6.5 (1963) 9502 (Oxyrhynchos, end August(?), 296), land declaration lodged with Valerianus Julianus alias Dioskourides πρ̣ωτοσ̣τάτῃ (*l.*5) of the area of Seryphis in the Oxyrhynchite nome.
- *P.Lond.* 3 (1907) 958 (Hermopolite nome, 28 Sept., 296), request concerning land addressed to a π. (*l.*3). The edd. of the *P.Lond.* text summarize it only on p.xlix; the information that it contains the word comes from Schwartz's article.
- *P.Oxy.* 44 (1976) 3184 (9 Jan., 297) consisting of two similar texts in both of which an address is made to Aurelius Asklepiades alias Achillion πρωτοστάτῃ (*l.*6 in both texts).
- *P.Cair.Isidor.* (1960) 64 (Karanis, *c*.298), petition addressed to a *strategos*, in which it is said that an approach concerning the matter had been made earlier to the πρωτοστάτῃ τῆς κώμης (10), to no avail. The noun here is 'doubtless equivalent to προστάτῃ' (edd. n., ad loc., referring to the phrase π̣[ρο]σ̣τάται κώμης Σούεως at *P.Oxy.* 10 [1914] 1275.7). It may be noted that occasionally προστάτης occurs as a false reading for πρωτοστάτης (see LSJ, s.v. προστάτης, init.).

These attestations all form a homogeneous group, both in time and in the meaning they share as a term for an official apparently mainly involved with land questions. The sense at Acts 24.5 is considerably more generalised, 'ring-leader', *vel sim.*

123. Request for prayer for healing

Heracleopolite nome mid-IV

ed.pr. — H.I. Bell, *P.Lond.* 6 (1924) 1926

τῷ τιμιοτάτῳ καὶ χρηστοφόρῳ
καὶ πάσης ἀρετῆς κεκοσμημένῳ ἄππα Πα-
φνούθις.
Οὐαλερία ἐν Χριστῷ χέρειν.
ἀξιῶ καὶ π̣α̣ρακαλῶ σε, τιμιώτατε πα-
τήρ̣, εἶνα̣ . . . ι . σ̣φηκιν ἐτήσῃς μοι
παρὰ τῷ Χριστῷ καὶ εἴασιν λάβω·
οὕτως π[ι]στεύω διὰ τῶν σῶν εὐχῶν
εἴασιν λαμβάνω, τῶν γὰρ ἀσκούν-
των καὶ θρησκευόντων ἀποκαλύν-
ματα δικνέοντε. μεγάλῳ γὰρ
νόσῳ περίκιμε δυσπνήας δινῆς.
οὕτως γὰρ πεπίστευκα καὶ πιστεύω
ὅτι ἐὰν εὔξῃ ἐπάνω μου εἴασιν
λαμβάνω. δέομε τῷ θεῷ δέομε
κέ σοι μνήσθητί μου ἐν τῇ ἁγίᾳ σου
προσευχῇ. ε̣ἰ κὲ ἐν σ̣ώματι̣ οὐκ ἶκα
παρὰ τοὺς πόδας σ[ο]υ ἐν πνεύματι
εἶκα πρ̣ὸς τοὺς πό[δ]α̣ς σου. προσα-
γ̣[ορε]ύ̣ω̣ τ̣ὰ̣[ς θυγατ]έ̣ρ̣α[ς] μ̣ου, καὶ
μνήσθητι αὐτῶν ἐν τῇ ἁγίᾳ σου
προσευχῇ, Βασσιανῆς καὶ Θεοκλίας.
ἀσπά[ζ]ετέ σε πολλὰ καὶ ὁ σύνβι-
ός μο̣[υ], καὶ εὔχ[ου] ἐπάνω αὐτῶ.
ἀσπ[άζ]ετέ σε δὲ καὶ ὅλος ὁ οἰκός
μου. [ ] ἐρ<ρ>ῶσθέ σε εὔχομε,
[τ]ιμιώτατε̣ πατήρ.

(*back*) τῷ τιμιοτάτῳ πατρὶ ἄππα Πα / / φνουτ[ίῳ] πα̣ρ̣ὰ τῆς θ̣υ̣γ̣α̣τ̣ρὸς
Οὐαλερίας.

A dark papyrus (13B x 27H cm.), badly worm-eaten and folded inwards from each side and once each from top and bottom. The script is clear but inelegant. Itacism abounds, as commonly, as do several other orthographical features. Read, e.g., ι for ει (εἴασιν, 7, 9, 14), ει for ι and αι for ε (περίκιμε, 12; δινῆς, 12), η for ι (ἶκα, 17). Read δεικνύονται (*l.*11). Grammatically, Παφνούθις (2) may be treated as indeclinable, or else is an error for the dative; cf. the address on the back where *ed.pr.* restores the oblique case ending, possibly without warrant. In *l.*12 νόσῳ may be treated as masculine, hence μεγάλῳ; or the latter may be an error for a feminine. In *l.*24 αὐτῶ reflects the common genitive/dative confusion.

Bib. — Tibiletti, *Lettere*, 185-86, no.28.

To the most honoured Apa Paphnutios, Christ-bearing and equipped with every virtue, Valeria sends greeting in Christ. | I ask and exhort you, most honoured father, that you request for me [help?] from Christ that I may receive healing; I believe that in this way through your prayers I am receiving healing, for by those who are ascetics and religious revelations are exhibited. | For I am overcome with a serious disease in the form of a terrible difficulty in breathing. For thus I have believed and I continue to believe that if you pray on my behalf I will receive healing. | I ask God and I ask you also: remember me in your holy intercession. Even though I am not physically present with you, I am present with you in spirit. | I mention my daughters: be mindful of them, too, in your holy intercession, that is Bassiane and Theokleia. My husband greets you warmly; and do pray for him. My whole household greets you too. | I pray for your health, most honoured father. (*Back*) To the most honoured father Apa Paphnutios from his daughter Valeria.

This letter is one of an archive of seven addressed to Paphnutios (*P.Lond.* 6.1923-1929; 1927 does not actually mention Paphnutios, but apparently it was found with the other six and *ed.pr.* has no doubt that it was also sent to him). Although this Paphnutios cannot be positively identified as a figure otherwise known, Bell has argued persuasively that he was an orthodox Catholic anchorite with monastic connections. The letters reveal that he was in touch with quite a wide circle of people, possibly including both Fl. Julius Ausonius, the Prefect of Augustamnica (*P.Lond.* 6.1924), and Athanasios, bishop of Alexandria (*P.Lond.* 6.1929); see Bell's commentary, 100, 115-18. The letters of the archive indicate that his correspondents held him in very high regard as a man of prayer and deep spirituality, and for the efficacy of his prayers for the healing of the sick. Compare the statement in *P.Lond.* 6.1928.14-15, ὅπου οὔτε ἀδελφοῦ οὔτε | τινὸς ἄλλου βοηθῆσαι̣ δύνα̣ται βοήθεια εἰ μὴ <ἥ> διὰ τοῦ κυρίου ἡμῶ(ν) | Χρηστοῦ διὰ τῶν ὑμῶ̣ν εὐχῶν προσδοκομένη ἐλπίς, 'where neither from a brother nor from any other person is it possible to derive real benefit except the hope which I expect by our Lord Christ through your prayers'. *P.Lond.* 1926 and two others from the collection (1928, 1929) are specifically concerned with requesting prayers for the healing of various physical conditions. There are of course other contemporary accounts of ascetics being sought out for their capacity to pray effectively for the sick: see, e.g., R.C. Gregg's recent edition (London, 1980) of Athanasios' *vita Antonii* (pp.74-78, 92). For a different request to a monastic to pray for someone see **61**.

P.Lond. 1926 raises for us the wider question of the tradition of Christian healing and the extent to which it may have continued beyond the Apostolic period. For a perceptive and stimulating review and analysis of the background to Christian healing in the NT period see the recent study of H.C. Kee, *Medicine, Miracle and Magic in NT Times* (Cambridge, 1986). The hints that we get from such passages as 1 Cor. 12.9, 28, 30 and Jas. 5.12-14 suggest that the exercise of some form of healing ministry became a fairly regular feature of at least some of the early Christian communities, and that particular individuals were seen to have a special gift or competence in this area. Unfortunately, our evidence for what went on after the end of the Apostolic age is slender and very scattered. There are some clues, however: Hippolytos' *Traditio Apostolica* 15 (early III) is concerned with regulations in relation to those who have received a gift of healing (see G. Dix, *The Apostolic Tradition of Hippolytus* [London, 1968^2]). There are occasional references in the writings of some of the Fathers, e.g., Irenaeus, *Haer.* II.31.2-3, 32.4-5; Justin, *Apol.* II.6; *Dial.* 30, 76, 85; Clement of Alexandria, *Paed.* 3.12; Tertullian, *Ad. Scap.* 4, etc.; cf. E. Frost, *Christian Healing* (London, 1949^2). Early liturgies occasionally have relevant material (cf. *Bishop Serapion's Prayer Book*, ed. J. Wordsworth [London, 1915]), as do also a number of papyrus letters, including the three from the Paphnutios correspondence

(*P.Lond.* 1926, 1928, 1929) and, e.g., *P.Oxy.* 6 (1908) 939; 8 (1911) 1161; and 31 (1966) 2609 (all dated IV). To these we must add two new fourth-century Christian papyri (drawn to my attention by B. Kramer) which refer to prayers for healing in a rather similar way to the Paphnutios letters (forthcoming in *Das Archiv des Nepheros und verwandte Texte: Papyri aus der Trierer und der Heidelberger Papyrussammlung*, edd. B. Kramer/J.C. Shelton/G.M. Browne). This evidence, despite its diverse nature, suggests that the tradition of Christian healing continued well into IV, and beyond. We might also refer to the evidence from amulets which, although disapproved of by the Church (serious attempts were made to stamp out their use in later IV), do reveal a strong, continuing belief by some sections of society in the power of Jesus to heal; cf. *P.Oxy.* 8 (1911) 1151 (V[?]); *P.L.Bat.* 19 (1978) 20 (provenance unknown, VI[?]) and *P.Turner* (1981) 49 (provenance unknown, V/VI), these last two discussed at *New Docs 1978*, **93**.

The letter of Valeria is of particular interest to Tibiletti in relation to the themes of belief, faith and prayer (see Tibiletti, *Lettere*, 117, 121). My own analysis of the theme of illness and healing in all the private letters designated by Tibiletti as certainly Christian or certainly non-Christian has indicated several things. First, Christian writers appear to display a greater interest than non-Christian writers in the subject of illness and related issues. Of the 104 letters which Tibiletti includes in the category of Christian, nine refer to illness: *P.Oxy.* 6 (1908) 939; 8 (1911) 1161; 31 (1966) 2601, 2609 (all dated IV); *P.Lond.* 6.1920 (provenance unstated, 330-40; Coptic), 1926 (printed above), 1928, 1929; and *SB* 6 (1958) 9605 (provenance unknown, early IV). In contrast, only three of the 92 letters held by Tibiletti to have been written by non-Christians make similar mention: *P.Oxy.* 6.935 (III); *P.Mich.* 8 (1951) 514 (provenance unstated, III), and *P.Herm.Rees* (1964) 2 (Hermopolis[?], IV).

Second, Christian writers typically describe the condition of people who are ill, whether themselves or others, in considerably more detail than writers whose religious affiliation is not Christian. The symptoms of an illness are detailed and its progress traced in only one of the three non-Christian texts (*P.Oxy.* 935), and then only briefly; but we find this sort of information in eight of the Christian letters (*P.Lond.* 6.1920 is the one exception). None of the non-Christian letters have, as their primary subject, a reference to the theme of illness and healing; but this is the case for four of the Christian letters (*P.Oxy.* 939; *P.Lond.* 6.1926, 1928, 1929), and it is an important secondary theme in another two (*P.Oxy.* 1161 and 2609).

Third, and this point is closely related to the previous one, Christian writers referring to illness use a striking range and breadth of terms, a significant number of which are rare in the papyri, or even elsewhere unattested. In the four Christian texts from Oxyrhynchos referring to illness six words are used uniquely: λευκωμάτιον, *P.Oxy.* 2601; νωθραίνω, *P.Oxy.* 2609; and from *P.Oxy.* 939 ἀνασφάλλω, ἀνεκτός, ἐπινόσως, and νοσηλός. Only the last two of these occur elsewhere in the papyri. As regards the Paphnutios correspondence, we have in *P.Lond.* 1929, for example, the terms ἀνωμαλέω (*l.*12), 'to be in bad health', attested only here in papyrus texts, and ἀτονώτατα (*l.*14), 'very weak health', attested only here as a superlative adverb; and possibly κάματος, here 'sickness' (*l.*12; see ed. n., ad loc.).

A fourth feature to be noted is that, while in two texts from writers whose religious affiliation is not Christian (*P.Oxy.* 935, *P.Herm.Rees* 2) we do not find evidence of a connection between illness, healing and the writer's gods, in at least six Christian texts which refer to illness there is a distinct difference of approach. The correspondents in these letters do not just make a connection between illness, healing and God but either actively seek divine healing through Christ or God or express their belief that this has occurred. There is a much more intense interest in the idea of divine healing in these Christian texts than ever appears in non-Christian ones. And there is no evidence among those private letters which reflect non-Christian religious affiliation for the existence of any figure exercising a gift of healing that is remotely comparable to Paphnutios whom we see in *P.Lond.* 1926, 1928, and 1929. Nor, indeed, is there any parallel in the sources, literary or documentary, relating to the Asklepian cult. There is, of course, a range of parallels that can be drawn between healing in the cult of Asklepios and Christian healing — cf. A. Oepke, *TDNT* 3 (1965) 194-215; H.C. Kee, *Miracle in the Early Christian World* (New Haven, 1983) 104-24 — but the sources do not ever suggest that Asklepios imparted a healing gift to a human agent. We do read of healings occurring through touching or licking by sacred snakes or dogs, but these were seen to be manifestations of the god: see Kee's article in B.F. Meyers/E.P. Sanders (edd.), *Jewish and Christian Self-Definition* III (London, 1982), 119-36.

The three texts from the Paphnutios archive are in fact something of an exception, even among Christian sources, in that they reflect a strong expectation of the possibility of healing even though the petitioners are not in physical proximity to Paphnutios. Valeria specifically indicates this in *ll.*17-19 of the text printed above. In the NT, there are some accounts of Jesus performing healings at a distance (Mt. 8.5-13; 15.21-28; Jn 4.46-53). In the first century Rabbi Chanina ben Dosa is also reported to have performed healings in this manner in the Babylonian Talmud (*Berakoth* 34b; Strack/Billerbeck, II.441). Cf. G. Vermes, *Jesus the Jew* (London, 1973) 72-78, especially 74.

If the ascetic Antony is any guide, it is very likely that Paphnutios' ministry of prayer for healing would have often involved, for those physically and financially able, actual face-to-face contact. But clearly there were others like Valeria who could not make the journey and who wrote requesting assistance. And that meant, of course, that neither of the two main rituals referred to in the NT which were used by the early Christians in the context of prayer for healing could be employed, the laying-on of hands and anointing with oil. We might note here that the regular NT formula in relation to laying-on of hands for healing uses χείρ in the plural and ἐπιτίθημι. However, T. Muraoka has pointed out to me that the Aramaic *Genesis Apocryphon* from Qumran (I BC?), which contains the only certain pre-Christian Jewish parallel to laying-on of hands for healing, may use 'hand' in the singular — the text is ambiguous at this point. In the Gospels the plural χεῖρες is always used except in two instances where others request healing of Jesus (Mt. 9.18; Mk. 7.32). In relation to the practice of anointing with oil, there is a tantalising reference to ἔλαιον in *P.Lond.* 6.1928.6; but the text is too damaged at that point to determine positively whether the oil is mentioned in relation to the healing being sought (see reference to this point in the chapter entitled 'Die Fürbitten des Priesters Nepheros und Jak. 5.14-15', in the forthcoming *Das Archiv des Nepheros . . .*, noted above). The conclusions of a recent study on the types of oil specified by *elaion* in the papyri would suggest that the *elaion* of *P.Lond.* 6.1928.6 may be olive oil, although it is not clear that the *elaion* of Jas. 5.14 is so restricted: see D.B. Sandy in *Atti del XVII Congresso Internazionale di Papirologia* (Naples, 1984) 1317-23. However, the fact that Paphnutios' correspondents do not expect the use of such rituals as the laying-on of hands and anointing with oil (at least not by Paphnutios personally) does not appear to lessen in any way the confidence which they have in the efficacy of his prayers and the likelihood of a positive outcome to their requests.

The detail given about the serious nature of the condition in *ll.*11-12 of Valeria's letter has some parallel in *P.Oxy.* 1161, another letter by a seriously ill female writer (δεινός is used again), and in *P.Oxy.* 939 (written by a man about a sick woman). While νόσος is fairly common in the NT, it is used to refer to illness or disease in a general way without reference to severity. In papyrus letters sickness in general is more frequently referred to by the terms ἀσθένεια and its related forms, never νόσος. The latter (and its related forms) is typically used when an illness of any severity is being described or referred to; this is illustrated in the two Oxyrhynchos texts referred to above, *P.Oxy.* 1161.8 and 939.6, 23. Either an adjective intensifies the meaning of the word — compare the phrase in *ll*.11-12 of the text printed above with the wording πυρετῷ μεγάλῳ at Lk. 4.38 — or a verb emphasises the seriousness of the condition. The verb περίκειμαι at *l*.12 in the *P.Lond.* text above serves to illustrate this, as does καταλαμβάνω at *P.Lond.* 1928.5, and ἐπείγω at *P.Oxy.* 8 (1911) 1121.9 (III). Another way of thinking about this difference between the NT and the papyri is that in the latter *nosos* is typically used of individuals, normally in the singular. *P.Lond.* 1929 is a partial exception to this as Athanasios is referring to the sickness being experienced by several members of his household. In the NT, on the other hand, *nosos* is used in a general sense (plural eight times, collective singular three times) to refer to the illnesses and diseases of those who sought healing from Jesus or — in Acts 19.12, the only occurrence of the word outside the Synoptics — from Paul. For a doctor who 'raised the sick' (νοσέοντας ἔγειρας) see **5**.

We might also note in *P.Lond.* 1926 the very significant Pauline phrase ἐν Χριστῷ, used here by Valeria in her opening salutation (*l*.4). It is much more common in Christian letters to find the phrase ἐν κυρίῳ θεῷ (typically abbreviated as *nomina sacra*). In fact, specific reference to the name of Christ is quite marked in each of the three *P.Lond.* 6 texts concerned with healing. It is of some interest that our writer uses both εὐχή (*l*.8) and προσευχή (*ll*.17, 22) in referring to the prayer that she hopes Paphnutios will make for her. The latter is by far the most common NT word for prayer, but the single instance of εὐχή occurs at Jas. 5.15 in the context of instructions for praying for the healing of the sick. It is possible that Valeria's use of εὐχή in close conjunction with the phrase ἴασιν λαμβάνω (*l*.9) may reflect this NT wording in James. In *l*.14 she also uses the verb εὔχομαι (again with ἴασιν λαμβάνω), which appears on one of only three occasions in the NT at Jas. 5.16 (with the meaning 'pray' rather than 'wish') in reference to prayer for healing the sick. This too, then, may suggest that Valeria had the James passage in mind in writing her request to Paphnutios. And it may be that some of the confidence that she expresses about the prospect of being healed may also derive from the very confident statement in James, καὶ ἡ εὐχὴ τῆς πίστεως σώσει τὸν κάμνοντα (5.15).

The verb πιστεύω is employed on three occasions in *P.Lond.* 1926 (*ll*.8, 13 *bis*), and is suggestive of a deep sense of confidence on Valeria's part as to the efficacy of the ascetic's prayers for healing. Perhaps the emphasis on faith in NT accounts of healings has led her to feel the need to stress her faith to Paphnutios. The wording πεπίστευκα καὶ πιστεύω (*l*.13) underlines this sense of confidence. Cf. the statement in another Christian text which refers to healing and which is also emphatic, although in a different way: *P.Oxy.* 31. 2601.32-33 (early IV), ἐγὼ γὰρ (*vac.*) εἶδον ἄλλους θεραπευθέντας, 'I myself have seen others cured'. It is possible but by no means certain that this refers to religious healing.

P.Lond. 1926 illustrates the development of the terminology of familial relationships amongst Christians. Valeria's opening address is to *apa* Paphnutios (*l*.2). But in the address on the back she adds πατρί (cf. *ll*.5-6, 27). The presence of the Greek and the Graecised Semitic words for father illustrates the process of institutionalisation of certain familial terms in the ecclesiastical context. *Apa* has effectively become a title, and to convey adequately her sense of deference to Paphnutios' pastoral ministry and holiness Valeria feels the need to use πατήρ in addition. In this regard, a comparison with the other letters of the archive is of interest. In *P.Lond.* 1924 and 1928 we find the same phrase which is used by Valeria in her letter, both in the opening salutation and in the address on the back. The form πατρὶ Παπνουτίῳ is used in the opening salutation and the address of both 1923 and 1929. Of the two remaining letters, we have no address for 1927 (the writer apparently forgets to insert Paphnutios' name and neither designation occurs); and while the form ἄπα Παπνουτίῳ occurs at the beginning of 1925 there is a lacuna before Paphnutios' name on the address on the back. This suggests, then, that there is nothing unusual about Valeria's form of address and that the formula πατὴρ ἄπα had become well established by this period.

After asking for prayer for herself, Valeria requests Paphnutios' intercession on behalf of her daughters and husband. The first editor found θυγατέρας problematic in *l.*20, not merely palaeographically but because he doubted whether, even if a correct reading, it could carry the meaning 'daughter' here 'in a spiritual or conventional sense' (n. ad loc.). But J.A.L. Lee points out to me that προσαγορεύω (19-20) is not confined to the meaning 'salute, greet', as Bell translates it; this rendering implies that the 'daughters' are with Paphnutios. For the sense 'mention' given in the translation above see BAGD, s.v., 2. This clarifies the situation: Valeria's daughters are with her. In the address on the back she states that the letter is παρὰ τῆς θυγατρὸς Οὐαλερίας. It is difficult to imagine that θυγατρός here is anything but a reference to a 'spiritual' daughter. A special relationship seems implied between Valeria and Paphnutios through her Christian faith. While there is no clear NT precedent for this use of 'daughter' in a spiritual sense, such a development is quite conceivable between Christians. Valeria passes on greetings from her husband (*ll.*23-24), although she does not name him, and from 'her whole household' (*ll.*25-26). We are left with the feeling that there may have been some quite close ties between Paphnutios and this particular family. There are similar references to family members and the whole household in *P.Lond.* 1929 (*ll.*11-12, 16-18), suggesting that such ties may have existed in this case also.

Finally, it is perhaps relevant to note here, too, the fatalistic *topos* that sickness and troubles are so inescapable that death can be welcomed as the end of them. *IG* XIV *Suppl.* 2461 (Massilia, Imperial period) is an epigram for a youth in which the deceased says 'now that I have obtained this tomb I have ceased from illness and labour and troubled toil; for these occur among the living' (6-8), λαχὼν τόδε σῆμα [π]έπαυμαι | νούσων καὶ καμάτοιο καὶ ἄχθεος ἠδὲ πόνοιο· | ταῦτα γὰρ ἐν ζωοῖσι. A similar sentiment occurs in *IGUR* 1146 (Rome, Imperial period; pl. on p.3), a funerary epigram where the bereaved seeks to be as positive as possible towards the deceased: 'no winter troubles you, no heat, no sickness disturbs you; no hunger possesses you, or thirst, since your life is no longer one of human desire' (9-13), οὐ χειμὼν λυπεῖ σ', οὐ καῦμα, | οὐ νοῦσος ἐνοχλεῖ, | οὐ πίνη σ', οὐ δίψος ἔχει σ', | ἀλλ' οὐδὲ ποθεινὸς | ἀνθρώπων ἔτι σοι βίοτος. This epitaph set up by a father for his seven-year-old daughter begins with the words οὐκ ἔθανες, Πρώτη, μετέβης | δ' ἐς ἀμίνονα χῶρον, 'you have not died, Prote, simply gone to a better place' (1-2).

(R.J.S. BARRETT-LENNARD)

124. Beloved brothers

Provenance unknown in Egypt IV/V

ed. pr. — D. Hagedorn, *P.Köln* 2.109 (pl.16)

τοῖς ἀγαπιτοῖς ἀδελφοῖς Παταα̣ὼ̣ρ
καὶ Λούττεος ἐν κυρ[ί]ῳ χαίριν.
πρὸ μὲν πάντων εὔχομαι τὴν ὑιγύαν
ὑμῶν παρὰ τῷ κυρίῳ θεῷ. ἀσπάζομαι
ὑμᾶς, ᾿Αβάριν καὶ Πανεισότις κ̣α̣ὶ̣ πάν-
τας τοὺς̣ ἀδελφ[οὺ]ς̣ ὑ̣μῶ̣ν, ἀσπά̣ζ̣ο̣μαι

. . . .[. .] .[. . .]ς̣. ἀσπάζετε
ὑμᾶς Πιτίμιο[ς κ]αὶ Ε[. . .]ωρος καὶ Παῦ-
λος καὶ Εἰακω̣ απ[.]ανεπλ̣ω̣ θεοῦ
θέλοντος τοῦ καιροῦ τοῦ θε[ρ]ι̣σ̣μ̣ο̣ῦ̣
προσδοκοῦμεν ὑμᾶς ἔρχεσθαι
παρ' ὑμᾶς. προνοήσασθαί μοι
ἕννα λέβιθα ἐρχόμενοι εἶνα
τοῦτό μοι ἀνίνκαι καὶ τὸ ψαλεί-
διον ἀνίνκαι, ὅτι ἐπροσεφώ̣νη-
σα αὐτὸ τῷ γν[α]φῖ. ἀσπά<ζε>τε ὑμᾶς
Πιβήχιος ὁ ἀδελφὸς Παπνου-
θίου. προνόησαί μοι ἕνα λέβ[ι̣θα]
εἰς τὴν σύναξιν. ἀσπάζομαι 'Απίν-
χιον, 'Εγώτεος καὶ ἄπα Μακάριον,
ἀσπάζομαι πάντας τοὺς ἀδελφοὺς
ἐν κυρίῳ θεῷ. ἐρρῶσθαι ὑμᾶς
εὔχομαι πολλοῖς
χ̣[ρόνο]ι̣[ς].
(*back*) τοῖς ἀγαπ[ι]τοῖς ἀδελφοῖς Παταὼρ καὶ Λο̣ύ̣[ττεος]
χαίριν.

Nearly complete letter, 15B x 21H cm. Read ε for αι and vice versa (7, 12, 16); ὑγίειαν (3), ἡμᾶς (12), λέβητα (13, 18), ἐνέγκαι (14, 15), and probably προνοήσ<ασθ>αι (= -ε, 18).

To the beloved brothers, Pataor also (known as) Loutteos (sends) greetings in the Lord.
5 Before everything (else) I pray before the Lord God for your health. I greet | you, Abaris, and Paneisotis, and all your brothers, I greet . . . Pitimios greets you as does E[ud?]oros
10 and Paul and Jacob . . . God | willing, we expect you to come to us at the time of the harvest. Take care to bring me a cauldron when you come, and bring the scissors,
15 | because I have mentioned it to the fuller. Pibechios, Paphnouthios' brother, greets you.
20 Take care (to bring) me a cauldron for the feast day. I greet Apinchios, | Egoteos, and Apa Makarios; I greet all your brothers in the Lord God. I pray you may be well for
25 a long time to come. | (*Back*) To the beloved brother Pataor also (known as) Loutteos (sends) greetings.

This letter is apparently being sent to members of a monastic community. Hagedorn believes that two senders are involved, Pataor and Loutteos; the possibility that the latter may be part of a patronymic is discounted by him (ed. n., ad loc.). But there is another possibility: Loutteos may be a byname of Pataor. Though it is not common, a mere καί between two names is occasionally employed to indicate the double name, e.g., the series of texts from *P.Sakaon* (1978) concerning Aurelios Athanasios καί Philadelphos (dealt with at *New Docs 1978*, **77**). Another instance from the current year's publications occurs in an Imperial-period inscription from Mylasa in Caria (*ed. pr.* — C. Şahin/H. Engelmann, *ZPE* 34 [1979] 215-16, no.3; pl.12b; cf. *AE* 612, *BE* 457), mentioning the priest of the cult of C. Marcius Censorinus, proconsul of Asia in 2/3 AD who died in the province. The priest's name is Diogenes son of Diogenes, (but) [by adoption] son of Aphroditos also known as Eirenaios, κ[αθ'] | [ὑοθ. 'Α]φροδε[ί]|τ̣ου καὶ Εἰρη|ναίου (*ll*.2-5). In the *P.Köln* letter, the fact that the verbs designating the sender are all first person singular (*ll*.3, 4, 6, 19, 21, 23; the plural in *l*.11 simply indicates that he is speaking on behalf of others) may encourage us to consider the possibility of a byname. An article on double names, forthcoming in the *Anchor Bible Dictionary* focuses heavily upon documentary parallels to the NT instances, examining the variety in phraseology as well as the types of such *supernomina* and reasons for their being accorded. Cf. *New Docs 1976*, **55**.

Though the presence of contracted *nomina sacra* is nearly always a sign of Christian authorship of a document, their absence as here (*ll*.4, 22) is no cause for doubting it. *Ll*.9-12 of this letter bear out the comment of K. Treu, who has pointed out to me in another context (*per litt.*) that the phrase θεοῦ θέλοντος 'is especially linked with travel plans'. For the sense of παρά + dative in *l*.4 cf. BAGD, s.v., II.2b. As is noted in *ed.pr.*, the sense required by προσφωνέω at *ll*.15-16 — note the double augment; cf. B.G. Mandilaras, *The Verb in the Greek Non-Literary Papyri* (Athens, 1973) §252 — is somewhat different from the meaning given in LSJ, s.v. It is perhaps a development of the notion given there 'make a report' (II.2), viz., 'I reported it (i.e., that you were bringing the scissors) to the fuller'. In any case, this is not how the verb is used in the NT. As Lampe, s.v., B, shows σύναξις became a technical term for the Eucharist (while still retaining its more general meaning, 'service'); but the less frequent use 'feast day' (ibid., C) seems more appropriate here, as λέβης is not attested in Lampe as having any use specific to Christian services.

For εἷς acting as an indefinite article (13, 18), cf. the several NT instances noted by BAGD, s.v., 3b; e.g., Mt. 8.19; 26.69. N. Turner, in Moulton's *Grammar of NT Greek,* III. *Syntax* (Edinburgh, 1963), 195-96, suggests that Matthew's usage without a following genitive in such passages as these two 'comes closer to Semitic [usage] than do Mk. or Lk., and is probably influenced by Heb. אֶחָד or Aramaic חַד'. Our papyrus letter shows that there is no warrant for seeing this use of εἷς as due specifically to Semitic influence.

The feature of greatest interest in the letter is the phrase ἀγαπητοὶ ἀδελφοί (*l*.1, and the address on the back). This term is most commonly employed within Christian circles in the papyri, by Christians of fellow believers. Christian papyrus letters also attest ἀγαπητός in combination with other words. Examples of these include ἀ. ἄπα (e.g., Naldini, no.82), κύριος ἀ. (e.g., Naldini, no.41), ἀ. πάπας (e.g., *P.Oxy.* 36 [1970] 2785, repr. as Tibiletti, *Lettere*, no.31), ἀ. πατήρ (e.g., Naldini, nos. 32 [E. Wipszycka, *JJP* 18 (1974) 215, disputes whether this text is Christian], 51, 67), τέκνον ἀ. (e.g., Naldini, no.43), ἀ. υἱός (e.g., Naldini, nos.5, 42, 43). Note also οἱ ἀγαπητοί used substantivally in Naldini, no.84. Clearly, several of these phrases take their cue from the NT, e.g., τέκνον ἀ. (1 Cor. 4.14, 17; Eph. 5.1; 2 Tim. 1.2). For οἱ ἀγαπητοί in a greeting context note the series of instances at Rom. 16.5, 8, 9, 12. The adjective used in conjunction with ἀδελφός is also found in the NT, e.g., Eph. 6.21; Philem. 16; Jas. 2.5; 2 Pet. 3.15. In contrast to these ἀ. υἱός is reserved in the Gospels and 2 Pet. 1.17 to be used of Jesus alone (the parable references at Mk. 12.6 and Lk. 20.13 are something of a 'halfway house' in this regard). The other combinations arose by analogy with these (ἀ. ἄπα, etc.).

To focus now upon the phrase which occurs in the *P.Köln* text with which we began, is its use restricted solely to Christian-to-Christian interchange (cf. Tibiletti, *Lettere* 29-30, 44-45)? The following list of instances gives us the basis from which an answer may be extrapolated.

1. *P.Alex.* (1964) 29 (provenance unknown, III; Naldini, no.19), short letter recommending 'our brother' (5) Diphilos to Maximos; name of sender not given. The letter concludes: ἐρρῶσθαί σε | εὔχομαι, | ἀγαπητὲ | ἀδελφὲ ἐν κ(υρί)ῳ (12-15); cf. [ἀγα]πητὲ ἀδελφέ (2).
2. *P.Grenf.* 2 (1897) 73 (= Kysis in the Great Oasis, late III/early IV; Naldini, no.21), letter from Psenosiris the presbyter to Apollo πρεσβυτέρῳ ἀγαπητῷ ἀδελφῷ | ἐν κ(υρί)ῳ (2-3), concerning their plans to move the body of a woman.

3. *SB* 16.1 (1985) 12304 (Nag Hammadi, late III/early IV; *ed.pr.* — K. Treu, *APF* 28 [1982] 53-54 [pl.3]), letter of recommendation from Herakleides *papas* το[ῖς κα]|τὰ τόπον συνλιτουργ[οῖς] | ἀγα<πη>τοῖς ἀδελφοῖς ἐν [κ(υρί)ῳ] | χαίρειν, 'to his fellow-servants in each locality, beloved brothers, greetings in [the Lord]' (1-4). The wording on the back (*ll.*14-17) carries the same formula, consistently omitting the syllable from ἀγαπητός, and even including χαίρειν.
4. *SB* 10.1 (1969) 10255 (provenance unknown, III/IV; Naldini, no.20), letter concerning the catechumen Serenos, addressed to Mensourios ἀγαπητῷ ἀδελφῷ | ἐν κ(υρί)ῳ (2-3).
5. *PSI* 3 (1914) 208 (Oxyrhynchos, III/IV; Naldini no.28), letter of recommendation from Sotas: χ̣αῖρε ἐν κ(υρί)ῳ, ἀγαπητὲ | [ἀδ]ελφὲ Πέτρε (1-2).
6. *PSI* 9 (1929) 1041 (Oxyrhynchos, III/IV; Naldini, no.29), parchment letter from the same Sotas to Paul asking him to receive several catechumens one of whom, Leon, is just beginning his instruction (καθηχούμενον | ἐν ἀρχῇ τοῦ εὐαγγελίου, 10-11): χαῖρε ἐν κ(υρί)ῳ ἀγαπητὲ | ἀδελφὲ Παῦλε (1-2; cf. ἀγαπητὲ ἀδε̣λ̣(φέ) in the closing formula at *l.*17). With the phrase in *ll.*10-11 cf. *P.Oxy.* 36.2785 (noted above), another letter of recommendation mentioning a man who is καθηχού|μενον ἐν τῇ Γενέσει (7-8).
7. *P.Herm.Rees* (1964) 4 (Hermopolis Magna, 317-24; Naldini, no.38), letter of John and Leon to Theophanes ἀγαπητῶι ἀδελφῶι (*l.*1; cf. Θεοφάνει ἀγαπητῶι in the address on the back, *l.*14). Rees (intro. n. to this text) doubts that the text is Christian; so also Wipszycka, *art.cit.*, 213-15, and Tibiletti, *Lettere*, 88. Naldini suggests (181) that at least those sending the letter may have been Christian.
8. *SB* 3.2 (1927) 7243 (provenance unknown, IV init.; Naldini, no.36), letter of Didyme and αἱ ἀδελφαί to Sophias ἀγαπητῇ [ἀ]δελφῇ (1-2).
9. *P.Abinn.* (1962) 6 (Philadelphia, 342-50), letter from Apa Mios τῷ ἀγ̣[απ]ητῷ ἀδε̣λ̣φῷ Abinnaios, requesting the loan of nets to catch gazelles which are getting into the crops.
10. *P.Abinn.* 7 (Philadelphia, 342-50; Tibiletti, *Lettere*, 179-80, no.25), letter from Apa Mios [τῷ] ἀγαπητῷ καὶ ἀ̣ληθῶς ἀδ[ε]λ̣[φ]ῷ Abinnaios (*l.*1), requesting a meeting the subject of which is couched in such guarded terms as to be obscure to us.
11. *P.Abinn.* 8 (Philadelphia, 342-50; Tibiletti, *Lettere*, 181-82, no.26 [pl.2]), letter from Apa Mios τῷ ἀγαπητῷ | ἀδελφῷ Abinnaios (1-2), concerning the despatch of some wine and other matters. Note also the concluding address, τῷ ἀγαπητῷ ἄδελφε (*sic*) 'Αμιννέῳ ἄπα Μιός (31).
12. *P.Abinn.*19 (Philadelphia, 342-50), letter to Abinnaios τῷ ἀγαπητῷ ἀδελφῷ (*back*, *l.*36), the beginning of which is very damaged, possibly from Mios. Cf. ἀγ]απη|τ̣ῷ[in *ll.*1-2. The writer requests that his brother-in-law be discharged from the army on compassionate grounds.
13. *P.Abinn.* 32 (Philadelphia, 342-50; *ed.pr.* — *P.Lond.* 2 (1898) 417; Naldini, no.40; Tibiletti, *Lettere*, 177-78, no.24), letter from Kaor, *papas* of Hermopolis τῷ δεσπότῃ μου καὶ ἀγαπητῷ | ἀδελφῷ Abinnaios (1-2). A translation of this letter is included in S.K. Stowers, *Letter Writing in Greco-Roman Antiquity* (Philadelphia, 1986) 161. This well preserved letter is similar in its general goal to Paul's letter to Philemon. Since Kaor is not free to come to see Abinnaios in person 'today', he writes on behalf of the soldier Paul, requesting Abinnaios to forgive him 'this once' for his desertion, π[ε]ρ̣[ὶ] Παύλῳ τοῦ στρατιότῃ | περὶ τῆς φυγῆς συνχωρῆσε | αὐτοῦ τοὔτω (*read* τοῦτο) τὸ ἅβαξ (*read* ἅπαξ) | ἐπειδὴ ἀσκολῶ ἐλθῖν πρὸ[ς] | σὲν αὐτὲ ἡμέρε (*read*, perhaps, αὐθημερόν) (*ll.*6-10). Confusion of the genitive and dative cases is very apparent here; several other examples are noted at **17** above. In view of his name this soldier is likely to be a Christian, thus making more understandable why Kaor intercedes for him. It may be this same Paul who is involved in a sheep-shearing and pig-stealing racket, along with some accomplices one of whom, named Peter, is also probably a Christian (*P.Abinn.* 48, dated 346). Like Kaor to Abinnaios, Paul addresses Philemon as his beloved brother (*vs.*1). The letter is full of subtle twists involving relative status, among which it should not be overlooked that when Paul urges Philemon to receive Onesimos back as a beloved brother (16) the implication is that Onesimos should be treated as an equal. For an interesting parallel to this note *P.Oxy.* 12 (1916) 1494 (IV init.), repr. in Tibiletti, *Lettere*, 169-70, no.21, in which Boethos sends his greetings to 'my sweetest sisters, Dionysodora and her slave Achillis', ἀσπάζομ<αι> τοὺς γλυκυ|τάτους μου ἀδελφούς, Διονυσο|δώραν καὶ τὴν δούλην αὐτῆς | 'Αχειλλίδαν (*ll.*9-12). The use of ἀδελφός, 'sister', should be noted.
14. *P.Heid.* 1 (1905) 6 (provenance unknown, mid-IV; *SB* 1 [1915] 2266; Naldini, no.41), letter of Justinus to [τῷ κυρίῳ] μου καὶ ἀγαπητῷ ἀδελφῷ Παπνουθίῳ χρηστοφόρ[ῳ] (*back*, *l.*26; cf. κύριέ μου | ἀγαπιτέ, 2-3; κύριε ἀγαπητ[έ], 25). For χρηστοφόρος 'Christ-bearing', cf. Naldini's n. ad loc., and Lampe, s.v. Χριστοφόρος, 1.

15. *P.Amh.* 2 (1901) 145 (provenance unknown, mid-IV; Naldini, no.49), letter from Apa Johannes to [τῷ ἀγ]απητῷ ἀδελφῷ καὶ ηὐλ[ο]γημένῳ | [ἐν] τῷ θεῷ Παύλῳ (1-2) 'the beloved and blessed brother in God, Paul'.
16. *PSI* 7 (1925) 830 (provenance unknown, IV; Naldini, no.46), letter of Antonius to τῷ ἀγ<απ>ητῷ ἀδελφῷ [±7] (*l*.1). The end of the text is lost. The adjective is the only indication of a possible Christian context. Cf. Wipszycka, 215.
17. *P.Oxy.* 8 (1911) 1162 (IV; Naldini, no.50), Λέων πρεσβύτερος τοῖς κατὰ | τόπον σ̣υ̣`ν´λ̣ι̣τουργοῖ[ς] πρεσβυτ[έ]|ροις καὶ διακώνοις ἀ[γ]απητοῖ[ς] | ἀδελφοῖς ἐν κ(υρί)ῳ θ(ε)ῷ | χαρᾷ χα[ί]ρειν (1-5), 'Leon the presbyter to his fellow-servants in the locality, presbyters and deacons, his beloved brothers, joyful greetings in the Lord God'.
18. *P.Iand.* 6 (1934) 100 (provenance unknown, IV; Naldini, no.87), letter of Bessemios τ̣ο̣ῖ̣ς̣ ἀγα̣π̣η̣[το]ῖς πατρά[σι] Δοΐλῳ καὶ | Οὐαλερίῳ καὶ τοῖς ἀδελφοῖ[ς Ἡρ]α̣κλείδῃ καὶ | Παησίῳ καὶ Ἁτρῇ. Formally, ἀγαπητός does not go with ἀδελφός here.
19. *SB* 3.2 (1927) 7269 (provenance unknown, IV/V; Naldini, no.94), Τύραννος τοῖς κατὰ τόπον | [ἀ]γαπητ[ο]ῖς ἀδελφοῖς ἐν κ(υρί)ῳ χαίρειν (*ll*.1-2), followed by a request to receive 'our brother' Eudaimon.
20. M. Hombert/C. Préaux, *CE* 13 (1938) 378 (provenance unknown, IV/V; Naldini, no.95), letter from John the deacon [τῷ ἀγα]π̣ιτῷ καὶ εὐλαβεστάτῳ | [ἀδ]ελφῷ Apa Horos (*ll*.1-3). Note also the address on the back, τῷ ἀγαπιτῷ καὶ εὐλαβεστάτῳ ἀδελφῷ ἄπα Ὥρου (*l*.30).
21. The item printed at the beginning of this entry.

There is only one item, no.7, which is problematical here; the rest are clearly Christian in authorship. But that single text needs to be seen in the wider context of papyri involving the jurist Theophanes (cf. *New Docs 1976*, **20**, for discussion of another letter mentioning him). He is known to have been a devotee of Hermes Trismegistos. Although Theophanes is not to be viewed as a Christian, that does not rule out the possibility that some of his private correspondence may have been with Christians, given his position. The names Johannes and Leon sit comfortably with the notion that the writers were Christians; and at *ll*.8-9 it is said that 'all the brothers with us greet you', perhaps suggestive of a monastic community. An analogy for no.7 is provided by the texts listed above which come from the Abinnaios archive. In the introduction to *P.Abinn.*, V. Martin implies (p.33) that he doubts whether Flavius Abinnaios was a Christian. He held a public position, that of *praefectus alae*, and a number of the letters relate to matters under his jurisdiction (military personnel, etc.). It should not be a matter for surprise that he was on familiar terms with Mios, a Christian of some rank within the Church. The openness of the latter about his faith, as expressed in the wording of nos.9-11 (and 12, if it is by him) should not be thought unexpected, given the mid-fourth century date. See further E.A. Judge/S.R. Pickering, *JbAC* 20 (1977) 57-59.

Yet is the use of the phrase ἀγαπητὸς ἀδελφός of both Theophanes and Abinnaios a stumbling-block? Would Christians use this designation of one who did not share their faith? The answer appears to be affirmative, and we should understand that the usage was more fluid than that of a tightly-applied technical term. While it was mostly used by Christians towards fellow Christians, apparently it could also be used by Christians on familiar terms with others from early-mid IV, once Christians were no longer under the impediment of having to be low-key about their faith. In no.13, also from the Abinnaios documents, the Christian *papas* Kaor also uses the phrase; but he is not on such terms of equality with Abinnaios in social status as Mios appears to be (*pace P.Lond.* 2.417, intro. n.).

If this interpretation of the phrase has merit, it follows that Antonius, the writer of no.16 in the list above, is a Christian, even though there is otherwise nothing to indicate this (*pace* Judge/Pickering, 69, that 'the phrase ἀγαπητὸς ἀδελφός seems not to constitute a clear signal'). On the other hand, *P.Ross.Georg.* 3 (1930, repr. 1966) 4 (Arsinoite nome, III) has the reading ἀσπάζο[με] | ὑ[μᾶς ἀγαπη]τ̣οὶ ἡμῶν at *ll*.27-28. Since there is a *proskynema* formula involving Isis and Apollo earlier in this letter (*ll*.3-5) we should rule out this text as being authored by a Christian (so Tibiletti, *Lettere*, 44). While it is true that a fourth-century Christian letter does include a *proskynema* formula, the relevant wording in that papyrus is much vaguer, making no reference to gods like Isis and Sarapis. Tibiletti sees the presence of the formula in that letter (*P.Mich.* inv. no. 346: *ed.pr.* — H.C. Youtie, *ZPE* 28 [1978] 265-68; cf. *New Docs 1978*, **52**) as a pagan reflex by a recent convert to Christianity. Though the supplement ἀγαπη]τοί is at best doubtful, it need not be excluded because the text is not of Christian authorship. Though the use of the specific phrase ἀ. ἀδελφός appears to be restricted to Christian correspondents, the adjective alone does occur in a wider range of texts. As merely one further example, note *P.Oxy.* 2 (1899) 235 (20-50 AD), a horoscope for Tryphon ἀγαπετέ (*l*.2; read -ητέ).

It is unrealistic to assume that men like Abinnaios and Theophanes had no contact with Christians in their official capacity. What is worthy of note is that these two individuals had a social network which included Christians on a level of some familiarity. This, together with the readiness of Christians like Mios to be so explicit about their faith when writing to non-Christians, is of considerable interest for the relations between Christians and their neighbours in the mid-fourth century.

The phrase with which we have been concerned here occurs in a number of Christian letters of recommendation: these are nos. 1, 3-6, 17, and 19 in the list above. The schematic form of these documents — excepting no.3, published a decade later; but it fits the pattern pretty closely (the identity of the recipients is not given) — is made plain in a useful article by K. Treu in *Zetesis. Bijdragen op het gebied van de klassieke Filologie, Filosofie, Byzantinistiek, Patrologie en Theologie aangeboden aan E. de Strijcker* (Antwerp, 1973) 629-36. A seventh papyrus which he also considers is *P.Oxy.* 36 (1970) 2785 (IV), in which ἀγαπητὲ πάπα occurs. The schematic form is: sender's and recipient's names, greetings 'in God' (*vel sim.*), name of the commended person, request that this brother/sister be helped (e.g., with accommodation), greetings from the sender's circle to the recipient's circle, farewell 'in Christ' (*vel sim.*). But not all letters of recommendation conform to this pattern, as Treu notes (635) in regard to *P.Oxy.* 31 (1966) 2603 (IV; Naldini, no.47). Although the writer of that text is alert to the basic pattern, his letter is both longer and displays more literary pretension. See **55** above for discussion of certain features of this papyrus. Of course, this genre of letter was not an exclusively Christian phenomenon: Paul was no innovator in writing such a letter as that to Philemon. See also his comments at 2 Cor. 3.1. The fact that the papyrus examples both predate and postdate the early IV AD persecutions show that they served a purpose not merely when Christians lacked official recognition. The continued use of such letters from later IV onwards testifies indirectly to the growth of schismatic groups within the Church. By the Byzantine period, these letters are still in use, but their form has altered to a much more florid style, in keeping with the times. An example of this from the present culling is *P.Köln* 112 (provenance unknown, V/VI; = *SB* 12.1 (1976) 10965; cf. Treu, *APF* 22 [1973] 391). In this document, both greeting and farewell formulae are dispensed with. *P.Oxy.* 51 (1984) 3643, a letter of recommendation which refers to Epicureanism, is reprinted above at **18**.

Treu's article is not noted by Tibiletti, *Lettere*, in his brief treatment of letters of this type. For earlier discussions see C.W. Keyes, *AJP* 56 (1935) 28-44; C.-H. Kim, *Form and Structure of the Familiar Greek Letter of Recommendation* (*SBLDS* 4; Missoula, 1972). Note also the more recent monograph by H. Cotton, *Documentary Letters of Recommendation in Latin from the Roman Empire* (*BeitrWge zur klassischen Philologie* 132; Königstein, 1981), which supplements Kim's collection with a further 19 items (53-54). Cotton's treatment is concise — only eight Latin documentary letters of recommendation survive — but provides several perceptive insights, e.g., on the relationship between documentary and literary letters of this type (4-7).

125. A Christian iconoclast

Ephesos V

ed. pr. — R. Heberdey *JÖAI* 8 (1905) Beiblatt, 69-70 (fig.)

[Δαίμ]ονος Ἀρ|τέμιδος καθελὼν | ἀπατήλιον εἶδος
| Δημέας ἀτρεκίης | ἄνθετο σῆμα τόδε,
| εἰδώλων ἐλατῆρα | θεὸν σταυρόν τε | γερέρων,
νικοφό|ρον Χριστοῦ σύν|βολον ἀθάνατον.

Epigram on a marble base, 54B x 90H x 43D cm. Vertical bars mark line divisions on the stone.

Bib. — **I.Eph.* IV.1351; Guarducci, *EG* IV.400-01 (fig.104, reproduced from *ed.pr.*); C. Foss, *Ephesos after Antiquity* (Cambridge, 1979) 32.

Having destroyed a deceitful image of demonic Artemis, Demeas set up this sign of truth, honouring both God the driver-away of idols, and the cross, that victorious, immortal symbol of Christ.

Tangible indications of the Artemis cult suffered severely at Ephesos at the hands of Christians from later IV onwards. This monument — we may infer that a cross was erected on the base — bears very self-conscious testimony to this iconoclastic wave. Though such activity had official sanction by the fifth-century, this private, individual initiative by the otherwise unknown Demeas of our inscription is likely to have been typical. Philosophical argument, used by the Apologists of the second century to give credibility to Christianity, now gave way to hammers and crowbars once it was no longer a question of defence.

Merely confining discussion to Ephesos, inscriptions survive in which only the name Artemis has been obliterated subsequently by Christians, e.g., *I.Eph.* II.508, 509 (92/3 and 103/4 respectively). In this latter, bilingual text, only the Greek form of the name was erased (*l.*5), the Latin equivalent in *l.*1 being left. Another instance, *I.Eph.* VII, 1.3263, is quoted at **28** above. Another way in which Christians at Ephesos indicated their dominance over the past was to inscribe crosses on to the foreheads of statues. In Selçuk Museum are two larger-than-life heads, of Augustus and Livia, each with a cross added later (cf. Foss, 32).

All non-Christian cults were targets, of course, not merely Ephesian Artemis. For example, S. Eugenios of Trapezos in Pontus was eulogised for destroying an altar of Mithras: see M.J. Vermaseren, *Corpus Inscriptionum Momumentorum Religionis Mithriacae*, I (The Hague, 1956) 48 no.14. On the subject of Mithraism and iconoclasm, it is pertinent to observe that the flourishing interest in Mithraic studies in the last decade has been accompanied by the rejection in some quarters of some of the fundamental methodology and research on it by F. Cumont, rightly recognised as the founder of modern Mithraic studies. Whether the pendulum will swing back to a steadier evaluation of Cumont's contribution in this area remains to be seen; though to say this is not to impugn the need for such 'demythologising'. Among recent publications on Mithraism the following may be noted in particular: *Mithraic Studies. Proceedings of the First International Congress of Mithraic Studies, Manchester 1971*, ed. J.R. Hinnells (2 vols; Manchester, 1975), in which the editor's introduction and the paper by R.L. Gordon (I.215-48) refer particularly to reassessments of Cumont. The mysteries of Mithras at Rome and Ostia are the main focus of U. Bianchi (ed.), *Mysteria Mithrae. Atti del Seminario internazionale, Roma/Ostia, Marzo 1978* (*EPRO* 80; Leiden, 1979). Within the wide range of papers a number of inscriptions and graffiti are discussed. M.J. Vermaseren has published studies on a number of Mithraea in four volumes entitled *Mithriaca* (*EPRO* 16; Leiden, 1971, 1974, 1978, 1982). As a final example of the range of recent Mithras-research mention may be included of M.P. Speidel, *Mithras-Orion. Greek Hero and Roman Army God* (*EPRO* 81; Leiden, 1980), the strictly limited aim of which is to explore the degree to which the myth of Orion lies behind that of Mithras.

126. A philosopher-nun

Nikaia — late Imperial

ed. pr. — M. Schede, *AM* 36 (1911) 103 no.14 (*non vidi*)

(*leaf*) Ἀττία φιλοσόφισσα·
παρθενίην δύσασα | φύγες κόσμου κακότητα,
| οὔνομα σεμ[ν]ώσασα θεῷ | πίστε<ι> τε ἀγά[π]ῃ τε·
ὧδέ σε | καὶ παράδεισος ἔχει ψυχήν | τε ἅγιος νοῦς
καὶ χορὸς ἔνθα | ἁγίων σὺν ἀγαλλομένοισι | [π]ροφήταις.
(*leaf*) χαῖρε, τέκνον γλυ|[κύ,] χαῖρε καὶ εἵλαθι σοῖς γενέται|[σιν]
[- - - παῖ]ς δὲ θεοῦ [- - -

Verse epitaph; vertical bars indicate line divisions on the stone.

Bib. — S. Şahin, **I.Nikaia* I.550.

Attia the philosopher. Putting on virginity you fled the world's wickedness, exalting God's name by your faith and love. So you and your soul are in Paradise, where are holy Nous | and the chorus of the saints with the rejoicing prophets. Farewell sweet child, farewell, and be benevolent to your parents . . . [child] of God . . .

Şahin points out that just as φιλόσοφος in a Christian text may mean 'ascetic, monk' (see Lampe, s.v., B and cf. C, 7, an adjectival use with the sense 'monastic') so this feminine form presumably means that Attia is a nun. This form — nowhere else attested? — is constructed by analogy with a word like διακόνισσα. That she is a nun is confirmed by the beginning of the poem where the striking metaphor of 'putting on virginity' is employed (for δύσασα we should understand ἐνδύσασα; so Şahin, ad loc.), followed by the reference to the ascetic life of withdrawal from the world. The figurative notion of 'putting on' is common in Paul (Rom. 13.14; Gal. 3.27; Eph. 4.24; 6.11, 14).

In *ll*.4-5 Attia is being associated with the saints and prophets, the latter probably referring to the OT figures who loomed large in early Christian thought and liturgy (witness the *Te Deum*), rather than to Christians who exercised the gift of prophecy within their congregation. If there is to be perceived an allusion to the NT here, the only place where 'saints and prophets' come into view together is in Rev., in contexts concerning their martyrdom (16.6; 18.24). Whether this is a hint that Attia was herself martyred is uncertain; although the possibility may be raised it should not be pressed. The wording of the text seems to me to be too explicit to allow us to think of a period as early as the mid-III or early IV AD persecutions. The intercessory role which she appears to be accorded in *l*.6 may instead make us think of V or later.

There is no need to understand ἅγιος νοῦς (*l*.4) as a mistake for an accusative, as Şahin conjectures. While we should not doubt that φιλοσόφισσα identifies Attia as a nun, the use of νοῦς here seems quite deliberate and brings to mind philosophical notions associated with that word. Specifically, as J.A.L. Lee points out to me, *nous* here is likely to be a way of referring to God: for numerous patristic examples of this usage see Lampe, s.v., F. It may then be that the deceased was a woman who had received some considerable education. For another example see *New Docs 1977*, **16**. At *New Docs 1978*, **14** it was noted that women are only infrequently praised for σοφία: in that place Pircher, no.18 (Sardis, II/I BC; also in Pfuhl/ Möbius I.418 [pl.69]) was discussed briefly. This famous funerary epigram for Menophila interprets a series of symbols carved on the stele: one of these is a book, which the poem explicitly indicates stands for wisdom, ἡ σοφία{μ} μὲν βίβλος (*l*.6). In *I.Eph*. IV.1063 (n.d.), a metrical prayer to Hestia on behalf of the *prytanis* and benefactor Tullia, the goddess is asked to grant children to her 'because of her unimpeachable modesty and wisdom', χάριν ἀχράντοιο | σωφροσύνης σοφίης τε (*ll*.7-8). A further instance worth recording here is *SEG* 22 (1967) 355, repr. at Guarducci, *EG* III (Rome, 1974) 190-91 (fig.76). This funerary epigram for the ten-year-old Tullia (near Olympia, III fin./IV init.) speaks of her as φιλόλογος (*l*.2). The epithet is used of children who loved study, as L. Robert has shown, *Hellenica* 13 (1965) 46-52; cf. briefly *New Docs 1976*, **74**, p.116. The word appears in the NT only as a name, at Rom. 16.15; it is so attested also at Pfuhl/Möbius II.1133 (Kapıkaya in Lydia, late Imperial).

Finally, the mention of ἀγάπη in the epigram for Attia (*l*.3) provides an opportunity to mention an early non-Christian occurrence of the noun. In *JACT Review* 3 (Autumn 1985) 2, K.J. Dover alludes briefly to a Red-Figure vase on which is a woman called Agape. This well-preserved vase (Leningrad inv. 644) is published in A.A. Peredolskaya, *Краснофигурные Аттические Вазы в Зрмитаже. Каталог* (*Catalogue of Red-Figure Vases in the Hermitage Museum*; Leningrad, 1967) 24-25 no.17 (pls. 14-15 and 166.2-7, the latter showing the writing on the vase); and is noted by J.D. Beazley, *Attic Red-Figure Vase Painters* (Oxford, 1963^2) I.16. The painter is Euphronios and the vase is to be dated *c*.505-500 BC. The pot depicts four naked *hetairai* at a *symposion*, most drinking wine and one playing a double aulos. As well as the artist's signature, and a toast by one of the girls to her lover, the names on the pot are Smikra ('Tiny'), Palaisto ('Tussler') Sekline and Agape. What is visible of this last name (written retrograde and in lettering of the period) is ΛΓΑΓ̣ . The etymology of the third name is unclear to me, but since the first two are clearly pet-names in an erotic context Agape should be so considered as well. It is true, of course, that the name was adopted by Christians (see *New Docs 1978*, **76**); and presumably the source of that popularisation is the NT use of the word as a noun. To that extent it is an analogous process to the adoption by Christians of names like Pistis, Eirene, Elpis, etc. Whether any 'line of descent' can be traced from the use of the name on the late VI BC vase is much more uncertain.

One other occurrence of the noun in a non-Jewish/Christian text has been posited: *P.Oxy.* 11 (1915) 1380, an early second-century invocation of Isis where deities in other places are said to be identified with her. At *ll.*109-10 the *P.Oxy.* editors read ἐν Ἰταλίᾳ ἀ[γά]πην θε|ῶν. S. West has persuasively emended this to ἀ[γα]θὴν θεόν (*JTS* 18 [1967] 142-43; ead., *JTS* 20 [1969] 228-30, responding to R.E. Witt's rejection of her emendation, *JTS* 19 [1968] 209-11). West and Witt do not discuss *ll.*27-28 of the same text, where the phrase ἐ]ν | Θώνι ἀγαπ[±11] occurs. The editors restored this as ἀγάπ[ην, i.e., that Isis was called 'love' at Thonis. But the same emendation by West for *l.*209 could fit here, ἀγαθ[ήν; or we may have the adjectival ἀγαπ[ητήν. Neither of these passages, therefore, provides evidence by which we can be confident that we do have a more nearly contemporary parallel to Jewish and Christian use of this noun. For useful discussion of ἀγάπη in the papyri see Tibiletti, *Lettere*, 100-02. A fuller, and rightly cautious evaluation of alleged attestations of the noun in documentary texts is provided by Spicq, *NLNT* I.15-30, especially 22-27.

127. Novatian Christians at Nikaia?

Nikaia late Imperial
ed. pr. — S. Şahin, *I.Nikaia* I.577 (pl.33)

Γεροντίων θεόφρων ἐκτήσατο τύμβον
ἑαυτῷ ἐξ οἰκίων πόνων ὁμώνυμος ὢν πατρὶ ἑαυ-
τοῦ θεμελί{ου}ους πήξας, πληρώσας οἰκοδομὴν
ἅπασαν σπουδέων, πατὴρ ἐὼν τῆς τῶν Εὐσεβῶν
ἐκκλησίας, σκέπην σώματι θνητῷ, ἀνάστασ<ι>ν προσ-
δεχόμενος, καὶ γυναικὶ Κυραδίῃ πιστοτάτῃ χριστοφό-
ρῳ, βιωσάσῃ [ἔ]τησιν κη΄, καὶ φιλτάτοις γλυκυτάτοις Εὐγενίῳ
Γεροντίῳ ἀλλὰ καὶ Λεωνίδῃ Χριστὸν ἐν στέρνοις ἔχουσιν.

Complete marble block, with somewhat irregular lettering in a *tabula ansata*. Read οἰκείων (2), σπουδαίων (4); in *l.*1 *ed.pr.* has ἔκτησα τὸ.
Bib. — **SEG* 1323; *BE* (1980) 517; *I.Nikaia* II, 1, pp.331-32.

Godly-minded Gerontion, having the same name as his father, acquired the tomb for himself by his own labours, after building its foundations. As father of the orthodox church, he filled with good people the whole edifice, | which is a shelter for his mortal body as he awaits the resurrection, and for his wife Kyradia the most faithful Christ-bearer who lived 28 years, and for his dearest, sweetest Eugenios Gerontios as well as Leonides, (who all) possess Christ in their breasts.

This epitaph is not merely explicit about the Christian faith of the family (expectation of the resurrection, etc.); certain phrases occur which sound as though they are tags specific to some particular group. The adjective θεόφρων (1) may be one of these markers: it is very rare in Classical Greek (see LSJ, s.v.), and not even common in Patristic literature, according to Lampe. The instance here may be our first documentary attestation. Another candidate for this group of distinctive words in the text is σπουδαῖος, common in the classical period of morally good people, but apparently very rare in the Patristic sphere (see Lampe, s.v.).

But there are two phrases which seem even more distinctive than these terms. The first, 'father of the orthodox church' — for εὐσεβής with this connotation see Lampe, s.v., 5 — parallels in Hellenistic Judaism 'father of the synagogue'. For discussion with references of this title see B.J. Brooten, *Women Leaders in the Ancient Synagogue* (*Brown Judaic Studies* 36; Chico, 1982) 64-71. Christophilopoulos, *Νομ. Ἐπιγ.* 1.19-20 discusses briefly the well known synagogue inscription from Stobi (*CIJ* 1.694; B. Lifshitz, *Donateurs et fondateurs dans les synagogues juives* [*Cahiers de la Revue Biblique* 7; Paris, 1967] no.10; Brooten, 258 n.135), which includes this title, ὁ πατὴρ τῆς ἐν | Στόβοις συναγωγῆς (*ll.*3-4). This Jewish title may itself be an adaptation of the honorific 'father of the *ekklesia*/*boule*/*polis*' which appears on inscriptions in Asia Minor. For useful discussion of πατὴρ τῆς πόλεως see C. Roueché, *GRBS* 20 (1979) 173-84. Apparently, though, Gerontion's title reflects his function as leader of this group, and is not merely honorific. The possibility is raised at *BE* (1980) 517 that in this wording we may have an allusion to the Novatians: this movement is known to have attained some popularity during IV-V in Asia Minor after Novatian and his followers largely lost support in mid-III N. Africa and Rome. Novatian came to prominence as a rival pope to Cornelius in Rome. The latter's correspondence with Fabius of Antioch shows that Eastern sympathy for Novatian was strong from the start. Yet if this inscription does belong to the fifth century and Gerontion wants to allude to his Novatianism — it was by then a fully institutionalised and respected church — it is odd (as G.W. Clarke points out to me *per litt.*, 1 Dec., 1986) that he does not use the established words of identification. As πατήρ only, Gerontion could not have held *clerical* office. Rather than Novatianism we have 'a group of self-conscious moral rigorists . . . This inscription seems too muted for a clear ascription to a proud and intransigent tradition' (Clarke, ibid.).

The final words of the text provide the other noteworthy phrase, which is reminiscent of Eph. 3.17, κατοικῆσαι τὸν Χριστὸν διὰ τῆς πίστεως ἐν ταῖς καρδίαις ὑμῶν. Though στέρνον itself is not found in the NT, it serves here as a synonym for καρδία.

Two other words may attract brief attention. Θεμέλιος (3) and οἰκοδομή (3) both occur literally and figuratively in the NT. Initial reading of this inscription suggests that the literal meaning is intended here for both nouns; but the possibility of a metaphorical usage ought not to be entirely excluded in this context. After speaking of acquiring the tomb, Gerontion proceeds to state what he has achieved as head of this congregation: by his own labours he has laid a foundation (i.e., established the group) and completed their edification (i.e., guided them to maturity). What tells against this interpretation is the word order: for on this understanding σκέπην (5) is far removed from τύμβον (1), with which it would have to be in apposition. Yet a literal understanding of the terms also has to deal with problematic word order: σκέπην is a long way from οἰκοδομήν (3), too. The clause in *l.*2, in which Gerontion mentions that his father's name was the same as his, interferes with the natural run of the sentence as well. The translation given above assumes a literal interpretation; certain alterations to the punctuation of the Greek text would be needed if a figurative understanding were to be given primacy. Figurative use of οἰκοδομή appears to be a Pauline innovation: see H.Pohlmann, 'Erbauung', *RAC* 5 (1962) 1043-70; cf. E.A.Judge, *TynB* 35 (1984) 23-24.

The use of πατήρ noted above as an honorific title is similar to its use as a respected address. On this see BAGD, s.v., 2b where several papyrus texts are noted. Another instance of this looser application of the noun occurs in *P.Oxy.Hels.* 48.22 (Oxyrhynchos, II/III; pl.35) at *l.*22 and in the address on the back of the letter (*l.*29). See the ed. n., ad loc.

128. *Refrigerium* at a funerary banquet

Tipasa in Numidia V/VI(?)

ed. pr. — M. Bouchenaki, *Fouilles de la nécropole occidentale de Tipasa* (*1968-1972*) (Algiers, 1975) 40-45 (*non vidi*)

in ☧o Deo
pax · et concordia · sit ·
convivio · nostro.

Polychrome mosaic (117B x 102H cm.), showing various types of fish swimming in the water above and below *ll.*2-3.
Bib. — H.-I. Marrou, *Ant.Afr.* 14 (1979) 261-69 (pls. 2, 3); **AE* 682.

In Christ our God may there be peace and unanimity at our banquet.

The Christian funerary *mensa* from N. Africa is a well-known phenomenon. But it was a feature which Christians adopted from their contemporaries and made distinctively their own: at *New Docs 1978*, **13**, attention was drawn to a non-Christian example from Mauretania, dated II[1].

Marrou specifies two features about this new example which make it noteworthy. First, the wording in *l.*2 implicitly acknowledges the bad reputation which funerary banquets had gained for drunkenness and disorder. Augustine was one of the Fathers who criticises its excesses (Marrou, 267-68).

Second, the portrayal of the fish indicates more than a gastronomic interest (Marrou, 268-69). In the centre of the mosaic surface there is a depression into which water was diverted from a basin less than a metre away, via a terracotta pipe. This served as a very tangible expression of the idea of *refrigerium*: cold water to provide refreshment for the dead. This notion — discussed briefly at *New Docs 1978*, **100**, p.145, in the context of the Osiris 'cold water' formula — did not originate among Christians, but was adopted by them so that it became a feature distinctive of N. African Christian funerary practice. It served both Christians and others as a suggestive image of happiness beyond death. One may compare the Tantalos story in Greek myth, though no direct line of descent should be presumed. Whether we should link in the request from the rich man to Abraham in the Gospel parable (Lk. 16.24), that he be given water, is less certain, but deserves some consideration. The wording is: . . . πέμψον Λάζαρον ἵνα βάψῃ τὸ ἄκρον τοῦ δακτύλου αὐτοῦ ὕδατος καὶ καταψύξῃ τὴν γλῶσσάν μου. In this regard, the presence of ἀνάψυξις at Acts 3.20 should be noted, since that noun is the equivalent of Latin *refrigerium* (even though the metaphor is different): ὅπως ἂν ἔλθωσιν καιροὶ ἀναψύξεως ἀπὸ προσώπου τοῦ κυρίου. The fact that both these sentences occur on the lips of Palestinian

Jews ought not to make us rule out a link with the notion known in Hellenistic paganism. T. Muraoka has drawn my attention to C. Meehan's article in *Hebrew Language Studies. Festschrift for Z. Ben-Ḥayyim* (Jerusalem, 1983) 379-82 (in Hebrew, *non vidi*), where the semantic link between 'cool'/'satisfaction' is well established in post-Biblical Hebrew and Jewish Aramaic.

These two words, καταψύχω and ἀνάψυξις, may take our attention for a moment. MM gives no documentary examples for καταψύχω, but BAGD has (under another siglum) noted *P.Cair.Zen.* 2 (1926, repr. 1971) 59155, a letter from Apollonios to Zenon (Philadelphia, 27 Dec., 256 BC), concerning the harvest in which he says: καὶ καταψύξας εὐθέως | κατάσπειρε τὸν τρίμηνον πυρόν (5-6), 'and when you have let it (the land) dry out, immediately sow the three month wheat'. This remains the only instance of the verb known in documentary texts; but unlike Lk. 16.24 the literal sense of the verb is lost. For here the writer is instructing Zenon about the land that has been flooded, after harvesting the early corn, to prepare it for the next sowing. As for ἀνάψυξις, MM has no entry, while BAGD merely signals 'pap.' In fact, this noun occurs in a Byzantine liturgical formula which is used on epitaphs from Nubia (*SB* 4 [1931] 7428.11, 7429.7, 7430.8), the Sudan (*SB* 5.2 [1938] 8235.9 [= *SEG* 8.875] and elsewhere, the earliest example of which is to be dated to the year 858. The formula occurs also on a papyrus from Nessana in Palestine (early VII), *P.Colt* 3 (1958) 96.5; but there the word is largely restored. The formula requests God to give the deceased repose in the bosoms of Abraham, Isaac and Jacob, ἐν τόπῳ φωτινῷ, ἐν τόπῳ ἀναψύξεως, κτλ, 'in a region of light, in a region of refreshment'. Kraemer's introductory n. to the *P.Colt* text is useful on the question of date and the variations in the formula. All these texts noted here — for others, see *WB* and Foraboschi, ad loc. — have adopted the word from a liturgical context. Whether the direct source for this use is the sole NT occurrence in Lk. 16.24 is, however, less than certain. But in any case, these attestations are too late to serve as illustrations of the NT *hapax*. As for the related verb, ἀναψύχω, BAGD offers three papyrus references to parallel the intransitive use at Rom. 15.32D. These are considerably closer in time to the NT: *P.Oxy.* 10 (1914) 1296.7 (III), a letter from Aurelius Dios to his father (quoted by MM, s.v.); *P.Osl.* 3 (1936) 153, a letter (early II) requesting news of the recipient's health so the sender may be relieved from anxiety, ἵνα καὶ ’γὼ{ι} | μεταλαββάνων ἀναψί|χω{ι} (*ll.*9-11; note the two false attempts at correctness, adding *iota*); and *SB* 1 (1915) 3939.28 (Roman period), an unusual letter on a wood tablet from a mummy requesting apparently that two people send a letter, 'in order that I may have repose', ἵνα καὶ ἐγὼ ἀναψύξω. In addition we may note *P.Würzb.* (1934) 21, col.A, *ll.*24-25, a letter from Antonia to her father (Oxyrhynchos, II) which becomes fragmentary at the relevant point, though the wording [ἀ]να|ψύξο πάλι is visible. On the form πάλι see **6**, above. It should be noted that in *SB* 5.2 (1938) 7872.12, a Christian letter of Constantinian date, the verb is entirely restored.

Finally, Marrou assembles (264-66) a useful collection of examples of the christogram serving as the Latin stem *Christ-*, followed by the case ending, as in *l.*1 of our text. These instances fill out one of the points made in a recent article on XP- in Latin and Old English MSS: G.H.R. Horsley/E.R. Waterhouse, *Scriptorium* 38 (1984) 211-30, at 216-17. This latter article was written without knowledge of Marrou's 1979 contribution; but in any case it takes his point rather further. Another instance which may be adduced from the present crop of texts occurs in *AE* 345 — *ed.pr.*: A. Recio Veganzones, *Riv.Ant.Crist.* 55 (1979) 49-53 (pl.2) — an epitaph (Lebrija, in Baetica, 482) for *Lucinus · famul<u>s* | XP*I* · *IħI*. The last three letters are to be resolved as *Ih(es)i*, and offer an analogous instance to *AE* 682 (at the start of this entry) in its transferral of the Greek abbreviation over into Latin.

129. Syncretistic tomb warning

Paiania (Attika) V

ed. pr. — M. Hatzidakis, *AD* 29 (1973/4 [1979]) *Chron.* 194 (pl.)

A
† κοιμητή-
ριον Εὐφιμί-
ας τῆς μιζο-
τέρας, γυνε-
κὸς νέας με´
τοῖς ἔτεσιν,
σώφρονος
κὲ τὴν χῖρα
ἐπάγρυπνο̣<ν>
ἐχούσης κα-
τὰ δύναμιν
εὐποιεῖν ⁝⁝⁝
ὃς ἂν δὲ οἱῴ̣-
ποτε χρόνῳ
ἢ τρόπῳ ἐπ[ι-]

B
χιρήσῃ θε[ῖ-]
νε ξένον
ἢ ἐντόπιο(ν)
ἢ συνγενῆ
αὐτῆς ἔχῃ
πρὸς [τὸ]ν
[θ]εὸν τὸν
[π]αντοκρά-
τορα κὲ πρὸ<ς>
τὰς ἐν οὐρανῷ
δυνάμις [κὲ]
πρὸς τὰς ἐ-
ν ἀέρι κὲ ἐν
[γῇ] κὲ κατα-
[χθ]ονίας

C
δυ<νά>μις καὶ
τὴν μερί-
δα μ(ε)τ(ὰ) τῶν
ἰρηκότων
Ἆρον σταύ-
ρωσον αὐ-
τόν· †
ἔχουσι δὲ
κὲ ο<ἱ> θεοφι-
λέστατοι
κατ᾽ ἐκίνου
κεροῦ κληρι-
κ̣οὶ πρὸς τὰς
προϊρημέ-

D
νας δυνά-
μ̣ις κὲ τὸ
ἀνάθεμα
κὲ τὸ κατά-
θεμα ἐὰν συ̣(γ)-
χωρήσωσιν̣
τεθῆνέ τι-
να ὡς ἴρητε
ἢ μετατεθῆ-
νε ἰς ἄλλον
τόπον τοὺς
ὧδε κιμέν(ους).

Marble stele found in a church. The text fills all four sides (A-D) of the stone, which tapers slightly towards the top.

Bib. — G. Touchais, *BCH* 103 (1979) 544-45 (pl.); *SEG* 250; *D. Feissel, *BCH* 104 (1980) 459-70; *BE* (1981) 254.

A **(*Cross*) Tomb of Euphemia the manager, a young | woman aged 45, modest, and one who turned her hand | without tiring to doing good to the utmost of her abilities.** B **Whoever at any time | or in any manner attempts to lay another (corpse) (here), whether a local resident or a relative | of hers, is to give account to almighty God, and to | the powers in heaven and those in the air, and to the powers on earth and** C **the | infernal ones; and (let him have) the portion with those who have said, | 'Away, crucify him!' (*cross*) And the most God-|beloved clergy at that time are also** D **answerable to the aforesaid | powers, and (lie under the same) imprecation and curse if they | allow anyone to be buried as has been said, or let be transferred to another | grave those who lie here.**

This inscription, for which Feissel provides an improved text and a comprehensive commentary, need not detain us long in view of its late date. As an epitaph it is unusual in that the monument is inscribed on all four sides; remarkable, too, is the imbalanced proportional length of the epitaph proper (*ll.*1-12) and the series of sanctions concerning tomb disturbance (*ll.*13-56). The name Euphemia occurs again in another Christian inscription, *SEG* 674, a much briefer epitaph (Byzantion in Thrace, V-VI). Two words found once only in the NT occur here, ἐντόπιος (*l.*18; cf. Acts 21.12), and κατάθεμα (*ll.*48-49; cf. Rev. 22.3); but their presence here indicates no debt to the NT. Quite what distinction is intended between ἀνάθεμα and κατάθεμα (*ll.*47-49) is difficult to perceive. For μειζότερος (3-4) see **67** above; Feissel (461-62) notes several other examples of this title with the meaning 'manager, steward'. For προσφιλής (39-40) see **83** above.

Yet the real interest of the epitaph is its syncretism. Undoubtedly Christian it is, and of a time when the Church is thoroughly a public institution in society. Yet here in a church is an imprecation involving answerability to God, to heavenly, earthly and infernal powers (*ll.*25-31). Feissel appositely draws attention (465) to the wording of Phil. 2.10, ἵνα ἐν τῷ ὀνόματι Ἰησοῦ πᾶν γόνυ κάμψῃ ἐπουρανίων καὶ ἐπιγείων καὶ καταχθονίων. It is not clear how the powers ἐν οὐρανῷ and those ἐν ἀέρι are to be distinguished: different grades of an angelic hierarchy, perhaps? The warning that those who disturb the tomb will share the lot of the Jews — the allusion in *ll.*35-37 is to Jn 19.15 — has received discussion previously, at *New Docs 1976*, **61**; *New Docs 1978*, **64**; **100**, p.146. From the texts read for the present Review cf. Pallas, *Monuments paléochrétiens*, 309, no.85c (Argos, VI?), which reprints a 'curse of Judas' funerary inscription. On the formula see further Feissel, 466.

The final section of the extended sanction begins at *l.*38, the cross at the end of *l.*37 serving as a punctuation indicator. The clergy at the time of any interference with the tomb are also held under threat. This last notion borrows for Christian cult the very common motif in civic life, that the current magistrates are responsible to ensure nothing untoward happens to civic monuments, etc. In this early Byzantine epitaph for Euphemia in Attika, therefore, we can detect the increasingly active role expected of the Christian clergy as civic functionaries.

What makes this funerary monument for Euphemia of Paiania unique is not its wording at certain points so much as its accumulation of so many curse elements. It is a virtual 'florilegium' of Chirstian funerary curse formulae (Feissel, 470). Elements drawn from the Christian heritage amalgamated with certain pagan expressions suggest to him that a fifth-century date is preperable to V/VI? as previously proposed by *ed.pr.*

130. Hospitality criticised

P.XV Congr. 20 (Oxyrhynchos(?), late III/early IV; pl.10), is a letter between Christians which was noted at *New Docs 1978*, **100**, p.144 for its θεία πρόνοια formula. But somewhat more of the document may be quoted here: πρὸ μὲν πάντων εὔχομαι τῇ θείᾳ προ|νοίᾳ ὅπως ἀπολάβῃς τὰ παρ' ἐμοῦ | γράμματα. ἀληθῶς θαυμάζω πῶς | τω{τη}σοῦτο ἐσφάλης ὡς σου τε|ξαμένου (*read* δεξ-) Ἡράκλει[ον] (*ll.*3-7), 'first and foremost I pray to divine providence that you may receive the letter from me. Truly I am amazed how great a blunder you made when you received Herakleios'. The letter then turns to other subjects. Although not too much should be read into this comment by Kollouthos to Ammonios, it brings to mind a NT passage such as 2 Jn 9-11 where the writer urges his readers not to receive the unorthodox person into their homes nor even greet him (μὴ λαμβάνετε αὐτὸν εἰς οἰκίαν, καὶ χαίρειν αὐτῷ μὴ λέγετε, *vs.*10).

131. Church property ownership in mid-IV Egypt again (cf. *New Docs 1978*, 104)

Mention of church property (οὐσίας ἐκκλη[σίας, *l*.4) occurs in *P.Strasb*. 693 (Antinoe, IV init.), a fragment of an administrative list of monies(?) received from various people. This phrase appears also in *P.Landlisten* (1978), *l*.534; cf. *New Docs 1978*, **104**. *P.Strasb*. 691 (Hermopolis) and 692 (Hermopolite nome) also have affinities with the *P.Landlisten* texts, for certain individuals mentioned in these short pieces are also listed in the latter. Some of these people named in *P.Strasb*. 691 appear to have church connections. But if all these *P.Strasb*. documents are indeed to be dated contemporary with *P.Landlisten* in virtue of their interconnections, then the suggestion of IV init. may be too early. At *New Docs 1978*, **104** it was noted that R. Bagnall has suggested that *P.Landlisten* be 'down-dated' to the 340s. More recently, W. van Gucht, *Atti del XVII Congresso internazionale di Papirologia* (Naples, 1984) 1135-40, argues from the bishops' names in *P.Landlisten* that those tax lists were written after 346/7.

Beside these landowning bishops we may set another who is an exact contemporary, Hierakapollon, who owns four ships: *P.Col*. 160.8, 21, 32, 64 (Karanis, 345-54), 161.2-3, 23-24 (Karanis, 345-51). Cf. the editor's discussion at p.103, especially n.28. For a useful general treatment of the town see E.K. Gazda (ed.), *Karanis, an Egyptian Town in Roman Times. Discoveries of the University of Michigan Expedition to Egypt (1924-1935)* (Ann Arbor, 1983).

Half a century later we have evidence, apparently, of wealthy Christians in NW Spain. The sole Christian text in F. Arias Vilas/P. Le Roux/A. Tranoy, (edd.), *Inscriptions romaines de la province de Lugo* (Paris, 1979) is no.92 (Quiroga, first decades of V; pl.31) which is an inscribed marble disk 94.5cm. in diameter. Bearing the inscription Αω surrounded by the elegiac couplet, Α☧ω *aurum vile tibi est arcenti* (read *arg-*) *pondera cedant*. (leaf) *plus est quod propria felicitate nites* ('Gold is worthless for you. Let quantities of money disappear. It is better that you shine with your own happiness'), the disk has been interpreted by the editors as the top of a table intended to receive offerings. All texts in this volume are in Latin.

132. A miniature Life of Mani

CMC (ET) provides a Greek text and facing translation of the first 99 pages of a fifth-century miniature parchment codex which bears the title περὶ τῆς γέννης τοῦ σώματος αὐτοῦ, 'Concerning the Origin of his Body'. Even though many of the 192 surviving pages are badly damaged or fragmentary, this book is remarkable in more ways than one.

First, it is the smallest codex ever found. Yet despite its dimensions (3.5B x 4.5H cm.), each page of this miniature work, whose provenance is probably Upper Egypt, contains 23 lines of very carefully written text. The hands of three different scribes can be discerned in its copying and corrections. L. Koenen/C. Römer, *Der Kölner Mani-Kodex. Abbildungen und diplomatische Text* (*PTA* 35; Bonn, 1985) provide (p.xxix) a photograph of an opened-out leaf of the codex at full size. The remainder of the *PTA* volume consists of a text with magnified photograph of the relevant parchment sheet. This publication is the first of a complete new edition of the *Cologne Mani Codex* (*P.Colon*. inv. 4780; cf. van Haelst, 1072): it will be followed by two further volumes, comprising an edited text, translation and indexes, and a commentary. Between the opening and restoration of the codex in the late 1960s and the 1985 volume, there has been much publication, above all by A. Henrichs/L. Koenen who have published the text with notes gradually in several volumes of *ZPE*: 19 (1975) 1-85; 32 (1978) 87-199; 44 (1981) 201-318; 48 (1982) 1-59. In addition to the bibliography (to 1979) provided by the *CMC* (ET) translators (6), some new readings are suggested by Koenen/Römer, *ZPE* 58 (1985) 47-54.

If its physical characteristics are remarkable, the contents of the document are of an interest for early schismatic Christianity which cannot be overrated. The work purports to give an account of the early life of Mani (216-76) in southern Babylonia, from after his third birthday until he was in his mid-20s. The anonymous author of the work was clearly a sympathetic insider, who includes various of the *ipsissima verba* of Mani himself. Mani's conversion, his break with the Baptists, and his first missionary journey are some of the narrative portions which may be especially noted; yet there is much gnostic theorising as well. The work provides us with our first evidence of the existence of a *Gospel of Mani*.

133. James the first Pope

This is a question reopened in a recent study by M. Hengel, in E. Grasser/O. Merk (edd.), *Glaube und Eschatologie. Festschrift für W.G. Kummel zum 80. Geburtstag* (Tübingen, 1985), 71-104. Further documentary attestation for this claim appears in *I. Eph.* IV.1290, a marble fragment from the Church of St. John. To the left of a cross may be read: - - - - | Ἰάκο|βος | α´ παπᾶ, the last line of which is resolved by the ed. as πρωτοπαπᾶ(ς). Apart from the question of date (not given in *I.Eph.*), the intriguing aspect about this text is why it should turn up in Ephesos.

134. Abgar and Jesus again (cf. *New Docs 1977*, 115)

Further epigraphical testimony to the factitious correspondence between King Abgar of Edessa and Jesus is reprinted in *I.Eph.* Ia.46 (V/VI), a text inscribed on the underside of the lintel of a house (52H x 155B cm.), no doubt for apotropaic purposes. The text agrees in essentials with that found in Eusebius, *HE* 1.13, although the two versions diverge in details at numerous points in Jesus' reply (*ll.*7-11); the only important difference is the inclusion in the Ephesos text (*l.*11) of a promise by Jesus of protection for Abgar's city. For more on the inviolability of Abgar's Edessa, see *l.*7 of the text reprinted at *New Docs 1977*, **115**, p.203. For bibliographical data on Edessa see *New Docs 1978*, **107**.

Belief in the protective power of this correspondence is further attested by the remains of two inscriptions from Philippi bearing copies of these letters, republished by Guarducci at *EG* IV.357-60 (V init.). These texts were found near a gate of the city through which the Via Egnatia passed, and Guarducci suggests that they were a talisman to defend the city from evil (358, 360). This text, too, included the promise of protection at the end (*ll.*12-13 in Guarducci's restoration; it is worth noting that the whole of Jesus' letter is restored on the basis of three small, non-contiguous fragments — the first four lines are entirely restored — and only a summary of Abgar's letter is given).

(A.L. CONNOLLY)

135. Christian texts in an anthology of Greek epigraphy

With the appearance of *EG* IV in 1978, M. Guarducci has rounded off a very large undertaking, a four-volume handbook on Greek epigraphy. The first appeared in 1967, and was devoted to the character and history of the discipline, and to Greek writing from its origins to the Imperial period. Volume II (1970) concentrated upon public inscriptions, and was balanced by the third volume four years later, which focused on private inscriptions. Some material from this third volume has proved relevant to refer to at various places of the present Review; for Guarducci deals there with such types of texts as votives, funeral monuments, foundation texts and manumissions. But it is the final volume (1978) which has mainly claimed attention, held over for treatment from *New Docs 1978*. Guarducci divides her attention almost equally between 'sacred pagan' inscriptions and those which give evidence of Christianity. Whereas the former are treated thematically (sacred laws, aretalogies, curse texts, amulets, etc.), the section on Christian texts is arranged on a regional basis.

In this volume perhaps 250 inscriptions are dealt with; a representative sample has been noted or occasionally reprinted in the present Review. But there is a considerable number of very well known Christian texts which there seems less warrant for reproducing. As merely three examples of these the following may be noted:

a. Inscribed funerary altar for Aberkios, bishop of Phrygian Hieropolis (*EG* IV.377-86, pls. 111a, b); dated by Guarducci *c*.170-200 (the text also appears as *IGM* 34 where it is dated III).

b. Funerary stele for bishop Metrodoros (Eumeneia in Phrygia, first decades of III): *EG* IV.386-88.

c. Fourth-century epigram for Pektorios (Augustodunum in Gaul): *EG* IV.487-94 (pl.150; cf. *SEG* 28 [1978] 825; *IG* XIV *Suppl.* 2525). This text is particularly notable for its employment of the ΙΧΘΥΣ acrostic as the initial letters of *ll.*1-5. This acrostic and the occurrence of the fish symbol in inscriptions continues to engage interest since F.J. Dölger's classic treatment over half a century ago. From the present year's culling we may note in passing the following relevant items: *EG* IV.473-75 (Cyrenaica, IV, 'probably prior to 365'), an acclamation to Philon τῷ διδασκάλῳ and his pupils, followed by the acrostic in *l.*5. In the catacomb of San Sebastian at Rome a graffito reads ΙΤΧΘΥC (*EG* IV.545-47; pl.170), which Guarducci dates III[1]. In *SEG* 1611 (Hesban in Palestine, mid-VI) a mosaic verse dedication uses the word in place of Χριστός: 'Eusebia provided (this mosaic?) for the salvation of the most pious elder Papion. Christ (ἰχθῦς), remember Philadelphos and all his household'. A Latin epitaph from Cornus in Sardinia (*AE* 311; late Imperial?) includes a fish sign in this text for a man aged *c*.80. An epitaph recorded as *I.Eph.* VI.2277 records merely the name of the deceased followed by a crudely carved fish; it is presumably on the basis of this that the editors interpret the man to have been a Christian. This is not the only possible interpretation of the design; see the discussion at **121** above. The sole inscription with a fish symbol in Pallas, *Monuments paléochrétiens* is one containing a 'curse of Judas' formula from Argos (85c, on p.309). Two instances of the fish symbol on Christian epitaphs may be noted from the publications of the year 1978: *TAM* IV, 1.363 (Karamatlı in Bithynia, late Imperial(?)); *SEG* 28 (1978) 512 (Demetrios in Thessaly, III fin./IV init.).

Guarducci's long experience in Greek epigraphy is in evidence in her selection of texts: she has a keen eye for monuments of considerable interest. The generous number of plates included is a very considerable gain from the book, too. Yet it is therefore all the more a disappointment that the commentaries on the inscriptions she selects are, for the most part, qualitatively in inverse proportion to the interest afforded by the texts themselves. Two further observations may be made. Jewish texts are well-nigh ignored, a major gap in her coverage. Second, there is noticeable in Guarducci's treatment of Christian texts a concern to date them as early as she can. Caution needs to be exercised, for the dating problems of particular inscriptions are not often enough dealt with by her in this book. As just one example, at **104** above it was noted that a lead sheet from Rhodes containing Ps. 79.2-16 — Guarducci, *EG* IV.365-68, where dated III — may be as late as V-VI.

136. In brief

(a) Graffito on an ossuary mentioning a **προσήλυτος**, Diogenes son of Zenon, from the 'Dominus Flevit' necropolis, Jerusalem: Guarducci, *EG* IV, pp.441-44 (fig. 131a), where dated I fin./II init. Beneath the text to the left Guarducci discerns a ☧ (fig.131b), probably to be dated II fin. It is doubtful whether this conjunction makes necessary the inference that Diogenes was a convert to Christianity; the question should be left open. For the noun in the NT cf. Mt. 23.15; Acts 2.11; 6.5; 13.43.

(b) *P.Bodmer* 10 (1959), consisting of **apocryphal correspondence between Paul and the saints of Corinth,** is reconsidered by T.W. Mackay, *Pap.Brux.* 18, pp.119-28. The language of this work includes quotations and paraphrases of both Pauline and other NT books. It is probably to be dated II (second quarter). Following the common practice of 'fathering' the authorship upon a well-known predecessor to give his work authority, the anonymous writer sought to draw attention to what he perceived to be incipient theological departures from the norms of the Primitive Church.

(c) **Valentinian(?) rites** mentioned in an inscription from Rome, dated II by Guarducci, *EG* IV.529-33 (fig.165). The four-line fragment appears to mention baptism, the Eucharist, praise of the Creator and the Son, and concludes with mention of the distinctively Valentinian terms σιγή and ἀλήθεια.

(d) **List of works of S. Hippolytos** inscribed on right side of a statue of him, seated: Guarducci, *EG* IV.535-45 (Rome, III^{1}, probably 222-35; figs.167-69).

(e) Commemoration of two people who are probably **Donatist martyrs** in a short Latin inscription (*AE* 689) from Amoura in Numidia, dated 322.

(f) **Anti-Arian slogan** on an inscription in a tomb which also contains frescoes: Pallas, *Monuments paléochrétiens*, 106-07 no.57 (Philippi, IV), κ(ύρι)ε ἐλέησον ἡμᾶς καὶ ἀνάστησον ἡμᾶς τοὺς ἐν τῇ ὀρθῇ πίστ<ει> ἐνθάδε κοιμηθέντας, 'Lord, have mercy on us and raise us who have fallen asleep here in the right faith'.

(g) A **gold finger ring**, *IMS* 140, found in a tomb (IV fin.) near Bela Palanka; on either side of a male bust is inscribed *in deo | vivas*. Though not a formulation exactly found in the NT, it is similar to some of them (e.g., Rom 6.11, ζῶντας δὲ τῷ θεῷ ἐν Χριστῷ Ἰησοῦ); and in view of the date it is at least possibly Christian.

(h) Prescriptions concerning **offerings to the Trinity on behalf of the dead**: Guarducci, *EG* IV. 339-44 (fig.90 on p.338). This 40-line inscription from Tanagra, dated IV fin./V init., is the longest Christian inscription known in Greek from the period down to that date.

(i) **V AD Christian epitaphs from N. Sinai**: A. Ovadiah in *Actes Constantza*, 429-30 (summary only). For Christians in this area see *New Docs 1977*, **116**.

(j) The formula **[†] ἀγαθῆι † τύχηι †** occurs at the beginning of a V/VI init. honorific inscription from Aphrodisias: *ed.pr.* — C. Roueché, *GRBS* 20 (1979) 173-85 (pl.); cf. *AE* 605; *SEG* 1070; *BE* (1980) 48. This phrase goes right back to Classical Greek usage, but appears here coexisting with Christian crosses a millennium later. The man who set up the inscription describes himself as πατὴρ τῆς | λαμπρ(οτάτης) Ἀφροδ(εισιέων) μητροπό(λεως) (*ll*.9-10). Roueché gives numerous parallels for the notion 'father of the *polis*'; for some analogous expressions in Judaism and Christianity see **127** above. This inscription will be reprinted in her publication as a *JRS* Supplementary volume of a corpus of the later Imperial-period inscriptions of Aphrodisias, due to appear in 1987.

(k) Mention in a Byzantine letter of a **house (οἶκος) which apparently functions as a monastery**: *P.Strasb.* 697.17-18 (provenance unknown, VI), with ed. n. ad loc. For a discussion of οἶκος, οἰκία, etc., along with various terms for architectural features of houses see G.Husson, *OIKIA. Le vocabulaire de la maison privée en Egypte d'après les papyrus grecs* (Paris, 1983).

(l) **Living conditions of Egyptian monastics,** as evidenced by papyri, archaeological finds and literary sources, is examined by G. Husson in *Hommages à la mémoire de S. Sauneron* II (Cairo, 1979) 191-207.

(m) **Abbreviation of the name Kyriake** in a Christian epitaph as Κ(υρ)ιακῆ⟪ς⟫ (genitive required, but the transcription has HN in ligature for the last two letters): *I.Nikaia* I.518 (cf. *SEG* 1325). Though no superior bar occurs over the contraction, we are to see the form as reflecting a flow-on from κύριος abbreviated as κ̅ς̅.

F. VARIA

137. Epigraphical surveys

Tod, *PGE*, collects and reprints unchanged a series of articles by M.N. Tod which reviewed recent publications of Greek epigraphy. These essays, seven in number, appeared initially in *JHS*, between vol.54 (1939) and vol.75 (1955). They constitute only the last third of Tod's contributions in this vein. The editor of the reprinted volume, A.N. Oikonomides, anticipates that the dozen articles covering the period 1914-1936 will appear in another collected volume, with detailed indexes making up a third. Neither of these has yet appeared, unfortunately. Certainly, Tod's series does require comprehensive indexing — as has now been done for all but the most recent volumes of *BE* — if the vast amount of material he surveyed so succinctly is to be accessible via his pages.

The surveys were organised regionally; accordingly, comment on Jewish and Christian texts is scattered throughout, and is not easy to locate without a close reading of every page. Occasionally Tod refers to items which I have not been able subsequently to locate; an instance is Z. Varga, *The World of The Hellenistic Inscriptions, Papyri and Ostraca, and the NT* (in Hungarian; Debrecen, 1942): *PGE* 121 (= *JHS* 67 [1947] 93). For the Greek inscriptions of Egypt and Nubia Tod wrote a separate series of shorter articles, which appeared in 17 instalments in *JEA* from vol.1 (1912/13) to vol.36 (1950). From vol.38 (1952) this series was taken over by P.M. Fraser, who continued it with more extensive articles, almost annually to vol.48 (1962).

The *JHS* enterprise was brought to an end by Tod's decision that, with the thorough-going, detailed and incisive treatment accorded texts on an annual basis by the Roberts in *BE*, and by the revival of *SEG* under A.G. Woodhead, 'my own work may well be deemed superfluous' (*PGE* 226 = *JHS* 75 [1955] 122). This was an over-modest assessment; for not only were his surveys comprehensive in their coverage, they were also distinguished stylistically by being both beautifully and charitably written. Yet Tod was correct in his perception of the *BE* series; and it is the superior utility of the latter which will probably ensure that *PGE* will not be read and mined as much as may otherwise have been the case.

As for *BE*, an era has come to an end with the death in May 1985 of L. Robert. Since 1938 he collaborated with his wife — R. Flacelière was also a co-collaborator in *BE* (1938) and (1939) — in producing near-annual surveys of the year's output in Greek epigraphy. *BE* was begun in *REG* exactly a century ago, but was put on to a new footing from vol.30 (1917) by P. Roussel (with the collaboration of others for certain numbers: G. Nicole for the first, A. Plassart for the review in *REG* 34 [1921], and Flacelière for that in vol.49 [1936]). Within a short period under the Roberts its scope soon expanded considerably. Their last such contribution was *BE* (1984). It is understood that J. Robert will no longer continue to work on the *BE*, and that it will continue under the editorship of P. Gauthier, aided by a team of colleagues. *BE Index* provides the second installment offering very comprehensive access to *BE* 1966-1973. *BE* 1938-1965 was covered by a three-volume index (Paris, 1973-75). In 1983 a third *Index du BE* appeared, treating *BE* 1974-1977. The indexes comprise Greek words, a concordance of publications dealt with, and a subject index.

Robert was to Greek epigraphy what Mommsen was to Roman history. His dominance of the discipline was complete; nowhere was this more evident than in his research on Asia Minor. Paradoxical though it may seem, he appears not to have been interested in epigraphy as an end in itself, but as a means to illuminate the milieux which spawned these texts in such quanitity and diversity. He had much to contribute, too, to numismatics; and though the term 'Historical Geography' may be especially associated by some with the name of W. M. Ramsay, yet it was Robert who did more than any other individual to make this area of research a sub-discipline in its own right. But the focus of his interest was not in these areas *per se*; it lay rather in the much larger question of Hellenism, its transferral, transformation and interaction with the indigenous cultures of Asia Minor and with Imperial Rome, especially in the East. The political and social institutions of these *poleis* lie at the heart of his work. Naturally, the first half-millennium of Christianity intersected with this constantly, and Robert gave frequent attention to its rise and increasingly overt self-testimony in Anatolia.

Yet for these subjects, as for almost all others, Robert did not provide any synthesis, that might have drawn together the many strands of detailed investigation into a coherent whole. It will be left to others to provide such works, based on the more than 30 books — and ten times that number of substantial articles — he produced. Although obituaries have appeared, one particular *desideratum* is that a thorough, but equally, a detached, evaluation of the whole gamut of Robert's output be provided, which will pinpoint the significance of his contribution for younger students of epigraphy and of Anatolia in the Imperial period.

BE 39, 40 provide cross-references to Greek inscriptions which concern Jews treated in *BE* (1979); *BE* 41, 42 do the same for Christian/Byzantine texts. It may be convenient to note here, too, those entries in *BE* that address the works treated in the present Review which have many hundreds of inscriptions. Inscriptions from Ephesos are dealt with at *BE* (1979) 396-412 (on pre-*I.Eph.* publications), (1981) 433-480 (on *I.Eph.* Ia-VI), (1982) 293-312 (on *I.Eph.* VII, 1 and 2), (1983) 335-340 (on new inscriptions not in *I.Eph.*; note especially no.335). Although the numeration in *I.Eph.* reaches 5115, there are many numbers unallocated, but also many (a) and (b) texts; an approximate total of inscriptions in *I.Eph.* would be *c.*3,540. Similarly, *I.Nikaia* has many of its 1597 numbers unallocated, the actual number of texts being just over 600. This latter collection of inscriptions is picked up in *BE* (1980) 502-518 (*I.Nikaia* I), (1982) 411, 413-15 (*I.Nikaia* II, 1), (1983) 420-423 (*I.Nikaia* II, 2). In the case of the *c.*2,500 items in Pfuhl/Möbius (the numerous (a) and (b) texts raise the number from the allocated 2323), *BE* deals with them at (1978) 19 (P/M I) and (1979) 11-24 (P/M II).

Finally, mention may be included here of a recently published bibliographical aid for Greek and Latin epigraphy: F. Bérard *et al.*, *Guide de l'épigraphiste. Bibliographie choisie des épigraphes antiques et médiévales* (Paris, 1986). This work is accurately compiled, carefully arranged, and usefully cross-referenced. A particular merit is the editors' inclusion of concise information about the contents of many of the publications listed (date range, provenance, main genres represented, etc.).

138. Epigraphical grammars

Grammars based on the papyri are able to cover their subject very adequately, based as they are on thousands of texts. The grammars of Mayser (for the Ptolemaic period) and of Gignac (covering the Roman and Byzantine material; the syntax volume, yet to appear, will be in two parts [F.T. Gignac, *per litt.*, 18.1.85]) appear to be rather better known to NT Studies than comparable epigraphical works. This reflects in part the greater awareness by NT researchers of the papyri than of inscriptions, an indirect legacy of Deissmann, MM, et al. Yet the value of a grammar based on the documentary texts which emanate from a tightly delimited region (such as a *polis*) will depend in part on the size of the corpus of texts available. Naturally, Attic inscriptions are one group for which something substantial can be done. L. Threatte has so far published the first volume of his *The Grammar of Attic Inscriptions* (Berlin, 1980), devoted to phonology. When this comprehensive enterprise reaches completion it will replace K. Meisterhans, *Grammatik der attischen Inschriften* (Berlin, 1900^3; repr. Hildesheim, 1971). The publication of the *I.Eph.* volumes renders a grammar of these inscriptions a *desideratum*: with some 3,500 texts in the corpus — the numbers reach beyond 5,100, but there are many gaps in the sequence, only partly compensated for by additional (a) or (b) texts — this body of evidence makes the attempt at a grammar worthwhile. Such an undertaking ought to be of considerable interest for those who study the NT, given that several of the books in the latter were written by individuals who spent some considerable time there. Yet the lack of provision of a date for so many of the texts in *I.Eph.* is an obstacle to that undertaking; for although diachronic questions may be of some interest, a synchronic study is likely to prove more fruitful. (It should be pointed out that although the editors do not give dates as often as they might, their notes occasionally provide references to other publications where the relevant text is dated.)

In contrast to the bulk of evidence from that city, the number of inscriptions from Erythrai is much slighter. H. Engelmann/R. Merkelbach, *Die Inschriften von Erythrai und Klazomenai* (*IK* 1, 2; Bonn, 1972, 1973) include *c.*430 texts from Erythrai. Those which fall within the two centuries from mid-V to mid-III BC provide the basis on which Garbrah, *Erythrae*, studies the phonology and morphology of this city in a clearly arranged monograph. In fact, he considers further matters not suggested by his subtitle: word-formation (128-31), as well as a small number of syntactical (132-37) and lexical questions (138-41). The reason for his cut-off date of mid-III BC is that by *c.*300 BC Ionic forms had largely been displaced by Attic ones, a process which had begun a century earlier (Garbrah, 145).

Since epigraphical grammars appear to be less well known in the NT field, it may be useful to list some of them here (not all seen by me). Perhaps the two best known are those from the turn of the century: E. Schweizer, *Grammatik der pergammenischen Inschriften* (Berlin, 1898); and E. Nachmanson, *Laute und Formen der magnetischen Inschriften* (Uppsala, 1903). Three more regional grammars appeared in the 1930s: A. Scherer, *Zur Laut- und Formenlehre den milesischen Inschriften* (Munich, 1934); B. Bondesson, *De sonis et formis titulorum Milesiorum Didymaeorumque* (Lund, 1936); E. Knitl, *Die Sprache des ionisches Kykladen nach den inschriftlichen Quellen* (Munich, 1938), dealing with selected features of phonology, morphology and syntax. From more recent times come J.J. Moralejo Alvarez, *Gramática de las inscripciones délficas* (Santiago de Compostela, 1973); G. Laminger-Pascher, *Index Grammaticus zu den griechischen Inschriften Kilikiens und Isauriens* (2 vols.; *Öst. Ak. der Wiss., ph.-hist. Kl. Sitzungsberichte* 284.3, 298.3; Vienna 1973, 1974); and C. Brixhe, *Le dialecte grec de Pamphylie. Documents et grammaire* (Paris, 1976). What is noteworthy is that locations in Asia Minor (whether specific cities or larger provinces) have elicited the majority of these publications.

139. In brief

(a) The entirety of *Pap.Brux.* 16 consists of a detailed reconsideration by E.G. Turner of the terms **recto/verso**, and of the larger question, the **nature of the papyrus roll**. This analysis lays bare the confusing way in which such words have been used differently by editors of papyrus texts. Turner suggests that 'front/back' should replace '*recto/verso*' for a sheet, and recommends 'inside/outside' be employed when speaking of a roll. A few more years will be needed to see whether this new terminology replaces the old, but there are signs in recent publications that it may.

(b) J. Kaimio, *The Romans and the Greek Language* (*Commentationes Humanarum Litterarum* 64; Helsinki, 1979; cf. *SEG* 1785) provides an excellent socio-linguistic analysis of **who used Greek in the Roman world, and why**. Inscriptions receive attention (especially 168-81, on Greek inscriptions erected by Romans). The discussion bears to some extent on the question of Greek in Palestine. A companion volume is promised, dealing with the position of other indigenous languages under the Empire. Cf. *Pap.Brux.* 18, pp.27-33, where Kaimio is concerned with the use of Latin in Roman Egypt. Worth mention also in connection with the indigenous languages of the Empire is the wide-ranging collection of contributions in G. Neumann/J. Untermann (edd.), *Die Sprachen im römischen Reich der Kaiserzeit* (*Bonner Jahrbücher Beiheft* 40; Köln, 1980) 215-39.

140. Other Christian texts encountered

The following Christian documentary texts were noted in publications of the year 1979 and others listed in the Abbreviations section of the Introduction, but have not been treated at all in this Review. ('Christian' here is used very broadly to refer to a text which may be distinguished by its content, or merely by the presence of certain signs, e.g., a cross on an official document.) Nearly all of these are late Roman or Byzantine in date. The insertion of a bracketed question mark indicates that there may be doubt about the claim that the text is Christian.

AE: 43, 44, 44 *bis*, 45, 235, 236, 241, 242, 308-12, 313(?), 314-16, 318-20, 322, 346, 347, 479, 480, 690, 691;

CPR: 22(?), 23, 27-29, 40, 44, 45, 47, 48, 50, 51, 58, 60;

Guarducci, *EG* IV: Attika — nos. 1, 3(?), 4, 5;
Peloponnese — nos. 1-2 (cf. *New Docs 1978*, **93**, **102**), 3, 5, 6;
Central Greece — nos. 1, 5-7;
N. Greece — nos. 1, 3, 4;
Aegean islands — nos. 3-6;
Asia Minor — nos. 3, 4, 6, 7, 10-14;
Crete — nos. 1-3;
Cyprus — nos. 1-3;
Cilicia — nos. 2, 3;
Syria — nos. 1-6;
Palestine — nos. 2, 4, 6;

Egypt — nos. 1, 2 (cf. *New Docs 1977*, **104**, p.178), 3-6;
Cyrenaica — nos. 1, 4;
Iberian peninsula — nos. 1, 2;
Gaul — nos. 2 (improbably Christian: see *New Docs 1976*, **23**), 3, 4;
N. Italy — nos. 2, 4-7;
Sicily — nos. 1, 2, 3 (?), 4;
Rome — nos. 2 (?), 5, 6, 7 (?);

Helbing, *AGI*: 10(?);

I.Apollonia: 3, 4, 29, 30, 36, 38, 45, 50, 61;

I.Eph.: II.317, 447, 453, 458, 494, 495, 543, 557, 570(3), 571(?), 572(1)(?), 580 (Christian crosses added later?);
IV.1191, 1192, 1195, 1196, 1280-85, 1289, 1291-95, 1297, 1298, 1300, 1301, 1304-09, 1313, 1320, 1322, 1323, 1331, 1332, 1336, 1338, 1339, 1347, 1349(?), 1352, 1355, 1357, 1358, 1360-64, 1366-68, 1370, 1373-76;
V.1534, 1674, 1983(?);
VI.2044, 2090, 2214(?), 2217d(?), 2223, 2223a, 2227, 2229(?), 2240, 2240a(?), 2253b, 2263, 2271, 2284, 2312b, 2409, 2580 (Latin), 2954;
VII, 1.3118, 3134, 3136, 3138c (Latin), 3286, 3288a, 3304, 3305, 3319;
VII, 2.3705, 3807, 3819, 3820c, 3823, 3842-45, 4128, 4129, 4131-34, 4138-50, 4201, 4202, 4204-09, 4211, 4214, 4216, 4219, 4220, 4223, 4226-28, 4233, 4237-42, 4244, 4247, 4249, 4250, 4270, 4281-83, 4302-05, 4307-18a, 4318c-4320, 4363, 5115. (Note that a number of other items in VII, 2 are listed as Christian by the editors — because of their provenance? — but lack any distinguishing features on the stone itself.)

IG XIV *Suppl.*: 2462, 2463, 2476, 2491, 2492, 2517, 2534(?), 2535, 2559-61, 2573.14, 2573.21; p.166 (*SEG* 13.434), pp.169-70 (*SEG* 19.648-51);

IGM: 111, 210;

IGUR: 1180(?), 1264(?), 1353(?), 1410(?);

IMS: 50-53, 58, 64, 77, 113, 115, 118, 132, 137, 138, 142;

I.Nikaia: I.450, 451, 460-68, 480-82, 489-91, 496, 498 (= *SEG* 1341), 499-501, 516, 518 (= *SEG* 1325), 530 (= *SEG* 1318), 531, 551, 553 (= *SEG* 1320), 554, 558 (= *SEG* 1322), 570, 572 (= *SEG* 1342), 574-76, 578 (= *SEG* 1324), 585 (= *SEG* 1339), 586, 587, 588 (= *SEG* 1340);
II, 1.802;
II, 2.1493;

P.Col.: 132(?), 167, 171 (see *New Docs 1976*, **81**);

P.Köln: 102, 104;

P.Laur.: 73, 75, 77, 80, 84, 88, 89, 91, 93, 95-97, 109-18, 121, 125;

P.Strasb.: 696, 699;

P.XV Congr.: 21, 23 (Coptic);

Pallas, *Monuments paléochrétiens*: 9 (pp.15-16, nn.29, 30), 17 *bis*, 29, 31, 32 (p.50), 39 (p.75), 41, 62c, 89d, 99 *bis* (p.310), 112, 129, 162, 166, 167d;

Pfuhl/Möbius: 1154 (alluded to briefly at *New Docs 1978*, **98**, as E. Gibson, *The 'Christians for Christians' Inscriptions of Phrygia* [Missoula, 1978] no.20), 1159 (= Gibson, no.12);

RIS: 3.255 (repr. at *New Docs 1977*, **101**, p.171);

SEG: 279, 302, 307, 308, 310-20, 322-27, 346, 372, 423, 430, 635, 636, 639-42, 644, 645, 665, 1010, 1059(?), 1117, 1139, 1227, 1269, 1530, 1534, 1589-95, 1601, 1602, 1609-10, 1660, 1662, 1664(b), 1664(d);

SIA II: p.224 (= *SEG* 3 [1927] 208);

SIA III: *IG* III, 2.x.1384, 1385, 1387, 1428, 3516a (*sic*), 3436-3508, 3510-24, 3526, 3528-44, 3547; Bayet, nos.1-37, 39-74, 76, 77, 79-104, 106, 108-17, 119-25; Creaghan/Raubitschek, nos. I-XIV, XVI-XXII, 1-12, 14-34. [It should be noted that there is considerable overlap between these items, especially between the *IG* texts and Bayet.]

Tibiletti, *Lettere*: 23, 33, 34 (= *P.Laur.* 2.42, repr. at *New Docs 1977*, **102**);

Tsigaridas, *Κατάλογος*: 2-7, 10-21, 23-44, 46-79.

141. Corrigenda to *New Docs 1976-1978*

The following corrigenda affecting clarity have been noticed, which have not already been listed in previous volumes of *New Docs* (*1977*, **121**; *1978*, **113**):

New Docs 1976

p.14, paragraph 3 *l.*17: for 'see **35**' read 'see **11**'.
p.37 Greek text *l.*30: for 'δεῇ' read 'δέῃ'.
p.54, Greek text *l.*7: for 'ἀπρόσκοπός ἱ-' read 'ἀπρόσκοπος ἵ-'.
p.55, paragraph 2, *l.*12: for 'ἰμήν' read 'ἥμην'.
p.97, paragraph 2 *l.*6: for 'Ps. 131.5-6' read 'Ps. 131.15-16'.
p.133, fourth last line: for 'αὐθυμέω' read 'εὐθυμέω'.
p.147, col. 1: for 'Ps. 131.5-6' read 'Ps. 131.15-16'.
p.148, index 2, col. 2: add †ἀναπλύνω — 88.
p.149, col. 2: add νεοφώτιστος — 88.
col. 3: πορίζω is out of alphabetical order.
col. 3: add asterisk beside Σαμαρίτης.

New Docs 1977

p.32, Greek text, *l.*27: for 'σοῦς' read 'σοὺς'.
p.62, first English paragraph, *l.*3: delete 'or ἐπιστόλιον'.
p.137, no.11, second last line: for 'no.7' read 'no.8'.
p.140, first new paragraph, *l.*5: for 'fifty-century' read 'fifth-century'.
p.219, index 3, s.v. Abgar: for '**116**' read '**115**'.
p.220, s.v. letters, Abgar/Jesus correspondence: for '**116**' read '**115**'.

New Docs 1978

p.3, s.v. *P.Hercul.* 2: for '*Papyri*' read '*Papiri*'.
p.25, *l.*5: for 'ἀγαπήν' read 'ἀγάπην'.
p.35, paragraph 4, *l.*1: for '*laudiato*' read '*laudatio*'.
p.39, **10**: date should read I^2, not 1^2; this same text is dated I/II at *I.Nikaia* I.192.
p.43, first paragraph, *l.*15: for 'Peteautos' read 'Peteaus'.
p.46, Greek text, *l.*3: for 'ἁμαρτίων' read 'ἁμαρτιῶν'. In *l.*2, ἐλευθέρᾳ σαυτοῦ 'should be here ἐλευθερᾶς αὐτοῦ with the well-known genitive-dative confusion' (G. Mussies, *per litt.* 9.8.85).
p.63, **26**, paragraph 1, *l.*10: for 'δίολου' read 'διόλου'.
p.64, **28**, *l.*4: for 'Sagallasos' read 'Sagalassos'.
p.65, **31**, *l.*1: for 'Lk. 2.52' read 'Lk. 2.51'.
p.67, **36**, paragraph 2, *l.*1: P.J. Sijpesteijn (*per litt.*, 2.9.85) points out that ἐπιπάλλοντα stands for ἐπιβάλλοντα, a common interchange in the papyri (and corrected in *P.Sakaon* 37).
p.69, **40**, last line: the sentence is unfinished: read 'where the noun σπάραγμα is mentioned (*c.*I AD?)'.
p.72, paragraph after the translation, *l.*5: for 'Lk. 1.68' read 'Lk. 24.21'.
p.88, **75**, second last line, for 'Octarian' read 'Octavian'.
p.98, **84**, sentence beginning 'It is possible that . . .' A.B. Shippee (*per litt.*, 24.3.86) points out that 'not only are the senses of the psalm and the inscription exactly opposite, but also the words of the inscription are found verbatim in Ps. 117.15 (LXX)'.
p.100, Greek text, A *verso* *l.*6: for {τὸ ὄνομα} read ⟦τὸ ὄνομα⟧.
p.104, no.3: for '04' read '*O.* 4'.
p.111, second last line, read βασιλεύς.

p.112, second last paragraph: K.Treu has rightly pointed out (*per litt.*) that the information given here is confused and inaccurate: 'However quires are made up, in any codex *recto* (or hairy side, for that matter) must precede as often as *verso*. The second part of a double leaf is necessarily the counterpart and opposite of the first'.

p.144, *l.*13: for 'π[ατ]ρῷων' read 'π[ατ]ρῴων'.

p.145, first paragraph, second last line: for '*regrigerium*' read '*refrigerium*'.

p.155, **102**, second paragraph, *l.*4: for 'θεότοκος' read 'θεοτόκος'.

p.157, last paragraph, *l.*1: for 'Diokoros' read 'Dioskoros'.

p.166, item (u): for 'possible' read 'possibly'.

p.171, last column: delete 'Lk. 1.68 — **46**', '2.52 — **31**'; add 'Lk. 2.51 — **31**, **32**', '24.21 — **46**'.

p.173, index 2, col. 2: add 'βιάζομαι — 6'.

p.174, col. 1: correct accent on θεοτόκος.
col. 3, s.v. φῶς: add '87'.
s.v. χριστιανός — add asterisk

p.176, col. 2, s.v. 'Names, Evangelos': add '18'.

INDEXES

1. Biblical passages

2. Words

This index does not register all occurrences of words in texts printed in this Review, but simply those words which receive some notice in an entry. Item numbers in bold type indicate more than a passing reference. An asterisk (*) indicates that comment is offered on the MM or BAGD entry, or occasionally on LSJ. New words are marked with a dagger (†).

A. Greek

B. Latin

3. Subjects

4. ECL, Patristic and Jewish Writers

5. Texts Discussed

Listed below are all texts new or old appearing in 1979 corpora and conspectus volumes and referred to in this work. Of other texts only those referred to in a more than passing manner are listed. Bold type indicates substantial discussion of a text at the item number given, or that a non-1979 text has been reprinted here. It is not the normal practice of this Review to suggest new readings or dates, but where they are offered an asterisk (*) beside the text in this index will indicate it.

NEW DOCUMENTS ILLUSTRATING EARLY CHRISTIANITY

New Documents 1976 (vol.1) pp.155; 1981 repr. 1984
ISBN 0 85837 481 1; 0 85837 899 X (pbk)

Some notable entries:

Invitations to the *kline* of Sarapis
A personalised Aretalogy of Isis
The regional *kanon* for requisitioned transport
The use of a double name
Nomina sacra in synagogue inscriptions
A deacon's work contract
The earliest attested monk
A Christian complains about assault

New Documents 1977 (vol.2) pp.224; 1982
ISBN 0 85837 508 7; 0 85837 509 5 (pbk)

Some notable entries:

Nursing contract
Doctors in the Graeco-Roman world
The purple trade, and the status of Lydia of Thyatira
Politarchs
Recent fragments of the Greek OT and NT on papyrus and parchment
Recent patristic (incl. Monophysite) texts
The earliest Christian silver hoard
The origin of the abbreviation *XMΓ* — a Christian cryptogram?

New Documents 1978 (vol.3) pp.182;
ISBN 0 85837 546 X; 0 85837 545 1 (pbk)

Some notable entries:

Joining the household of Caesar
The 'good news' of a wedding
Expiation and the cult of Men
Cities of the Revelation
The 'prodigal son' parable spiritualized
The Lord's Prayer in a necropolis
Credal formula in a Christian amulet against fever
Christian inscriptions from Phrygia
Divine Providence in a letter of Judas